Readings

in

Chinese

Literary

Thought

Harvard-

Yenching

Institute

Monograph

Series

30

Readings in Chinese Literary Thought

Stephen Owen

Published by the

Council on East Asian Studies

Harvard University

Distributed by

Harvard University Press

Cambridge, Massachusetts

and London   1992

The Harvard-Yenching Institute, founded in 1928 and headquartered at Harvard University, is a foundation dedicated to the advancement of higher education in the humanities and social sciences in East and Southeast Asia. The Institute supports advanced research at Harvard by faculty members of certain Asian universities, and doctoral studies at Harvard and other universities by junior faculty at the same universities. It also supports East Asian studies at Harvard through contributions to the Harvard-Yenching Library and publication of the *Harvard Journal of Asiatic Studies* and books on premodern East Asian history and literature.

Library of Congress Cataloging-in-Publication Data

Readings in Chinese literary thought / [edited by] Stephen Owen.
    p. cm.—(Harvard-Yenching Institute monograph series; 30)
    Engish and Chinese.
    Includes bibliographical references and index.
    ISBN 0-674-74920-0
    1. Chinese literature—History and criticism—Theory, etc.
I. Owen, Stephen, 1946– . II. Series.
PL2262.2.R4 1992
895'.109—dc20   92-19554
                                  CIP

Book design by Adrianne Onderdonk Dudden
Index by Patricia Carlson

Contents

Preface

This book has reached unexpected proportions. It is a wise thing to let some projects sit for years and mature, until they become subtle like fine wine. But there are other projects which grow like those monsters of old science fiction movies, swallowing everything that passes by, ever growing. I will admit this book wants something of the *labor limae*, the Horatian "work of the file" that smoothes writing as a sculptor polishes his stone; but it has seen the cruder work of the ax many times, with great formless chunks hacked off time and again. Still it has kept growing. Those chunks hacked off lie scattered around, ominously pulsing and already increasing; but it is hoped that publication will cage the material of the parent book once and for all.

The book took its first form a decade ago in a course taught at Yale, a course in which I innocently hoped to present Chinese literary theory to students of Western literatures. The summer before the course I found myself doing far more translation than I had ever intended. Over the next ten years the manuscript of translations and commentaries continued to grow, until it reached proportions that are an organizational nightmare. However, it is still painfully inadequate: inadequate both in the texts omitted and in the commentary on the texts included. I have entitled the book "Readings In . . . " so as not to make a promise I do not fulfill: It is not a survey of all the important texts of Chinese literary thought; it does not even include enough of those texts, particularly in the later period, to provide continuity. All I can promise is that the texts included are, in some way or other, important or representative. Furthermore, read together, they tell an abbreviated story of the development of some of the important issues in Chinese literary theory and criticism. My colleagues in the field have continued to tell me "You can't leave out X." My apologies, but X has been left out, and much more. Aware of such omissions, I have made the form of the book an open structure, putting in place a few landmarks in a tradition of more than two millennia. Such an open structure can allow for myself or others to fill in some of the spaces at a later date.

I owe thanks to the students in various courses in Chinese literary theory, taught over the years. Thanks also go to K'o Ch'ing-ming of National Taiwan University, who patiently went over the drafts of the early chapters with me, correcting errors and some of my more outrageous judgments. Another round of corrections and suggestions came from my readers, Pauline Yu of Columbia University and Tim Wixted of Arizona State University. Professor Wixted's voluminous annotations, going far beyond a reader's usual obligations were particularly helpful. I also owe special thanks to the Guggenheim Foundation for its support and to the American Council of Learned Societies that provided a small additional grant to enable me to be finish off this monster. My graduate assistant Eileen Chou was invaluable in providing characters when the manuscript was being readied for the typesetter. And thanks are, as always, due to my wife Phyllis who endured the long labor and my grumblings.

Readings
in
Chinese
Literary
Thought

Introduction

In its tradition of literary thought, a civilization tries to interpret the relation between its literature and its other concerns: to explain the role literature plays in that civilization and to describe literature and literary works in terms that have resonance in other areas of intellectual and social life.[1] Such an activity is, admittedly, not one of the more obvious projects that a civilization may undertake. The existence of a tradition of literary thought presupposes that literature's nature, role, and values are not self-evident, that literature is a problematic area of human endeavor which requires some explanation and justification. These motives underlying a tradition of literary thought ensure that the relation between such a tradition and literary texts themselves is not transparent. The interpretations offered by such a tradition can never be a direct way to understand a great literary work, but they do offer an oblique and essential insight into broad areas of concern, desires, and repressed possibilities that lie behind both the writing and reading of literature.

If we conceive of the relation between literary works and their readers using the metaphor of an implicit contract, then in the tradition of literary thought we do not find the contract itself but rather an attempt to make the contract explicit and thereby to limit and control it. In order to appreciate the force of the texts of literary thought, it is essential never to take them simply at face value. For example, if a work such as the "Great Preface" to the *Book of Songs* tells us that a poem offers immediate access to the cares of a human mind regarding a particular historical moment in society, the existence of such a claim is at the same moment the mark of an anxiety that the poem might be, in some way, deceptive, or perhaps simply irrelevant: the theoretical statement tells us what a poem ought to be. In such texts we can discover the tradition's unquestioned assumptions, the range of variation within those assumptions, and the tradition's most powerful desires and fears.

The force of a tradition of literary thought acts in ways other than setting guidelines for how texts should be understood. Although a tradition of literary thought has its own history independent of the history of the literature on which it reflects, in many periods it is bound in an intense, if often oblique productive relation to literary works; this is, what poets actually do can never be perfectly extricated from what poets believe they ought to be doing. Such a relation is never a simple one: no major poet simply obeys the prescriptions or simply embodies the descriptions found in theoretical texts; but sometimes major poets believe they are following theoretical injunctions, or try their best to follow the theoretical injunctions, or react violently against the theoretical injunctions. Every great work has an implicit poetics that relates in some way to an explicit poetics (if one has developed in the civilization); and that relation becomes part of the poem.

To grasp such forces operating in a literary work, one must understand that tradition's explicit poetics and the true nature of the challenge presented in the poetics. The tradition of literary thought teaches us to pay attention to certain aspects of literary works that we might otherwise overlook; but at the same time we often see clearly what an interpretive tradition tries to conceal: these are not aspects of the text to which no attention is given, but dangerous possibilities that interpretation tries to deny or hide and which, in their suppression, become all the more powerful. In short, if the relation between literary works and literary thought is never simple, it is always intense; and the more attention is paid to a certain feature or question, the more we recognize that it represents a problem.

This much the tradition of Chinese literary thought shares with its Western counterpart. Beyond that point we find mainly differences: in the kinds of assertions made, in the genres, and in the basic structure of literary thought. We will take these questions up as we encounter them in particular texts, but a few general issues may be outlined here.

In many ways a tradition of literary thought is constituted by a set of words, of "terms," which have their own long histories, complex resonances, and force. Such words do not constitute a collection of autonomous containers of meaning, but are part of a mutually defining system that evolves in time and has links to conceptual vocabulary in other areas of human endeavor. Not only do these terms acquire meaning by their relation to one another, each term carries a history of prior usage in particular theoretical texts, and the efficacy of each term is continually reinforced by association with particular phenomena in literary texts; moreover, each term has a degree of latitude for variation and the possibility of idiosyncratic redefinition.

Though educated readers are, as the linguists say, "competent" in the use of such terms, no one, either in the English-speaking or Chinese-speaking tradition, knows what those terms "mean." No one knows what a plot "is," but almost everyone knows one when they see one. This problem with the meaning of terms is, of course, not limited to literary thought; and in the Western tradition literary thought joins in the larger cultural aspiration for "definition," the hope to stabilize meanings and thereby control words.

Since the quest for definition has been one of the deepest and most enduring projects of Western literary thought, its virtual absence in Chinese literary thought (as well as in other aspects of Chinese intellectual history) will be surprising. Brief, often canonical definitions of the central terms may be offered in passing; but the systematic attempt to explain terms occurs only very rarely, late in the tradition (in the fourteenth century) and on the very lowest level of literary studies (in other words, definition was not a goal that was considered important in its own right, but was offered to students of poetry, who were truly not "competent" in the use of those words).

As in other areas of Chinese intellectual history, the significance of key words is stabilized by their use in texts that everyone knows. Modern scholars, both Chinese and Western, often lament the "vagueness" of Chinese conceptual vocabulary. In fact, it is not a whit more vague than most of the conceptual vocabulary of European languages; but in the Chinese tradition conceptual precision was not a value and therefore no one need maintain the pleasant illusion that a precise technical vocabulary existed. As the Western reader recognizes "plots" and "tragedies" and *mimêsis* and "representation," the Chinese reader may not have been able to say exactly what *hsü* or *wen* or *chih* were, but he knew them when he saw them. The difference is this: In the Western tradition there has always been a tension between the desire for precise definition on the one hand, and on the other hand, a desire for "resonance" in literary terms (their application to various frames of reference, which inevitably works against precise definition). In the Chinese tradition only "resonance" was a value.

The second reason that Chinese terms often sound vague to Western ears is that they simply do not correspond to phenomena that the Western reader has learned to recognize. For example, the term *t'i*, which applies to styles, genres, and forms of all kinds, may strike many readers as impossibly broad; but the Chinese term embodies a distinction, and hence a concern, that is absent in the roughly corresponding English terms: in this case, *t'i* refers to normative style, generic norm, and other aspects of normative form, in distinction from the particular levels on which a norm is worked out in individual texts (e.g., *t'i* as "style" is always a normative type of style rather than the particular style of a text). The term *hsü* is "empty" or "plastic," referring to substances like air or water that conform to "solid" shapes; it is extended to refer to the changing fluidity of the emotions and the way they may be "invested" in solid things. This commonplace of traditional Chinese psychology, poetics, and linguistics can be made comprehensible to a Western reader; but it is, quite obviously, not a part of the Western tradition's conceptual repertoire. Each tradition has its own areas of great conceptual strength. The reader disposed to be dismissive will observe the incapacity of the Chinese tradition to account for aspects of literature that seem absolutely essential in the Western tradition. The Western reader disposed to be impressed by the Chinese tradition will find only strengths: for example, the rich vocabulary for operations of mood and mind that are often without counterpart in English. Both would be correct. In the commentaries that follow, comparisons will be made, but they are given for the sake of understanding rather than comparative evaluation: each tradition follows its own set of questions and tries to account for a very different tradition of literary texts.

Throughout the commentaries and in the glossary, I have tried to discuss the usage of important terms. In doing so, I must acknowledge the difficulty of generalizing about nearly three millennia of semantic changes in these words. It is hoped that between the brief general discussions in the glossary and the more detailed and particular discussion of terms in specific usages in the commentary, the English-speaking reader can develop some sense of how these terms can be plausible categories of literary description.

In addition to the problem of terms, classical Chinese discourse employs structures of argument that are often quite perplexing for the Western reader. An argument that is pellucid and subtle in classical Chinese often emerges in English translation as disjointed and incomprehensible. We may roughly distinguish three overlapping kinds of argument. The most primitive structure, seen in the "Great Preface" to the *Book of Songs*, is the aggregation of elements around a center (and seems in the case of the "Great Preface" to be less a mode of argument than a way of organizing a disparate body of received material). As with pedagogic traditions of commentary and subcommentary, the oldest and most authoritative statement is given first, with supplements and amplifications added in a roughly hierarchical progression of degrees of importance, generality, historical priority, and so forth. In this kind of "argument" the progression of the text is essentially a gradual building up of the significance and consequences of the primary text. Since this is not so much a constructed sequence of dependent statements as an assemblage of thematically related passages (albeit assembled according to a set of governing principles), these texts are often genuinely disjointed.

The most important structure of argument in earlier writing is rhetorical diaresis, which can be seen both in "The Poetic Exposition on Literature" and in the chapters of the *Wen-hsin tiao-lung* 文心雕龍. This is "analysis" in its root sense, in which a topic is broken into its component parts, then continuously subdivided until the matter is covered. Since this procedure is not entirely unfamiliar to students of Aristotle, it should be added that in the Chinese case the topic statements of the various segments are not explicit (as they are in the Aristotelian tradition), so that one must be able to recognize implicitly when the subheadings of A have been completed and one is shifting to B. Such arguments are sometimes rigidly structured—one might even say too rigidly structured—and their disjointedness in English translation is only too apparent. In the commentaries to both "The Poetic Exposition on Literature" and in the *Wen-hsin tiao-lung*, I have tried to clarify such arguments.

Some texts present no difficulties in argumentation, and some texts simply transcend the issue: there is no problem in following the polemical fustian of Yen Yü's "Ts'ang-lang's Remarks on Poetry," while the idea of argumentation is not really applicable to the wispy associations that loosely bind each of "The Twenty-Four Categories of Poetry." However, there is a third kind of argument, of which Yeh Hsieh's "Origins of Poetry" provides a late classical example in its most sophisticated and fully developed form. Yeh Hsieh aims at a lucidly linear exposition, yet the explicit terms of logical exposition in classical Chinese are considerably fewer in number and looser than in English. This is not to say that the argument itself is looser, simply that the recognition of a tight argument is left to the trained reader. Because a determinate sequence of conditions is implicit in the Chinese, I have supplied them explicitly in the English translation. The degree of explicit subordination required to produce good English would have produced an agonizingly tedious classical Chinese (Yeh Hsieh already approaches bad style by the degree of subordination he uses).

On the largest scale, the history of Chinese literary thought seems to have followed a pattern similar to that of its Western counterpart, beginning with the repetition, elaboration, and variation of a set of commonplace notions, universally held to be true; then moving to contesting groups, each representing clusters of positions derived from the commonplace notions of the earlier tradition; and finally to individually developed theoretical positions. The modern reader of Renaissance and eighteenth-century literary theory quickly learns to see through the mandatory recapitulation of commonplaces (for example, that poetry should be *dulce et utile*) to the particular twist (if any) given in the text in question; one also learns to recognize whether the twist is purposeful or unconscious. The Chinese tradition had its own set of conventional pieties, which return in theoretical texts again and again. Because these commonplaces are unfamiliar to the Western reader, however, they deserve close examination; for in them we find the most basic concerns and shared assumptions of the tradition.

The transition out of the period of authority can be roughly characterized as the phase when the theorist is no longer simply stating a universally recognized "truth" but rather "a position": this usually coincides precisely with a statement on the part of the theorist that he is, indeed, "telling the truth." This transition is, of course, not a point in time but an ongoing process occurring over many centuries. Although in the Chinese case we might trace it back as early as the factional literary disputes of the early sixth century, the stridently polemical voice of Yen Yü in the thirteenth century is perhaps the first "position" set against some of the most cherished commonplaces of the tradition. And Yen Yü is one of the first theorists to assure us that he is, indeed, telling the "real truth." This second phase is most clearly marked in the factionalism of literary groups during the sixteenth and early seventeenth centuries. By the time we reach Wang Fu-chih and Yeh Hsieh in the mid and late seventeenth century, we have "literary thought" in the modern sense, a critic genuinely "thinking through" a set of problems.

THE SOURCES OF LITERARY THOUGHT

Literary thought is often treated as if it were a disembodied set of ideas, whose articulation in texts is only a fortunate accident of history. In fact, no such disembodied ideas exist. What we call literary thought is a group of diverse texts, which in turn belong to distinct genres. The genres of a tradition of literary thought exert a profound influence on the nature of the discourse: such genres are distinct categories of occasion that call for certain kinds of things to be said in certain ways. The difference between Aristotle and Horace writing on literature is in no small degree the difference between a formal *techné*, expounded in what seems to be the format of a lecture, and a verse epistle. The inclination of these two classical writers to these two distinct genres bespeaks a difference in disposition that is more profound than any difference in "position." Even modern academic critics, for whom consistency of position is a sacrosanct value, will write very different sorts of comments in a preface to an anthology, a book review, and an academic book of criticism.

In the latter part of the Chinese tradition a consistently articulated position, defined against the positions of opponents, played no less a role in writing on literature than it does in the modern West. The historical inertia of the various genres of such writing, however, tended to color and modify such "positions," situating them in the history and conventions of each critical genre. A rough survey of the major kinds of sources follows.

Classics, Early Prose, and the "Literature of Knowledge" (Tzu)

There are many brief references to literary and aesthetic matters in the Confucian Classics. As one might expect, such comments developed immense canonical authority later in the tradition and often served as the core statements of received truth on which the later critic would build. In addition to passages referring directly to literary issues, however, statements on psychology, moral philosophy, and hermeneutics made in the Classics often appear in later writing on literature and are no less important. While the Confucian Classics generally stress the ways in which language can be an adequate manifestation of inner life and the social world around the writer, the early Taoist texts contain important counter-arguments regarding the inadequacy of language. From the late Warring States through the Ch'ing dynasty, there was a genre of collected discourses, the *tzu* 子, which promised a relatively systematic coverage of all knowledge or of some particular branch of knowledge (statecraft, historiography, and, in the case of *Wen-hsin tiao-lung*, literature itself).[2] Such works usually contained one or more chapters on language, literature, or persuasive rhetoric. Such works are the closest in form to the Western "treatise," and their individual chapters are roughly identical with the detached "discourse" (*lun* 論), one of the genres of Chinese literary prose belonging to the belles lettres.

The Genres of Literary Prose and Poetry

1. *Poems on poetry:* There are many subtraditions here. The most immediate association in Chinese is a form known as "poems on poetry," *yung-shih shih* 詠詩詩; these are usually quatrains offering terse, allusive comments on specific poets and their literary historical relations rather than treating questions of theory. A group of quatrains by the T'ang poet Tu Fu (712–770) are usually considered the precursor of this form (although characterizations of the works of other poets in T'ang social poems was far more important in establishing the form). The standard late classical version of the form took shape in the Southern Sung and found its most famous example in a series of quatrains by the Chin poet Yuan Hao-wen (1190–1257). Outside such quatrain series, this kind of comment on the style of individual poets was very common in classical poetry. Another subtradition of poems on poetry celebrates the conditions of composition—primarily the question of spontaneity and the organic relation between state of mind and the poem. Ssu-k'ung T'u's (837–908) "Twenty-Four Categories of Poetry" and its later imitations constitute yet another and quite anomalous subtradition: here we have poetic evocations of sets of moods or qualities.

2. *Prefaces:* Prefaces form one of the largest groups of sources for Chinese literary thought. These were written for groups of poems composed by several people on a given occasion, for anthologies, and for the works of single authors. In the collected works of a single author the composition of the preface was often entrusted to the most eminent authority on literature whom the author (or his offspring) could persuade to write it, although adding one's own preface became increasingly common after the T'ang. The form of prefaces varies greatly, but the attempt was usually made to reconcile the author's style with larger issues of literary theory and poetics or received commonplaces. Here can be found some of the most interesting elaborations and variations on received values. Anthology prefaces are often important sources for literary historiography and generic theory.

3. *Letters:* These often contain full discussions of theoretical issues, but

usually declare one's "position" to the person addressed, sometimes polemically and sometimes not.

4. *Essays:* These are usually brief (usually one to five pages of Chinese, roughly two to twelve pages of English), systematic expositions of some question or position taken by the author. Individual essays are found in literary prose, but the essay is also the generic form of chapters in longer works, classified as the "literature of knowledge."

5. *Colophons:* These are especially important from the eleventh century onward. Besides containing important bibliographical information, colophons often contain comments on the history of literary reception and the writer's style.

Informal Prose

There is no clear dividing line between literary and informal prose, with the exception that "literary" genres are included in an author's collected works, *chi*, while informal prose generally is not. Colophons, mentioned above, are a marginal genre, sometimes included in collected works and sometimes not. As the name I have given the category suggests, lightness and informality, the quality of offhand comment, is prized here (though the form may sometimes be used, as by Wang Fu-chih, to work out complex theoretical arguments). Collections of informal prose usually consist of short entries (rarely longer than a page of Chinese) ranging from literary theory to prosody to philology to literary history. *Shih-hua*, "remarks on poetry," appear first in the eleventh century and constitute the largest category of occasional prose on literature. Almost a thousand *shih-hua* from before the twentieth century survive (in addition to fragments of lost ones preserved in *shih-hua* anthologies), and they are still written today. There is a great variety in the kinds of *shih-hua*: some represent a serious attempt to write the history of poetry, while others (the very best, in my opinion) are a peculiar art form in their own right, embodying the style of thought of the *shih-hua* writer. *Shih-hua* is itself a specialized subform of *pi-chi*, "random notes," of which there are thousands. *Pi-chi* differ from *shih-hua* only in the variety of topics on which they offer comment, among which literature is included; in addition to comments on literature, however, these *pi-chi* may contain political comments, advice on flower arranging and making tea, discourses on difficult points in history, and everything else imaginable in every conceivable combination. Although *pi-chi* often group comments in broad categories, they share an aesthetics of casualness and randomness with *shih-hua*. There are also specialized subforms of *pi-chi* for comment on art-song (*tz'u-hua*), on popular song and drama (*ch'ü-hua*), on the poetic exposition (*fu-hua*), and on prose (*wen-hua*): these also represent an immense volume of critical writing.

Technical Manuals

Technical works were considered a low critical form, in earlier periods teaching composition, but later often attempting to give a general understanding of the poetics of a genre (using "poetics" in its proper sense as a description of the normative qualities of the literary work in regard to its being "made"). Here is where one looks for a systematic exposition of traditional poetics, at the same time recognizing that such systematic exposition was usually considered a dubious activity and inherently unsophisticated. As there were distinct subforms of literary prose for different literary genres, there were distinct categories of technical manuals for poetry, song (tz'u), popular song (ch'ü), and rhymed and unrhymed prose. Because of their importance in pedagogy such works were very widespread; but these books were often poorly printed and little attention was given to their preservation, with the result that many have been lost or survive in only single copies. Such technical works borrowed shamelessly from one another; their sources are often either not cited or improperly cited; and the texts are often unreliable, containing frequent misprints and miscitations. Within these technical works are many distinct kinds of comment, including:

1. *Lists of prohibitions, things to be done, areas on which a writer should concentrate, categories of various sorts, sets of terms.*

2. *Chü-t'u*, or collections of couplets, grouped either under some complex hierarchy of poets (e.g., *Shih-jen chu-k'o t'u* 詩人主客圖) or under categories of mood (e.g., *T'ang-jen chü-fa* 唐人句法 in *Shih-jen yü-hsieh* 詩人玉屑). These *chü-t'u*, linking descriptive terms to poetic examples, provide one way to develop a sense of the vocabulary of moods in Chinese criticism.

3. *Exemplary analyses of poems*, that teach the *fa**, the "technique" of the poet.

4. *Discussions of normative development in various genres*, either in terms of the development of a theme or of its phases of mood or time. Such discussions are sometimes nothing more than collections of quotations from more sophisticated critics or popularized restatements.

5. *Discussions of terms*. Attempts to discuss important terms occur only in a few cases, modeled on the *Pei-hsi tzu-yi* 北溪字義, an attempt to discuss the basic concepts of neo-Confucianism; needless to say, the attempts to explain literary terms are far less sophisticated than their neo-Confucian model.

Critical Anthologies and Interpretive Editions

Important in these works are the prefaces, *tu-fa* 讀法 (instructions on how to read), interpretive comments interspersed with poems and sometimes interpretive essays after poems, and marginalia (*mei-p'i* 眉批). In the Ming and Ch'ing such works often contain long introductions on reading and criticism. It should be pointed out that many of the greatest scholars and critics preferred marginalia, while systematic interpretation was reserved for pedagogic hacks. The *tu-fa* are of great interest to those interested in literary hermeneutics.

Scholarship on the Book of Songs

Though intersecting at many points with "secular" poetics and literary theory, the tradition of interpretation on the *Book of Songs* is a distinct tradition in its own right, with its own specialized terms and questions evolving over a period of two millennia. Some of the most sophisticated traditional criticism can be found here, in works such as Wang Fu-chih's *Shih kuang-chuan* 詩廣傳; but the force of such criticism is contingent on understanding the history of the issues involved and the history of the interpretation of particular poems; thus it is largely inaccessible to Western readers.

Other

In addition to the above sources for literary thought, there is a large body of biographical material, both in the standard histories and elsewhere, books of anecdotes purporting to tell the occasions of poems, and literary scholarship. Most of these sources contain critical material, and many contain theoretical material.

THE PLAN OF THIS WORK

This work is addressed primarily to two audiences: first, to scholars of Western literature who wish to understand something of a tradition of non-Western literary thought; and second, to students beginning the study of traditional Chinese literature. The works covered in this volume are all, in some way, classics of traditional literary theory; but the determination of such "classics" has, in several cases, been a product of the reconsideration of the critical tradition during the Ch'ing and modern times.

To place these works in context, it is important to recognize the sheer size and complexity of premodern Chinese literary theory, criticism, and allied writing on literature. One set of recent anthologies, quoting passages from the genres of "literary prose and poetry" (discussed above), consists of eleven volumes averaging between three and five hundred pages each (keeping in mind that a page of classical Chinese can be between two and five pages of English). These anthologies do not even touch on the nearly one thousand works of premodern *shih-hua*, "remarks on poetry," or on technical manuals. Another recent work is a three-hundred-page list of the titles of essays, prefaces, and poems. A true history of Chinese literary thought and a genuinely representative anthology are equally impractical because of the great bulk that would be required, not only for the translations, but also for the annotations, the explanation of issues and terms, and the necessary background discussions of a large and changing tradition of literary works.

To present this material in English, some radical principle of selectivity is obviously necessary. One solution, adopted by the late James J. Y. Liu in *Chinese Theories of Literature,* was to identify a taxonomy of approaches and to excerpt primary texts to illustrate each. A more conservative solution was that adopted by John Timothy Wixted in *Poems on Poetry: Literary Criticism by Yuan Hao-wen (1190–1257):* in a book of nearly five hundred pages, Wixted traces the background of these thirty quatrains back to their sources in poetry and literary discussion. The remarkable depth of Wixted's learning carries this book far beyond mere annotation. Yet a third solution, the best and most insightful to date, has been offered by Pauline Yu in her recent *Reading of Imagery in the Chinese Tradition.* Yu takes one central issue—how the tradition understood the operation of poetic "meaning"—and traces it through the T'ang and beyond.

The present anthology of translations and commentaries is a fourth solution to the problem. It does not set itself against the works above, but rather seeks to complement them. By its very nature it is a solution doomed to a certain ponderousness. It tells a story of literary thought through texts. Because of inevitable omissions (the price paid for examining complete works rather than excerpts), that story, however intricate, is still grossly simplified. Yet the story is a true one and, I believe, the essential one. But even if its centrality is accepted, the reader should understand that it is only one possible synopsis of a main plot, which is large, complicated, and surrounded by an array of subplots.

To tell this story properly through the texts means respecting those texts, which are very different in kind. To address the problem of the diversity of these texts, one can either aim for a consistency in presentation that does violence to some of the texts, or one can sacrifice consistency of treatment for the peculiar demands of each text. For better or worse I have chosen the latter course.

A story should be clear at the beginning. Out of all the richness and complexity of early writing that forms the background of Chinese literary thought, in the first chapter I have selected and discussed only a few passages at length in the form of an essay, in order to set forth clearly issues that will arise in later texts. Many other texts from this period (most of which are very short) will appear in later chapters as we take up specific problems. More than any other chapter, this represents merely one interpretation of early literary thought.

The form of the commentary will be consistent—a passage of the original text followed by a translation and then by a discussion of the issues. The nature of the commentary will vary, however, according to the requirements of the texts treated. To offer general statements on the "theory" of "The Poetic Exposition on Literature" without facing its philological details would be as frivolous as a full philological commentary on Ou-yang Hsiu's "Remarks on Poetry" would be an academic evasion of its real interest. Whatever "ideas" the texts embody, those ideas cannot be separated from the differing natures of each text. For this reason I have chosen the form of commentary rather than a more synthetic approach.

While most of the works treated fall more or less under the rubric of "literary theory," at least two of the works—Ts'ao P'i's "Discourse on Literature" and Ou-yang Hsiu's "Remarks on Poetry"—are, each in its peculiar way, literary thought as literature. I have treated them as such. In two other cases, Lu Chi's "Poetic Exposition on Literature" and Ssu-k'ung T'u's "Twenty-Four Categories of Poetry" (both in verse and each "literary" in a different sense), "literary thought" cannot be separated from very complicated philological issues. In these cases any broader interpretation must be bound up with precise discussion of lines and words, with due consideration given to the effort and erudition of those Chinese scholars who have attempted to resolve the problems. If the reader is distressed by the loss of the "story" in such philological details, he must blame Lu Chi and Ssu-k'ung T'u for the way they wrote. There are lucid English translations of both works; and readers who not wish to confront in detail how problematic our understanding of these works is, may content themselves with those other translations.

The remaining chapters offer texts that can be treated more conventionally; they address philological issues when these arise, but primarily carry the story. Although the works treated are only a few spots in a tradition of nearly two and a half millennia, the commentary structure is an open form that can permit future supplement and the addition of other works.

When I was undertaking this work, there was a moment when I imagined myself translating Aristotle's *Poetics*, with explanatory discussions, into classical Chinese for a premodern audience. The historical depth and great volume of the exegetical traditions surrounding the "Great Preface," "The Poetic Exposition on Literature," *Wen-hsin tiao-lung*, "The Twenty-Four Categories of Poetry," and to some degree "Ts'ang-lang's Remarks on Poetry" are equaled in the Western tradition of literary thought only by the *Poetics*. Like the *Poetics* these works are inextricable from the history of their interpretation.

It would be quite easy to offer a simple and elegant translation of the *Poetics*, recasting its terms and arguments in familiar Chinese terms. The result would be a pleasant, at times incomprehensible and at times naive version of a Chinese argument on literary structure. One might go beyond that, attempting to explain the original Greek words and how they differed from the Chinese concepts; here we would have a problem because the precise force of the Greek words is in many cases a matter of great scholarly debate and ultimately inseparable from the history of the interpretation of those words in Latin and the vernaculars (as well as being inseparable from the transformations of those words as they were naturalized within the literary traditions of the vernaculars). I can imagine some of the moments: *dio kai philosophôteron kai spoudaioteron poiêsis historias estin*: "For poetry is both more philosophical and more serious than history." I would translate: *shih (poiêsis) chih yü shih, li sheng erh chin yeh*: "As for poetry's relation to history, it excels in natural principle and is [the] serious [one]." Such a statement would be virtually nonsensical to my premodern readers of classical Chinese: after all, history perfectly embodies *li* (principle), but the role of "natural principle" in poetry is decidedly problematic. It would take a good deal of space to explain what Aristotle meant by "poetry," "philosophy," and "history"; in each case the understanding of those terms would be radically different in the Chinese version.

As a scholar, I would feel somewhat uneasy in presenting the *Poetics* as if the only problems were those of translation, as if there were no deep disagreements about the interpretation of that text within the Western tradition. I would therefore next present my readers with a survey of the interpretive questions that are so central to the *Poetics*, from the early scholiasts (let me pretend for the sake of argument that the *Poetics* had a scholiastic tradition) to Robortello to Lessing to Else and other modern scholars. Keep in mind that all this time I am translating from a conceptual vocabulary evolving over two millennia into a tradition with an entirely different set of conceptual terms. The new problems and new meanings of words that arise over those two millennia all sound pretty much alike from the perspective of my premodern Chinese readers. At some point my reader will groan and give up in despair.

The inversion of this small fantasy is precisely the problem faced in translating these Chinese texts into English. On the one hand, a Western literary scholar who wants to understand a truly different tradition of literary thought will want to avoid the kind of translation that makes everything different into something comfortably familiar. On the other hand, there is an invisible line in exegesis, beyond which the texts begin to recede into a welter of complications. Certain arguments may be individually very interesting, but in the aggregate they can overwhelm the text and the discussion. In the following exegeses I have decided to confront the Chinese exegetical tradition fully in only two cases: in "The Poetic Exposition on Literature" and in "The Twenty-Four Categories of Poetry." I have made this decision both because of their particular difficulties and to give examples of the kind of interpretive problems that arise in classical Chinese; even so, I have only scratched the surface of the exegetical tradition in the discussions of passages. Elsewhere, while I myself have had to confront the exegetical tradition, I have decided, except in a few cases, to keep it largely out of the discussions. I will not attempt to justify every decision I make, nor will I offer all the alternatives.

In most cases I have decided in favor of a literal awkwardness in translation that will permit the English reader to see something of how the original

Chinese text works. This relative literalness is not attractive; but in texts of thought, especially from the Chinese, grace in translation is usually a mark of vast concessions to the conceptual habits of the translation's audience. There are appealing previous translations of many of the works translated in this volume; yet from them it is sometimes impossible to form more than a rudimentary sense of what the Chinese theorist is saying. Arguments that are deep and precise in Chinese often appear in English as vacuous and disjointed generalities. The only remedy for this is exegesis, and the translations are given not to stand on their own but to work together with the commentaries.

There is also no graceful way to handle the problem of the technical terminology of traditional Chinese poetics. As is the case in Western literary thought, the descriptive and prescriptive force of Chinese literary thought cannot be separated from this complex body of terms, which were located in a historically evolving structure that at different periods allowed different degrees of individual variation. These terms may often sound odd and exotic; but the reader should always keep in mind that, like the central terms of Western tradition, these surprising historical growths were largely taken for granted as the normal way to conceive of literary phenomena, and they were used as if they referred to something self-evident. Since their meanings derive from their use in a variety of particular contexts and from a set of relations to other terms, they have no true equivalents in the terminology of Western poetics.[3] They can never seem as natural and obvious to an English reader as they did to a Chinese reader, nor will their mutual associations ever come as readily. Moreover, the English reader will never have developed a sense of concrete referentiality when he encounters these terms, something achieved by repeated association with particular facets of particular literary texts. By encountering them again and again in a wide variety of theoretical texts, however, the English reader can gain some sense of their functional meaning. The device of including romanizations after the translations of important terms, however awkward, is to be a continual reminder that the Chinese word translated does not really mean the same thing as its English translation.

In the translations and commentary, some of the most important of these terms appear with a conventional English translation followed by the romanized Chinese term, given in parentheses. When the romanized term is marked by an asterisk, the term occurs in the Glossary. A few of the terms will be given only in romanization. I have not judged it reasonable to note the Chinese term every time it is used, and I am certain many readers will feel I have done so far too often; however, cases where I have not added the romanization are usually those in which a particular translation of a term has been established in context, and the rest of that passage simply continues to use the same term.

One of the most difficult choices was between maintaining a single conventional English translation for a particular Chinese term and varying the translation according to context. I have made an uneasy compromise here, adjudicating the demands of the text being translated. A term like *ch'i** is almost invariably given in romanization. The term *pien**, when used alone, is almost always rendered "mutation" in order to call attention to its precise implications and distinguish it from other terms of change, although that often produces awkwardness in translation. *Yi* is usually rendered "concept," even when it is awkward; but there are certain cases when it must be rendered differently. For some terms I offer a wide variety of translations depending on context. In short, I have tried to make these decisions term by term and text by text, with my primary goal being to give an English reader insight into the Chinese argument rather than graceful English. Much has been written about the best possible English translation for many of these terms; but there is no best translation, only good explanations. Every translation is weighted in some way that does an essential violence to the Chinese concept; this will be true in the central conceptual terms of any tradition; these terms are important to the civilization, they bear a complex history, and they are embedded in texts shared by the civilization. Most of these terms do not belong exclusively to Chinese literary thought; rather they are shared by all branches of Chinese thought, but will take on slightly different associations depending on the frame of reference in which they are used.

Another insurmountable problem is the continual reference to writers and works with which the reader is not familiar. Even if I were to include a full anthology of Chinese literature to accompany this volume, the qualities referred to in those literary works would usually be lost in translation. Dates have been provided in many cases to give the reader a rough sense of the time frame.

Another practical problem concerns those questions that recur throughout the works discussed in this volume. In order to give each commentary coherence, a certain amount of repetition will be unavoidable in summarizing issues discussed in greater detail elsewhere.

For the convenience of English readers I will give a short English bibliography, organized by chapters, listing selected alternative translations and secondary works in Western languages. The fuller bibliography of Chinese and Japanese works provides not only the sources used in the volume but also a more general bibliographical introduction for students of Chinese.

Texts from the Early Period

子曰。視其所以。觀其所由。察其所安。人焉廋哉。人焉廋哉。

He said, "Look to how it is. Consider from what it comes. Examine in what a person would be at rest. How can a person remain hidden?—how can someone remain hidden?"

Analects II.10

The *Analects* contains many passages in which Confucius offers judgments on the poems of the *Book of Songs*, on *wen**, and other topics which lead directly into the concerns of traditional Chinese literary thought. In their authoritative recurrence and exegesis, these comments were immensely influential in the tradition; but if we seek in them the profundity of Plato's critique of poetry or Aristotle's exposition, we will be disappointed. Moreover, the deepest forces in the development of Chinese literary thought were not Confucius' comments on literary matters per se, but the larger concerns of Confucian thought embodied in the *Analects*. The passage above, which makes no direct reference to literature or writing, announces a problem that remains with Chinese literary thought to the modern era.

As often in later Chinese literary thought, we find here a triadic sequence of stages rather than a bipolar structure of signification, which we find in Western language theory and in concepts of *mimêsis* or representation. Confucius enjoins us first to observe the quality of an act ("how it is," "the that-by-which" 其所以), then to consider the motives or originating circumstances ("from what it comes" 其所由), and finally, to infer the conditions in which the agent would be "at rest" (其所安). Of course, Confucius is here concerned with recognizing moral qualities and the character of a person. He promises us that a certain kind of attention will enable us to observe a person's true nature, which would otherwise remain concealed.

The question raised in this passage involves a special problem of knowledge. It is not a truly "epistemological" problem because it is not concerned with the nature of knowledge in its own right, the question of knowledge as it is posed in some of the Platonic dialogues. Nevertheless, this problem of knowing is in many ways the counterpart of the epistemological questions raised in early Greek thought. The question that Confucius initiates is one of "recognizing" the good in a particular case, rather than "knowing" what the Good is. Chinese literary thought began its development around this question of knowledge, a special kind of knowing as in "knowing a person" or "knowing the conditions of the age." This problem of knowledge is predicated on multiple levels of concealment, and it leads to a hermeneutics that promises to reveal the complex conditions that inform human actions and utterances. Chinese literary thought is grounded in this hermeneutics, just as Western literary thought is grounded in a poetics (what a poem "is" with regard to its being made). Ultimately a traditional poetics grew out of the Chinese concern for hermeneutics, just as Western literary hermeneutics grew out of its poetics; but in both cases the original concern shaped the later transformation.

This passage from the *Analects* makes some basic assumptions that are worth examining. First, there are inner and outer truths: there is the possibility of misunderstanding the inner by observing the outer (the possibility of hiddenness), but there is also the assumption that some particular quality of attention to the outer will allow perfect access to the inner. This presumes that there is a necessary correlation between a particular inner condition and its external manifestation. The relation between inner and outer is one of manifestation, what is inside making its way outward (a notion of process leading to a presence implicit in "from what it comes"). The outer does not voluntarily "represent" the inner: for example, an embarrassed expression on a face does not "represent" the feeling of embarrassment and the originating circumstance "from which it comes"; rather the expression involuntarily discloses the feeling, and the disclosure of the feeling implicates originating circumstances. Finally, the most subtle assumption in the passage: what is manifest is not an idea or a thing but a situation, a human disposition, and an active relation between the two. What is manifest is ongoing and belongs entirely to the realm of Becoming.

Alêtheia, "disclosedness" (the Greek word often translated as "truth"), became implicated in the notion of a world of deceptive appearances and something absolutely True behind them, an opposition of Becoming and Being. This was one of Plato's central concerns and has remained, in many transformations and concealments, at the heart of Western metaphysics. "Being" as such was an inconceivable issue for Confucius, but he would have understood very well the form of the relation, *alêtheia*, truth as disclosedness. Both traditions worked with an opposition between deceptive appearances and something valid behind the surfaces; but their divergence in the construction of the opposition is central to the differences between the two traditions, in literary thought as in all other thought.

Crudely stated, Plato's attention was directed to the transience, variance, and contingency of particular phenomena, measured against the permanence, invariance, and self-subsistence of a Form. Confucius' attention was directed to a different but related question: not the failure of appearance to correspond to the stable term, but the fact that what is inner does indeed inform what is outer (appearance), that there is indeed some necessary relation between the two. For Plato a beautiful person "referred" him to the form of Beauty; Confucius would have noticed rather that beauty is indeed immanent in a person, that it appears on the surface, and that a particular quality of attention is necessary to perceive it. The two traditions worked with fundamentally different (later incommensurate) terms, but one term is shared: "concealment," the possibility of misjudgment, most powerfully threatened by deception and lies; and the secret concern for deception and lies is inseparable from a concern with language.

The Platonic movement from Form to phenomenon (loosely corresponding to the Chinese movement between inner and outer) is one of fixed models and making after models. For this reason the *poiêma*, the literary "thing made," becomes tertiary and disturbing in the Platonic scheme of things. The counterpart of "making" in the *Analects* passage above and in most Chinese literary thought is "manifestation": everything that is inner—the nature of a person or the principles which inform the world—has an innate tendency to become outward and manifest. Aristotle would have liked something of the sort, but his manifestation was a qualitative approximation in *phusis* (the nature of something as a process of becoming) of the entelechy of the thing (that is, the fully realized form of some entity toward which it develops). In the Confucian version a complicated confluence of circumstance may veil any particular inner truth; but if one but knows how to look, that inner truth is immanent in the outer phenomenon.

In this construction of inner and outer, we can see the origins of a rich non-fictional literature. There is a level of mere surface; if we look closely, we can see why it is the way it is, its origins in circumstance. But the third level is the most interesting: on that level we can also see the conditions under which a person would be "at rest." That is, in this surface we can also infer the stable and constant dimensions of a human nature free of the buffetings of the lived world. This is true for Confucius in observing persons; it is also true in reading a literary text, which—to remind the Western reader of a simple and all-important fact—always comes from a person.

敢問夫子惡乎長。曰。我知言。我善養吾浩然之氣。

. . . .

何謂知言。曰。詖辭。知其所蔽。淫辭。知其所陷。邪辭。知其所離。遁辭。知其所窮。

Kung-sun Ch'ou: "What, sir, is your excellence?"

Mencius: "I understand language and have mastered the fostering of boundless and surging *ch'i*."

. . . .

"What do you mean by 'understanding language'?"

"When someone's words are one-sided, I understand how his mind is clouded. When someone's words are loose and extravagant, I understand the pitfalls into which that person has fallen. When someone's words are warped, I understand wherein the person has strayed. When someone's words are evasive, I understand how the person has been pushed to his limit."

Mencius II.A. 2.xi, xvii

Confucius' imperative to observe behavior, motive, and basic disposition is fulfilled in a special way in Mencius' claim to "understand language," *chih-yen** 知言. Language is the ultimate form of outwardness, and it embodies most perfectly, yet problematically, the correspondence between inner and outer.

For Confucius, the moral quality of the act itself was insufficient to know the person: look to what it comes from—a good act may be done from selfish motives or a bad act may have mitigating circumstances; and through considering these, the person may be known. As Mencius says (IV.A.17), someone who would not give his hand to his sister-in-law if she were drowning is a wolf. And yet one should not touch the hand of one's sister-in-law. Even in a good act with good motives or in a bad act with bad motives, we might discover some quality of discomfort in the person, and in that way, too, we might see something of the person's true nature: "examine in what a person would be at rest."

In the same way Mencius' "understanding language" is not simply an understanding of the meaning of words and certainly not an understanding that merely reflects or reproduces what the speaker thinks the words say. Mencius' knowledge of language is a knowledge of what the words reveal about the speaker, what they make manifest. "When someone's words are one-sided, I understand how his mind is clouded": no dictionary or grammar or philosophical reflection on a concept will teach this kind of "understanding language." Words become only a surface whose shape reveals what lies within. Mencius' list of different kinds of language shows that the trained listener can make fine discriminations. Most important, what the speaker reveals in his words is involuntary—perhaps not at all what he would wish to have revealed. Error and deception are not autonomous categories here, but are subsumed under understanding the person: they are nothing more than manifestations of ignorance or the desire to deceive and as such become important pieces of evidence for us when we listen to someone speak. Recognizing the truth or accepting error, being deceived or not being deceived rest with the capacities of the listener.

Here at the beginning of Chinese literary thought, we should take careful note of the direction in which we are being led. The observer/listener/reader is defined very differently from a "member of an audience." Even our English term *member* silently teaches us that only the collective "body" is the complete organism: the hope of reception that resides in the text cannot be fulfilled by a single reader. The Western notion of the work's "audience" has its own history, and we cannot fully grasp the concept without uncovering something of that history. Plato was deeply disturbed and shocked by the way in which a person became a "member of an audience," swept away in a peculiar frenzy when viewing a tragedy. Nor were Plato's worries entirely without foundation: that same member of the Athenian audience stood in the Agora, listened to rousing speeches, and in a burst of unthinking enthusiasm sent a generation off to die beneath the walls of Syracuse.

When Socrates was ready to demolish the self-understanding of the rhetor Ion, he noted the power of the rhetor to cast the audience into a state of *ekplexis*, "being out of their wits." Later, in the Roman period, the author of *On the Sublime* was dissatisfied with the literature of his own age, feeling its impotence in comparison to the great works of the past, and its inability to raise its audience to *ekstasis*, "standing outside of" the self. The Western notion of an "audience" situates the reader/listener as an anonymous member of a collective entity; his license, even exercised in solitude, has something of the freedom of becoming lost in the enthusiasm of the mob. Such freedom remained something sought from literature, a longing to be swept away, *ekstasis*. The notion of aesthetic experience as it developed in the eighteenth century, may have been a much gentler and disinterested play of the faculties, but it still presumed that art provided a mode of experience that was separate, free from the appetites and moral imperatives of the ordinary world.[1]

Mencius' "understanding language" characterized the ancestor of a very different kind of reader, someone not seeking a unique mode of experience for its own sake, but rather attempting to understand another person. In the germinal stages of such "understanding language," moral judgment and moral education were the primary concerns, but eventually the interest of the reader grew into a broader and more complex attempt to understand the Other. This initial construction of an art of reading was fraught with problems—no more and no less than those in a literary tradition founded on *mimêsis/*

representation—and in due time those problems worked their way to the surface, with many resolutions offered.

In the construction of the literary art that grew from these beginnings, if a text stirred the reader's emotions strongly, it was because of the writer and his age; the experience did not involve a closed relation between the reader and the text. And even though a text might pass through the hands of millions of readers, it was always looking for one person—this person or that—who "understands language."

咸丘蒙曰。舜之不臣堯。則吾既得聞命矣。詩云。普天之下。莫非王土。率土之濱。莫非王臣。而舜既為天子矣。敢問瞽瞍之非臣如何。

曰。是詩也。非是之謂也。勞於王事而不得養父母也。曰。此莫非王事。我獨賢勞也。故說詩者。不以文害辭。不以辭害志。以意逆志。是為得之。

Hsien-ch'iu Meng said, "I have accepted your declaration that the Sage-King Shun did not consider Yao [who abdicated the throne in favor of Shun] to be his subject. Yet there is a poem in the *Book of Songs*:

> Of all that is under Heaven,
> No place is not the king's land;
> And to the farthest shores of all the land,
> No man is not the king's subject.

I would like to ask how it could be that, when Shun became emperor, the Blind Old Man [Shun's father] would not be considered his subject?"

Mencius replied, "This poem is not talking about that. Rather the poem concerns the inability to care for one's parents when laboring in the king's business. It says, 'Everything is the king's business [and should be a responsibility shared by all], yet I [alone] labor here virtuously.' In explaining the poems of the *Book of Songs*, one must not permit the literary patterning (*wen**) to affect adversely [the understanding of] the statement (*tz'u**); and one must not permit [our understanding of] the statement to affect adversely [our understanding of] what was on the writer's mind (*chih**). We use our understanding (*yi**) to trace it back to what was [originally] in the writer's mind (*chih**)—this is how to grasp it".

Mencius V.A. 4.ii

We have a thorny ethical problem: when Sage-King Yao abdicated the throne to Sage-King Shun, was Yao then Shun's subject; and furthermore, was Shun's father then Shun's subject (an unthinkable situation in which two orders of hierarchy are at odds)? Mencius has made an exception to the king's suzerainty in these cases, but Hsien-ch'iu Meng cites the *Book of Songs* as an authority to prove that there are no exceptions. Mencius attacks Hsien-ch'iu

Meng's interpretation (but does not question the authority of the *Book of Songs* to decide such issues): the *Song* in question arises from a particular situation in which an officer is caught between conflicting claims of duty to the king and duty to his parents. The "king's business" is the duty of all, but he feels as if he alone were charged with completing it. However questionable the particular interpretation may be, the way in which Mencius interprets is significant.

Hsien-ch'iu Meng is a failed reader, and the way in which he fails is precisely by his inability to follow the instructions for understanding given by Confucius in the *Analects*. For Hsien-ch'iu Meng, the words of the passage in the *Book of Songs* mean what they say: he looks to "how it is." For Mencius, the reason they were said gives meaning to the words of the passage; meaning grows out of a particular (if ultimately doubtful) circumstance. That is, Mencius considers "from what it comes." Mencius is able to give the passage a general meaning; but the general meaning can arise only by working through a level of circumstantial intention, understanding the words as a relation to the particular circumstance in which the words were produced. The critique offered by Mencius here is not simply directed against misreading a part by failing to consider the whole; rather it announces a central assumption in the traditional theory of language and literature, that motive or circumstantial origin is an inseparable component of meaning.

As Confucius' instructions for "knowing persons" are here transferred to reading poems, some important new terms appear. Here also the process by which inner becomes outer, the process of manifestation, is described in stages. The outermost stage is *wen**, "literary patterning," in later contexts, "writing."

Wen* should be an organic outgrowth of some situation or inner state, but Mencius is made aware of a danger, a danger only implicit in the earlier *Analects* passage: the process of manifestation may give rise to distortion and misunderstanding. To understand the poems of the *Book of Songs*, one must possess a special capacity to know "what was really meant" by the speaker, not simply what the poem might seem to say.

Mencius has assumed here a distinction between literary language (*wen**) and plain language (*tz'u**, the "statement").[2] In doing so he may have had in mind the kind of exegetical paraphrase of early texts which was already being practiced and which was later to become a prominent feature of the Chinese scholastic tradition. More significant, *tz'u** is conceived as an intermediate phase between *wen** and *chih** ("what was on the writer's mind"). Since the phases of interpretation that Mencius describes are the mirror image of the process of *chih**'s manifestation in language, we can see that *wen** and not *tz'u** is the fully realized form. This is an early suggestion of an important assumption later in the tradition: that *wen**—the patterned, literary word and the written word—is not a figuration or deformation of plain language, but the full and final form of language. Although it is most open to misunderstanding, *wen** is also the entelechy of language.

Prior to *tz'u** is *chih**. Reading well, we discover not "meaning" but *chih**, "what is/was intently on the mind." *Chih** is a condition of mind (*hsin**) that subsumes the ordinary possibilities of "meaning" in language, both literal and figurative, but which goes beyond them. The language of the *Book of Songs* is not an index of "what is said" (literal meaning) or even of "what is meant" (potentially encompassing the possibility of both figurative and literal meaning); rather language is an index of what was said and meant in relation to **why** it was said and **why** the speaker meant to say it. Confucius' injunction in the *Analects* should show how such a theory of language could come into being. The process of understanding is quite simply to follow the serial stages back to their source; and since complex series raise greater possibilities of error, they require a special kind of reader.

Without indulging in an elaborate comparison between early Chinese language theory and Western language theory, we might note that versions of the same simple semiotic model of sign/meaning appear at an early stage both in the West and in China (as in *Kung-sun Lung-tzu* 公孫龍子). It is a primitive and highly imperfect model for describing the real operations of language, and a model which the Western intellectual tradition has continually refined without entirely escaping. The apparent disappearance of language theory in China is, in fact, nothing more than the failure and abandonment of that simple model: the theory of signs was replaced by a more sophisticated model for the operations of language—*chih**. *Chih** integrates motive and circumstance with those purely normative operations of signification to which the study of "language" is limited in the Western tradition. This is not, as it might seem, replacing linguistics with psychology; rather it is recognizing the fact that no language has ever been produced except through some psyche and in some particular circumstance. Attention to that obvious truth made it exceedingly difficult to conceive of the operations of language impersonally. Thus, we do not find in the Chinese tradition the emphasis placed on certain great linguistic and philosophical projects of the Western tradition: grammar, philosophical definition (which would remain stable for all language users), a quasi-mathematical language of perfect "accuracy."

詩言志。歌詠言。

The Poem (*shih**) articulates what is on the mind intently (*chih**); song makes language (*yen*) last long.

Book of Documents (Shu ching), "Canon of Shun"

This is the canonical statement of what poetry "is." Even if modern scholarship no longer credits the attribution of the statement to the legendary antiquity of Shun, still it is probably the earliest definition of *shih* 詩. More important than its true historical provenance is the fact that it was understood to be the primary and most authoritative statement on *shih* throughout the traditional period. It should be emphasized that this is not "a theory" of poetry: it is almost as authoritative as if God had delivered a brief definition of poetry in Genesis. Not only is it canon, its authority is strengthened by the fact that it is an etymological (or more properly, pseudo-etymological) definition, arrived at by dividing the character *shih* into its component parts. Thus, whenever someone looked at the character and wondered what this thing *shih* might be, that person would see the components *yen* 言 and *chih** 志 (actually 寺, which was interpreted as *chih** by a pseudo-etymology). Together, *yen-chih** is the exact formulation given above: "articulates" "what is on the mind intently." Such an etymological definition gives the statement a special claim to truth. This definition can no more be rejected than the statement, "A poem is something made": both are tautological by etymology (*poiêma*, "a poem" from *poein*, "to make"). "The poem articulates what is on the mind intently" must remain the given assumption under which all later poetic theory develops or with which it must be reconciled. Within this definition there remained great latitude for development, variation, and dispute; but the definition itself is taken for granted: one cannot say "The poem does not articulate what is on the mind intently."

If we translate *shih* as "poem," it is merely for the sake of convenience. *Shih* is not a "poem"; *shih* is not a "thing made" in the same way one makes a bed or a painting or a shoe. A *shih* can be worked on, polished, and crafted; but that has nothing to do with what a *shih* fundamentally "is." This difference in definition between a poem and a *shih* has immense consequences: it affects how, in each tradition, the relations between a person and a text will be understood and taught; moreover, it affects how poets in each tradition behave. Perhaps the greatest consequence lies in the question of control: if we take a text to be a "poem," a "made" text, then it is the object of its maker's will; it is not the person himself but rather something he has "made." Since the Romantic period many writers of lyric have tried to move toward a "poetry" like *shih*; but when they write about poetry, their concerns show the marks of their struggles with the ancient notion of poetry as something "made"—we read of masks, personae, distance, artistic control.

If, on the other hand, we take a text to be *shih*, the author's crafting of the text is not essential to what a *shih* "is" (in the same way that a Western teacher of poetry may tell the naive student that the poet's state of mind may be interesting, but that it is not essential to what a poem "is"). The writer of *shih* cannot claim the same quality of control over his text that a poet does. As a result the *shih* is not the "object" of its writer; it **is** the writer, the outside of an inside. When Mencius hears "one-sided words" (see p. 22), he hears the attempt to control language: the very attempt presents itself to the good reader precisely as an "attempting," which in turn raises questions of motive. In short, this canonical statement on *shih*, an assumption that remained with the form for two and a half millenia, assures us that *shih* is, in some way, what was in the mind of the person. Even though some poets and some schools of poetry hoped that Western poetry could do the same, the concept of poetry does not, implicitly, make that promise in itself.

What is this "inside" that we find in *shih*? It is *chih**, traditionally defined as "that to which the mind goes." The first aspect of *chih** we should note is that it is prearticulate, a true "state of mind," qualified by a degree of intensity and an object. When it finds language adequate to it, it becomes *shih*. One of the most misleading translations from Chinese to English is the conventional translation of *chih** as "intention." *Chih** may be "intent" in the sense of English "being intent upon something"; but it is not "intention," either in the popular or the philosophical sense of the term. "Intention" is voluntary; a moment's reflection will reveal how deeply the notion of "intention" is implicated in the Western concern with free will. *Chih** may have a level of the voluntary, but the concept privileges the involuntary origins of any act of volition: *chih** occurs because one is stirred by something in the external world. One may have the "intention" to express one's *chih**; one may "intend" that one's *chih** appear to others in a certain way. But for one who "understands language" like Mencius, the *chih** perceived in reading the *shih* will be true *chih**, whether or not that is what the writer "intends" to be revealed.

A second problem with the translation of *chih** as "intention" is that *intention*, as it is used in regard to literature, is always the "intention" to make a poem in a certain way: its object is the literary artifact. *Chih**, on the other hand, is a relation to some object, event, or possibility in the living world outside of poetry. *Chih** is a subjective relation to some content, a relation of a certain intensity and of a certain quality. *Chih** is that condition when the mind is fixed on something, a "preoccupation." *Chih** is tensional, yearning for both resolution and for external manifestation. Very often *chih** takes on a public, political sense as "ambition"—the desire to do something or accomplish something in the political sphere. In other cases it has a broader moral frame of reference, as "goals" or "values to be realized." Ultimately the ethical and political dimensions of *chih** became so strong in the tradition that most writers on literature preferred to substitute other terms as the source of the poem in the psyche, especially *ch'ing**, "the affections."

This canonical definition of *chih** makes it an activity of human beings in general. There is nothing here of poetry's restriction to a special class of humanity whose profession or vocation makes them "poets." Later writers in the Western tradition will call weak poetry "verse" and maintain an absolute division between the greatest writing and anything less. The Chinese tradition, after wrestling with the problems of value inherent in the canonical definition, will still admit continuity of degree between the greatest poetry and social "versifying."

The second clause of the canonical definition is equally interesting. Here, too, the statement is tautological, based on dividing the character *yung* 詠 (to "intone") into *yung* 永 ("prolong") and *yen* 言 ("language").[3] The statement probably referred originally to "intoning," stretching out the words in the act of singing. But commentators play on the meaning "lasting long," transferring it to another aspect of song, its capacity to be preserved, carried afar, and transmitted. Through the patterning of song, a text becomes fixed and repeatable. Unlike speech, which disappears as soon as it is uttered, song is one of the earliest examples of the fixed text; and that repeatability is a miracle. This capacity of language to be preserved through time and over space occurs in *wen**, "literary patterning" and the "written word." This capacity of prolongation, "going far," became one of the determinative characteristics of *wen**.

仲尼曰。志有之。言以足志。文以足言。

不言。誰知其志。言之無文。行而不遠。

Confucius said, "There is a record[4] of someone's thoughts which says: the language (*yen*) is to be adequate to what is on the person's mind (*chih**), and the patterning (*wen**) is to be adequate to the language. If a person does not use language, who will know what is on his mind? If the language lacks patterning, it will not go far.

Tso chuan 左傳, 25th year of Duke Hsiang

This saying, attributed to Confucius, citing a source now unknown, belongs to the extensive Confucian apocrypha; but it is an important collateral text for the canonical definition, "The Poem articulates what is intently on the mind." In this passage *chih** is given as the origin not just of poetry, but of any language that must be made known to others. Moreover, in this passage, *wen** is brought into the equation.

Like the three stages of understanding given by Confucius ("how it is," "from what it comes," "in what a person would be at rest"), and closer still to Mencius' hermeneutic triad ("literary patterning," "statement," and "what was on the writer's mind," *chih**), this passage also sets up a triadic process of manifestation: from *chih**, to *yen*, to *wen**. In this it remains consistent with Confucian language theory; but the passage develops language theory in a significant way, turning the process around and changing the structure of a hermeneutics to the structure of a productive "poetics."

In the passages from the *Analects* and the *Mencius* it was assumed that those who observed a person correctly, listened to language well, or became good readers of the *Book of Songs*, could know the inner from the outer: there was assumed to exist an involuntary and necessary correspondence between interior nature and its exterior manifestation. But suppose a person wants to be known, to have his inner nature and *chih** revealed to others. Suppose that in doing so a person seeks to advance in the political world, or to be admired, or simply to be understood. In such a case there is a motive for discourse and for "literature," *wen**: it comes into being to make the self known. In this passage manifest *chih** would be understood primarily as the ethical disposition of the speaker. But as Chinese literature grew, aspects of the self revealed in literature increased; but this did not alter the fact that literature was still understood essentially as a way of knowing persons.

If a person speaks to be known, the revelation of self is voluntary, even though the precise quality of what is revealed remains essentially involuntary. This latter point is important: if the writer were to create a mask or project a wishful image of the self—the essential assumption made in Western lyric, whose roots are essentially dramatic—then that writer would (theoretically) be revealed precisely as someone creating a mask or projecting a wishful image of the self, with all the complex motives that attend on such acts. The assumption remains that inner truth is visible in its outer manifestation.

One speaks to have one's *chih** known, and the words take on "literary patterning," *wen**, so that they can have extension, can "go far." *Wen** is a mode necessary in adequately fixing an utterance—in the written word or in memorable form—so that it can be carried beyond the momentary wind that blows across the face. *Wen** becomes necessary if one hopes to be understood in another place and another time. *Wen** does not seek the vast, anonymous audiences of a "poem" (in the Western sense), but it does address the problem of the distance of the unique auditor. This capacity to "go far" applies to many frames of reference in distance—space, history, social standing.

Once again we may note that ordinary "language," *yen*, is given as a mediating and imperfect term in the process of manifestation. One cannot develop a theory of literarity as linguistic deviation here: *wen** is the ultimate and fully adequate manifestation of *chih**; *yen* is only an intermediate stage, adequate only for local goals.

"In the Beginning was the Word" is Hellenistic, not Chinese; likewise, its logocentric descendants are not Chinese. Here the assumption is a prearticulate *chih** that is primary and may or may not come out. *Chih** has semantic content, but it is more than its semantic content: it is also a relation to that content, a quality of care (just as someone's shouting "Help!" in distress implicates an immediate concern on the part of the speaker and a claim on the listener that goes beyond the semantic content of a request for aid). If *chih** becomes manifest in language, such care, with its complex circumstantial ground, is immanent in the utterance.

The "language," *yen* or *wen**, that "comes out" of those prelinguistic states does not "represent" those states; it brings them out for the sake of someone else, in order that they might be known. The correspondence between inner and outer is not a question; it is an assumption. Nevertheless, the question of adequacy does arise. The outer cannot "mismanifest" the inner, but one may worry that the manifestation is unequal to the fullness and power of the inner state.

子曰。書不盡言。言不盡意。然則聖人之意。其不可見乎。子曰。聖人立象以盡意。設卦
以盡情偽。繫辭焉以盡其言。

He said, "What is written does not give the fullness of what is/was said (*yen*);
what is/was said does not give the fullness of the concept in the mind (*yi**)."

"If this is so, then does it mean that that the concepts in the minds of the
Sages cannot be perceived?"

He said, "The Sages established the Images (*hsiang**) [of the *Book of
Changes*] to give the fullness of the concepts in their minds, and they set up the
hexagrams to give the fullness of what is true and false in a situation (*ch'ing**);
to these they appended statements (*tz'u**) to give the fullness of what was
said . . . "

Book of Changes, Hsi-tz'u chuan

The passage above has a purely local application to the *Book of Changes*; but
elements of it, particularly the first statement (attributed to Confucius) were
so frequently cited in later literary thought that the passage became part of
the canonical repertoire of every writer and reader. We have already seen a
model of linguistic operation in which circumstance and motive are integrated with a literal and/or figurative level of "meaning." This model of
language makes possible a special "epistemology" concerned with knowing
people. The *Hsi-tz'u chuan* passage expands upon this model, announcing
a problem inherent in the process of manifestation and suggesting a way
in which knowledge other than the knowledge of people can occur through
language.

In the first statement the speaker, presumed to be Confucius, sets up a
model of essential inadequacy in the triadic process of manifestation; then in
his response to the questioner, he shows how the structure of the *Book of
Changes* resolves the problem. Since the initial statement of linguistic inadequacy had a life in the tradition virtually independent of the response offered
to the interlocutor's question, we may consider it independently.

As the "inner" term in a model of language, *yi** (translated as "concept in
the mind") is very different from *chih** ("what is intently on the mind"). *Yi**
does not encompass circumstance, motive, and an intense emotional relation
to some "content": *yi** is voluntary (and thus is sometimes properly translated as "will" or "intention"). In the frame of reference of a human speech
act, it becomes something like "what was meant" or "what someone had in
mind." Although *yi** was commonly used of ordinary human beings, its application here to the Sages is particularly apt; for the Sages, unlike other mor-
tals, have no hidden inner motives but are in every way what they appear to
be. As a unifying minimalization of some putative content that transcends
the particular words of an utterance, *yi** most closely approaches "meaning"

or "concept" in the Western sense (and on that level is close to, and in some periods interchangeable with another *yi** 義, "a truth"). However, even though *yi** has this level of relative dissociation from a particular act of the human mind, it never quite achieves the full level of abstraction or collectivization we find in Western terms such as *meaning, concept,* or *idea.* It is "concept" as it is being grasped by a human mind—"what is meant" rather than "Meaning."

In the formulation, "what is written does not give the fullness of what is said; what is said does not give the fullness of the concept in the mind," we find something new but not entirely unexpected. The relation of inner *yi**, speaking, and writing is a process of successive diminishment: more is meant than is spoken; more is conveyed in speech—with its gestures, inflections, living context—than can be written down. Thus the written word becomes as Han Yü 韓愈 (768–824) will later describe it, an irreducible "essence." The relations between inner and outer are conceived in terms of "adequacy," *tsu* (as in the *Tso chuan* passage given previously) or as here in terms of "giving the fullness of," *chin,* or "not giving the fullness of," *pu-chin.*

As we will see, the tradition divides here between those who believe that the inner can indeed be known from the diminished outer manifestation, and those who believe that an absolute breach exists, that "essence" resides in something absolutely inner that cannot be recovered through language.

Those disposed to believe that the inner can indeed be known from the outer will follow Mencius' instructions and trace the words back to their source, where they will find more than appears on the surface of the written text. Reading and understanding becomes a process of following words back to their origins, and in doing so, restoring the fullness which necessarily resides beneath the diminished text. Modern Western theorists often call language essentially "metaphorical" because the Western theory of signs is essentially metaphorical: the word "stands in for" the thing. The central assumption in Confucian language theory (excluding those early, failed attempts to develop a theory of signs) is that language is essentially synecdochal: an inner whole manifests a necessarily diminished surface, and through that peculiar "part" the whole may be known.

The subtle "concepts" of the *Book of Changes,* grasped by the minds of the Sages, threaten to elude language altogether, they stand close to that breach between inner and outer that would make understanding impossible. "Confucius" resolves the problem and accounts for the format of the *Book of Changes* by interposing the notion of *Hsiang** ("Images") between *yi** and language.[5] We might turn here to the "Elucidation of the Image," *Ming Hsiang** 明象 by the philosopher Wang Pi (王弼; 226–249), who plays a set of exegetical variations on the triadic structure of "concept" (*yi**), "image" (*hsiang**) and "language" (*yen*).[6]

夫象者出意者也。言者明象者也。盡意莫若象。盡象莫若言。言生於象。故可尋言以觀象。象生於意。故可尋象以觀意。意以象盡。象以言著。

The Image is what brings out concept; language is what clarifies (*ming*) the Image. Nothing can equal Image in giving the fullness of concept; nothing can equal language in giving the fullness of Image. Language was born of the Image, thus we seek in language in order to observe the Image. Image was born of concept, thus we seek in Image in order to observe the concept. Concept is fully given in Image; Image is overt in Language.

Wang Pi, "Elucidation of the Image," Ming Hsiang

The rhetoric of Chinese exegesis encourages running through serial relations in several directions to clarify the exact terms of those relations. What Wang Pi discovers in doing this has important implications for understanding the *Book of Changes*, for a general theory of language, and particularly for poetry.

On the level of the *Book of Changes*, the *yi** or conceptual value of a hexagram is immanent in and accessible only through the *Hsiang**. Thus the hexagram *Ch'ien* is the "dragon," embodying active force and the capacity to undergo all transformations. *Ken* is the "mountain," a powerful stillness that attends upon action. The *yi** of the hexagrams can be explained in words, as I have started to do above, but the words will keep accumulating without ever "giving the fullness of" the significance of the hexagram. Yet the *yi** of the hexagram is immanent in the Image, which can be spoken of in words.[7]

On the level of a theory of language, Wang Pi's passage suggests that words do not name "things"; words are a stage in the processes of mind, "born from" the images of things. Although Wang Pi's intentions are confined to the problematic relations between the hexagrams and their associated Images, we may extend his theory to a more general description of the workings of language. The word *bowl* does not name this bowl or that bowl; rather bowl exists as a concept (*yi**) from which emerges a generalized image (*hsiang**) of "bowl," and the word is a name given the image. Here we have an initial move away from a purely psychological theory of language; Wang Pi's theory of universal categories make it possible to speak of a concept of "bowl," apart from this or that particular bowl or how one happens to feel about bowls in general.

There were, in early China, theories of language as "naming things." We suspect that one important reason such linguistic speculation never got beyond the most rudimentary stages was the increasingly psychological interpretation of language. Wang Pi might not entirely approve of our extension of his passage, but our elaboration remains true in this respect: readers tended to understand words not as neutral descriptions of the world, but as acts of mind in reference to the world. *Yi** never quite reaches the level of "idea," which has an existence entirely independent of anyone's conceiving of it. Even here, as *yi** is pushed toward the notion of pre-existent idea, the interlocutor in the *Hsi-tz'u chuan* passage reminds us that even these *yi** have an empirical location, the "concepts in the minds of the Sages."

The necessary mediation of "image" between concept and language has important consequences for poetry and for other literature. When the poet observes the forms of the world around him, the infinite particularity of the physical world can be reduced to some essential minimum, into categorical "images," and thence, into categorical language. The poet and his readers can assume that those images are the natural embodiment of *yi**, the "conception" of how the world "is." Thus poetic "imagery" (which should be clearly distinguished from "imagery" as the term is applied in Western literary studies) may be the immanence of "concept"; and this assumption carries the immense authority of the *Book of Changes*.

This notion of "image" is essential to understanding the role of "description" in Chinese literature. Description here is not an intentional act, as it is usually understood in Western literary thought; it is not a construct for some artistic purpose. From one side, description may be the form of the writer's attention, the way he perceives, revealing his state of mind (*ch'ing**) or "what is intently on his mind" (*chih**). From the other side, description is a structure of "images," the visible form of "concept" immanent in the world; and it is only through these images that "concept" can be adequately manifest in words.

孟子謂萬章曰。一鄉之善士。斯友一鄉之善士。一國之善士。斯友一國之善士。天下之善士。斯友天下之善士。以友天下之善士為未足。又尚論古之人。頌其詩。讀其書。不知其人可乎。是以論其世也。是尚友也。

Mencius said to Wan-chang, "A good *shih* in one small community will befriend the other good *shih* of that community. The good *shih* of a single state will befriend the other good *shih* of that state. The good *shih* of the whole world will befriend the other good *shih* of the whole world. But if befriending the good *shih* of the whole world is not enough, then one may go on further to consider the ancients. Yet is it acceptable to recite their poems and read their books without knowing what kind of persons they were? Therefore one considers the age in which they lived. This is 'going on further to make friends.'"

Mencius V.B.8.ii

The term *shih* once referred to a class of military retainers that stood midway between the aristocracy and the peasantry. By Mencius' time *shih* had come to refer to the educated class, custodians of culture, and the administrators of states. The *shih* were still intermediate between the aristocracy and the peasantry, but the category had become at least partially open to anyone who acquired the skills of the *shih* and who shared their values. In effect, this describes the educated elite throughout the traditional period, and it was to this group that classical Chinese literature primarily belonged.

In many ways this passage represents the consequences of the theories of language and literature presented in the preceding texts. A peculiar hermeneutic circle develops between the ability to understand a text and knowing others: one knows the other through texts, but the text is comprehensible only by knowing the other. Ultimately, however, the relation between reader and writer is a social one. Reading is located in a hierarchical sequence of social relations; it is different in degree but not in kind from making friends with others in a small community. The question of adequacy recurs here in a different mode, in those who find their sphere of like-minded people too narrow and constantly reach out to an ever larger scope. Writing and reading bypass the limitations of death and establish civilization as the living community, in its largest sense, through time.

One reads the ancients not to wrest some knowledge or wisdom from them but to "know what kind of persons they were." And such knowledge can come only from understanding them in the context of their lives, a context built out of other texts. Knowledge may come from such reading, but that knowledge is inseparable from the person. The ground of literature is here a kind of ethical curiosity that is both social and sociable.

Counterstatement

桓公讀書於堂上。輪扁斲輪於堂下。釋椎鑿而上。問桓公曰。「敢問。公之所讀何言邪？」

公曰。「聖人之言也。」

曰。「聖人在乎？」

公曰。「已死矣。」

曰。「然則君子所讀者。古人之糟魄已夫！」

桓公曰。「寡人讀書。輪人安得議乎！有說則可。無說則死。」

輪扁曰。「臣也以臣之事觀之。斲輪。徐則甘而不固。疾則苦而不入。不徐不疾。得之於手而應於心。口不能言。有數存焉於其間。臣不能以喻臣之子。臣之子亦不能受之於臣。是以行年七十而老斲輪。古之人與其不可傳也死矣。然則君之所讀者。古人之糟魄已夫！」

Duke Huan was reading in his hall. Wheelwright Pien, who was cutting a wheel just outside the hall, put aside his hammer and chisel and went in. There he asked Duke Huan, "What do those books you are reading say?" The duke answered, "These are the words of the Sages." The wheelwright said, "Are the Sages still around?" And the duke answered, "They're dead." Then the wheelwright said, "Well, what you're reading then is no more than the dregs of the ancients." The duke: "When I, a prince, read, how is it that a wheelwright dares come and dispute with me! If you have an explanation, fine. If you don't have an explanation, you die!" Then Wheelwright Pien said, "I tend to look at it in terms of my own work: when you cut a wheel, if you go too slowly, it slides and doesn't stick fast; if you go too quickly, it jumps and doesn't go in. Neither too slowly nor too quickly—you achieve it in your hands, and those respond to the mind. I can't put it into words, but there is some fixed principle there. I can't teach it to my son, and my son can't get instruction in it from me. I've gone on this way for seventy years and have grown old in cutting wheels. The ancients have died and, along with them, that which cannot be transmitted. Therefore what you are reading is nothing more than the dregs of the ancients."

"The Way of Heaven," *Chuang-tzu*

And perhaps language doesn't work, gives no access to what is really important in the person. The challenge of Wheelwright Pien haunts the literary tradition and makes writers ever more ingenious in inscribing the essential self in writing. Chuang-tzu's dark mockery drives the tradition of Chinese literary thought as surely as Plato's attack drives the Western theoretical tradition. In both traditions all theoretical writing on literature contains a strong element of a "defense."

The "Great Preface"

The "Great Preface," *Ta-hsü* 大序, to the *Book of Songs* was the most authoritative statement on the nature and function of poetry in traditional China. Not only was it to be the beginning of every student's study of the *Book of Songs* from the Eastern Han through the Sung, its concerns and terminology became an essential part of writing about poetry and learning about poetry. It was one text on the nature of poetry that everyone knew from the end of the Han on; and even when the "Great Preface" came under harsh attack in later ages, many positions in it remained almost universally accepted.

In the *Book of Songs*, a short "Lesser Preface," *Hsiao-hsü* 小序, preceding each poem announces its provenance and original purpose; and the "Great Preface," as we now have it, has been integrated into or replaces the "Lesser Preface" to the first poem.[1] It is uncertain exactly when the "Great Preface" reached its present form, but we can be reasonably sure that it was no later than the first century A.D. Many readers accepted the "Great Preface" as the work of Confucius' disciple Tzu-hsia and thus saw in it an unbroken tradition of teaching about the *Book of Songs* that could be traced back to Confucius himself. A more learned and skeptical tradition took the "Great Preface" as the work of one Wei Hung, a scholar of the first century A.D. It is probably anachronistic, to apply the concept of "composition" (except in its root sense of "putting together") to the "Great Preface"; rather, the "Great Preface" is a loose synthesis of shared "truths" about the *Book of Songs*, truths which were the common possession of traditionalists (whom we now call "Confucians") in the Warring States and Western Han periods. In their oral transmission these truths were continually being reformulated; the moment when they were written down as the "Great Preface" may be considered that stage in their transmission when reformulation changed into exegesis.

The actual origins of the "Great Preface" are less important than its influence. The history of the interpretation of the "Great Preface" and of those scholars who began to challenge its authority in the Sung is a subject of immense complexity and beyond the scope of the present study.[2] In the following commentary we will simply try to place the "Great Preface" in the context of the earlier texts considered in the preceding section. We will give the "Great Preface" in its original context, as part of the "Lesser Preface" to the first poem of the *Book of Songs* (*Kuan-chü*), traditionally understood as celebrating the virtue of the Queen Consort of King Wen of the Chou Dynasty.

In contrast to the theoretical treatise (a Greek *technologia*), which draws from particular texts only to illustrate deductive arguments, this most influential statement on the nature of poetry in the Chinese tradition is presented in the form of exegesis of a particular text, answering general questions that will arise in the reading of *Kuan-chü* and other poems of the *Book of Songs*. If the highest values in Western traditions of discourse on literature are to be found in the genre of the treatise, which promises to tell us what poetry is in its "essence," to name its "parts" and the "force" that inheres in each part (taking Aristotle's *Poetics* as the paradigm), the model of authority in the Chinese tradition is inductive, going from specific poems to larger questions that follow from reading those poems. There are "treatises" in the Chinese tradition of discourse on literature, but until recent times these have lacked both the authority and the allure of critical comments grounded in response to specific texts.

THE "GREAT PREFACE" TO THE BOOK OF SONGS

關雎。后妃之德也。風之始也。所以風天下而正夫婦也。故用之鄉人焉。用之邦國焉。風。風也。教也。風以動之。教以化之。

Kuan-chü is the virtue (*tê**) of the Queen Consort and the beginning of the *Feng**. It is the means by which the world is influenced (*feng**) and by which the relations between husband and wife are made correct (*cheng**). Thus it is used in smaller communities, and it is used in larger states. "Airs" are "Influence";[3] it is "to teach." By influence it stirs them; by teaching it transforms them.

The root meaning of feng* is "wind". The term (finding a fortuitous counterpart in the English word airs) is also applied to the first of the four sections of the Book of Songs, the "Airs of the States," Kuo-feng 國風. By a dying and constantly revived metaphor of the way in which the wind sways the grass and plants, feng* also refers to "influence."[4] Feng* also applies to local customs or folkways (perhaps extending "influence" or "currents" to the way in which a particular community exerts social influence or the way in which social influence is exerted by higher authorities on a community). Finally, feng* 風 is related to and sometimes interchangeable with feng* 諷, "to criticize," the attempt to "influence" in a more limited sense. This rich semantic range of feng* is essential to the opening exposition of the Kuan-chü in this passage. The statement "Kuan-chü is . . . the beginning of feng*" works on several levels. First, it is a simple statement that Kuan-chü is the first poem in the Feng* section of the Book of Songs.[5] On a second level, the statement tells us that the Kuan-chü is the beginning of a process of "influence," a program of moral education implicit in the structure given the Book of Songs by its legendary editor, Confucius. Finally, on the level of historical reference, the song embodies the beginning of King Wen's "influence" and the course of moral civilization manifest in the history of the Chou Dynasty.

A theory of manifestation and of the perfect correspondence between inner and outer can lead to two movements, both of which are developed in the "Preface." Either the inner informs the outer manifestation, or the outer can be used to shape what lies within. The first of these movements is the production of the text, the manifestation of the inner condition of mind in the outer text, and the ability to know the inner through the outer. This movement, discussed in the previous chapter, is further elaborated in the next section of the "Great Preface."

The second movement—the regulatory and paradigmatic—is developed here. When people read and recite the Kuan-chü, not only do they recognize the "values" (chih*) of King Wen's consort, and thereby King Wen's role in forming the ideal marriage, but their own responses are also shaped by the values presented. The poems of the Book of Songs were meant to give paradigmatic expression to human feeling; and those who learned and recited the Songs would naturally internalize correct values. Thus through the dissemination of this poem, "the relations between husband and wife are made correct." Just as the inner state of mind becomes manifest in the outer (the poem), so the outer poem can also shape the inner state.

The role of the Songs in a process of moral education is sustained by stressing the semantic element of "influence," hence "teaching," in feng*. To assign this role to the Songs was not entirely new, but rather was an ethical, Confucian transformation of one of the oldest uses of the Songs in early oratory. The Songs were employed in roughly three ways in early oratory and in the prose essays that grew out of the tradition: first, to prove a point, by citing one of the Songs as authority; second, to express what the speaker "was intent upon" (chih*); and third, to persuade by "stirring" (hsing*) the emotions of the listeners in favor of the point of view presented by the orator.

In the third case of "stirring" (hsing*), it was assumed that the outer poem could be used to affect the inner disposition of the listener. Yet the orators assumed further that the suasive force of the Song had no inherent moral direction and could be directed to whatever purpose the orator might choose. Against this assumption of the emotional efficacy and ethical neutrality of the Book of Songs, there developed a Confucian counter-tradition, expressed here in the "Preface," that a particular moral force inhered in each poem of the Book of Songs. A particular moral force in a given poem could be determined and validated in only two ways: either by showing that it was the poem's "original" intent, thus by tracing the poem to its historical origins; or by showing its "editorial intent," that is, by determining why Confucius included it in the Book of Songs. This Confucian imperative to stabilize the ethical force of each poem of the Book of Songs led ultimately to the explanation that poetry was produced not as involuntary manifestation but as voluntary composition (or editing) for the sake of moral persuasion. We might call this a "didactic intention," so long as we realize that the purpose here is not to make people understand the Good, but rather to internalize the Good involuntarily so that it becomes "natural" for them. There is a hint of this in the present passage, when it speaks of the poem as a "means by which the world is influenced." As in the West, there will be millennia of conflict between the assumptions of voluntary and involuntary forces in the production of the poem.

詩者。志之所之也。在心為志。發言為詩。

The poem is that to which what is intently on the mind (chih*) goes. In the mind (hsin*) it is "being intent" (chih*); coming out in language (yen), it is a poem.

The immediate reference of "the poem" is, of course, the poems of the Book of Songs, but the passage becomes the canonical definition for all subsequent poetry. What poetry "is" and "should be" in the future is assumed immanent in the Book of Songs.

We should first consider how this statement differs from the definition of poetry given in the Book of Documents, namely, "the poem articulates what is intently on the mind" (shih* yen chih*). The "Great Preface" gives us a reformulation of that definition, but no reformulation is neutral: although acts of reformulation and paraphrase implicitly claim to be conceptually identical with their predecessor texts, they actually conceal some essential swerve. "The poem articulates what is intently on the mind" is a definition by process or action: the poem *is* what the poem does. On the other hand, "the poem is that to which what is intently on the mind goes" is a definition by equivalence: the definition is not as an action but in a restatement of the essence of *shih* in regard to its origins. In the "Great Preface" *shih* is explained as a "movement," a spatialization of poetic process in conformity to the fully established paradigm of "inner" (*nei* 內) and "outer" (*wai* 外). This becomes the ground of the psychology of poetic theory and links the movement in the production of the poem to the "extensive" aspect of communication in *shih* (*shih* is said to "go far").

The spatialization of poetic production in a "going" creates a model of movement across the boundaries between inner and outer. Thus we have the remarkable amplification in the next sentences: "In the mind it is *chih**; coming out in language, it is a poem." Now we have a "something," an X, which may be *chih** or *shih* depending on where it is located. This is very different indeed from the statement on *shih* in the *Book of Documents*: *shih* is not simply the "articulation" of *chih**; it *is chih**. This model of metamorphosis in spatial movement has another implication: when this X goes from its *chih** state to its *shih* state, there is a hint that the *chih** is evacuated and the tension inherent in *chih** is dissipated. This hint will be developed in later writers, speaking of the therapeutic necessity of poetry.

Poetry here is described in essentially psychological terms, not a "psychology of art," but art's place in a more broadly conceived psychology. This psychological definition was easily accommodated to the ethical and political interpretation of the *Book of Songs*; but because the human mind can be stirred in situations neither ethical nor political, the psychological definition was easily extended. It was likewise easily accommodated by the cosmological poetics of the *Wen-hsin tiao-lung* and other later theoretical works: the tensional disequilibrium of *chih**, which seeks to "go out" into the poem, was treated as a special case of the universal tendency of all things to move from latency to manifestation.

情動於中而形於言。言之不足。故嗟歎之。嗟歎之不足。故永歌之。永歌之不足。不知手之舞之。足之蹈之也。

The affections (*ch'ing**) are stirred within and take on form (*hsing**) in words (*yen**). If words alone are inadequate, we speak them out in sighs. If sighing is inadequate, we sing them. If singing them is inadequate, unconsciously our hands dance them and our feet tap them.

This passage is grounded in a psychology also developed in the "Record of Music" (*Yüeh-chi*) and in the writings of various Warring States philosophers. Humans are born in a state of equilibrium and silence. The affections, *ch'ing**, are stirred by outer things; but these stirrings are amorphous and prearticulate. Language gives shape to these amorphous affections, a bounded externality.

The passage places poetry within this theory of the relation between the affections and language by assuming a hierarchy of inner intensities and a parallel hierarchy of manifestations adequate to them. We should take careful note of the implication here: ordinary language and poetry have no inherent qualitative difference; they are differentiated only quantitatively by the degrees of intensity and complexity of the affections within. This hierarchy of degrees can be most clearly understood by resorting to physiological theories of *ch'i**, "breath" or "energy." In ordinary language *ch'i** or breath is expelled in the act of speaking. In more difficult emotional situations, still more breath comes out, creating a "sighing" intonation in speech. Singing (and later the chanting of poetry) is placed at the next degree of intensity in the expulsion of *ch'i**. Finally, when the mouth can no longer accommodate the accumulation of it, *ch'i** courses through the veins, throwing the body into movement, into dance.

In telling us what poetry "is," the passage tells us what poetry "should be." We learn that it is grounded in physiological processes, that it is physically "natural": poetry belongs to humanity in general; there is no qualitative difference between poets and non-poets (though there may be quantitative differences in the capacity to be stirred). The passage is traditionally taken to refer to the production of a poem, but we are uncertain whether it describes composing one's own poem or reciting a poem that already exists; that is, the essence of poetry resides in the situation of recitation and the immanence of the reciter's affections in the process; the question of who "owns" a particular poem is not raised. Finally, the "unconsciously" (*pu-chih* 不知) of the final clause makes explicit what had previously been only implicit: poetic expression is involuntary. That involuntariness is a guarantee of its authenticity and opens it completely to the hermeneutics in Mencius' "having knowledge of language" and Confucius' instructions to "look to how it is."

Unfortunately, three things soon became apparent. First, not everybody was a poet. Second, those who could write poetry could do so out of the mere intention to write a poem, without any deep inner compulsion or psychological necessity. Third, the composition of poetry could be a self-serving act, projecting an inauthentic image of the self to others. Throughout the history of Chinese literary thought, there have been subtle struggles between the realities of poetry and the values articulated in the "Great Preface."

Literary theory arises because a need is felt to justify poetry. The more voluminous and complex a tradition of literary thought is, the more the literature of that tradition is threatened by some challenge (often unstated) to its worth. In the poetry of the prophets and psalmodists of Israel and in early Greek poetry, a claim of divine inspiration gave poetry an authority for its being. But beginning with Aristotle in the West, as faith in divine authority receded and poetry came under rationalistic and utilitarian attack, there developed the attempt to give poetry a philosophical authority. Similarly, an intensely utilitarian current ran through pre-Han and Han thought, and classical exegesis became the means for traditionalists to justify the value of texts whose authority had once been simply taken for granted. Divine authority was never granted to poetry in the Chinese tradition (which is one reason it developed in such different directions from Western poetry). Instead, authority was granted to poetry by claiming that it was psychologically and physiologically "natural." The psychology of the "Great Preface" is elaborated to prove poetry's naturalness (the physiological aptness of "sighing," obviously an involuntary act, is given as an intermediate state between speaking and singing to support this "proof"). Poetry is thus sited in human nature and, in the following passage, in the larger context of human society.

情發於聲。聲成文謂之音。治世之音安以樂。其政和。亂世之音怨以怒。其政乖。亡國之音哀以思。其民困。

The affections (ch'ing*) emerge in sounds; when those sounds have patterning (wen*), they are called "tones." The tones of a well-managed age are at rest and happy; its government is balanced. The tones of an age of turmoil are bitter and full of anger; its government is perverse. The tones of a ruined state are filled with lament and brooding; its people are in difficulty.

Next we turn to the medium of this process of manifestation. The movement of the affections produces sheng*, "sound" or "voice," language's mode of externality. The more intense stirrings of the affections produce poetry and song, whose mode of externality is yin*, "tone." What differentiates "tone" from "sound" is wen*, "patterning." And we may recall that wen* is the quality which, as Confucius tells us in the Tso chuan passage, permits extension, "going far."

We should give some attention to how the argument of the "Great Preface" is developing. Beginning with a reformulation of the canonical definition of poetry in the Book of Documents, the "Great Preface" amplifies the process in both directions, going ever farther into the sequence of conditions out of which the poem originates (in this passage) and its consequences (in the following passage).

The affections, ch'ing*, are stirred; and when that stirring is intense, continuous, and directed to some end or goal, the tensional condition chih* occurs, which manifests itself externally as shih. Because of chih*'s increasingly strong political associations as "ambition," later ages would come to feel a strong opposition between "what the mind is intent upon" (chih*) and the affections (ch'ing*); but in the formative period of the "Preface," the late Warring States and Western Han, the two terms are closely related in a unified psychology: *ch'ing** is the stirring of mind in itself; *chih** is the mind's relation to some goal that follows from such stirring. The next stage in building this paradigm of poetic production is to ask what it is that stirs the affections. In this period the exegesis of the classics was largely concerned with the history of the Chou Dynasty as a normative model for the social order. Thus, the political and social conditions of an age are given as the primary external condition that stirs the affections, but it is obvious that other outer circumstances can do so as well. In later poetic theory, a large variety are given as the center or part of the origin of the poetic process— some moment in human relations (e.g., parting), the cycle of the seasons, an ancient site, some principle recognized in the landscape.

At this point we should remember that the description of the origins and consequences of poetic process are given here for the sake of a hermeneutics; that is, these passages are telling us how to understand the *Kuan-chü* and other poems of the *Book of Songs*. In the passage above we learn that in reading the poem we know the condition of the age (cf. Mencius on "going on further to make friends"). In poetry we know those conditions through heightened responses, which carry enough energy to cause language to become "patterned," *wen**, which, as Confucius tells us, made it possible for these poems to "go far" and come down to us.

Although we may know an earlier world through the poems of the *Book of Songs*, the Classic is not descriptive history. Even in this most historical interpretation of the nature of poetry, the past world that we encounter through the poem is radically mediated by the mind of one person. We do not apprehend that world directly, but rather know it through the way it affected the poet. As the "Great Preface" says later of the *Feng**: "they are rooted in a single person."

This inner mediation of a particular mind had important consequences for the development of poetry. How do we know the originating circumstance from which the poem arose?—not by specific representations of those circumstances, either literal or figurative, but by a mood: "at rest" (*an* 安), "bitter" (*yüan* 怨), "filled with lament" (*ai* 哀). Mood, closely associated with the effects of music, became an important part of Chinese literary and aesthetic thought. Moods are not open to easy analysis, but neither are they vague. Later Chinese literary thought developed a complex vocabulary of moods, which, though overlapping, were immediately recognizable. From the theory of poetry developing here, it should be obvious why mood would become a central aesthetic category: mood is an integral of the mind's operations, not simply "what" a person says, but some integral embodying the person's relation to the statement. It is a way of unifying "how it is," "from what it comes," and "in what a person would be at rest."

故正得失。動天地。感鬼神。莫近於詩。先王以是經夫婦。成孝敬。厚人倫。美教化。移風俗。

Thus to correct (*cheng**) [the presentation of] achievements (*tê**) and failures, to move Heaven and Earth, to stir the gods and spirits, there is nothing more apposite than poetry. By it the former kings managed the relations between husbands and wives, perfected the respect due to parents and superiors, gave depth to human relations, beautifully taught and transformed the people, and changed local customs.

This passage shifts back from the question of knowing to the regulatory function of poetry. Not only does poetry result from the affections being "moved," *tung* 動, poetry "moves" others as well—in this case, Heaven and Earth. Poetry "stirs," *kan**, as well as originating from some stirring. A Newtonian physics is at work here, a transmission of equal force. Considering this power, the "Great Preface" shifts from poetry as the involuntary manifestation of a state of mind to poetry as an instrument of civilization, something "apposite," *chin* 近, "close at hand," either for the task or for the ease of use.

We see the regulatory power of poetry in a full range of human relations: husband and wife, parent and child, superior and inferior, and other relations. Finally we see its most general function, as an instrument of *chiao-hua**, "teaching and transforming," with the effect of "changing local customs" over all the world.

Poetry occupied a very important place in the Confucian cultural program, but its instruction is not supposed to be coercive. Instead, according to the K'ung Ying-ta commentary, when combined with their music, the poems of the *Book of Songs* were supposed to influence people to good behavior unconsciously: listeners apprehended and thus came to share a virtuous state of mind, and the motions of their own affections would be shaped by that experience. But this Edenic power was possible only in those days when the poems still had their music; in this later age, with the original music lost and only the naked texts remaining, commentary is required to show the virtue that was then immanent in all the poems.

故詩有六義焉。一曰風。二曰賦。三曰比。四曰興。五曰雅。六曰頌。

Thus there are six principles (*yi**) in the poems: 1) Airs (*feng**); 2) exposition (*fu*); 3) comparison (*pi**); 4) affective image, (*hsing**); 5) Odes (*ya**); 6) Hymns (*sung*).

Much ink has been spilled to explain why the "Six Principles" (*liu-yi**) are presented in this sequence.[6] The problem is that two essentially distinct orders have been mixed together. "Airs" (*feng**), "Odes," and "Hymns" are the three main divisions of the *Book of Songs*. *Fu*, *pi**, and *hsing** are three modes of presentation under which any poem in the collection might be clas-

sified (though the Mao commentary notes only those poems that are hsing*).
Fu, "exposition," is any unfigured sequence. If in the fu mode a speaker describes a swiftly flowing stream, that stream is taken to be present in the
scene, perhaps one that the speaker of the poem must cross. Fu encompasses
direct description, narration, and explanation of what is on the speaker's
mind.[7] Pi*, "comparison," means that the central images of the poem are
simile or metaphor; the reader anticipates figuration.

The category hsing*, "affective image," has drawn the most attention
from both traditional theorists and modern scholars. Hsing* is an image
whose primary function is not signification but, rather, the stirring of a particular affection or mood: hsing* does not "refer to" that mood; it generates
it. Hsing* is therefore not a rhetorical figure in the proper sense of the term.
Furthermore, the privilege of hsing* over fu and pi* in part explains why
traditional China did not develop a complex classification system of rhetorical figures, such as we find in the West. Instead there develop classifications
of moods, with categories of scene and circumstance appropriate to each.
This vocabulary of moods follows from the conception of language as the
manifestation of some integral state of mind, just as the Western rhetoric
of schemes and tropes follows from a conception of language as sign and
referent.[8]

上以風化下。下以風刺上。主文而譎諫。言之者無罪。聞之者足以戒。故曰風。

By feng* those above transform those below; also by feng* those below criticize those above. When an admonition is given that is governed by patterning (wen*), the one who speaks it has no culpability, yet it remains adequate
to warn those who hear it. In this we have feng*.

Feng* is used here in the sense of "influence" (social superior to social inferior) and in the sense of "criticism" (social inferior to social superior). In
either case the capacity of feng* to "go far" is here defined as a movement
between social classes.

Just as in the Western tradition fictionality or poiesis is granted special
license to violate social taboo, so wen* is supposed to place its user in a
protected domain, free from the culpability normally attendant on criticizing
authority. Wen* does not conceal the message (the listener or reader still
recognizes it clearly enough to take warning), but it protects socially dangerous discourse. It is unclear precisely why this should be the case, unless the
claim of involuntarism in the production of such poems frees the speaker
from the usual requirements of respectful decorum. The clause, "the one who
speaks has no culpability," became very important for later writers of social
criticism (even though the authorities did not always respect the right of
literary sanctuary).

至于王道衰。禮義廢。政教失。國異政。家殊俗。而變風變雅作矣。國史明乎得失之迹。傷人倫之廢。哀刑政之苛。吟詠情性以風其上。達於事變。而懷其舊俗者也。故變風發乎情。止乎禮義。發乎情。民之性也。止乎禮義。先王之澤也。

When the royal Way declined rites and moral principles (*yi**) were abandoned; the power of government to teach failed; the government of the states changed; the customs of the family were altered. And at this point the mutated (*pien**) *feng** and the mutated *ya** were written. The historians of the states understood clearly the marks of success and failure; they were pained by the abandonment of proper human relations and lamented the severity of punishments and governance. They sang their feelings (*hsing*-ch'ing**) to criticize (*feng**) those above, understanding the changes (*pien**) that had taken place and thinking about former customs. Thus the mutated *feng** (*pien-feng**) emerge from the affections (*ch'ing**), but they go no further than rites and moral principles. That they should emerge from the affections is human nature (*hsing**); that they go no further than rites and moral principles is the beneficent influence of the former kings.

Chinese literary historical process was often described in terms of the movement between "proper" (*cheng**) and "mutated" (*pien**). These terms are replete with value judgment and in this context are firmly linked to issues of moral history. *Cheng** describes the stability of a government and society functioning properly, a stability that is manifest in the "tone" of the poems of that age. *Pien** appears in this context as a falling away, a "devolution," in which the growing imbalances in society manifest themselves in poetry. These terms never became entirely free of value judgments that were ultimately rooted in moral history; in later ages, however, there was some attempt to use them in a purely literary sense. In this context *cheng** might represent the norm of some genre, the *pien** would be a falling away from that norm; these processes of attaining a norm and subsequent devolution might operate independent from the moral history of dynasties.

A thorny problem follows from the description of poetry in the "Great Preface," a problem that the passage above attempts to address and resolve. If the "mutated *feng**" come from a period of moral decline, they will simply manifest moral decline; in that case the value of such poems as ethical paradigms becomes suspect. The "Great Preface" solves this problem by the mediation of the "historians of the states," given as the putative writers of "mutated *feng**." Thus we are to read "mutated *feng**" not simply as manifestations of moral decline, but rather as responses by virtuous men to the problem of moral decline. If we read a love poem from the *Book of Songs* in which the lovers are obviously not following the proper courtship and marriage rites, we are to read it as having a tone of disapproval and criticism, to read it from the point of view of a virtuous man who sees this present behavior in the context of "former customs." This bit of exegetical ingenuity keeps the interpretation of the *Book of Songs* consonant with Confucius' dictum that in all its three hundred poems there are "no warped thoughts" (*Analects* II.2). It should be added that when the great classical exegete Chu Hsi (1130–1200) made his authoritative reinterpretation of the *Book of Songs*, he did away with the mediation of the historians of the states as the writers of the "mutated" *Songs* and took the poems as direct manifestations of the times (thus a poem revealing a breakdown of rites would come directly from those infected by the decadence of the age). As a result of this reasonable revision, Chu Hsi was forced to reinterpret Confucius' statement on the absence of "warped thoughts" by explaining that the proper judgment of the poem resides in the moral capacity of the reader (thus bringing the interpretation closer to Mencius' "having knowledge of language").

The mediation of the "historians of the states" created another problem for the writer(s) of the "Great Preface." That the poems were produced spontaneously by human nature had to be reaffirmed; but it was recognized that the affections, once stirred, tended to go to imbalance and excess. The historians of the states, living in a corrupt age, must have had natural responses distinct from others in the times. Their responses were both moral and natural because they had internalized the "rites and moral principles" which came from the "beneficent influence of the former kings." These internalized values placed a decent limit on the motions of the affections. Essential here is the fact that in the Confucian tradition emotion and moral judgment were not set in antithesis; natural response was given high value, and a moral judgment had to be produced spontaneously in order to be valid. Morality, in the form of "rites and moral principles (*yi**)," was a limit of moderation applied to a concept of the affections as a motion from stillness to excess; this moral limit bounded and gave normative expression to the affections. Thus a claim could be made that in the *Book of Songs* even the "mutated *feng**" were spontaneous and completely natural, while at the same time remaining morally paradigmatic.

The final section of the "Great Preface" distinguishes the three generic divisions of the *Book of Songs*, with the further division of the Odes into "Greater" and "Lesser." The four sections ("*Feng**," "Lesser Odes," "Greater Odes," and "Hymns") yield the "Four Beginnings," *Ssu-shih* 四始. These are four levels on which the moral history of the Chou is played out, each level or section being a sequence that moves from "proper" into "mutation."

是以一國之事。繫一人之本。謂之風。言天下之事。形四方之風。謂之雅。雅者正也。言王政之所由廢興也。政有小大。故有小雅焉。有大雅焉。頌者。美盛德之形容。以其成功告於神明者也。是謂四始。詩之至也。

Thus the affairs of a single state, rooted in [the experience of] a single person are called *Feng**. To speak of the affairs of the whole world and to describe customs (*feng**) common to all places is called *Ya**. *Ya** means "proper" (*cheng**). These show the source of either flourishing or ruin in the royal government. Government has its greater and lesser aspects; thus we have a "Greater *Ya**" and a "Lesser *Ya**." The "Hymns" (*Sung*) give the outward shapes of praising full virtue, and they inform the spirits about the accomplishment of great deeds. These are called the "Four Beginnings" and are the ultimate perfection of the poems.

SUPPLEMENT
Selections from Hsün-tzu, "On Music"

夫樂者樂也。人情之所必不免也。故人不能無樂。樂則必發於聲音。形於動靜。而人之道
聲音動靜性術之變盡是矣。故人不能不樂。樂則不能無形。形而不為道。則不能無亂。先
王惡其亂也。故制雅頌之聲以道之。使其聲足以樂而不流。使其文足以辨而不息。使其曲
直繁省廉肉節奏足以感動人之善心。使夫邪汙之氣無由得接焉。是先王立樂之方也。

. . . .

故聽其頌雅之聲而志意得廣焉。執其干戚。習其俯仰屈伸。而容貌得莊焉。行其綴兆。要
其節奏。而行列得正焉。進退得齊焉。…故樂者天下之大齊也。中和之紀也。人情之所必
不免也。

. . . .

夫聲樂之入人也深。其化人也速。故先王謹為之文。樂中平則民和而不流。樂肅莊則民齊
而不亂。

Music is delight,[9] which is inevitable in the human affections (*ch'ing**). A person cannot help but have delight; and such delight always emerges in sounds and takes on form in movement.[10] In the Way of man, sounds and movements and the mutations (*pien**) in his nature are all to be found here [in music]. As a person cannot but feel delight, that delight cannot but take on form. Nevertheless, if that form is not guided,[11] then it will necessarily be disorderly. The kings of old hated such disorder and thus organized the sounds [or notes] of the Odes (*Ya**) and Hymns [of the *Book of Songs*] to provide guidance. They made the sounds [i.e., the music of the Odes and Hymns] adequate for showing delight without letting it run into dissolution;[12] they made the texts (*wen**)[13] [of the Odes and Hymns] adequate to make proper distinctions without leading people into corruption. They made the various aspects of performance—tremolo and sustained notes, symphony and solo, lushness and austerity, and the rhythms—adequate to stir the good in people's hearts. They made this so that there was no way that a corrupt *ch'i** would be able to reach people. This was the way in which the kings of old established music.

. . . .

When a person listens to the sounds of the Odes and Hymns, his intentions (*chih*-yi**) are broadened. When a person takes up shield and ax [for the war dance] and practices its moves, his appearance and bearing will achieve gravity from it. When he moves in the proper order and to the proper places in the dance, and when his movements keep to the rhythm, a sense of correct rank and order will come from it, and a knowledge of when to advance and when to withdraw will be in balance . . . Thus music is the supreme balancer of the world,[14] the guideline of a medial harmony, and something that cannot be dispensed with for the human affections.[15]

. . . .

Musical sounds penetrate deeply into a person, and they transform a person swiftly. Thus the kings of old used great caution in giving them pattern [or texts, *wen**]. If the music is even, then the people will be in harmony and not slip into dissolution. If the music is grave and stern, then the people will be balanced and avoid disorder . . .

SUPPLEMENT
Selections from the "Record of Music"

The *Book of Rites* (*Li chi* 禮記) has only the most tenuous claim to the status of a Confucian Classic. It is a Western Han miscellany of largely Confucian texts from the Warring States and Han. Among its "chapters" is a treatise on the origins of, functions of, and relations between music and rites: the *Yüeh chi* 樂記 or "Record of Music." Much of the material in this work appears, only slightly recast, in the "Treatise on Music," *Yüeh shu* 樂書, in the *Historical Records* (*Shih chi* 史記) of Ssu-ma Ch'ien 司馬遷 (145–86? B.C.). In both of these texts we find again some of the material that went into the making of the "Great Preface," along with a fuller elaboration of the psychology on which the "Great Preface" is based.

The "Record of Music" and the "Great Preface" share a concern for reconciling the spontaneous expression of feeling and its normative regulation. As the "mutated *feng**," composed by the "historians of the states," are generated spontaneously but stop at decent norms, so here "rites" are the natural expression of human feeling that finds a normative and limiting form. Out of this comes the beautiful distinction between the roles of music and rites in ceremony: rites assert the distinction of roles in human relations, while music overcomes these distinctions and unifies the participants.

凡音之起。由人心生也。人心之動物使之然也。感於物而動。故形於聲。聲相應。故生變。變成文。謂之音。比音而樂之。及干戚羽旄。謂之樂。樂者。音之所由生也。其本在人心之感於物也。是故其哀心感者。其聲噍以殺。其樂心感者。其聲嘽以緩。其喜心感者。其聲發以散。其怒心感者。其聲粗以厲。其心敬心感者。其聲直以廉。其愛心感者。

其聲和以柔。六者非性也。感於物而后動。是故先王慎所以感之者。故禮以道其志。樂以和其聲。政以一其行。刑以防其姦。禮樂刑政。其極一也。所以同民心。而出治道也。

All tones (*yin*) that arise are generated from the human mind (*hsin**). When the human mind is moved (*tung**), some external thing (*wu**) has caused it. Stirred (*kan**) by external things into movement, it takes on form (*hsing**) in sound. When these sounds respond (*ying*) to one another, mutations (*pien**, i.e., changes from one sound to another) arise; and when these mutations constitute a pattern (*wen**),[16] they are called "tones." When such tones are set side by side and played on musical instruments, with shield and battle-ax for military dances or with feathered pennons for civil dances, it is called "music."

Music originates from tone. Its root (*pen*) lies in the human mind's being stirred (*kan**) by external things. Thus, when a mind that is miserable is stirred, its sound is vexed and anxious. When a mind that is happy is stirred, its sound is relaxed and leisurely. When a mind that is delighted is stirred, its sound pours out and scatters. When a wrathful mind is stirred, its sound is crude and harsh. When a respectful mind is stirred, its sound is upright and pure. When a doting mind is stirred, its sound is agreeable and yielding. These six conditions are not in innate nature (*hsing**): they are set in motion only after being stirred by external things. Thus the former kings exercised caution in what might cause stirring. For this reasons we have rites to guide what is intently on the mind (*chih**); we have music to bring those sounds into harmony (*ho*); we have government to unify action; and we have punishment to prevent transgression. Rites, music, government, and punishment are ultimately one and the same—a means to unify the people's minds and correctly execute the Way.

One problem arises in the phrasing of the six conditions of mind: we might expect that the response of the mind would follow from the nature of what stirred it; that is, "when the mind is stirred by something happy . . . ," and so on. That is a possible interpretation of the passage, but the phrasing of the Chinese suggests that the mind has been previously disposed to one of these conditions, and the stirring brings it out. In no case, of course, are these six conditions innate.

凡音者生人心者也。情動於中。故形於聲。聲成文謂之音。是故治世之音安以樂。其政和。亂世之音怨以怒。其政乖。亡國之音哀以思。其民困。聲音之道與政通矣。

. . . .

All tones are generated from the human mind. The affections (*ch'ing**) are moved within and take on form in sound. When these sounds have patterning (wen*), they are called "tones." The tones of a well-managed age are at rest and happy: its government is balanced (ho). The tones of an age of turmoil are bitter and full of anger: its government is perverse. The tones of a ruined state are filled with lament and brooding: its people are in difficulty. The way of sounds and tones (sheng-yin) communicates (t'ung*) with [the quality of] governance.

[Section omitted elaborating the correspondences between the five notes and government offices and social problems implicit in some musical disorder in each of the notes.]

Note the near identity of this passage with statements in the "Great Preface": "The affections (ch'ing*) are stirred within and take on form (hsing*) in words (yen)"; and "the affections (ch'ing*) emerge in sounds; when those sounds have patterning (wen*), they are called 'tones.'" The two works also have in common passages on the correlation between the quality of music and the social situation of the age in which it was produced. These seem to be widely held commonplaces, often reworked and amplified with ever new variations to account for new terms and situations, moving ever deeper into origins and consequences. This movement of continuous repetition around a center was one common form of exposition.

凡音者生於人心者也。樂者通倫理者也。是故知聲而不知音者。禽獸是也。知音而不知樂者。眾庶是也。惟君子為能知樂。是故審聲以知音。審音以知樂。審樂以知政。而治道備矣。是故不知聲者。不可與言音。不知音者。不可與言樂。知樂。則幾於禮矣。禮樂皆得。謂之有德。德者得也。

All tones are generated from the human mind. Music is that which communicates (t'ung*, "carries through") human relations and natural principles (li*). The birds and beasts understand sounds but do not understand tones. The common people understand tones but do not understand music. Only the superior person (chün-tzu) is capable of understanding music. Thus one examines sounds to understand tone; one examines tone to understand music; one examines music to understand government, and then the proper execution of the Way is complete. Thus one who does not understand sounds can share no discourse on tones; one who does not understand tones can share no discourse on music. When someone understands music, that person is almost at the point of understanding rites. And when rites and music are both attained (tê*), it is called Tê* ["virtue" or "attainment"], for Tê* is an "attaining" (tê*).

Presumably the "examination of music to understand government" follows from the earlier passage in which, from listening to music, a person can tell the condition of society. One might point out here how, in traditional arguments such as this, stages of a process are closely related to hierarchies.

是故樂之隆非極音也。食饗之禮非致味也。清廟之瑟朱弦而疏越。壹倡而三歎。有遺音者矣。大饗之禮。尚玄酒而俎腥魚。大羹不和。有遺味者矣。是故先王之制禮樂也。非以極口腹耳目之欲也。將以敎民平好惡。而反人道之正也。

The true glory of music is not the extreme of tone; the rites of the Great Banquet are not the ultimate in flavor (wei*). The zither used in performing "Pure Temple" [one of the Hymns in the *Book of Songs*] has red strings and few sounding holes. One sings, and three join in harmony; there are tones which are omitted. In the rite of the Great Banquet, one values water [literally "the mysterious liquor"] and platters of raw meat and fish; the great broth is not seasoned [*ho*, "harmonized"]; there are flavors which are omitted. We can see from this that when the former kings set the prescriptions for music and rites, they did not take the desires of mouth, belly, ears, and eyes to their extremes, in order thereby to teach people to weigh likes and dislikes in the balance and lead the people back to what is proper (*cheng**).

Here the aesthetics of omission, so important in later Chinese literary thought, is given its earliest enunciation, in an ethical context. The perfect music holds back from overwhelming force; the sense that something is omitted brings response from others, draws them in. The phrase "one sings, and three join in harmony" will come to be commonly used for precisely such aesthetic restraint as engages others. In its original context here in the "Record of Music," however, that restraint has an ethical rather than an aesthetic force. Omission is the embodiment of the principle of proper limits in sensuous satisfaction.

人生而靜。天之性也。感於物而動。性之欲也。物至知知。然後好惡形焉。好惡無節於內。知誘於外。不能反躬。天理滅矣。夫物之感人無窮。而人之好惡無節。則是物至而人化物也。人化物也者。滅天理而窮人欲者也。於是有悖逆詐偽之心。有淫泆作亂之事。是故強者脅弱。眾者暴寡。知者詐愚。勇者苦怯。疾病不養。老幼孤獨不得其所。此大亂之道也。

A human being is born calm: this is his innate nature (*hsing**) endowed by Heaven. To be stirred by external things and set in motion is desire occurring within that innate nature. Only after things encounter conscious knowledge do likes and dislike take shape (*hsing*). When likes and dislikes have no proper measure within, and when knowing is enticed from without, the person becomes incapable of self-reflection, and the Heaven-granted principle (*T'ien-li**) of one's being perishes. When external things stir a person endlessly and when that person's likes and dislikes are without proper measure, then when external things come before a person, the person is transformed (*hua**) by those things. When a person is transformed by things, it destroys the Heaven-granted principle of that person's being and lets him follow all human desires to their limit. Out of this comes the refractory and deceitful mind; out of this come occurrences (*shih**) of wallowing excess and turmoil. Then the powerful coerce the weak; the many oppress the few; the smart deceive the stupid; the brave make the timid suffer; the sick are not cared for; old and young and orphans have no place—this is the Way of supreme turbulence.

This is a distinctly Hobbesian view of human society, with its Chinese roots in the Confucianism of Hsün-tzu. Here traditional morality exists to place limits on the disruptive force of human desire. The phrase translated as "conscious knowledge" is literally "knowing knowing," *chih-chih* 知知.

是故先王之制禮樂。人為之節。衰麻哭泣。所以節喪紀也。鐘鼓干戚。所以和安樂也。昏姻冠笄。所以別男女也。射鄉食饗。所以正交接也。禮節民心。樂和民聲。政以行之。刑以防之。禮樂刑政。四達而不悖。則王道備矣。

樂者為同。禮者為異。同則相親。異則相敬。樂勝則流。禮勝則離。合情飾貌者。禮樂之事也。禮義立。則貴賤等矣。樂文同。則上下和矣。好惡著。則賢不肖別矣。刑禁暴。爵舉賢。則政均矣。仁以愛之。義以正之。如此。則民治行矣。

For this reason the former kings set the prescriptions of rites and music and established proper measures for the people. By weeping in mourning clothes of hemp, they gave proper measure to funerals. By bell and drum, shield and battle-ax [for military dances] they gave harmony (*ho*) to expressions of happiness. By the cap and hairpin of the marriage ceremony, they distinguished male and female. By festive games and banquets they formed the correct associations between men. Rites gave the proper measure to the people's minds; music made harmony in human sounds; government carried things out; punishments prevented [transgression]. When these four were fully achieved and not refractory, the royal way was complete.

Music unifies; rites set things apart. In unifying there is a mutual drawing close; in setting things apart there is mutual respect. If music overwhelms, there is a dissolving;[17] if rites overwhelm, there is division. To bring the affections into accord and to adorn their outward appearance is the function (*shih**) of music and rites. When rites and ceremonies are established, then noble and commoner find their own levels; when music unifies them, then those above and those below are joined in harmony. When likes and dislikes have this manifest form, then the good person and the unworthy person can be distinguished. By punishments one prevents oppression; by rewards one raises up the good; if these prevail, then government is balanced. By fellow-feeling one shows love; by moral principles (*yi**) one corrects them, and in this way the management of the people proceeds.

If the Confucianism of *Hsün-tzu* seeks to control dangerous forces, Han Confucianism seeks to hold opposing forces in balance. Rites define functions in social relations and thus are a system of distinctions. As a system of distinctions, however, rites always threaten to pull people apart and set them in opposition to one another. That dangerous force in rites is countered by music, which is shared by all participants in a ceremony; it is music that makes them feel like a unified body. Yet that impulse to unity threatens to destroy distinctions, and thus it is counterbalanced by rites.

樂由中出。禮自外作。樂由中出故情。禮自外作故文。

Music comes from within; rites are formed without. Since music comes from within, it belongs to genuine affections (*ch'ing**); since rites are formed without, they have patterning (*wen**).[18]

Here we can see clearly how the balance between music and rites parallels the theory of poetry, which likewise has its origins within, in the affections, and finds bounded external expression in something with "pattern," *wen**.

大樂必易。大禮必簡。樂至則無怨。禮至則不爭。揖讓而治天下者。禮樂之謂也。暴民不作。諸侯賓服。兵革不試。五刑不用。百姓無患。天子不怒。如此則樂達矣。四海之內。合父子之親。明長幼之序。以敬天子。如此則禮行矣。
大樂與天地同和。大禮與天地同節。和故百物不失。節故祀天祭地。明則有禮樂。幽則有鬼神。如此則四海之內。合敬同愛矣。禮者殊事合敬者也。樂者異文合愛者也。禮樂之情同。故明王以相沿也。故事與時並。名與功偕。

The supreme music must be easy; the supreme rites must be simple. When music is perfect, there is no rancor; when rites are perfect, there is no contention. To bow and yield, yet govern the world is the true meaning of rites and music. There is no oppression of the people; the feudal lords submit; armor is not worn; the five punishments are not used; no calamity befalls the masses; the Son of Heaven feels no wrath—when things are thus, music has been perfected. Within the four seas fathers and sons are joined in affection, the precedence between elder and younger is kept clear, and respect is shown to the Son of Heaven—when things are like this, rites are in practice.

The supreme music shares the harmony of Heaven and Earth. The supreme rites share the proper measure of Heaven and Earth. In the harmony of the former, none of the hundred things fail; in the proper measure of the latter, the sacrifices are offered to Heaven and Earth. In their manifest aspect, they are rites and music; in their unseen aspect, they are spiritual beings. When things are like this, then all within four seas are brought together in respect and love. Though acts differ in the performance of a rite, these acts share the quality of respect. Though music has different patterns, these are brought together in the quality of love. Since the affections involved in music and rites remain the same, wise kings have followed them. Thus when act and occasion are matched, fame and accomplishment are joined.

This rapturous Confucian vision of society, functioning in harmony with human nature and universal nature through music and rites, is not directly related to literature. However, it provides an essential background for the interest, recurring throughout the history of Chinese literary thought, in the coincidence of genuine feeling and form.

A Discourse on Literature

Ts'ao P'i's 曹丕 (187–226) "Discourse on Literature," *Lun-wen* 論文, was not originally a separate essay on letters, but rather a chapter from his *Authoritative Discourses, Tien-lun* 典論. This work, initially in twenty chapters, composed when Ts'ao P'i was first chosen as Crown Prince (217–218), exists now only in fragments.[1] The present version of "A Discourse on Literature" survived because of its inclusion in the famous Liang anthology, the *Wen hsüan*. Other fragments from the "Discourse," moreover, not included in the present version, have been preserved independently elsewhere and suggest that the *Wen hsüan* version of the "Discourse" is incomplete.[2] *Authoritative Discourses* belonged to a long tradition of collected discourses on general knowledge, and such collections usually included at least one essay treating some aspect of language or writing.[3] The "Discourse," however, is structurally unique. Ts'ao P'i wrote in the "plain style" advocated by Wang Ch'ung 王充 in his collected discourses, the *Lun-heng* 論衡; but there are forces at work in "A Discourse on Literature" that twist the line of thought at key points and produce an argument more quirky and personal than anything in the lucidly magistral expositions of Wang Ch'ung.

Han literary thought continued directly from that of the Warring States period and was primarily concerned with writing's role in maintaining social ethics, particularly applying to a court literature that directed and restrained the actions of a prince. One consequence of this dominant interest was a predisposition to view the domain of writing as an integral whole, with no clear division between "literary" and "non-literary" works, except as a distinction in relative degrees of ornamentation. Immense changes in the nature and concept of literature were occurring in the last decades of the Han, the period known as the Chien-an; but most reflective statements on literature in the period remained within the scope of earlier Han issues. In Ts'ao P'i's "Discourse" these changes begin to find expression.

From his final reference to Hsü Kan's 徐幹 *Discourses on the Mean, Chung-lun* 中論, it is clear that Ts'ao P'i still considered collected discourses (including his own *Authoritative Discourses*) within the scope of *wen**, "literature" or "belles lettres" (later such discursive prose would be classified as *tzu* 子, "the literature of knowledge"). From his enumeration of genres in the "Discourse," however, we see that the idea of *wen** (encompassing poetry, poetic expositions or *fu*, and short prose forms) had attained roughly the range it would maintain throughout the rest of the history of traditional Chinese civilization. Moreover, even though Ts'ao P'i echoed the old Han themes throughout the "Discourse," the central issues he raises surrounding *wen** were no longer the venerable Han concerns regarding the conflict between moral force and the seductive, potentially immoral forces that may be carried in writing. Literature is by no means treated as an autonomous art in the "Discourse," but Ts'ao P'i's primary concern is not ethics; rather he is interested in how personality comes to be inscribed in writing, what makes writing compelling rather than morally "good," and the immortality that a writer may hope to achieve.

"A Discourse on Literature" is not a profound work of literary theory. Its primary historical interest is the way it articulates new concerns that are obvious in the literature of the period and in other areas of intellectual activity. It is clear, however, that Ts'ao P'i's sense of his own self-worth is very much caught up in this statement on literature. The associations he makes in the piece, moreover, make us aware of an unusual mind at work; and the primary value of the "Discourse" is perhaps as a literary work in its own right.

A DISCOURSE ON LITERATURE

文人相輕。自古而然。傅毅之於班固。伯仲之間耳。而固小之。與弟超書曰。武仲以能屬文為蘭臺令史。下筆不能自休。

Literary men disparage one another—it's always been that way. The relation between Fu Yi [d. 90] and Pan Ku [32–92] was nothing less than the relation of a younger brother to an elder brother.[4] Yet Pan Ku belittled him, writing in a letter to his elder brother Pan Chao [33–108]: "Wu-chung [Fu Yi] became

Imperial Librarian through his facility in composition: whenever he used his writing brush, he couldn't stop himself."[5]

The opening is abrupt and unexpected, as if Ts'ao P'i were remarking on some event outside the text, offering a general proposition and historical example to prove the truth of his observation. It is an essay that begins with a tinge of contempt for literary men, who belittle one another in courting princely favor; yet the essay ends in awe at their achievements, as political power yields place to the power of writing. The historical anecdote that Ts'ao P'i cites links writing to political advancement (though the final value ascribed to writing in the "Discourse" turns out to be quite different), and the belittling seems to arise from envy: writing gains something for the individual, an aggrandizement of self that others may also desire.[6] And in the anecdote, in order to attain the object of desire (office), there is a peculiar ratio between motivated action (the possibility of writing in order to get office) and lack of control ("he couldn't stop himself").

夫人善於自見。而文非一體。鮮能備善。是以各以所長相輕所短。里語曰。家有弊帚。享之千金。斯不自見之患也。

People are good at [or fond of] making themselves known; but since literature (wen*) is not of one form (t'i*) alone, few can be good at everything.[7] Thus each person disparages that in which he is weak by the criterion of those things in which he is strong. There is a village saying: "The worn-out broom that belongs to my own household is worth a thousand in gold." Such is the ill consequence of a lack of self-awareness.

The idea of "making oneself known" through literature is the volitional variation on the canonical statement that "poetry articulates what is intently on the mind (chih*)." It passes, however, beyond the simple desire to be understood (see pp. 29–30) to a broader desire for later ages to understand "who you were." This motive for writing had an antecedent in Ssu-ma Ch'ien's comment that Yü Ch'ing was unable to write in order "to make himself known to later generations."[8] In Ts'ao P'i's variation on this motive, it is unclear in precisely what sense a person wants to be known (i.e., whether it is merely to have fame, or to have one's abilities recognized, or to be understood as a person in some profound sense), but it is clear that the possibility is a powerful motive. For Ts'ao P'i that motive is dangerous and corrupting. Ts'ao P'i is the prince from whom writers seek recognition; but instead of recognizing any degree of talent or particular quality, he notices first of all the desire to be known itself and the power of that desire to distort the writer's judgment.

The distortion of judgment follows from partiality to oneself and to one's own particular skills. The issue of partiality becomes closely connected with the developing concept of personality type. Here at the beginning of Ts'ao P'i's argument, writing is merely the means of "making oneself known" and thereby valued. As we said, it is not yet clear precisely what the writer hopes will be recognized and valued—some quantitative degree of talent or some differentiated sense of identity (such as personality type, the "kind" of person he is). A skill in and thus a partiality for a certain kind of writing (t'i*) shifts imperceptibly to the association of a given type of personality with a particular t'i* in writing. Instead of being a mere area of a particular writer's skill, the literary t'i* comes to seem to possess an organic affinity with a certain type of personality. From this it follows, however, that such a manifestation of typological identity is also the appearance of partiality and limitation.

"[S]ince literature is not of one form alone, few can be good at everything." There is some limited totality of "kinds of writing" (t'i*) whose "full complement" (pei) can theoretically be attained (however rare such attainment may be). Ts'ao P'i has set up two levels of value, one involving a particular excellence (whose limitation is inseparable from individual or typological identity), and the other involving comprehensive excellence, in which all particular excellences are combined (a capacity associated with the Sage/ruler). To possess a particular excellence blinds a person to the value of others and to one's own limitations. The comprehensive excellence of the Sage/ruler, who needs to assign individual abilities to their appropriate government functions, must encompass and appreciate each particular excellence, rejecting the notion of the superiority of any one particular excellence over another; yet at the same time in his own superiority he may show contempt for the inherent limitation of any single particular excellence.

今之文人。魯國孔融文舉。廣陵陳琳孔璋。山陽王粲仲宣。北海徐幹偉長。陳留阮瑀元瑜。汝南應瑒德璉。東平劉楨公幹。斯七子者。於學無所遺。於辭無所假。咸以自騁驥騄於千里。仰齊足而並馳。以此相服。亦良難矣。

The literary men of this day are K'ung Jung [153–208], called Wen-chü, of the state of Lu; Ch'en Lin [d. 217], called K'ung-chang, of Kuang-ling; Wang Ts'an [177–217], called Chung-hsüan, of Shang-yang; Hsü Kan [170–217], called Wei-ch'ang, of Pei-hai; Juan Yü [ca. 165–212], called Yüan-yü, of Ch'en-liu; Ying Ch'ang [d. 217], called Tê-lien, of Ju-nan; and Liu Chen [d. 217], called Kung-kan, of Tung-p'ing. These seven masters have omitted nothing in their learning, have no borrowed colors in their diction (tz'u*). Yet they have found it most difficult to all gallop together a thousand leagues, side by side with equal pace on their mighty steeds, and thus to pay one another due respect.[9]

Following Ts'ao P'i's previous observations, this catalogue of writers strongly suggests that each has his own partial strengths and that each is blind to his own weaknesses. Their inability of "gallop side by side with equal pace" carries the submerged metaphor of a horse race: all aspire to "win," to be recognized (by the ruler or posterity), yet all are perfectly equal in their powers. Each has only some partial excellence; none is "complete," for completion would put them beyond the capacity of envy. Yet each is complete in learning and the originality of his writing. Therefore the locus of their limitation must lie elsewhere, in some predisposition for a certain kind of writing, a predisposition that transcends mastery, skill, and originality. Ts'ao P'i's argument carries him inexorably closer to an important event in Chinese literary thought, the identification of a "kind of writing" (t'i*) with a kind of person, a personality type (t'i*)

蓋君子審己以度人。故能免於斯累而作論文

A superior person (chün-tzu) examines himself to measure others; and thus he is able to avoid such entanglements [e.g., envy and blindness to the worth of others]. Thus I have written a discourse on literature.

The impartial observer would find in the Seven Masters only cause for admiration; but as they watch one another from within the "horse race" there is only envy and competition. Perfection may be achieved in one kind of writing, but none of those kinds is inherently superior to any other. Implicit here is the idea that the only true perfection is the completion of all "kinds." Completion can be achieved only by transcending the limitations implicit in a particular excellence, with which the notion of typological identity (i.e., definition of a person as a personality type) is becoming bound up. One must try to be more than what one already is—to embody and therefore be able to recognize the full complement of variations. The means of achieving this is "self-examination," tzu-shen 自審, leading to self-awareness, tzu-chien 自見, and the knowledge of one's limitations. As soon as one recognizes a limitation for what it is, something in the self has already transcended it. Only the chün-tzu can do this; since the Seven Masters cannot, they are not chün-tzu. A tactful silence in the argument tells us that Ts'ao P'i, heir and son of the overlord Ts'ao Ts'ao, is the chün-tzu (literally the "son of the prince"), who can avoid the entanglement and correctly evaluate others.[10]

Had Ts'ao P'i truly been a chün-tzu, his "Discourse on Literature" might have been a more morally paradigmatic work; but it would have lacked precisely that undercurrent of personal concerns which gives the piece its value for us. The Prince criticizes the Seven Masters for criticizing one another, while we note that "self-examination" is singularly lacking in the "Discourse," that disparagement of individual writers is only thinly veiled throughout, and that the "Discourse" closes with the passionate desire to make the individual self known through literature.

王粲長於辭賦。徐幹時有齊氣。然粲之匹也。如粲之初征。登樓。槐賦。征思。幹之玄猿。漏巵。圓扇。橘賦。雖張蔡不過也。然於他文。未能稱是。琳瑀之章表書記。今之雋也。

Wang Ts'an excels in poetic expositions (*fu*); even though Hsü Kan at times shows languid *ch'i**, still he is Wang Ts'an's match.[11] Even Chang Heng [78–139] and Ts'ai Yung [132–192] do not surpass works like Wang Ts'an's "Beginning of the Journey," "Climbing a Tower," "The Locust Tree," or "Thoughts on Travel"; or works like Hsü Kan's "The Black Gibbon," "The Syphon," "The Circular Fan," or "The Orange Tree." Yet their other writings are no match for these. In regard to memorials, letters, and records, those of Ch'en Lin and Juan Yü are preeminent in the present.

Strong here is the evaluative impulse, the duty and prerogative of the prince—to measure the men of his own age, one against another and against the giants of preceding ages. The entire discourse is replete with the terms of valuation, from the opening assertion that literary men disparage one another to the later claim that *ch'i** is what is most valuable for the success of a work as a whole. At the center of this world of valuing lies the Confucian imperative to "know persons," *chih jen* 知人, which first appears in Confucius' fine judgments of character and personality in the *Analects*, and in Ts'ao P'i's own age begins to develop into a fascination with personality appraisal.

Evaluative comparisons begin to pour out, at first restricted to excellence in purely literary matters, but soon shifting unconsciously to more general qualities that apply equally to the person and to the writing.

應瑒和而不壯。劉楨壯而不密。孔融體氣高妙。有過人者。然不能持論。理不勝辭。以至於雜以嘲戲。及其所善。楊班儔也

Ying Ch'ang is agreeable but lacks vigor. Liu Chen is vigorous but holds nothing concealed [*mi*; i.e., in reserve]. K'ung Jung's form (*t'i**) and *ch'i** are lofty and subtle, with something in them that surpasses all the others; but he cannot sustain an argument, and the principle (*li**) in his work is not up to the diction (*tz'u**), to the point that he mixes his writing with playfulness and spoofing. At his best he rivals Yang Hsiung [53 B.C.–A.D. 18] and Pan Ku.

It is important to develop a relatively precise sense of these terms of manner. "Agreeable" or "harmonious," *ho* 和, describes the manner of human behavior, music, weather, cuisine, and so forth, in which two or more entities are thrown into relation and neither entity asserts its identity vis-à-vis the other(s). Thus in the case of Ying Ch'ang, we have a strong sense of his "compliance" with us, his fitting in; there is no intimidating force in his words or the personality behind them.

"Vigor," *chuang* 壯, is the compensating term in which Ying Ch'ang is deficient. *Chuang* characterizes a man in his prime, and is associated with strength and assertiveness. In this case, the reader strongly senses the separate personality of the writer as against his own. One may admire and feel in awe of such force, but one does not feel an easy closeness with it. *Chuang* is the virtue antithetical to *ho*; but the virtue which compensates for the deficiencies of *chuang* is *mi*, not *ho*.

Mi 密 means "concealed" or "hidden." Here it is a positive quality, indicating some "reserve," some hidden richness of thought or personality, a quality entirely lacking in the pure outwardness of *chuang*.

Note that in this passage Ts'ao P'i has shifted to terms that may describe both a literary work and a personality. Throughout the Chinese literary tradition, as in certain phases of Western literature, readers identified the style or manner of the text with the personality of its author. Although current literary opinion considers such an identification misguided, the truth or falsity of the identification is less important than the fact that both readers and writer took it to be true. The powerful intuition of personality in style was a historical fact and a deeply held value.

Consider the form of contrast and distinction here: "agreeable but lacks vigor . . . vigorous but holds nothing concealed." We have here not binary antitheses, but a set of serial variations in which a quality, carried to its extreme, creates a lack that is supplied by the next quality in the series. Y is the compensation for deficiencies inherent in the fulfillment of X, but Z is the compensation for deficiencies inherent in the fulfillment of Y. This pattern of serial compensation, given in an attenuated form here, is based on theories of the sequence of the hexagrams in the *Book of Changes*.[12] The *Book of Changes* offers a powerful structural model of personality typology: each individual character phase, even in its perfection, is inherently incomplete; completion exists only in the "full complement" of all the particular phases. The Seven Masters are much like hexagrams, each generating a deficiency in the very perfection of some inherent quality.

In this passage we find an early version of the dichotomy between form and content. K'ung Jung's "form" (*t'i**) and *ch'i** are superior, but he cannot maintain an argument.[13] The unity of formal style and energy in a work is here seen as separable from some sense of discursive order (I hesitate to call this discursive order "logic," but the passage presumes a sense of necessary sequence in argument that roughly corresponds to the idea of "logical" coherence in the Western tradition). The parallel statement clarifies this: "the principle (*li**) . . . is not up to the diction (*tz'u**). It links the capacity to sustain an argument (*ch'ih-lun* 持論) with *li**, the principles of order that operate in the world, but can somehow fail to operate in texts. On the other side of the antithesis, diction (*tz'u**) is the level on which form (*t'i**) and *ch'i** are manifest.

常人貴遠賤近。向聲背實。又患闇於自見。謂己為賢

Ordinary people value what is far away and feel contempt for what is close at hand. They favor repute (*sheng*) and turn their backs on substance (*shih**). Moreover, they suffer the ill consequences of ignorance in self-awareness, claiming to be men of great worth.

Ts'ao P'i gradually shifts his argument from a mere overvaluing of self to an overwhelming concern for reputation that leaves men indifferent or blind in regard to their true nature. What is "far away" is related to "repute" (*sheng*), which depends on literature's capacity to "go far" (a capacity that Ts'ao P'i takes up in a positive way at the end of the "Discourse on Literature," seduced there by the very values he criticizes here). The value of literature here is balanced precariously between a revelation of the inner person (how the qualities revealed in a text truly and adequately manifest a person's nature, including its limitations) and the concealment of the inner person (the hope that an excellence will appear to others simply as an excellence, without revealing corresponding deficiencies).

夫文本同而末異。蓋奏議宜雅。書論宜理。銘誄尚實。詩賦欲麗。此四科不同。故能之者偏也。惟通才能備其體

Literature (*wen**) is the same at the root (*pen**), but differs in its branches [*mo*, a "branch tip," the later stages of a process]. Generally speaking, memorials and disquisitions should have dignity (*ya**); letters and memorials should be based on natural principle (*li**); inscriptions and eulogy value the facts (*shih**); poetry and poetic exposition (*fu*) aspire to beauty (*li**). Each of these four categories is different, so that a writer's ability will favor some over others. Only a comprehensive talent (*t'ung**-*ts'ai**) can achieve the full complement (*pei*) of these forms (*t'i**).

This is one of the earliest statements of Chinese genre theory. The structure and assumptions made in the passage are ultimately more interesting than the particular distinctions made. Generic categories are the precise counterparts of categories of human personality: there is some prior unity "at the root," but that unity devolves into a multiplicity of particulars. The ultimate mastery would be a "comprehensive talent" that can reunify difference, not as a simple unity but as a capacity to pass through all variations. This capacity obviously parallels Ts'ao P'i's own aspirations to be the "prince," the *chün-tzu*, who "comprehends" all the limited and particular abilities of the writers who seek his favor.

The passion to provide an orderly enumeration of forms and techniques recurs throughout traditional Chinese literary criticism. This impulse embodies a hope to limit and control divergence by establishing a fixed number (*shu**) of normative categories, each with its own unifying characteristics.[14] The model for treating these questions of unity and multiplicity is traditional cosmogony, a history of binary division. Here we note that the number of forms is a multiple of two and that each characteristic has two different forms associated with it. Genre theory is, "at root," lineage, an orderly system of identities filiated on a historical ground.

Generic typology and the typology of personality arose together in traditional China, and they are unified by a largely shared vocabulary of manner and quality (in the list of qualities above, this is most apparent in *ya**, "dignity" or "grace," which can qualify style, behavior, and personality equally).[15] Each pair of forms is adequately characterized by a quality proper to it. Thus a given personality type will manifest a corresponding manner and will appear at his best in those forms in which his manner is naturally appropriate.

文以氣為主。氣之清濁有體。不可力強而致。譬諸音樂。曲度雖均。節奏同檢。至於引氣不齊。巧拙有素。雖在父兄。不能以移子弟。

In literature *ch'i** is the dominant factor. *Ch'i** has its normative forms (*t'i**)— clear and murky. It is not to be brought by force. Compare it to music: though melodies be equal and though the rhythms follow the rules, when it comes to an inequality in drawing on a reserve of *ch'i**, we have grounds to distinguish skill and clumsiness. Although it may reside in a father, he cannot transfer it to his son; nor can an elder brother transfer it to the younger.

Before entering a detailed discussion of this famous passage, we should take note of several things. First, it was an age in which literary works were always recited or delivered out loud; moreover, there are good indications that some forms of literary works were composed orally and extemporaneously, then written down from memory. This fact greatly strengthens the analogy made in this passage between literary composition and musical performance. Second, although the music in question had melodic, structural, and rhythmic rules, a performance would have been far more improvisatory than a performance of a fully scored piece of Western music from the past two centuries. Finally, the analogy drawn is clearly to flute or wind music; thus the importance of "breath" or *ch'i** is literal as well as figurative.

Traditional Chinese thought tended to place value on terms that unified the abstract and the physical, or mental processes and physiological processes. Indo-European conceptual vocabulary grows from the "death" of metaphors (and the atemporality of abstractions is closely related to the atemporality of death). In the Chinese tradition, too, terms from the sensuous physical world were extended into the non-sensuous, but without "dying," surrendering their "root" reference to the sensuous.[16] *Ch'i** is grounded in physiological "breath" and physical "air," but it carries a weight that goes far beyond the apparently physical. *Ch'i** comes from "within" the writer, carried to the "outside" in the breath used in recitation (where it may become the "wind," *feng** that "influences" the listener). The *ch'i** in a person has both quantity and quality. It is not a natural endowment like *ts'ai**, "talent," though a capacity for some quantity of *ch'i** may be innate. *Ch'i** cannot be learned or forced; it can, however, be "nurtured," *yang* 養, stored up and depleted in use. Finally, *ch'i** is itself a "something" and not simply the energy impelling or infusing a something.[17]

*Ch'i** may be a "something," but it is an ongoing something, something in process. For this reason the analogy to improvisatory music is one of crucial importance. The relation implied here between artistic control and its product differs greatly from the common assumptions of Western poetics and even from the assumptions of poets in the late classical period in China. The terminological and procedural assumptions of Western poetics (especially visible in clichés and in popular discourse on poetry) posit complete artistic intention prior to the text: the text is given atemporally as an "object" determined before the object is realized in composition. Such assumptions about poetry have, of course, been seriously questioned in the Western tradition, but such questioning defines itself against and sustains the normative assumptions. We might add here that the perfection of Western musical notation grew precisely from the desire to textualize music, to assert and preserve the composer's control over the work, to make a piece of music a "thing" and thus absolutely repeatable (it is at this point that a performance begins to be conceived as an "interpretation").

In contrast to the objectification of the text, a notion of improvisatory performance engages the ongoing constructive powers of the composer-performer, who exerts control in action rather than the atemporal control of a maker over his object (a relation whose secret model is transcendent divinity). This ongoing control of act rather than object is the mode in which *ch'i** is used, both in music and poetry. That a poem can be written down and transmitted is a miracle equal to the capacity to record an improvisatory performance. And if we later hear a recording of the performance or read the poem, we can recognize the quality of the poet-performer's *ch'i**—the constants of that quality, the mood of the moment, and how he handles the demands of the ongoing performance.

Assumptions of the text as object also existed in traditional China; such assumptions contended with the notion of text as performance and eventually overcame it. There remained, however, a powerful nostalgia for the per-

formative, ongoing text. Later concepts in poetics such as *huo-fa**, "lively
rules," are attempts to recover the performative text (or more properly, the
impression of such a text) in a world where it could no longer be taken for
granted. Far more than in the West, the Chinese tradition recognized, or
hoped to recognize, the poem as an event in time. *Ch'i**, moreover, gives a
text an animate unity (as opposed to the master metaphor of textiles, which
yields a sense of poetic unity much closer to the Western). In later theoretical
writing the unity of *ch'i** will often be described as *yi-ch'i** 一氣, "in a single
breath": it is the momentum and continuity of ongoing movement. The
T'ang writer Li Tê-yü 李德裕 (787–850) in his "Discourse on Letters," *Wen-
chang lun* 文章論, explained this passage as follows:

魏文典論稱。文以氣為主。氣之清濁有體。斯言盡之矣。然氣不可不貫。不貫則雖有
英辭麗藻如編珠綴玉。不得為全璞之寶矣。鼓氣以勢壯為美。勢不可以不息。不息則
流宕而忘返。亦猶絲竹繁奏必有希聲窈眇。聽之者悅聞。如川流迅激必有洄洑逶迤。
觀之者不厭。

Emperor Wen of the Wei [Ts'ao P'i] in his *Authoritative Discourses* said: "In
literature *ch'i** is the dominant factor. *Ch'i** has its normative forms—clear
and murky." These lines say it all. But the *ch'i** must penetrate through continuously. If it does not penetrate through continuously, then even the most
splendid phrases and fine flourishes will be like pearls or pieces of jade on a
string: they will not attain the condition of a single, complete jewel. It is
loveliest when the *ch'i** is driven with forceful vigor, but that force must
necessarily come to rest. If it doesn't come to rest, then it will be swept away
and never return; it is also like woodwinds and stringed instruments played in
concert: there must be some very faint tones for subtlety, so that the audience
will hear it with pleasure. It is like a swiftly flowing stream: there must be
whirling eddies and meanderings so that the viewer will not get bored with
it.[18]

*Ch'i** is that by which all other elements which contribute to the formation
of a poem—talent, learning, personality, the affections—are animated. Thus,
"in literature *ch'i** is the dominant factor"—everything else remains inert
without it.

If we want to hear the human being in any discourse, even in a "Discourse
on Literature," we must pay close attention to the joints of the discourse, to
those points where its movement falters and it jumps. The transition between this passage and the final paragraph is particularly rich in conflicting
impulses; and that conflict makes Ts'ao P'i's "Discourse on Literature" great,
without being theoretically profound. His passage on the impossibility of
transmitting *ch'i** from father to son or brother to brother unmistakably
echoes the story in the *Chuang-tzu* of the Wheelwright Pien, who tells his
duke that the writings of the Sages are only the "dregs" of their being: like his
skill in wheel-making, which is performed by instinct and cannot be passed
on, the Sages' essence is precisely that which eludes the written word.[19]

Although Ts'ao here wanted to speak only of the untransmissibility of *ch'i** as the most essential quality in writing, the story tells of writing's own incapacity to transmit what is most essential in a person: the echoes of the story of Wheelwright Pien threaten Ts'ao's whole "Discourse." Ts'ao P'i wants very much to be the *t'ung**-*ts'ai**, the "comprehensive talent." Its value is stated explicitly in the "Discourse on Literature" and implicitly in the experimental variety of his own poetry. Ts'ao P'i wants to be the Sage, the comprehensive judge of men who transcends all merely partial excellence. He longs to make all this permanently manifest in his own writing. But if, as Wheelwright Pien says, words—even the words of a Sage—are mere "dregs," then all this is in vain: his true achievements will not be adequately transmitted. To that threat Ts'ao P'i responds with a grand declaration.

蓋文章經國之大業。不朽之盛事。年壽有時而盡。榮樂止乎其身。二者必至之常期。未若文章之無窮。

I would say that literary works (*wen**-*chang**) are the supreme achievement in the business of state, a splendor that does not decay. A time will come when a person's life ends; glory and pleasure go no further than this body. To carry both to eternity, there is nothing to compare with the unending permanence of the literary work.

First we must recall the old promises that through words and literary works a person's inner nature might be known: Mencius' "understanding words"; Confucius' "if a person does not use language, who will know what is on his mind?"; the canonical statement "the poem articulates what is on the mind intently"; or the *Book of Changes'* (*Hsi-tz'u chuan*), "the affections of the Sages are revealed in their statements." Add to these the assertions in *Mencius*, "The Great Preface," and "The Record of Music," that the quality of an age and of a government is manifest in poetry. Then suppose that the person who reflects on these received truths is someone who will be a future ruler, one who is the heir of the Lord Protector, and one who will finally end the fiction of Han rule and establish himself as the emperor of the new Wei dynasty: that person is the present writer Ts'ao P'i. And he must wonder how future ages will know how he governed, the moral legitimacy of his rule. How will the future know who he was? Only the literary works of his age will be the truly perfect and transmissible outcome of all his accomplishments. These works will be his true *yeh*, translated above as "achievements"; *yeh* is "patrimony," something one stores up and transmits to one's posterity; it is a term used for capital, property, learning, merit (the accumulated merit, *yeh*, of an official might be passed on to his children and increased or dissipated by their own acts).[20] In later ages *yeh* is Buddhist *karma*, an accumulation of good or evil deeds that determines one's next life. At this point Ts'ao P'i realizes that literary works are the ultimate *yeh* of government, the sole trustworthy legacy free of the decay that attends upon the vegetative cycles of dynasties. A frivolous heir can dissipate a person's wealth; barbarians can lay waste your land; only in literature might there be a reliable transmission of a person's accomplishments, that "splendor," *sheng-shih* 盛事 (literally "an event of full flowering"), that admits no decay. Or are those texts only the "dregs"?

One peculiarity here deserves note: according to the passage, what is transmitted is *jung-lo* 榮樂, "glory and pleasure." It is the *lo* 樂, the "pleasure," which first gives us pause; for the "pleasure" experienced in this life would seem to be one of the things that would not be transmitted. On further reflection, we discover that *jung* 榮, "glory," is much the same. And we realize that Ts'ao P'i does not conceive of either as purely private sensations: for Ts'ao P'i both conditions exist in being recognized and appreciated by others. The pleasure of a banquet is not in what I alone am doing—there would be less, perhaps no joy in eating and drinking alone—but rather it is a pleasure in collective enjoyment and making one's delight visible to others. If that pleasure is permanently recognized, the pleasure is, in a strange way, permanent itself, even though I may not be present. The experience of "glory" is an even clearer example of this: it is not a purely private sensation, but rather a satisfaction contingent on recognition by others. Thus the literary work that embodies present "glory and pleasure" seems to Ts'ao P'i to preserve not simply the knowledge of the condition, but the condition itself.

But a problem remains: "literary men disparage one another." Having described the jealousies, the vanity, and the one-sided capacities of the literary men around him, how can Ts'ao P'i trust men like them with the perfect transmission of his achievements? Perfect transmission would require someone who unites all partial excellences. Trustworthy transmission can thus come only from the prince himself.

是以古之作者。寄身於翰墨。見意於篇籍。不假良史之辭。不託飛馳之勢。而聲名自傳於後。

So writers of ancient times entrusted their persons to ink and the brush, and let their thoughts be seen in their compositions; depending neither on a good historian nor on momentum from a powerful patron, their reputations were handed down to posterity on their own force.

When His Majesty [Ts'ao P'i] was first in the Eastern Palace [as Crown Prince], a great pestilence came and people were wasting away. His Majesty was deeply moved, and wrote in a letter to Wang Lang, a man whom he had long respected: "Alive we have a form six feet in length; dead we have soil enough for a casket. Only by establishing his virtue and spreading his reputation can a man avoid perishing. Next to that the best thing is to be a writer. Pestilences arise often; men sicken and die. Who am I that I can live out my full span of years?"[21]

The fear of death permeates the last part of "A Discourse on Literature." When Ts'ao P'i speaks of "entrusting their persons," he uses the term *chi-shen* 寄身, a word from the vocabulary of battle (a brave soldier "entrusts his person" to the sword). As is fitting, then, for the heir of Ts'ao Ts'ao, the greatest of the warlords, Ts'ao P'i here speaks of writing in terms of a bold risking of the self.

In the preceding passage, Ts'ao P'i had looked to "a splendor which does not decay," and that phrasing inescapably recalls the ancient *sententia* from the *Tso chuan* (Hsiang 24) of "the three things that do not decay," *san pu hsiu* 三不朽: "establishing oneself by virtue," *li-tê* 立德; "establishing oneself by deeds," *li-kung* 立功; and "establishing oneself by words," *li-yen* 立言. Ts'ao P'i offers a us a triad—the work of a historian, the momentum from a patron, and compositions from one's own brush—but only one of these can ensure transmission of the three things that do not decay. Even a good historian who records a man's virtues, deeds, and words may overlook some excellence in his subject. The "momentum from a powerful patron" (literally, a "headlong gallop," a metaphor for political patronage) may provide opportunities for deeds; but establishing oneself in this way may be thwarted by one-sided people who can value only the qualities they themselves possess. Only in his own writing, "establishing himself by words," can a man take full charge of his own immortality.

故西伯幽而演易。周旦顯而制禮。不以隱約而弗務。不以康樂而加思。夫然則古人賤尺璧而重寸陰。懼乎時之過已。而人多不強力。貧賤則懾於饑寒。富貴則流於逸樂。遂營目前之務。而遺千載之功。日月逝於上。體貌衰於下。忽然與萬物遷化。斯志士之大痛也。融等已逝。惟幹著論成一家言。

The Earl of the West [later made King Wen of the Chou], when imprisoned, amplified the *Book of Changes*; the Duke of Chou, though in his glory, prescribed the Rites. The former did not ignore this [the importance of literary work] in spite of hardship; the latter was not distracted by health and pleasure. From this we can see how the ancients thought nothing of large jade disks [marks of wealth], but valued each moment, fearful lest their time pass them by.

Yet people usually do not exert themselves: in poverty and low station they fear the hunger and cold; amid wealth and honor they drift with the distractions of pleasure. They busy themselves with the demands of what lies right before their eyes, and neglect an accomplishment lasting a thousand years. Overhead, the days and months pass away from us; here below, face and body waste away. Suddenly we will move off into transformation with all the other things of the world—this is the greatest pain for a person with high aspirations (*chih**). K'ung Jung and the others have already passed away, and only the discourses composed by Hsü Kan are the fully realized work of an individual writer.

The "Discourse" runs on to its melancholy conclusion: lives are wasted in common worries and bustlings, passing away into silence and the future's forgetfulness, with few caring enough to secure their immortality. The voice in the passage carries something of the tone of a Christian moralist, expressing pastoral concern that the flocks of the church are not sufficiently concerned for their immortal souls. Of all the writers Ts'ao P'i has known, only Hsü Kan has written well enough to "establish himself" and be remembered.

There is an emotional intensity in Ts'ao P'i's "Discourse on Literature"—partially in the elegiac reflection on his dead friends and partially in fear for his own immortality—that drives this work, as if "in one breath," *yi-ch'i* 一氣, and carries it through sharp shifts in mood and antithetical positions. He ends as he began, evaluating. In the beginning of the "Discourse" the "Seven Masters" galloped with an "equal pace," neck and neck; now most have fallen behind, leaving only Hsü Kan at the finish line.[22] Ts'ao P'i began contemptuously, commenting on their competitive passion for recognition and reputation; he ends lamenting them and discovering the highest of values precisely in such a quest for literary immortality.[23] Along the way he criticizes them for "valuing what is far away and feeling contempt for what is close at hand . . . favoring repute and turning their backs on substance"; he ends yearning himself for what is far away and for reputation in future ages. Now they are criticized for "busy(ing) themselves with the demands of what lies right before their eyes, and neglect(ing) an accomplishment lasting a thousand years." He has told us that "*ch'i** is the dominant factor in literature" and "is not to be brought about by force" *pu k'o li-ch'iang erh chih* 不可力強而致; he closes lamenting that people "do not exert themselves" *pu ch'iang li* 不強力, do not apply themselves seriously enough to literature (the same characters with the order of the compound reversed). And we must wonder what has happened in the writing of this "Discourse on Literature" to so change his tone and position.

Somehow in writing about these literary men, former companions, many of whom are now dead, he comes to share their values; by the end of the work we find him writing from precisely the position that he was coolly evaluating in the opening. The greatness of "A Discourse on Literature" lies precisely in the way that princely and magistral voice is driven by its reflections into a desperate hope in the power of literature. And if we trace back to where the voice bends in a new direction, we find that moment of turning in the disturbing echo of Wheelwright Pien. His questions of transmission to a son or brother are of concern to Ts'ao P'i, heir of Ts'ao Ts'ao, who had been both a poet and the most powerful man in China. And not only is Ts'ao P'i Ts'ao

Ts'ao's heir, he is also the elder brother of Ts'ao Chih, who was widely regarded as the greatest writer of the day. Suddenly Ts'ao P'i finds himself in the position of the Seven Masters, surrounded by competitors; and at this moment he puts aside the magistral voice and enters the competition, praising the power of literature and enjoining a fierce devotion to the pursuit as necessary to win undying fame. "A Discourse on Literature" is perhaps the best piece Ts'ao P'i ever wrote, and its power comes from anxieties that cut Ts'ao P'i to the core.

The Poetic Exposition on Literature

Both in literature and in literary thought, we encounter now and then a work of such originality that it could not have been anticipated from the works that preceded it. "The Poetic Exposition on Literature" (*Wen fu* 文賦) by Lu Chi 陸機 (261–303) is such a work. Not only had nothing like it ever been written concerning literature, Lu Chi himself never wrote anything else quite like it. By his time there was already a set of established questions regarding literature and an established vocabulary of terms with which to address those questions. But Lu Chi took up genuinely new questions, and the vocabulary he used to address those questions was drawn from a variety of sources, a vocabulary whose application to literature still remains, in many cases, problematic. Ts'ao P'i's "Discourse on Literature" was a personal, even idiosyncratic organization of literary issues; as unique as it was, however, it was still comprehensible as a transformation of certain old questions regarding writing. Lu Chi makes occasional raids on that older tradition of literary thought, but the greater part of "The Poetic Exposition on Literature" deals with aspects of the writing process that had never before been seriously considered. Much in later literary thought, especially in the literary thought of the Southern Dynasties, consists of following through questions first raised by Lu Chi.

   "The Poetic Exposition on Literature" is a work that is both literature and literary thought; and at least part of its originality follows from the conjunction of the topic ("literature," wen*), which would normally have been treated discursively, as in "A Discourse on Literature," and the form of the poetic exposition (fu 賦). Two aspects of the poetic exposition in the Tsin seem to have exerted a particularly powerful influence on the shape of "The Poetic Exposition on Literature" and thus contributed to its originality: first, the tendency to situate the topic of a poetic exposition in some cosmological frame of reference and to understand the topic as a construct of balanced members or as an orderly process; second, the conventional techniques of rhetorical amplification which, though much less stringent than the formal structure of chapters in Liu Hsieh's later Wen-hsin tiao-lung (ca. 500), nevertheless had their own analytic momentum, which exerted pressure on Lu Chi to develop the topic in certain directions.

Many scholars have noted how Lu Chi moved away from the usual issues of literature, such as its ethical purpose, its social grounds, and the inscription of personality; instead we find in "The Poetic Exposition on Literature" an interest in the Neo-Taoist theory of mind and the cosmological grounds on which the operations of mind are understood. As a model for the orderly unfolding of the compositional process, this had scarcely been touched on by earlier writers. In the "Record of Music," mind is caught amid uncontrollable stirrings from external things; in Lu Chi's "Poetic Exposition on Literature," mind wanders through the microcosm within, looking for encounters that will be the origins of a literary work.

These new interests are in part shaped by one kind of contemporary poetic exposition, such poetic expositions do what Lu Chi says a poetic exposition should do: "give the normative form of the thing" (t'i*-wu*), and place its topic in the largest and most universal context.[1] To give just one example, a master of the preceding generation, Ch'eng-kung Sui 成公綏 (231–273) had written a poetic exposition on "Heaven and Earth," as well as one on "Whistling," treating the latter as the primordial music generated from the ch'i* of the human body. "The Poetic Exposition on Literature" is very much in this tradition of the physiological-philosophical treatment of a topic, with the more circumstantial and personal voice of the preface serving as one proper way to introduce such a topic.

We will remark details of the structure of rhetorical exposition in the commentary. Here, however, we may take note of four basic structural principles. First, the macrostructures of discourse are often organized around the conventional taxonomy of a thing or process: its parts or stages. In contrast to poetry (shih), which tends to treat something as it is encountered in the world in some particular circumstance, the poetic exposition (fu) tends to describe the way the thing "is" or "should be." Thus, in the case of "The Poetic Exposition on Literature," we have first the preconditions for writing, then the meditation before the act of writing some particular work, then the considerations involved in the act of composition itself.

Second, arguments tend to be built on diaresis (antithetical divisions of each issue) and the aggregation of antithetical terms. For example, in the preface the problem of writing is broken down by diaresis, into "concepts" not being adequate for the things of the world, and writing not being adequate to express the concepts; this distinction aggregates with another antithesis between one's own thought and what one learns through reading (presumably because reading enables a person to become skillful enough to present his concepts adequately in writing); this further aggregates with an antithesis between present (one's own thinking) and past (what is encountered in reading). Although the alignments are often less clear than in these exemplary cases, there is a strong tendency to antithetical division and to joining each member of an antithesis with a member from a previous antithesis.

A third rhetorical structure is resumptive amplification: after an antithesis has been announced, each member is developed, sometimes repeatedly in different contexts. This structure can be schematically presented: AB/AAA/BBB/AAA/BBB.

The fourth and final principle, while closely related to diaresis, is less a rhetorical structure than a general impulse of thought: this is the compensatory countermovement. Whenever Lu Chi develops one position fully, he shows an almost instinctive anxiety regarding its one-sidedness and immediately compensates with a counterstatement. What appears to be contradiction in "The Poetic Exposition on Literature" is often a sequence of movements and compensatory countermovements.

"The Poetic Exposition on Literature" cannot be understood apart from its genre. In its early stages, the poetic exposition (*fu*) was an epideictic form (i.e., the rhetoric of verbal display) that made extensive use of catalogues and lists. Its aim was always to "give the full measure of," to say all that could be said about its topic. This generic legacy survives even in such a late and sophisticated work as "The Poetic Exposition on Literature." The genre is not adapted to linear exposition; rather, in seeking to say all there is to say about a topic, it can cheerfully allow contradictory impulses to exist together in close proximity. Lu Chi usually presents a relatively consistent position; but when there are contradictory elements in the exposition, the attentive reader will note that these are often treated as complements to one another.

Lu Chi was born during the Three Kingdoms Period into an important military family of the state of Wu. When he was about twenty, the northern kingdom of Tsin conquered Wu and briefly reunified China. Some ten years later Lu Chi and his brother Lu Yün 陸雲 (262–303) made their way to the Tsin capital of Lo-yang, where they soon came to enjoy the literary and political patronage of Chang Hua 張華 (232–300), the leading cultural figure of the day. Lu Chi was a prolific writer and soon became a very popular one. Although most of his literary work came to seem somewhat leaden in later ages, his status as a major poet and prose stylist was very high during the

Southern Dynasties and even in the T'ang. Only a small part of his original collected works survives, but it remains one of the largest individual collections from the Western Tsin. In the context of such popularity, "The Poetic Exposition on Literature" was well known in subsequent centuries and exerted a powerful influence on the development of literary thought in the Southern Dynasties. In the *Wen-hsin tiao-lung* Liu Hsieh often criticizes Lu Chi; but as commentators on "The Poetic Exposition on Literature" have frequently pointed out, many elements in Liu Hsieh's own work are developed directly from short passages in "The Poetic Exposition on Literature."

The date of the composition of "The Poetic Exposition on Literature" is a matter of fierce scholarly debate. A line in a song by the T'ang poet Tu Fu says that Lu Chi wrote it when he was twenty (or in his twenties), that is, in the early 280s. Since many more texts of the period were extant in Tu Fu's age than now, it is hard entirely to discount such precision (though it is also true that unreliable biographical anecdotes circulated freely in the T'ang, and Tu Fu, if he had heard that Lu Chi wrote "The Poetic Exposition on Literature" at twenty, would not have hesitated to repeat the story). In the other camp, an ambiguous reference in a letter by Lu Chi's brother suggests the date of composition was around the year 300.[2]

A NOTE ON THE FORM OF COMMENTARY AND DOCUMENTATION

"The Poetic Exposition on Literature" cannot be understood without a detailed attention to its particular uses of words, for which there is an extensive commentarial tradition. After translating a passage, I will discuss in detail particular words, phrases, or pairings of phrases. The premodern commentarial tradition, beginning with the T'ang commentaries to the *Wen hsüan* by Li Shan and the "Five Officers," the Wu-ch'en commentrary, has been collected in Chang Shao-k'ang's *Wen fu chi-shih*, given in the bibliography. Here and in other modern line-by-line commentaries, I will not give page numbers, unless the comment is elsewhere than under the line in discussion. For convenience the excellent commentary in the *Wen Chin Nan-pei-ch'ao wen-hsüeh shih ts'an-k'ao tzu-liao* will be referred to simply as *TL* (*tzu-liao*). Other modern commentaries will be identified by their authors' names; full documentation for these works can be found in Section I.D.1 of the Bibliography.

THE POETIC EXPOSITION ON LITERATURE
Preface (Section A)

余每觀才士之所作。竊有以得其用心。夫其放言遣辭艮多變矣。妍蚩好惡。可得而言。

Whenever I consider what is made by persons of talent (*ts'ai**), there is something within me that lets me grasp their strenuous efforts (or "use of mind," *yung-hsin**). Though there are indeed many mutations (*pien**) in the way they let loose their words (*yen*) and expel phrases (*tz'u**), still we can grasp and speak of value and beauty in them.

What is made, *so-tso*: The application of the verb "make," *tso*, to the composition of literary works came into common usage in the Han and perhaps earlier.[3] This application of *tso* to literary works was closely related to a more primordial "making" associated with the ancient Sages and the formation of the Classics (see below). However, "making" in this context should not be confused with *poiêsis* and its lineage in Western literary thought ("fictions," "creation"). In the *Poetics* 1451B, Aristotle is adamant on the point that the poet/maker is a "maker of plots" (*poiêtês muthôn*) rather than a "maker of verses" (*poiêtês metrôn*). In Aristotle *poiêsis*, an internally complete structure of necessity unfolding in a story, applies regardless of whether that story is a received myth (Aristotle uses the term *muthos* both as "myth" or "story," and as "plot") or an invented one. That is, literary "making" or *poiêsis* is something entirely distinct from the question of the referential truth of what is said. Thus the versified philosophy of Empedocles is excluded from *poiêsis* on the grounds that it is versifying rather than "making" a plot. Empedocles would, however, be eligible for the original, sagely sense of *tso*, again not because he made verses but because he gave paradigmatic verbal formulations to "what is." This original sense of *tso*, as practiced by the Sages, is to say what is true or right in authoritative, paradigmatic words. It is in this sense of "formulating" that *tso* is used in *Analects* VII.1, where Confucius modestly disclaims his sagely status by saying of himself: "I transmit but do not make," *shu erh pu tso* 述而不作. The ancient Sages "make," put the way the world works into words. In the "Record of Music," the meaning of *tso* is clarified in an amplification of the distinction between "making" and "transmitting": "Those who know the disposition of Rites and Music are capable of making; those who comprehend the texts (*wen**) of Rites and Music are capable of transmitting. Those who make are known as Sages; those who transmit are known as ones who understand (*ming* 明)." Given the fact that the Sage only formulates a prior knowledge of "the disposition of Rites and Music," he operates on a more empirical level than the "maker of plots" (Aristotle) who reformulates old stories according to transcendent laws of necessity and probability. The Aristotelian maker (*poiêtês*) rewrites a story according to how it "ought to have been"; the Sage maker (*tso-che*) formulates how things both should be and historically were. By the Han, this grander sense of sagely "making" had diminished (as indeed *poiêsis* had in Western civilization) to a weaker and broader sense of "writing" or "composition." Although *tso* bears some comparison to Aristotelian *poiêsis*, *tso* never picked up the full sense of fictionality. This was especially true in regard to the idea of creating *ex nihilo* "another world" or heterocosm, on the model of the creative God, as we begin to find in discussions of poetry in the late Middle Ages and Renaissance.

There is something within me that lets me grasp, *ch'ieh yu yi tê*: Ch'eng Hui-ch'ang in *Wen-lun yao-ch'üan* cites *Analects* VII.1 for the polite and self-deprecatory *ch'ieh*, untranslated but carrying something of the force of "I dare say . . . " The use of *ch'ieh* was not uncommon in Lu Chi's time; but because *Analects* VII.1 is the primary source for the opposition between "making" (*tso*) and "transmitting," it seems that here Lu Chi is lightly assuming the voice of Confucius and his role of "transmitting but not making." The kind of exposition of the literary art that Lu Chi gives in this piece would fall roughly in the domain of *shu* 述, "transmission" in the sense of "exegesis." The choice of *tê* ("to grasp" or "attain") instead of some other verb of understanding, suggests that Lu Chi not only recognizes their strenuous efforts, but also takes them to heart. The capacity to understand others, in this case to grasp the mind or efforts of others behind their writing, has a deep resonance among the Confucian virtues, from Mencius' "understanding language" back to *Analects* I.16: "He said, 'It does not trouble me that others do not understand me; what troubles me is not understanding others.'"

Strenuous efforts (or "use of mind"), *yung-hsin**: Lu Chi continues lightly to echo the voice of Confucius, here *Analects* XVII.22: "He said, 'One who fills himself with food all day and exerts strenuous efforts at nothing is a problem indeed" 子曰。飽食終日無所用心難矣哉. *Yung-hsin*, literally "to employ one's heart/mind," had long been used in the sense of "exerting strenuous effort" (as in *Mencius* I.A.3); but considering the special role of *hsin**, "mind," in the definition and discussion of literature, it seems likely here that Lu Chi is playing on the literal sense of the phrase.[4] A similar play on the phrase (probably echoing Lu Chi's) can be found in the "Afterword" of the *Wen-hsin tiao-lung*: "The patterned/literary mind (*wen**-*hsin**) means the use of mind (or 'intense effort') in writing" (see p. 292). Implicit in the notion of *yung-hsin** as "strenuous effort" is the assumption that composition is an intentional and voluntary act. This assumption recurs throughout "The Poetic Exposition on Literature," and it is significant: the role of voluntarism in composition had usually been absent or muted in earlier discussion of the role of "mind" in composition.

Mutations, *pien**: Among the many terms for "change," *pien** usually carries the sense of variation from a norm, sometimes carrying the pejorative sense of "deviation." Based in the tradition of commentary to the *Book of Songs*, *pien** was the most common term used to describe literary historical change. Lu Chi is using it here in as neutral a sense as possible, and the term becomes largely neutral in later discussions of literary change in the fifth and sixth centuries.

Let loose their words and expel phrases, *fang-yen ch'ien-tz'u:* This is a common rhetorical form based on the division and recombination of two synonymous compounds (AB and XY becoming AX and BY: *fang-ch'ien* and *yen-tz'u* becoming the formulation above). Here the second verb-object compound, *ch'ien-tz'u,* receives its force from the established meaning of the first compound, *fang-yen.* Once again the source is the *Analects* (XVIII.8) where *fang-yen,* "let loose one's words," means "to speak as one pleases"; this implies a lack of restraint and rashness, though the rash words on which Confucius comments are matched by a purity of behavior. Lu Chi's adoption of the phrase suggests a boldness in language that creates rich variation (*pien**).

Beauty and value, *yen-ch'ih hao-e:* This phrase is literally translated "beauty and ugliness, good and bad." Caution is required regarding the many Chinese descriptives that get translated as "beauty." *Yen* is an alluring feminine beauty; *ch'ih* is both ugliness and doltishness. If we want to understand the concept of 'beauty' in the Kantian sense, then *yen* would be more properly translated as "attractiveness." *Hao-e,* "good and bad," appeals to a relatively general sense of value.

In poetic expositions of this period, "prefaces," *hsü* 序, often establish the circumstantial ground of a literary work: what stirred the writer to do this particular work, his qualifications for the task, the failures or limitations of previous writers on the subject. Although Lu Chi voices his self-doubts at the end of "The Poetic Exposition on Literature," most of the main body of the work describes the question of writing in its most general case. Here in the preface, however, Lu Chi speaks of his own capacities and motives, which are the grounds for his composition of "The Poetic Exposition on Literature." And as is appropriate when speaking of purely circumstantial questions (as opposed to what "the writer" does), Lu Chi makes reference here to Confucian issues of transmission and knowing others.

Two rather different claims are made in the first sentence of the preface. First, Lu Chi says that he can "appreciate their effort," can see how much effort went into their writing, and, more important, can see precisely how that effort went in: "use of mind" or "strenuous effort" (*yung-hsin*) in this sense is craft. The second claim is more archaic, and its established authority sustains the initial foray into this new concern with literature as craft. The archaic claim is that Lu Chi can know the operations of the author's mind from reading his work. The distinction here between writer as writer and writer as person is crucial to the development of the new literary theory of the Tsin and Southern Dynasties. When we read a work like Wang Ts'an's (177–217) famous poetic exposition "Climbing a Tower," *Teng-lou fu* 登樓賦, do we perceive in it Wang Ts'an's feelings on climbing a tower and gazing toward his home, or do we perceive Wang Ts'an trying to write about his feelings on climbing a tower and gazing toward his home? The second case places the act of writing and its particular problems in the foreground. The ambiguity of the opening sentence permits Lu Chi to forestall a decision between these two very different interests; but as the exposition progresses, Lu Chi increasingly shows that his true interest lies in the second case, the question of writing.

Rich multiplicity, both in the world and in literary expression, fascinates Lu Chi throughout "The Poetic Exposition on Literature." Here he shows awareness of the chief danger inherent in such variability: the lack of normative criteria that permit evaluation. Lu Chi, in fact, never really offers any standards of judgment, except in the most general way; but the recognition of their necessity survives as an impulse. Thus whenever he speaks admiringly of the infinite variety of images in the world or of words used—the lure of daring and freedom that accompanies the new voluntarism in composition— he usually compensates by speaking of the possibilities of failure, of dangers and the necessity of restraint and limits.

Note that the first criterion by which Lu Chi sets himself up as critic and theorist is his capacity as a reader with insight. The second criterion by which he claims the critic's role is his position as a self conscious author.

Preface (Section B)

每自屬文。尤見其情。恒患意不稱物。文不逮意。蓋非知之難。能之難也。

And whenever I myself compose a literary piece, I perceive full well their state of mind (or "the situation," ch'ing*). I constantly fear failure in my conceptions' (yi*) not being equal to the things of the world (wu*), and in my writing's (wen*) not being equal to my conceptions. I suppose it is not the understanding that is difficult, but rather the difficulty lies in being able to do it well.

Whenever I myself compose a literary piece, mei tzu chu wen: The repetition of mei, "whenever," sets up an antithetical balance with the preceding section: "On the one hand, whenever I read . . . ; on the other hand, whenever I compose . . . " (see Ch'ien Chung-shu, pp. 1176–1177). Chu is a less weighted term than tso 作, "to make": chu implies the "putting together" of words and phrases, in exact correspondence to the Latin root of "compose."

I perceive full well their state of mind (or "the situation"), yu chien ch'i ch'ing: "Full well" or "especially well," yu, implies that in composition the problems become even clearer than in reading. This prepares us for the apothegm, "it is not the understanding that is difficult, but rather the difficulty lies in being able to do it well." Ch'i ch'ing may be the "state of mind" experienced by other writers on encountering the difficulties of composition (thus demanding "strenuous efforts," yung-hsin*, on their part). However, it may also echo the broader sense of yung-hsin* as "use of mind," and thus may be a claim to have insight into their "state of mind" in a more general sense.[5]

The context inclines us to the first of these interpretations, that Lu Chi becomes aware of their feelings about the difficulties of composition; but behind his phrasing are echoes of older texts (such as "The state of mind of the Sages can be seen in their words" 聖人之情見乎辭 from the *Hsi-tz'u chuan*) which would support the more general interpretation of *ch'ing**, "state of mind." In essence, Lu Chi is building a new attention to literary and compositional issues (perceiving Wang Ts'an trying to write about his feelings on climbing the tower) on the base of older notions of the perfect transparency of the literary text (perceiving Wang Ts'an's feelings on climbing the tower).

I constantly fear failure, *heng huan*: Literally, "I am constantly troubled (lest). . . " This is perhaps the earliest statement of anxiety regarding the success of composition, though such anxiety follows quite naturally from the "horse race" of competition before the evaluating prince, described in Ts'ao P'i's "Discourse on Literature." This anxiety is closely related to the shift in interest described above, from the extraliterary circumstances that are manifest through composition to the act of composition itself. In reference to the preceding comments on "knowing others," it is worth noting that "troubled," *huan*, here is the same quality of anxiety felt by Confucius in *Analects* I.16: "He said, 'It does not trouble me that others do not understand me; what troubles me is not understanding others.'"

My conceptions' not being equal to the things of the world, and my writing's not being adequate for my conceptions, *yi pu ch'eng wu, wu pu tai yi*: T'ang Ta-yüan (*Wen-fu chi-shih*, p. 4) offers an important observation here, associating the relation between conceptions and the things of the world with "thought," and the relation between writing and conceptions with "learning" or the experience of reading. This antithesis, between personal thought and reading, becomes one of the central oppositions around which the main body of the poetic exposition is developed. Kuo Shao-yü has attempted to discriminate between the many senses of *yi**.[6] While we may express the same reservations here that we expressed about the scholarly debate over the meaning of *ch'i** in "A Discourse on Literature," we can agree with Kuo's conclusion, that *yi** here is an individuated act of mind, someone "forming an idea" about the world. Thus what we see in a particular work is not a universal "concept" or *yi**, but rather a particular way of understanding that implicates the individuality of the writer. Ch'ien Chung-shu cites a number of earlier and later examples in which operations of reference are described in terms of a tripartite structure. Ch'ien's example from the Mohist Canon includes "singling out," *chü* 舉 (literally "raising up" out of a field of possibility), "name," *ming* 名, and "substance," *shih* 實. In fact, as Chang Shao-k'ang points out in *Wen-fu chi-shih* (p. 5), the similarity is only in the tripartite structure per se: the Mohist "singling out" is the semiotic operation relating "name" and "substance." In contrast, Lu Chi's formulation has *yi** ("conception") as an individual act of subjective structuring that mediates between *wu** ("the things of the world") and *wen** ("writing"). In Mohist linguistic theory the communality of language would require that everyone "raise up" the same class of things using the same "name"; the structuring (rather than naming) function of yi* is individual and not repeatable. In Mohist linguistics the relation between "name" and "substance" is purely conventional and is thus neither adequate nor inadequate (i.e., words are not claimed to have any organic relation to the things they name); in contrast, the individual yi* is measured against the inherent structure of things and thus can be judged adequate or inadequate. The passages from *Wen-hsin tiao-lung* cited by Ch'ien Chung-shu are more to the point and probably reflect the influence of this passage.

The source of Lu Chi's tripartite structure of reference is most likely one not cited by Ch'ien Chung-shu, but rather the process of adequate manifestation, moving from yi* ("conception") to hsiang* ("image") to yen ("words") described in Wang Pi's "Elucidation of the Images," *Ming Hsiang* (see above pp. 33–34). This source is conflated with the radical statement of the essentially inadequate relation between words, writing, and concept in the *Book of Changes, Hsi-tz'u chuan* (see above p. 31). As early as the time of Hsü Ling (507–583) Lu Chi's passage above was associated with that famous passage from the *Hsi-tz'u chuan* (*Wen-fu chi-shih*, p. 5). Although the terms of the process described by Wang Pi are very different from those in Lu Chi's preface, the essential question of adequacy in serial manifestation is shared by both texts. From Wang Pi would come the sense that the structure of reference (or more properly, of "manifestation") is tripartite, occurring in necessary stages, each one seeking to be adequate to the stage before. Lu Chi combines serial adequacy with a disposition from early texts in literary thought to understand that process as a transformation from the "external," *wai* 外 ("things of the world") to the "internal," *nei* 內 ("conception"), then again to the "external" ("writing"). Such transformations between external and internal are most prominent in the "Great Preface" to the *Book of Songs* and in the "Record of Music" in the *Li chi*. Lu Chi's formulation, however, swerves in some interesting ways from these canonical texts:

1. In the canonical texts the transformational series between internal and external is usually described as an involuntary process, proceeding through some natural force from the world experienced to mind and thence to language, writing, or poetry. In the passage from Lu Chi, the anxiety of composition drives the process in the opposite direction, becoming more a structure of reference than one of manifestation. "Conception" reaches toward the fullness of the "things of the world" and sometimes fails; "writing" reaches toward the fullness of "conception" and sometimes fails.

2. As the relation is reformulated, the old question of adequacy is intensified. The canonical expression of this formulation is found in the *Hsi tz'u chuan*: "What is written does not exhaust what is said; what is said does not exhaust conception (or 'what was meant')." The questions of fullness, diminution in expression, and degrees of adequacy are central to traditional Chinese theories of literary manifestation and reference. They constitute a

problem continually refined and readdressed, corresponding both in magnitude and provenance to the great Platonic critique of the secondariness or tertiariness of *mimêsis*. What is given in the *Hsi-tz'u chuan* as a rule of impossibility becomes in Lu Chi's preface a possibility, and hence a source of anxiety. The terms Lu Chi uses are *ch'eng*, "to equal on a balance" (translated as "being equal to"), and *tai*, "to reach up to" (translated as "being adequate for").

3. Of the three terms Lu Chi uses, the one that differs in the most interesting way from those in the "Great Preface" and the "Record of Music" is the mediating term, the "internal" (*nei*) term. In the "Record of Music" the internal term is *ch'ing**, "state of mind" or "emotion"; in the "Great Preface" the internal term is *chih**, "what is intently on one's mind." In Lu Chi's preface the mediating, internal term is *yi**, "conception"; and this choice clearly reveals the new voluntarism and accompanying sense of reflective distance in composition. Writing has become an act of will, something proposed in the mind before enactment, and thus open to reflection. Unlike *ch'ing** and *chih** (which must be instigated by something external), "conception," *yi**, is not essentially passive and affective. *Yi** is both a mental act of relating of "things of the world" and a sense of the significance immanent in those relations. To take the famous aphorism of the *Huai-nan-tzu* 淮南子, "when a single leaf falls, all the world knows it's autumn." According to the "Great Preface" and "Record of Music," the single falling leaf, a "thing of the world," would be an essentially affective force, stirring the inner person, and later emerging as a poem or as music; Lu Chi, instead, would have it that a writer observes this "thing of the world" and forms a "conception" of its relation to other things and the implications of that relation. We should take particular note that the involuntary emotional force has not disappeared altogether; rather it has been transferred to the anxiety of composition—whether or not "conception" can adequately grasp the fullness of the "things of the world."

I suppose it is not the understanding that is difficult, but rather the difficulty lies in being able to do it well, *kai fei chih chih nan, neng chih nan yeh.* Ch'ien Chung-shu correctly identifies the *Tso chuan* as the source of what was no doubt a commonplace, and at the same time points out that Lu Chi could not possibly have known the passage from the *Book of Documents* forgery that is cited in the Li Shan commentary to *Wen hsüan*. One may detect a slight refinement over the *Tso chuan* source and its subsequent variations in Lu Chi's substitution of *neng*, "to do well," for *hsing* 行, "to do," "to carry out." Lu Chi's concern is excellence rather than mere doing. I take the opposition here to be between knowing how to write well and actually doing so.[7] Ch'ien Chung-shu, however, gives this passage as the source for another passage in the "Spirit Thought" chapter of *Wen-hsin tiao-lung*: "Whenever a person grasps the writing brush, the *ch'i** is doubled even before the words come. But when a piece is complete, it goes no further than half of that with which the mind began" (see p. 206 below). This suggests that Ch'ien Ching-shu understands this passage from "The Poetic Exposition on Literature" as an antithesis between what one "knows" of the world and the ability to put that knowledge on paper. This is close to the standard Romantic position, as in Shelley's "Defense of Poetry": "for the mind in creation is as a fading coal, which some invisible influence, like an inconstant wind, awakens to transitory brightness . . . Could this influence be durable in its original purity and force, it is impossible to predict the greatness of the results; but when composition begins, inspiration is already on the decline, and the most glorious poetry that has ever been communicated to the world is probably a feeble shadow of the original conceptions of the poet."[8] Such an interpretation of the passage in "A Poetic Exposition on Literature" creates inevitable difficulties in the following lines, leading to ingenious attempts at solutions by various scholiasts. That is, if Lu Chi claims an absolute difficulty between knowing what one wants to write and actually writing it, then how can he claim here to "have minutely exhausted the subtleties of the subject"? But if the difficulty lies between "knowing how to" (which can be adequately presented in the "Poetic Exposition") and actually writing a literary work, then he is free to say that here he has said everything that might be said about the topic, with the qualification that this does not guarantee that the reader of the "Poetic Exposition" will be able to write brilliantly after thoroughly comprehending this work.

Preface (Section C)

故作文賦以述先士之盛藻。因論作文之利害所由。他日殆可謂曲盡其妙。

Thus I write (*tso*) "A Poetic Exposition on Literature": first to transmit (*shu*) the splendid intricacy of craft (*tsao*) of previous writers, and second, thereby to discuss the origins of success and failure in the act of writing (*tso-wen**). I hope that at some time it will be known for minutely exhausting the subtleties of the subject.

Transmit, *shu*: This is a good example of how the force of *tso*, "to make," has been weakened (see section A). Here *shu* and *tso* are no longer antithetical terms as they were in *Analects* VII.1; instead, Lu Chi "makes" precisely in order to "transmit."

I hope that at some time it will be known for minutely exhausting the subtleties of the subject. This sentence has disturbed various scholars: the reason, one suspects, is the indecorous vanity in the most obvious construction of this sentence. To restore to Lu Chi a modicum of proper modesty, scholars like Yü Cheng-hsieh (cited in Ch'ien Chung-shu; and *Wen-fu chi-shih*, p. 8) would take *wei* 謂, "to be said to," as an interpolation and suggest an interpretation that Lu Chi hopes some future writer will "minutely exhaust the subtleties." This interpretation is followed by Ch'eng Hui-ch'ang. Ch'ien Chung-shu suggests that Lu Chi is referring to previous writers who "can be said to have virtually exhausted all the subtleties [of writing]." Although this relieves the potential vanity of the statement, it remains a rather forced interpretation of the lines. The interpretation I have given in the translation is the oldest, most natural, and most widely accepted one, derived ultimately from the T'ang Wu-ch'en commentary to the *Wen hsüan*. Despite its vanity, it is consonant with the last statement of the preface: "What can be put into words is all here." To boast of the thoroughness and originality of one's achievements was commonplace in prefaces of Western Tsin poetic expositions, such as Ch'eng-kung Sui's *T'ien-ti fu* 天地賦 and Tso Ssu's 左思 *San-tu fu* 三都賦. The way in which Lu Chi conceives his procedures is worth our attention: the central terms are *chin*, "exhaust" (one of the main terms used in the question of adequacy) and *miao**, the "subtleties," the "fine points." The goal of Lu Chi's exposition is not some definition or structure that determines the essence of a topic, but rather exhausting a field; perfect understanding must involve an understanding of detail. Aristotelian expository procedure offers an excellent contrast: one delimits a topic by differentiating it from a field of related topics, then proceeds to distinguish the essential divisions and subdivisions within the topic; the goal in that case is to identify only those divisions which follow necessarily from essence—the very opposite of "exhausting the subtleties." Lu Chi offers no definition of "literature" (no marking of boundaries by which this phenomenon can be distinguished from "non-literature"); instead of a set of internally complete sections, we have several sets of oppositions repeated in various frames of reference and amplified in ever-increasing detail.

We can see the initial movements of these procedures already in the preface. Lu Chi begins with an opposition between reading the works of others and writing himself; this strategy of opposition is repeated in the antithesis between knowing and "being able to do it well." It reappears here in the goal of "transmitting the splendid intricacy of craft of previous writers" and "discussing the origins of success and failure in the act of writing." In this final case, "thereby," *yin* 因, links knowing and doing; and that tentative relation between the two is embodied in the problematic metaphor of the ax-handle in the following, final passage of the preface.

Preface (Section D)

至於操斧伐柯。雖取則不遠。若夫隨手之變。良難以辭逐。蓋所能言者具於此云爾

When it comes to taking an ax in hand to chop an ax-handle, the model is not far from you; however, it is hard indeed for language (*tz'u**) to follow the movements (*pien**, "mutations") of the hand. What can be put into words is all here.

Taking an ax in hand to chop an ax-handle, the model is not far from you, *ts'ao fu fa k'o, sui ch'ü tse pu yüan.* This is a free restatement of the aphorism at the beginning of *Book of Songs* 158:

> To chop an ax-handle, to chop an ax-handle,
> The model is not far.

By Lu Chi's time this aphorism had become common wisdom and was often cited in prose, with no direct reference to its source in the *Book of Songs*. *Sui,* "although," (translated as "however" and transferred to the head of the second predicate) grants the truth of the aphorism, but prepares for a problematic refinement or alternative case.

It is hard indeed for language to follow the movements of the hand, *sui shou chih pien, liang nan yi tz'u chu.* Most commentators here cite the story of Wheelwright Pien, as told in the *T'ien Tao* 天道 chapter of the *Chuang-tzu* (see above p. 35). The wheelwright argues for the essential untransmissibility of the Way of the Sages on the model of the prereflective and intuitive mastery of his own craft: "you achieve it in your hands, and those respond to the mind. I can't put it into words, but there is some fixed principle there. I can't teach it to my son, and my son can't get instruction in it from me." Although the parable is clearly relevant to Lu Chi's statement here at some level, there is no direct verbal allusion.

As is often the case in classical arguments, one linguistic level is clear, but the finer linguistic level, requiring the choice of one of several possible determinations, is far from clear. The first question is whether the second predicate ("however . . . ") is an extension of the example given in the first predicate: that is, is Lu Chi referring here specifically to the movements of the hand in chopping an ax-handle? If this is indeed the case, the weight of the antithesis lies in the difference between a static model (an ax-handle in hand when one chops another ax-handle) and any performance involving change and movement, as in the execution of something according to a model. This, of course, would follow from the opposition between "knowing how to" and actually doing. If, on the other hand, the second predicate refers directly to Wheelright Pien and does not directly extend the metaphor of the ax-handle, then we have not an antithesis between model and execution, but between two different kinds of acts—those which have clear models at hand and those which are based on intuitive knowledge. Although these two alternatives can be reconciled to some degree, they are essentially different: the former stresses the difficulty of all performance; the latter stresses the difficulty of a certain kind of performance. A third possibility, which does not exclude either of the others, is to place the heaviest weight on the inability of language to convey the "movements of the hand." In this case, when one has an ax-handle in hand, one can readily chop another ax-handle; but that process cannot be described in language (doing may be more difficult than knowing, but describing the doing is virtually impossible). In this case the stress is not on the difference between model and execution, but between the intuitive execution of an act and a description of that execution.

The example is ambiguous; the application to the context at hand is equally so. Lu Chi may be speaking of the difference between those activities that have static models, like chopping ax-handles, and other activities, like writing, that are intuitive and performative, and thus untransmissible. A second possibility, remote but attractive, is that Lu Chi is obliquely referring to his own work here, whose literary qualities are an "ax-handle in the hand" and offer a more immediate and intuitive model for his readers than a less literary attempt to describe the writing process.[9] A third possibility is that Lu Chi is referring specifically in the first predicate to "previous writers," thus continuing his established antithesis between reading and writing, knowing and doing: in this case the sense here becomes something like "the models for writing are right here before me, but it is impossible to describe exactly how they did it".[10] The fourth possibility, which stresses the antithesis between a rough, static model (the ax-handle) and the fine points of the act, would lead to the final statement of limitation: some of it can be expressed in words, but not all of it, not the most subtle motions of composition.

---

1   佇中區以玄覽
2   頤情志於典墳

---

1   He stands in the very center, observes in the darkness,
2   Nourishes feeling (ch'ing*) and intent (chih*) in the ancient canons.

Line 1: As the T'ang scholar Li Shan, the most authoritative early commentator on "The Poetic Exposition on Literature," notes, chu means "to stand for a long time"; it often carries a note of expectation. The most common word for "stand," li 立, would stress location, taking a particular place. Chu stresses duration, with the implication that the inner journey is something eagerly awaited.

Chung-ch'ü, translated as "the very center," is the "central region," sometimes referring to the capital (as it is taken by the Wu-ch'en commentary), but here referring to a central position in the world or cosmos (Ch'eng Hui-ch'ang, cited in TL).[11]

Observes in darkness, hsüan-lan: Li Shan cites Lao-tzu for this phrase and gives the Ho-shang kung 河上公 exegesis of the usage (which would probably have been known to Lu Chi): "the mind resides in a dark and mysterious place, there observes and knows all things; this is called 'observing in darkness.'" The Wu-ch'en commentary, followed by Ch'ien Chung-shu, wants to take this as "to observe literary works from afar." Ch'ien would take this couplet as referring to the reading process, matched by the experience of the world in the second couplet (lines 3–4). But he misses the rhetorical structure: the first couplet involves an initial antithesis between an imaginative experience of the things of the world (A) and reading (B): the topic of the first line is subsequently amplified in lines 3–8; the topic of the second line is amplified in lines 9–12 (see below). This expository form AB/AA/BB is more common than the primitive AA/BB form proposed by Ch'ien Chung-shu. Furthermore, the less mundane interpretation of "the very center" is supported by the repeated injunctions in *Lao-tzu* to cleave to the empty center.

Hsüan-lan was originally a technical term of spiritual experience; and along with other words of roughly the same class, it acquired a loose, secular frame of reference in the Han, becoming something like "imagination." This set of terms of spiritual vision and spirit journeying became the model for operations of the literary imagination, as in the chapter on "Spirit Thought" in the *Wen-hsin tiao-lung*: "Thus when one broods fixedly and in silence, thought reaches to a thousand years in the past; and as one's countenance stirs ever so slightly, vision has crossed over ten thousand leagues" (see p. 202 below). Throughout "The Poetic Exposition on Literature," when Lu Chi speaks of encountering the "things of the world" (*wu**), he is referring to an imaginative encounter, an "envisioning." That the model of mystical experience remains very strong in this early stage of conceiving the literary imagination is witnessed by the demand that the writer occupy "the very center."[12] The shift from purely empirical "things of the world" implicit in earlier literary thought (e.g., in the "Record of Music") to these "things of the world" discovered in a spirit journey within the mind parallels the shift from the involuntarism of earlier literary thought to Lu Chi's voluntarism.

From Aristotle on, the long and complex history of the theory of the imagination in the West is based on the metaphor of forming pictures in the mind. It should be obvious how such a model easily accommodates itself to the idea of original creation (as late as Dilthey the idea of the poetic imagination was based on the recombination of images of experience according to principles not found in reality). In contrast, in the model of the spirit journey, consciousness actually "encounters" objects; these objects are conceived as having existence autonomous from consciousness, even though they are discovered within the microcosm of the self. This in turn accommodates itself to the traditional Chinese notion of literary "making," *tso*, as the verbal formulation of that which has prior existence in the world. Great literary traditions grow out of the possibility of the lie, the concepts of truth and falsehood that come into being with language. We still live with the legacy of the Greek solution in the idea of *poiêsis*, the "fiction," the untruth that is in some way true without making a literal truth-claim. China found another solution, not fictionality but a strange "interior empiricism," and thus developed a richer and more interesting notion of literal truth.

Line 2: Nourishes feeling and intent, *yi ch'ing* chih**: *Ch'ing** "feeling," tends to be the passive and receptive aspect of "mind," *hsin**; here it has a capacity to be nourished or fed, and in this sense is perhaps closest to English "sensitivity." Although also stirred by things, *chih** is an active component of mind, that which "goes out" or "goes toward" something. This opposition between receptive and active is amplified in lines 7–8 (although there the general category *hsin** takes the role of the more purely receptive *ch'ing**). These two faculties, *ch'ing* and *chih**, are neither wholly innate not wholly learned; they are capacities that can be "nourished," and here, nourished by reading.

Although no doubt both *ch'ing** and *chih** are stirred by reading, that stirring in itself is less significant than developing the capacity to be stirred. This capacity is put to use when speculatively encountering the "things of the world" and when engaged in one's own composition.

The ancient canons, *tien-fen*: The "five *Tien*" and the "three *Fen*" were mythical writings of the Sage Emperors of high antiquity. Here they are used as a general reference to old, authoritative writings.

In the rhetorical structure of "The Poetic Exposition on Literature," this couplet opens the main body of the work by responding to the double anxiety of "my conceptions' not being equal to the things of the world" and "my writing's not being adequate for my conceptions."[13] "Observation" of the things of the world (in the spirit journey or imagination) is a means to resolve the potential inadequacy of one's conceptions. Reading, to develop a sense of the correspondences between words and feelings, is a means to resolve the potential inadequacy of one's writing. This double requirement of experience and reading remains strong in the Chinese theoretical tradition. The "Spirit Thought" chapter of *Wen-hsin tiao-lung* amplifies this into five preconditions of composition: 1) vacancy and calm (corresponding here to the position in "the very center"), 2) learning, 3) understanding natural principle (*li**), 4) experience, and 5) knowledge of earlier literature. The third and fourth of these correspond roughly to Lu Chi's "observing in darkness"; the second and fifth would be the sort of things obtained from the "ancient canons."

3   遵四時以歎逝
4   瞻萬物而思紛
5   悲落葉於勁秋
6   喜柔條於芳春
7   心懍懍以懷霜
8   志眇眇而臨雲

3	He moves along with the four seasons and sighs at their passing on,
4	Peers on all the things of the world, broods on their profusion,
5	Grieves for the falling leaves in strong autumn,
6	Rejoices in the pliant branches in sweet spring;
7	His mind shivers, taking the frost to heart;
8	His intent is remote, looking down on the clouds.

Lines 3–4: Moves along with . . . peers. . . , *tsun . . . chan*: In parallel constructions such as this, the semantic field of a word is determined not only by the syntagm in which it occurs, but also by the parallel term. Often such parallel terms collapse into a common complementary compound, and in such cases the mutual definition of each term is clear. However, an uncommon antithesis such as this one stresses some essential difference, in this case between a passive participation in natural cycles (*tsun* implies acquiescence) and the distance of observation and reflection. This opposition is sustained by the further opposition between the objects of the verbs: thus the "four seasons" encompass the poet as well as things, while the "things of the world" refer specifically to that which is external to the self (e.g., *wu*-wo* 物我, "things and self," object and subject). This opposition between participation in change and reflective knowledge of change is further supported by the opposition between the verbs: the immediately affective "sighs" set against the more reflective (though also affective) "broods," *ssu**.

Sighs at their passing on, *t'an-shih*: This phrase constitutes the title of another poetic exposition by Lu Chi, a lugubrious elegy on the impermanence of things. *Shih*, like "to pass on," is a polite way of referring to death.

"Passing on . . . profusion . . . , *shih . . . fen*: This uncommon opposition is a rhetorical variation within a common family of antithetical compounds, best represented by *sheng-shuai* 盛衰 ("splendor" or "full flowering" and "decline"), which is associated with the cycles of fortune, dynasties, the seasons and their vegetation, and human life. Thus "passing on" is related to autumn and winter, and is picked up by line 5 "profusion" is associated with spring and summer, and is picked up in line 6.

Broods on their profusion, *ssu*-fen*: Most commentators choose to violate parallelism here and read "my thoughts become (as) profuse."[14] *Ssu**, here translated as "brood," is a verb of thought, often carrying the implication of care, and sometimes the implication of longing or desire. The things of the world, in all their splendid profusion, are "on his mind"; but it is unclear whether he is anxious about their future passing or desires a similar profusion in himself.

Lines 5–6: Grieves . . . rejoices . . . , *pei . . . hsi*: Li Shan reads *chia* 嘉, "consider excellent," "admire," in place of "rejoice." The two terms, *pei-hsi*, as they appear in the antithesis here, constitute the primary antithesis in "emotion," *ch'ing**; and used together, they circumscribe the full range of emotion. This is an essential point in understanding parallelism in both Chinese poetry and prose. Classical Chinese forms its counterparts of abstract categories often from established antitheses (e.g., *yüan-chin* 遠近, "far-near," "distance"); therefore the division of such terms in parallel construction often indicates the full range of distinction in a categorical abstraction, and not simply the two specific extremes. Thus, while the determinations made by the specific propositions are true (he "grieves" in autumn and does not "rejoice"), the couplet implicates a full range of emotional response to the cycles of nature.

Line 7–8: *Lin-lin* 懍懍 (also written 凜) evokes the mood of encountering something fearsome, awesome, or cold; hence "shivers." *Huai*, translated as "take to heart," combines the sense of physically "embracing to one's breast" and the psychological sense of "caring for," "having on one's mind." The line emphasizes the genuineness of affective response: thinking of the frost, he feels a genuine shiver of cold/awe/fear. Frost was associated with purity, moral severity, punishment and destruction, and, of course, with autumn, the season for exercising those qualities (cf. 1. 15).

Clouds do not have a determinate association with spring, thus breaking the symmetry of alternation between autumn and spring in the two preceding couplets and initiated in this couplet with the mention of frost. This line is based on the common qualification of "intent," *chih**, as "lofty" (*kao* 高) or "far-reaching" (*yüan* 遠). "Mind," *hsin** (more properly *ch'ing**, the affections) responds passively to external impulses ("shivers" in the preceding line); the active counterpart and outcome of being stirred is *chih**, "intent," which "goes out" (the old etymological gloss for *chih** being "that to which mind goes" 心之所至也). In this line "intent" goes so far and so high that it is above the clouds. This "going out" of intent is one form of spirit's "going out" in imagination. Note the perspectival distance of "intent" from the speaking subject in the modal descriptive *miao-miao*, describing the quality of something that is tiny and faint in the distance.

These eight lines treat the problem of "conceptions' not being equal to the things of the world" and amplify the resolution of that problem by "observing in darkness," *hsüan-lan*. The question is an epistemological one, and it is resolved here much as it is resolved in the chapter "The Sensuous Colors of Physical Things" in *Wen-hsin tiao-lung*: we can adequately know (form conceptions about) the things of the world because we are an organic part of nature as well as being aware of nature; we "follow along with the seasons" as well as being aware of the things of the seasons. Our participation in nature is attested by the affective power that nature has over us: grieving, rejoicing, shivering. The repeated antitheses—grieve and rejoice, autumn and spring— emphasize a full range of responses to a full range of changes. The modern reader will certainly find these associations learned rather than organic; we no longer believe that each season and each thing has an inherent mood that we share; but this does not change the fact that such associations may be experienced as if they were organic.

The final couplet of the passage, moving from passive stirring to active response in "being intent," takes us to the condition of composition, in which "being intent" plays a central role. The language continually links physical states and emotional states ("taking the frost to heart," "intent is remote") in order to reinforce the correspondence between outer and inner; thus the condition of "being intent," which goes out and becomes the literary composition, will be stamped by the same correspondence. We might note that even though Lu Chi emphasizes the voluntary and self-conscious dimension of composition in his anxiety about his "conceptions' not being equal to the things of the world," the only way he can resolve that anxiety is by appealing to older notions of involuntary affect, the power of outer things to impel the human mind involuntarily.

Lu Chi's alternation between seasons and between moods here indicates that he is making a general proposition and not referring to the world at hand. And it is about such a capacity for generalization that Lu Chi is writing: the full range of nature's changes can be known speculatively as well as directly and empirically; this is the function of "observing in darkness," *hsüan-lan*. These "things of the world" which conception hopes to equal are not experienced by the outer senses; they are known through a journey within the self. Now, having amplified the speculative experience of things, Lu Chi may be expected to treat the parallel term, the necessity of reading.

9	詠世德之駿烈
10	誦先人之清芬
11	游文章之林府
12	嘉麗藻之彬彬

9   He sings of the blazing splendor of moral power (*tê*) inherited by this age,
10   Chants of the pure fragrance (or "reputation") of predecessors,
11   Roams in the groves and treasure houses of literary works,
12   Admires the perfect balance of their intricate and lovely craft.

Lines 9–10: Sings of...chants..., *yung...sung...*: *Sung* was often interchanged with another *sung* 頌, also applied to chanting recitation, but often carrying the implication of "praise." This raises the question whether ancient and modern worthies are the object of his own writing, or whether he is reciting their works. Line 9 inclines slightly to the former interpretation, while line 10 inclines slightly to the latter possibility. In terms of the rhetorical amplification, these lines should treat his experience of earlier literature rather than what he writes about (the stage of actual composition is many lines ahead).

Blazing splendor . . . pure fragrance . . . , *chün-lieh ch'ing-fen . . .* : *Lieh,* "blaze," often refers to a brightly manifest excellence. *Fen,* "fragrance," is a member of a group of olfactory metaphors associated with reputation. The opposition, involving direct and indirect perception (with "fragrance" the source can be absent), is an appropriate distinction between the ways in which we apprehend present and past excellence.

Moral power inherited by this age . . . predecessors, *shih-tê, hsien-min*: Both of these phrases are taken from the *Book of Songs*.[15] My interpretation of this as an alternation between present and past is based on one possible interpretation of *shih-tê,* as a moral force accumulated by generations of predecessors and possessed by people in the present. To "sing of" this might also be to write about the past, those predecessors in whom such moral force was accumulated. The source passage in the *Book of Songs* would support either interpretation.[16] What weighs the interpretation strongly in favor of reference to the present is the common attributive use of *shih* in Lu Chi's time to mean "of this age."

Lines 11–12: "Roams," *yu**: see Glossary.

Groves and treasure houses, *lin-fu*: These are two standard metaphors for the received corpus of writing. Wu-ch'en overingeniously distinguishes between the "grove," as referring to the amount, and "treasure house," referring to value.

Intricate and lovely craft, *li-tsao* (Wu-ch'en reads *tsao-li*): Note the repetition of *tsao* from the Preface, Section C; such repetitions help sustain the chain of antitheses. Here, as before, this marks reading of earlier literary works, as opposed to the experience of the things of the world.

Perfect balance, *pin-pin. Pin-pin* is virtually defined by its use in *Analects* VI.16: "Only when refinement (*wen**) and substance (*chih**) are in perfect balance do we have a gentleman" 文質彬彬然後君子. In the context of the *Analects,* "refinement" (*wen**, "patterning") and "substance" refer to behavior and character; but they became central terms in literary thought. Lu Chi is still able to use *pin-pin,* "perfect balance," in conjunction with "intricate and lovely craft," *li-tsao*; in later literary theory "intricate and lovely craft" would suggest an imbalance, a preponderance and perhaps an excess of *wen**, "patterning," "refinement."

This section treats the experience of earlier literature as an answer to the danger that "writing not be adequate for the conceptions." The experience of reading earlier works gives one the capacity to express one's own conceptions. The exposition here is less interesting than that of the preceding section. Note that here the reader's "roaming" corresponds to the spirit journey in the experience of things.

13	慨投篇而援筆
14	聊宣之乎斯文

13	With strong feeling he puts aside the book and takes his writing brush
14	To make it manifest in literature.

Line 13: "With strong feeling, he puts aside his book," *k'ai t'ou p'ien*: Although "strong feeling" must follow from both the experience of things and reading, its position here suggests that reading is the immediate stimulus for the process of composition.[17]

Line 14: "To make it manifest," *hsüan chih*: Manifestation (encompassing *hsüan* and other, allied terms such as *ming* 明, "make bright") is the movement from interior to exterior and the essential conceptual ground of all literary activity. The related terms that we gather under the rubric of "manifestation" have a stature roughly equivalent to the lineage of *mimêsis* ("imitation," and in its later transformations, "representation") in Western literary thought. Manifestation may be somewhat closer to the Romantic idea of "expression"; however, one qualification should be added: in China the poet never occupied the role of the rhapsode in "Ion" or the role of the aeolian harp among the Romantics; that is, the poet is never simply a vessel through which divinity or some grand force of the universe manifests itself. Even the closest formulation, that of "Its Origins in the Way" in *Wen-hsin tiao-lung*, has the manifestation of universal pattern mediated by conscious mind. Properly, manifestation should be the organic "outcome" of what lies within, that is, *hsin**, "mind"/"heart" ("expression" as in the sense of "the expression on someone's face," a condition that may reveal, but does not "imitate" inner life as an act of voluntary self-expression). Here, as a volitional act, it follows immediately from an intense mood ("with strong feeling").

Literature, *ssu-wen*: This is an *Analects* usage, referring to "culture" in a broad sense, as received from ancient texts and traditions. By the Han this phrase had come to be used in a loose sense as "belles lettres"; Lu Chi's use of the compound is in that spirit, referring to "literature," but lending an archaic authority to the activity.[18]

Lines 13 and 14 conclude the first section of "The Poetic Exposition," treating the two preconditions for composition: imaginative experience of the "things of the world" and the experience of literature. Although more elaborate lists of preconditions are given in later theoretical texts, Lu Chi diverges significantly from the assumptions made in the earliest texts of literary thought on the preconditions of writing. These early traditions, finding their fullest expression in the "Record of Music" and in the "Great Preface" to the *Book of Songs*, assume that composition follows from a state of mind involuntarily stirred by a direct experience of the world (even the more purposive theories of the origins of the *Book of Songs*, tracing their composition to the moral intentions of the "historians of the states," depend on an initial response to the condition of the age rather than a desire to write a poem). Lu Chi retains vestiges of the notion of emotional stirring, but substitutes a voluntary and speculative experience of the "things of the world," attained by a spirit journey within the self. Equally important, Lu Chi adds the experience of other literature as a precondition to composition; and in this we have an early acknowledgment of the historicity of literature that inevitably accompanies a shift to "the intention to write a poem," as opposed to a response to the outer world. The role which such necessary experience of earlier literature should play—the degree to which the language of the Other mediates the language of the self—eventually raised problems that have remained with Chinese literary thought down to modern times. Western poetics began in the Greek notion of *technê*, an "art" in the sense of a system of production whereby a certain thing could be made (*poiêsis*); indeed, the term "poetics," *poiêtikê*, is originally an attributive modifying *technê*. This led to an analysis of the object of production ("a thing made," *poiêma*, a "poem") into its component parts. The term for a description of that system of production is, properly, a *technologia*. In essence this is the status of Aristotle's *Poetics*, and in a more diffuse way, of the *Peri Hupsous* attributed to Longinus (which explicitly calls itself a technologia). Although in the later tradition a "poetics" became a description of what the thing "is" rather than how it can be "done," the way of thinking about what it "is" had deep roots in the idea of production.

There were later Chinese critical genres that came very close to the Western genre of *technologia* (e.g., *shih-fa**, "methods for poetry"). But Lu Chi's poetic exposition and the majority of traditional Chinese theoretical works make very different assumptions: they describe the stages in a process of coming-to-be, not the relation of a "maker" to a "thing made"; there is no analysis of component parts. Although some of the things Lu Chi describes in his poetic exposition could be elements of a *technê*, more often composition is made possible by achieving an orderly series of preconditions: background, states of mind, and areas of attention. These preconditions facilitate a thing's coming-to-be, rather than describing the structure or blueprint of the made thing itself. In the Chinese tradition, identifying the stages of a process answers the question of what a phenomenon "is," just as the analysis (literally "dividing" into component parts) in a poetics answers the same question in the Western tradition. Any analysis must begin with boundary questions, questions of definition, to set the object of description apart from other phenomena; from this imperative arises the concept of the "extraliterary" (e.g., Aristotle's initial exclusion of Empedocles' verse from the category poetry, and the contrast with history and philosophy later in the *Poetics*) and a deep distrust of the intrusion of the "extraliterary" into poetry. In contrast, the identification of stages in a process must show how the process begins, especially how it begins out of something else. Its concerns are not with boundaries and definitions but with the clarification of relations and the establishment of grounds for the event. Lu Chi is remarkable in not tracing literature in some way back to the lived, extraliterary world; but he does obey the imperative to establish the preconditions of composition—in his own peculiarly private way, alone in his speculative imagination and with his books.

---

15 其始也。皆收視反聽。
16 耽思傍訊。
17 精騖八極。
18 心遊萬仞。

15 Thus it begins: retraction of vision, reversion of listening,
16 Absorbed in thought, seeking all around,
17 My essence galloping to the world's eight bounds,
18 My mind roaming ten thousand yards, up and down.

Lines 15–16: "Thus it begins," ch'i shih yeh is an extrametrical phrase used as a paragraph marker in poetic expositions. The preceding lines described the preconditions of writing; this "beginning," the next stage, seems to be the process of meditation or speculation that precedes an individual act of composition.

Retraction of vision, reversion of listening, shou-shih fan-t'ing: There is a complicated relation between this and similar passages in "The Poetic Exposition on Literature" and Taoist quietism, both in its early versions in Lao-tzu and Chuang-tzu, and in its Neo-Taoist versions elaborated by Lu Chi's contemporaries. Most Chinese exegetes since Li Shan and the Wu-ch'en commentary interpret this passage as a cutting off of sense perceptions, taking shou ("retract") in a common usage as "cease," and apparently taking fan ("revert") as the attention of listening "reverting" to nonattention. Chinese theorists often spoke of the necessity of cutting oneself off from the determinations of the lived world in order to write. Of uncertain date but close in time to Lu Chi, "The Miscellaneous Records of the Western Capital," Hsi-ching tsa-chi 西京雜記, contains an anecdote about the great Western Han writer of poetic expositions, Ssu-ma Hsiang-ju, which not only speaks of the writer's disengagement from the ordinary world but also describes the writing process in a grand manner similar to that of Lu Chi:

When Ssu-ma Hsiang-ju wrote the Shang-lin Park poetic exposition, his thoughts (yi*-ssu*) were dispersed, and he no longer paid attention to external things. He drew in all Heaven and Earth, commingled past and present; suddenly he would be as if sleeping, then in a flash he would bestir himself. After a hundred days it was finished. His friend Sheng Lan asked him about the writing of a poetic exposition, and Hsiang-ju said, ". . . the mind of a writer of poetic expositions encompasses all the universe and makes general observations of things and people. But this is something attained within; it cannot be grasped and transmitted."[19]

The cosmic scope of the writer's thoughts here is similar to what we find in Lu Chi, but the initial concentration in order to write is described in somewhat more mundane terms: he didn't "pay attention to external things." Others, however, described something very much like a state of Taoist vacuity as the precondition for composition. For example, in the "Spirit Thought" chapter in *Wen-hsin tiao-lung* we read: "Thus in molding literary thought, the most important thing is emptiness and stillness within. Dredge clear the inner organs and wash the spirit pure." *Wen fu chi-shih* cites a passage from *Chuang-tzu* (chapter 11) that can serve as an excellent example of the Taoist model behind Lu Chi's description. In it an allegorical sage, Kuang-ch'eng-tzu (Master of Extensive Perfection), is advising the Yellow Emperor on how to achieve long life:

> The essence of the perfected Way is dark and mysterious; the ultimate in the perfected Way is a murkiness and absolute silence. There is no seeing and no listening, clasping one's spirit in stillness; then the body will be right. There must be stillness and clarity, with nothing troubling your body, and then you can achieve long life. When the eyes see nothing, and the ears hear nothing, and the mind knows nothing, your spirit will protect your body, and your body will achieve long life. Take care of what is within you and close off what lies outside you: much knowledge brings destruction. Then I will lead you to a place above, the supreme brightness . . .

There is no question that in his own lines Lu Chi is using a Taoist model of spiritual movement, from cutting off the outer world to a dark stillness and finally to inner light. But it is important to distinguish between a useful, attractive model for the operations of mind in literary composition and true Taoist values. We might note that Lu Chi never rejects knowledge, that rejection being essential to the Taoist spiritual project. Lu Chi is simply transferring the Taoist spiritual model to the writer's quest for words and ideas. In place of the Taoist negation of perception, Lu Chi chooses a somewhat different phrasing, one more appropriate for his purposes: reversion or inversion of the senses. Ch'eng Hui-ch'ang cites a source for this phrasing in the *Shih chi* 史記 (*Historical Records*): "Reversion of listening is called quickness of mind; internalized vision is called understanding."[20] This source passage and the context in the present exposition suggest that the meaning is not a vacuity achieved by "cutting off" the senses, but rather a true "inversion" of the senses—looking and listening within the microcosm of the self.

Lines 17–18: Li Shan takes "essence," *ching*, as "spirit," in the sense of individual consciousness. It is given in parallel with "mind," *hsin**.

Seeking all around, *p'ang-hsün*: *P'ang*, literally "on the side(s)," is here used as "all around," "everywhere." *P'an-hsün* is a neologism modeled on similar compounds such as *p'ang-ch'iu* 傍求, "to search everywhere" (see Ch'ien Chung-shu, pp. 1183–1185). The seeking here is obviously interior, in the microcosm of mind.

The world's eight bounds . . . ten thousand yards (up and down) . . . , *pa-chi*, *wan-jen*: *Pa-chi* are the eight directions carried to their extremes; the phrase is used to refer to the horizontal limits of the world and all within. *Wan-jen* (which is literally closer to twenty-five thousand yards) emphasizes the distance up and down. The opposition is between an extreme range of horizontal and vertical movement.

The reflective process before writing demands an "inversion" of the senses, which becomes an intense quest within. In the spirit journey the mind operates under none of the limitations imposed on the external, bodily senses. This sense of absolute mastery goes with the voluntarism of the inner quest; but still, whatever he "thinks of" is treated as something "encountered," not something invented or made.

19	其致也。情瞳曨而彌鮮
20	物昭晰而互進。
21	傾羣言之瀝液。
22	漱六藝之芳潤。
23	浮天淵以安流。
24	濯下泉而潛浸。

19　And when it is attained: light gathers about moods (*ch'ing**) and they grow
　　　in brightness,
20　Things (*wu**) become luminous and draw one another forward;
21　I quaff the word-hoard's spray of droplets,
22　And roll in my mouth the sweet moisture of the Classics;
23　I drift between Heaven and the abyss, at rest in the current,
24　I bathe in the falling stream, immersed in its waters;

Lines 19–20: Light gathers . . . becomes luminous, *t'ung-lung . . . chao-che*: These two descriptive compounds suggest different stages of brightening. *T'ung-lung* is a hint of light, as just before sunrise; *chao-che* is full brightness. Recall that the initial condition was "observing in darkness," *hsüan-lan* (although *hsüan* is not "dark" in the sense of "hard to see," but rather the "mysterious dark color" of the Heavens); when speculative consciousness encounters an object, there is a brightening. As in the West, consciousness, knowing, and perception are spoken of in light metaphors (both dead metaphors and active ones). The strongest of these terms is *ming* 明, "to be bright" and transitively, "to brighten," hence "to admit understanding" and "to understand." In the passage from the *Chuang-tzu* quoted above, *ming* is the term used to name the goal of the spiritual progress, "the supreme brightness." Consciousness seems to cast light on its object. *TL* stresses the metaphoric model of sunrise here and is probably correct, but it is also possible to think of a lamp revealing something in darkness.

Moods . . . thing, *ch'ing** . . . *wu**: Lu Chi's treatment of *ch'ing** ("mood," "emotion," "the affections") in this couplet is anomalous in traditional Chinese psychology and epistemology (and occurs here probably out of a need to find a parallel for "things.") *Ch'ing** is usually an aspect of *hsin**, "mind," a condition of perception rather than an object of perception. "Things" (*wu**) are said to stir *ch'ing**. But in this couplet it is clear that the first stirrings of *ch'ing** are treated as objects for consciousness, discovered in the spirit journey. This problem might seem to be somewhat resolved if we were to take *ch'ing** in its other sense as "circumstance"; but even in this usage *ch'ing** is properly a condition of knowing and perception rather than an object of it.

Lines 21–22: The Wu-ch'en commentary explains "word-hoard," *ch'ün-yen* as "all books" 羣書; Ch'eng Hui-ch'ang explains it as "the philosophers" 諸子百家. But Li Shan is certainly correct in the citation of Yang Hsiung's *Fa-yen*, where *ch'ün-yen* means something like "all available words." The translation of "word-hoard" is somewhat misleading in that *ch'ün-yen* does not mean sourceless "vocabulary items"; rather it means "all that has been said or written and the words available therein."

The classics, *liu-yi*: *Liu-yi* is literally the "six arts." Li Shan is incorrect in citing the traditional "six arts" (rites, music, archery, charioteering, writing, and arithmetic). Ch'ien Chung-shu engages in a long explanation to prove that *liu-yi* may be "the Classics" (although *TL*'s citation of Ho Cho shows that this interpretation has been around since the Ch'ing). *Liu-yi* may also be a very loose phrase, suggesting the kinds of things an educated person should know, as opposed to the words necessary to describe them, *ch'ün-yen*. One cannot help here recalling Socrates' interrogation of Ion on the *technê* of poetry, that if a poem presents a description of charioteering, would not the *technê* of charioteering be better by a charioteer than by a poet?

Lines 23–24: *T'ien-yüan*, translated as "between Heaven and the abyss," may also be interpreted as "Heaven's gulf" (Wu-ch'en), an asterism or mythological place to be discovered in the imaginative journey through the cosmos while "observing in darkness." I have followed Li Shan in taking it as "the range between Heaven and the lowest watery depths": it is this sense which is amplified in the following couplet (ll. 25–26), repeating *yüan*, there translated as "the deepest pool." I have followed the Wu-ch'en commentary and later Hsu Wen-yü in taking the topic here and in the following line to be the movement of spirit thought. Many commentators, however, have taken the topic to be the "phrases" referred to in the following couplet, phrases that come from afar, drifting in the currents, waiting to be caught.

Falling stream, *hsia-ch'üan*: This is a phrase from *Book of Songs* 153, with relatively little resonance here. Its other meaning as "the underworld" is also inappropriate in this context.

To summarize the situation: The writer who has accomplished the necessary preconditions of composition begins a "search within" to find the "stuff" that goes into the generation of a work of literature—"things," moods, words, and knowledge. These elements are presented as roughly coordinate. That is, it is not that "things" provoke moods or that words name things, but rather that all seem to be encountered, mixed together in an inner search. This will lead to the model of the writer as one who "composes" or "arranges" the elements. This section describes the primary encounter with such "stuff": a movement from darkness to light, from emptiness to plenitude, from active searching to being swept along and inundated. A mood "dawns"; things appear; then we have ever more things in a flood of presence.

The metaphor of light for the activities of consciousness should be familiar to Western readers (even though Lu Chi's extension of it is striking). Less familiar are the metaphors of eating and drinking, and the related "flood" metaphors; these are very powerful in the Chinese tradition (and in other parts of Lu Chi's poetic exposition). As sight and hearing are turned inward for the spirit journey, what is encountered is "quaffed" and "rolled in the mouth"—savored and swallowed. Knowing is not only light, it is also ingestion. Since language and, in particular, learning are often spoken of in metaphors of ingestion, when Lu Chi turns from moods and things to the encounter with words and learning, it is appropriate that he shift metaphor sets. The word "moisture," *jun* 潤, often implies the power to make fertile, an apt way to describe the effect of "absorbing" the Classics (or knowledge in a more general sense). With the happy illogic of a metaphorical paradigm, the "spray of droplets" and "sweet moisture" become a flood that sweeps him along in his speculative journey through the inner cosmos, and eventually pours over him in a "falling stream." Before he was a seeker, anxious about finding something; now he can drift passively, happily overwhelmed by a plenitude.

The poetic exposition constantly moves between antitheses: between inner and outer in both directions, between active and passive, between things and words, between emptiness and fullness. The argument develops by complementarity and compensation. Earlier the experience of things was set against the experience of reading; here when things are mentioned (l. 20), a statement on words must follow (l. 21). When there is active movement, "intense brooding, seeking all around," it will resolve itself with the poet "at rest in the current"; from being passively "at rest in the current," the poet will turn in the next couplet to active metaphors of fishing and hunting. As a genre, the poetic exposition (*fu*) aims at inclusion rather than exclusion, a totality rather than unity; reconciling contradiction—though moves are sometimes made in that direction—is less important than compensating for one-sidedness. In addition to giving the inventory of a totality, these antithetical movements are also essential to the description of processes; and since it is a process of composition being described here (rather than the anatomy of a "thing"), the process will be understood as movements between opposed terms.

---

25 於是沈辭怫悅。若游魚銜鈎。而出重淵之深。
26 浮藻聯翩。若翰鳥纓繳。而墜層雲之峻。

25   Then, phrases from the depths emerge struggling as when the swimming
         fish, hooks in their mouths, emerge from the bottom of the deepest
         pool;
26   and drifting intricacies of craft flutter down, as when the winging bird,
         caught by stringed arrow, plummets from the tiered clouds.

Phrases from the depths, *ch'en-tz'u**: Ch'en-tz'u is literally "sunken phrases." In addition to continuing the water metaphor of the preceding lines, *ch'en* has two strong associations here: first, "deep in the self" (e.g., *ch'en-ssu* 沈思, "sinking thought," "brooding"); second, "hidden," something to be drawn to awareness by this fisher of words.

Emerge struggling, *fu-yüeh*: This is a descriptive compound glossed by Li Shan as "the manner of being hard to bring forth." The Wu-ch'en commentary amplifies the compound preposterously, explaining *fu* as "the manner of not yet having emerged," and *yüeh* as "the manner of faintly emerging." Ch'en Chuo (*Wen fu chi-shih*) explains this by another, homophonous compound that describes fish, either hiding deep in the waters, or, as seems better in this context, hard to draw up.

Drifting intricacies of craft, *fu-tsao*: For *tsao* ("intricacies of craft"), see Preface, Section C, and line 12. Used as a modifier, "drifting," *fu*, usually suggests insubstantiality, even frivolity. Although *fu* often carries negative implications, its use here is positive, a "lightness" appropriate to intricate craft. It also lightly continues the water metaphor.

Drifting between Heaven and the abyss: The poet reverts here to the active, seeking mode as a fisher and fowler, "catching" words and rhetorical graces. From an initial location in a central position (l. 1), the poet travels to the limits of the cosmos (ll. 17–18), and in this couplet returns to a central position between water and sky. The baroque ornamentation of the metaphors here, while familiar enough to Western readers, is uncommon and extreme in the Chinese context. These metaphors suggest a particular relation to language: the words and phrases used in composition have an existence apart from the poet; they are neither made nor used, but "taken" by skill and good fortune (note also that the eating metaphor lies in the background of these metaphors of prey). Like the things of the world, language is encountered. The consequences of this model for a concept of originality are apparent in the two following couplets.

27	收百世之闕文。
28	採千載之遺韻。
29	謝朝華於已披。
30	啟夕秀於未振。

27	He gathers in writing (*wen**) omitted by a hundred generations,
28	Picks rhymes neglected for a thousand years;
29	It falls away—that splendid flowering of dawn, already unfurled,
30	But there opens the unblown budding of evening.

Liness 27–28: Gathers in ... picks, *shou ... ts'ai:* To complement the fishing and fowling metaphors of the preceding lines, the language here is of harvesting: *shou* is the word for harvesting grain, and *ts'ai* is the term used for gathering vegetables and fruit. Such words support the set of food metaphors.

Writing omitted, *ch'üeh-wen:* All commentators refer this to *Analects* XV.25, a passage that refers to the practice of leaving a blank in a text when the truth of a topic was unknown; "Even in my time a historian would omit writing something ... Nowadays that's gone." This is as good an example as one can find of how a classical phrase can be reused without reference to its source context. Were it a serious echo of the *Analects* passage, it would be a most unfortunate one. Confucius is praising a quality of human character that will prevent a person from writing anything of which the person is not certain; Lu Chi here wants to fill in those blank spaces, to write down what was not written before. While there is a profound difference between the historian and the literary man, one can be certain that Confucius would have seen Lu Chi's advice as an example of the fact that "nowadays [such restraint] is gone."

Rhymes, *yün:* Since the great seventeenth-century scholar Ku Yen-wu erroneously singled out this passage as the first discussion of rhymes in Chinese, the passage has been discussed intensely. Most scholars have pointed out either that there were earlier discussions of rhymes, or that rhymes per se was not what Lu Chi meant here. As Ch'ien Chung-shu points out, this does not refer literally to avoiding rhymes used before, but rather to avoiding borrowing from earlier writing. We may, with Ch'ien, take this as specifically "rhymed writings," or we may interpret *yün* in a general sense as "manner," what "chimes with" others.

Lines 29–30: In parallel with *ch'i*, "open," and in this context, *hsieh* translated as "it falls away," should refer to the falling of flowers. The more frequent interpretation of *hsieh*, however, is not impossible: the poet "rejects" (*hsieh*) the blossom already blown, and "brings to open" (*ch'i*) the bud of evening.

This passage, speaking of something like "originality," makes interesting presumptions, which are consonant with the notion of "capturing" words and rhetorical graces: all the possibilities of verbal expression already exist and have always existed; earlier writers have simply "neglected" them or "omitted" to use them.[21] Since language is encountered, one looks to encounter what has never been encountered before. Language is treated as an organic growth, but one that is external to the poet and available to him in his quasi-agricultural work.

As he "gathers in" and "picks," the poet gleans what has been overlooked; but the vegetative metaphor suggests yet another category of concern— timeliness. This concern is amplified in the flower couplet. Not only are words and phrases "picked," they also blossom in their own season; the poet should avoid the full-blown blossom (i.e., a phrase used before) in favor of the fresh bud. Language itself is understood as a process of becoming: the phrase picked in the bud **will** blossom, but the full blown flower **will** fade and fall. There is here a desire for freshness in language, but there is something more: as elsewhere in the tradition, there is an attention to incompletion and incipience—that which holds the potential for further growth and change. All that is in "full flower" contains the promise of overripeness and rotting. It is perhaps too much to say that the phrase "picked in the bud" will "blossom" later when the reader encounters the text, but that sense of potential in reserve is an important aesthetic quality.

Lu Chi is intensely aware of the "hundred generations" and the "thousand years" which lie behind him, whose words have blossomed and now are fading. He feels a strong sense of belatedness and identifies his own world with the evening. The concern for "originality" manifested here can occur in a tradition only when there is great disquietude at the magnitude of what has been written before.

31   觀古今於須臾

32   撫四海於一瞬

31	He observes all past and present in a single moment,
32	Touches all the world in the blink of an eye.

This couplet summarizes the spirit journey and brings to a conclusion this section on encountering and gathering material before writing. On the spirit journey, the poet can instantly encompass all time (in the Chinese sense conceived as past and present) and space.[22] This process includes reflective consideration (*kuan*, "observes"), which is emotionally neutral, and encounters that are more emotionally engaged (*fu*, "touches" or "caresses," sometimes with a strong association of "care").

33	然後選義按部。
34	考辭就班。
35	抱景者咸叩。
36	懷響者畢彈。

33	Only afterward he selects ideas, setting out categories,
34	Tests phrases, putting them in their ranks,
35	Striking open all that contains light,
36	Plucking everything that embraces sound within.

Lines 33–34: Selects ideas . . . tests phrases, *hsüan-yi** *. . . k'ao-tz'u*: Placed in parallel construction, "select" and "test" are the language of evaluating the qualifications of aspirants to government service. The thoroughness with which the poet inspects the flood of words and ideas that seek to be used is the thoroughness of someone charged with seeking talent for government service (*yung* 用, "use"). When Lu Chi must speak of evaluation and judgment, this is the model that would come most readily to mind, related to the contemporary practice known as *p'in-t'i jen-wu* 品題人物, "evaluating and categorizing persons and things to judge where they would best fit in" (although Lu Chi touches on the more particular aspects of *p'in-t'i jen-wu* only very lightly in his poetic exposition). Note how the poet's attitude shifts from anxious seeking to plenitude to reflective judgment. The *yi** ("idea," "principle," "a truth") used in this line is very close to *yi**, "conception"; but *yi**, "a truth," is more of a constant principle independent of a particular exercise of mind and, because it is a truth, carries strong overtones of positive moral value (Confucian philosophy often calls moral principles *yi**, "truths").[23] Coordinate with *tz'u**, "phrases," and given as an object of judgment, this *yi**, "a truth," is more appropriate than *yi**, "conception." Hsü Fu-kuan sees the particular sequence of these lines as significant: he believes this means that the writer is first supposed to arrange the ideas, then select the phrasing.

Setting out categories . . . putting them in their ranks, *an-pu . . . chiu-pan*: These phrases also belong to the language of political judgment, making assignments that match a particular talent to an office. *An-pu*, used to describe the establishment of a military table of organization, describes the creation of a structure of functions (in Chinese *wei* 位, a hollow "position" which may be held by different individuals). Hsü Fu-kuan points out that *pu*, "category," is the term used for the divisions in the early lexicographical work, the *Shuo-wen* 說文 by Hsü Shen (ca. A.D. 100); such divisions are semantic categories and would be closely related to the formation of antitheses in parallelism.[24] *Chiu-pan*, the act of assigning individual persons to appropriate positions, complements *an-pu*. The metaphor of government structure seems to be applied thus: one selects and frames a structure of preexisting "ideas" (or "truths," *yi**), then assigns individual phrases to appropriate places in that structure (the phrases culled in the inner search). This political metaphor suggests something of the dispassionate judgment so often assumed in Western neo-classicism; but the analogy breaks down when we consider that this is not the sculptor's *limae labor* ("the labor of the file" that Horace enjoins), but rather the model of a structure of relations between elements, each with is own autonomous disposition, like human beings in a political structure.[25]

Lines 35–36: That (which) contains light . . . that (which) embraces sound within, *pao-ying-che . . . huai-hsiang-che*: Compounds and antitheses based on sight and sound often comprehend a full range of sensuous attributes (see commentary to ll. 5–6). "Contain," *pao*, and "embrace within," *huai*, refer not only to the possession of these attributes, but also to "withholding" them, requiring the poet's active intervention to bring them forth. Embedded in this antithesis is the common compound *huai-pao* 懷抱, a person's "cherished feelings," often withheld from expression. Although this couplet speaks primarily of bringing out and putting to use the latent qualities of the things of the world, the metaphor of political judgment and assignment remains strong: someone charged with seeking out talent for office is enjoined to discover and bring out hidden (or withheld) capacities in those examined and to put those capacities to appropriate use. There is disagreement regarding the frame of reference here. The phrases may refer to the sensuous qualities of things (although Chang Shao-k'ang disagrees strongly with this possibility). It may refer to rhetorical "flash" (in Chinese, rhetorical flourishes are often described as light and color emanating from the text) and the auditory qualities of a text. Or it may be, as Huang K'an and Chang Shao-k'ang suggest, the development of "poetic ideas," bring out their latent possibilities.

Striking open, *k'ou*: Originally meaning "knock," *k'ou* early took on the extended sense of to "bring forth," as in *Analects* IX.7.

This important passage concerns the ordering process that must follow the encounter with plenitude. The dominant model is one of building a government out of an unorganized body of persons with various kinds of potential. One must build a structure of positions or functions, then judiciously match individual capacity with function, taking great care to discover everything and overlook nothing. Like a founding emperor (conventionally called a "Sage"), the poet does not create out of nothing, but rather uses what is available to give natural order to chaos.

The preface echoed the voice of Confucius (the Sage) in several places; and, in Lu Chi's time, the spirit journey could easily be associated with the cosmic authority of an emperor (Sage), imperial panegyric having often been based on the spirit journey, as in the "Great Man," *Ta-jen fu* 大人賦, by the Western Han writer Ssu-ma Hsiang-ju 司馬相如. Following the associative transformations of the writer as Sage, in this section we have the model of discovering talent to form a government. It should be stressed that any analogy between the actions of a poet and those of the Emperor-Sage are very subdued and nowhere explicit.

In Western literary thought, divinity was a recurrent model for the work of a poet, from the god's control of poetic utterance in *Ion* to the long lineage of "creation" theory, in which the poet as "maker" was equated with the Maker, that began in the early Renaissance. Lu Chi looks to a very different, but equally powerful model, to the Sage and his utopian state: this model promises a human understanding which makes it possible to enact the counterpart of Nature's harmonious order, where everything is living relation.

The structure of categories (*pu*) that informs a composition is not conceived as a logical or persuasive "argument," but rather as a system of productive differences and relations. This section seems to address the question of "conceptions' being equal to the things of the world"; the writer is supposed to organize a literary structure that corresponds to the structure of Nature. It is important to note that words and things have their own inherent natures: their qualities in a literary work are not something that is "given" by the poet. Rather the poet orders them according to their natures and "calls forth" their latent qualities. The following section amplifies with illustrations of some of the essential relations which organize the literary work just as they organize Nature.

37	或因枝以振葉。
38	或沿波以討源。
39	或本隱以之顯。
40	或求易而得難。
41	或虎變而獸擾。
42	或龍見而鳥瀾。
43	或妥帖而易施。
44	或岨峿而不安。

37	He may rely on the branches to shake the leaves,
38	Or follow the waves upstream to find the source;
39	He may trace what is hidden as the root and reach the manifest,
40	Or seek the simple and obtain the difficult.
41	It may be that the tiger shows its stripes and beasts are thrown into agitation,
42	Or a dragon may appear and birds fly off in waves around it.
43	It may be steady and sure, simply enacted,
44	Or tortuously hard, no ease in it.

Lines 37–38: The antithetical pair of relations comprehended in this couplet was so common that it would have been immediately recognized by all readers, thus establishing expectations regarding the structural significance of the less common examples in the lines that follow. Branches to leaves is a movement from origin to consequence; waves to source is the contrary movement from consequence back to origin. Relations between origin and consequence (often expressed in Chinese as *pen-mo* 本末, "root and branch-tip") constitute an essential category of *yi**, "conception," and include temporal, causal, and hierarchical value relations. The question arises whether Lu Chi intended these and the following relations to apply to the internal structuring of the text or to operations of significance: is the movement from origin to consequence the way of developing an idea within a text, or is it how "meaning" means (that is, when the text mentions something that might be taken as an origin, will the reader think of the consequence—as in T'ang poems when the poet mentions wind and flowering trees, the reader is to think of the fall of the flowers)? The T'ang Wu-ch'en commentary seems to take it as an operation of meaning: "One writes of the branches and thinks of the leaves." And indeed "relies on the branches to shake the leaves" does suggest an operation of meaning: by means of one movement a second movement is implicated. But the etiological movement of "following the waves upstream to find the source" suggests the structural development within the text, investigating a phenomenon back to its origins. It may be that we have here a Chinese rhetorical figure known as *hu-wen* 互文 : "A is X; B is Y" may be understood "A and B are X and Y." If this is the case, Lu Chi might be lightly implicating both operations in one general principle: these relations that inform "conception" may apply both to the structure of the composition and to how one may understand any particular element in that structure.

Lines 39–40: The paradigm in lines 37–38 is a movement between origin and consequence; a similar paradigm of change is given to the opposites in this couplet. The relation described here seems to refer to a term that resolves into its opposite: 1) in the movement of the discourse; or 2) through movement in the process of understanding (for example, a difficult point that becomes clear when examined, or a clear point that reveals hidden complexities);[26] or perhaps in this case, 3) through a movement in the act of composition. As the movement between origins and consequences (*pen-mo*) describes one essential category of relations, the same is true of the movements between the "hidden" (or "obscure" or "latent") and "manifest." The origin of this line is in Ssu-ma Ch'ien's evaluative comment on the "Biography of Ssu-ma Hsiang-ju" in the *Shih chi*: "The *Book of Changes* takes what is hidden as the root and reaches the manifest."[27] The scholiasts explain this as the latent (and also obscure) principles of the *Book of Changes* that become manifest in human affairs. If Lu Chi has this source text strongly in mind, then he would be suggesting that a literary work may be obscure or its significance latent, only unfolding in its application. An opposition similar to Lu Chi's *yin* and *hsien* occurs in the chapter "Latent and the Out-Standing" of *Wen-hsin tiao-lung*; but there *yin* and *hsiu* refer to two distinct qualities in a text, qualities closely related to affect and significance. In the chapter "The One Who Knows the Tone," when Liu Hsieh refers to the reading process, he uses the same terms Lu Chi uses here: "in the case of reading a work of literature, one opens the text and enters the affections [of the writer], goes against the current to find the source; and though it may [at first] be hidden, it will certainly become manifest."

Considering this discourse of obscurity and obviousness, ease and difficulty, it is perhaps not improper to carry the question back to the lines themselves. Lu Chi's lines read easily in Chinese, but a modicum of reflection (on the original) or a quick survey of the Chinese exegetes assures us that the lines have so many possibilities of interpretation that no single one of them, however attractive, can completely win out over the aggregate of other readings. To offer a few examples of divergence on the line about ease and difficulty: Hsü Fu-kuan takes it as understanding something basic and applying it to what is difficult ("either first to investigate the hidden, then with that as a basis, to move to the resonances; or first to investigate what is easy, then move from the easy to resolve difficulties"). Chang Shao-k'ang thinks the second line refers to seeking an easy phrasing and thereby getting the kind of line that is "hard to obtain" (i.e., very good). Others interpret it as an attempt to achieve simplicity that ends up becoming obscure (a bad outcome). It could be the difficulty of writing simply; it could be getting into difficult points when trying to deal with something apparently simple. For each of these possibilities we would subtly adjust the translation; but the Chinese original holds them all in a happy suspension, in a line that is apparently pellucid. Often the sense of "The Poetic Exposition on Literature" dissolves on reflection, both because the language is exceedingly elliptical and because its usages usually lack the rigid precedents that eventually become so essential in determining the meaning of a sentence in classical Chinese.

Lines 41–42: This couplet is notoriously obscure. Li Shan is correct in referring the first line to the hexagram *Ko* in the *Book of Changes*: "The Great

Man shows his stripes [literally, "does a tiger-mutation"]; the pattern (wen*) is gleaming." This metaphor for nurturing oneself in seclusion is based in the folk belief that the tiger will hide away and let its pelt brighten, so that it can later emerge with its stripes clearly visible, showing itself for the powerful beast it is. Important here is the play on "pattern," wen*, which is the adequate external manifestation of inner nature, be it in the stripes of a tiger or in a literary work. Without reviewing the full history of the dispute over these lines, let me say that Ch'ien Chung-shu's interpretation is the most cogent; his interpretation of jao as "submissive" is, however, forced (even though in line with Li Shan). The ordinary sense of jao as "disturbed" or "agitated" is quite the appropriate response to a tiger showing itself in its true colors. The verbal or adjectival use of lan, "waves," is most unusual, and must refer, as Ch'ien Chung-shu suggests, to the sea birds flying off in droves when a dragon shows itself.[28]

After clarifying some of the images, we must wonder to what kind of relation they refer. In both cases a new, powerful element, something with the capacity for transformation, enters the scene, establishing a hierarchy, changing the stance of previous members of the scene by showing itself. In general terms, the relation described seems to involve a change in value by juxtaposition, so that the appearance of a particular element in a composition (in this case, a powerful image, line, thought, etc.) revalues what went before. The relation seems to correspond to lines 127–128:

> Set a suggestive phrase in an essential spot,
> And it will be a riding crop for the whole piece.

Or in lines 153–154:

> Thorn bushes and medlars need not be cut down—
> They too can become glorious by the roosting kingfisher.

The interest in the "strong image" or "strong line" is here probably a more general relation of relative value through juxtaposition.[29]

Lines 43–44: This opposition between steady ease of movement and difficulty is a fundamental antithesis, but less complex than the preceding ones. As with the preceding couplets, it may apply to the internal development of a piece, to the process of understanding, or to composition. Applied to composition, it recurs several times later in the poetic exposition.

Note that Lu Chi's "rhetoric" is indeed comprised of something like lexis ("word choice") and taxis ("arrangement"); but the differences are striking and significant. The poet encounters things and words (and perhaps "moods," ch'ing*, as well) in an abundant and happy disorder. From these he selects and organizes according to the fundamental rules of relation and transformation. All this is accomplished in the mind before writing; composition can occur only when this stage is complete.

45	罄澄心以凝思。
46	眇眾慮而為言。
47	籠天地於形內。
48	挫萬物於筆端。
49	始躑躅於燥吻。
50	終流離於濡翰。

45	He empties the limpid mind, fixes his thoughts,
46	Fuses all his concerns together and makes words.
47	He cages Heaven and Earth in fixed shape,
48	Crushes all things beneath the brush's tip.
49	At first it hesitates on his dry lips,
50	But finally flows freely through the moist pen.

Empties the limpid mind, *ch'ing ch'eng hsin*: In the preceding stage of meditation before composition, the poet's mind was anything but limpid and empty. The modifier "limpid" may best be understood here as the result of the emptying process: "he empties the mind so that it becomes limpid." Each of the three stages—attainment of the preconditions of composition, meditation before composition, and here, composition itself—repeats the essential process, beginning in emptiness and proceeding to fullness.

Fixes his thoughts, *ning-ssu*: This is the compound for "concentration": thoughts that had previously been moving about, now become "fixed" on a single point.

Fuses all his concerns together, *miao chung-lü*: This very difficult phrase is based, as Li Shan notes, on a passage in the *Shuo-kua* 說卦, "Discourses on the Trigrams," in the *Book of Changes*: "Spirit [in]fuses (*miao**) all things and works in them" 神也者, 妙萬物而為言者也." A proper understanding of Lu Chi's line depends on just how Lu Chi understood the *Shuo-kua* passage, and particularly on how he understood the use of *miao**. He may have understood *miao** as "fine" or "subtle," in the sense of what is as if seen remotely or in miniature. In any case, the early commentaries on the *Shuo-kua* are not precise enough to clarify the passage fully and give us a precise sense of how Lu Chi would have read it. Hsü Fu-kuan and some other modern exegetes take *miao** in a philosophical sense as a perfection in union, a fusion in which all differences disappear. In this context it does seem highly likely that Lu Chi understood *wei-yen*, "works in them," as "makes language." The *Shuo-kua* passage seems to describe how spirit operates in even the finest (*miao**) transformations of things, thus fulfilling and unifying them. If this is the case, the compositional parallel would be that the poet begins writing only after having drawn all the individual elements (described in the preceding section) into a seamless unity. A far simpler alternative would be simply to ignore the *Shuo-kua* passage, take *miao** in a transitive sense of its common meaning of "remote," and construe the line: "he puts all concerns far from him" (or in the very similar interpretation of Chang Feng-yi and Fang T'ing-kuei, "transcends the concerns of ordinary people"). Considering Lu Chi's interest in and familiarity with the *Book of Changes*, however, it seems he would not be ignorant of such an attractive source passage.

He cages Heaven and Earth in fixed shape: Li Shan cites *Huai-nan-tzu* 淮南子: "Ultimate Unity encompasses [encages] Heaven and Earth" 太一者, 牢籠天 地也. The statement of mastery in the following line leads me here to the stronger, more literal rendering of *lung* "cage." The Wu-ch'en commentary suggests that "fixed shape," *hsing** 形, is here the "form" of a literary work; but *hsing** is not commonly used in this way, and it seems that Lu Chi's statement is more directly cosmogonic.[30]

This is a remarkable passage, suggesting through the allusion, that the poet is the counterpart of *T'ai-yi* 太一, the deified principle of "Ultimate Unity." Along with the statement attributed to Ssu-ma Hsiang-ju in the *Hsi-ching tsa-chi* (see commentary to l. 15 above), this and a few other roughly contemporary statements constitute the beginning of a tradition in Chinese literary thought in which the poet becomes equivalent to the forces of Ongoing Creation (*Tsao-hua**). In contrast to Lu Chi's other versions of the poet—the anxious seeker, the vessel through which things become manifest, the Sage-Emperor organizing an orderly society of words and ideas—this notion of the poet as *Tsao-hua** is much closer to the Western notion of literary "creation." The similarity can, however, be deceptive. The stress here is not on voluntary creation *ex nihilo*, but on a comprehensive and animate whole in which the operations of a poet's mind reenact the animate totality of Nature. The work is a heterocosm, "another world" or "second nature"; but it is one of ultimate realism, reenacting the principles that inform this world. The poet's quasi-divine power lies in his capacity to carry out these complex processes, not in invention. The central difference between this vision and the Western concept of literary "creation" lies in the Western concept of free will and its relation to creative divinity: from the late Middle Ages on, the poet's work was explicitly compared to God's free creation of the universe. Lu Chi does exult in the writer's power, but it is the power to **be** Nature, not to make that "second nature" whose identity comes from its distinction from the first Nature.

In fixed shape, *hsing**-nei*: *Hsing**, here translated as "fixed shape," is the corporeality that all things possess. Earth and all things already have *hsing**; whether Heaven has *hsing** is a matter of dispute (but if it does, it is round). But Lu Chi is not referring to Heaven and Earth per se, but rather to an entire world. There seem to be two possibilities for "caging in fixed shape": First, Lu Chi may be referring not to the abstraction of "literary form," but to the physical text and the physical "shape" of the characters; thus a whole world is captured in these ink-shapes. The second possibility is a reference to an envisagement, through a text, of quasi-corporeal forms and relations: if a poet wrote of "clouds blowing through the sky," these are not mere words but indices of a determinate envisagement. Through the poet's power, as through the power of *Tsao-hua**, these things, which existed only in potential, become physical and have the relations of physicality.

We should stress the impulse toward limitation and stasis in this and the following line: "cages" and "crushes." The outer world is always in transformation, coming-to-be. Given in written language, the things of the world are torn out of transformation and fixed: in a text the words "autumn leaf" will never fall to the ground and decay, to be replaced by a spring leaf six months later. The poet not only puts things in fixed form, he "cages" them there in a particular form. That very power of transmutation in which the poet exults also fails to recreate the outer world in its most important attribute—the capacity for change. From this arises a problem which Lu Chi will address later in the poetic exposition.

Lines 48: The antithesis between "all things" and "Heaven and Earth" comprehends the totality of the external world. This is a remarkable sense of violent power over some "thing," which passes through mind and emerges in the written character, "flattened" under the tip of the bent brush. This flattening and crushing that occurs in the physical act of writing adds to the impression that the things of the outer world have been transmuted into an inanimate stasis.[31]

Lines 49–50: The traditional antithesis that governs this couplet is *t'ung**-*se* 通塞, "passage through and blockage." The unwritten composition swells within the poet, hangs blocked at the "exit" (the lips, for the composition is first recited), then flows out through the writing brush. The opposition between "dry" and "moist" links this process to barrenness followed by fertility. The metaphors of liquid and ingestion earlier are completed in the overtone (certainly not consciously intended) of urination or ejaculation, as the liquid flows out from the writing brush. If something is "taken in" and "stored up" (common metaphors for experience and study), then something must finally "come out." This pattern of storage and sudden discharge became a favorite model for the psychology of composition, as five centuries later in Han Yü's famous "Letter in Response to Li Yi": "[After much study] what my mind has chosen pours out through my hand in a swift stream . . . and only when it has gone on like this for years does it become a wild flood . . . *Ch'i** is water; words are the things that float upon it; when the water is in flood, then all floating things large and small are borne up upon it; such also is the relation between *ch'i** and words."[32] Supporting the sexual metaphor in Lu Chi's lines is the close relation in provenance, sense, and sound (which in Lu Chi's time may have been even closer) of *tzu* 字, the "written character" (also meaning "nurture," "give birth to") and *tzu* 子, "child" or "seed." There is a minor tradition in later literary thought that uses the metaphor of offspring for a writer's work; and there is a more powerful tradition that speaks of the literary work as a human body (as in the Western treatment of the poem as *sômaton*, the "little body"). But *tzu* in the sense of "seed" may be related to one of the most powerful of traditional metaphors for the literary work, the literary work as tree, developed in the following couplet.

51　理扶質以立幹。

52　文垂條而結繁。

51　　Natural principle (*li**) supports the substance (*chih**), a tree's trunk;

52　　Pattern (*wen**) hangs down in the branches, a net of lushness.

Through the tree metaphor this couplet outlines the organic relations between some of the most basic terms in Chinese literary thought: "natural principle" (*li**), "substance (*chih**), and "pattern" (*wen**). For convenience the Western reader may think of the relation between form and content as a point of departure, but the particular implications of this tree metaphor make the Chinese ideas quite different.

First we should note that a diachronic relation is immanent in the synchronic relation described: the essential structure of the tree and of a literary work is their process of formation; describing their parts is also tracing their coming-to-be. "Natural principle" is anterior to the trunk/substance; trunk/substance precedes the twigs and leaves that grow from it. The movement between these terms is also a process of "becoming outward"; and investigating the terms is a contrary movement "inward."

Li*, "natural principle," is the universal structure that inheres in any living, formative process: it is not "treeness" but "treeing," "elming," "oaking-in-bad-soil-without-enough-water" (though *li** is conceived as something unitary and universal operating in the particular case). *Chih**, "substance," is the "stuff" of the tree, its inner materiality, which is informed by *li**. Even though the emergence of twigs and leaves is also governed by *li**, they do not have the claim to "be" the material tree; thus if we looked at a leafless winter oak or an oak from which all the branches had been cut, we would still say, "That is an oak" (as we would not say looking at a pile of oak leaves or oak twigs). The trunk has "priority," both in the process of coming-to-be and in the hierarchical claim to "be" the tree.

Wen*, "pattern," is the lavish exterior of leaves and twigs and branches, that which is most visible. Setting aside the botanical fact that we see something of the trunk in most trees (though if we follow the Wu-ch'en commentary and take *kan* as "root" rather than "trunk," we have something truly concealed), the point here is that the pattern of leaves and branches surrounds the trunk, at once concealing it, and at the same time revealing its shape and nature. Wen*, the "pattern" of leaves and branches, is the final stage of growth (ignoring a few more botanical facts), the most exterior stage of "becoming outward," that to which a tree grows. To the untutored eyes, li* and chih* are concealed in the lush intricacy of wen*; there is the illusion of the autonomous and arbitrary in forms that are, in fact, highly determinate. The tutored eye sees li* and chih* immanent in wen*; in fact, li* and chih* (as inner materiality) can be perfectly manifest only in wen*. These three terms form an organic whole: none can be complete or vital without the others. I should point out here that the relation is nowhere worked out with this completeness in Chinese texts (except in Yeh Hsieh's "Origins of Poetry" in the Ch'ing); but such a system of relations can be loosely extrapolated from a wide range of uses of this metaphor.

Wen* is, of course, the profuse intricacy of a literary text, "literariness." Most important, the organic tree metaphor redeems wen* from the complex issues of secondariness inherent in concepts of mimêsis and later, of "representation." Wen*, the literary text, is the outside of an inside, the final stage of a process. The inside can be known through wen*, but wen* does not "represent" the inside any more than the expression on a person's face "represents" a state of mind. Wen* is posterior to li* and chih*, but it is necessary to their completion. Something imitated or represented can exist independently of the imitation/representation (and in the modern version, the quondam "representation" can exist without anything represented: the strange flight from secondariness into self-referentiality); but li* and chih* cannot be complete without wen*: the inside must have its organic outside or it is "bare," incomplete. The purpose of this comparison is not to show superiority in the traditional understanding of wen* over Western concepts of mimêsis or representation; it is simply to demonstrate that issues that have been central to the long tradition of Western literary thought will not, and indeed cannot arise here. Other problems—substantial problems—do, however, arise.

The question remains exactly of what is wen* the outside. The most elegant answer is given in the theory of poetry, shih 詩: as in the "Great Preface," the literary text is the outside of a certain kind of state of mind, a state of mind qualified by the condition of "being intent upon," chih*. But wen* is a much broader term, encompassing a wide range of non-fictional prose; and in these uses the theory of being an organic "outside" is much harder to justify. Suppose one were to write of an event in history: li* would be the "principle" that informed the event; chih* would be the event itself, the "facts." Wen*, in the sense of "text," would be that which made the event manifest to those on the outside, in other places and times. One can easily argue that the event "was" whether it was written about or not; but for this event to "be" for others, to have continued existence and not be forgotten, it depends on the manifest outwardness of wen*. Difficulties arise because of the broad semantic range of wen*, from "written text" to "ornamentation." Thus there are variations: a very sparse chronicle will often be spoken of as being *chih**, "substantial," giving the "bare facts" (even though as a written text it will also be spoken of as *wen**), and contrasted with other texts that have the quality of *wen**, more "ornamented" or "literary." The fuzziness of the term *wen**, which is the hope of an organic relation between the world and literary writing, is the strength of Chinese literary thought before the Sung. Many theorists in the Sung decided against an organic relation, claiming that *wen** was only a vehicle to carry the Way: it was necessary for transmitting the Way, but was not itself the outer shape of the Way. This was the symptom of a profound loss of faith in writing.

53　信情貌之不差。
54　故每變而在顏。
55　思涉樂其必笑。
56　方言哀而已歎。

53　　Truly mood and manner are never uncoordinate:
54　　Each mutation is right there on the face.
55　　When thought fares through joy, there will surely be laughter;
56　　When we speak of lament, sighs have already come.

Ch'ing, here translated as "mood," is the condition of mind whenever it is stirred by something. But even if the mind were in a state of perfect balance, a condition of being "without *ch'ing**," that also would be visible in a person's manner. "Manner," *mao*, is the ground of sensuous variation in appearance, especially the "expression" on a person's face. It would not be improper to translate the line as "mood and the expression on a face." *Mao* is often used in glossing descriptive compounds: "the manner of . . ." (e.g., of rugged mountains, the sun just coming out, a look of uncertainty). Thus *mao* is neither static form (*hsing**) nor coloration (*se**) but a quality of appearance that reveals some attribute (in this case, *ch'ing**). Ch'en Shih-hsiang's translation, "should never fail to correspond," misses the radical quality of the indicative here: the two "never do fail to correspond."

Mutation, *pien**: Reference here is made to the changes in mood or emotion, *ch'ing**.

Fares through, *she*: The use of this verb with a mood or emotion is relatively unusual and probably derives from its extended sense as something like "experience," "to pass through" and thus "to have been in" something. Ch'ien Chung-shu takes this as reviewing an experience of joy in reflective consideration. There is nothing in the verb itself to demand such an interpretation; and while the statement would indeed be true of remembrance and reading, it is no less true of an original experience of the world.

There will surely be laughter, *pi-hsiao*: Ch'ien Chung-shu takes this as the response that comes from reflection on an earlier time of joy, also suggesting that those who read will laugh as well. This is possible. There is little, however, to indicate that the lines do anything more than reaffirm the perfect coordination between state of mind and outer manner. The phrasing here makes it very possible to take this as the affective response of the reader as well. It is also remotely possible that, in conjunction with the following line, *pi-hsiao* means "[When thoughts fare through joy,] it is necessary that one have [actually] laughed"; that is, real experience is a necessary precondition for reliving that experience "recollected in tranquility" or for creating an affect in presenting that experience.[33]

When we speak of lament, sighs have already come: Ch'ien Chung-shu takes these as the sighs of recollected experience that precede actual writing; in this case, however, it seems we ought to read these as the sighs of a genuine emotional response that must precede writing lament. Hidden here is the sequence of manifestation in the "Great Preface": first the experience (joy) followed by expression in sound (laughter); then an expression in mere sound (sighs) followed by expression in words.

Lu Chi here asserts the principle on which the great tree metaphor and indeed all early Chinese literary thought is founded: there is a perfect correspondence between inside and outside. Since this principle would have been awkward to illustrate through the tree metaphor, Lu Chi shifts to something much closer to the actual situation of literature, the relation between *ch'ing** ("mood," "emotion") and manner or the expression on the human face. The principle articulated here is directly opposed to one of the deepest assumptions in Western literary thought, that truth can appear best when displaced into a fiction or into the mask of another. This Western assumption finds an extreme and oddly personal expression in Oscar Wilde's famous aphorism: "Man is least himself when he talks in his own person. Give him a mask, and he will tell you the truth."[34]

Not only is every mood apparent in writing, every "mutation" (*pien**) in mood appears as a change in outer expression. It is not paradoxical to say that Lu Chi's assertion of perfect correspondence is no less a response to the threat of deceptive appearances than Oscar Wilde's theory of the mask: both traditions (including the brief Western swerve toward the Chinese position with the interest in "sincerity" in the nineteenth century) base literature on an answer to the danger of deception and untruth. Lu Chi's radical claim in these lines is a hopeful promise: if only one knows how to look or read, the true inner state will be revealed. If one looks at a deceiving appearance, one should be able to see "the act of concealing one's true emotions"; the skilled viewer or reader will not be deceived. One can always read the inner state from the surface; if there is deception, both the deception and its motives will be part of what one sees. We take Lu Chi's lines here in the context of Mencius' claim to "understand language" (II.A.2.xvii; see above pp. 22-23).

While Lu Chi's principle of perfect correspondence can comprehend the problematic case of attempted deception, he speaks here in terms of the direct, unproblematic examples. He uses the two primary emotions to encompass the full range of emotion (see commentary to ll. 5–6 above). In doing so Lu Chi seems to be articulating another fundamental principle, the reproduction of mood in the process of manifestation: the originating mood inheres in the texts and recurs in reading the text, and perhaps, as Ch'ien Chung-shu suggests, in reflection on the originating experience that occurs before writing.

That the original state of mind or mood (ch'ing*) is reproduced through the text is another hopeful promise. If we read this to mean that convincing literary presentation can originate only in genuine emotion, it might be marginally tenable. But if we take it to mean that the writer's state of mind is reproduced perfectly and accurately in the reader, then we have a promise more fraught with difficulties than the principle of perfect correspondence between inner and outer.

---

57   或操觚以率爾。
58   或含毫而邈然。

57   He may have grasped the tablet and dashed it off lightly,
58   Or may have held the brush in his lips, [his mind] far in the distance.

This antithesis between instant composition and slow, reflective composition has parallels throughout "The Poetic Exposition on Literature" (and in the later dispute in Buddhism between instant and gradual enlightenment). As is often the case in Chinese rhetoric, antithetical terms that in alternation define a process may also appear as synchronic alternatives. We have already seen a version of the antithesis in this couplet given as describing the stages of a process: first the leisurely spirit journey that led to a storing up of material, which then hung for a moment on the writer's dry lips; then the pouring-out through the writing brush. Here this antithesis between gradual and instantaneous appears as alternative modes of writing (cf. also ll. 221–224, 229–230, 235–248). We might note further that the gradualist position corresponds roughly to the tree metaphor, while instantaneous manifestation corresponds to the changing moods appearing immediately on the face.

---

59   伊茲事之可樂。
60   固聖賢之所欽。

59   In this event can be found joy,
60   Firmly held in honor by Sages and men of worth.

This general comment marks a transition and may echo the tradition that Sages "make" (*tso* 作), while "men of worth" (*hsien* 賢) "transmit" (*shu* 述; see Preface, Section C). The union of joy and ethical valuing ("held in honor") has deep resonance in the Confucian tradition. Note that here Lu Chi is referring specifically to the "event" (*shih**), the act of writing, not to the product.

There is a rich discourse of joy in the Chinese tradition, beginning with the first entry in the *Analects*. Ch'ien Chung-shu cites a number of examples in which writing is given as a means to release a person from sorrow; but this is quite different from the simple pleasure of the activity. One passage, however, cited by Ch'ien Chung-shu is quite apt in this context, a fragment of a letter by Ts'ao Chih (192–232): " . . . so I followed my whim and wrote this letter, first holding back my good cheer as I grasped the brush, then with a great laugh letting the words come out: this may even be the ultimate in pleasure." As in the eighteenth century in the West, in China literature is often associated with play, or rather a liberty and ease of movement, a "wandering away" from the limitations and demands of the world. In *Analects* VII.6, after various injunctions on duty and moral action, Confucius concludes "wander freely in the arts," *yu** *yü yi* 遊於藝. Although by *yi*, "arts," Confucius meant a variety of noble pastimes that probably did not encompass the composition of literary works, the meaning of the word had shifted by the Han; thereafter, for most people, literature was the first thing to come to mind when thinking of Confucius' phrase.

61　課虛無以責有。

62　叩寂寞而求音。

61　A trial of void and nothing to demand of it being,

62　A knock upon silence, seeking sound.

Line 61: The use of *k'o* ("try," "test," "evaluate against a standard") is remarkable here, and none of its common usages fit the sense comfortably. Less active than in the following line, the writer here seems to "put void and nothing to the test" to see whether *it* can produce being, as it did in the primordial cosmogony. It may be, however, that the writer himself is making the attempt, "put to the task," in the void. "Void and nothing," *hsü-wu* 虛無, was, by some accounts, the original condition of the universe out of which "being" or "presence" (the "there-is"), *yu* 有, occurred.

This passage is of particular comparative interest because it explicitly refers to a second cosmogony and creation *ex nihilo*, both recurring concerns in Western literary thought. A close examination of this passage, however, shows that the poet seems to be more the midwife of this second creation than its maker. He compels (or tries to compel) nothingness again to produce being—he "puts it to the test"—but the role of his will is limited: if something is produced, his will plays a role in the fact *that* something is produced and perhaps even in *what* is produced; but the will does not itself do the producing. The description of the role of the "creative" poet differs here from the Western notion of second creation found in such Renaissance works as Boccaccio's *De geneologia deorum*, Julius Caesar Scaliger's *Poetics*, and Sir Philip Sidney's "Apology for Poetry," not only in its lack of a theological model, but also in its conception of self. Obviously this literary "being" (*yu*) that is produced does indeed emerge out of the self in Lu Chi's version, but "mind" (*hsin**), in which consciousness and volition are located, is not the whole of the inner self; "mind" rather moves in a microcosmic void and from that draws forth the "being" that is the literary work.

Line 62: Although the poet is here in a more active, productive relation, he is still "seeking" rather than "making": as in the preceding line, sound here comes into being through an active relation between mind and something else within the self. Note that the "knocking," *k'ou*, is the same word as "striking open" in line 35.

Both in China and in the West, cosmogony has been one of the most powerful models for understanding the genesis of the literary text, just as nature has been one of the most powerful models for understanding the dynamics of the text. In traditional Chinese intellectual culture the dominant view of cosmogony was the spontaneous generation of being (more properly "presence," the "there-is") out of nothingness ("absence," the "there-is-not"). Unlike the primordial cosmogony, however, literary "cosmogony" requires the conscious mind, and its role in the process will be a problematic one. Lu Chi's solution to this problem is an ingenious one: mind is neither "creator" nor mere bystander, but rather an "initiator," an agent who sets in motion and governs a natural process, calling forth being and sound.

---

63   函緜邈於尺素。
64   吐滂沛乎寸心。

63   He contains remote distances on a sheet of writing silk,
64   Emits a boundless torrent from the speck of mind.

Contains, *han*: Li Shan explains this by a *Book of Songs* gloss, equating this *han* with *han* 含, "to hold within." This *han*, however, carries a slightly different semantic force, particularly appropriate to the context here: "to admit," "to be big enough to contain."

A sheet of writing silk, *ch'ih-su*: Later *ch'ih-su* came to mean simply "a letter"; here it retains its force as a physical object, "a foot (*ch'ih*) of silk" on which any kind of work can be written. The measurement *ch'ih* (in Lu Chi's time about 24 cm., though intended loosely rather than precisely) is still literal enough to make the line oxymoronic.

Speck of mind, *ts'un-hsin*: A *ts'un* was about 2.4 cm.; the mind, the seat of consciousness, was popularly conceived as being a "square *ts'un*" 方寸 in dimension.

In the preceding couplet the antitheses were arranged as a movement of process: presence generated out of absence, sound generated out of silence. In this couplet the antitheses are arranged oxymoronically, as opposites: vast space contained in a foot, a torrent out of a "speck." The earlier metaphors of ingestion and expulsion find a counterpart here in movements of contraction and expansion, in which the poet and the text are nexi. The vastness of the outer world seems to enter the minute space of mind; out of that minute space a torrent of words or thought emerges; that torrent, and its origins in the vastness of the universe, are again contracted into the "foot" of writing silk. Lu Chi began his poetic exposition concerned with one stage of the compositional process "being adequate" for the preceding stage. One aspect of the question of adequacy is qualitative; this aspect is addressed in the theory of correspondence given earlier. Perhaps the more serious aspect of the question of adequacy is quantitative: Lu Chi is fascinated by the multiplicity and complexity of the outer world, and he must wonder by what principle such richness can be reduced to the limitations of the text. These movements of contraction and expansion, by which the vast can be contained in the tiny and by which the tiny can reproduce the vast, are essential in solving the problem of quantitative adequacy and anticipate the role of understanding as the organic expansion of the limited text.

---

65 言恢之而彌廣。

66 思按之而逾深。

65 Language gives it breadth, expanding and expanding;

66 Thought pursues it, growing deeper and deeper.

Both the grammar and the sense of this couplet are extremely difficult. I have followed the Wu-ch'en commentary in taking "language" and "thought" as the subjects of their respective verbs (the Wu-ch'en commentator's paraphrase is literally "extends it by language" with the second line interpreted in parallel); but many commentators take "language" and "thought" as the objects of the verbs: "Language—give it breadth . . . ; thought—curb/pursue it . . . "[35]

Pursues, *an*: *An* here may mean either "restrain" or "investigate." This leads to a rough division in the possible interpretations of the line: either thought curbs the expansion of language by an intensive process of organization that counterbalances language's extensive movement (*copia*); or one should extend the treatment in language and at the same time pursue the thought ever deeper. If we take "thought" as the object of *an* interpreted as "restrained," then a movement of mind which is obviously held back gives a sense of depth, of unspoken possibilities.

The difficulties of this couplet are, in miniature, the difficulties of "The Poetic Exposition on Literature" as a whole: because the lines use familiar antitheses, they follow smoothly on first reading; but reflection yields a welter of possibilities that obscure any easy "sense" one might find in the couplet. The terms of the couplet are obviously related to the motif of "expansion" and "contraction," treated from lines 61 to 70: language is related to extension, while the "depths" pursued by thought would be associated with the intensive movement of contraction. One characteristic feature of the *taxis* of Chinese rhetoric is that the order of presentation follows the presumed order of process: first things are given first. Thus (using the kind of observations made in later rhetorical analysis), the statement "The boy was out of breath because he ran so fast" would be an "inversion" (*tao* 倒); the normal order should be "He ran so fast, he was out of breath." If this couplet referred to composition, the proper sequence of presentation would have been "thought," *ssu* (with allied terms such as "conception," *yi**), then "language," *yen*. The sequence as given here leads to a possible interpretation of the couplet (roughly followed by Ch'en Shih-hsiang) in which "thought," *ssu*, refers to the process of reading and understanding the text: first we have language, expanding either in copiousness of treatment or in its associations; as that occurs, the reader pursues the significance ever more deeply.

On the other hand, we may choose not to grant any significance to the sequence here: "language," then "thought." Thought, "pursuing" a question to its depths, may occur in the process of a copious treatment in language: "as the words extend ever more broadly, the thought is pursued ever more deeply." If we take *an* as "restrain," it may refer to a compensatory balancing that is mentioned elsewhere in the poetic exposition: words seem to have an innate tendency to profusion, requiring a compensatory restraint on the part of thought (cf. the section beginning at l. 33 and ll. 75–76). There are other legitimate possibilities. In a couplet such as this, it is impossible securely to adjudicate Lu Chi's intentions: the reader comes to this couplet with expectations derived from what he has read before, both earlier in this poetic exposition and elsewhere, and his "natural" reading of the couplet will support those expectations. Given its ambiguity, the couplet is not going to tell a reader what that reader does not want to hear.

My own opinion is that the strong associations of fragrance and "wind" (*feng**) with the affective power of literature in the following couplets tend to weight these lines toward reference to literature's affect. Following the rhythms of Lu Chi's exposition, we pass from a fullness of things in the outer (or inner) world to a contraction in the "speck" of mind and on the "sheet of writing silk"; the next stage of the process would be an expansion, occurring in reading, engaging the extensive associations of limited words and thought's pursuit of the intensive concentration of significance in the words. In the following couplet that movement of expansion is carried still further.

67	播芳桂之馥馥。
68	發青條之森森。
69	粲風飛而猋豎。
70	鬱雲起乎翰林。

67	It spreads the rich scent of drooping blossoms,
68	Produces the dark density of green twigs:
69	Sparkling, the breezes fly and whirling gusts commence;
70	Swelling, clouds rise from the forest of writing brushes.

Speaking of this final stage in the literary process, Lu Chi returns to the tree metaphor, specifically to the outer pattern of leaves and branches, which is the domain of *wen** (l. 52). Later, the language of vegetation was to become very important in the development of a vocabulary of styles and moods (e.g., *ku* 枯, "bare and leafless," a spare, rugged style). Here, the fragrance of blossoming trees provides a metaphor for good reputation, which is born on the "wind" or "breeze," *feng**, the primary term for literature's influence or affective power. From the constriction into the "speck of mind" and into the written word (whose "characters," *tzu* 字, may be associated with *tzu* 子, "seed"), there grows this lush forest in all its intricate outwardness, a "forest of writing brushes," the world of literature. These lines conclude the first section of "The Poetic Exposition on Literature," passing from the preconditions of writing, to the process of reflection before an actual composition, to this vision of intricate lushness, whose fragrance is born outward on the breeze.

71	體有萬殊。
72	物無一量。
73	紛紜揮霍。
74	形難為狀。

71	There are ten thousand different normative forms,
72	The things of the world have no single measure:
73	Jumbled and jostling, fleeting past,
74	Their shapes are hard to describe.

Normative forms, *t'i**: All commentators take this as the "normative forms of literature," *wen*-t'i**; that is, either as genres, categories of occasion and theme (subgenres), and normative styles (thinking perhaps of Ts'ao P'i's "literature is not of one form"), or as the variations that must occur in any particular form to treat adequately the variety of its possible topics (in the latter case we would translate the line "in a form there are ten thousand differences). Given the common coordinate construction between literature and the things of the world (both of which provide materials for the poet to select), such an interpretation cannot be entirely excluded at this stage. Ch'eng Hui-ch'ang explains the relation between lines 71 to 72 by saying "the divergent paths of literary forms arise from the distinctions that exist in the images of things (*wu*-hsiang**)"; that is, the diversity of normative forms in literature arises from the categorical diversity of the things of the world. There are two problems with this interpretation: first, the "normative forms of literature" (*wen*-t'i**) are usually spoken of in smaller and limited numbers (although the infinite variability of a particular form is often discussed); second, the things of the world have *t'i**, "normative forms," just as literature does (see ll. 99–100, commentary). If the *t'i** here refers to the normative categories of form in things, then "ten thousand" is no exaggeration. Moreover, the passage as a whole seems to be restricted to the difficulty of describing the transient, ever-changing shapes of things. Note also that in compound *t'i*-wu** ("to give the normative forms of things") is the definition of the poetic exposition (*fu*) as a genre (l. 86). Thus it seems best here to take *t'i** (as Ch'en Shih-hsiang does) as referring to the "normative forms" of things in the world, rather than to the "forms" of literature.[36]

No single measure, *wu yi liang*: This simply means that things are various, with no measure of quantification or qualification that can apply equally to all (size, color, number, etc.).

Jumbled and jostling, fleeting past, *fen-yün hui-ho*: These are two descriptive compounds, the first giving the quality of disorder and numerousness, the second giving the quality of swift movement.

Shapes, *hsing**: This is the "fixed shape" of line 47, in which the poet "cages Heaven and Earth." The usages of various words for "form" in classical Chinese overlap, but there are significant differences in their semantic tendencies. To give some rough examples of these tendencies: *t'i**, "normative form," would be the word used for body in the phrase "the human body"; *shen* 身 would be the "body" in the phrase "my body"; looking at someone's body in a particular stance at a particular moment, one might identify it as *t'i**, the normative category which is the human body. If something "has form" or "has shape" (or conversely, if it is "formless"), however, *hsing** would be the appropriate word. If a piece of wood were carved into the likeness of a human being, *jen-hsing** 人形 would be the appropriate compound, though that would not be the "human form," *jen-t'i**. Thus *hsing** tends to refer to form in general and especially to external appearance; t'i* tends to refer to a particular normative form or the concept of normative form, and tends to comprehend the totality of form of what a thing "is," rather than simply its appearance.

Describe, *chuang*: *Chuang* is yet another form word, referring to "manner" or "stance"; here, used as a verb, it means something like "to catch the manner of," thus "to describe." Here and throughout "The Poetic Exposition on Literature" there is a fascination with the infinite variety and constant change of the external world, accompanied by a sense of language's inadequacy to make that variety manifest. Stated in Western terms, the external world is one of Becoming, while the world of language is one of Being (containing the profound intuition that Being is somehow essentially a linguistic event). Composition is a translation from the world of Becoming into the world of Being; it is an act of mastery (ll. 47–48) and an act of granting permanence (ll. 251–262), but it is also an act fraught with the danger that in some basic way language may fail adequately to present the essential character of the external world.

---

75 辭程才以效伎
76 意司契而為匠

75   Diction displays its talents in a contest of artfulness;
76   Concept holds the creditor's contract and is the craftsman.

Diction, *tz'u**: *Tz'u** has a much less limited range than English "diction": it may vary from language in general, to the particular utterance, to "phrases," to "flowery language." Used here in opposition to "concept," *yi**, *tz'u** is treated not as a product of "concept," but rather as a rhetorical elaboration driven by its own impulses, an operation that must be brought under control by "concept."

A contest of artfulness, *hsiao chi*: Li Shan and many subsequent commentators take *hsiao* as "present" or "show," thus rendering the line: "Language displays talent and shows artfulness." While this is a legitimate extension of *hsiao*, I prefer the root sense of "emulation and competition": displays of craft were often spoken of in terms of competition. Thus it is as if each phrase (*tz'u**) is trying to be more lovely than the last.[37] The implicit danger of disorder and disharmony in such competition is answered by the next line.

Concept holds the creditor's contract, *yi ssu-ch'i*: *Ssu-ch'i* is to take the creditor's half of a tally in a financial contract. Already in *Lao-tzu* LXXIX the phrase is used figuratively: "One of virtue holds the creditor's contract," though he makes no exactions from the people.[38] As Lu Chi uses the phrase, it means "being in control" in a limited, rather than in an absolute sense—

something like English "to have the upper hand." The relation of concept to language is one of a governing authority: concept is neither the creator nor something that exercises absolute control; rather it has the authority to govern, organize, and restrain language's tendency to showiness. The submerged metaphor of government appears also in the term *chiang*, here used in its basic sense as "craftsman," but often applied to the skillful application of authority by a statesman.

The translation given above is weighted to emphasize the dangerous autonomy of diction, but it might also be translated so as to stress the divided impulses of the writer:

> Through diction he displays his talent and competes in artfulness;
> Through concept he holds the creditor's contract and acts as the craftsman.

There is a similarity in manner between the things of the world and language (and perhaps literary forms as well): both are lush and varied; both are hard to get under control in their richness. The primary means for limitation and organization is "concept," *yi**. Previously Lu Chi had spoken of his anxiety regarding the adequacy of his concepts for the complexity of the things of the world; now the function of concept is to govern that multiplicity. The writer's consciousness is filled with populous provinces of things and words, attractive in their richness, but always threatening chaos; thus the writer's task is a form of governance—to get this teeming complexity to work together in orderly fashion. Through the course of Lu Chi's poetic exposition, "concept," *yi**, undergoes interesting transformations, beginning as a general principle of organization, gradually acquiring (as here) a sense of conscious control and intention, finally to become something very much like "intended, unifying meaning" (see commentary to ll. 123–132).

77	在有無而僶俛
78	當淺深而不讓
79	雖離方而遯圓
80	期窮形而盡相

77	There he strives between being and nothing,
78	In deep or shallow, not giving up.
79	Though it may depart from the geometry of circle and square,
80	He hopes to exhaust the limits of shape and countenance.

Line 77: This and the following line are very obscure. Ch'ien Chung-shu rightly points out that "being" ("presence," the "there-is") and "nothing" ("absence," the "there-is-not") refer back to the moment of the literary work's generation (l. 61). Considering the lines that follow, however, this is not an unqualified cosmogony, but rather one in which the poet hopes to adequately manifest the things of the world.

Line 78: Ch'eng Hui-ch'ang gives a plausible explanation of this line by citing *Book of Songs* 35:

> Where the water was deep,
> I crossed it with a raft or boat;
> Where the water was shallow,
> I swam it and waded through it.

The application of these lines to the present context would be that the poet will not give up under any circumstances. The chief attraction of this interpretation is that it makes some sense of a line that is otherwise very obscure. There is, however, little to strongly support this interpretation.[39]

Line 79: As Li Shan points out, the "circle and square" are metonymy for the "compass and carpenter's square." The "circle and square" imply fixed and constant norms of treatment, as they imply norms of ethics and behavior.[40] The point of the line is that in order to capture the particular circumstances of the things of the world, it is permitted to transgress fixed and constant norms given beforehand (an analogy might be the ratio in size between parts of the body in anatomical drawing; to draw a particular body, one may find that one has to depart from the normative ratios). On the one hand, Lu Chi may here be referring to purely literary norms; for instance, a poetic exposition (*fu*) should treat its topic in a certain way; but in certain topics (the present case of "literature" being an excellent example), the writer should be willing to deviate from those norms. On the other hand, "circle and square" might carry their common ethical implications; in this case the license might be to complicate normative judgments when describing persons and events. Whatever the uncertain practical application of this principle, Lu Chi is emphasizing that it is the particularity of the object that should govern its treatment.

This section (ll. 71–80) construes the literary art as essentially descriptive, or more properly, "making manifest the things of the world." In their subtlety, multiplicity, and constant change, things elude us; to present them properly, one must bring the impulses to showy diction under control, strive hard, and keep to the object, even if it means deviating from some norm.

81	故夫誇目者尚奢
82	愜心者貴當
83	言窮者無隘
84	論達者唯曠

81   Thus to make a brave display for the eyes, prize extravagance;
82   To content the mind, value the apposite.
83   That the words run out is no impediment:
84   Discourse attains its ends only in broadening.

The significant difficulties of this passage are an excellent illustration of Chinese rhetoric in action. As in several cases discussed previously, understanding the lines is radically contingent on what the reader expects the passage to say; those expectations are derived from the reader's established assumptions before he begins to read and, consequently, from the way he has construed earlier passages. The central issues are: first, whether lines 81 and 82 are complementary or contrary; second, whether *yen ch'iung che* should be taken as "that the words run out" or as "one who speaks of being in hardship," and in the parallel line, whether to take *lun ta che* as "discourse attains its ends" or "one who discusses his success."

Let me begin by quoting Ch'ien Chung-shu's evaluation of Li Shan's comments:

> According to Li Shan's commentary, "Since these two situations vary, the way in which the writing is done is also different; thus someone who wants to make a brave display for the eyes prizes extravagance (*she* 奢) in his writing, while someone who wants to satisfy the mind values appositeness (*tang* 當) in his writing. When one speaks of being in difficulty and in a lowly position, one always speaks from a sense of confinement;[41] when one discusses success, there is always an expansiveness in the way that person speaks." Ho Cho 何焯 makes the following evaluative comment on this: "Lines 81 and 82: the commentary [Li Shan's] is in error." Li Shan's commentary is in error in all four lines, and Ho Cho has not pointed out these errors completely. Ho is correct in saying that the two lines, "a brave display for the eyes" and "content the mind" are to be taken together as a single situation. The "So" here follows strictly from "He hopes to exhaust the limits of shape and countenance": we can clearly recognize the continuity in the thread of discourse. The *ch'iung* in *yen ch'iung* is *ch'iung* in the sense of "exhaust the limits of," as in "exhaust the limits of shape"—not *ch'iung* in the sense of "poor" or "hardship," as in "the grievances of the people in hardship." Likewise, the *ta* of *lun ta* is *ta* in the sense of "perfect," as in "a perfect explanation"—not *ta* in the sense of "successful," as in the phrase "a successful man's understanding of what is ordained." Both refer to the momentum of writing and have nothing to do with one's mood being high or low. When one "exhausts the limits of shape and countenance," the language easily spreads out in all its intricacy—that is "extravagance." But when one is "extravagant" in language, the purpose is, in fact, to seek appositeness. "To content the mind" is precisely what he "hopes" in the preceding line. "Only in broadening" and "no impediment" have the same meaning and are both amplifications of "extravagance." Not to be hampered and to "exhaust one's words," to be unrestrainedly free in "perfectly" expanding one's

purport—these are what it would mean to have an "extravagant" style for the sake of "appositeness," and thus the mind's "hopes" may be "contented."[42]

In Li Shan's time "extravagance" (*she*) would have carried strongly pejorative overtones and would have seemed a clear opposite of "appositeness" (*tang*): thus the T'ang critic reads lines 81 and 82 as opposites. Given his personality and the spirit of the twentieth century, Ch'ien Chung-shu would have "appositeness" follow from "extravagance": thus he reads line 82 as the fulfillment of line 81. If we examine the aesthetic values of Lu Chi's age, we discover that there is sometimes a sense "extravagance" being pejorative, but that in other cases the language of dazzling lushness can have a positive value. Thus we have no clear indication here whether the couplet is complementary or oppositional.[43]

Without rejecting either Ch'ien Chung-shu's or Li Shan's interpretations as reasonable possibilities, I would like to propose a third interpretation, which I believe better catches the manner of Lu Chi's exposition. I would agree with Li Shan that "extravagance" and "appositeness" are contraries, but they may embody two contradictory impulses in writing rather than two different kinds of writers; moreover, I suspect that both are treated positively. Lu Chi's poetic exposition progresses by balancings and compensations: a statement in one direction often must be qualified, held in check, by a statement in the opposite direction. Thus "departing from the geometry of circle and square"—a necessity that Lu Chi freely admits—leads naturally to "extravagance"; he does indeed enjoin us to extravagance, but restrains its potential for excess by a contrary demand for the apposite.

In lines 83 and 84, I again depart from Li Shan and Ch'ien Chung-shu. *TL* cites Sun K'uang 孫鑛, who explains these lines as "though the words are exhausted, there is meaning left over" and "a discourse attaining its ends arises from a breadth of knowledge." In his interpretation of line 83, Sun K'uang appeals to one of the most cherished principles of traditional Chinese literary thought from the ninth century on: after the words are exhausted, there is "lingering significance." Ch'ien Chung-shu correctly associates this use of *ch'iung* as "exhaust," "run out," with its usage a few lines earlier in line 79; but it would be more natural to read this sentence as Sun does ("that the words be exhausted/run out") than to read it as Ch'ien Chung-shu does ("that the words exhaust it"; i.e., exhaustively describe shape and countenance). Not only is Sun's reading of the line more natural, it corresponds to Lu Chi's earlier fascination with the interplay between the vast and limited: all things and Heaven and Earth contained in writing (ll. 47–48); limitless space confined to the small space of writing silk (l. 63); a boundless torrent emerging from the speck of consciousness (l. 65). Growing out of Lu Chi's fascination with rhythms of expansion and contraction, this line would be the first theoretical statement in the tradition of how meaning may expand beyond the text. To paraphrase the lines: "That the words run out when attempting to give the exhaustive presentation of shape and countenance is no impediment to achieving your goal, because the goal is achieved only beyond words."

Sun K'uang is also surely correct in at least the first half of his interpretation of line 84: the *ta* here seems an unmistakable echo of *Analects* XV.40 "Words should attain their ends and that's all" 辭達而已矣. The ideological prejudice that Lu Chi is not "Confucian" and therefore would not cite the *Analects* is given the lie by repeated echoes of the *Analects* throughout "The Poetic Exposition on Literature." All commentators take *k'uang* 曠 in the sense of *kuang* 廣, "broad and expansive." Sun K'uang's interpretation of that "breadth" as a "breadth" of learning would be another conventional expectation of late classical poetics, but an association not entirely relevant to this context. *Kuang*, (廣, "broad and expansive,") appears in a similar context in line 65: "Language gives it breadth, expanding and expanding." Ch'ien Chung-shu's interpretation of *k'uang* lies close to this sense ("discourse achieves a perfect treatment only in being extensive"); but this fits into the context only by, what seems to me, an untenable interpretation of the preceding line. I would thus like to take the "broadening" to follow from the absence of impediment after the words are done, a "broadening" of significance that occurs in the process of understanding, by which the discourse "attains its ends."

To summarize, I would like to take these lines and their context as follows: "Even if it requires departing from the norms, one should aspire to capture the fullness and particularity of what one is writing about; extravagance of description will give the reader a sense of the intricate externality of the thing; but one must also take care to satisfy the mind with the aptness of a description. It will, of course, be impossible to put everything about your topic into words (a fact whose truth in regard to writing about literature has already been confessed in the Preface); however, even when the words run out, you will find that is no impediment to fully capturing your subject: a discourse achieves its ends (which was the goal of all writing as stated by Confucius) only in having the significance expand beyond the words."

Note especially the antithesis between *yen*, "language," and *lun*, "discourse." *Yen* here is essentially "utterance," limited to the words actually used. *Lun* is a complete discourse (or "argument"), a totality that may go well beyond the particular assertions (the sense of the individual utterances, *yen*) contained within it and through which it is constituted. The very variety of interpretations here is precisely an example of how a "discourse attains its ends"—even contradictory ends—beyond the limitations of the words. It is precisely the elliptical quality of classical Chinese and classical Chinese arguments that lent a special force to the idea of "meaning beyond the words" in traditional literary theory. At the same time, in the various interpretations offered for these lines, we have seen how much room for disagreement is left to the exegetes who seek to bring a discourse, achieved "beyond words," back into the limited realm of words.

85	詩緣情而綺靡。
86	賦體物而瀏亮。
87	碑披文以相質。
88	誄纏緜而悽愴。
89	銘博約而溫潤。
90	箴頓挫而清壯。
91	頌優游以彬蔚。
92	論精微而朗暢。
93	奏平徹以閑雅。
94	說煒燁而譎誑。

85   The poem (*shih*) follows from the affections (*ch'ing**) and is sensuously intricate;

86   Poetic exposition (*fu*) gives the normative forms of things (*t'i*-wu**) and is clear and bright;

87   Stele inscription (*pei*) unfurls pattern (*wen**) to match substance (*chih**);

88   Threnody (*lei*) swells with pent-up sorrow;

89   Inscription (*ming*) is broad and concise, warm and gentle;

90   Admonition (*chen*) represses, being clear and forceful;

92   Ode (*sung*) moves with a grand ease, being lush;

92   Essay (*lun*) treats essentials and fine points, lucidly and expansively;

93   Memorial to the throne (*tsou*) is even and incisive, calm and dignified;

94   Persuasion (*shui*) is flashy, delusory and entrancing.

Line 85: Li Shan relates this to the etymological definition of *shih* in the *Shu ching* and its amplification in the "Great Preface" to the *Book of Songs*: "The poem is the means to articulate what is intently on the mind, therefore he says 'following from feeling.'" Lu Chi's line is indeed grounded in the traditional etymological definition of *shih*, but the substitution of *ch'ing** ("feeling," "state of mind," etc.) for *chih** ("what is intently on the mind") is significant, and has been the subject of much discussion as a watershed in the understanding of poetry. As it was used in the canonical definition of *shih*, in the *Book of Documents* and in the "Great Preface" to the *Book of Songs*, *chih** probably had a broad psychological meaning, in which social and ethical concerns were inextricable from the general concerns of mind; from that broad sense of *chih**, which never entirely disappeared, comes the broad translation used here: "what is intently on the mind." The Eastern Han tradition of *Book of Songs* exegesis was, however, beginning to limit the focus of *chih** to a much more narrow political and ethical referent: "what is on the mind intently, with special reference to one's political ambitions, social values, and personal goals." Such a limited focus might have been adequate for the poems of the *Book of Songs*, as Lu Chi understood them; but such a strictly limited notion of *chih** would have been too narrow for poetry (*shih*) as it was practiced in Lu Chi's time. By substituting *ch'ing** for *chih** here, Lu Chi "broadens" the originary definition of *shih* to account more perfectly for poetry's true range. *Ch'i-mi*, the descriptive applied to the quality of *shih*, is difficult to define, and particularly difficult in this period before the term had acquired a rich history of usage. The *ch'i* is the determinate semantic element in the compound; the *mi* was added probably primarily for euphonic reasons, though it carried a strong semantic sense of "delicacy." It was roughly during Lu Chi's time, during the Wei and Tsin, that the word *ch'i* began to be transferred from a patterned silk, whose patterns (*wen**) were not woven into the fabric, to a descriptive term for any attractive and intricate pattern. At this stage *ch'i* compounds have none of the pejorative associations that they later acquired (associations that caused many Ming and Ch'ing critics to attack this line harshly). One example of such compounds is *ch'i-li* 綺麗, slightly older than *ch'i-mi* which later came to suggest a seductive, but essentially frivolous, beauty.[44] *Ch'i-mi* described something brightly colored, intricate, and alluring; and these were precisely the qualities strongly associated with "feeling," *ch'ing**.[45] Note that the essential attribute of poetry here is not principle (*li**) or the individual's engagement in social reality (although that is by no means excluded), but rather capturing the "quality" of inner life.

Line 86: The central problem in this line is the meaning of *t'i**-*wu**, translated as "gives the normative forms of things." By Lu Chi's time, poetic expositions tended to treat one "thing," *wu**; and the "thing" was usually presented as a normative category, rather than as a particular. Thus if "wren" were the topic, one would write on "the wren," rather than seeing any particular wren. Poetic expositions that were rooted in particular occasions (as many in this period were) tended to treat the experience in normative rather than in particular terms. Thus when Lu Chi's contemporary Tso Ssu 左思 wrote a poetic exposition on the "Three Capitals," *San-tu fu* 三都賦, the remedy he proposed to counter the fantasy and hyperbole in the capital *fu* of his predecessors was the close consultation of written sources: in a poetic exposition the interest was in the shared knowledge regarding the capitals rather than a personal experience of them. This notion of "normative form" or "normative embodiment" is implicit in *t'i**. Thus the writer of a poetic exposition "gives the normative embodiment of the thing," describing its parts, its essential aspects, and the stages of its coming-to-be. Most commentators take *t'i**-*wu** in a reductive sense as simply "describe the thing." Hsü Fu-kuan, however, goes beyond this nicely, interpreting the phrase to mean "expresses a thing and joins with the thing to make one form (*t'i**)," by which he means that the form of the topic or "thing" under consideration gives form to the poetic exposition. The quality proper to such an act is *liu-liang* 劉亮, "clear and bright": to make those normative qualities as if present and clearly perceived. Suggestiveness and personal associations held in reserve were not virtues in poetic expositions.[46]

Line 87: One way to understand the qualities given as "proper" to each genre is to consider their opposites. The danger that might threaten the poem is to be flat, to fail to capture the intricacy of inner life, perhaps by simply stating categories of feeling ("I am sad"); the failure of the poetic exposition would be to leave the thing hidden, not brightly manifest before us. The danger of the stele inscription would be another kind of failure of correspondence: some deed or a lifetime of deeds requires commemoration; the deeds will be hidden from us unless manifested in wen*; the stele inscription writer must steer a course between flattery and omission of what is essential; he must write in a way adequate for the deed commemorated. For the relation between wen* and chih*, see commentary to lines 51–52. Hsiang, translated as "to match," deserves comment: hsiang basically means "assist," "to join with as a pair."[47] The use of hsiang here admits the priority of chih* ("substance," "the facts," what was really done and the way a person really was), at the same time suggesting that wen* is necessary for completion. Ch'ien Chung-shu suggests the inclusion of the [often] unrhymed stele inscription in this list shows that Lu Chi is using wen* in its earlier sense of "belles lettres" in a broad sense, rather than in its narrower sense of "rhymed writings," (as the Southern Dynasties later tried to limit—unsuccessfully—the meaning of wen*).

Line 88: Ch'an-mien, "swells with pent-up," belongs to a group of compounds describing the emotions, especially sad emotions, in terms of a swelling or tangling up inside. Ch'an-mien is more literally, "all twisted and tied." Ch'an-mien is also a member of a large families of metaphors, living and dead, in which emotions are described in terms of threads (ultimately related to the pun on ssu 絲, "thread," and ssu 思, "thought," "longing"). This family of metaphors supports another common metaphor for the literary work as a fabric of some sort, especially as an intricate piece of brocade. Note that the quality proper to threnody responds to the greatest danger that besets the genre, that of "frigidity" or lack of genuine emotion.

Line 89: "Broad and concise," po-yüeh, is, of course, oxymoronic; Li Shan gives a reasonable explanation, saying that "the matters [treated] are broad, but the writing is concise." Since inscriptions were often done on smaller objects such as ritual vessels, mirrors, and swords, we may have here an interesting case in which the material circumstances of the genre affect the stylistic qualities proper to it. "Warm and gentle," wen-jun, describes the quality of personality appropriate to a "gentleman," chün-tzu; it involves a softness and compliance, and is often associated with the Confucian value of jen 仁, "kindness" or "fellow feeling." There is nothing inherent in inscription to make wen-jun a quality particularly appropriate to it; its appearance here seems to be a balance for the more severe qualities of admonition in the following line.

Line 90: *Tun-tso,* translated as "represses," is an interesting and important term, which in later usage gathered a much broader range of significance (as a quality of movement in various kinds of performance and in the "movement" of a literary text). *Tun-tso* describes a rapid shift "downward" between opposite states, a sudden repression—from rapid and frenzied movement to stillness, from the joyous to the pensive, and so on. Such a shift is quite appropriate to the effect of an admonition. Rather than stressing *tun-tso's* affect in the social function of the genre, some commentators take the compound as simply the restrained or indirect manner of the literary work itself.

Line 91: *Yu-yu,* translated freely as "moves with grand ease," describes a calm, unflustered manner, appropriate to the dignity of *sung* ("ode"), often a rhymed work of praise or celebration. *Pin-wei,* translated as "lush," is probably an original usage here and combines two distinct semantic elements. *Pin* is taken from the reduplicative compound *pin-pin* 彬彬, the perfect balance between *wen** and *chih** (see commentary to line 12; *pin-pin* can be divided and *pin* used in new compound formations, as here, but *pin* cannot properly stand alone). *Wei* suggests a rich, vegetative luxuriance.

Line 92: This is the only truly discursive genre of the group, and it is a genre comparatively independent of occasion. Like *pin-wei* above, *ching-wei,* translated as "treats the essentials and fine points," is a compound in which the two elements retain a degree of semantic autonomy (in contrast, in many compounds, such as *yu-yu,* 1. 91, the semantic values of the individual characters either disappear entirely or survive only as overtones). *Ching* is the "essence" of something; *wei* describes what is "detailed" or "minute." In this case, *wei* may be either a complementary quality of "treating the essence of something" (if the essence is "subtle") or it may be an opposite. Of the two elements of *lang-ch'ang, lang* "clearly," is an obvious virtue (a "brightness" that is perspicuous); *ch'ang* "expansively" is the opposite of "concise" (l. 89) and permits a mode of exposition that would be called "leisurely" in English (though this is only relative: the normally elliptical mode of Chinese exposition makes an "expansive" exposition austerely concise in English).

Line 93: "Even and incisive," *p'ing-ch'e,* is explained by the Wu-ch'en commentary as "making the words agreeable and communicating the idea." *P'ing,* "even," may refer to the manner of presentation (as the Wu-ch'en commentary takes it) or it may refer to an "evenhandedness" in the presentation of opinion within the memorial. *Ch'e,* literally "penetrating through," lies somewhere between simply "communicating" and being "incisive." It seems that these qualities respond to the dangers inherent in memorials to the throne—a strident pleading of a case or "beating around the bush."

Line 94: The description of persuasion, *shui,* is the negative image of the qualities of a good memorial to the throne. Luminosity is generally a positive stylistic quality, but *wei-yeh* suggests a dazzling radiance that blinds rather than makes perspicuous (cf. *wei-wei* 煒煒). The Wu-ch'en commentary, followed by several later commentators, takes *wei-yeh* as simply "bright and perspicuous"; but this is unlikely. *Chüeh-k'uang*, translated as "delusory and entrancing," is a strongly negative descriptive, implying something that is both strange and deceiving. In the case of *shui*, alone among the genres listed, Lu Chi gives the bad qualities that persuasions do have, rather than the positive qualities they ought to have.

Lu Chi's list of genres is important in the development of Chinese genre theory, an intermediary between the simpler list given in Ts'ao P'i's "Discourse on Literature" and the extensive treatment of genres given in the first half of *Wen-hsin tiao-lung*.[48] There are many interesting questions that might be raised in regard to this passage: the problematic distinction between *wen** and "plain writing" (*pi* 筆), discussed at length in Ch'ien Chung-shu; the relation of this list to earlier and later lists of genres and to actual practice; the qualities appropriate to each individual genre, as discussed above.

What seems of paramount importance, however, is the way in which Lu Chi is thinking about genre. In contrast to Liu Hsieh, who "traces the genre to its root," both etymologically and in earlier writing, Lu Chi follows in the tradition of Ts'ao P'i's "Discourse on Literature," linking each genre to a quality proper to it. What seems to distinguish genres here is neither formal properties nor purpose (although in practice such distinctions are very strong), but rather modes or manners. Genres are *t'i**, "normative forms"; categories of quality are also thought of as *t'i**. Indeed some of the categories of quality used above (and even more close variations on those categories) appear in later lists of *t'i**. What is happening here is the development of a rudimentary sense that there are two orders of *t'i**: one that is "generic" and another that is stylistic or modal. The most appropriate way to describe a genre/*t'i** is to match it with an appropriate mode/*t'i**. Given the fact that there is a clear awareness of different orders of *t'i**, the impulse to retain one single categorical term, *t'i**, shows the desire to have a theoretical vocabulary with the widest possible range of reference—to retain broad, unifying levels that comprehend all fine distinctions.

Note that in the qualities of manner we find an intermingling of qualities located in the writer and qualities of affect. The blurring of the distinction between transitive and intransitive modes reinforces this; for example, the writer of a threnody "swells with pent-up sorrow" and presumably creates the same affect in the reader or listener. The only case where there is a clear distinction between writer's mind and reader's mind is in the only genre presented pejoratively, a genre of deception, the *shui* or "persuasion": the persuader deludes but is not himself deluded. The use of the other, positive terms of manner or quality contributes to one of the primary goals of Chinese literary theory: the promise of an adequate transfer of a state of mind from writer to reader. Negative terms are, on the contrary, terms of deception, in which the writer manipulates the response of the reader.

95	雖區分之在茲。
96	亦禁邪而制放。
97	要辭達而理舉。
98	故無取乎冗長。

95　Though fine distinctions are being made in these,

96　They prohibit deviation and restrain impulsiveness.

97　Require that your words attain their ends, that the principle (*li**) come
　　　forth;

98　Have nothing at all to do with long-winded excess.

Prohibit deviation, *chin-hsieh*: Commentators disagree as to whether "deviation" here is literary or moral. It is difficult entirely to suppress the moral dimension of the term *hsieh*, "deviation"; and I suspect that deviation from the generic proprieties described above would suggest a willfulness and license with overtones of some ethical failure. In this context, however, *chin-hsieh* is clearly not a simple injunction against moral deviation. The phrase seems to echo and to transpose into primarily literary associations the statement of Confucius in *Analects* II.2: "He said, The *Songs* are three hundred, and one phrase [from them] covers them all: unswerving in thought."

Require that your words attain their ends, *yao tz'u ta*: This embeds Confucius' famous statement in *Analects* XV.40, quoted earlier: "Words should attain their ends and that's all." This demand, made in various forms in various traditions of literary theory, is extremely problematic, begging more questions than it answers: it raises questions as to the precise nature of the ends of writing, and questions about what is, in fact, necessary. Read in conjunction with the preceding passage, the familiar principle suggests, in this case, that the ends of discourse can be best attained by maintaining the proper distinctions of generic mode. On the other hand, linked to the following line, the principle may be taken in its simplest and most common sense: concision. *Yao*, "require," is a strong demand.

That principle comes forth, *li chü*: TL takes *chü* "come forth" (literally "rise up" or "be raised up"), as "complete." The Wu-ch'en commentary takes it as I have here. See also Preface, Section B, for the use of *chü* in early theories of linguistic reference. *Li chü* seems to define the "ends" that one's words should attain: words should stop when the principle is clear. (Some alternative "ends" of discourse might be the successful accomplishment of a persuasion or internal completeness of structure.) The phrase does not mean that principle is "named" (presuming that naming of principle is possible), but rather that it is adequately "indicated" (one sense of *chü*) or immanent in the literary text. To give an example using the ever popular tree metaphor: a few essential strokes, in painting or in poetry, could "indicate" a willow tree in a certain kind of topography in a certain kind of weather; the goal is neither a photographic presentation of the tree nor an abstraction, but rather a minimal presentation of externals in which the principle is immanent and can be recognized.

Long-winded excess, *jung-chang*: Although this line is the earliest attested use of the term in this sense, *jung-chang* became the standard term in classical Chinese for "diffuseness" or "long-windedness": it combines a sense of excessive verbiage with disorder.

Ch'ien Chung-shu makes the excellent observation that in these lines we have a counterbalance to the license given in line 70 to "depart from the geometry of circle and square." He also takes the demand for concision here as a balance for his interpretation of line 84 as an encouragement to copiousness. He describes this balancing process as "giving free rein, then reining in, preserving by opposition each from the dangers inherent in the other." This is an apt description of much of the structure of the "Poetic Exposition on Literature" and indeed of the structure of argumentation in many classical Chinese works. These four lines end the long section begun on line 71. It is certainly true that the daring license granted in line 79 is counterbalanced by the list of modes appropriate for each genre, the knowledge of which allows one to "prohibit deviation and restrain impulsiveness" and not overstep the mark. The closing advice to use no more words than is absolutely necessary tries to mediate between the encouragement to license and the injunction to restraint.

99	其為物也多姿。
100	其為體也屢遷。
101	其會意也尚巧。
102	其遣言也貴妍。

99 As things (*wu**), there are many postures;

100 As normative forms (*t'i**), there are frequent shiftings.

101 In forming conceptions (*yi**), value clever craft;

102 In expelling words, honor the alluring.

Lines 99–100: The first couplet is extremely ambiguous. The Wu-ch'en commentary wants to take "things" (*wu**) as referring to the "normative forms of literature" (*wen*-t'i**); in the context of this work (and in the context of the usage of *wu** in Chinese literary theory) such an interpretation would be most unusual. The reason the Wu-ch'en commentary is led to such a dubious interpretation of *wu** is probably the double "as" construction (*ch'i wei . . . ch'i wei*, literally "its being an X" or "its acting as an X"), which may suggest that there is one entity appearing in two different aspects in the two lines of the couplet.

This couplet, beginning a new section, seems clearly to refer back to the terms at the beginning of the previous section (ll. 71–72); and the way we understand the use of *t'i** and *wu** there will determine how we take them here. If we take the *t'i** of line 71 as referring to the "normative forms of things" (*wu**-*t'i**) rather than to the "normative forms of literature" (*wen**-*t'i**), we should do so again in this couplet. Such an interpretation would solve the problem of the double "as" construction. In this interpretation, the couplet would be restating the complexity of the outer world of things, in preparation for further comment on the difficulty of adequately presenting it in writing. In this case *wu** would refer to particular "things," which appear in infinitely varied "postures" (*tzu* 姿, "bearing" or "manner," the stance of a particular thing at a particular moment); *t'i** would refer to the identity of things by categorical differences. Thus, on the one hand, if we were looking at a willow leaf, it would assume a rich variety of "postures," depending on whether the wind was blowing or not, whether there was mist, how the light was shining, whether it was autumn or summer, and so on. On the other hand, as a "normative form" (*t'i**) the willow leaf would have identity not by its "posture" of the moment but as a category "willow leaf," defined against willow twigs, oak leaves, and so forth. Following such an interpretation, the couplet would be amplifying the idea of the "multiplicity of the world" by an antithesis between the determination of a particular thing by its internal and circumstantial variations and by its categorical relations. In face of such overwhelming complexity, the writer must worry about his conceptions' being adequate for things (see Preface, Section B); and this is the question addressed in line 101.

I believe that the above interpretation is correct, but the majority of commentators follow a third possibility, first stated by Li Shan: *wu** refers to the variety of the things of the world, while *t'i** refers to the forms and genres of literature listed above (ll. 85–94). The point of this interpretation would be that things and the normative forms of literature are both various, and it is hard to get them to come together. I suspect that the reason Li Shan made this interpretation and the reason that so many later commentators followed it was the increasingly common use of *t'i** in reference to literary "forms." Although *t'i** was used in this sense in Lu Chi's time, its technical application to literature had not yet hardened, and it still retained a much broader frame of reference. The history of a language is often the history of increasingly restrictive reference, growing out of repeated usage. The semantic shifts in the word *t'i** justify not following the majority of commentators in this case; but there are, in addition, two further reasons to reject the interpretation of *t'i** as the "normative forms of literature": first, such an interpretation ignores the presumed unity of some entity that appears in two distinct aspects in the double "as" clause; second, it violates the smooth progression from "things" to "conceptions" to written expressions (ll. 99–102), which recapitulates the triadic progression first articulated in Preface, Section B.

Shiftings, *ch'ien*: Note that the differentiation in "normative forms," *t'i**, is often described as a process of movement from one to another, rather than as static differentiation.

Forming conceptions, *hui-yi*: *Hui-yi** is often used as "understanding" or "getting the gist" in reading; here it is "understanding" the things of the world in the ability to "form conceptions" when considering them.[49]

Clever craft, *ch'iao*: The common pejorative overtones of *ch'iao* are clearly absent here. There is an implicit conflict here that echoes the earlier conflict between voluntarism and involuntarism in composition. The line responds to the concern, stated in Preface, Section B, that "conceptions [may] not be equal to the things of the world." The determinate nature of the things of the world should in turn determine the conceptions formed about them and serve as a standard to judge the success of such conceptions. For example, if a falling leaf suggests autumn and the approaching end of the seasonal cycle, nature's order determines the validity of the human conception regarding it. But "clever craft," *ch'iao*, refers to the writer's own wit and suggests an altogether different standard of judgment.

Expelling words, *ch'ien yen*: See Preface, Section A, *fang-yen ch'ien-tz'u* 放言遣辭. The reference here is to diction, *lexis*.

The alluring, *yen*: *Yen* is the term translated as "beauty" in Preface, Section A.

Beginning a new section on problems and advice, these four lines summarize the situation that brings about compositional problems: the multiplicity of the things of the world, the difficulty in forming conceptions about them, and the difficulty of finding language adequate for those conceptions. The frequent echoes of the Preface give these introductory lines a sense of going back and "resuming" the basic issues of the topic. Two terms are offered to resolve the problems in forming conceptions and finding words: *ch'iao*, "clever craft," for conceptions; and *yen*, "allure," for diction. These two literary qualities correspond to the two most commonly mentioned aspects of the things of the world: their lush complexity and their sensuous attractiveness.

---

103   暨音聲之迭代。
104   若五色之相宣。

105	雖逝止之無常。
106	固崎錡之難便。
107	苟達變而識次。
108	猶開流以納泉。
109	如失機而後會。
110	恆操末以續顛。
111	謬玄黃之秩敘。
112	故淟涊而不鮮。

103	When it comes to the alternation of sounds,
104	They are like the five colors, setting each other off:
105	Though there is no constancy in their passing on or halting—
106	A rocky path, that cannot be made easy—
107	Still, if one grasps mutation and understands succession,
108	It is like opening a channel to receive a stream.
109	But if you miss the occasion and bring things together too late,
110	You will always have the beginning following the end.
111	Error in the relative positions of Purple [Heaven] and Brown [Earth],
112	Brings mere muddiness and no vividness.

Sounds, *yin-sheng*: This is the general term for sounds, especially musical sounds, which can be in harmony. Some commentators want to take this as an early indication of interest in tonal balancing, which became an important feature of versification several centuries later. This is not impossible; but to conceive of such a vague sense of tonal balance as *sheng-lü* 聲律, "tonal regulation," would be anachronistic and inappropriate. The line clearly refers to euphony in a broad sense, which may or may not include some rudimentary sense of tonal balance. Most likely, the appreciation of euphonic qualities cannot be distinguished from the semantic and stylistic qualities of the words: as an embroidered figure is both defined and made vivid by a relation of colors, so the alternation of sounds both creates meaning and is euphonic. This is apparent in *hsiang-hsüan*, "setting each other off," literally "making each other manifest." Meaning, the determination of semantic values, appears in the relation of sounds. The embroidery analogy is helpful: the design is conceived not as a shape with the colors "filled in," but rather as a relation of colors. For example, in "The Affections and Coloration," in *Wen-hsin tiao-lung*, we read: "The pattern of shapes is that of the five colors," which is to say that shape is not an "outline" but rather a relation of color areas. Thus in language the alternation of sounds articulates a "sound shape" that has meaning and beauty in the context of its sound relations.

Note that literature is always conceived as being voiced, never as something read silently. Although some commentators have gone too far in seeing this as the beginning of tonal regulation, Hsü Fu-kuan offers a more moderate and credible alternative to the broad interpretation above. He lays stress on "alternation," and since the alternation of level and deflected tones became the basis of tonal balancing, he suggests that this is an incipient attention to this question as a central criterion in euphony. He further suggests that the fact that there were as yet no tonal rules leads to description of precariousness in the following lines.

Alternation, *tieh-tai*: The disposition of the Chinese intellectual tradition to take note of ongoing processes made Lu Chi intensely aware of the literary work as an event in time, rather than the static relation one finds in the visual art of embroidery. Relations in literature are always relations of succession and alternation: the poet cannot manipulate the parts of a static "thing," but rather must contend with something that is ongoing.

The five colors, *wu-se*: There are the traditional Chinese primary colors: red, blue/green, yellow/brown, white, and black. Lu Chi probably has embroidery in mind here, but it is possible that painting, too, would be comprehended in the generality of the line.

Lines 105–106: The Li Shan paraphrase is of interest here: "There is no constancy in their passing or halting of words; rather the movement is only what suits the state of mind (*ch'ing**); but because of the many mutations (*pien**) of normative forms (*t'i**), it is a rocky road that cannot be made easy." That is, the movement of language (sounds) follows *ch'ing** and thus is as variable and unpredictable as the movement of *ch'ing** itself; yet at the same time there are constantly changing norms which must be taken into account, and this makes the movement still more difficult. Here Li Shan takes line 106 as the apodosis; I have followed *TL* and others in delaying the apodosis to lines 107–108.

Commentators differ here as to whether these and the following lines refer only to questions of euphony or to euphony together with concept and language, the question raised in the preceding couplet. Since these lines articulate principles basic to all aspects of composition, I think that the broader interpretation is correct. First we must wonder exactly what is meant by "passing on or halting"; it is clearly "language," but we are uncertain precisely what aspect of language is intended. It may be the rhythms of exposition, the topic (suggested by ll. 109–110); it may be the cadences of the language; or it may be the cadences of voicing the text, pausing on certain words for emphasis and mood, a salient feature of modern recitation technique. The lack of "constants," *ch'ang* 常, means that there are no permanent rules for what to do at what point. I take line 106 to be in apposition to this: the fact that there are no constants makes the movement of "passing on or halting" a metaphorically "rocky path" (*ch'i-ch'i*, a descriptive of quality for something that is rugged and insecure). Since there are no constants to guide one, it is very easy to err (ll. 109–113).

Line 107: *TL* takes *tz'u* as "come to rest" rather than "succession," thus linking "mutation" with "passing on" (l. 105) and *tz'u* ("coming to rest") with "halting" (l. 105). This interpretation has the merit of preserving the rhetorical order of exposition, but it would be an unusual usage of *tz'u* in a context like this. To understand *tz'u* as "succession" or "sequence" seems preferable. *Ta pien**, translated as "grasp mutation," is more literally "achieve perfection in mutation." *Shih tz'u* is to "recognize the proper sequence." The way to negotiate this very difficult process of the ongoing movement of language is a sure sense of changes and sequences. We might think of an analogy to Lu Chi's sense of process here in skiing on a wooded slope: once committed to the process, one must contend with what is unexpected and oncoming; there are no easy constants, no certain determinations decided beforehand that can let a person know what to do at what point; nevertheless, there are general principles of "mutation" and "sequence" that permit instant and intuitive decisions about shifts in weight and balancing, oncoming turns and choices that must be made on the spot.

Line 108: Earlier the spirit was immersed in a flood within (ll. 21–24; in composition the flood pours forth (l. 64); here the flow must be managed. In this we have a hint of the theme of the poet as Sage-King: channeling the great rivers to prevent floods was the mythical labor of the Sage-King Yü in antiquity, and waterworks remained an important part of the imperial government. As in many of the earlier metaphors for poetic activity, the poet is not isolated in the act of composition: he "contends with" forces that have their own momentum. The sense of ongoing movement is strong. The poet must not only act in the right way, he must act in the right way at the right moment.

Line 109–110: *Chi**, translated as the "occasion," was originally the "trigger mechanism of a crossbow" and was extended to the "springs" or subtle initiating motion of any process. One must know to act at a certain moment in order to initiate a process that will lead to a certain conclusion. Although the meaning "trigger mechanism of a crossbow" is not present here, it is a useful analogy for the function of *chi**: to hit a moving target requires not only aim but knowledge of when to pull the trigger; likewise, in composition one must act at precisely the right moment to initiate or turn a particular process. *Hui*, translated as "bring things together," is the same verb used earlier (l. 101) in the compound *hui-yi** "forming conceptions." As the second element of the title of the *Fu-hui* 附會 chapter of *Wen-hsin tiao-lung*, *hui* is the active principle of "unifying" a work, bringing it all together. This should be clearly distinguished from an atemporal concept of "unity" in a literary work; *hui* rather is an event and act within the text, the intuition of proper sequencing that creates unified movement, and especially concluding acts that "bring things together." To miss the proper moment to "bring things together" is to invert the proper sequences. Such inversion is referred to here as "having the beginning following the end": literally "you will grasp the end (*mo**, "branch tip," i.e., consequence) and have the head follow it."

"Purple and Brown," *hsüan-huang*: These two colors are metonymic for Heaven and Earth respectively. The relative positions of Heaven and Earth, one above and one below, are taken as the fixed and constant standard.

The image of poetic action offered in these lines is a rich one: words and conceptions come forth in a flood, capable of going anywhere and governed by no rules. The role of the poet is to manage their motion; and while there are no rules that govern the spontaneous outpouring of words and conceptions, the structure of the poet's management of that flood can be measured against constant principles of sequence, change, and order. To return to the analogy of skiing down a wooded slope: there are countless ways to get gracefully from the top to the bottom and countless ways to fail. One is carried by momentum, and each channeling of that momentum responds to the continual variations of topography and circumstance. And while it is essential to recognize that the complete sequence of movements cannot be determined in advance, in each act there *are* constant principles of movement—general rules of turning, balancing, slowing down or speeding up. This analogy is more apt than the equally performative analogy of dance, where the unity of the whole is often given from the beginning rather than won in the act itself. In contrast the poet is "contending with" an ongoing flood of words and concepts and giving them order.

A knowledge of the principles of change and sequence enables a poet to guide that process. The sounds he uses have meaning and beauty only in relation to other sounds, just as the juxtaposition of colors in an embroidery articulates the design. Failure occurs in the inversion of some organic relation, or, in the significant metaphor of the last line of the passage, in a blurring of relations, a "muddying" of colors that destroys "vividness" (*hsien*).

The sections that follow (i.e., ll. 113–186) consider a series of failings and their remedies. Buried in the structure of Lu Chi's poetic exposition is the venerable rhetorical scheme of *ch'ang-tuan* 長短: persuading someone by giving the strong points of one position and then the weak points of the opposing position. Lu Chi has been giving positive directions on how one should proceed in composition; here he turns to the failings and dangers one may encounter. In these descriptions we can often see important facets of Lu Chi's literary values through their negative images in his descriptions of failings.

113	或仰逼於先條
114	或俯侵於後章
115	或辭害而理比
116	或言順而義妨

117	離之則雙美
118	合之則兩傷
119	考殿最於錙銖
120	定去留於毫芒
121	苟銓衡之所裁
122	固應繩其必當

113	At times you may transgress against a previous section,
114	Or trespass ahead to some later part.
115	At times your diction may be faulty, though the principle follows its proper course,
116	Or the language proceeds smoothly, though the idea (*yi**) is blocked.
117	Avoid both [these situations] and the beauty is doubled;
118	If the two occur together, twice the damage.
119	Consider relative merits by the tiniest measures;
120	Decide on rejecting or retaining by a hair's breadth:
121	If what has been trimmed to the most accurate measure
122	Truly follows the straight line, then it must be suitable.

Lines 113–114: *T'iao*: (literally "branch" and lamely translated as "section" above) is glossed by Li Shan as *k'o-t'iao* 科條, literally legal "statutes"; but he goes on to explain the line in terms of a purely literary sense of order, an understanding of what must come first and what must follow. All subsequent commentators have ignored the legal metaphor. The choice of a technical legal term as a gloss here is very persuasive because the antithesis forms the compound *t'iao-chang** 條章, legal "statutes and sections." Thus if we were reading line 113 in isolation, we would probably take it as: "At times one may transgress the [literary] statutes laid down by our predecessors." But lines 113 and 114 must be read in parallel: not only would the notion of "transgressing" laws set by future writers make very little sense, *hou-chang** should probably refer to a "later section" of an individual work. Thus we must read the language of precedence and posteriority here in terms of the exposition of an individual work. But the legal overtones of *t'iao-chang** cannot be suppressed entirely: it seems that *chang** is the pivotal word, with Lu Chi playing on literary "sections" as statutory "sections," thus generating an antithesis in *t'iao*, "statute," as a metaphor for part of the literary work, especially insofar as that part regulates what must be done later in the work. This constitutes one of the earliest examples of the language of law as a metaphor for literature (later encompassing a rich matrix of terms such as *fa**, *lü* 律, and *fan* 犯, but not including either *t'iao* or *chang** in this sense). *Pi*, "transgress," and *ch'in*, "trespass," are compounded as *ch'in-pi* 侵逼, the "transgression" that occurs with an invasion or, more appropriate here, with a crime. The point of the couplet seems to be that exposition has it "laws": transgression of those laws may refer either to a failure of consistency (statement B may violate statement A) or a failure to say the right thing at the right time.

Earlier in the tradition of discourse on literature, a work might be criticized for lacking proper ethical purpose (as we find in the Han critic Yang Hsiung 揚雄); and Ts'ao P'i offered general criticisms regarding the limitations of certain writers. The attention to violations and faults, which ultimately came to play such a powerful role in writing about poetry, appears first in the Western Tsin, especially in the work of Lu Chi and of his brother Lu Yün. This attention to violations and faults goes together with a new unease about writing, the omnipresent dangers of failure that haunt "The Poetic Exposition on Literature." Ts'ao P'i had simply wanted to write something that could survive for eternity. Lu Chi wants to avoid humiliating blunders. As the judgment of faults in the Western critical tradition was strongly (though not exclusively) associated with a public forum, the theater, so in China apprehension at the possibility of error is linked to the role literature was coming to play in social relations. At least since the time of Ts'ao P'i, literature had been becoming increasingly the activity of a group; and there was a recognized group of writers in the Western Tsin capital of Lo-yang. Generous praise was offered solely on the grounds of literary talent (Chang Hua 張華 quipped that the young Lu Chi was the greatest prize taken in the conquest of Wu); reputations were made, not by the emperor but by a consensus of connoisseurs; but there was also the danger of failure and rejection. We begin to read comments of the sort not often seen before: Lu Yün writes to his brother, "Your 'Nine Griefs' has many fine phrases and a person can really become absorbed reciting it; but the rhymes are a bit off... " Or Lu Yün asks Lu Chi to read over his own work: "I'd like to add or take out things—just a few words here and there—I don't expect you to do a lot. My sense of sounds is a Southern one, and I'd like you to fix them."[51] As small and informal as these comments are, they indicate the arrival of an entirely new era in literature.

Lines 113–116: The parallel terms *tz'u** ("diction") and *yen* ("language") together form the compound *yen-tz'u**, referring to "language" in a broad sense. Likewise the parallel terms *li** ("principle") and *yi** ("a truth") together form the compound *yi**-*li**, referring not only to "moral principle," but also to the "meaning" or "significance" of language. Depending on the context and the conventional relations of the terms involved, parallel terms may sometimes stress distinction (see commentary to ll. 3–4) or they may collapse into a compound with an essentially unitary meaning. The latter case occurs here: it would not be inappropriate to use "language" (*yen* or *tz'u** or a compound) and "significance" (*yi** and *li** compounded) in both lines. *Hai*, translated as "faulty," is literally "to do harm" or "to damage"; terms of damage were a common way of speaking of the failure of language to convey an idea clearly. Lu Chi's use of *hai* here and the phrasing *tz'u** *hai* comes from *Mencius* V.A.4.2 (as Lu Chi would have understood it): "In explaining the poems of the *Book of Songs*, one must not permit the parts (*wen**) to affect adversely (*hai*) the sense of the whole (*tz'u**); and one must not permit the sense of the whole to affect adversely [our understanding of] what was on the writer's mind (*chih**)."

Two hidden compounds govern this use of *pi*, "follows its course": *pi-yi**, "to follow the right," and *shun-pi*, "to follow along naturally" (*shun* is "proceed smoothly" in the next line).[53] Note that *fang* 坊, "be blocked," and *hai*, "faulty," can be similarly compounded as *fang-hai*. Couplets like this one are constructed of divided compounds; the more restricted semantic value of these compounds often limits the wider semantic range of the individual characters. Thus a word like *pi* might be taken in many ways in the context of the single line, but the familiar compounds it forms with other characters in the couplet restrict its possible range of meaning. The flat redundancy of this couplet is as clear as the message it conveys; and the assumptions made in the couplet should be quite familiar to Western readers: there are two independent "tracks" in writing, one of language and one of meaning, which may succeed or fail independently of one another.

Lines 117–118: This is gratuitous quantification of failure, which itself fails by the standards set in the preceding couplet: we do not know whether the dangers are the "faulty diction" and "blocked idea" of lines 115–116, or the violations referred to in lines 113–114 together with those in lines 115–116.

Lines 119–120: "Relative merits," *tien-tsui*, are, as Li Shan points out, lesser and greater degrees of merit as adjudicated by the Han court. Again Lu Chi uses the imperial "judge of men" as a model for the writer's judgment of words. "The tiniest measures" are literally two small measurements of weight, a *tzu* 錙 and a *chu* 銖. A "hair's breadth," *hao-mang*, is a dead metaphor for something very fine, combining "hair" with the "tassel floss" of grain.

Follows the straight line, *ying-sheng*: *Ying-sheng* is literally "corresponds to the cord [used to draw a straight line]." Note that Lu Chi does not hesitate to mix metaphors. Such metaphors of weights and measures were commonly applied to judgments of deeds and character when choosing men for office: a hint of the model of governance is still present.

Little in these lines calls for comment, except for their tone. Western readers, making the inevitable analogies with their own tradition, may feel some discomfort here. Lu Chi earlier sounded much like a Romantic theorist, speaking of literary cosmogony, organic unity, the poet as a nexus through which the intricate multiplicity of the world becomes manifest. All of a sudden he shifts to general advice on practical matters in a tone that is virtually Horatian. Combined with this advice is a passion for judgment, a confidence in our ability consciously to perfect a text, which we associate with Neo-

Classicism. The earlier movements in the poetic exposition stress the positive generation of the text; the later movements are negative, and largely concerned with the avoidance of errors in composition. Lu Chi includes both because both are, from different points of view, true. We should not ignore the fact that the notion of the text as a spontaneously produced organism, at most channeled in process, does indeed run at cross purposes to the notion that the text is a construct of reflective judgment. But Lu Chi's impulse, which may be the impulse of the poetic exposition as a genre, is to include, not to "discriminate" and take a position. As one might expect, these antithetical impulses are given to us as different stages of composition, the earlier stages producing material to be "trimmed" and judged by the later stage. And as earlier, the sequence of stages is a compensatory movement: whenever Lu Chi has "given free rein," he then feels the need to "rein in."

123	或文繁理富
124	而意不指適
125	極無兩致
126	盡不可益
127	立片言而居要
128	乃一篇之警策
129	雖眾辭之有條
130	必待茲而效績
131	亮功多而累寡
132	故取足而不易

123	It may be that the pattern (*wen**) is lush and the principle (*li**) rich,
124	But in terms of concept (*yi**), it does not really have a point.
125	Reaching its limit, there is no second significance;
126	Exhausted, it will be unable to increase.
127	Set a suggestive phrase in an essential spot,
128	And it will be a riding crop for the whole piece:
129	Even though the word-hoard follows the statutes,
130	One must have this to compete for great merit.
131	The accomplishment will be great and the complications few.
132	So choose just what is enough and do not change it.

Lines 123–124: *Pu chih ti*, translated as "not really have a point," is explained by the Wu-ch'en commentary as "the work does not hit the matter it is aiming at," or alternatively, that its central point is not clear (Hsü Fu-kuan). In a long discussion Ch'ien Chung-shu takes the phrase as I have: that is, not that it does not "hit the matter it is aiming at," but rather that it really has no central point. I suspect that *chih-ti* is, in fact, the common compound *chih-*

che 指摘, "to choose and in doing so make clear distinctions." This would maintain the language of selection in regard to concept (cf. l. 33), especially with the overtones of governance, "selecting" those worthy for office. In this case the line would be translated: "But the concept has not been chosen with care."

This passage is of particular interest because it shows the difference between a simple dichotomy between content and expression and Lu Chi's tripartite scheme (in this case, with *li**, "principle," taking the place of *wu**, "things"). It is not surprising that *wen** be lush (*fan*, the language of vegetation) and the *yi**, "concept," still be inadequate. It is surprising, however, that "concept" can be inadequate despite a richness of *li**, "principle," in the text. *Yi** seems to function as a unifying structure that draws the propositions of the text together into some "point." Thus Lu Chi is noting that it is possible to say true and important things (richness of principle), without some conceptual unity in mind that organizes them to some end.

Lines 125–126: This is one of the most elusive couplets in the whole work. As Ch'ien Chung-shu points out, Li Shan's explanation does not help much. It is possible to take this couplet as enjoining the writer to precision and an avoidance of ambiguity (a wondrously ambiguous and imprecise encouragement to precision): "When it reaches its limit [point], it [should] have no ambiguity; when the words are done, one should not be able to add to them." This interpretation is followed by Chen Shih-hsiang and, roughly, by Ch'ien Chung-shu. It seems to me more likely that the couplet refers to the words' being "exhausted" without the discourse's having achieved an adequate presentation of "concept." In this vein the Wu-ch'en commentary paraphrases: "it reaches the point of exhaustion/ending without being able satisfactorily to make its point." The paraphrase in *TL* suggests something similar. The *chih* of "no second significance" (*wu liang chih*) is the *chih* of *chih-yi** 致意, "to get one's point across."

If we follow the Wu-ch'en commentary and *TL*, as I have done, the implications are interesting. The fulfillment of "concept," the unifying point that draws the text together, occurs in the domain of "second significance," *liang-chih*, and "increasing," *yi* 益; it is somehow beyond the surface meaning of the text; it is "that to which the text goes" (perhaps implicit in *chih-ti* 指適, and sustained by the riding metaphor in l. 128). Such an interpretation is consistent with my interpretation of line 84 and with the fascination with extension in lines 63–66; moreover, it is sustained in the following couplet.[54] If the significance of the text is "exhausted" with the words, the point of "concept" will not be reached.

Lines 127–128: As Li Shan points out, *p'ien-yen*, translated as "suggestive expression," comes from *Analects* XII.12: "From a hint (*p'ien-yen*) able to resolve disputes—that was Yu." *P'ien-yen*, is a "partial expression," incomplete in itself, but leading a person of understanding to a comprehension of the whole. Its application to the situation in the preceding four lines is that concept can be indicated by a partial expression ("suggestive expression"), incomplete in itself but directing the discerning reader to the unifying point of the piece. This supports the interpretation of "second significance" and "increase" in the preceding couplet as positive values and not as ambiguity to be avoided. "The riding crop" ("the whip that shocks into motion") is discussed at length by Ch'ien Chung-shu, taking note of the common metaphor of riding in reference to literature. Lu Chi's troping on the metaphor here seems to be that the "suggestive phrase" whips the piece into motion, gives it energy and direction, and speeds it toward the unifying point.[55] Ching 警 is used here in the sense of ching 驚. Ch'ien Chung-shu correctly distinguishes ching-ts'e from the later term ching-chü 警句, "startling lines"; yet that later usage can be ultimately traced to the use of ching in this passage.

Word-hoard, *chung-tz'u*: *Chung-tz'u* is used very much like *ch'ün-yen* 羣言; see commentary to line 21.

Follow the statutes, *yu-t'iao*: *T'iao*, "branches" or "statutes," is the problematic term discussed at length in the commentary to line 113. *Yu-t'iao* is both "to have rules or statutes" and "to have branches." In the latter sense it echoes the tree metaphor earlier: the piece may follow the proper sequence of growth. In the former sense, it responds to line 113: the piece must show regard for the rules. But the orderliness implied in *yu-t'iao* is not enough, for the work must also have a suggestiveness that gives vigor to the whole. This sounds much like the commonplace concession of Western Neo-Classicism, that genius must go beyond the rules.

To compete for great merit, *hsiao-chi*: See commentary to line 75. Not only do the words compete for excellence and attention, the work as a whole is part of an implicit competition. Since Ts'ao P'i's "Discourse on Literature," the language of competition and reward had come to play an important role in literary discussion. From the Western Han (and if one takes the orators of the pre-Ch'in period into account, from a much earlier time) literary skill had been a means to achieve social and political position. Lu Chi surely intends "merit" in a non-political sense of "literary success"; but he conceives of literary success on the political model of competition, being singled out and rewarded. Furthermore, he transfers this model to the writer's relation to his words: as the writer might become the object of judgment by the emperor (political success) or by society (literary success), so in the act of composition the writer himself becomes the judge, and the words become the objects of his judgments.

Choose just what is enough, *ch'ü tsu*: The recurrent theme of minimalization (seen earlier in the advocacy of concision) further supports the interpretation of the preceding lines as referring to a minimal surface text, beyond which lies more extensive concept.

It is characteristic of Lu Chi's argument that one virtue or the remedy for one danger leads to a consideration of a new danger. In the preceding section he had addressed the danger that principle or phrasing may be imperfect; but success in these two problematic aspects of writing is not, in itself, adequate for good writing; there must also be "concept," *yi**, some unifying sense of purpose or significance in the writing. Even though the impulse to add *yi** (to the previous dichotomy between principle and phrasing) comes from the triadic structure of composition announced in the preface and developed in the first part of the main body of the poetic exposition, the meaning of "concept" here has been extended from its earlier function. In those earlier usages "concept" had been a structure of relations mediating between the things of the world and writing (*wen**); thus it might be seen as a grasp of some particular aspect of "principle," *li** (and seems to be so described in ll. 37–44). In the passage above *yi** has become something like "unifying significance," to which the text should point but which lies beyond what is stated explicitly in any particular part of the text (if it could be stated explicitly, the passage on the "suggestive phrase" would be inexplicable in the context).

*Li**, "principle," is both content and structure that belongs to Nature. As content, it is a proposition that has a particular claim to being true (e.g., leaves fall in autumn); as structure, it is a "natural" organization of exposition, whose authority (but not necessarily the particular structures) corresponds roughly to a Western notion of "logical development" or "logical consistency." When Lu Chi speaks of principle's being rich, he means that the writer says true things and puts them together in a proper, natural way. He realizes, however, that this is obviously not adequate to produce good writing. The addition of *yi**—or more precisely, of the deferral of *yi**—promises to account more perfectly for good or interesting writing. Although in some cases *yi** has an almost abstract sense of "concept," it is usually a particular act of mind (to the extent that a phrase like *T'ien yi** 天意, "Heaven's will," tends to anthropomorphize Heaven). In the Preface *yi** had been a formation of "concept" that grasped the "things of the world," *wu**, presumably according to *li**. Here it has become a structuring act of mind in the writer *in contrast to* "principle," *li**, which belongs to Nature. *Yi** is a unifying concept to which the text points, discovered in the momentum of the words and not as a proposition.

Here and elsewhere in "The Poetic Exposition on Literature" Lu Chi is making incipient moves towards a notion that was to become one of the most salient characteristics of later literary thought: meaning is an event that occurs "beyond words" and "after the words have ended." Without that sense of some significance, flavor, or whatever beyond the surface of the text, the literary work seems flat.[56] The use of *p'ien-yen*, the "suggestive expression" or literally "partial expression," marks the incompleteness of the surface text; and it is such language, recognized as somehow incomplete, that is the "riding crop," giving the text energy and forward momentum.

133	或藻思綺合。
134	清麗芊眠。
135	炳若縟繡。
136	悽若繁絃。
137	必所擬之不殊。
138	乃闇合乎曩篇。
139	雖杼軸於予懷。
140	怵他人之我先。
141	苟傷廉而愆義。
142	亦雖愛而必捐。

133	It may be that your intricately crafted thoughts cohere, finely patterned,
134	A lucid loveliness, gloriously bright,
135	Shimmering like a many-colored brocade,
136	Or deeply moving like a flurry of strings.
137	Then suppose you find what you aim at lacks distinction—
138	Your work unwittingly corresponds to some long-ago piece.
139	Even if the shuttle and loom were in my own feelings,
140	I must dread lest others have preceded me;
141	If it damages integrity and transgresses what is right,
142	Though I begrudge doing so, I must cast it from me.

Line 133: "Intricately crafted thoughts," *tsao-ssu** refer to the process of thought involved in composition, a process concerned with the "intricate craft," *tsao*, of literature. In a common rhetorical figure, the object of the thoughts is transferred to the position of modifier. The use of *ssu**, "thoughts," evokes here the venerable pun on *ssu* 絲, "silken threads," developed in the fabric metaphor in this line (*ch'i* 綺) and in lines 135 and 139. For the association of *ch'i*, "fine patterns," see line 85, commentary. *Ho*, translated as "cohere" recurs in line 138, where it is translated "coincide." The "coherence of thoughts," *ho-ssu**, is precisely the concern of the preceding section; thus the transition between the sections would be something like: "even if you succeed in giving the work coherent concept, there is yet another danger."

Line 134: *Ch'ing*, "lucid" or "clear," became a common positive attribute in Chinese aesthetics. Its negative counterpart is a "muddiness" in which forms lose their outlines and colors are mixed (although a positive antithesis to "clarity" develops later, a lovely mistiness). The provenance of the descriptive term "gloriously bright" (ch'ien-mien, which Li Shan glosses as "full of light and color") applies to flourishing vegetation; it is one of the many terms of vegetation extended to the description of style.

Line 136: *Ch'i*, translated as "deeply moving," is a term for deep sorrow. Often when one definite emotion must represent all the emotions, a term of sorrow is chosen. The English "deeply moving" bears some similarity to this, being a term for sad or serious feelings that suggests emotion in general. A "flurry of strings," *fan-hsien*, is playing the strings of one or more instruments in concert or in quick succession; the association is with intense feeling.

Lines 137–138: The central problem in this couplet is how to take *so-ni*, in which the term *ni* can mean either "take as one's model" in the general sense of aspiring to a goal or "imitate" in the more particular sense of copying. The Wu-ch'en commentary paraphrases *so-ni* as "the work," thus implicitly taking *ni* in the former sense of "what is aspired to" or "what is intended." Following this commentarial tradition, I have translated *so-ni* as "what you aim at," taking *ni* in the sense of "the work as you would like it to be." *TL* and Ch'ien Chung-shu, however, take *ni* as "imitate"; this interpretation is plausible, but it creates problems in the next lines, which seem to refer to the discovery of accidental identity with an earlier work as something to be avoided. Compounding the difficulties here, Ch'ien Chung-shu wants to take *pi* ("necessarily") as "if" or "supposing"; this leads to a translation something like "If you do not aim for distinction in what you take for imitation, then unwittingly your work will coincide . . . " How in such a case the correspondence with an earlier work could be "unwitting" is left unexplained. *An*, translated here as "unwitting," is literally "hidden" or "unperceived," in this case initially unperceived by the writer. Note the repetition of *ho* 合, "correspond," from line 133 where it is translated as "cohere."

Line 139: Resemblance to an earlier work can occur even if there was no intent to imitate. The mind is a weaver working with *ssu* 絲 "threads" or *ssu* 思 "thoughts." Note the use of *yü* 予, the first person pronoun usually omitted, to emphasize "one's own."

Lines 141–142: Even if a passage's similarity to an earlier work is recognized only after the passage has been written or conceived, it still must be rejected. One's integrity is compromised not by intentional plagiarism, but by permitting the duplication of something from an earlier work that might lead others to suspect plagiarism. In later Chinese literary thought the problematic relation between individual identity and composition was more fully explored, and the position Lu Chi had taken here was reversed: a situation in which the writer "accidentally coincided with the ancients" was a happy moment when the spontaneous and individual elements of composition matched the universal and hence recurrent.[57]

This radical demand for originality, apparently made even on the level of phrases, is most unusual and certainly not true of the Chinese literary tradition as a whole (or of any other literary tradition), where intertextual borrowing is the norm. One might, however, add that in this particular poetic exposition, Lu Chi himself tends to conform to the demand he makes here: the uniqueness of the work in the tradition and its almost impenetrable difficulty arise largely from Lu Chi's original phrases. Plagiarism *was* an issue in the Chinese literary tradition (cf. Ch'ien Ching-shu on these lines) but not a common or central one.[58] The charge of plagiarism was raised only in regard to whole poems and sometimes couplets; here, however, the idea of unwittingly reproducing an earlier text can only refer to phrases, sentences, or a line of argument.

This statement on originality generates anxiety about a corresponding danger, the "solitude" of something that is too original.

143	或苕發穎豎。
144	離眾絕致。
145	形不可逐。
146	響難為係。
147	塊孤立而特峙。
148	非常音之所緯。
149	心牢落而無偶。
150	意徘徊而不能揥。
151	石韞玉而山暉。
152	水懷珠而川媚。
153	彼榛楛之勿翦。
154	亦蒙榮於集翠。
155	綴下里於白雪。
156	吾亦濟夫所偉。

143	It may be that a blossom comes forth, a spike of grain stands upright,
144	Separated from the crowd, isolated from the sense:
145	A shape no shadow can follow,
146	A sound to which no echo can be linked.
147	It stands there towering, solitary and immobile,
148	Not woven in with the constant tones.
149	Mind is in a desolate expanse, nothing corresponds;
150	Conception circles aimlessly, unable to leave it.
151	The mountain shimmers when jade is in the stone,

152	The stream is alluring when its waters bear pearls;
153	Thorn bushes and medlars need not be cut down—
154	They, too, can become glorious by the roosting kingfisher.
155	If we link an art song with a popular tune,
156	We may augment what makes it exceptional.

Line 143: This line seems to be based on the dead metaphor *hsiu* 秀, a "high ear of grain," which by Lu Chi's time was applied to anything that "stood out" or was "outstanding." "Blossom," *t'iao*, was originally a reed blossom, and had come to refer generally to something flowering, though the kind of flowering that rises above the rest of the plant (as opposed to, say, blossoms on a flowering tree). Both *t'iao* and the spike of grain are *hsiu*, "out-standing," and as such they present a danger of discontinuity.

Line 144: "Separate from the crowd," *li-chung*, carries not only the implication of the line's or phrase's separation from the overall argument of the piece, it also carries a strong sense of unique excellence.

Isolated from the sense, *chüeh-chih*: *Chih* is an interesting term; its root meaning of "go to" or "bring" is extended to a quality of inclination or direction in thought, manner, or feeling, a "conveying" (in later classical Chinese its force is weakened to merely "mood," "feeling," "import"). *Chüeh* can mean either "cut off" or "superb," "peerless." I have followed Li Shan in construing *chih* as "conveying thought," *chih-ssu** 致思 (i.e., the argument), and the phrase *chüeh-chih* as "cut off from the thrust of the argument." This maintains the parallelism of Lu Chi's own argument and takes *chih* in a way consistent with Tsin usage. Another possible interpretation, offered in *TL*, is to take *chüeh-chih* as "a peerless manner." There is no problem with the sense of such an interpretation; but it should be regarded with suspicion, not only because it twists the parallelism somewhat, but also because it yields too easily to the late classical usage of *chih*.

Lines 145–146: This couplet rests on the idea that all phenomena should have natural correspondences, as shape is followed by a shadow or sound is followed by an echo. A passage that is an isolated beauty will have no such contiguous patterns or echoings. I have taken the isolated beauty to be the "shape" or "sound," with no "shadow" or "echo" later in the text to balance and continue it. Possibly, however, the isolated beauty might be interpreted as the shadow itself, in which case we would construe line 145 as "it cannot follow any shape," that is, it is so elusive that it has no ground in tangible reality. The problem with such an interpretation is that line 146, on echo and sound, is most naturally translated as above (it would be possible but forced to take it as "an echo not linked to any sound"); and parallelism would dispose us to take the elements of the two lines in analogous relations. The interpretation followed by the translation emphasizes that the uniqueness of an isolated beauty "stops" discourse (cf. ll. 149–150) because there is no way to continue or match it. The second, less likely interpretation would emphasize only the elusiveness of isolated beauty.

Line 147: *K'uai,* translated as immobile, also suggests solitude.

Line 148: "Constant tones," *ch'ang-yin,* are also "ordinary tones." Their commonplaceness contrasts with the uniqueness of the isolated beauty, while their being "constant" bespeaks a comprehensible coherence in the text from which the isolated beauty stands apart. "Woven in," *wei,* is literally "to be made the woof in a weaving."

Line 149: *Lao-lo* (or, alternatively, according to Li Shan, *liao-lo* 寥落) describes the quality of a vast, unpopulated expanse of land and a state of mind, a melancholy isolation that is appropriate to being in such a location. This condition is clear in "nothing corresponds," *wu-ou*: "without mate, match, or parallel." This line reveals much about Chinese aesthetic values and the affect of parallelism: an isolated beauty, however splendid in itself, looks around for a shadow or echo, a "match"; unable to find anything, it suddenly assumes the melancholy isolation of a solitary figure in a vast wasteland. Hsü Fu-kuan takes this and the following line as referring to the response of the reader, who does not know what to "relate," *ou,* the solitary beauty to.

Line 150: *T'i* is alternatively glossed in Li Shan as "leave" 禘 (or "get rid of"). Ch'eng Hui-ch'ang takes *t'i* in its usual sense of "pick" or "select," leading to an interpretation of the line as "conception is unable to accept it into [select it for] the work," with conception's reluctance dispelled by the following lines. Hsü Fu-kuan, continuing his interpretation of these lines as referring to the reader, takes *t'i* as "get," so that the reader is unable to "get anything out of it." The Wu-ch'en commentary reads *ch'ih* 摡, meaning "remove," yielding basically the same sense as the alternative Li Shan interpretation of *t'i*. "Circles aimlessly," *p'ai-huai,* is a movement that embodies hesitation and uncertainty, "pacing back and forth," or in the standard classical gloss, "the manner of moving without getting anywhere."

Lines 151–152: Li Shan cites "Encouraging Study" in the *Hsün-tzu:* "When jade is in a mountain, the vegetation will be moist and fertile; when pearls are in the depths, the shore will never dry up." Lu Chi may or may not be alluding to the *Hsün-tzu* specifically, but he is certainly alluding to some variation on this saying: as these rare things, jade and pearls, impart fertility and moisture to their surroundings, so the isolated beauty, though not part of the common fabric or landscape of the text, still can give a richness and beauty to the rest.

Lines 153–154: Much dispute has arisen regarding the interpretation and truth of this couplet. *Chen-hu* are two kinds of scrubby trees, used in *Book of Songs* 239 in association with a lush richness appropriately qualifying great virtue; in other contexts, however, *chen-hu* represents a kind of underbrush that ought to be cut away. In that latter sense Li Shan takes this as another version of the "constant/ordinary tones" mentioned earlier, that is, as something undesirable that needs to be somehow redeemed.

Another problem arises in the interpretation of *chi-ts'ui*. This may be taken as a "roosting kingfisher" as above (Hsü Wen-yü, cited in *TL*); or it may be taken as the "massed azure" of the vegetation of "thorn bushes and medlars" (Wu-ch'en). This latter interpretation, while philologically plausible, simply does not fit the sense of this passage, forcing an improbable equation of the isolated beauty with "thorn bushes and medlars."

In the chapter "Casting and Paring" in the *Wen-hsin tiao-lung*, Liu Hsieh takes Lu Chi to task for his wordiness. He makes specific reference to this passage and comments that Lu Chi "had no heart to pare away lushness" (see pp. 249). It must be said in fairness to Lu Chi, that Liu Hsieh seems to have entirely missed the point of this couplet. It is not that Lu Chi thinks a literary piece should be filled with superfluous verbiage, but rather that there is a virtue in alternating a plain style with something more lively.

The metaphor of the kingfisher roosting in thorn bushes would seem to make roughly the same point as the jade in the mountain or the pearls in the stream: there are points of exceptional beauty, discontinuous with the material as a whole, which nevertheless lend verve and beauty to the whole. Although we are tempted to take it this way, there remains one serious problem: the issue, as it is posed in the couplet, is not removing the kingfisher (the isolated beauty), but rather removing all the underbrush that frames it. Thus we might take this line as a complement to the preceding lines: not only should the isolated beauty (pearls and jade) be kept, but so should the ordinary background that is made beautiful by its presence.

Line 155: Literally this line reads, "If we link *Hsia-li* to *Pai-hsüeh*," alluding to two melodies mentioned in "Responses to the Questions of the King of Ch'u," *Tui Ch'u-wang wen* 對楚王問, attributed to Sung Yü. From that source *Hsia-li Pa-jen* 下里巴人 became a commonplace example of a song that was popular and low, while *Yang-ch'un pai-hsüeh* 陽春白雪 became the corresponding example of a song of exquisite beauty that could be appreciated by only a few. Lu Chi's appreciations of mixed modes and his interest in intensification by contrast is reminiscent of arguments made for the mixed modes of Shakespearean drama, proposed from Dryden through the nineteenth century.

This passage raises interesting questions regarding the sense of unity. The capacity of a passage to fit in with the whole piece (the unifying conception addressed in ll. 123–126) is not a simple integration with a linear argument but the need for another element that corresponds (l. 149). Thus, while there is a sense of overall unity, an individual passage enters such coherence through balance, echoes, and parallelism. It is a lack of such corresponding elements that makes a particular passage truly discontinuous. In other words, the overall coherence of a work occurs not through a necessary and linear sequence of propositions, but rather through a complex structure of balances and correspondences. The structure of this poetic exposition itself is an excellent example of this principle: a complex sequence of amplifications organized as balancing and compensatory moves. While an unmatched and thus discontinuous passage violates this sense of unity, Lu Chi allows a fine one to remain in the work, as something that enriches the work and gives it force by variety, contrast, and its own intrinsic beauty (obviously there would be no point in defending an undistinguished passage). In making this allowance Lu Chi implicitly recognizes the danger in a structure of echoes, balances, and compensations: a potential blandness and flatness. It is perhaps ironic that in making his point that balancing correspondences are not always necessary, Lu Chi feels the need to round off his point with a balancing and compensatory counterpoint: that one should also add the ordinary to a work that is, on the whole, elevated.

The following section of his poetic exposition (ll. 157–86) takes up five distinct faults in composition. Before commenting on them individually, two points of general interest should be raised: the arrangement of the terms of positive value (whose absence defines a fault) and the provenance of those terms.

The arrangement of the terms is derived from a Han (and perhaps earlier) structural model to account for relations between the hexagrams in the *Book of Changes*. A hexagram was conceived as the abstract ideogram of a condition that passed from a phase of incipience to a phase of excess. A condition in the phase of excess creates a corresponding absence or lack, for which another hexagram arises as compensation. A sequence in this form appears as A but lacking in B, B but lacking in C, C but lacking in D, and so on. In his "Discourse on Literature" Ts'ao P'i used a fragment of such a sequence to describe the relations between the style (*t'i**) of several of the Seven Masters (see pp. 62–63 above).[59] Lu Chi uses the same form here: each fault is in fact the danger that may be present in the excess of the preceding virtue; or each virtue contains within itself the seeds of the subsequent fault. Thus a writer may have "clear song, but nothing responds"; perfecting "response" may lead to a failure in "harmony"; perfecting "harmony" may lead to a failure in "emotion"; achieving "emotion" may lead to a failure in "dignity"; the perfection of "dignity" may lead to a failure in "allure." Such potential faults are not to be corrected by some golden mean, but rather by a structure of compensatory movements, such as we find in Lu Chi's own poetic exposition: it would not be a static condition of "balance," but rather a complex series of "balancings," each tendency requiring a countermotion to redeem it from foundering in the excess of its own virtue.

A musical metaphor is present in the elaboration of the five faults. Jao Tsung-yi has shown the provenance of the five main terms in the special vocabulary of music, particularly in discussion of playing the ch'in.[60] Although the metaphors that dominate this section are musical (and perhaps grow out of the musical reference in ll. 155–156), it should not be forgotten that all these terms had a rich range of literary and other associations, and were not exclusively musical.

157	或託言於短韻。
158	對窮迹而孤興。
159	俯寂寞而無友。
160	仰寥廓而莫承。
161	譬偏絃之獨張。
162	含清唱而靡應。

157   Suppose you put your words in too short a rhyme;
158   They face the end of their tracks, a solitary stirring.
159   They look down into a dismal stillness, lack companion;
160   They look up into vast space and continue nothing.
161   Compare it to a string of limited range, strung alone—
162   Within it lies clear song, but nothing responds.

Line 157: In explaining "too short a rhyme," *tuan-yün*, Li Shan is clearly correct in his interpretation as "too short a composition"; that is to say, a composition needs a degree of amplitude for resonance.[64] Although short poetic forms eventually came to play a very powerful role in Chinese poetry (as Lu Chi could never have foreseen), this demand for resonance remained, transformed into an intensive rather than extensive resonance. Chang Shao-k'ang is correct in spirit, if perhaps not in the letter of his interpretation, when he says that this has nothing essential to do with brevity per se but rather with a lack of variation that leaves no room for interplay.

They face the end of their tracks, *tui ch'iung-chi,* uses the common spatialization of the text as a movement, a movement which here ends too abruptly. The phrasing of the passage gives us to understand that the lack of amplitude causes lack of response (*ying**); but clearly it is the need for intratextual response in itself that is the real problem, and one could just as easily say that the lack of response between elements in the text is what defines insufficient amplitude. This abrupt closure of a text, a negative quality, contrasts strongly with the hints earlier in "The Poetic Exposition on

Literature" of the text's continuing on and expanding after the words are done (e.g., l. 84). Here we can see that the possibility of such expansion must be based on intratextual resonances, parallels, movements and countermovements, everything that creates interesting relations within the text. The monolithic text simply ends, and its solitude (even its unity) is seen as a lack.

A solitary stirring, *ku-hsing**: As *TL* points out, the *hsing** here can be taken either as the text's "coming forth" with insufficient amplitude, or something in the text's "stirring" a feeling to which the text, in its insufficiency, provides no response.

Lines 159–160: "They look down," *fu*, and "they look up," *yang*, are the proper terms for "what follows" and "what precedes" in the linear movement of the text (and here looking forward and backward into the blank spaces that surround the inadequate text). In addition, however, the image suggests the anthropomorphic solitude of a figure alone in the wilderness.

Dismal stillness, *chi-mo*: This common modal compound later suggests simply a gloomy desolation, but here, amid the auditory imagery of the passage, it strongly retains its original semantic element of "silence."

Continue nothing, *mo ch'eng*: This phrase might also be translated as "nothing continues [them]," meaning that nothing continues the words that look up into vast space; but the fact that the words are "looking up" (i.e., backward in the text) into "a vast space" strongly suggests that nothing was given beforehand for them to continue. The term *ch'eng*, "continue," was to become an important term for a relation of "building on" or "developing" an earlier passage. Ultimately *ch'eng* became ossified as the technical term for the second couplet of a regulated verse and the second line of a quatrain: the "development."[62]

Lines 161–162: Each of the "five faults" closes with an analogy to music, or more precisely here, to playing the *ch'in*. It should be stressed that making an explicit analogy, here using verbs of comparison, implies the consciousness of a *distinction* between the literary and musical, a distinction that was not made in the "Great Preface," where the literary and the musical were treated as the same thing. *P'ien*, translated as "of limited range," is literally "one-sided" as opposed to "comprehensive": the single string cannot equal the range of a full set of strings. Ch'ien Chung-shu's explanation of "getting a line, but not being able to complete the whole piece" misses the point: the concern of this passage is with an inherent limitation of short forms (a limitation that was overcome in later poetry), not a limitation of talent in using a form.

Within it lies, *han*: This is not the positive "reserve" of later poetics, but rather a potential that is unrealized and should be realized. It might be pointed out that short forms overcame the limitations discussed here precisely by a transformation of the quality of *han*, from something "unrealized" and therefore lost to an "unrealized reserve" whose possibilities can be intuited in the text.

Nothing responds, *mi ying*: *Ying** is a technical musical term here, but one with a very broad range of usage outside of the frame of reference of music. It is the term for "sympathetic resonance," or as Chang Shao-k'ang points out, notes of the same pitch (as when a singer is accompanied by an instrument). Beneath this passage lies the famous statement in the "Record of Music" that in the ideal music "one sings and three join in harmony" (see p. 53). In the "Record of Music," however, this refers to a reserve in the forcefulness of performance, leaving something to be fulfilled through the response of the listeners; Lu Chi here requires that the response occur within the text itself. Perhaps the most interesting aspect of this passage is the reinforcement of the notion that the text is an event in time, like a musical performance, rather than a "thing": the work is not to be conceived as a simultaneous whole. One part must be finished for another part to "respond." We might schematize that temporal relation as: A is unconditioned by B; B is conditioned by A; C is conditioned by A and B; and so forth. Without the temporality of response, there are qualities of limitation, even of loneliness in the text. The temporal interplay of voices is the formal recreation of the sociability of the external human world and the organic relations of the natural world.[63]

163	或寄辭於瘁音。
164	言徒靡而弗華。
165	混姸蚩而成體。
166	累良質而為瑕。
167	象下管之偏疢。
168	故雖應而不和。

163	Suppose you entrust your lines to dreary tones:
164	The words will have pointless languor and want splendor;
165	A form constituted of lovely and ugly mixed,
166	Good substance encumbered by blemishes.
167	Likened to pipes in the lower part of the hall played too fast—
168	Though there is response, there is no harmony.

Line 163: "Dreary," *ts'ui* 瘁, also written 悴 and used in the common compound *ch'iao-ts'ui* 憔悴 ("haggard"), clearly suggests an unfavorable quality, though precisely how this quality of "sickly," "worn out," or "dreary" fits into the subsequent musical analogy is uncertain. Perhaps it refers to a kind of overenergetic performance that soon leads to exhaustion and confusion. Ch'eng Hui-ch'ang suggests that it refers to a structureless muddle that lacks "bone," ku*: such a form would be associated with dissipation. The Wu-ch'en commentary's suggestion that this means composition on an unworthy subject is clearly wrong.

Line 164: In the phrase "pointless languor," t'u mi, Li Shan glosses mi as "lovely," mei 美; The Wu-ch'en commentary and TL take it as "extravagant." Mi is an interesting term, suggesting "delicacy," "compliance" or "going along with," leading to associations of "indulgence" and a sensuality associated with women. Its version of "beauty" is a delicate, languid beauty. There is a suggestion of intimacy here that contrasts with the solitude described in the preceding section, but which, in itself, is inadequate . "Splendor," hua, is the contrasting quality: a beauty that is vibrant, sparkling, and colorful.

Line 165: Such a form, t'i*, is constituted of attractive and unattractive qualities, the latter destroying the effect of the former. But here Lu Chi alters the emphasis to lead to his concluding point: the conflict between good and bad aspects of such a mode becomes a more general lack of harmony, which could occur even in an improper mixture of good qualities.

Lines 167–168: This is a fascinating example of the role of memorized classical phrases in forming discourse. To maintain the parallelism in each of the five faults, Lu Chi searches for new terms of similitude and here comes up with hsiang, "to liken," "to resemble." This leads him in turn to think on another use of the word hsiang as an ancient military dance, the "Semblance Dance." This usage of hsiang recalls a passage in the Book of Rites, "High in the hall they sing 'The Pure Temple' [from the Book of Songs], while the pipes in the lower part of the hall play the hsiang of [King Wen's] military exploits." The second part of that passage reads in Chinese hsia-kuan hsiang-wu 下管象式. Thus Lu Chi's choice of the term hsiang in the sense of "liken" leads to the association of hsia-kuan. However interesting this may be in the psychology of composition, one should not thereby infer, as TL does, that the hsiang dance is being played here: even though a military dance might well be played overenergetically, this would be a kind of music entirely different from the mode suggested in the first four lines of the passage. Hsü Fu-kuan extrapolates from the Book of Rites passage, where singers sing "The Pure Temple" from the Book or Songs while dancers dance the hsiang, to suggest that the problem addressed is figured in the very musical performance described: singers and dancers respond to one another but cannot keep in harmony.

In the preceding passage the danger was of isolation, lacking "response," ying. The antithesis is a plenitude of response, but such a plenitude is itself in danger of lacking an orderly relation between the parts, of lacking *ho*, "harmony." The concept of *ho*, "harmony," merits some attention. Like *ying* it suggests elements related in sequence rather than acting simultaneously as implied by the modern English use of "harmony." Unlike *ying*, however, *ho* implies notes of different pitches, so that we have a unity in difference. Thus in "The Rules of Sound" chapter of *Wen-hsin tiao-lung* we read, "when different tones follow one another, it is called harmony." *Ho* is a relation in which each element has a distinct identity yet contributes to a greater whole. It suggests a natural orderliness, a response that is also a "joining with."

169	或遺理以存異。
170	徒尋虛以逐微。
171	言寡情而鮮愛。
172	辭浮漂而不歸。
173	猶絃么而徽急。
174	故雖和而不悲。

169	Suppose you disregard natural principle and keep what is strange,
170	Pointless quest for the empty, pursuit of the over-subtle:
171	The words will lack feeling, be short on love,
172	Your lines will drift aimlessly to no end.
173	As when the strings are too thin and the bridges set too tight,
174	There may be harmony, but no strong emotion.

Line 169: The term missing here to clarify the opposition between "natural principle," *li**, and the "strange," *yi*, is the word *ch'ang* 常. *Ch'ang* is both that which is "constant" and that which is "ordinary." As "constant," *ch'ang* is an essential property of *li**; as "ordinary," *ch'ang* is the antithesis of the "strange." The danger addressed here is a mode that disdains the concrete, the close-at-hand, and that which can be readily shared with others. Lu Chi's choice of the term *li** in this context supports a mode of treatment that is not simply "ordinary," but "the way things naturally are."

Line 170: "Empty," *hsü**, combines the notions of insubstantiality, elusiveness, and otherworldliness. *TL* and Hsü Fu-kuan point out the resonance of the term *hsü** in Neo-Taoist speculation, popular in this period.

Lines 171–172: To "lack feeling," *kua-ch'ing**, would be a condition to which Neo-Taoist adepts would aspire. "Love," *ai*, is the stronger term, suggesting intense emotional attachment and desire, thus even more to be rejected by the Neo-Taoist inclination to an ethereal purity.[64] From the "Great Preface" on, poetry in particular had become associated with "feeling" or the "affections," *ch'ing**. Although Neo-Taoist intellectual trends of the period might disapprove of amplifying the buffetings of the affections in poetry, this was, nevertheless, the domain of poetry ("poetry follows from the affections"). For someone like Lu Chi, a person for whom literature was central, the presence of true feeling would be requisite. The opposition between feeling and no feeling had a counterpart in a quality of movement, movement either in life or in a text. Chuang-tzu and his spiritual progeny in the Neo-Taoists of the late Eastern Han, Wei, and Tsin valued a condition of "drifting aimlessly," moving without motives or goals, without any attachments that bind a person, as "feeling" and "love" do. A discourse that "drifted aimlessly" would be "to no end," *pu-kuei*, literally "not returning"; that is, it would be a discourse that does not "return" to the substantial world and its attachments (*kuei* was often used much like colloquial English "gravitates toward"). *Kuei* was also used in traditional hermeneutic vocabulary much like English "to have a point," to have some purpose or consequence that governed the understanding of the text. Even though the affections, *ch'ing**, were spoken of as being "empty," *hsü**, they grow out of relation to the concrete living world and remain tied to it. Lu Chi sees a danger in the possibility that the literary work might break its ties of attachment to the world.

Many commentators offer a somewhat different interpretation of this condition; rather than Taoist detachment, they take it as frivolity and mere cleverness, a kind of play that avoids anything serious. Since metaphors of drifting and emptiness are also applied to this very different mode, it is equally tenable as an interpretation for the passage.

Line 173: The metaphor here is of a string strung so tightly that the range of its pitch is high and the sound it produces is faint, tinny, and without resonance.

Line 174: *Pei*, "strong emotion," is literally "grief"; but like *ch'i* in line 136 above, *pei* is used to exemplify the full range of human feeling. In moral history, to which music and literature are bound according to the "Great Preface" and "Record of Music," *pei* is normally given as a negative quality, associated with the dissolution of customs and the "tones of a ruined state." In this context, however, Lu Chi is clearly using *pei* as a positive value and for the moment entirely disregarding any correspondences it might have to moral history (though we should note how that context returns in the negative phase, in the next passage on the *Sang-chien*).

The musical analogy here clarifies the role of this danger in the developing structure of values. "Response," the possibility of complex internal relations, is the first term of value and the ground upon which other values are possible; "harmony" assures order in response; but these categories are still purely internal. The addition of *pei*, "deep feeling," requires that the harmonious order, endangered by an excessive internal purity, be able to reach out and touch listeners or readers. Although now detached from its ground in moral and social history, the musical or literary performance is not a separate domain: it grows out of the human affections and must "return" to them. The values go beyond the internal relations of the performance to locate the event of art in a community who can share such feelings. But, of course, this movement toward others has its own dangers.

175　或奔放以諧合。
176　務嘈囋而妖冶。
177　徒悅目而偶俗。
178　固聲高而曲下。
179　寤防露與桑間。
180　又雖悲而不雅。

175　But suppose you let yourself go rushing into choral unisons,
176　Devote yourself to the bewitching beauty of an orgy of sound:
177　Pointlessly you please the eye, match the common taste,
178　The sound may be loud indeed, but the tune inferior.
179　Be aware of *Fang-lu* and *Sang-chien*—
180　Though strong emotion is present, it may lack dignity.

Line 175: "Choral unisons," *hsieh-ho*, refers to voices singing together without any dissonance, probably in unison. Musically this would be the opposite of the preceding condition, from ethereal singularity to losing oneself in the collective.

Line 176: As *TL* notes, "an orgy of sound," *ts'ao-tsa*, is a descriptive binome, glossed in the *Fang-yen*, 方言, a Han dictionary of dialect terms, as a popular and local word for many voices speaking together. Other glosses provided by later commentators stress qualities of loudness and vulgarity. The Wu-ch'en commentary extends the Dionysiac aspect of this, explaining *ts'ao-tsa* as "sensually alluring sounds," and other uses of the binome in the period support this. This sense is confirmed by its conjunction with *yao-yeh* 妖冶, "bewitching beauty," with strong implications of seduction and loss of restraint. Rock music is often *ts'ao-tsa*.

Line 179: *TL* offers an excellent summary of the scholarly debate surrounding this line. *Sang-chien* 桑間, "Among the Mulberries," was a popular song (or class of songs) referred to in the "Record of Music" of the *Book of Rites* as "the tones of a ruined state," *wang-kuo chih yin yeh* 亡國之音也. The "Geographical Treatise," *Ti-li chih* 地理志, of the *Han History* associates the song with illicit sexual encounters. Thus it is obvious that this song is the kind of thing Lu Chi had in mind as an art that engages "strong emotion" but "lacks dignity." There is uncertainty, however, as to what *Fang-lu* 防露, "Keeping

Off the Dew," is. It is possible that *Fang-lu* is given as the example of a dignified (*ya**) composition, leading to the interpretation of the line: "be aware of the difference between *Fang-lu* and *Sang-chien.*" Li Shan, however, links *Fang-lu* to the "Seven Remonstrances" 七諫 attributed to the Western Han writer Tung-fang So, thus referring it to the exile of Ch'ü Yüan, the "tones of a ruined state," and the mode *pei* 悲, appropriate for such tones. Thus the other possibility is that *Fang-lu* is yet another example of a song that has "strong emotion" (*pei*) but lacks dignity. I have accepted the latter interpretation as the most plausible.

Strong emotion, *Pei,* turns away from ethereal singularity and reaches out to embrace others, first as a positive value in itself, but then moving toward a danger of something like a Dionysiac loss of restraint and dissolution of identity, associated with the dissolution both of the polity and of sexual mores. "Dignity," *ya**, imposes a degree of restraint on this impulse, moving back towards barriers of identity and especially of hierarchical distinction. Strong emotion compensates for the failures implicit in an excess of harmony, while dignity compensates for the dangers implicit in an excess of strong emotion. Even though harmony and dignity are both in a negative relation to strong emotion, they are not, however, equivalents: they are negations of different phases of *pei.* Harmony stresses orderly place within relation, while dignity stresses restraint, hierarchy, and distinction. The subsequent movement of compensation will, of course, be a movement to reestablish desire, an impulse across the barriers of restraint implicit in dignity.

181	或清虛以婉約。
182	每除煩而去濫。
183	闕大羹之遺味。
184	同朱絃之清氾。
185	雖一唱而三嘆。
186	固既雅而不豔。

181	Suppose you have a chaste indifference and graceful restraint,
182	Always cutting away complexity, getting rid of excess:
183	It will lack that "flavor omitted" of the ceremonial broth;
184	It will be the same as the chaste reverberations of a temple zither.
185	Even though "one sings and three join in harmony,"
186	Dignity you may have, but no allure.

Chaste indifference: *ch'ing-hsü**, is literally "pure and empty," suggesting a lack of engagement. There are close similarities between this danger and the failure described in lines 169–174.

Graceful restraint, *wan-yüeh,* suggests a maidenly modesty and humility, compliance as a positive quality, whereas the "complexity" and "excess" of the following line suggest seductive sensuousness. Thus this mode—extreme *ya**, roughly equivalent to "fastidiousness"—is at pains to avoid any hint of such seductive qualities.

Lines 183–185: These lines refer to the passage on the aesthetics of omission in the "Record of Music," where the ceremonial music and banquet constitute the ultimate in *ya** (see p. 53). At first the potential excess of *ya** seems to fail the standard for the perfection of *ya** described in the "Record of Music": unlike the ceremonial broth, the excessive *ya** will be so restrained it will not even leave the sense of "flavor omitted." But Lu Chi quickly shifts to ceremonial music as the very embodiment of a dreary fastidiousness. The "temple zither" is literally the "red strings" mentioned in the "Record of Music." Such music, even though it does result in "three sighing" in response to its restraint, is inadequate.

Line 186: "Allure," *yen,* is the quality that compensates for a dignity that has degenerated into fastidiousness. An excess of restraint leads to a sense of distance, and that distance has its compensation in a movement not *into* dissolution, but *toward* dissolution: sensuous and sensual attraction. Thus the full sequence of the five values that are linked to the five faults are: 1) "response," *ying,* a ground of the possibility of intratextual relations; 2) "harmony," *ho,* where each element of response is not only itself but also contributory to a relational whole; 3) "strong feeling," *pei,* a movement out from the text to touch a common ground in human emotion; 4) "dignity," *ya**, a restraint that enforces hierarchy and distinction in relations; 5) "allure," *yen,* a sensual attractiveness that draws us toward the text. This structure of values is a complex elaboration of the antithesis between music and rites announced in the "Record of Music": music unifies while rites make distinctions. All the conditions of the five values are forms of coming together and holding apart; this is the central issue in literature and music, as it is in relations between humans, a complex balancing back and forth between isolation and absorption.

187	若夫豐約之裁。
188	俯仰之形。
189	因宜適變。
190	曲有微情。
191	或言拙而喻巧。
192	或理朴而詞輕。
193	或襲故而彌新。
194	或沿濁而更清。

195	或覽之而必察。
196	或研之而後精。
197	譬猶舞者赴節以投袂。
198	歌者應絃而遣聲。
199	是蓋輪扁所不得言。
200	故亦非華說之所能精。

187	In the way it is cut, either terse or elaborate,
188	In form, descending or ascending:
189	One moves into mutations according to what is appropriate,
190	And the fine turns have the most subtle moods.
191	Sometimes the language is artless, but the lesson artful;
192	Sometimes the principle is plain, and the diction light;
193	Sometimes following what is old yields something very new;
194	Sometimes moving with murkiness gives renewed clarity;
195	Sometimes a glancing overview brings requisite insight;
196	Sometimes the essence follows only after laborious honing.
197	Liken it to the dancer, flinging her sleeves to the rhythm,
198	Or to the singer, sending out her voice in response to the strings.
199	It is this that Wheelwright Pien could not put into words,
200	Nor is even the most glittering discourse able to catch its essence.

Line 187: "Cut to pattern," *ts'ai*, is a term for the craftsmanship involved in the "making" of a literary work, based on the metaphor of cutting cloth in making clothing. Paired with *jung* 鎔, the "casting" of metal in a mold, *ts'ai* is given an entire chapter, "Casting and Paring," in the *Wen-hsin tiao-lung*. Since the notion of working to a static pattern is in conflict with the rest of this passage (which treats the text as a process of changes, in which one must respond to the moment), we should stress the interest in the continuum between amplitude and terseness, which is central to the concept of *ts'ai*: rather than simply "cutting to pattern," the writer, as he moves through the text, must know where to linger, amplify, and fill in detail and where to restrain such impulses, where to "cut back" (*ts'ai*) and be terse. We may note the association of amplitude or verbal "lushness" with sensuality and the association of "terseness" with a sense of personal restraint.

Line 188: *TL* glosses *hsing**, "shape" or "form," as the author's active "forming," *hsing**-*ch'eng* 形成. The problem here lies in the meaning of "descending or ascending," *fu-yang*, literally "looking down and looking up." *TL* glosses this plausibly as the "momentum of *ch'i**," *ch'i**-*shih**, decrescendos and crescendos of energy. But since *fu-yang* is also used for the internal relations of sequence in a text, the compound might refer to a forward movement, "looking ahead" within the work, and a retrograde or retrospective movement, "looking back" to what had been said previously.

Line 189: See the commentary to lines 103–112 for a fuller discussion of the compositional process as a movement guided in accordance with principles of change and transformation. Line 189 seems to refer to the ranges of alternatives established in the preceding couplet; that is, one should vary between terseness and elaboration, or between crescendos and decrescendos, according to a sense of what it proper.

Line 190: "Fine turns," *ch'ü*, refers to the subtle shifts in direction that occur in the process of mutation, *pien**. Such "fine turns" may be contrasted with sharper changes of reversal or movement in a new direction. A subtle shift in mood (*ch'ing**) in the writer may be the motive for engaging in a mutation, but it seems more likely that this is rather the effect of such subtle changes. These "turns" occur in all aspects of the work: mood, argument, tempo, force, and so on. In these turns appear "subtle moods," either in the affections (*ch'ing**) conveyed or in the circumstances (*ch'ing**) presented. Presumably the gross categories of *ch'ing**—joy, anger, sorrow, and so on—can be conveyed statically: but for the finer, more "subtle" (*wei* 微) distinctions, conveying the authentic movements of mind/heart (*hsin**), continual change and turning is necessary.

Line 191: "Artless," *cho*, and "artful," *ch'iao*, are a common antithesis. Both can have either a positive or a pejorative sense. Both terms are probably positive in this context, although "artless," *cho*, may assume that someone would look down on such a style. *Cho* is "clumsy" and "guileless." One is tempted to render it as "naive"; but *cho* misses the precise theoretical sense of "naive" as used by Schiller in that writers of Lu Chi's age were quite self-conscious about being *cho* and would not hesitate to claim to possess such a quality. *Yü*, here translated "the lesson," is the term often translated as "allegory": this term is as close as Chinese comes to the notion of an "intended message," prior to and independent of the text and transmitted through it. The transformations described in the preceding lines clearly referred to the internal movements of the text; as so often in early Chinese writing on literature, Lu Chi here conflates intratextual movement with the movement of understanding or affect, in this case a "layering" of the text with intended message beneath. As with a good parable, what seems very simple on the surface reveals itself to be complex in the process of understanding.

Line 192: "Plain," *p'u* (originally "unfinished wood" with the bark still on it) is an important term in the *Lao-tzu*. *P'u* applies to "natural principle," *li**, just as "artless," *cho*, applies to human character and behavior. "Light," *ch'ing* 輕 however, does not form a clear antithesis to *p'u*, except in the fact that *p'u* is substantial or serious while *ch'ing* implies unconcern. "Light," *ch'ing*, can be linked to "artful," *ch'iao*, even though *ch'ing* stresses lack of seriousness and disengagement. Although the shifting of terms in this line to some degree twists the force of the opposition, the line is still meant to be the chiasmatic antithesis of the preceding line: language artless: lesson artful / principle plain: diction light.

Lines 193–194: These two lines continue the interchange between antitheses, though we do not know if these antithetical movements occur in the internal movement of the text or in the processes of composition or understanding. *Hsi* translated as "following," is a term to describe adhering closely or imitating—actions that in this case yield their opposites, variation and innovation. "Murky," *cho*, and "clear," *ch'ing*, constitute an antithesis commonly applied to the quality of *ch'i**, but it may also apply to moral and conceptual qualities (see Ts'ao P'i, "Discourse on Literature," pp. 65–66 above). "Murky," *cho*, tends to be a pejorative term.

Lines 195–196: It is unclear whether these lines apply to the process of reflection during composition or during reading. This antithesis of ease and difficulty occurs throughout the work. The first of these lines would seem to mean "sometimes a glancing overview brings the necessity of [further] examination" (Chang Feng-yi 張鳳翼, cited in Chang Shao-k'ang, offers an interpretation in this vein); but since such an interpretation would spoil the implicit antithesis between the two lines (in the *huo . . . huo . . .* construction), the Wu-ch'en commentary, Ch'eng Hui-ch'ang, and *TL* have taken the interpretation given in the translation.

Lines 197–198: These two beautiful similes stress the ongoing, almost improvisatory process of the text. The relation here is less organic than the images of shadow and echo in lines 145 and 146; but in the transformation of the organic metaphor, it admits the existence of a performative skill. Moreover, shadow and echo referred to the inner relations of the text as a whole, while these similes refer to compositional process and the apprehension of that process in reading. The ability to compose would depend on understanding the principles of transformation, as described in line 107, and thus to know instinctively where and how to move at any given moment. But if the writer is in the position of dancer and singer, what occupies the position of the music or musician that gives the rhythm or plays the strings? One answer can be found in the "stirring, response" (*kan-ying*) pattern of line 221, which presumes some experience, some movement of the affections, or the internal momentum of the text that may serve as a stimulus.

Lines 199–200: Wheelwright Pien was the figure in the *Chuang-tzu* who offered Duke Huan of Ch'i a critique of the limits of language, using the example of his own craft to show a performative skill that could not be put into words and transmitted (see pp. 35–36 above). Wheelwright Pien's intuitive movement of the hands echoes the movement of the dancer's sleeves and the oblique reference to Wheelwright Pien and the limitations of language in the Preface, Section D.

Glittering discourse, *hua-shuo*: This description aptly applies to Lu Chi's own poetic exposition. The use of "even," *yi* and "catch its essence," *ching*, may be somewhat playful or ironic. It seems to make a mock appeal to the consideration that although someone as "artless," *cho*, as Wheelwright Pien might not be able to put it into words, a more flashy, elaborate discourse *might* hope to do so; but even such an elaborate discourse fails the task. The irony would lie in the reader's recognition of the counter-value, that precisely because of his "artlessness" Wheelwright Pien could explain the situation far better than "glittering discourse," *hua-shuo*. The use of *ching*, "catch its essence," strengthens the probability of irony, since *ching* as a quality lies at the opposite end of the stylistic spectrum from *hua*, "glittering" or "ornate." This reflexive comment on the inability to explain the true "essence," *ching*, of the art of words in words refers us back to the Preface, Section D. Note that Achilles Fang emends the last character of this couplet to *ming* 明, "make clear," to avoid repetition with line 196.

Throughout "The Poetic Exposition on Literature" Lu Chi shows a consistent fascination with the subtleties of change and motion, the *miao**. More than anything else, the writer's art is seen as a mastery of movement, and such mastery can be embodied but not objectified in words. Skill is shown in "timely" action, an ability to proceed well through the unforeseeable, a concern that has largely disappeared from the repertoire of modern thought, with its obsession with predictability and control of events.

201	普辭條與文律。
202	良余膺之所服。
203	練世情之常尤。
204	識前修之所淑。
205	雖濬發於巧心。
206	或受嗤於拙目。
207	彼瓊敷與玉藻。
208	若中原之有菽。
209	同橐籥之罔窮。
210	與天地乎並育。
211	雖紛藹於此世。
212	嗟不盈於予掬。
213	患挈瓶之屢空。
214	病昌言之難屬。
215	故踸踔於短韻。

216	放庸音以足曲。
217	恒遺恨以終篇。
218	豈懷盈而自足。
219	懼蒙塵於叩缶。
220	顧取笑乎鳴玉。

201	The overall statutes of phrasing and writing's regulations
202	Are things to which my heart has submitted.
203	I have a fine sense of the constant transgressions in the disposition of this age,
204	And recognize what is pure in former worthies.
205	Although something may emerge from the depth of the artful mind,
206	It may still be ridiculed in the eyes of the artless.
207	Such agate flourishes and filigree of jade
208	Are like the wild beans on the central plain,
209	Never exhausted, like the Great Bellows,
210	All nurtured together with Heaven and Earth.
211	Yet however abundant they are in this age,
212	I sigh that they do not fill *my* open hand.
213	My misfortunes is to have a pint-sized capacity, often empty,
214	And I suffer at the difficulty of continuing the apt words of the past.
215	So I limp along in rhymes too short,
216	Give forth ordinary tones to complete my songs,
217	And always some regret remains at the end of a piece—
218	Never is my heart full, never am I satisfied.
219	I am frightened that this vessel will be tapped as it lies in the dust,
220	And will surely be laughed at by the ringing jade.

Line 201: "Statutes," *t'iao*, is the legal term discussed in the commentary to lines 113 and 129. Here in parallel with "regulation," *lü*, its legal sense is dominant over its other meaning, "branches." This line is a *hu-wen* 互文, a Chinese rhetorical category in which corresponding terms of a parallel construction are interchangeable with no variation in meaning: instead of *tz'u*-*t'iao* and *wen*-*lü*, we could just as easily have *wen*-*t'iao* and *tz'u*-*lü*. The Wu-ch'en commentary takes *t'iao* as "branchings," encompassing generic and historical lineages of writing. Chang Feng-yi 張鳳翼, cited in Chang Shao-k'ang, suggests that this refers to the organic structure of the work, and Hsü Wen-yü 許文雨, also cited in Chang Shao-k'ang, relates this to the old metaphor of literature as a grove. As fond as Lu Chi is of the organic tree metaphor, he also conceives of writing in terms of rules and transgressions; and this is the concern dominant in the first part of the passage. As Ch'eng Hui-ch'ang points out, the Wu-ch'en commentary's interpretation of *wen-lü*

as tonal regulations is anachronistic. Lu Chi certainly assumes there are strict rules in writing (no doubt encompassing his own sense of euphony), but this sense of "law" is a general and uncodified one and does not anticipate the appearance of explicit codes of poetics in the following centuries.

Line 202: The use of *fu*, translated as "submit," is open to other interpretations. "Take to heart" is the most likely alternative.

Line 203: "Have a fine sense," *lien*, is to have a "trained" or "practiced" sense; that is, he knows by studious experience. "Constant transgressions," *ch'ang-yu*, might also be taken as a nominalized considerative verb: "I have a fine sense of what this age constantly considers a [literary] transgression." The phrase might also be taken as "constants and transgressions." In both of these latter interpretations, Lu Chi would be claiming to understand both the excellences of the ancients as well as the refinements of modern times. As translated above, it contrasts the success of the ancients with the failings of the moderns. "The disposition of the age," *shih-ch'ing**, perhaps would support the considerative interpretation of *yu*, "[consider as] a transgression," in that *ch'ing** would more appropriately apply to the response to error than to the locus of errors of the kind to which Lu Chi is referring. But the following couplet, on the fear of being misvalued, supports the interpretation given in the translation.

Lines 205–206: In contrast to line 119, here the "artless," *cho*, is pejorative, and the "artful," *ch'iao*, is clearly positive. This may be an example of how the "disposition of the age" fails to appreciate what is truly valuable. Note that what is valuable is located within, while misprision occurs in the ability of those outside to perceive what lies within. Further, we should note that the presumed source of the literary work is here the "artful mind," *ch'iao-hsin**, not *chih**, "what is intently on the mind," a relation to something outside the realm of art. Fang T'ing-kuei 方廷珪, cited in Chang Shao-k'ang, takes "what emerges from the artful mind" as referring specifically to works by "former worthies": although this follows reasonably in the rhetorical structure here and is certainly included by the line, it seems too restrictive for the general statement made here.

Lines 207–208: *Fu*, translated as "flourishes," means primarily "unroll" or "extend"; it takes on the sense of some intricate vegetative profuseness, much like *tsao* 藻, a vegetative intricacy commonly extended to literature. The metaphor of gems is often applied to fine writing, although the seme "rareness" in the gem metaphor is set in contrast to the seme "commonness" in the beans, extended from the vegetative metaphor of *fu* and *tsao*. The proverbial commonness of the beans on the central plains has a literary source in *Book of Songs*, where it is appropriately combined with an exhortation to learning in order to become as good as one's predecessors:

On the central plains are bean vines,
The common people pick them.
The moth bears children,
But the wasp carries them away.
Teach your children
So that in excellence they may equal you.

Book of Songs 196

The commonness of the wild beans suggests, in Lu Chi's usage, the easy availability of the material of literary excellence. We may note that Lu Chi uses a commonsense reading of this passage, unencumbered by the established exegeses of the Classic.

Lines 209–210: The "Great Bellows," *t'o-yüeh*, is the image used in *Lao-tzu* V to describe the inexhaustible generative processes of nature and the constant movement of *ch'i** (the "air" in the bellows).[65] Taken together, this couplet and the preceding one are a new version of the organic metaphor: instead of the inner nature of the work being a vegetative organism, here the "stuff" of literature is generated inexhaustibly everywhere, ready to be "culled" (note the recurrence of selection as the essential act in composition).

Lines 211–212: "Abundant," *fen-ai*, is a descriptive of vegetative density, here applied to the "beans" of literary excellence. As Ch'ien Chung-shu points out, this is the point where Lu Chi's poetic exposition turns from confidence to explicit self-doubt, from control to helplessness, from fullness to dearth.

Lines 213–214: "Pint-sized capacity," *ch'ieh-p'ing*, is literally a "small water pitcher," a phrase used in the *Tso chuan*, Chao 7, as a metaphor for small capacity. Not only does Lu Chi suffer dearth personally amid all this abundance, he also has little ability. "Apt words," *ch'ang-yen* (also, and perhaps more properly explained as "glorious words") was a phrase from the *Book of Documents* in common use; here it refers to the greatness of past writing (hence the interpolation of the word "past" into the translation). After commenting on his inadequacy in regard to present possibility, Lu Chi turns to his inadequacy in comparison to past accomplishments. This sense of present decline in face of past literary greatness, which was to become a powerful motif in Chinese literary thought (as it was in Western literary thought) may be contrasted to Ts'ao P'i's confidence that the excellence of writers of his own age was in no way inferior to the great Eastern Han predecessors.

Line 215: "Limp along," *chen-chuo*, is a stumbling, shambling gait. I have taken the reading *tuan-yün*; but *TL*, Ch'eng Hui-ch'ang, Ch'ien Chung-shu, and Chang Shao-k'ang all prefer the reading *tuan-yüan* 短垣, "a low earthen wall," which, if one walked along it, would cause a stumbling gait. The main objection to the reading *tuan-yün*, "rhymes too short," is that it repeats line 158. This is not persuasive because Lu Chi often brings back earlier topics. There it is a general problem; here it is his problem. Sun Chih-tsu 孫志祖, cited in Chang Shao-k'ang, argues persuasively against the emendation. The question of insufficient amplitude is sustained in the following lines and fits in with the larger question of adequacy, raised in many frames of reference throughout the work. Hence the Wu-ch'en commentary's paraphrase: "he feels bogged down in short pieces," thus longing for scope.

Lines 219–220: As in line 213, crockery is used here as a metaphor for capacity; its smallness is revealed by tapping it. To be "covered in dust" is to be in a low situation and unused. In contrast, "ringing jade" is a metaphor commonly applied to excellent writing.

Pride and self-doubt are a bound pair: where one appears, the other will not be hidden far away. As Lu Chi breaks into criticism of his contemporaries, who will not be able to understand his excellence, he wobbles on the heights of exultation and immediately sinks into self-criticism and self-doubt. Ch'ien Chung-shu points out the places here and in the following passages where he gives an inversion of the values he espoused earlier. Although this passage has contradictory impulses, it embodies those satisfying psychological motions prized in classical writing: "I understand the true values, those of the ancients, as most moderns do not; they mock what is truly good, even though literary excellence is to be found easily in this age; yet I don't find it; thus my [real] failings will be mocked by the excellence of my contemporaries." The inversion of the argument here is a small-scale variation on the balance of impulse and counter-impulse that runs throughout the piece.

The argument of the next large section is a four-part examination of "inspiration," its general principles (ll. 221–226), its fullness (ll. 227–234), the effects of its absence (ll. 235–242), and a summation of the experience of its power and vagaries (ll. 243–248).

221	若夫應感之會。
222	通塞之紀。
223	來不可遏。
224	去不可止。
225	藏若景滅。
226	行猶響起。

221	At the conjunction of stirring and response,
222	At the demarcation between blockage and passage,
223	What comes cannot be halted,
224	What goes off cannot be stopped.

225   When it hides, it is like a shadow disappearing,
226   When it moves, it is like an echo rising.

Lines 221–222: This locates the crucial moment of composition in its beginning, standing between the reflection before writing described in the first part of the work and the subsequent points of attention enjoined in the compositional process. This is essentially the same point described in lines 45 to 50, but now this nexus has become a point of crisis. At the "conjunction" or "meeting," *hui*, between "being stirred," *kan**, and "active response," *ying**, there is an uncontrollable space where the sequence of occurrences in composition may be "blocked," *se*, or "pass through," *t'ung**. Since this moment of initiation is beyond control (perhaps the moment when the analogy to the movements of Wheelwright Pien's hands is most operative), Lu Chi can offer no advice here: he can only tell us "how it is."[66]

Lines 223–224: This couplet rephrases a passage in *Chuang-tzu* XXI where Shu-sun Ao explains why he took no joy in the glory of high office and felt no sorrow in losing it. Lu Chi's worry about the uncontrollability of inspiration is, of course, at odds with the aloof indifference prized in the source text; but such unconsciously ironic inversions of application were not uncommon in literary quotation from the *Chuang-tzu* from the Eastern Han through the T'ang. Another famous example of such misapplication is the quotation from *Chuang-tzu* in the very opening of the "Spirit Thought" chapter of the *Wen-hsin tiao-lung* (see pp. 201–202 below).

Lines 225–226: *TL* glosses *ying* as "light," but in conjunction with *hsiang*, "echo" or "resonance," "shadow" seems to be the better interpretation (cf. ll. 145–146).

Out of the epistemological concerns of Confucian hermeneutics, Chinese literary thought tended to focus on the determinate and involuntary aspects of composition. In "The Poetic Exposition on Literature," Lu Chi strongly shifts toward composition as a voluntary act and its structure as controlled. Here, however, toward the end of the work, involuntarism recurs, not in the content of what is made manifest, but in whether the desired compositional process will "flow" or not. The person who spoke "one-sidedly" to Mencius with his "knowledge of words" might well be uneasy about what he would involuntarily reveal of himself; but in that case what would have been revealed would have been a defect of character. Troping on this, Lu Chi, who defines himself as a writer, is in danger of having his limits as a writer exposed at this conjunction, where involuntary forces govern utterance.

---

227   方天機之駿利。
228   夫何紛而不理。

229 思風發於胸臆。
230 言泉流於唇齒。
231 紛葳蕤以馺遝。
232 唯毫素之所擬。
233 文徽徽以溢目。
234 音泠泠以盈耳。

227 When Heaven's motive impulses move swiftly on the best course,
228 What confusion is there that cannot be put in order?
229 Winds of thought rise in the breast,
230 A stream of words flows through lips and teeth,
231 Burgeoning in tumultuous succession,
232 Something only the writing brush and silk can imitate.
233 Writing gleams, overflows the eyes:
234 The tones splash on, filling the ears.

Line 227: Heaven's motive impulses, *T'ien-chi**, refer to the initiation and the initiatory impulses of a process in nature, something that is subtle and elusive at the beginning but that follows through powerfully. When literary "response," *ying**, comes, it comes in this manner, as a spontaneously unfolding natural process that gathers momentum. Hsü Fu-kuan properly stresses the unconscious and incomprehensible aspect of this natural force.

Move swiftly on the best course is a free rendering of *chün-li. Li* here is what is most "advantageous," the course of action or of movement that offers the least resistance. The modifying *chün* suggest superiority, size, and speed.

Line 228: *Fen*, translated as "confusion," usually describes a tangled, disorderly profusion. Here it is given as a negative quality requiring ordering: but a few lines later, in line 231, it is used in a positive sense as the "burgeoning" of inspiration.

Put in order is the transitive verbal use of *li**, "natural principle."

Lines 229–230: In the parallel between "winds of thought," *ssu*-feng** and "stream of words," *yen-ch'üan*, the sequence from "thought" to "words" marks the process of outward manifestation. The images of wind and the stream, which figure prominently throughout the poetic exposition, are central metaphors in describing the ongoing, flowing quality that is valued both in composition and presumed to inhere in the text itself.

Line 232: *Ni* is "to imitate" (see l. 137, commentary), but the two terms essential to the concept of imitation are the movement of thought and words on the one hand, and the act of writing on the other. This is a supremely Shelleyan notion of the creative process, inspiration flowing furiously and the writing hand trying to catch it before it disappears. But we should note that it is not some pre-verbal "poetic idea" that gets "imitated," but rather oral words moving in synchronization with thought that must be "imitated" in written words.

In line 222 the antithetical terms "passage" and "blockage" were raised. The section above amplifies "passage," *t'ung** and successful "response," *ying*. As a natural process, composition is described in terms of a natural burgeoning to the point of being flooded by bounty. From this vision of fullness we next turn to the complementary term "blockage," *se*, a vision of dearth.

235	及其六情底滯。
236	志往神留。
237	兀若枯木。
238	豁若涸流。
239	攬營魂以探賾。
240	頓精爽而自求。
241	理翳翳而愈伏。
242	思乙乙其若抽。

235	But when the six affections are stalled and hampered,
236	When mind strains toward something, but spirit remains unmoved,
237	One is immobile as a bare, leafless tree,
238	Gaping empty like a dried-up stream.
239	One draws the soul to search secret recesses,
240	Gathers vital forces to seek from oneself;
241	But natural principle is hidden and sinks away ever farther,
242	Thought struggles to emerge, as if dragged.

Line 235: The particular affections that constitute "the six affections," *liu-ch'ing** 六情 differ in various lists, but they are usually given in pairs, such as being pleased and anger, sorrow and joy, love and hate. Categorical concepts that can be comprehended by a single antithesis are usually expressed by a single two-character compound. Categories like "the affections," which obviously admit more than a single antithesis, are often given a stock enumerator; thus "the hundred plants" are simply "plants"; "the six affections" are simply "the affections."

Line 236: This is literally "*chih** goes and spirit stays." According to the traditional etymological definition, *chih** is "that to which mind goes": here there is an object and a directional energy, but "spirit," *shen**, does not convey it. This situation is, of course, wanting to write about something but not being able to.

Lines 237–238: The common metaphors of vegetation and flowing water recur here, but as absences. While Lu Chi does not hesitate to make use of *Chuang-tzu* when it suits him, here the image of the barren tree, a positive image in *Chuang-tzu*, is seen as a profound loss of natural vitality. *Wu*, "immobile" combines the unmoving, the unfeeling, and the inanimate.

Lines 239–240: Here is a failed return to the voluntarism which opened "The Poetic Exposition on Literature," an acknowledgement that knowing and doing all the correct preliminaries is not adequate. Where before the process operated naturally, now there is conscious effort, "seeking in the self."

Soul, *ying-hun*, is a vague and general term for some undefined aspect of the psyche. Some texts read *ch'iung-hun*, "solitary soul"; but this forms a less perfect parallel to the corresponding term in line 240, *ching-shuang*, translated as "vital forces." However distinct such terms and compounds may have been in the pre-Ch'in period, and however much philosophers and glossarists of Lu Chi's own time may have tried to limit their meaning, in poetic expositions and in parallelistic prose such terminological fine points are rarely preserved.

To search secret recesses: *T'an-tse*, is a term for investigating anything mysterious and hidden.

To seek from oneself: *Tzu-ch'iu* may well mean "to seek all alone"; but it may also be, as translated here, the attempt to find inspiration in the depths of self, echoing the implications of *t'an-tse*.[67]

Lines 241–242: "Natural principle," *li**, is clearly the hidden thing sought. *Ya-ya* 乙乙 describes the quality of something coming forth with difficulty. *Ch'ou* 抽 may be either "pulling out" or "pushing out," as in "sprouting." It is probably the "thoughts," *ssu**, themselves that are having such difficulty emerging or being drawn out; but it may be that "thoughts" are having difficulty, struggling to bring out hidden natural principle.

243	是以或竭情而多悔。
244	或率意而寡尤。
245	雖茲物之在我。
246	非余力之所勠。
247	故時撫空懷而自惋。
248	吾未識夫開塞之所由。

243	Thus at times I wear out my feelings, and much is regretted;
244	At other times I follow the bent of my thoughts with few transgressions.
245	Although this thing is in the self,
246	It is not within the scope of my concentrated forces.
247	At times I consider the emptiness in my heart and turn against myself,
248	That I do not know the means to open this blockage.

Line 243: The writer "wears out his feelings," *chieh-ch'ing**, in his efforts at trying to write. The regret follows either from not getting anything or from writing something bad despite one's efforts.

Line 244: "Follow the bent of my thoughts," *shuai-yi**, is a set phrase meaning "to follow one's whim"; but in this context, the technical sense of *yi** is brought to the fore—hence, to go effortlessly with one's literary concepts as they arise.

Lines 245–246: The "thing," *wu**, is presumably the literary work, which already exists hidden in the "self," *wo*, the "I"; or, as Fang T'ing-kuei, cited in Chang Shao-k'ang, suggests, it is *wen**-*chi**, the "springs of the literary work." This description of discovering the literary work hidden within the self is reminiscent of some pre-Romantic descriptions of composition, as in Edward Young's "Conjectures on Original Composition"; but in the pre-Romantic inner quest, what is discovered is the hidden self; in Lu Chi what is discovered is a more universal natural principle of which the self is the container. Moreover, the emergence of natural principle, or its "presenting itself" for voluntary discovery by the determined writer, is initiated by forces within natural principle itself, forces within the self that are not subject to conscious control.[68]

Concentrated forces, *lu-li* 勁力 (here syntactically divided as *fei yü li chih so lu*) is a strenuous effort, collective or individual.

Line 247: "Consider the emptiness in my heart," *fu k'ung-huai*, can be taken physically, "I stroke my empty breast"; but *fu-huai* was commonly extended to mean "reflect on what is in one's heart." In this case, "what is in one's heart" is qualified as "empty."[69]

The closing section is a peroration. Most complete poetic expositions (*fu*) have a formal coda, separated from the main body of the text by a phrase that can usually be translated "the Coda says . . . " Although Lu Chi's concluding section is not so marked, it clearly serves the same function. Like formal codas, the peroration here is elevated in diction and almost lyrical.

249	伊茲文之為用。
250	固眾理之所因。
251	恢萬里而無閡。
252	通億載而為津。
253	俯貽則於來葉。
254	仰觀象乎古人。
255	濟文武於將墜。
256	宣風聲於不泯。
257	塗無遠而不彌。
258	理無微而弗綸。
259	配霑潤於雲雨。
260	象變化乎鬼神。
261	被金石而德廣。
262	流管絃而日新。

249	The functioning of literature lies in being
250	The means for all natural principle.
251	It spreads across ten thousand leagues, nothing bars it;
252	It passes through a million years, a ford across.
253	Looking ahead, it grants models to coming generations;
254	Looking back, it contemplates images in the ancients.
255	It succours the Way of the ancient kings, on the point of falling;
256	It manifests reputation, does not let it be lost.
257	No path lies so far it cannot be integrated;
258	No principle so subtle it cannot be woven in.
259	Peer of clouds and rain with their fertile moisture,
260	Semblance of divinity in transformation.
261	When it covers metal and stone, virtue is spread;
262	Flowing through strings and flutes, it is daily renewed.

Lines 249–250: Later thinkers would divide phenomena into the categories of *t'i**, "normative form," and *yung* 用, "function." The functional definition of the poetic exposition was "to give the normative form of things," *t'i*-wu** (l. 86), which is precisely what Lu Chi has done for *wen** in his own idiosyncratic way. It is therefore fitting that here in the conclusion he turns to "function," *yung*. Literature is the "means," *so-yin* (literally "the that-depending-on-which") of *li**, "natural principle." All commentators agree that manifestation is the end for which *li** depends on *wen** as the means; that is, *li** "is," but for it to be manifest and knowable, it must appear through *wen**. We are not certain whether *wen** in this case is restricted to literature (thus knowable to mind) or is the broader sense of *wen** as "pat-

tern," immanent in all things (as Liu Hsieh claims in the first chapter of *Wen-hsin tiao-lung*). Lu Chi qualifies *li** as *chung-li**, "aggregated natural principles," "all natural principle." *Li** is both universal and particular in particular things and events. All depend on *wen** to be manifest; and as Lu Chi says a few lines later, none are beyond the competence of *wen** (this despite the disclaimer in the Preface, Section D).

Line 252: A ford across, *wei chin*: Ever since Confucius sent Tzu-lu to "ask of the ford" (*Analects* XVIII.6), the language of fording and crossing over was used for the transmission of the Way in the world, especially its transmission though time. Lu Chi's transfer of this principle to a kind of personal immortality is well stated by Hsü Fu-kuan's paraphrase: "The human spirit can pass through (*t'ung**) a million years, and literature (*wen**) is its ford." This kind of extension, both in space and time, is what is meant by the attribute *yüan*, "far," in this context translated as "far-reaching."

Lines 253–254: As elsewhere, *fu-yang*, literally "looking down and looking up," is looking ahead and backward in time (as earlier it was looking back to earlier passages and anticipating passages to come).

Model, *tse*, is a norm or regulation, especially with moral associations. In this closing section Lu Chi increasingly turns to the terms and values of the tradition of Confucian ethics.

Contemplates the images, *kuan-hsiang** is what the Sages who compiled the *Book of Changes* were said to have done: clearly what Lu Chi means here is that one can contemplate the "images," either those of the *Book of Changes* or in general, in the writings of the ancients.

Line 255: The "ancient kings" are literally "Wen and Wu," the founders of the Chou. This passage echoes *Analects* XIX.22 where Kung-sun Ch'ao asks the disciple Tzu-kung where Confucius studied, and Tzu-kung replies, "The Way of Kings Wen and Wu has not yet fallen to the earth; it is among men." Of course, in Lu Chi's late age that ancient Way was even more gravely imperiled and would have to depend on the written word for transmission. Thus Lu Chi changes the "not yet fallen," *wei-chui* 未墜, of the *Analects* to the more precarious *chiang-chui*, "about to fall," "on the point of falling."

Line 256: "Reputation" here is *feng**-*sheng*, "wind and sound," influence and repute. Li Shan cites the *Pi-ming* 畢命 chapter of the *Book of Documents* in which the Chou King K'ang instructs his eastern viceroy, the Duke of Pi, to "make manifest the good and make the evil suffer, establishing the influence and reputation [of such]." Such archaic echoes lend authority to this peroration.

Lines 257–258: "Integrated" and "woven in" together form the compound *mi-lun* 彌綸, a common politico-philosophical term based on the weaving metaphor; *mi-lun* is to draw everything together into one unified "network." The notion of literature as a unifying structure of culture is central here. The notion of a "far path" may suggest authorization for literature to treat topics outside the norm

Line 259: "Clouds and rain," *yün-yü*, was already a euphemism for sexual intercourse, here linked to the function of the Sage or emperor, whose benevolence functions as the fertilizing rains. Literature transmits that good, life-giving influence.

Line 260: "Transformation," *pien*-hua* is characteristic of all nature, but especially characteristic of spiritual beings. Literature shares that power of swift metamorphosis, both in itself and in its effects.

Lines 261–262: "Metal and stone," *chin-shih* refer to inscriptions by which past virtue, *tê**, is made known. Thus "metal and stone" became a standard metonymy for permanence in writing. Performance of texts to the accompaniment of "strings and flutes" is a reenactment that makes the old text always new.

Lu Chi's ringing praise of the function of literature centers on its mediating role in making manifest to others what is in danger of being hidden, in joining things that are separate or in danger of becoming separate: it joins old and new, near and far, latent and manifest, publishes the virtue of one to many, and so forth. Lu Chi clearly understands the written word, *wen**, as the means by which civilization is held together.

Wen-hsin tiao-lung

Wen-hsin tiao-lung 文心雕龍 is an anomaly in the history of Chinese literary thought, a systematic treatise on literature, as it was conceived around the turn of the sixth century.[1] At the time of its composition, the author, Liu Hsieh 劉勰 (ca. 465–522), was not himself an experienced or well-known writer; as a lay-scholar in a Buddhist temple, his views on literature had not been formed in the great aristocratic salons of the day, salons whose continuous debate on literary issues formed the background of virtually all other critical writing of the period.[2] *Wen-hsin tiao-lung* is said to have been composed when Liu Hsieh was a young man (in his thirties), as an attempt to gain the attention of the literary arbiters of the salons and thereby to secure for himself an appointment in the entourage of one of the royal princes.[3] Liu Hsieh's biography indicates that the work was fortunate in having met the approval of Shen Yüeh 沈約 (441–513), the most influential literary man of the age. Shen Yüeh was not impressed enough by it to mention it in his own writings, but his support seems a likely explanation for Liu Hsieh's obtaining a series of minor appointments in the entourages of various princes, culminating in a good position at one of the most prestigious courts, that of the Liang Crown Prince, Hsiao T'ung 蕭統 (501–531). In Hsiao T'ung's court the great anthology, *Wen hsüan*, 文選 was compiled; and it has been suggested that Liu Hsieh may have exerted some influence on its composition.[4] After having been ordered by the emperor to edit the religious scholarship left behind by his former teacher Seng-yu, Liu Hsieh returned to the monastery and finally took Buddhist vows.

In the contemporary literary world of the Ch'i and Liang, Liu Hsieh was, at best, a minor figure. Although Liu Hsieh often treated the same issues and disputes that recurred in other criticism of the period, there is no evidence that *Wen-hsin tiao-lung* itself was particularly influential or much read.[5] It is more difficult to properly evaluate the influence of *Wen-hsin tiao-lung* on later generations. We know that the book never disappeared from circulation. A partial T'ang manuscript version was recovered in the Tun-huang materials—certainly the only work of literary criticism in that heterogenous library (and perhaps included because of Liu Hsieh's prestige in the Buddhist tradition). From the T'ang through the Ming, there is a substantial and continuous corpus of references and echoes.[6] Before the Ch'ing, however, the work was only infrequently cited as an authority in important works of criticism and theory, and it clearly had nothing like the stature it is now accorded. Interest in *Wen-hsin tiao-lung* grew substantially during the Ch'ing; and in modern times (largely under the influence of the high value that the Western tradition places on a systematic poetics), the book has received an unparalleled attention.[7]

The way in which Liu Hsieh deploys his vast erudition and superb rhetorical training has more the flavor of the temple school and library than of the social world of literary composition, criticism, and dispute—the world of coteries and salons that produced all other criticism in the period. The fact that *Wen-hsin tiao-lung* gives a full and relatively orderly account of many key concepts in traditional literary theory ensures the importance of the work; but, as is often the case, its greatest virtues are also its greatest shortcomings. It has a distinctly "academic" quality. In place of the intemperate convictions and subtle judgments that came from the experience of the masters of the salons, *Wen-hsin tiao-lung* sets in motion the machine of fifth-century rhetoric and analytic technique. Liu Hsieh's genius is the skill with which he operates this expository machine.

Liu Hsieh follows conventional (if not rigid) rules of exposition: tracing the origins of a term or genre, developing each element of a compound, drawing analogies from other uses of the term, mentioning important source passages, and building highly structured sets of illustrative examples. Those techniques of exposition often govern what is said.[8] Many of his comments seem not so much "considered" as forced upon him by the inertia of exposition. The plausibility of such points derives from an implicit faith that such a rhetorical exposition and analysis accurately reflect how things indeed "are." The need to produce a parallel clause or fill a predetermined structure can often generate a brilliant observation. However, such gifts of the expository machine are neither the shared assumptions of Chinese literary theory nor the personal beliefs and considered opinions of Liu Hsieh (though they remain within the scope of both); they are "thought" in the sense of applying analytic rules to some object. In this aspect the rhetoric of Wen-hsin tiao-lung is close to the formal expository procedures in Aristotle's Poetics and other Western treatises in the philosophical tradition: it produces positions to which the theorist is forced by the "logic" of the argument—positions which, though obtained by methodological compulsion, prove to be quite interesting.[9]

To avoid the serious problems of interpretation presented by the title, I have chosen to leave it in romanization throughout.[10] In the "Afterword" (Chapter 50) Liu Hsieh gives his own remarkably unhelpful explanation of the title. The title is made up of two components. The first is wen*-hsin*, "the literary mind" or "to make the mind literary/cultivated/patterned," or "to consider mind in regard to the question of wen*," or (translating Liu Hsieh's explanation literally) "the use/effort of mind in literature." The second element, tiao-lung, literally "carve dragons," refers in some way to the craft of literature. It seems to be a positive transformation of an old pejorative term for literary craft, tiao-ch'ung 雕蟲, "to carve insects" (a "dragon," as a reptile, was classified under the general category of ch'ung, "insects," but its position in that generally lowly category raises it to the sublime).[11] Liu Hsieh clearly wants to dissociate his idea of craft from the pejorative associations that hover around all terms for craft in Chinese. The complete title may be read as a single predicate, something like "the literary mind carves dragons" (i.e., the way in which the more philosophical and psychological aspects of the tradition are realized in technical craft). Or, with a slightly different emphasis, the title may be taken as two separate coordinate clauses, as Vincent Shih translates "The Literary Mind and the Carving of Dragons" (i.e., the philosophical and psychological aspects of literature as well as, or as opposed to, the craft). The English reader need only keep in mind that there is a potential tension between these two elements and that the second element, "dragon-carving," is the more problematic, a hopefully positive term for ornamental craft, which Liu Hsieh alternately attacks and defends throughout the work.

Wen-hsin tiao-lung consists of forty-nine regular chapters, and a concluding afterword, which concerns his motives in the composition of the book and its structure. After four opening chapters on the Way, the Sage, the Classics, and the Apocrypha (the latter being a good example of the compulsion of form, the Confucian Apocrypha having no importance whatsoever in the work except as a complement for the chapter on the Classics), Liu treats the major genres. Although there are moments of great interest in these generic chapters, I have left them untranslated since they make continual reference to works and authors with which the Western reader will not be familiar and, in many cases, in which he would have no interest even if he were.

Beginning with Chapter 26, there follows a remarkable series of chapters on basic concepts of literary thought. Here we should offer a caution: some of these topics were burning issues of the day; some are the oldest concerns of Chinese literary thought; but there are also some which seem to have been included to fill out the projected number of chapters (the number fifty having special significance in the *Book of Changes*).

Rather than offering here a synthesis of Liu Hsieh's philosophical orientation or his views on topics such as "literary creation," genre, or style, I have preferred to work within Liu Hsieh's own categories and to attempt to explain them. In contrast to "The Poetic Exposition on Literature," where inclusiveness was a more powerful imperative than consistency, *Wen-hsin tiao-lung* does indeed attempt to give a complete and internally self-consistent overview of literature. Inconsistencies do remain, in no small part the products of Liu Hsieh's expository procedures. But we encounter an entirely new level of problem when we reinterpret his categories under the very different rubric of modern literary categories. To insist on modern categories (e.g., "Liu Hsieh's theory of literary creation") blurs the distinctions that were of importance to Liu himself. Since we are writing in English, using modern terms, this problem is with us, whether we like it or not. But the form of commentary, unlike the synthetic essay, compels us continually to honor the difference between Liu Hsieh's categories of literary discourse and our own.

CHAPTER 1
Its Source in the Way, Yuan-tao 原道

The project of "Its Source in the Way" is nothing less than to show how literature is generated from the basic workings of the universe.[12] Liu Hsieh accomplishes this in several ways. First, he uses the term *wen** in the broadest sense possible, freely mixing its many frames of reference in order to enforce the point that *wen**, as used in terms such as "astronomy" (*T'ien-wen** 天文, Heaven's pattern) and "topography" (*ti-wen** 地文, Earth's pattern), is the same as *wen** when used by Confucius to refer to cultivation and traditional forms of polite behavior, which in turn is the same as *wen** as "the written word" and *wen** as "literature." For Liu Hsieh the historical provenance of a word is a single semantic center; and all modern usages are extensions, elaborations, limitations, or, at worst, deviations. Thus the shifting frames of reference of *wen** serve to reveal the secret and primordial unity that lies behind the apparent diversity in its usage.

The second way Liu Hsieh links *wen** to the cosmic order is by building his argument with phrases and whole lines from the most authoritative texts of Chinese cosmology, especially from the *Hsi-tz'u chuan* 繫辭傳 ("Appended Comments"), a cosmological tract appended to the *Book of Changes* and attributed to Confucius.[13] Throughout the chapter the reader encounters familiar and authoritative passages, understood now with *wen** as the explicit or implicit topic or frame of reference.[14] Finally, Liu Hsieh distributes his references and quotations to make an argument that is rather original, at least in its opening phases: in the cosmogonic process of differentiation, each separate thing that comes into being manifests an external pattern (*wen**) proper to it; and such pattern appears on the ground of its essential characteristic. Since the essential characteristic of human beings is mind, the *wen** proper to human beings will be manifest through mind, knowing and responding to the world, and making that mediation again manifest to mind in *wen**, literary writing (there is a touch of Hegel's aesthetics behind Liu Hsieh's florid rhetoric).

When Ts'ao P'i stated grandly that "literary works are the supreme achievement in the business of state, a splendor that does not decay," his was a claim explicitly set against the fear of death and of posterity's misprision or forgetfulness. In the same way Liu Hsieh's grand claim of literature's basis in nature is made to oppose a threatening alternative: there is always the possibility that literature (*wen**) is **not** essential, but rather mere adornment, something added. Liu Hsieh himself often speaks of literature as a "carving" of some other material. Again and again Liu stresses the "naturalness" (*Tzu-jan**, the so-of-itself-ness) in the manifestation of *wen**, warning us away from doubts he anticipates: "These are in no way external adornments: they are of Nature (*Tzu-jan**)." Thus in this chapter Liu Hsieh acts as literature's genealogist, tracing a family tree to show that literature has a good lineage, going all the way back to the origins of the universe.

文之為德也大矣。與天地並生者何哉。夫玄黃色雜。方圓體分。日月疊璧。以垂麗天之象。山川煥綺。以鋪理地之形。此蓋道之文也。

As an inner power (*tê**), pattern (*wen**) is very great indeed,[15] born together with Heaven and Earth. And how is this? All colors are compounded of two primary colors, the purple that is Heaven and the brown that is Earth. All forms are distinguished through two primary forms, Earth's squareness and Heaven's circularity.[16] The sun and moon are successive disks of jade, showing to those below images (*hsiang**) that cleave to Heaven.[17] Rivers and mountains are glittering finery, unrolling forms that give order (*li**) to Earth.[18] These are the pattern of the Way.[19]

As an inner power (*tê) pattern (*wen**) is very great indeed, born together with Heaven and Earth.** To say that *wen** has *tê** is to speak of positive and compelling qualities that inhere in it, qualities whose force can be attributed to *wen**'s venerable lineage. If the danger is that literature is superfluous, a parvenu dressed in outward finery and usurping our attention, then Liu Hsieh must show that it was present from the very beginning. But unfortunately the phrase that came immediately to Liu Hsieh's mind to affirm that ancient lineage was the wrong phrase, a phrase used by one ancient, Chuang-tzu, who scoffed at both genealogy and seriousness, someone who claimed that "no one lives longer than an infant dead before its time; no one dies younger than P'eng-tsu [renowned for his long life]; Heaven and Earth were born together with me, and all the things of the world are one with me" (*Ch'i-wu lun* 齊物論 in *Chuang-tzu*). Liu Hsieh wants to demonstrate literature's value by showing that it is coeval with Heaven and Earth, but he does so in words that mock the authority of origins.

All colors are compounded of two primary colors, the purple that is Heaven and the brown that is Earth. All forms are distinguished through two primary forms, Earth's squareness and Heaven's circularity. Color and shape are the two primordial categories for differentiating appearances; both are external manifestations and both belong to the domain of *wen**. Since the cosmogonic process proceeds by division, all the more complex categories of shape and color will derive from these two primordial pairs. Before the division of Heaven and Earth occurred, there was no shape and no color; with the moment of division, shape and color are produced, and they are *wen**.

Next Liu Hsieh proceeds to the more conventional *wen** in Heaven and Earth: "astronomy," the "pattern of Heaven," and "topography," the "pattern of Earth." As pattern begins to be imprinted everywhere in this newly formed world and becomes increasingly elaborate, Liu Hsieh's own language becomes increasingly ornamented (appropriately since "ornamentation" is part of the semantic range of *wen**): the heavenly bodies are called "disks of jade" and the landscape "glittering finery." Actual jade disks (*pi*) were symbolic counterparts of Heaven and the heavenly bodies; they reproduced precisely the *hsiang**, the "images," which Heaven manifested to those below. Everywhere Liu Hsieh's choice of words binds together different frames of reference to suggest their common ground: it was quite proper to describe a landscape by a fabric metaphor such as "finery," *ch'i*; yet that same word was an important element in many compounds describing the intricacy and "fineness" of a literary work. To speak of Heaven and Earth as having *wen**, "pattern," was not a radical proposal; but to speak of "the *wen** of the Way" was radical. The Way (*Tao*) is usually understood on a high level of abstraction (*hsing-erh-shang* 形而上), a rightness of natural process; it does not in itself possess particular determinate qualities, but rather is the "way" in which particular determinate qualities occur. Thus, from Liu Hsieh's argument, it would be straightforward to say that *wen** appears **through** the way that Heaven and Earth come into being. But Liu Hsieh wants to say more: he wants *wen** to be not simply the consequence of any particular natural process, but rather the visible externality of natural process itself.

仰觀吐曜。俯察含章。高卑定位。故兩儀既生矣。惟人參之。性靈所鍾。是謂三才。為五行之秀。實天地之心。心生而言立。言立而文明。自然之道也。

Considering the radiance emitted above, and reflecting on the loveliness (chang*) that inhered below,[20] the positions of high and low were determined, and the two standards were generated.[21] Only the human being, endowed with the divine spark of consciousness (hsing*-ling),[22] ranks as a third with this pair. And they were called the Triad [Heaven, Earth, and human beings]. The human being is the flower (hsiu) of the elements: in fact, the mind (hsin*) of Heaven and Earth.[23] When mind came into being, language was established; and with the establishment of language, pattern became manifest [ming, "bright," "comprehending," "admitting comprehension"].[24] This is the natural course of things, the Way.

The position of human beings in the structure of Heaven and Earth had always been a problem for Chinese thinkers. In certain ways the human being was "of" Heaven and Earth, a part of nature and manifesting within the species those binary divisions that corresponded to the binary divisions of the cosmic order (e.g., high and low, male and female). However, residing in a space "between" Heaven and Earth, human beings also constituted a third term; and they transcended the structure of division by knowing it. Hsün-tzu, for one, argued strongly for the human difference from nature, and such difference was a function of understanding and the capacity for voluntary action.

In the peculiar natural philosophy of Wen-hsin tiao-lung the impulse within natural process to make inherent distinctions manifest already implies the necessity that mind arise; manifestation is complete only if there is a subject to recognize it and know it. Mind is that for which manifestation occurs. Mind, in its turn, implies the necessity of language as a form of manifestation unique and proper to mind itself. Language is the fulfillment of the process, the knowing that makes known, and that fulfillent will be human wen*.

傍及萬品。動植皆文。龍鳳以藻繪呈瑞。虎豹以炳蔚凝姿。雲霞雕色。有踰畫工之妙。草木賁華。無待錦匠之奇。夫豈外飾。蓋自然耳。至於林籟結響。調如竽瑟。泉石激韻。和若球鍠。故形立則章成矣。聲發則文生矣。夫以無識之物。鬱然有彩。有心之器。其無文歟。

If we consider further the thousands of categories of things, each plant and animal has its own pattern. Dragon and phoenix display auspicious omens by their intricacy and bright colors; the visual appearance of a tiger is determined by its stripes, and that of a leopard, by its spots. The sculpted forms and colors of the clouds possess a subtlety that transcends the painter's craft; the intricate luxuriance of trees and plants does not depend upon the wondrous skill of an embroiderer.[25] These are in no way external adornments: they are of Nature

(*Tzu-jan**). And when we consider the resonances created by the vents in the forest,[26] they blend like zithers and ocarinas; the tones stirred by streams running over stones have a harmony like that of chimes and bells. Thus when shape is established, a unit (*chang**) is complete; when sound emerges, pattern (*wen**) is generated. Given the fact that these things which lack the power of recognition may still possess such lush colors, how can this vessel of mind (*hsin**) lack a pattern appropriate to it?

In this paragraph Liu Hsieh arranges conventional cosmological assumptions for rhetorical effect. The sequence of Heaven, Earth, and human beings ("the vessel of mind") was a commonplace hierarchy, and the momentum of that descending sequence would naturally carry Liu Hsieh beyond the Triad to the remaining things of the world, lower on the hierarchy of being but also displaying lush patterning. In describing the chain of being, however, Liu Hsieh omitted mention of "human *wen**" in its proper place, an omission every reader would have recognized. He returns to it here in the conclusion: if absolutely everything else has *wen**, human beings must as well. This permits him to stress the distinction of human *wen** from the surface patterns of other phenomena. It is clear that, in contrast to nature's gaudier displays, our rather plain bodies lack the splendor appropriate to human *wen**. Our human *wen** appears through our determinate characteristic, "mind," for which the body is only a "vessel."

Another interesting move in the exposition is embedding the standard term for literary works, *wen**-*chang** (as separate characters with broad frames of reference) in the description of the natural world. The reader is not simply given the proposition that literature, "human *wen**," is natural; the reader and Liu Hsieh discover it within the natural world: there, too, we find *wen**-*chang**.

人文之元。肇自太極。幽贊神明。易象惟先。庖犧畫其始。仲尼翼其終。而乾坤兩位。獨制文言。言之文也。天地之心哉。若迺河圖孕乎八卦。洛書韞乎九疇。玉版金鏤之實。丹文綠牒之華。誰其尸之。亦神理而已。

自鳥跡代繩。文字始炳。炎暤遺事。紀在三墳。而年世渺邈。聲采靡追。唐虞文章。則煥乎始盛。元首載歌。既發吟詠之志。益稷陳謨。亦垂敷奏之風。夏后氏興。業峻鴻績。九序惟歌。勳德彌縟。逮及商周。文勝其質。雅頌所被。英華日新。文王患憂。繇辭炳曜。符采複隱。精義堅深。重以公旦多材。振其徽烈。剬詩緝頌。斧藻羣言。至夫子繼聖。獨秀前哲。鎔鈞六經。必金聲而玉振。雕琢情性。組織辭令。木鐸起而千里應。席珍流而萬世響。寫天地之輝光。曉生民之耳目矣。

The origins of human pattern (*jen-wen**) began in the Primordial.[27] The Images (*Hsiang**) of the *Book of Changes* were first to bring to light spiritual presences (shen*-ming. "spirit-brightness") that lie concealed. Fu Hsi marked out the initial stages [by producing the trigrams of the Changes], and Confucius added the Wings [exegetical and cosmological tracts accompanying the Changes] to bring the work to a conclusion. Only for the two positions of Ch'ien and K'un did Confucius make the "Patterned Words."[28] For is not pattern in words "the mind of Heaven and Earth"?! And then it came to pass that the "Yellow River Diagram" became imprinted with the eight trigrams;[29] and the "Lo River Writing" contained the Nine Divisions.[30] No person was responsible for these, which are the fruit (shih*, "solids") of jade tablets inlaid with gold, the flower of green strips with red writing (wen*): they came from the basic principle (li*) of spirit (shen*).

When the "tracks of birds" took the place of knotted cords,[31] the written word first appeared in its glory. The events that occurred in the reigns of Yen-ti and Shen-nung were recorded in the "Three Monuments"; but that age is murky and remote, and its sounds and colors cannot be sought.[32] It was in the literary writings (wen*-chang*) of Yao and Shun that the first splendid flourishing occurred.[33] The song of "The Leader" [a verse in the Book of Documents] initiated singing intent [the origin of poetry]. The expostulation offered in the Yi-chi [chapter of the Book of Documents] handed down to us the custom (feng*) of memorials to the throne. Then rose up the Lords of Hsia [the dynasty before the Shang], whose achievements were towering and whose merit was vast; when "the nine sequences were put into song," their deeds and virtue were even more fully elaborated.[34] When it reached the dynasties of Shang and Chou, patterning became greater than substance (chih*). Whatever the Ya* and Sung [of the Book of Songs] covered is daily renewed in all its splendor. The "Comments" [to the Book of Changes composed] by King Wen of Chou in the time of his troubles [when imprisoned by the Shang] still gleam, like streaked jade, multifarious and cryptic, the essential principles firm and deep. In addition to this there was the Duke of Chou with his great talent, who displayed his goodness and endeavors in fashioning Songs and compiling the Hymns (Sung, of the Book of Songs), master of intricate wordcraft. Then came Confucius, successor of the Sages, uniquely outstanding among former wise men; he molded the Six Classics so that they would ring like metal and jade and would sculpt human nature (hsing*-ch'ing*) in the interweaving of their words. The sound of the wooden bell-clapper arose, and was answered from a thousand leagues around;[35] the treasures at his table [his writings] flow forth and resound for ten thousand generations: he delineated the radiance of Heaven and Earth, and opened up the eyes and ears of all the people.

After demonstrating the emergence of pattern in nature and asking how "this vessel of mind [could] lack a pattern appropriate to it," Liu Hsieh traces the origin of human wen*, both as writing and as a manifestation of the cosmic order. This origin of human wen* is to be found in the trigrams of the *Book of Changes*, glyphs that are explicitly given as schematizations of the basic situations in nature. Just as single characters are less determinate in their reference than compounds and offer broad, original categorical identities, so the hexagrams of the *Book of Changes* are still broader and less determinate than single characters; the hexagrams themselves are like character compounds, being made up of two trigrams, which are in turn still broader and less determinate than the hexagrams. The process of wen*'s evolution leads from the trigrams, and thence to the hexagrams, then to characters, and finally to character compounds; this process parallels a cosmogony of increasing division, elaboration, and determination.

The boundary between nature's wen* and human wen* is a point of crisis, and here Liu Hsieh must stress the organic emergence of human wen*. The primordial glyphs of the trigrams are the "prints" of nature's structure, just as in later times the ordinary characters of the written language were created on the model of the prints of birds. The discovery of the glyphs is usually attributed to the studious and privileged observations of the Sage-Kings of remote antiquity; but nature, too, seems anxious to produce such patterns for the use of humanity and sends forth the "Yellow River Diagram" and the "Lo River Writing," at which moment sagely scholarship passes over into revelation, sent by a providential Heaven.

The pattern of literary history Liu Hsieh presents here is a story he tells again and again throughout *Wen-hsin tiao-lung* (and it is a story that literary historians still cling to). This story is one of mysterious origins, no longer accessible. Origins are followed by a period of perfect simplicity and transparency of representation in the earliest extant texts. Then begins a process of complication and increased patterning. Liu Hsieh does not complete this literary historical story here; but in many other chapters we can read how patterning goes swiftly to excess, carrying literature ever further from its simple roots. Even today a more elaborate text is often assumed to be later than a less elaborate one, despite the fact that the very earliest texts, the texts used to validate this mythic law of literary history, have long been recognized to be forgeries, their simplicity shaped to conform to the very cultural narrative that they prove.

It is crucial in this chapter that Liu Hsieh suppress comment on the phases of excessive wen*, literary patterning (although the momentum of development is clear when the *Book of Songs* is characterized as a point when "patterning became greater than substance"). The premise of the chapter is that wen* is not mere adornment, but is rather the outside that corresponds perfectly to some inside. Liu Hsieh's true intention is that this is what wen* **should** be. Were he here to go into those phases when "patterning" leaves behind substance, he would be admitting that *wen** may indeed be mere adornment, something added and unnecessary.

爰自風姓。暨於孔氏。玄聖創典。素王述訓。莫不原道心以敷章。研神理而設教。取象乎河洛。問數乎蓍龜。觀天文以極變。察人文以成化。然後能經緯區宇。彌綸彝憲。發輝事業。彪炳辭義。故知道沿聖以垂文。聖因文而明道。旁通而無滯。日用而不匱。易曰。鼓天下之動者存乎辭。辭之所以能鼓天下者。迺道之文也。

From Fu Hsi, the mysterious Sage who founded the canon, up to the time of Confucius, the uncrowned king who transmitted the teaching, all took for their source the mind of the Way to set forth their writings (*chang**), and they investigated the principle of spirit (*shen**-*li**) to establish their teaching. They took the Images from the Yellow River Diagram and the Lo River Writing, and they consulted both milfoil and tortoise carapaces about fate [methods of divination]. They observed the pattern of the heavens (*T'ien-wen**, "astronomy," "astrology") to know the full range of mutations; and they investigated human pattern (*jen-wen**, "culture," "literature") to perfect their transforming [i.e., to civilize the people]. Only then could they establish the warp and woof of the cosmos, completing and unifying its great ordinances, and they accomplished a patrimony of great deeds, leaving truths (*yi**) shining in their words.

Thus we know that the Way sent down its pattern (*wen**) through the Sages, and that the Sages made the Way manifest in their patterns (*wen**, "writing"). It extends everywhere with no obstruction, and is applied every day and never found wanting. The *Book of Changes* says, "That which stirs the world into movement is preserved in language."[36] That by which language can stir all the world into movement is the pattern of the Way.

The peroration recapitulates the history of *wen** from its human beginnings down to its point of perfection in Confucius, whose *wen** is both perfect and permanent, a standard against which all subsequent *wen** is mere elaboration or decline.

道心惟微。神理設教。光采元聖。炳燿仁孝。龍圖獻體。龜書呈貌。天文斯觀。民胥以傚。

Supporting Verse
　　The mind of the Way is subtle,
　　The principle of spirit establishes teaching.
　　Luminous is that Primal Sage,

In whom fellow-feeling and fillal piety gleam.

The diagram on the Yellow River dragon offered the form;

The writing on the tortoise showed its appearance.

Here the pattern of Heaven can be observed,

For all the people to emulate.

CHAPTER 2

Revering the Classics, Tsung-ching 宗經

"Revering the Classics"[37] is not one of the easier chapters of *Wen-hsin tiao-lung* for a Western reader to appreciate: in addition to constant references to the rich and complex lore of classical studies, the chapter contains much florid and conventional piety. Beneath the lore and the rhetorical flourishes, however, "Revering the Classics" overlaps and extends the history of human *wen** that was first presented in "Its Source in the Way." In this version of the history, proliferation and elaboration began immediately after the simple origins of human *wen** and quickly came to a stage where the essentials were buried. At this point the great editor Confucius appeared, cutting away the excess to reveal the kernel of constant values and literary models that are the Confucian Classics.

Like his contemporary Chung Jung, Liu Hsieh plays the role of literary genealogist.[38] As with the great families of the Southern Dynasties, value and authority in literature demanded a clear line of descent. Chung Jung traced some of the earlier poets back to the *Book of Songs*, but his efforts were primarily directed to delineating the stylistic genealogies of the preceding four centuries. For Liu Hsieh literature's genealogy must go back to the origins of the universe, but more immediately to the Five Classics: the *Book or Documents*, the *Book of Songs*, the *Book of Changes*, the *Spring and Autumn Annals*, and the *Rites*.

Demonstrating literature's ancestry in the Classics is equally important for Liu Hsieh's sense of the value of his own project in *Wen-hsin tiao-lung*. In the "Afterword" he tells of an ambition to be a scholar of the Classics; this ambition was renounced out of despair of adding anything new and significant to the classical scholarship already in existence. It was at this point he decided to turn to literary studies, precisely on the grounds that in his own time literature is the proper successor to the Classics. Thus, by analogy, the literary scholar is the proper successor to the great classical commentators.

三極彝訓。其書曰經。經也者。恆久之至道。不刊之鴻教也。故象天地。效鬼神。參物序制人紀。洞性靈之奧區。極文章之骨髓者也。

There are unalterable teachings regarding the Three Ultimates [Heaven, Earth, and human beings], which, written down, are known as the Classics. The

Classics are the perfection of the Way, permanent and enduring, the grandest form of instruction and one that is never eradicated. They are works that take their image from Heaven and Earth, investigate the [realm of] the spirits and gods,[39] give consideration to the order of things (wu*),[40] determine the standards for human beings, penetrate the secret recesses of the soul (hsing*-ling), and reach all the way to the bone and marrow of literary works (wen*-chang*).

The list of functions and attributes here is reminiscent of the shorter list of such functions in the "Great Preface" to the Book of Songs. (see p. 45 above). The role of such lists is essentially an amplification of the attribute yüan 遠, "far-reaching," something before us that extends into many frames of reference.

As with the character wen* there is a comprehensive source that unfolds into more limited and determinate areas. Literature was often described as mo 末, "what comes last," sometimes "of the present," the final phase of a sequence (and thus carrying the implication of "minor importance"). Literature and allied activities are often the last term in sets of cultural activities, as in the famous passage in Analects VII.6: "He said, 'Set your intent (chih*) upon the Way; take firm hold on virtue (tê*); rely on fellow-feeling; wander freely (yu*) in the arts.'" In Liu Hsieh's list of applications above, literature is the last thing into which the Classics extend—the "present" concern, however "minor," that can be traced back to those great origins.[41]

皇世三墳。帝代五典。重以八索。申以九邱。歲歷緜暖。條流紛糅。自夫子刪述。而大寶咸耀。於是易張十翼。書標七觀。詩列四始。禮正五經。春秋五例。義既埏乎性情。辭亦匠於文理。故能開學養正。昭明有融。然而道心惟微。聖謨卓絕。牆宇重峻。而吐納自深。譬萬鈞之洪鍾。無錚錚之細響矣。

The Three Monuments of the Primordial Reigns and the Five Canons of the period of the Emperors[42] were enlarged by the Eight Investigations[43] and were extended by the Nine Masses.[44] With the passage of the years these grew remote and dark, with branches and streams multiplying and mixing. Ever since the Master edited and transmitted them, however, the great treasures have revealed their radiance. Then the Book of Changes spread its Ten Wings,[45] the Book of Documents set forth the Seven Things for Consideration,[46] the Book of Songs arrayed their Four Beginnings,[47] the Book of Rites gave the proper form of the Five Enduring [Rites],[48] and the Spring and Autumn Annals had their Five Examples.[49] Since the truths (yi*) [contained in the Classics] shape[50] human nature and the affections (hsing*-ch'ing*), and since the language (tz'u*) is the most finely wrought in the principles of literature (wen*-li*), they initiate learning and nurture what is proper, "and their radiance also endures."[51] However, the mind of the Way (Tao*-hsin*) is subtle, and the deliberations of the Sage are peerless; his walls and roof are layered and lofty: what is given forth and received there is deep.[52] Compare it to a great bell of ten thousand pounds: there are no delicate, tinkling echoes.

The texts of remote antiquity survived only as scattered names and a presumption that they must have been concise and essential. Liu Hsieh has projected into antiquity a process of literary evolution following the same pattern that he saw in the literature of more recent times. Originally there were only a few texts, which were increased and enlarged by the addition of new texts, until the originals became "remote and dark" in the sheer abundance of "branches and streams multiplying and mixing." Then Confucius appeared, returning to the essential origins of the Classics by an editorial work known as *shan* 刪, "cutting away." This refers to the legend that Confucius selected the three hundred poems of the *Book of Songs* out of an original three thousand, and according to some sources, performed a similar operation on the *Book of Documents*.

Editorial selection is one of the paradigmatic acts of Chinese civilization, recovering what is basic, original, and essential out of excessive multiplicity. "Essentials" are often "essential points" that can be enumerated, and the sets of enumerated features ascribed to each Classic are an attempt to regulate multiplicity. Such lists of essential categories have been an enduring feature of Chinese pedagogy, and they can be best understood as a counterbalance to the fascination with the sheer fecundity of words and concepts. The "cutting away," Confucius' editorial work, was to make the basic truths visible and to establish an intelligible and permanent mean between primordial unity (the Way) and a late world of multiplicity.

But unfortunately, the Classics are not easy to understand. As there is continual balancing movement between limited number (*shu**) and ungoverned multiplicity, so there are similar balances between hidden depths and that which is manifest to all. The Classics may be the origins and roots of all human norms, including those of literature; but as roots, they may lie deep out of sight and require devoted study.

夫易惟談天。入神致用。故繫稱旨遠辭文。言中事隱。韋編三絕。固哲人之驪淵也。

The *Book of Changes* talks of Heaven (or "Nature"); it "enters the realm of spirit (*shen**) and applies it [in the human realm"].[53] Thus the *Hsi-tz'u chuan* claims that precepts [of the *Book of Changes*] are far-reaching and its phrases (*tz'u**) are refined (*wen**), that its words hit the mark and the events (*shih**) [implied in it] are hidden. [When Confucius studied the *Book of Changes* late in his life,] the leather straps [binding the bamboo slips on which the *Book of Changes* was written] broke three times [from the intensity of his study of the work][54]: truly for our wise Sage this [the *Book of Changes*] was the abyss in which the black dragon [held the precious pearl beneath its chin].[55]

In this passage and the following paragraphs, Liu Hsieh takes each Classic up in turn, discussing its particular strengths and suggesting that in their conjunction, these various strengths present a full and orderly complement of essential values. The descriptions of the *Book of Changes*, the *Book of Songs*, and the *Spring and Autumn Annals* are the most significant for contemporary and later literary values.

The long two-part essay on cosmology, the *Hsi-tz'u chuan* 繫辭傳 (two of the "ten wings" of the *Book of Changes*) is an important model and source for Liu Hsieh. This text, more than almost any other, explained how the universe as a whole functioned. But most important for Liu Hsieh was the way it demonstrated the secret order of how things unfold into the empirical world. Thus, as we will see later, it is the origin of genres that explain and amplify, exegesis in the highest sense. One phrase from the *Hsi-tz'u chuan*, cited above by Liu Hsieh, became particularly important in later poetics: this is "enters the realm of spirit" (*ju-shen**). In "Ts'ang-lang's Remarks on Poetry" of the thirteenth century, this term is given as the highest value in poetry. There the significance of the phrase is somewhat different in that it omits the complementary phrase from the *Hsi-tz'u chuan*: "and makes application of it [in the human realm]." In this earlier period "spirit," *shen**, is not a value in itself; rather such imperceptible mysteries are important as means to account for the empirical.

書實記言。而訓詁茫昧。通乎爾雅。則文意曉然。故子夏歎書。昭昭若日月之明。離離如星辰之行。言昭灼也。

詩主言志。詁訓同書。摛風裁興。藻辭譎喻。溫柔在誦。故最附深衷矣。

禮以立體。據事制範。章條纖曲。執而後顯。採擿片言。莫非寶也。

春秋辨理。一字見義。五石六鷁。以詳略成文。雉門兩觀。以先後顯旨。其婉章志晦。諒以邃矣。尚書則覽文如詭。而尋理即暢。春秋則觀辭立曉。而訪義方隱。此聖人殊致。表裏之異體者也。

The *Book of Documents* gives a factual (*shih**) record of words,[56] yet in regard to philological questions it is obscure; however, if one comprehends (*t'ung**) the *Erh-ya* [an ancient lexicon], then the meaning of the writing (*wen**-*yi**) will be lucid. Thus it was that [Confucius' disciple] Tzu-hsia exclaimed of the *Book of Documents*: "Shining as the alternating brightness of sun and moon, clear before us as the intricate movements of the stars and planets."[57] What he says is obvious.

The *Book of Songs* articulates what is intently on the mind (*yen-chih**), but it is the same as the *Book of Documents* in the question of philological problems. In the way it presents the *Feng**, *Ya**, and *Sung*, and forms exposition (*fu*), comparison (*pi*), and affective images (*hsing**),[58] its elegant phrasing is elusive and suggestive;[59] there is a gentleness in the recitation [of the *Songs*], and thus they touch our inner lives most deeply.

The *Rites* are to establish normative forms (*t'i**) and determine the pattern according to the matter at hand. Their statutes are minute and have fine variations; they become obvious only after carrying them out. Every partial phrase in them is a gem.

The *Spring and Autumn Annals* make discriminations of principles (*li**), and the significance (*yi**) is revealed in [the usage of] individual words.[60] [In the passages about the] five stones and six albatrosses, he [Confucius] wrote giving details about one and omitting the details about the other.[61] [In the passage about the] two watchtowers at Chih Gate, the significance is shown by the sequence.[62] "Finely phrased composition, the intent obscure":[63] truly the work is profound. As for the *Book of Documents*, it seems strange when you read over it; but when you seek the principles (*li**) [behind it], they are spread out clearly before you. When it comes to the *Spring and Autumn Annals*, however, when you read the lines, you understand them immediately; but then when you look for the significance (*yi**), it is hidden. Such are the different stances taken in the writings of the Sage, different forms (*t'i**), one exterior, one interior.

Each of the Classics offers a different kind of model, a distinct form (*t'i**) with its own virtues. The virtue of the *Book of Documents* is its clarity, despite lexical difficulty. The virtue of the *Book of Songs* is its ability to touch its readers most completely and most inwardly: it is a text less for understanding than for moving and shaping its readers. As texts, the *Rites* are not terribly interesting; they are only the blueprints for action, and their true value can only be appreciated in performance. The *Spring and Autumn Annals* is the model of perfect usage, both in the choice and arrangement of words; it shows that judgment and understanding can be perfectly inscribed in language and transmitted through it.

For the Western reader, the structures of interpretation in *Wen-hsin tiao-lung* are often of more interest than the particular judgments made. There are two easy cases: one Classic, the *Book of Songs*, offers a norm for texts whose affect is immediate; another, the *Rites*—Liu uses the collective term for the various classics of ritual—is a norm for texts that can be realized only in *praxis*. But there are also two Classics that establish norms for texts that require "understanding," an event that occurs in time and moves between opposite qualities.[64] The mirror opposition between the *Book of Documents* and the *Spring and Autumn Annals* is a doubled pairing of the principles of the "latent" (*yin*) and "overt" or "out-standing" (*hsiu*), treated in Chapter 40. Each of the two Classics comprises opposite ratios of these principles: the obscure becomes clear or the clear becomes obscure. We often find a similar presumption of inversion in later criticism of poetry: the linguistically dense poem may be presumed shallow, while the simple and pellucid poem may be presumed to to hold a wealth of subtle significance "held in reserve." But the structural assumption of movement between opposite qualities transcends its particular application here and recurs in different forms in the following passage.

至根柢槃深。枝葉峻茂。辭約而旨豐。事近而喻遠。是以往者雖舊。餘味日新。後進追取而非晚。前修文用而未先。可謂太山徧雨。河潤千里者也。

[The Classics] have roots that coil deep, with leaves and branches that are lofty and lush: the diction (*tz'u**) is terse, but the purport (*chih*) is rich; the events (*shih**) treated may be close at hand, but they imply things that are far-reaching. Thus, though they come from far in the past, the flavor (*wei**) that remains in them is renewed daily. The later-born seek within them and learn from them, without thinking it too late [for the Classics to be of use]; earlier worthies have long used them, not thinking it was too soon. We can call them a Mount T'ai that sends rains everywhere or a Yellow River that irrigates a thousand leagues.[65]

The word for Classics, *ching* 經, means "constant," "passing through"; it is also the "warp" of a weaving. The Classics are not revealed scripture (rather, they are discoveries made by particularly gifted individuals); but like scripture they are the appearance of permanent truths in a particular historical moment. The structure by which that original "point" in time extends to permanence repeats itself on many levels: terseness to extensive significance, matters close at hand to far-reaching implications; the one unfolds into the many.

故論說辭序。則易統其首。詔策章奏。則書發其源。賦頌歌讚。則詩立其本。銘誄箴祝。則禮總其端。紀傳銘檄。則春秋為根。並窮高以樹表。極遠以啟疆。所以百家騰躍。終入環內者也。若稟經以製式。酌雅以富言。是仰山而鑄銅。煮海而為鹽也。

The *Book of Changes* is the unifying point of origin for the discourse (*lun*), the exposition (*shuo*), the comment (*tz'u**), and the preface (*hsü*).[66] The *Book of Documents* is the fountainhead for the edict (*chao*), rescript (*ts'e*), declaration to the throne (*chang*), and memorial to the throne (*tsou*). The *Book of Songs* is the root of poetic exposition (*fu*), ode (*sung*), song (*ko*), and adjunct verse (*tsan*).

The *Rites* are the general beginning of the inscription (*ming*), eulogy (*lei*), admonition (*chen*), and prayer (*chu*). The *Spring and Autumn Annals* is the basis of the record (*chi*), the biography (*chuan*), the oath (*meng*), and the dispatch (*hsi*). Together they establish the very highest standards possible and open up the most far-reaching territories. Thus, when the hundreds of masters go bounding off, they ultimately end up within the scope [of the Classics]. If one determines one's pattern by endowing it with the Classics, and if one consults the *Erh-ya* [the ancient lexicon] to enrich one's vocabulary, this is looking to a mountain to smelt copper or boiling the sea to get salt.[67]

Having described the Classics as a full complement of distinct primary forms (*t'i**), Liu Hsieh now filiates all the major literary genres to their appropriate Classic. As we have seen, the originary form that unifies any set of divisions is a region of inexhaustible fertility. Functioning in isolation, one of the later literary genres (*t'i**) will be in danger of being exhausted or "drying up." The capacity to achieve new things in literature ("daily renewal") can be achieved only by reasserting connection with the parent Classic and returning to its fertile source.

故文能宗經。體有六義。一則情深而不詭。二則風清而不雜。三則事信而不誕。四則義直而不回。五則體約而不蕪。六則文麗而不淫。揚子比雕玉以作器。謂五經之含文也。
夫文以行立。行以文傳。四教所先。符采相濟。勵德樹聲。莫不師聖。而建言修辭。鮮克宗經。是以楚豔漢侈。流弊不還。正末歸本。不其懿歟。

Thus if a person is able to show reverence for the Classics in his writing, his normative form (*t'i**) will have the following six principles:[68] a depth in the affections (*ch'ing**) without deceptiveness; the affective force (*feng**) clear and unadulterated; the events (*shih**) trustworthy and not false; the principles (*yi**) upright and not bending around; the normative form (*t'i**) terse and not overgrown [with weeds]; the literary quality (*wen**) beautiful and not lewd. Yang Hsiung [53 B.C.–A.D. 18] compared it to carving jade to form a vessel, by which he meant that the Five Classics were replete with *wen**.[69] Writing (*wen**) is established by [the quality of] a person's actions, and those actions in turn are transmitted by writing. Placing *wen** at the head of the Four Things Taught,[70] was to assist the jade-like pattern [of the other three]. All who enact virtue and establish their repute take the Sage as a teacher. Yet when they would set up words and polish their language (*tz'u**), few know to revere the Classics. For this reason the sensuality of Ch'u [literature] and the extravagances of Han [literature] dwindled to baseness and did not turn back [toward their origins]. Wouldn't it be wonderful if we could correct the later phases (*mo*) and return to the root?

Here at the end of the chapter is the first appearance of a concern that recurs throughout *Wen-hsin tiao-lung*: there is a process of evolution that is in danger of losing sight of origins. Although the beginnings of this theme can be traced back to the Han, it was among Liu Hsieh and his contemporaries that it took on the form that would be repeated in different versions throughout the rest of the history of traditional Chinese literature. One function of literary theory became to force contemporary writers to recognize origins and, in doing so, to reestablish continuity.

三極彝道。訓深稽古。致化歸一。分教斯五。性靈鎔匠。文章奧府。淵哉鑠乎。羣言之祖。

Supporting Verse

    The permanent instruction regarding the Three Ultimates:
    The depth of this Way comes from study of the ancient.
    The transformation accomplished is unitary,
    But their teaching is divided into Five [Classics],
    Which are the formative craftsmen of the [human] spirit,
    And the mysterious treasure house of literary works.
    Deep indeed, and gleaming!
    These the ancestors of all words.

CHAPTER 26
Spirit Thought, Shen*-ssu* 神思

The concerns of this chapter on spirit thought reveal the profound influence of Lu Chi's "Poetic Exposition on Literature" on *Wen-hsin tiao-lung*.[71] At various points throughout his work, Liu Hsieh sharply criticizes Lu Chi; but such attacks seem merely Liu Hsieh's attempt to assert his own distinction against the powerful influence of this famous predecessor, who was widely regarded as one of the greatest writers of his era. It was Lu Chi who first elaborated the archaic model of the spirit journey to describe the operations of mind in planning a composition. And Liu Hsieh, while describing the process far more fully than Lu Chi, rarely departs significantly from him. Moreover, as in "The Poetic Exposition on Literature," the discussion of spirit thought is given first place in in the sequence of questions of composition (in Liu Hsieh's case, first in the sequence of theoretical chapters), suggesting the "priority" of spirit thought, both in importance and in the process of composition.

古人云。形在江海之上。心存魏闕之下。神思之謂也。文之思也。其神遠矣。故寂然凝慮。思接千載。悄焉動容。視通慢里。吟詠之間。吐納珠玉之聲。眉睫之前。卷舒風雲之色。其思理之致乎。

Long ago someone spoke of "the physical form's being by the rivers and lakes, but the mind's remaining at the foot of the palace towers of Wei."[72] This is what is meant by spirit thought (*shen*-ssu**). And spirit goes far indeed in the thought that occurs in writing (*wen**). When we silently focus our concerns, thought may reach to a thousand years in the past; and as our countenance stirs ever so gently, our vision may cross (*t'ung**) ten thousand leagues. The sounds of pearls and jade are given forth while chanting and singing; right before our eyelashes, the color (*se**) of windblown clouds unfurls. This is accomplished by the basic principle of thought (*ssu*-li**).

Perhaps to deflect the reader's immediate association of this topic with Lu Chi, Liu Hsieh opens this chapter in an unusual way, with a reference to the *Chuang-tzu*, thus giving the idea of "spirit thought" a pedigree in an age long before that of Lu Chi. But the quotation is grossly misapplied; and it is tempting to read much into the choice of such a twisted example, given as the sole definition of spirit thought, especially since it is given at the beginning of the chapter where it was usual to treat definitions and origins of a topic. We might consider that Liu Hsieh, living in the lower Yangtse region, is another person whose "physical form is by the rivers and lakes" (conventionally referring to the general region that was the center of the Southern Dynasties); we might recall that Lu Chi was another native of that region, who went north to the capital of the Tsin in Lo-yang, directly west of the capital of the old state of Wei (and if Liu Hsieh associated Wei with the dynasty, the capital would be still closer). We should perhaps avoid distinguishing any particular motives in the unusual ineptness of the opening allusion, but we may suspect pressures that were, at least in part, personal.

故思理為妙。神與物遊。神居胸臆。而志氣統其關鍵。物沿耳目。而辭令管其樞機。樞機方通。則物無隱貌。關鍵將塞。則神有遯心。

When the basic principle of thought is at its most subtle, the spirit wanders with things. The spirit dwells in the breast; intent (*chih**) and *ch'i** control the bolt to its gate [to let it out].[73] Things come in through the ear and eye; in this, language controls the hinge and trigger. When hinge and trigger permit passage, no things have hidden appearance; when the bolt to the gate is closed, then spirit is concealed.

This is one of the most important and fully discussed passages in *Wen-hsin tiao-lung*. There is some question whether some of its more interesting propositions follow from Liu Hsieh's clear intentions or from the force of parallel exposition. But whatever their provenance, these propositions are most suggestive. It should be noted that when I discuss words below, I am not implying that Liu Hsieh is necessarily using them with cautious precision; rather, in using terms that are laden with implications from past usage (implications that are not at all obvious in English translation), he is, in fact, making statements that provide interesting insights.

When the basic principle of thought is at its most subtle, the spirit wanders with things. We have seen that the "basic principle of thought" (ssu*-li*) is the capacity, in an act of spirit thought, to go beyond the determinate empirical circumstances in which the writer finds himself. As in the spirit journey in "The Poetic Exposition on Literature," in this process the mind encounters "things" (wu*). Later commentators often paraphrase this as a relation between thought and a scene before one's physical eyes; but Liu Hsieh is working very much in the tradition of Lu Chi: although there is nothing here that precludes empirical observation (indeed Liu Hsieh seems to be shifting towards the empirical when he says that "things come in through the ear and eye"), the initial model is one of imagination disjoined from the empirical scene before the writer. The phrasing used by Liu Hsieh here may assume the possibility of a gross form of "spirit thought" in which the things are seen simply as objects.[74] But in its "finest" or "most subtle" form (miao*, presuming the fine points and subtle changes, that which is essential but invisible to the ordinary senses), "spirit wanders with things." The "with" (yü 與) is an essential relation. When writing on the idea of the Sage, it was often said that the Sage is "with" things; that is, the Sage neither loses himself in things nor does he see them as mere objects, but rather he participates "with them." Commentators often speak of this passage in "Spirit Thought" as the fusion (chiao-jung 交融) between self and scene, a union prized in later poetics; certainly that later notion of the mutual determination of self and other is an outgrowth of the values implicit here. But Liu Hsieh's version is somewhat closer to the older Confucian ideal of the Sage: not so much a fusion (in which the autonomous identity of each disappears) as a tentative association, poised between unity and difference. It is essential to recognize that the writer in the condition of spirit thought is not merely knowing or observing; he is "sharing" in a system of things.

Wanders, yu*, is a term as weighted as "with." Yu* is to "go without direction, purpose, or end." Encountering things, the mind does not "go to" any end, but rather "goes along with." Yu* strongly implies a freedom and an absence of motive. As Liu Hsieh says later in "The Sensuous Colors of Physical Things," the poet rolls round and round in the course of things (sui wu* yi wan-chuan 隨物以宛轉, "follow things and turns around and around.").

The spirit dwells in the breast; intent (chih*) and ch'i* control the bolt to its gate. Things come in through the ear and eye; in this, language controls the hinge and trigger. Imagination is a spirit journey, a movement through space;

thus we have the traveler ("spirit," *shen**), the motive and direction of its motion (*chih**), and the energy that makes motion possible (*ch'i**). Having previously discussed free "wandering with things," Liu Hsieh must turn to the question of control; and control is located in the initiation of the movement of spirit. The parallel line can suggest one of two things: either that language is necessary for the recognition of things (the gatekeeper that allows or denies things access to consciousness), or that a store of language is requisite to expressing the experience of things in writing. The former is an attractive and radical possibility, suggested by the phrasing of the line itself (in which language is linked with things "coming in"). However, the following passage, with its demand for a store of learning as in "The Poetic Exposition on Literature," suggests that the second interpretation is correct: language is necessary to reveal things to others, not to recognize things oneself. The amplifying passage, "when hinge and trigger permit passage, no things have hidden appearance," can also be taken either way: that is, they are not hidden from the writer or not kept hidden from potential readers.

是以陶鈞文思。貴在虛靜。疏瀹五藏。澡雪精神。積學以儲寶。酌理以富才。研閱以窮照。馴致以懌辭。然後使玄解之宰。尋聲律而定墨。獨照之匠。闚意象而運斤。此蓋馭文之首術。謀篇之大端。

Thus in shaping and turning [as on a potter's wheel] literary thought (*wen**-*ssu**), the most important thing is emptiness and stillness within. Dredge clear the inner organs and wash the spirit pure.[75] Amass learning to build a treasure house; consult principle (*li**) to enrich talent; investigate and experience to know all that appears [literally "exhaust what shines"]; guide it along to spin the words out. Only then can the butcher, who cuts things apart mysteriously, set the pattern according to the rules of sound; and the uniquely discerning carpenter wield his ax with his eye to the concept–image (*yi**-*hsiang**).[76] This is the foremost technique in directing the course of *wen**, the major point for planning a piece.

Liu Hsieh follows Lu particularly closely in this chapter, first enumerating the preconditions to be achieved before composition, preconditions to be followed by spontaneous action. First, there is inner stillness, cutting off external determinations and concerns, followed by a list of capacities that one needs to have developed within: learning, understanding of principle, and experience. The intuitive action that is a consequence of meeting these preconditions is an old value in the tradition (and in this case an issue **not** addressed by Lu Chi): intuitive action will obey the rules perfectly; it will "set the pattern according to the rules of sound"—a swift, unself-conscious act that conforms perfectly to established norms. Perhaps the oldest statement of this value is in *Analects* II.4, in which Confucius describes himself at seventy as "following his heart's desire without transgressing the strict standard." This Chinese version of "free conformity to law," or perhaps "intuitive conformity to law," became, in various versions, quite important in the later theoretical tradition. It should be added that it is unclear whether the intuitive action described in this section is the act of composition itself (as the passage seems to suggest in its own right) or the operation of spirit thought (which interpretation will make the next passage follow more smoothly).

We should also note here the appearance of a compound that was to become an important technical term in later theory and criticism: "concept-image," *yi*-hsiang**. While this term does not yet have the weight of associations it was to develop in later criticism, the germ of the later notion is already present. We may note that it is something which the craftsman considers as he acts, a prior envisagement from which the work follows. Had the Chinese been using concepts of *mimêsis* or representation, it would have been easy at this point to say that the actual artwork "represents" the prior "envisagement." The possibility is not excluded; it is simply not addressed. In later criticism, a reader in his turn will perceive the *yi*-hsiang** in the text. *Yi*-hsiang** is the sketchy outline (from the fuzziness and lack of detail in the concept of *hsiang**, a normative schematization of the thing) of what is intended, though there is felt to be a special beauty and richness in that indeterminacy and lack of detail.

夫神思方運。萬塗競萌。規矩虛位。刻鏤無形。登山則情滿於山。觀海則意溢於海。我才之多少。將與風雲而並驅矣。

When spirit thought is set in motion, ten thousand paths sprout before it; rules and regulations are still hollow positions; and the cutting or carving as yet has no form.[77] If one climbs a mountain, one's affections (*ch'ing**) are filled by the mountain; if one contemplates the sea, one's concepts (*yi**) are brought to brimming over by the sea.[78] And, according to the measure of talent in the self, one may speed off together with the wind and clouds.

The freedom and multiple possibilities (ten thousand paths) that appear in the operation of spirit thought are contrasted in the next section with the limitations that may come in actually trying to put the experience into writing. What is most interesting in this passage is the relation between self and world implicit in "If one climbs a mountain, one's affections (*ch'ing**) are filled by the mountain; if one contemplates the sea, then one's concepts (*yi**) are brought to brimming over by the sea." *Wen-hsin tiao-lung* occupies an intermediate stage in the theory of the relation between mind and the world, a question all important in Chinese literary thought. In pre-Ch'in and Han literary psychology, mind (*hsin**) is stirred (*kan**) to response (*ying**) by social circumstance or the things of the world (*wu**) (this earlier idea is recapitulated and elaborated at the beginning of "The Sensuous Colors of Physical Things"). In the Sung we see the development of a model later known as *ch'ing*-ching* chiao-jung* 情景交融, the "fusion of scene and the affections," in which both self and world are mutually determined.[79] In "The Poetic Exposition on Literature" the literary mind ranges through the world of things, but retains an artistic autonomy and is essentially unaffected by them. The "stuff" that is the material of the poem is spoken of as something acquired—searched out, plucked, gathered, and hoarded, but not infusing the consciousness of the poet. This incipient notion of artistic distance would have been difficult to sustain in the context of Chinese literary thought, and Liu Hsieh offers various ways to restore a relation between self and things that is both natural and a ground for literary work. Earlier in this chapter we saw the very beautiful model of the mind being "with" things, a model that recurs elsewhere in *Wen-hsin tiao-lung*. Here we have a somewhat different relation, in which the self (both the receptive "affections," *ch'ing**, and the volitional or concept-forming *yi**) is "filled" by the external scene. This is different from the archaic notion of "stirring" in that the phrasing here suggests some correspondence between the external object and the content of what consequently lies in the affections. On one level, this is quantitative: the mountain and the sea are vast things and they "fill" the *ch'ing** and *yi**. But especially in the water metaphor ("brimming over") of the second image, it seems that the scene itself enters the mind on its own force and exists there as a mental counterpart of the external scene (this would be true even of things encountered in spirit travels). That process of transference is partially implicit in the earlier usage of "concept-image," *yi*-hsiang**. Note that in the last sentence of this passage, Liu Hsieh returns to the model of being "with" things.

方其搦翰。氣倍辭前。暨乎篇成。半折心始。何則。意翻空而易奇。言徵實而難巧也。是之意授於思。言授於意。密則無際。疏則千里。或理在方寸而求之域表。或義在咫尺而思隔山河。是以秉心養術。無務苦慮。含章司契。不必勞情也。

Whenever a person grasps the writing brush, the *ch'i** is doubled even before the words come. But when a piece is complete, it goes no further than half of that with which the mind began. Why is this? When concepts soar across the empty sky, they easily become wondrous; but it is hard to be artful by giving them substantial (*shih**) expression in words. Thus concept (*yi**) is received from thought (*ssu**), and language in turn is received from concept. These [language and concept] may be so close that there is no boundary between them, or so remote that they seem a thousand leagues from one another. Sometimes the principle (*li**) lies within the speck of mind, yet one seeks it far beyond the world; sometimes a truth (*yi**) is only a foot away, but thought goes beyond mountains and rivers in pursuit of it. Thus if one grasps the mind and nourishes its techniques, it will not be requisite to brood painfully. If you retain the design within and retain control of the creditor's half of the contract (*ssu-ch'i*),[80] you need not force the affections to suffer.

As in "The Poetic Exposition on Literature," Liu Hsieh here is painfully conscious of the difference between intent and execution. One begins eagerly, with a surplus of *ch'i**, but ends up with something that seems to fall far short of the envisagement in mind. The explanation shows that actual writing is different from spirit thought: concepts, *yi**, are free, soaring across the sky, wandering "with" things; but words are somehow *shih**, "substantial" and limited. Rather than representation, the relation between words and concepts is *cheng*, translated lamely as "give it expression," but actually "to testify," "to show proof," to offer some adequate evidence of an inner experience that cannot be publicly recognized.

These problematic relations lead Liu Hsieh to his own version of the venerable tripartite scheme to link language to mind and the world. Here "thought," *ssu**, is the first term, an activity that is indeterminate and constantly moving. This leads to "concept," *yi**, a mediating construct that limits and determines the fluidity of thought. The final term is language. And as so often in such sequences of manifestation, there may be problems and losses in the movement between the stages. Liu Hsieh seems to offer alternatives here, but in fact suggests that a gap in this process is a failure, that the answer should always be close at hand. Despite his instinct that the relation between thought and language should always be easy and direct, the rhetoric suggests alternatives; in the next section, he takes up those alternatives through examples of slow and quick composition, an opposition closely related to the controversy between instant and gradual enlightenment in Buddhism.[81]

人之稟才。遲速異分。文之制體。大小殊功。相如含筆而腐毫。揚雄輟翰而驚夢。桓譚疾
感於苦思。王充氣竭於思慮。張衡研京以十年。左思練都以一紀。雖有巨文。亦思之緩
也。淮南崇朝而賦騷。枚臯應詔而成賦。子建援牘如口誦。仲宣舉筆似宿構。阮瑀據案而
制書。禰衡當食而草奏。雖有短篇。亦思之速也。
若夫駿發之士。心總要術。敏在慮前。應機立斷。覃思之人。情饒岐路。鑒在疑後。研慮
方定。機敏故造次而成功。慮疑故愈久而致績。難易雖殊。並資博練。若學淺而空遲。才
疏而徒速。以斯成器。未之前聞。是以臨篇綴慮。必有二患。理鬱者苦貧。辭溺者傷亂。
然則博見為饋貧之糧。貫一為拯亂之藥。博而能一。亦有助乎心力矣。
若情數詭雜。體變遷貿。拙辭或孕於巧義。庸事或萌於新意。視布於麻。雖云未費。杼軸
獻功。煥然乃珍。

People are endowed with different allotments of talent, some swift and some slow. And the forms (*t'i**) of literary work differ in the achievement, some of large magnitude and some small. Ssu-ma Hsiang-ju [179–117 B.C.] ruined the hairs of his writing brush by holding it in his mouth; Yang Hsiung [53 B.C.– A.D. 18], when he couldn't write, kept waking up from dreams; Huan T'an [ca. 30 B.C.–A.D. 41] put so much effort into thinking he became sick; Wang Ch'ung's [27–ca. 97] *ch'i** was used up in brooding; Chang Heng [78–139] polished his [poetic exposition] "The Capitals" for ten years; Tso Ssu [ca. 250– 305] refined his [poetic exposition] "The Great Cities" for a dozen. Though these are all immense works, they are also [examples of] slowness of thought.

In contrast, the Prince of Huai-nan [179–122 B.C.] composed his *Sao* in the space of a morning; Mei Kao [Western Han] completed a poetic exposition as soon as he received the royal command; Ts'ao Chih [192–232] would take a writing tablet and recite extempore; Wang Ts'an [177–217] lifted his writing brush as if he had already done several drafts beforehand; Juan Yü [ca. 165– 212] wrote letters in the saddle; Mi Heng [173–198] could draft a memorial at dinner. Even though these are short works, they are also [examples of] quickness of thought.

The mind of a sharp-witted person combines all the essential techniques; and his very quickness preempts reflection, making instant decisions in response to the demands of the moment (*chi**). The state of mind (*ch'ing**) of someone who broods deeply is filled with forking paths: he sees clearly only after uncertainties and makes his determination only after thoughtful reflection. When one is quick of mind in response to the demands of the moment, the accomplishment is brought about hastily; when reflection is full of uncertainties, it takes a much longer time to achieve one's goals.

Although ease and difficulty differ, both depend on perfecting oneself on a broad scope. If learning is shallow, the latter type is slow in vain; if talent is diffuse, the former type is swift to no good end. One never hears of great accomplishment by the likes of these.[82] There are two sources of danger as you approach a piece and compose your reflections: if principle remains blocked, there is poverty [of content]; if language gets bogged down, there is confusion. In such cases, broad experience is the provision that can feed poverty [of content], and continuity is the medicine that can save one from confusion. To have breadth and still to be able to provide continuity aids the force of mind.

The variety of states of mind (*ch'ing**) may be peculiar and mixed; the mutations of normative form (*t'i*-pien**) shift just as often. Plain and simple diction may be made pregnant by some artful truth (*yi**); commonplace matters may be brought to sprout by fresh concepts. Compare hempen cloth to threads of hemp—though some might say the latter are of little value, when shuttle and loom set their achievement before us, it is prized for its glittering brightness.

The final paragraph above draws heavily on Lu Chi's "Poetic Exposition on Literature," and shows a discontinuity of argument closer to Lu than is generally characteristic of Liu Hsieh. It is not at all clear what the transformations of forms and states of mind have to do with rescuing the bland by some timely flourish. Likewise, the qualifications regarding the limits of language and conscious technique in the next paragraph comes directly from Lu Chi.

至於思表纖旨。文外曲致。言所不追。筆固知止。至精而後闡其妙。至變而後通其數。伊摯不能言鼎。輪扁不能語斤。其微矣乎。

But when it comes to those tenuous implications beyond the reach of thought, the fine variations in sentiment beyond the the text (wen*), these are things that language cannot pursue, and where the writing brush knows well to halt. That subtlety can be brought to light only by reaching ultimate essence; that order (shu*) can be comprehended (t'ung*) only by reaching the ultimate in mutation (pien*). Yi Yin could not tell of the art of the cauldron;[83] Wheelwright Pien could not speak of the ax. These are the real fine points.

Let us quote the relevant passages from "The Poetic Exposition on Literature," first from the preface: "When it comes to taking an ax in hand to chop an ax-handle, the model is not far from you; however, it is hard indeed for language to follow the movements of the hand. What can be put into words is all here." Then towards the end, lines 197–200:

> Liken it to the dancer, flinging her sleeves to the rhythm,
> Or to the singer, sending out her voice in response to the strings.
> It is this that Wheelwright Pien could not put into words,
> Nor is even the most glittering discourse able to catch its essence.

Although there are difficulties in both passages, Lu Chi is clearly referring to the prereflective aspects of the act of composition, aspects that cannot be expressed in words. Liu Hsieh is using similar terms, but the frame of reference is far less clear. The last part of the paragraph seems to return to Lu Chi's interest in accounting for composition, but the first part is more problematic. It may be making a general statement on the limitations of writing: the subtleties of what is dimly perceived in spirit thought ("tenuous implications beyond the reach of thought") cannot be transmitted in literature. Or it may refer to the limitations of writing about writing: there are subtleties conveyed in literary writing, though not in explicit words, which the critic cannot explain ("fine variations in sentiment beyond the text"). We remain uncertain whether it is the writer's brush that must stop (faced with wonders he cannot describe) or the critic's (finding in the text wonders he cannot describe). The decision here is less important than the promise that there is some wonder, either on the margins of thought or the margins of writing, which is the goal of a perfected attention that "reaches the ultimate in mutation."

神用象通。情變所孕。物以貌求。心以理應。刻鏤聲律。萌芽比興。結慮司契。垂帷制勝。

Supporting Verse
    Spirit gets through by images (*hsiang**),
    Giving birth to mutations of the affections.[84]
    Things are sought by their outer appearance,
    But the response of mind is for basic principle.
    Craftsmanship is given to the rules of sound,
    It sprouts in comparisons and affective images:
    Drawing one's thoughts together, take the creditor's half of the contract,
    And behind hanging tent-flaps determine victories.[85]

CHAPTER 27
Nature and Form, T'i-hsing 體性

"Nature and Form" takes up two of the central concerns in Chinese literary thought: how the internal characteristics of the individual writer become manifest in writing and the status of normative categories. As so often in Liu Hsieh, these questions are addressed by a single character term that permits shifting frames of reference. In this case the central term is *t'i**, normative form. On the most general level any individuating nature (*hsing**) will become manifest in a particular normative form; for instance, "human nature" (*jen-hsing**) produces the "human form" (*jen-t'i**). Human mind (*hsin**) admits further categorical distinctions in typologies of personality; and such differences will be manifest in *wen**, mind's externality, which is literature. We should stress that even though Liu Hsieh is speaking here primarily of categories of personality, the principle is an exceedingly broad one and can easily be applied to literary historical periods, kinds of social situations, and other categories, all of which will be said to have their own *t'i**.

The question of the relation between categorical norm and absolute particularity is a central issue in Chinese literary thought, as it is not in Western literary thought (except perhaps in the interpretation of poetry as the universal unfolding itself in the particular). English and European languages find no difficulty in using the word "style" to refer both to a normative style, such as the "classical style," and to the particular stylistic traits of a given work. In Chinese, these two are kept quite distinct: *t'i** is always normative style, while the particular style of a given work is described with a variety of terms, all following from the variability of *t'i** according to particular circumstances. The concept of *t'i** stresses a norm that is inherent and prior to any particular manifestation; it carries a force that participates in the unfolding of a particular manifestation, and it can be identified within a particular manifestation; but it is not itself the particularity of that manifestation. On the other hand, Western literary thought makes a sharp distinction between style and genre; at this stage in Chinese literary thought, no such distinction is made; both are *t'i**. Even later in the tradition, when distinctions between normative style and genre begin to be made, it is carried out within the concept of *t'i**: for example, "the various *t'i** distinguished by the criterion of period." To preserve this focus of interest, we have chosen the awkward locution "normative form" for *t'i**.

夫情動而言形。理發而文見。蓋沿隱以至顯。因內而符外者也。

When the affections (*ch'ing**) are stirred, language gives them [external] form (*hsing**);[86] when inherent principle (*li**) comes forth, pattern (*wen**) is manifest. We follow a course from what is latent and arrive at the manifest.[87] According to what lies within, there is correlation to what lies without.

The opening paragraph of a chapter of *Wen-hsin tiao-lung* lays the groundwork for the question to be discussed, often relating the question to accepted assumptions or to a recapitulation of earlier points. Here, in what is perhaps its most succinct and direct form, the theory of manifestation and correlation is given. Language, the human capacity that follows from the existence of mind, is the "outside" of the affections (*ch'ing**); *wen** is the outside of principle (*li**), which is the position established in "Its Source in the Way." All internal terms move to external manifestation, and there is perfect correspondence between the inner and outer terms. These are the articles of faith and ground rules on which the mainstream of Chinese literary thought is founded.

The central terms of this process, given in the title, are *hsing**, "individuating nature" (to be kept distinct from the *hsing** in the paragraph above meaning "external form") and *t'i**, "normative form." *Hsing**, "individuating nature," is the internal term, some natural endowment that determines the category of an entity and from which certain qualities follow. *Jen-hsing** 人性 is "human nature," the innate qualities that separate a human from other creatures. *T'i** is the term that is given as the external counterpart of *hsing**, some normative manifestation whose determinations correspond to the determinations of *hsing**. Thus a person who is, say, modest "by nature" (*hsing**) will have a certain "style," *t'i**, of writing and behavior. This is not to say that such a person might not, on certain occasions, be brash; furthermore, there are higher degrees of determination and particularity in that person's individual nature and in a given circumstance. *Hsing** and *t'i** are simply the large categories of identity on which these more particular determinations are based. And, as we will see, there is a strong impulse to limit the number of these large categories and to find an internal order in that number.

In this chapter, *t'i** lies between a normative category of personality and of literary style; but it can be applied to any normative category, the most common being genre. Partially through this range of meaning, Chinese criticism often came to associate individual writers with the genres in which they excelled. But *t'i** can be applied to almost any norm. In a later chapter, Liu Hsieh discusses "latency" (*yin*), a sense that something is hidden beneath the text; when he thinks of it as a "kind" of writing, he calls it a *t'i**.

然才有庸儁。氣有剛柔。學有淺深。習有雅鄭。並情性所鑠。陶染所凝。是以筆區雲譎。文苑波詭者矣。故辭理庸儁。莫能翻其才。風趣剛柔。寧或改其氣。事義淺深。未聞乖其學。體式雅鄭。鮮有反其習。各師成心。其異如面。

But talent (*ts'ai**) varies between mediocrity and excellence; *ch'i** varies between the firm and the yielding; learning varies between the shallow and the profound; practice [or "habit"] varies between the crude and the gracious. These all are smelted in the forge by one's nature and disposition (*hsing**-*ch'ing**), and fused by how a person has been shaped and influenced. Thus, there are extraordinary cloud shapes in the realm of the writing brush, and in the garden of letters, strange waves.

But no one can countervail against the measure of talent evidenced in the mediocrity or excellence of the principles (*li**) or the use of language (*tz'u**). No one can alter the quality of *ch'i** in the firm or yielding disposition of someone's manner (*feng**-*ch'ü**).[88] I've never heard of anyone running contrary to the degree of learning apparent in the shallowness or profundity of [knowledge of] events and truths (*yi**). Few reverse habits of crudeness or grace in form (*t'i**). Each person takes as his master his mind as it has been fully formed, and these are as different as faces.

From the universal principles in the opening sentences, Liu Hsieh here sets forth the categories through which differentiation occurs. The four categories are roughly divided into two pairs, one pair being innate (talent and the quality of *ch'i**) and the other acquired (learning and habit). Each category admits its own range of antithetical qualities.

It is important to note that Liu Hsieh is speaking here of the stage when an individual's character is fully formed, and at this stage none of the four are open to human freedom; that is, what a person has learned is given as a historical determinacy just as innate qualities are a natural determinacy. Liu

Hsieh stresses this in the second paragraph above, ruling out all hope of self-transformation (and laying the groundwork for the description of learning to write in the later part of the chapter). The innate terms are said to be "smelted" in the forge of a person's nature, probably emphasizing the perfect integration of the two first categories. Then they are "fused" or "hardened" together with "learning" and "habit" in the history of a person's growth. The metaphor of metallurgy stresses the firmness of those determinations.

Traditional Chinese ontogenies such as this try to move from unified origins to the infinite variations and differences of the empirical world. Essential in this process is a mediating structure with a fixed number of norms: hence the eight *t'i** given in the next passage. There is always a leap between that fixed "number" and the vision of infinite variety: here the "extraordinary (*chüeh*, "weird") cloud shapes" and "strange waves," both being standard images of infinite plasticity and transformation. The fascination with infinite variety and fixed norms is a Janus face, each opposing vector of attention balancing the dangers inherent in the other. Similar alternations between limitation and ungoverned transformation can be seen in "The Poetic Exposition on Literature."

Somehow in the admixture of these categories we achieve infinite variety: "Each person takes as his master his mind as it has been fully formed, and these are as different as faces." The face simile (cf. "The Poetic Exposition on Literature" ll. 53–54) is a powerful model: it is the outside that shows the inside; it has recognizable categorical groupings while allowing for absolute individuation; and it is something that can retain individuality through complex transformations bound to the contingencies of the moment. Each person takes that established identity "as his master": this is a remarkable statement, and as a pungently aphoristic formulation of a universally recognized but often suppressed truth, it became one of the few phrases in *Wen-hsin tiao-lung* that entered the repertoire of the culture. In the background we can hear Ts'ao P'i, also concerned with categorical differentiation, observing how people prize their own strengths. The "master" or "teacher," *shih*, is supposed to be the authoritative other who can redirect the momentum of a person's development; but in the adult, that momentum is beyond outside influence.

From absolute individuation, Liu Hsieh turns back to the limited "number" of norms that will govern differentiation and make it comprehensible.

若總其歸塗。則數窮八體。一曰典雅。二曰遠奧。三曰精約。四曰顯附。五曰繁縟。六曰壯麗。七曰新奇。八曰輕靡。典雅者。鎔式經誥。方軌儒門者也。遠奧者。馥采典文。經理玄宗者也。精約者。覈字省句。剖析毫釐者也。顯附者。辭直義暢。切理厭心者也。繁縟者。博喻釀采。煒燁枝派者也。壯麗者。高論宏裁。卓爍異采者也。新奇者。擯古競今。危側趣詭者也。輕靡者。浮文弱植。縹緲附俗者也。故雅與奇反。奧與顯殊。繁與約舛。壯與輕乖。文辭根葉。苑囿其中矣。

If we can generalize about the paths followed,[89] we find that the number (shu*) is complete in eight normative forms: tien-ya*, decorous [or "having the quality of canonical writing"] and dignified; yüan-ao, obscure and far-reaching; ching-yüeh, terse and essential; hsien-fu, obvious and consecutive; fan-ju, lush and profuse; chuang-li, vigorous and lovely; hsin-ch'i, novel and unusual; ch'ing-mi, light and delicate. The decorous and dignified form is one that takes its mold from the Classics and Pronouncements and rides in company with the Confucian school. The obscure and far-reaching form is one whose bright colors (ts'ai*) are covered over, whose writing is decorous, and one that devotes itself to the mysterious doctrines.[90] The terse and essential form is one that examines every word and reflects on each line, making discriminations by the finest measures.[91] The obvious and consecutive form is one in which the language is direct and where the truths (yi*) are spread out before us, satisfying the mind by adherence to natural principle (li*). The lush and profuse form is one with broad implications (yü) in its variegated colors, whose branches and tributaries sparkle and gleam. The vigorous and lovely form is one whose lofty discourses and grand judgments have superlative flash and rare colors. The novel and unusual form is one that rejects the old and rushes instead after what is modern; off-balance, it shows delight in the bizarre. The light and delicate form is one whose insubstantial ornament (wen*) is not securely planted, whose airy vagueness is close to the common taste. We see that the dignified is set in opposition to the unusual; the obscure differs from the obvious; the lush and terse are at odds; the vigorous and light go against one another. Such is the root and leaf of literature (wen*-tz'u*), and the garden of letters contains them all.

Each of these normative forms is quite distinct and recognizable as such in the context of the Chinese tradition. We might note the procedures briefly: from infinite variation, Liu Hsieh returns to name a fixed "number," then each of these is briefly amplified, after which he turns back again to show the internal unity of the eight, reducing the fixed "number" to four pairs. If the reader is accustomed to the rhythms of a Chinese argument by this point, he can anticipate the next move: a return toward infinite variation.

若夫八體屢遷。功以學成。才力居中。肇自血氣。氣以實志。志以定言。吐納英華。莫非情性。

These eight forms often shift,[92] but success in each is accomplished by learning. The force of one's talent (ts'ai*-li) is located within and begins with ch'i* in the blood; ch'i* solidifies [or "actualizes," shih*] that upon which one is intent (chih*); and that upon which one is intent determines language. The splendor that is given forth in this process is always a person's affections and nature (*hsing**-*ch'ing**).

Liu Hsieh returns to affirm the organic bond between a person's physiological and psychological nature, a literary work, and the mediating normative forms, at the same time drawing in the grounds of differentiation discussed earlier: learning, talent, and *ch'i**. *Hsi*, "habit" or "practice," is a problem point, a locus of change, and Liu Hsieh will take it up later. The normative forms shift, let us say from situation to situation; and successful use of a form depends on learning. It is remotely possible that the first statement of the passage means that a person depends on talent to make successful use of the form that matches his nature. But the most natural way to read the line raises a possibility that Liu Hsieh will take up later: that it is possible for a person to write successfully in different forms. This strongly recalls Ts'ao P'i's notion of the *t'ung'-ts'ai**, the "comprehensive talent," one who can pass through and comprehend all the variations. Since Liu Hsieh has already strongly affirmed limitation, that "each person takes as his master his mind as it has been fully formed, " he will have to discover the possibility of the *t'ung**-*ts'ai** elsewhere, in a proper education. This is the beginning of an interest that we see often in later poetics, as in Yen Yü's "Ts'ang-lang's Remarks on Poetry": success in poetry depends upon a process of learning in which the initial orientation is of the utmost importance.

Liu Hsieh's literary physiology is a combination of conventional physiology and some suggestive lines from the *Tso chuan*.[93] *Ts'ai** is a pure capacity, without any force of its own. To manifest itself, it requires *ch'i**; and in Chinese physiology, *ch'i** is carried in the blood stream, a vital essence that is both energy and "stuff." Given capacity (*ts'ai**) and energy (*ch'i**), the other requisite term is direction; and this is supplied by *chih**, "that upon which the mind is intent." Without talent and *ch'i**, *chih** is only an "empty" form of direction: *ch'i** fills it and makes it actual. When all these occur together, they emerge in language. Finally Liu Hsieh makes the recursive move, concluding that all the force and beauty we see in literary works follows directly from the inner condition. At this point in the structure of a *Wen-hsin tiao-lung* chapter, it is appropriate for Liu Hsieh to offer a set of examples to prove his point. This he does in the following section, in a series of twelve perfectly parallel judgments.

是以賈生俊發。故文潔而體清。長卿傲誕。故理侈而辭溢。子雲沈寂。故志隱而味深。子政簡易。故趣昭而事博。孟堅雅懿。故裁密而思靡。平子淹通。故慮周而藻密。仲宣躁銳故穎出而才果。公幹氣褊。故言壯而情駭。嗣宗俶儻。故響逸而調遠。叔夜儁俠。故興高而采烈。安仁輕敏。故鋒發而韻流。士衡矜重。故情繁而辭隱。觸類以推。表裏必符。豈非自然之恆資。才氣之大略哉。

Chia Yi [200–168 B.C.] came forth grandly; thus his writing (*wen**) was terse and its form (*t'i**) lucid.

Ssu-ma Hsiang-ju was proud and brash, thus in natural principle (*li**) he was extravagant and in diction (*tz'u**) excessive.

Yang Hsiung was brooding and still; thus his intent (*chih**) was latent and the flavor (*wei**) deep.

Liu Hsiang [77–6 B.C.] was plain and simple, thus his interest (*ch'ü**) was patent and the [factual] matters (*shih**) were extensive.

Pan Ku [32–92] was dignified and virtuous; thus his cutting to pattern was careful and his thought attained the delicate points.

Chang Heng was profound and comprehensive (*t'ung**); thus his considerations were all-encompassing and his rhetoric dense.

Wang Ts'an was rash and competitive;[94] thus his work was sharp-witted and his talent daring.

Hsü Kan's [170–217] *ch'i** was narrowly focused; thus his words were vigorous and his sentiments (*ch'ing**) were startling.

Juan Chi [210–263] was unrestrained; thus the resonance of his work was aloof and the tone far away.

Hsi K'ang [223–262] was bold and heroic; thus his being stirred (*hsing**) was lofty and the colors (*ts'ai**) blazing.

P'an Yüeh [247–300] was airy and clever, thus the pointedness of his works was in the open, and his rhymes were diffuse.

Lu Chi was grave and serious, thus his sentiments (*ch'ing**) are richly complex and the language (*tz'u**) cryptic.

Investigating each by his kind, we see that outside and inside necessarily correspond. What else can this be other than the constant endowment of Nature (*Tzu-jan**), the general case of the operations of talent and *ch'i**.

It is perhaps ungenerous to note that while the number of normative forms is strictly limited to eight, we are here offered twelve examples, of which only a few clearly correspond to the eight forms. The passage above belongs to a basic form of Chinese criticism for the judgment of personality and style (in other arts as well as writing), and it bears many similarities to the descriptions of individual poetic style in the roughly contemporary "Categories of Poets" by Chung Jung 鍾嶸. In certain ways such paragraph-lists anticipate the lists of variations under a given category in popular criticism of the T'ang and later ages. The terminology used for such appraisals of personality and style has a unique combination of vagueness and precision that always accompanies the perfectly chosen descriptive word: such a word refers to one quality that the competent reader will recognize as distinct from any other descriptive; but because of its very precision, it eludes "definition." It is language used in such a way that all terms of paraphrase are, *a priori*, "not quite it." Such precisions make it virtually impossible fully to grasp the term after fourteen hundred years. The formula of appraisal that Liu Hsieh uses is first to state the name and general manner of the person. Then, using a formal marker of consequence ("thus"), he derives two particular qualities characterizing two aspects of the writer's work. The most important consequence of the formula is perhaps the structural repetition, which reinforces the conclusion that there is always a perfect correspondence between the nature of the person and the qualities of that person's writing. It should also be noted that exactly the same kinds of words are used to describe both personality and style.

夫才有天資。學慎始習。斲梓染絲。功在初化。器成綵定。難可翻移。故童子雕琢。必先雅製。沿根討葉。思轉自圓。八體雖殊。會通合數。得其環中。則輻輳相成。故宜摹體以定習。因性以練才。文之司南。用此道也。

Talent is endowed by Heaven; but in learning, we must take care for early practice: as in carving *tzu* wood or dying silk, success resides in the initial transformation (*hua**). When a vessel is formed or a color is set, it is hard to alter or reverse it. Thus when a child learns to carve, he must first learn dignified (*ya**) construction. Following the roots, we reach the leaves; and the revolutions of thoughts achieve a perfect circle. Though the eight forms differ, there is a way of merging them that comprehends all. If you attain the center of the ring, all the spokes meet there to make the wheel.[95] Thus it is fitting that one imitate normative forms in order to fix practice; then, according to individuating nature, he refines his talent. The compass of *wen** points along this path.

As in Ts'ao P'i's "Discourse on Literature," the discussion of categories of difference leads to the possibility of reunification, the *t'ung**-ts'ai**, the "comprehensive talent." The fact that an adult's *t'i** is determined casts Liu Hsieh back to a a literary education in which a young person's practice may be directed. The metaphors of carving and dyeing are important: "talent," *ts'ai** 才, is essentially the same word as "material" or "timber," *ts'ai** 材; and once the process of carving has begun, future choices are limited by the work already done. In the same way, a person has a "basic color," *pen**-se**, which can be dyed; but all subsequent dyeings and additions of color must work on the color applied previously. But how can any "direction" be given that does not inherently limit? Liu Hsieh offers two answers, which, though not in conflict, are weighted very differently. First, in the range of normative forms, some have priority over others, "elder brothers": the "dignified," *ya**, mode is one such. And by choosing to begin with a form that has "priority," the student may learn the list as a lineage, "following the roots to reach the leaves," thus learning all the forms. In this way, synchronic difference is made diachronic. But this progression must engage a new notion of practice, one in which stages do not pile on top of preceding stages like a series of eight dyes applied in sequence to one piece of cloth. To resolve this problem, Liu Hsieh shifts the metaphor to one in which the student stands apart from any single determination, stands at the center of the wheel and can conditionally enter into any limited form. But we must note what has happened; now instead of normative form following organically from individuating nature, normative form has become a role to play: "Thus it is fitting that one imitate normative forms in order to fix practice." The balancing clause, "according to individuating nature, he refines his talent," is ambiguous: it may be that Liu Hsieh is saying that the student refines his talent "according to the individuating nature of that form"; but it is also possible that Liu is trying to return here to some notion of individuality prior to education, in which case we would translate it "according to *his* individuating nature." And we note that "talent," previously an endowment from Heaven that could not be changed, has now become something open to "refinement." Liu Hsieh concludes in the same confident, authoritative voice with which he began, but he has trapped himself in some of the oldest questions of the tradition: the relation of learning and natural behavior, the capacity to be both many and one. Yet that confident voice is secretly aware of the difficulty, and tries once more to smooth it over, making a statement in the penultimate line of the adjunct verse that pretends to resolve the issue.

才性異區。文辭繁詭。辭為膚根。志實骨髓。雅麗黼黻。淫巧朱紫。習亦凝真。功沿漸靡。

Supporting Verse
    Talents with individual natures have differing realms,
    The forms of literature are profuse and various.
    The words used are skin and sinew,
    Intent is solid bone and marrow.
    Patterned ritual robes have dignity and beauty;
    Vermilion and purple are a corrupting artfulness;[96]
    Yet practice may firmly set what is genuine,
    And from that true accomplishment gradually follows.

CHAPTER 28
Wind and Bone, Feng*-ku* 風骨

The compound "wind and bone," *feng*-ku**, has a long and complicated history in Chinese discourse on literature. That history begins prior to *Wen-hsin tiao-lung*, but the most common associations of the term developed only later.[97] Originally and in this chapter, feng*-ku* was a quality that could or should be found in all literature; later its presence came to suggest one particular quality, an affective directness that marked a poetic lineage traced back to the poetry of Chien-an and Wei (the last decade of the second century and the first half of the third century). "Wind," feng*, carried a heavy freight of associations from the exegetical tradition surrounding the *Book of Songs*. "Bone," ku*, originally related to physiognomy, had less of a history by the time of Liu Hsieh, but was already becoming an established term in aesthetics. The history of these terms is not, however, of central importance to understanding this chapter: Liu Hsieh transforms them, and by the logic of presumed antithetical relation in many of his chapter titles, directs them along paths rather different from the ways they were used, both independently and in compound, in earlier and later periods. Though compelled by the rhetorical structure of his chapters to define the terms against one another, he must at the same time account for them as a unity (since the terms were already a compound) and treat them as complementary, naming a positive quality that a work should have.

詩總六義。風冠其首。斯乃化感之本源。志氣之符契也。是以怊悵述情。必始乎風。沈吟鋪辭。莫先於骨。故辭之待骨。如體之樹骸。情之含風。猶形之包氣。緒言端直。則文骨成焉。意氣駿爽。則文風生焉。若豐藻克贍。風骨不飛。則振采失鮮。負聲無力。是以綴慮裁篇。務盈守氣。剛健既實。輝光乃新。其為文用。譬征鳥之使翼也。

The *Book of Songs* encompasses "Six Principles," of which "wind" (feng*, the "Airs" section) is the first. This is the original source of stirring (kan*) and transformation (hua*), and it is the counterpart of intent (chih*) and ch'i*.[98] The transmission of the disconsolate feelings (ch'ing*) always begins with wind; but nothing has priority over bone's disposing the words (tz'u*), as one intones them thoughtfully.[99] The way in which the words depend upon bone is like the way in which the skeleton is set in the [human] form (t'i*). And the quality of wind contained in the affections is like the way our shape holds ch'i* within it. When words are put together straight through, then the bone of writing (wen*-ku*) is complete therein; when concept (yi*) and ch'i* are swift and vigorous, then the wind of writing (wen*-feng*) is born therein.[100] If a piece of writing is abundantly supplied with elegant phrasing, but lacks wind and bone to fly, then it loses all luster when it shows its coloration (ts'ai*) and lacks the force to carry any resonance.[101] Thus in composing one's reflections and in cutting a piece to pattern, it is essential to conserve a plenitude of ch'i*. Only when its firm strength has become solid (shih*) will its radiance be fresh. We may compare its [wind and bone] function in literature to the way in which a bird of prey uses its wings.

Liu Hsieh begins his argument, as he often does, by invoking origins, in this case the affective function of *feng** in the *Book of Songs*, as interpreted by the "Great Preface": "'Airs' are 'Influence'; it is 'to teach.' By influence it stirs them; by teaching it transforms them." But Liu Hsieh was a master at twisting his authoritative source passages to his own use. The echoes of the great Confucian project of moral education are soon revealed to be concern with a more general affective power in literature. Classical exegetes had agreed that the positioning of *Feng** as the first of the "Six Principles" was a mark of its primary importance. Liu Hsieh cites this solely for the purpose of proving that *feng** is indeed important; he has no intention of asserting that *feng** is any more important than *ku* or than the categories in the other chapters. Much is made of Liu Hsieh's "Confucian" point of view; there are indeed aspects of *Wen-hsin tiao-lung* that can be properly characterized as "Confucian," but in many cases Liu Hsieh is simply borrowing the authority of canonical texts to support much broader positions. Confucian *feng** had an ethical center; *feng** here does not.

For Liu Hsieh *feng** is essentially the affective force of a literary work, the "wind" that is "vital breath," *ch'i**, set in motion and directed outward. In this sense it is, as he says, "the original source of stirring and transformation." *Chih**, which gives direction (as the mind is directed to something by "being intent upon" it), and *ch'i**, which imparts energy, find their external counterpart in *feng** (which is externalized and energized *ch'i** with direction). The analogy between the affections (*ch'ing**) containing *feng** and the body ("shape," *hsing**) containing *ch'i** shifts the model but clarifies the term: *ch'i** is what gives the body motion and force. In the same way when we perceive the affections in a literary work, it is the affective power of *feng** that animates it.

"Bone" is an animate integrity in the text, something that holds it together, as the skeleton holds the body together, a structure that allows for motion. Its virtues are unity and hardness. Commentators often identify it with a structural unity of argument; but it is also a manner, an unalterable sequence of propositions that seems to possess firm strength, and, as one would say in English, "holds together."

The image of the bird of prey is significant: wind and bone in conjunction are complementary qualities of animate force, but in themselves they lack sensuous allure or attractiveness; they constitute that quality in a work that moves us without necessarily attracting us. In the appreciation that follows from attraction, duration is important: one "plays with" the text or "rolls it over" (*wan* 玩). With "wind and bone" the effect is immediate and it leaves an "impression" (in the root sense), distinct from (though not necessarily excluding) the reflective distance of appreciation, which is the attraction that follows from "coloration."

故練於骨者。析辭必精。深乎風者。述情必顯。捶字堅而難移。結響凝而不滯。此風骨之力也。若瘠義肥辭。繁雜失統。則無骨之徵也。思不環周。索莫乏氣。則無風之驗也。

One who has refined the bone of the work must keep to the essentials in argument;[102] one who has attained depth in wind must transmit the affections clearly. In the first case, the words have been pounded so firmly that they cannot be moved; in the second case, the resonance will be knit fixedly and not get bogged down—this is the force of wind and bone. If the truths (*yi**) are emaciated but the phrasing fat—a profusion indiscriminately mixed and lacking all governing coherence—then we see no evidence of bone. If the thought (*ssu**) does not go full circle—dull, lifeless, lacking *ch'i**—then we see no evidence of wind.

Having defined each term, Liu Hsieh now shows their mutual dependence: each one fails in some essential way without the other. Note that both qualities are associated with motion. "Wind," in particular, keeps the text from getting "bogged down." "Bone", by holding a shape, keeps the text from scattering or meandering.

昔潘勗錫魏。思摹經典。羣才韜筆。乃其骨髓峻也。相如賦仙。氣號淩雲。蔚為辭宗。迺其風力遒也。能鑒斯要。可以定文。茲術或違。無務繁采。故魏文稱文以氣為主。氣之清濁有體。不可力強而致。故其論孔融。則云體氣高妙。論徐幹。則云時有齊氣。論劉楨。則云有逸氣。公幹亦云。孔氏卓卓。信含異氣。筆墨之性。殆不可勝。並重氣之旨也。夫翬翟備色而翾翥百步。肌豐而力沈也。鷹隼乏采而翰飛戾天。骨勁而氣猛也。文章才力。有似于此。若風骨乏采。則鷙集翰林。采乏風骨。則雉竄文囿。唯藻耀而高翔。固文筆之鳴鳳也。

Long ago when P'an Hsü [ca. 165–215] wrote [on behalf of of the Han Emperor] a Grant of Honor for the Duke of Wei [Ts'ao Ts'ao, 155–220], his literary thought aspired to emulate the Classical canons, and all other persons of talent hid their writing brushes: this was due to the excellence of bone and marrow in his work. When Ssu-ma Hsiang-ju wrote his poetic exposition on the immortal ["The Poetic Exposition on the Great Man," presented to Han Wu-ti], people declared that his *ch'i** passed up over the clouds, and they found splendor in his mastery of language (*tz'u**): this was the firmness of the force of wind in his work. If a person sees the essential points clearly here, he can perfect his writing; but should he stray from this technique, there's nothing to be gained from lush coloration (*ts'ai**). For this reason, Ts'ao P'i claimed, "In literature *ch'i** is the dominant factor. *Ch'i** has its normative forms—clear and murky. It is not to be brought by force." Thus when he discussed K'ung

Jung, he said that his "form and *ch'i** are lofty and subtle." And when he discussed Hsü Kan, he said that "at times he shows languid *ch'i**."[103] In discussing Liu Chen, Ts'ao P'i says that he has "an untrammeled *ch'i**";[104] and Liu Chen himself said, "K'ung Jung is superlative and truly has an unusual *ch'i** within him; it would hardly be possible to surpass him in the nature of his brushwork." All of them laid stress on the significance of *ch'i**. The pheasant has a full complement of colors, but it can flutter only a hundred paces—its force gives out because its flesh is fat. A falcon lacks bright colors, but it flies high, to the very heavens—its bone is sturdy and its *ch'i** is fierce. The force of talent in literary works bears resemblance to these examples. If wind and bone lack bright coloration, we have a bird of prey roosting in the forest of letters. And if bright colors lack wind and bone, we have a pheasant hiding away in the literary garden. Only with glittering rhetoric and high soaring do we really have a singing phoenix in writing.

Liu Hsieh's examples show that his notion of "wind" is very close to the quality of *ch'i**, as stressed by Ts'ao P'i, among others. In another chapter (which I have not translated), Liu Hsieh himself discusses "The Nurturing of *Ch'i**"; but in this case, *ch'i** is the potential force stored up in the self; he reserves the term "wind" for that force in affective action.

Liu Hsieh manages to draw wind and bone together into a complementary unity by contrasting them with a third quality, rhetorical flourish or "bright coloration" (*ts'ai**), a topic he will take up in a later chapter. *Ts'ai** is the term of allure. But although what has *ts'ai** attracts us, it does not exert any active, transformative force upon us in its own right: one might say it "flatters" our predispositions. Liu Hsieh's expository procedures are particularly clear in this sequence of three terms. First two terms, "wind" and "bone," are defined against one another, then reconciled to a unity. This unity, however, implies a deficiency on another level, a deficiency supplied by the introduction of *ts'ai**, "coloration." This leads to yet another level of complementary unity, of force (wind and bone) and allure (coloration) combined, in the image of the phoenix.

若夫鎔鑄經典之範。翔集子史之術。洞曉情變。曲昭文體。然後能孚甲新意。雕畫奇辭。
昭體故意新而不亂。曉變故辭奇而不黷。若骨采未圓。風辭未練。而跨略舊規。馳騖新
作。雖獲巧意。危敗亦多。豈空結奇字。紕繆而成經矣。周書云。辭尚體要。弗惟好異。
蓋防文濫也。然文術多門。各適所好。明者弗授。學者弗師。於是習華隨侈。流遁忘反。
若能確乎正式。使文明以健。則風清骨峻。篇體光華。能研諸慮。何遠之有哉。

When one casts and molds according to the model of the Classics, or soars and roosts among the techniques of the thinkers and historians, then one will comprehend the mutations of the affections (*ch'ing**-*pien**), and one will have revealed the forms of literature (wen*-t'i*) in their minute particulars. Only then can one cause fresh concepts (yi*) to sprout; only then can one carve out and paint wondrous phrasing (tz'u*). Having the forms revealed means that concepts will be fresh but not in disarray; comprehending the mutations means that phrasing will be wondrous without getting muddy. But if bone and coloration are not fully perfected, if wind and phrasing are not polished, and a writer strides proudly over all former rules to go rushing after fresh creations—in such cases, even though one may attain some clever concept, danger and ruin usually follow. A hollow construction of strange words, full of error, cannot become a Classic. The *Book of Documents* says, "In diction value embodying the essentials; do not develop a passion for [mere] difference." This is to prevent excess in literature.

There are many ways into the techniques of literature, and each person suits his own preferences. Those who understand are not taught; those who study have no teacher. Therefore one who becomes habituated to glitter and goes off into excess will drift away and never return. But if one can become firm in the proper models and make his writing bright [*ming*, "showing comprehension and manifestly comprehensible"] and firm, then the wind will be clear, and the bone, splendid; and the form of the piece will shimmer. Accomplishment will not be far to anyone who works at these considerations.

贊曰。情與氣偕。辭共體並。文明以健。珪璋乃聘。蔚彼風力。嚴此骨鯁。才鋒峻立。符采克炳。

Supporting Verse
>When affections and ch'i* are are joined together,
>When phrasing goes together with form,
>"The writing is bright and firm,"
>A fine piece of jade is presented.[105]
>The force of wind is rich,
>The boniness is stern.
>Talent's spearhead stands high,
>And matching coloration gleams.

CHAPTER 29
Continuity and Mutation, T'ung-pien 通變

The terms "continuity" (t'ung*) and "mutation" (pien*) belong to the technical vocabulary describing the operations of hexagrams in the *Book of Changes*. T'ung* occurs when a broken or unbroken line retains its character in the next position (i.e., in the upward reading of the lines that is both the synchronic and diachronic structure of the hexagram); pien* occurs when the quality of the line changes to its opposite. These same terms are further used to describe more complex operations in the relations of the hexagrams. Most significant for Liu Hsieh's discussion, *t'ung** and *pien** became key concepts in the "philosophy" of the *Book of Changes* as expounded in the appendix, the *Hsi-tz'u chuan*. As often with such paired concepts, the relation between the two terms is fluid. At times they are antithetical; at times, complementary; at times, identified. We read in the *Hsi-tz'u chuan*: "to transform and to interrupt [a process] are what we mean by 'mutation' (*pien**); to push forward and carry it out is what we mean by 'continuity' (*t'ung**)." *Hsi-tz'u chuan* also observes, however, that "in the *Book of Changes*, when it [i.e., a phase of process, a line of a hexagram, a hexagram itself] is exhausted, it mutates; by mutation it achieves continuity ("carries on," *t'ung**); by continuity it endures long." In Liu Hsieh's chapter, at times we have "continuity versus mutation"; at times we have "achieving continuity by mutation"; at times we have "carrying through (*t'ung**) mutation.[106]

Not only is the relation between the terms fluid, their application is very broad. Although Liu Hsieh draws his examples from literary history, the terms can refer to very different aspects of literature: to the development of a single work, or to an author's oeuvre as a whole, or to the variation between authors in a particular period.

夫設文之體有常。變文之數無方。何以明其然耶。凡詩賦書記。名理相因。此有常之體也。文辭氣力。通變則久。此無方之數也。名理有常。體必資於故實。通變無方。數必酌於新聲。故能騁無窮之路。飲不竭之源。然綆短者銜渴。足疲者輟塗。非文理之數盡。乃通變之術疏耳。故論文之方。譬諸草木。根幹麗士而同性。臭味晞陽而異品矣。

Although there are constants in the forms (*t'i**) in which literature is given, there is no limit to the mutations (*pien**) they may undergo. How can we understand why this is so? In the poem, in the poetic exposition, in the letter, and in the memoir, the name and the basic principle (*li**) depend on one another: these are examples of forms (*t'i**) in which there are constants. But phrasing (*wen*-tz'u**) and the force of *ch'i** endure long only by continuities (*t'ung**) and mutations (*pien**):[107] of these there are limitless numbers.

Since there are constants in name and basic principle, the forms are necessarily endowed with some prior substance;[108] but since the continuities and mutations are limitless, their number must always be infused with new sounds. In this way, we can gallop along an endless road yet drink from an inexhaustible source. The person whose well-rope is too short will suffer thirst; the person whose feet tire will stop on the road—in such cases, it is not that the variety of principle in literature (*wen*-li**) has been exhausted, but rather that the technique of continuity and mutation is weak. Literature may be discussed through an analogy to plants and trees: root and trunk cleave to the soil and share a common nature [i.e., each species or category]; but according to the exposure to sunlight, the kinds of fragrance and flavor will differ.[109]

One of the central issues in Chinese literary thought is the relation between norm and particular. This relation is usually explained as a process of change from a primordial unity to some orderly structure of norms, and thence to the infinite variety of the world. Continuous binary division is one structure that accounts for this fragmentation of the world, so that the particular relates to its normative category on the model of a family lineage. A variation on the structure of binary division, the variation that Liu Hsieh chooses here, is to limit the process of division to the production of one orderly structure of norms (e.g., the Classics or the eight normative styles in "Nature and Form"), and to explain the particularity of the world as infinite variation upon those norms.

The opening of the "Continuity and Mutation" chapter addresses precisely this question of norm and variation. In Chapter 27, "Nature and Form," *t'i** were normative styles; here, as the examples of poem, poetic exposition, letter, and memoir make clear, *t'i** refers to what we would call genre. Each genre or *t'i** is based on some natural principle (*li**) that is revealed in its name. For example, the name for the poem or poetry (*shih*), by pseudo-etymological diaresis of the character, is held to incorporate the canonical definition that "the poem articulates what is intently on the mind"; thus the *t'i** or genre "poetry" follows from a natural principle operating in the human psyche.

The paired primary terms, *tung** and *pien**, are joined together by the introduction of a third term, a "constant" (in this case, *t'i**) that includes both possibilities. It is important to distinguish "continuity" (*t'ung**) from the "constant" *t'i** (and allied concepts such as [basic] "principle," *li**). "Constants" retain identity through time and variation yet possess a degree of indeterminacy or flexibility that allows for both "continuity" and "mutation." *T'ung** is precisely the element of "continuing": its content might be points of identity with previous phases, or it might be the more abstract "capacity to continue," which is achieved by mutation itself (this latter version following from the dictum in the *Hsi-tz'u chuan* that "when it is exhausted, it mutates; by mutation it carries on"). But *t'ung** is particularized, as the constant *t'i** are not. There are two possible truths about change as it occurs in literature: either it is driven by its own internal laws or it occurs in response to external circumstance. The conclusion of the passage above suggests the latter truth, which is embodied in another passage from the *Hsi-tz'u chuan*: "Mutation and continuity occur according to the requirements of the moment." That is, the operation of these principles demands a flexibility in responding to a given situation, just as plants and trees dispose themselves most advantageously to make the best of their surroundings. But the rules of exposition will lead Liu Hsieh to consider the more problematic alternative truth, that change is an internal law that carries the history of literature ever farther away from its origins. In the following passage, he continues the point above: the core or root remains the same, while external expression changes; but that soon turns into a different historical story.

是以九代詠歌。志合文別。黃歌斷竹。質之至也。唐歌在昔。則廣於黃世。虞歌卿雲。則文於唐時。夏歌雕牆。縟於虞代。商周篇什。麗於夏年。至於序志述時。其揆一也。暨楚之騷文。矩式周人。漢之賦頌。影寫楚世。魏之篇制。顧慕漢風。晉之辭章。瞻望魏采。推而論之。則黃唐淳而質。虞夏質而辨。商周麗而雅。楚漢侈而豔。魏晉淺而綺。宋初訛而新。從質及訛。彌近彌澹。何則。競今疏古。風味氣衰也。今才穎之士。刻意學文。多略漢篇。師範宋集。雖古今備閱。然近附而遠疏矣。夫青生於藍。絳生於蒨。雖踰本色。不能復化。桓君山云。予見新進麗文。美而無採。及見劉揚言辭。常輒有得。此其驗也。故練青濯絳。必歸藍蒨。矯訛翻淺。還宗經誥。斯斟酌乎質文之間。而櫽括乎雅俗之際。可與言通變矣。

In the songs of all nine dynasties, we find unities in what the human mind may be intent upon; but we also find that the external expression (wen*) differs.[110] The song from the period of the Yellow Emperor, which began "Cut the bamboo," was the ultimate in plainness (chih*).[111] The song Tsai-hsi from the reign of Yao is more extensive than the one from the Yellow Emperor's reign.[112] The song "Auspicious Clouds" from the reign of Shun is still more highly patterned (wen*) than that of Yao's reign. And the song from the time of the Hsia Dynasty [which contains the phrase] "decorated walls" is more lush than what we find in Shun's reign. The pieces and suites of pieces from the Shang and Chou [i.e., the *Book of Songs*] are more beautiful (li*) than the works of the days of the Hsia. However, in telling what was on their minds (chih*) and in describing the times, these were all of the same measure. The *Sao* writings of Ch'u take their model from the Chou writers, and the poetic expositions and odes of the Han are a reflection of the times of Ch'u. The compositions of the Wei dynasty look back with admiration to the manner (feng*) of the Han, and the literary works of the Tsin have their eyes on the bright colors of the Wei. Considering this from a broad perspective, [we conclude that] the ages of the Yellow Emperor and Yao were plain and pure, the ages of Shun and Yü were plain but more articulated, the Shang and Chou had a dignified loveliness, the Ch'u and Han works were excessive and sensuous, the Wei and Tsin were shallow and decorative. In the Liu-Sung dynasty, things first became deceptive and a hunger for novelty appeared. From substantive plainness (chih*) on to falseness—the nearer we come to our own times, the more insipid literature becomes. The reason is that people compete for what is contemporary and hold themselves apart from what is ancient: wind is in its final stages and ch'i* declines.

When the most brilliantly talented scholars of this day shape their concepts and study wen*, they usually overlook the works of the Han and take the collected writings of the Liu-Sung period as their model. Even if they have made a thorough survey of past and present writing, still they adhere to what is close to them and distance themselves from what is remote.[113]

The color blue comes from the indigo; maroon comes from the madder: though these colors go beyond the original color (se*), they cannot be further transformed. Huan T'an once said, "I have seen lovely beautiful works offered up recently; I take nothing from them, however lovely they are. But when I see the words of Yang Hsiung and Liu Hsin, I always find something right away." This is a good illustration of what I mean: to get a refined blue and a purified maroon, one must return to the indigo and madder. To straighten the false and confute shallowness, one must return to a reverence for the Classics. One can speak of continuity and mutation only with someone who deliberates carefully between substance (or "plainness," chih*) and pattern (wen*) and who applies the wood-straightener at the juncture between dignity and common-ness.

"Continuity" (t'ung*) and "mutation" (pien*) are broad terms, and they lead Liu Hsieh in several directions. In the section that follows, t'ung* and pien* will refer to a general "kind" of scene that admits varied treatment, as writers look back to their predecessors. In the passage above, however, the terms are used in a truly literary historical frame of reference. The popular literary historical myth of increasing complexity and elaboration in literary writing (a myth parallel to the cosmogony based on binary division towards intricate multiplicity) underlies Liu Hsieh's description of the earliest songs up to the time of the Book of Songs. The "mutations" described are counterbalanced by an affirmation of their unity and continuity: "in telling what was on their minds (chih*) and in describing the times, these were all of the same measure." The next sequence, beginning with the rhapsodies of Ch'u (third century B.C.) and continuing down through the Tsin, is first described in terms of continuity, with each period modeling itself on the preceding period. But when he goes back to consider that history from the large point of view, Liu Hsieh finds only differences, differences that begin to show signs of decline in the Ch'u kingdom and the Han dynasty. In later periods the impulse to model oneself on immediate predecessors produces ever-increasing degrees of failure. Finally Liu Hsieh comes to the recent past, the period beginning with the Liu-Sung, when a new twist occurs: the hunger for novelty, and eagerness for mutation, without the balancing element of continuity. The "wind" of influence and tradition that impels literary history seems to be giving out. From this came the "modern" condition, involving a radical break with the past. Out of this description, we see one of the most important models for change in Wen-hsin tiao-lung and in much later literary thought:

the notion of *pen-se**, "original color." All things have original qualities that permit change and variation, but such variation must occur on the primary ground. Serial variation (X + A, then [X + A] + B, then [X + A + B] + C, etc.) leads, on the model of dyeing, to mere muddiness. On another model (X to A; A to B; B to C, etc.) it leads to an increasing distance from the primary ground, an attenuation of the original qualities that are grounded in natural principle. The proper model of change, which allows for infinite transformation without loss, is continual variation of the original ground (X + A, then X + B, then X + C, etc.). This brings Liu Hsieh back to one of his favorite themes, reverence for the Classics. As the once unified universe unfolded itself into a plurality of norms, then halted division, so literary history has a legitimate process of elaboration and ornamentation to the point at which normative texts are established; these texts are Classics, *ching,* which means "constants." The existence of these Classics does not halt history and change, but they govern the nature of change, defining all variation against those fixed points.

夫跨張聲貌。則漢初已極。自茲厥後。循環相因。雖軒翥出轍。而終入籠內。枚乘七發云。通望兮東海。虹洞兮蒼天。相如上林云。視之無端。察之無涯。日出東沼。月生西陂。馬融廣成云。天地虹洞。固無端涯。大明出東。月生西陂。揚雄校獵云。出入日月。天與地沓。張衡西京云。日月於是乎出入。象扶桑於濛汜。此並廣寓極狀。而五家如一。諸如此類。莫不相循。參伍因革。通變之數也。

The expansive description (*k'ua-chang*) of sounds and the appearances of things reached an extreme early in the Han;[114] thereafter writers followed along as if on a ring: though they might soar high above the wheel tracks [of their predecessors], in the final analysis they remained within the same scope. In the "Seven Stimuli" Mei Sheng wrote:

> My gaze passes far to the Eastern Sea,
> Stretching on continuously to the grey heavens.

In his poetic exposition on Shang-lin Park, Ssu-ma Hsiang-ju wrote:

> I look on limitlessness,
> Examiner of the unbounded,
> Where the sun emerges from its pool in the east,
> And the moon appears over slopes in the west.

Ma Jung, in his panegyric on Kuang-ch'eng Palace, wrote:

> Heaven and Earth, a continuous expanse,
> No limit, no boundary at all:
> A mighty gleaming emerges in the east,
> And the moon appears over slopes in the west.

Yang Hsiung, in his poetic exposition on the Stockade Hunt, wrote:

> Emerging, sinking—sun and the moon,
> And Heaven, remote from the Earth.

Finally, in the poetic exposition on the Western Capital, Chang Heng wrote:

> Then sun and moon emerge and sink back in—
> Images of the Fu-sang Tree [in the far east] and Meng-ssu Pool [in the farthest west].

All five writers are one in describing an immensity. There are many cases of the same sort, and writers always follow one another. Sometimes following, sometimes breaking with precedent—in the intricate mingling of the two is the number of continuity and mutation.

Note that, although in several cases these writers use or vary a predecessor's phrase, the sequence of examples presents different versions of the same kind of scene rather than a serial progression.

是以規略文統。宜宏大體。先博覽以精閱。總綱紀而攝契。然後拓衢路。置關鍵。長轡遠馭。從容按節。憑情以會通。負氣以適變。采如宛虹之奮鬐。光若長離之振翼。迺穎脫之文矣。若乃齷齪於偏解。矜激乎一致。此庭間之迴驟。豈萬里之逸步哉。

To get the general structure of the unity of the literary tradition, one should give broad consideration to its overall form (*t'i*):[115] first, by wide reading to examine the essentials, then by a synthesis of the general principles in order to unify the work. Only after this can one open up highways and paths, and establish securely the bolt on the gates,[116] first galloping afar with loose reins, then ambling and slowing one's rhythm. Relying on his affections (*ch'ing*), one will achieve continuity (*t'ung*); depending on *ch'i* one will move to mutation (*pien*). The work will be brightly colored like the upraised crest of a rainbow and will shake its wings like the redbird. This will be writing that breaks free of confinement. But if one is all cramped up in some one-sided comprehension and boasts excitely of some single accomplishment, then it is circular galloping in a small yard—not the unfettered pace that goes thousands of leagues.

Note the similarity between the passage above and the close of the chapter on "Form and Nature." This is the venerable theme of the "comprehensive talent," which is found earlier in Ts'ao P'i's "Discourse on Literature." There is a relation between the return to origins, to the constant norm that is the "original color," and the capacity to pass through a full range of variations. These primary forms seem more general and open than their variations; and one argument against linear change is that it traps a person in historical determinism, following a single direction or course that leads to one-sidedness. The constant norm is the "center of the wheel" from which movement in all directions becomes possible: from that point which remains "constant" for us, one can perpetually begin. The linguistic analogy might be the difference between using single characters, the primordial word that has many frames of reference, and the compound, a later development that limits the frame of reference and semantic range.

Oddly enough the closing metaphors invert the conventional images: a capacity for infinite variation, achieved by staying close to the original form (described as "the center of the ring" in "Nature and Form") becomes a realized linear motion in the horse "that goes a thousand leagues." In contrast, the limitation that follows from being carried in one direction away from the source is described as "circular galloping in a small yard." Yet the inversion is appropriate, preparing the way for the treatment of "momentum" (shih*) in the following section.

文律運周。日新其業。變則其久。通則不乏。趨時必果。乘機無怯。望今制奇。參古定法。

Supporting Verse

> The rule of literature is to move in full cycle,
> Its accomplishment is found in daily renewal:
> By mutation it can last long;
> By continuity nothing is wanting.
> To seize the right time brings sure decision,
> To take the occasion (*chi**) means no anxiety.
> Looking to the present, construct the marvelous;
> Keep the past in mind to make its laws secure.

CHAPTER 30
Determination of Momentum, Ting-shih 定勢

The term *shih**, translated in the title as "momentum," already had a complex history of usage by the time Liu Hsieh adopted it to play a key role in his sequence of chapters on the unfolding of a literary work. *Shih** is a force that inheres in some thing or event and directs its movement along "the path of least resistance," *li* 利. *Shih** was used in early political discourse as "power," the force that inhered in the actions or disposition of a state or ruler. If we were to describe a political situation in English as "things are looking ominous," early Chinese discourse would most likely have used *shih**, the "momentum of the situation." "Tendency" is sometimes an appropriate translation, though "tendency" lacks the forcefulness and the unfolding temporality of *shih**. In the *Sun-tzu* 孫子, a pre-Ch'in military text, *shih** was an important conceptual term applied to the movements of battle, with advice on how to make best use the "momentum," both of one's own troops and those of the enemy. The concept remained important in the martial arts. The earliest use of *shih** in the realm of aesthetics came in its application to calligraphy (in the second century A.D.), where written characters and the brushstrokes that composed them seemed clearly to embody "lines of force." Thereafter *shih** became a basic category of calligraphic discourse.

It is uncertain when the term was first transferred to literature. Liu Hsieh cites an early third century usage, but there it seems to suggest mere "forcefulness," a particular quality to be described quantitatively, rather than a category admitting distinct qualities. Liu Hsieh's usage of *shih** in this chapter is sophisticated and quite distinct from the term's earlier application in literary, calligraphic, and military discourse. Moreover, Liu Hsieh's is the first written work we have that treats *shih** as an important aspect of literature. The term helps him to solve a very specific problem: how normative forms *(t'i**)* unfold in time, why certain kinds of writing do display or should display certain particular qualities. Instead of using *shih** as a rubric under which a group of kinetic qualities can be named and listed (as it often was in discussions of calligraphy), Liu Hsieh considers the theoretical place of the category itself in relation to *t'i** and *hsing**.

Some attention might be given to the verbal element *ting* 定, "determination." The proper qualities and the proper unfolding of a text are not free, but are "determined" by the given normative form *(t'i**)*. As "Continuity and Mutation" resolved the problem of how norm becomes particular by a notion of infinite variation on a primordial ground, here the discussion considers the way in which normative form determines a particular unfolding.

In the beginning of the chapter, this determinate unfolding is described as an organic process: determinations follow naturally from *t'i**. In other parts of the chapter, however, composition is given as a voluntary act; and in this case there may be a conflict between the "tendencies" *(shih**)* of the literary form or situation and the "tendencies" of the writer. Here "determination" becomes voluntary rather than automatic, and it requires mastery and judgment on the part of the writer, the ability to recognize exactly how something should be according to the demands of the moment and the ability to carry it through. To meet such demands, the tendency *(shih**)* of a particular personality type *(t'i**)* must be re-educated and broadened in order to respond to the direction *(shih**)* of treatment required by a particular occasion and form *(t'i**)*. One of the virtues of Chinese discourse on literature is the way in which its terms are shared by, and thus unify several frames of reference; yet this often creates unresolved difficulties. In this case, the chapter begins with human feelings that lead naturally to a particular *shih** in the text; the chapter ends with advice to the writer to broaden his mastery and overcome his limited natural inclinations in order to be able to respond properly to the demands of the form. It is not impossible to reconcile the two positions, but Liu Hsieh does not do so.

夫情致異區。文變殊術。莫不因情立體。即體成勢也。勢者。乘利而為制也。如機發矢直。澗曲湍回。自然之趣也。圓者規體。其勢也自轉。方者矩形。其勢也自安。文章體勢。如斯而已。

The particular affections that are felt (ch'ing*-chih) differ in kind; there are various techniques in the mutations of literature (wen*-pien*); but in all cases the normative form (t'i*) is set in accordance with the affective state (or "circumstance," ch'ing*); then according to the normative form, a momentum (shih*) is given. Momentum is formed by following the path of least resistance.[118] It is the inclination (ch'ü*) of Nature (Tzu-jan*), like the straightness of a crossbow bolt released from the trigger mechanism (chi*), or the circling movement of swift eddies at the bend of a mountain stream. What is round [referring especially to Heaven] sets the model of a normative form, and, accordingly, its momentum is to rotate on its own accord. What is square [referring especially to Earth] takes that shape as its basis, and its momentum is to be at rest. This is precisely how normative form and momentum operate in a literary work.

The problem with a category such as "normative form" is its atemporality and generality: it can allow us to group phenomena under large headings, but it cannot explain how and why texts unfold in the particular as they do. The concept of "mutation" is one solution to the problem, allowing for a form to shift through variations while retaining its primordial and essential unity. Shih*, "momentum" or "force," is another solution: by its "shape" every normative form has an inherent disposition or tendency to move in a certain way, to show certain qualities, and to unfold itself along certain lines into particulars.

As he often does, Liu Hsieh opens the chapter by recapitulating the relations between terms established in earlier chapters: here it is the relation between the affections and the variations in normative form. But the question of a general "disposition" (stressed in the chapter on "Nature and Form") is gradually being shifted to more particular circumstances as the determining ground of the text's unfolding. We should note that in the opening line Liu Hsieh chooses the compound ch'ing*-chih, translated as "the particular affections that are felt." This refers to one's "sentiments" in a specific circumstance, whereas the single word ch'ing* may have the more categorical sense of one's "disposition" or "the affections" in general. These sentiments are, of course, highly variable, and in that variability they find counterparts in the variations of writing (wen*-pien*). The second usage of ch'ing* (now as a single character) shades over into its other sense as "circumstance," engaging the connection between the choice of a form and a particular situation (it is worth noting that most of the "forms" that Liu Hsieh treats in his chapters on genres, not translated here, are connected to specific kinds of occasion). Then Liu Hsieh links the terms in the process of manifestation: a particular ch'ing* (mood, or situation) leads to a particular version of t'i*, and from the t'i* a given momentum follows.

Although momentum is strongly associated with movements and events in time, we are uncertain whether the "event" in which shih* shows itself is the production of the text (an overall quality that "follows from" the circumstantially determined t'i*), or the internal "movement" of the text.[119] The metaphor of the crossbow bolt and the stream here are important: the text, like other moving things in the world, tends to follow along the path of least resistance, determined by the direction of the initial impulse (the crossbow bolt) and by the medium through which it moves (eddies in a stream). The analogy of the crossbow bolt is a "solid" (shih*) moving through an "empty" (hsü*) medium; the analogy of the stream is something "empty" (water) moving through a "solid."

是以模經為式者。自入典雅之懿。效騷命篇者。必歸豔逸之華。綜意淺切者。類乏醞藉。斷辭辨約者。率乖繁縟。譬激水不漪。槁木無陰。自然之勢也。

Whoever takes the Classics as his model will naturally come into the excellence of the decorous and dignified mode.[120] Whoever decides that his work should imitate the Li Sao will always come to the splendor of a sensuous and unrestrained mode (yen-yi). Cases in which concepts (yi*) are brought together in a shallow and obvious way will, according to that kind of mode, lack a fullness of reserve.[121] Cases where the phrasing of an argument is too concise or clear-cut will generally fail in abundance. These are likewise the momentum of Nature, just as swift waters form no ripples or a barren tree gives no shade.[122]

Here momentum seems to refer to some overall quality or manner of the text that follows from the form (taking as the model the Classics or the Li Sao, a long poem from the third century B.C.) or the normative style ("shallow and obvious," "too concise or clear-cut"). "Momentum" is a term of process; and in traditional thought, qualities tend to develop towards a negative extreme; hence one of the first considerations in shih* is the danger or limitation to which a given quality of momentum tends.

是以繪事圖色。文辭盡情。色糅而犬馬殊形。情交而雅俗異勢。鎔範所擬。各有司匠。雖無嚴郛。難得踰越。然淵乎文者。並總羣勢。奇正雖反。必兼解以俱通。剛柔雖殊。必隨

時而適用。若愛典而惡華。則兼通之理偏。似夏人爭弓矢。執一不可以獨射也。若雅鄭而共篇。則總一之勢離。是楚人鬻矛譽楯。兩難得而俱售也。是以括囊雜體。功在銓別。宮商朱紫。隨勢各配。

As in the act of painting we work with colors (*se**, or "outward appearance"), so literary language gives the full measure of the affections (*ch'ing**). By combinations of colors, horses and dogs take on their various shapes; by the intercourse of the affections, dignified and common modes differ in their momentum.[123] Each matrix in which we propose to cast has its own skill to be mastered; and although its domain is not strictly bounded, there are still aspects that should not be trespassed. The attainment of depth in literature means that one has comprehended all the different kinds of momentum: the unusual may stand in opposition to the proper, but one must understand both and be able to carry both through (*t'ung**); firm and yielding may differ, but one must be able to apply each according to the demands of the moment. Suppose you love the decorous (*tien**) and detest the ornate, in regard to your capacity to carry both through, your [comprehension of] principle (*li**) is one-sided; and it is like the two men of Hsia, the one boasting of his arrow and the other of his bow—since each had only one, neither could shoot. On the other hand, if one puts the [severely classical] Odes [of the *Book of Songs*] together in the same piece with the [sensual] music of Cheng, the unity of the momentum becomes divided; and this is like that man of Ch'u who tried to sell his spear [claiming that it could pierce anything], while at the same time singing the praises of his impenetrable buckler—he found it was difficult to put both on the market at the same time. While you must have all the normative forms at your command, accomplishment is to be found in judicious distinction. Whether the note *kung* or *shang* is to be played, whether the color red or purple is to be used—each will be appropriate according to the momentum.

In this passage we encounter, in passing, one of the most striking assumptions made about literature in *Wen-hsin tiao-lung*: the notion that the affections (*ch'ing**), rather than language, are the medium of a literary work in the same way that bodies of color are the medium of painting. When Liu Hsieh thinks of language as the mere externality of *ch'ing**, he is again reminiscent of Hegel (for whom language is the mere externality of mind, and not in itself the medium of the literary work). The source of Liu Hsieh's assumption can be traced back to the "Great Preface" of the *Book of Songs*, where the poem is simply the outward manifestation of *chih**. Liu Hsieh does not speak of the relation between language and the affections consistently in these terms, nor can it ever be an unproblematic assumption. But the very survival of such a notion, particularly in the sophisticated world of discourse on literature in the Southern Dynasties, is striking. It is a notion of language that Schiller described as characteristic of "naive" poets, in which language is perfectly transparent: "It is a manner of expression of the sort in which the sign disappears entirely into the thing signified and in which language still leaves the thoughts it expresses bare, so that one could not represent them any other way without simultaneously concealing them; it is this mode of writing that is generally called one of genius and replete with spirit."[124] For Liu Hsieh the term that is "expressed" is, of course, not "thoughts" but ch'ing* (which will incorporate thoughts, fused with the state of mind in which they occur); but the principle is the same as with Schiller's "naive" poets: when you read the text, you are not reading language; you are reading ch'ing*.

When Liu Hsieh writes, "by the intercourse of the affections, dignified and common modes differ in their momentum," we must not let the conventional hierarchy of value ("dignified and common") distract us from the kernel of the statement, namely, that any particular quality in a work comes from a unique "coming together" of the affections, and such a quality imparts a distinct momentum to the work that can be judged according to standards. In certain ways Liu Hsieh is also reminiscent of Longinus in his constant alternation between the involuntary and the voluntary aspects of the work. In the case of Longinus the magical quality of the Sublime, which seems beyond human control, is balanced by the promise of a technê, a learnable skill, which will enable a writer to achieve it voluntarily. In his beautiful discussion of a lyric by Sappho, Longinus begins by praising her skill in conjoining emotions to give the "impression" of passion; but then, citing a passage, he speaks as if Sappho herself really felt the emotions and were carried away by them; finally he falls out of the illusion and returns to the praise of her manipulation of the affections. As in the Chinese tradition, attention is focused on an unknowable question: whether the text cannot help exposing the human heart or is a construct by which that (potentially deceptive) impression is created. Liu Hsieh begins by grounding form in the feeling of the moment (ch'ing*-chih), which leads in turn to some natural momentum; in this passage he tells us instead that we should "master" all the normative forms in order to use them when they are required. To reconcile the two divergent impulses, we could say that mastery of a style creates a capacity that lets us respond appropriately to the natural feeling of the moment. But there remains a tension between the voluntary and involuntary that remained one of the deepest and most enduring problems in Chinese literary thought.

The venerable opposition between one-sidedness and the "comprehensive talent" returns here in a new guise. Any particular stylistic affinity is limitation. The parable of the two men of Hsia suggests that successful action can only follow from the combination of differences. This immediately suggests a corresponding danger: the admixture of inappropriate differences, and the second parable of the man of Ch'u refers to joining things that are mutually exclusive. In short, one must have a range of mastery in order to respond to the demands of the moment, but the moment must indeed determine the response rather than having the writer give us a mere show of his mastery.

A section of the chapter on the different qualities of momentum appropriate to various genres has been omitted here.

此循體而成勢。隨變而立功者也。雖復契會相參。節文互雜。譬五色之錦。各以本采為地矣。

In these cases the momentum is perfected according to the normative form ($t'i^*$), and achievement comes from following the mutations. And although division and reconciliation are mixed together,[125] though rhythm and pattern be diverse—just as a brocade is made up of many colors—each piece has a basic coloration as its ground.

The mixing of analogical models in the relation between the concept of "basic coloration" (in this case *pen-ts'ai** rather than the more common *pen-se**) and "momentum" should not obscure the point that some normative origin must remain immanent in the unfolding of particular qualities. Variation, change, and movement are valid only if they retain contact with some source. The fear of loss of origins is repeated in many frames of reference.

桓譚稱文家各有所慕。或好浮華而不知實覈。或美眾多而不見要約。陳思亦云。世之作者。或好煩文博採。深沈其旨者。或好離言辨句。分毫析釐者。所習不同。所務各異。言勢殊也。

Huan T'an claimed that each writer yearns for some particular quality: some are fond of insubstantial glitter and do not understand what is worth consideration for its factual truth (*shih**); some find beauty in multiplicity without seeing what is essential and terse. In the same vein, Ts'ao Chih [192–232] said that some of the writers of his age were fond of complexity and of drawing from a wide range of sources, imparting a concealing depth to the significance of their words; others preferred the words perfectly clear and their lines finely argued, making discriminating judgments by the finest standards. Habits are not the same, and likewise each person differs in where his efforts are directed; these are distinctions in the momentum of words.

Here "momentum" is very much the inclination to certain qualities that follows from a particular type ($t'i^*$) of personality. In each case the inclination of a personality type is at the same time a limitation, which Liu Hsieh will try to remedy by proposing that writers learn to follow differing directions of momentum.

劉楨云。文之體勢實有強弱。使其辭已盡而勢有餘。天下一人耳。不可得也。公幹所談。頗亦兼氣。然文之任勢。勢有剛柔。不必壯言慷慨。乃稱勢也。

Liu Chen [d. 217] said that in the momentum of normative forms there is indeed a distinction between the strong and the weak,[126] and that there was only one person in the whole world who could make his words conclude while leaving a surplus of momentum, something that no one else could achieve.[127] Liu Chen was probably integrating *ch'i** into what he was saying here. However, the momentum carried in a literary work (*wen**) may be either hard or soft; the term "momentum" is not applied only to vigorous words and strong emotions.

Clearly in Liu Chen's usage the concept of *shih** had been primarily quantitative, a degree of force carried in the words. Liu Hsieh is careful to distinguish his own use of the term as a category of quality from that earlier usage, which he associates with *ch'i**. A "soft" *shih** may be a positive quality, a tentative or leisurely and winding motion of mind. In contrast, Liu Chen's "weak *shih**" is simply a lack of force (like a lack of *ch'i**), and the highest value is to possess such a surplus of force that it carries on after the words.

又陸雲自稱往日論文。先辭而後情。尚勢而不取悅澤。及張公論文。則欲宗其言。夫情固先辭。勢實須澤。可謂先迷後能從善矣。

　　自近代辭人。率好詭巧。原其為體。訛勢所變。厭黷舊式。故穿鑿取新。察其訛意。似難而實無他術也。反正而已。故文反正為乏。辭反正為奇。效奇之法。必顛倒文句。上字而抑下。中辭而出外。回互不常。則新色耳。

Lu Yün [262–303] even said that when he used to discuss literature, he gave priority to language (*tz'u**) and second place to the affections, valued momentum and did not concern himself with making it attractive; but when he heard Chang Hua's [232–300] discussions of literature [which preferred the alternative values], he was inclined to accept the authority of Chang's words. Of course, the affections have priority over language, and the momentum really must have something attractive; at first he was in error, but later was able to go in the right direction.

In recent times writers have generally showed a liking for the bizarre and artful. If we look to the origins of that form, it was in a mutation to a momentum inclined to the delusory.[128] They grew sick of the old models and adopted whatever novelty they could get by any contrivance. If we examine their delusory concepts (*yi**), what seems difficult is, in fact, nothing but an inversion of the proper. When literature (*wen**) inverts the proper, it is wanting;[129] when language (*tz'u**) inverts the proper, it is extraordinary.[130] The method they use to get the extraordinary is always changing the word order of a sentence, placing the words that belong at the beginning at the end, placing the language belonging in the middle on the outer edges, turning everything around from the normative—that's the "new look."

Liu Hsieh commonly denounces contemporary writing, but this precise identification of one of their objectionable stylistic traits has interesting ramifications in literary ideology. Classical Chinese is a positional language. Traditional comments on literature understood positional sentence structure as an order that was "natural" on logical rather than purely linguistic grounds. For example, in the proposition "the boy hit the ball," the boy is given first, then the action, then the object of the action. There was an assumption that linguistic sequence was the natural sequence of the event in the world. Within this broad assumption, a degree of flexibility was permitted, so that a "natural sequence" could follow the action of the mind or hierarchies of value, as well as the sequence of events in the external world.[131] This principle was extended to the sequence of clauses in sentences and to the organization of sentences within the discourse as a whole. "Because he practiced, the boy hit the ball" would be "proper," *cheng**; the two events are given in their proper order. "The boy hit the ball because he had practiced" would be an "inversion" (*tien-tao* 顛倒).[132] Although questions of sequencing in literature were more fully developed by later writers on style (primarily those writing on prose), the issue was already clearly articulated in commentary on the *Spring and Autumn Annals*. Stylistic inversion for the sake of novelty is, for Liu Hsieh, loaded with questions of value: it is a willful rejection of the "proper" simply because one is "sick of it" (*yen-tu*). As such, it seems to threaten the essential correlation between literature and the natural order of things. Here we see problems arising in the assumption that language gives a transparent access to the affections (though at times Liu Hsieh preserves the assumption by suggesting that such hunger for stylistic novelty is the manifestation of a particular shallowness in the personality, *t'i**, of the writer).

夫通衢夷坦。而多行捷徑者。趨近故也。正文明白。而常務反言者。適俗故也。然密會者以意新得巧。苟異者以失體成怪。舊練之才。則執正以馭奇。新學之銳。則逐奇而失正。勢流不反。則文體遂弊。秉茲情術。可無思耶。

Broad thoroughfares are level, yet many take short-cuts: this is because they rush to what is closest.[133] Proper writing (*cheng**-*wen**) is perfectly clear, but such writers as these always strive for inverted language: this is to suit the common fashion. Those who have a truly close understanding are successful in their artistry by [genuinely] novel concepts, while those who perversely seek difference for its own sake get the normative form wrong and achieve mere strangeness. A talent trained in the old ways can maintain the proper and still make good use of something extraordinary,[134] while a sharp wit with new learning goes chasing after the extraordinary and loses the proper. When the momentum drifts on without returning, the forms of literature (*wen*-*t'i**) sink into ruin. Can anyone who grasps the [present] circumstance and its techniques help worrying about it?

All of a sudden Liu Hsieh shifts to *shih** in another of its senses, the "tendencies" of the age, which in this case are not good.

形生勢成。始末相承。湍迴似規。矢激如繩。因利騁節。情采自凝。枉轡學步。力止壽陵。

Supporting Verse

> When shape is born, a momentum is formed:
> There is a continuity between beginning and end.
> Eddies circle like a compass,
> A crossbow bolt bursts forth straight as a ruler.
> The pace gallops along the path of least resistance,
> The affections and coloration become fixed of themselves.
> But if one pulls the bridle aside to imitate the pace of others,
> His force will be no greater than that of the boy of Shou-ling.[135]

CHAPTER 31
The Affections and Coloration, Ch'ing–ts'ai 情采

The pairing of "affections" (*ch'ing**) and "coloration" (*ts'ai**) is yet another version of the correspondence between "inner" and "outer" qualities. As was often the case, such a paradigm served to stabilize and define one or both of the constituent terms (allowing that such a term could appear in other pairings that would shift and enlarge the term's significance). "Coloration" was used in earlier and later literary criticism, but nowhere with the frequency with which it appeared in *Wen-hsin tiao-lung*, and nowhere else was it a technical category that would have merited the separate treatment it received here. Its primary meaning was a flashy appearance, often constituted of many bright colors. *Ts'ai** was associated with literary ornamentation, especially in its capacity to attract and allure a reader. By devoting his chapter to a pairing of *ts'ai** with the more common category *ch'ing**, Liu Hsieh has given it a special importance as *ch'ing**'s external complement. Commonly compounded with *wen** as *wen*-ts'ai**, its role in this chapter is very much like that of *wen** itself in one of its more restrictive senses: ornamental patterning (with the qualification that in this sense "ornament" must be presumed necessary).

聖賢書辭。總稱文章。非采而何。夫水性虛而淪漪結。木體實而花萼振。文附質也。虎豹無文。則鞹同犬羊。犀兕有皮。而色資丹漆。質待文也。若乃綜述性靈。敷寫器象。鏤心鳥跡之中。織辭魚網之上。其為彪炳。縟采名矣。

The writings of Sages and good men are collectively called "literary works" (*wen*-chang**), and what is this but coloration?[136] The nature (*hsing**) of water is its plasticity (*hsü**, "empty"), and ripples form in it. The normative form of wood is solid (*shih**), and flowers blossom on it. In both cases the pattern [shown externally] (*wen**) is contingent upon substance (*chih**). On the other hand, if tigers and leopards had no patterns, their bare hides would be the same as those of dogs and sheep;[137] rhinoceroses and wild bulls have skins, but the color they have depends upon red lacquer.[138] In these cases the substance (*chih**) is dependent on the patterning. When it comes to the overall transmission of our spiritual nature (*hsing*-ling*) or the ample delineation of images of things [literally "vessels"],[139] we inscribe our minds in the "tracks of birds" [the written word] and weave phrases on fishnet [paper]. And the brilliant glitter of this is given the name "lush coloration."

Liu Hsieh begins the chapter by providing a respectable genealogy for *ts'ai**, filiating it to values in the Classics and affirming, as he so often does, its organic relation to the nature of the thing. He offers the expected conclusion, from the examples of trees and water, that intricate surfaces are contingent on the basic nature of the thing. Since this chapter is in part a defense of *ts'ai**, however, Liu Hsieh offers the counter-case in a series of remarkable allusions: the nature of a thing may be contingent on its external patterning. This radical—and in the context of the tradition, not altogether credible—inversion of the usual hierarchy is a defense against the most common criticism of all *wen**: that it may be superfluous ornament.

The next, and less problematic, argument is a development of the position taken in "Its Source in the Way." *Wen** is the outward appearance of something's essential nature, and human *wen** is the outward appearance of mind. Mind is "inscribed" in written characters: the term used is *lou*, "carved in," just as an artisan might carve the shapes of creatures without "spiritual nature." But the relation is not mimetic: the word used in this case is "transmit," *shu*, the term of continuation and extension used by Confucius who "transmitted but did not make" (*Analects* VII.1). For conveying what is external to mind ("the images of things" or literally "of vessels"), the relation is somewhat more mimetic: the term used here is *hsieh*, translated as "delineate." *Hsieh* was a word with a complicated semantic range, from "pour out" or "divulge" to something like "reflect," and, by Liu Hsieh's time, to "copy," as in making a copy of a text. Perhaps the dominant element in *hsieh* is the reappearance of something in a different medium or on a different ground: things are transferred from the world to words.

The luminous world of mind and things is put down "in black and white" (as we say); Liu Hsieh wants to stress the point that this "black-and-white" transcription has its own glitter that conveys the quality of the original. Such allure, embodied in language, is *ts'ai**, "coloration." Although this allure is embodied "in" language, however, it is not an allure "of" language: it is, precisely, the allure of feeling (*ch'ing**).

故立文之道。其理有三。一曰形文。五色是也。二曰聲文。五音是也。三曰情文。五性是也。五色雜而成黼黻。五音比而成韶夏。五性發而為辭章。神理之數也。

There are three basic principles (*li**) in the Way of setting forth pattern (*wen**). The first is the pattern of shapes, which is constituted of the five colors (*se**). The second is the pattern of sounds constituted of the five tones. The third is the pattern of the affections (*ch'ing**) constituted of the five "natures" (*hsing**).[140] A mixture of the five colors forms the patterns of imperial brocade. The conjunction of the five sounds forms the Shao-hsia [a legendary piece of ceremonial music]. The five natures come forth and they are pieces of language (*tzu*-chang**). This is the fixed number (*shu**) of divine principle (*shen*-li**).

This is the most direct statement of Liu Hsieh's remarkable notion that the affections (*ch'ing**) are literally the medium of literature, just as color is the medium of embroidery and sound is the medium of music. Rather than serving itself as the medium, language is the product, in the same way that a piece of brocade or a musical work are products in their respective media. But in this model, Liu Hsieh returns to the problem of voluntarism that recurs throughout *Wen-hsin tiao-lung*: he speaks of the affections as objects, to be manipulated and presented (the human affections used as an embroiderer chooses colored threads to make a pattern or a composer uses tones for music). At the same time he wants the affections to be the condition of the presenting subject that appears involuntarily in the presentation.

孝經垂典。喪言不文。故知君子常言未嘗質也。老子疾偽。故稱美言不信。而五千精妙。則非棄美矣。莊周云辯雕萬物。謂藻飾也。韓非云豔采辯說。謂綺麗也。綺麗以豔說。藻飾以辯雕。文辭之變。於斯極矣。研味孝老。則知文質附乎性情。詳覽莊韓。則見華實過

乎淫侈。若擇源於涇渭之流。接彎於邪正之路。亦可以馭文采矣。夫鉛黛所以飾容。而盼
倩生於淑姿。文采所以飾言。而辯麗本於情性。故情者。文之經。辭者。理之緯。經正而
後緯成。理定而後辭暢。此立文之本源也。

The *Book of Filial Piety* has given us an authoritative statement that language at
funerals should not be patterned (*wen**); we conclude from this that in ordinary times the language of a superior person is never plain (*chih**).[141] Lao-tzu
hated falseness, and thus claimed "Beautiful words are not to be trusted";[142]
yet his five-thousand word [book] gives us the subtle essences (*ching-miao**),
by which we can see that he himself did not reject beauty. Chuang-tzu speaks
of [how the ancient kings had] "a discrimination that adorned the thousands of
things," by which he meant fancy ornament.[143] Han Fei speaks of "alluring
and brightly colored arguments," by which he meant an intricate loveliness.[144]
However, an intricate loveliness in "alluring arguments" and fancy ornament
in "a discrimination that adorns" represent an extreme in the devolution
(*pien**) of writing (*wen**-tz'u**). If we reflect studiously on the flavor (*wei**) of
what was said in the *Book of Filial Piety* and by Lao-tzu, we realize that pattern
and plainness (*wen**-chih**) are contingent upon one's nature and the state of the
affections (*hsing**-ch'ing**); on the other hand, if we look carefully over what
was said by Chuang-tzu and Han Fei, we see that flower and fruit (*hua-shih**,
"floweriness and substance") have gone past the mark into excess and dis-
soluteness. If we select well between the sources of the [clear river] Ching and
the [muddy river] Wei, if we guide the halter, choosing between the paths of
what is proper (*cheng**) and what is warped,[145] then we can guide the coloration of pattern (*wen**-ts'ai**).

Mascara is a means to adorn the face, but the glance and the dimpled smile
arise from a pure loveliness of manner. Likewise the coloration of pattern is a
means to adorn words, but the beauty of an argument has its basis in the
affections and individuating nature (*ch'ing**-hsing**). Thus the affections are the
warp of pattern (*wen**), and diction (*tz'u**) is principle's woof. The woof can
be formed only after the warp is straight; diction can expand itself only after
principle is set. This is the origin and basis of setting forth pattern (or "literature," *wen**).

Liu Hsieh's chapters are often less true thought than a sonata of variations on
a term or problem into which are woven recurrent ideological motifs. There
is a desire that "coloration" be an essential glow on the surface of any inner
condition; at the same time, there is the mirroring anxiety that rhetorical
"coloration" might be mere ornament and inessential. Here true beauty
comes only from within; and the external term, diction (in this case, the
literary qualities of the phrasing) and coloration, can only enhance it, even
though though they are as necessary to the fabric as the woof is to the cloth.

昔詩人什篇。為情而造文。辭人賦頌。為文而造情。何以明其然。蓋風雅之興。志思蓄憤。而吟詠情性。以諷其上。此為情而造文也。諸子之徒。心非鬱陶。苟馳夸飾。鬻聲釣世。此為文而造情也。故為情者要約而寫真。為文者淫麗而煩濫。而後之作者。採濫忽真。遠棄風雅。近師辭賦。故體情之製日疏。逐文之篇愈盛。故有志深軒冕。而汎詠皋壤。心纏機務。而虛述人外。真宰弗存。翩其反矣。夫桃李不言而成蹊。有實存也。男子樹蘭而不芳。無其情也。夫以草木之微。依情待實。況乎文章。述志為本。言與志反。文豈足徵。

The works of the former poets of the *Book of Songs* are *wen** produced for the sake of how they felt (*ch'ing**). In contrast, the poetic expositions and panegyrics of the [later] rhetors produced feeling (*ch'ing**) for the sake of *wen**. How am I aware this is so? What stirred (*hsing**) the Airs (*Feng**) and Odes (*Ya**) was a repressed intensity in their thoughts and what they were intent upon (*chih**-ssu**); and "they sang forth their affections and their natures" to criticize those in power.[146] This is producing *wen** for the sake of feeling. The philosophers and their ilk felt no swelling emotion, yet made an illicit display of hyperbolic ornament to buy themselves fame and fish for glory in the age. This is producing feeling for the sake of *wen**. That which exists for the sake of one's feelings is concise, essential, and depicts what is genuine. That which exists for the sake of *wen** is seductively beautiful and excessive. Later writers chose the excessive and overlooked the genuine, cast the Airs and Odes from them, taking their masters closer at hand, from the writers of poetic expositions. Thus works that embody the affections get daily more scarce, and pieces that go chasing after *wen** become ever more abundant. The consequence is that there are some whose ambitions (*chih**) lie deep among great carriages and crowns, but who will chant idly of the moorlands; some whose minds are embroiled in stratagems and duties will vainly describe that which transcends the mundane world. In such people that something which is truly in control of the self no longer survives:[147] they fly swiftly in the opposite direction. Peach and plum trees, though they never speak, have paths beaten to them; it is because they bear fruit.[148] And if a male plants an orchid, it will not be fragrant: men lack the right quality of the affections.[149] If even lesser things like plants and trees depend on circumstance (or "the affections," *ch'ing**) and substance (or "fruit," *shih**), it is all the more so in works of literature, whose very basis is the transmission of that upon which mind is intent. If the words contradict that upon which mind is intent, what is to be proved by writing?

In his *Fa-yen* the Han writer Yang Hsiung made the following distinction between the poets of the *Book of Songs* and the rhetors of later ages: "*Fu* [the technique of exposition] in the poets of the *Book of Songs* was beautiful in order to give the normative rule; *fu* [exposition and the genre, "poetic exposition"] among the rhetors was beautiful in order to seduce." What was, in Yang Hsiung and in most Han criticism, a question of the ethics of literature's social purposes has here been transformed into an opposition between genuineness and falseness. The question of ethics has not disappeared, but it has been placed in the background by the question of authenticity.

Liu Hsieh is here making explicit a question that had been implicit in the tradition for a long time. The assumption of authenticity was central to the "Great Preface" of the *Book of Songs*: the *Songs* are involuntary expressions of how people really felt. On the other hand, the writings of the rhetors (orators and writers of poetic expositions) were often described in terms of deception, with the implicit presumption that the person who leads others astray himself knows better. Here the question of authenticity versus writing as a value in itself is clearly formulated: in the case of the *Book of Songs*, the poem follows from prior emotion (*ch'ing**), and the reader discovers the real emotions of the writer in the text; in the case of the rhetors, the affective qualities of the work are manipulated to make the reader admire the literary work for its own sake and the writer purely as writer. This argument against rhetoric is a familiar one in the Western tradition, nor is the alternative of authenticity altogether absent in the West. But the West offered a third model for the literary work: the poem, whose fictionality was itself an oblique and mysterious truth.

Liu Hsieh states the principle of authenticity clearly; but elsewhere in *Wen-hsin tiao-lung* (as in the following chapter on "Casting and Paring"), he often phrases his arguments in such a way as to suggest quite the opposite: that the affective quality (*ch'ing**) of a work is something consciously chosen.

是以聯辭結采。將欲明理。采濫辭詭。則心理愈翳。固知翠綸桂餌。反所以失魚。言隱榮華。殆謂此也。是以衣錦褧衣。惡文太章。賁象窮白。貴乎反本。夫能設模以位理。擬地以置心。心定而後結音。理正而後摛藻。使文不滅質。博不溺心。正采耀乎朱藍。間色屏於紅紫。乃可謂雕琢其章。彬彬君子矣。

Thus when we compose words (*tz'u**) and form coloration, our aim should be to clarify natural principle (*li**). The more excessive the coloration and the more bizarre the words, then the more the principles in the mind (*hsin*-li**) will be concealed. It is well known that a fishing line of kingfisher feathers and cassia as the bait turns out to be a way not to catch fish.[150] This is what is meant by the saying [of Chuang-tzu]: "Words are hidden by flash and glitter." Thus the line [from the *Book of Songs*], "Robed in brocade covered by a plain shift," expresses hostility to excess showiness of pattern. The Image of the hexagram *Pi* treats whiteness as the ultimate color: here a reversion to basics is valued. Set a model that gives principle (*li**) a place, determine a ground on which mind can stand securely; then only after mind is set firmly, the tones form, and only after principle is proper (*cheng**), ornament is applied. Keep the pattern (*wen**) from destroying the substance (*chih**); keep breadth [of learning] from engulfing mind; the proper coloration (*cheng**-*ts'ai**) will gleam in red and indigo, the interspersed colors will exclude the pink and purple [garish colors]: after all this, we can say that the piece (*chang**) is carved and chiseled, [the work of] a superior person in whom pattern and substance are in balance.[151]

言以文遠。誠哉斯驗。心術既形。英華乃贍。吳錦好渝。舜英徒豔。繁采寡情。味之必厭。

Supporting Verse
   "By pattern words go far":[152]
   We can see the proof that this is true.
   When mind's ways take on outer shape,
   The splendor is ample.
   But the brocades of Wu bleed and fade easily,
   The kapok's blossom are alluring in vain.[153]
   Dense coloration that lacks feeling
   Will always cloy when we savor (*wei**) it.

CHAPTER 32
Casting and Paring, Jung-ts'ai 鎔裁

The preceding group of six chapters treated the most general theoretical concepts in the genesis of a literary work. With "Casting and Paring" there begins a cluster of eight chapters that treat the technical aspects of composition. "Casting and Paring" is followed by chapters on "Sound Qualities" (*Sheng-lü* 聲律), "Paragraph and Period" (*Chang-chü* 章句), "Parallel Phrasing" (*Li*-tz'u'** 麗辭), "Comparison and Affective Image" (*Pi*-hsing** 比興), "Ornamentation by Overstatement" (*K'ua-shih* 夸飾), "References" (*Shih*-lei** 事類), and "Word Choice" (*Lien-tzu* 練字). While the idea of literature as organic process is constantly recapitulated in chapter openings and conclusions, the primary concern of these chapters is the reflective judgment that should be exercised by the literary craftsman.

Both "casting" (*jung*) and "paring" (*ts'ai*) are terms of artisanship. *Jung* belongs to the technical vocabulary of metallurgy, metal cast in a mold; and in this literary application it refers to the way in which the relatively amorphous interior elements of composition (the affections, thoughts, etc.) must be given in normative form. "Paring," *ts'ai*, is more properly translated "cutting to pattern," based on the metaphor of cutting cloth for making clothes; in this case all excesses are trimmed away.

Of the two terms, "paring" is the more fully amplified and it is the term with particular resonance in earlier literary thought. In "The Poetic Exposition on Literature," Lu Chi sometimes marveled how the natural processes that generate a literary work seem to have an inherent tendency to profusion; Liu Hsieh agrees and takes Lu Chi to task for allowing such excesses to remain in his work. Beneath the metaphors of metallurgy and making clothes in "Casting and Paring," there is a submerged agrarian model: the first concern is growth, an organic process which can be helped along but which is not entirely within the scope of human volition (e.g., the "coloration," discussed in the preceding chapter, which must emerge from authentic feeling); once growth occurs, however, there is a danger of excess—the weeds and the crowding of plants that threaten a healthy crop. In this phase the instrumental will can work freely: the necessary cutting back is completely in the domain of skill. Later in the chapter, the demands of exposition lead Liu Hsieh to acknowledge a form of talent whose excellence is "copiousness" (to counterbalance a talent whose strength is concision); but there is no question that Liu prefers concision.

情理設位。文采行乎其中。剛柔以立本。變通以趨時。立本有體。意或偏長。趨時無方。辭或繁雜。蹊要所司。職在鎔裁。櫽括情理。矯揉文采也。規範本體謂之鎔。剪截浮詞謂之裁。裁則蕪穢不生。鎔則綱領昭暢。譬繩墨之審分。斧斤之斲削矣。駢拇枝指。由侈於性。附贅懸肬。實侈於形。一意兩出。義之駢枝也。同辭重句。文之肬贅也。

When the places of the affections and basic principle have been set, then pattern and coloration move in their midst.[154] "The basis is established as either firm or yielding; then mutation or continuity occur, according to the requirements of the moment".[155] There are normative forms by which "the basis (*pen*, "root") may be established," but the concepts may incline too far in one direction or another. There is no limited rule in "answering the requirements of the moment," yet language may be too dense or mixed. To command the key points along this path, one must attend to casting and paring. To do so one must apply the straightedge to the principles of the affections (*ch'ing*-li**), and one must regulate the coloration of pattern (*wen*-ts'ai**). To take the basic normative form as one's model is called "casting."[156] To cut away superfluous (*fu*, "floating") diction is called "paring." If one pares, no weeds will grow; if one casts, the main lines of the discourse will be visible and extend. These may be compared, on the one hand, to the reflective judgments of divisions made in using the straightedge and, on the other hand, to the way in which an ax is used to cut something down to size. Webbed toes or an extra finger comes from some superfluity in nature; tumors and bulbous protrusions are truly a superfluity in the [human] form.[157] When the same idea appears twice [in a work], it is the webbed toe or extra finger of some truth; identical wording and redundant sentences are the tumors and bulbous protrusions of writing.

From the *Hsi-tz'u chuan* Liu Hsieh derives a formula for any successful process: "establishing the basis" and "answering the requirements of the moment." But successful process has an inherent fecundity whose consequences are disturbing. The ensuing tendency to shapelessness and excess is not the fault of the writer but the natural outcome of doing things correctly. Desert suddenly becomes jungle, and the writer had wanted fertile and orderly croplands in between the two extremes. The writer wants to "get his point across" (*t'ung**); he wants "the main lines of the discourse (*kang-ling*) to be visible and extend"; lushness blocks passage. Against such profusion, the writer must guide the act of "paring back" by normative models—the geometry of the straightedge or the human body—whereby elements of abundance can be judged excrescences. Behind this rejection of excess and demand for concision is the canonical injunction of *Analects* XV.40 "Words should attain their ends and that's all."

凡思緒初發。辭采苦雜。心非權衡。勢必輕重。是以草創鴻筆。先標三準。履端於始。則設情以位體。舉正於中。則酌事以取類。歸餘於終。則撮辭以舉要。然後舒華布實。獻替節文。繩墨以外。美材既斲。故能首尾圓合。條貫統序。若術不素定。而委心逐辭。異端叢至。駢贅必多。

Whenever thoughts first emerge, there is a problem in the way the coloration of the language (*tz'u*-ts'ai**) is all mixed together; the mind lacks an even balance, so the momentum always is too light or too heavy. Thus, to write a masterwork, you must first set up three standards: in the first stage, establish the feeling (*ch'ing**) in order to set the normative form in its place; in the second stage, consult events (*shih**) in order to match categories;[158] in the final stage, gather the phrases (*tz'u**) together in order to bring out the essentials. Only then can you spread forth the flowers and fruit (*hua-shih**), giving measure to your writing by decisions about what to use and what not to use. Then, when you cut away from the excellent timber whatever lies beyond the straightedge, the beginning and end can come together perfectly, with an orderly sequence all the way through. But if your technique is not determined from the start and you go chasing after phrases however you please, then outlandish principles will come in masses, and you will always have many webbed toes and tumors.

Even in the "organic" phases described in the previous chapters, Liu Hsieh not only explained the inherent operations of *wen**, he also gave writers advice on how to manipulate and make use of those operations for best advantage: nurturing abilities, mastering many forms, returning to originary norms, and so on. But in many of these chapters on craft, Liu Hsieh insinuates authorial control even more deeply into the process. When Liu Hsieh spoke of "producing *wen** for the sake of feeling" in "The Affections and Coloration," he presumed that "feeling" (*ch'ing**) simply happened, that it was given beforehand, without consideration of the *wen** that might grow from it. Although it is perhaps not in absolute contradiction to a demand for authenticity, the instrumentalist formulation above seems dangerously close to "producing feeling for the sake of *wen**": "in the first stage, establish the feeling in order to set the normative form in its place." We had known that "normative form" follows from feeling, but we had not been told to determine the feeling in order to produce the desired normative form. In the earlier chapters we had something like a farmer's almanac for literature, advising us how to act in a timely fashion; in this chapter we are given an instruction book with steps to follow.

故三準既定。次討字句。句有可削。足見其疎。字不得減。乃知其密。精論要語。極略之體。游心竄句。極繁之體。謂繁與略。隨分所好。引而申之。則兩句敷為一章。約以貫之。則一章刪成兩句。思瞻者善敷。才覈者善刪。善刪者字去而意留。善敷者辭殊而意顯。字刪而意闕。則短乏而非覈。辭敷而言重。則蕪穢而非瞻。

　　昔謝艾王濟。西河文士。張俊以為艾繁而不可刪。濟略而不可益。若二子者。可謂練鎔裁而曉繁略矣。至如士衡才優。而綴辭尤繁。士龍思劣。而雅好清省。及雲之論機。亟恨其多。而稱清新相接。不以為病。蓋崇友于耳。夫美錦製衣。脩短有度。雖翫其采。不倍領袖。巧猶難繁。況在乎拙。而文賦以為榛楛勿剪。庸音足曲。其識非不鑒。乃情苦芟繁也。

When these three standards are set, next give careful consideration to words and sentences. If there are sentences that can be excised, we can tell that the writing is too loose. If not a word can be deleted, we know that it is dense. An argument that gets the essence and indispensable words characterize the supremely terse style (*t'i**); "a mind wandering at its leisure through intricately carved sentences" characterizes the supremely lush style.[159] The lush and the terse are preferences that follow from the [writer's] nature. If one is disposed to draw matters out, then a couple of sentences can be elaborated into a whole work; if one is disposed to terse unity, then a whole work can be cut back into a couple of sentences. A person whose thoughts are abundant is a master of elaboration; one whose talent is intensive is a master at cutting things back. The master at cutting things down gets rid of words while preserving the idea (*yi**), while the master of elaboration uses different language (*tz'u**) so that the idea is crystal clear. But if the idea disappears when the words are cut back, then it is deficiency of talent and not intensive depth; if the words are redundant when the language is elaborated, it is a jungle and not abundance.

Some time ago [in the Tsin] there were two literary men of Hsi-ho, Hsieh Ai and Wang Chi. In the opinion of [their contemporary] Chang Chün, Ai was lush, yet nothing could be cut out of his work; Chi, on the other hand, was terse, but nothing could be added to his work. Writers like these two may be described as well-versed in casting and paring—they are the cognoscenti of lushness and terseness. Lu Chi's talent was superior, but there was an inordinate lushness in his compositions. The thought of his brother, Lu Yün, was inferior; but Lu Yün always favored clarity and brevity. When Lu Yün wrote about Lu Chi, he repeatedly deplored his brother's excesses; yet he claimed that [in Lu Chi's work] clarity and novelty were conjoined, and because of such conjunction, he really could not consider Lu Chi's excesses a fault. This is probably nothing more than a brother's proper show of respect. When one cuts clothes out of lovely brocade, there are strict measures of length. However much one may delight in the brocade's bright colors, one cannot, simply for that reason, double the [length of] sleeves and put the collar into disorder. If even such artful writing [as Lu Chi's] has problems with lushness, just think how it will be for a clumsy writer. In the "Poetic Exposition on Literature," it was Lu Chi's opinion that "thorn bushes and medlars need not be cut down" and that "ordinary tones complete the song." It was not that his comprehension was unclear; rather it was that he had no heart to pare away lushness.

Wen-hsin tiao-lung was trapped between two opposing modes of discourse, each of which pulled Liu Hsieh's exposition in very different directions. The first mode, familiar to Western readers, was the attempt to argue a single point; this required proofs (either by logic or authority) and required that some alternative be disproved or devalued.[160] The second mode was deeply ingrained in the antithetical rhetoric that Liu Hsieh employed: this mode was essentially descriptive, either dividing and subdividing each topic into component pairs or developing the exposition by serial compensations.[161] The impulses to complementarity and compensation often worked against the exclusiveness required in arguing for a single point. We have seen this second mode in a relatively pure form in "The Poetic Exposition on Literature." We also note that the position of this chapter, on cutting back and restriction, is in some ways a compensation for the opulence implicit in "The Affections and Coloration."

In the passages above, we can clearly see the clash between these two modes of discourse. In the opening section of this chapter, Liu Hsieh argued forcefully against any redundancy: "When the same idea appears twice [in a work], it is the webbed toe or extra finger of some truth; identical wording and redundant sentences are the tumors and bulbous protrusions of writing." This is an argument for a single position: the most concise writing is the best. But the rules of antithetical exposition demand that there be a complementary pair of good styles: a lush style *and* a terse style. Therefore, in the first paragraph of the section above, Liu Hsieh is compelled to speak favorably of the lush style; and he does so in precisely the same terms he had previously applied to unnecessary excess.[162]

As Liu Hsieh felt the need to describe an antithetical pair of styles, he was also aware of the conflict; and, in the next paragraph, he tried to resolve it by citing the example of Hsieh Ai—which was a remarkably obscure example, dredged up solely for the sake of Chang Chün's comment. In Hsieh Ai (or at least in Chang Chün's claim about Hsieh Ai), two values are conjoined: he "was lush yet nothing could be cut out of his work." In effect, Liu Hsieh has escaped the problem by citing an authority, evading the obvious fact that "lushness" in this case must mean something rather different from Liu's earlier description of "a couplet of sentences . . . elaborated into a whole work." But the citation of authority allows Liu to return to his primary point on the value of concision and roundly to condemn Lu Chi, not only for the lushness of his own work, but for apparently licensing looseness in "The Poetic Exposition on Literature," and quoting Lu Chi's own lines (ll. 153 and 216) against him.

As he often does at the end, Liu Hsieh reasserts the organic model, even though it does not follow from the preceding argument. The truth of "casting and paring" is contained in the metaphor of cutting clothing above, not in the closing figure of the living body.

夫百節成體。共資榮衛。萬趣會文。不離辭情。若情周而不繁。辭運而不濫。非夫鎔裁。何以行之乎。

A hundred jointed segments constitute a body/form (*t'i**), and they all depend on the circulation of blood and *ch'i**. Likewise, thousands of impulses (*ch'ü**) conjoin in a literary work, but none can depart from language and the affections (or "giving linguistic expression to the affections," *tz'u*-ch'ing**). Except by casting and paring, how can one make the affections complete without getting over-lush, and make the language function without letting it go to excess?

篇章戶牖。左右相瞰。辭如川流。溢則汎濫。權衡損益。斟酌濃淡。芟繁剪穢。弛於負擔。

Supporting Verse

 Each work has windows and doors
 That look back and forth on one another.
 The language is like the current of a stream:
 If it floods, it flows over its banks.
 Weigh additions and excisions on the balance;
 Deliberate whether it's too dense or too thin.
 Pare away lushness, cut down the weeds
 To lighten the burden you carry.

CHAPTER 34
Paragraph and Period (Stanza and Line,) Chang-chü 章句

"Paragraph and Period" treats two basic levels of division in both poetry and prose, and it contains one of the fullest discussions of the counterpart of "sentences" in early Chinese writing. To fully appreciate such a discussion, the modern reader must suspend the common assumption that grammar is a self-evident descriptive category in all traditions. Traditional Chinese writing on language differs radically from the grammar-based descriptions of language that appeared in the Indian and European traditions. There was no concept of "sentence" in classical Chinese (nor, for that matter, any concept of grammar, nouns, verbs, etc.); if we use this term, we use it as an anachronistic convenience.[163]

A *chü* is a "period" (as the term is used in the description of prose). Until recent times, most Chinese texts were usually given without punctuation; and as a reader went through the text, he would add dots (*tien*) to mark off the natural pauses and groupings of words: these are *chü*, "periods." Sometimes *chü* make complete sentences; sometimes they are merely clauses; a series of descriptive compounds or nouns often constitute a *chü* in poetic expositions and descriptive prose; and *chü* are also the "lines" of a poem. Most printed texts made divisions of "paragraphs," *chang**, but some did not (early editions of *Wen-hsin tiao-lung* were not divided into *chang**, and a comparison of modern editions often reveals significant differences in the division of paragraphs—although on another level the chapters themselves are *chang**). Learning how to punctuate and how to recognize paragraphs and the grouping of characters in periods was called *chang**-chü*, "paragraphing and making periods," which is the title of this chapter in its pedagogic sense. *Chang**-chü* was the earliest form of studying literary texts, such as the Classics, and it remained the most elementary form. In extant writings before Liu Hsieh, the term *chang**-chü* is commonly used in reference to reading and study; *Wen-hsin tiao-lung* is the first extant occasion when it is given as a consideration in composition.

Exactly the same terms were applied to the divisions of poetry: in the translation below one could substitute "stanza" for "paragraph," and "line" or "couplet" for "period."

夫設情有宅。置言有位。宅情曰章。位言曰句。故章者。明也。句者。局也。局言者。聯字以分疆。明情者。總義以包體。區畛相異。而衢路交通矣。

In setting forth the affections there are lodgings;[164] in setting down language, there are positions.[165] The lodging given to [a particular] affection is known as a "unit" (*chang**, "paragraph," "stanza," "chapter"); setting the positions of language is known as period-making (*chü*). [Etymologically] *chang** means "to make clear," and *chü* means "to close off." In "closing off language," we link words together and define boundaries; in "making clear the affections," we gather together some truth (*yi**) and embrace it in a form (*t'i**). The bounded areas are distinct from one another, but highways and roads permit intercourse and passage through (*t'ung**).

Liu Hsieh's discussion of these two concepts is persuasive in its simplicity and probably derives from commonplaces of Classical studies.[166] A *chü* simply gathers a group of words together into one bounded unit, "closed off" from what precedes and what follows; a *chü* requires simply that these words be read together. Since the "grammar" or construction of a passage can change significantly depending on how the *chü* are marked (radically different readings of a passage can be produced by slight shifts in the punctuation dots), this is the basic organizational principle: grouping words and separating them from other words.[167] The model here is a division of the text into "containers," large ones containing small ones. Since *chü* are often not complete predicates and since their meaning is usually determined by the context of the rest of the paragraph, they are merely containers of words.[168] By the rhythms they impose on the words they join, these "containers" produce probabilities of relation, but they are not in themselves units of meaning.[169] *Chang**, on the other hand, are units of meaning, or as Liu Hsieh says, of a particular affection, *ch'ing** (recalling that the interplay of *ch'ing** is the medium of a literary work).

The way in which *chü* and *chang** work together to produce meaning is described in terms of roads, moving through a series of distinct territories (as opposed to a structure of contingent relations). Liu Hsieh had a complex vocabulary available to him with which to treat questions such as the relation between language and the psyche or the way in which some primary norm unfolds into the particular; here, however, there was no received terminology by which he could address complex issues of *taxis*. The organization of a text is conceived in the most general and indeterminate way, as enabling passage (*t'ung**) from one "point" to another. Yet it should be pointed out that such a structure of highly indeterminate relations is all too appropriate for the realities of Chinese *taxis* (particularly in the prose of this era), where one passes from period to period without explicit subordination and often without even implicit determinate relations; in many ways Liu Hsieh's description is quite accurate: the sense of a passage seems to emerge out of the aggregation of many periods.

夫人之立言。因字而生句。積句而成章。積章而成篇。篇之彪炳。章無疵也。章之明靡。句無玷也。句之清英。字不妄也。振本而末從。知一而萬畢矣。

When a person sets down language,[170] periods (*chü*) are produced out of written characters (*tzu*); the accumulation of periods makes a paragraph (*chang**); the accumulation of paragraphs forms a whole work. The brilliance of the whole work lies in the flawlessness of the paragraphs; the luminosity of the paragraph resides in the lack of imperfections in the periods; the clarity of the periods lies in the lack of falseness in the words (*tzu*, the "characters"). From a stirring of the root, the branch tips follow suit; if one thing is known, all is encompassed.

Within this description of language is a variation on an archaic structure of argument, closely related to traditional cosmogony: one builds from the most basic element to the fully elaborated; here the character is the basis, aggregating into units of increasing dimension. The structure of generation is also a structure of contingency, in which each prior phase governs the success or failure of the phase that follows. In "Nature and Form" we saw a literary pedagogy based on another variation of the same pattern: "When a vessel is formed or a color is set, it is hard to alter or reverse it. Thus when a child learns to carve, he must first learn dignified (*ya**) construction. Following the roots, we reach the leaves; and the revolutions of thoughts achieve a perfect circle." Success follows from proper beginnings; and it is therefore essential to understand where those beginnings are, to identify what is most basic.

From early descriptions of composing dramatic poetry to the modern idea of an outline, the Western tradition emphasizes moving from the general to the detail; we find a similar process advocated in some later works in Chinese poetics and elsewhere in *Wen-hsin tiao-lung*. Here, however, the value of the whole is a generated aggregate of true and precise words. The principle of choosing the right word as the basis of good discourse is closely related to the hermeneutic tradition surrounding the *Spring and Autumn Annals*, in which "significance is shown in single words."[171] That same tradition is also the beginning of an ideology of syntax as a natural *taxis* that follows the order of perception or the structure of an event.[172]

夫裁文匠筆。篇有小大。離章合句。調有緩急。隨變適會。莫見定準。句司數字。待相接以為用。章總一義。須意窮而成體。其控引情理。送迎際會。譬舞容迴環。而有綴兆之位。歌聲靡曼。而有抗墜之節也。

In literary craftsmanship, works vary in size; in the division of paragraphs and the joining of periods, there are distinctions of speed in the melody. There are no predetermined standards in following mutations and meeting the right occasion. A period governs several words and depends on their connection for its ability to function. A paragraph encompasses a single truth (*yi**); here the concept (*yi**) must be exhausted, and the form, complete. In the way they draw in the affections and principle, meeting each and sending it off at the right moment, it is like the circling movement of dancers, each with his or her own position on the dance platform, or like a singer's voice delicately holding the notes, with clear sections of swelling and diminuendo.

Note how easily Liu Hsieh moves from the relatively wooden model of containers and territories traversed by roads to the animate model of music, based on process and an instinctive sense of subtle changes and transformation. The interest in acting at the right moment is reminiscent of Lu Chi's "Poetic Exposition on Literature," where the metaphors of the singer and dancer also figure prominently. As in that earlier work, mastery here is an instinctive ability to carry out a process in time. Like Wheelwright Pien, Liu Hsieh cannot say how to do it, nor does he try: all he can say is that it must be done "just so," responding intuitively to the demands of the moment.

尋詩人擬喻。雖斷章取義。然章句在篇。如繭之抽緒。原始要終。體必鱗次。啟行之辭。逆萌中篇之意。絕筆之言。追媵前句之旨。故能外文綺交。內義脈注。跗萼相衝。首尾一體。

If we consider the way in which the poets of the *Book of Songs* made metaphorical references, even though they may sometimes have made their point (*yi**) in detached stanzas,[173] still the stanzas (*chang**) and lines (*chü*) in a piece are like silk drawn from a cocoon, starting from the beginning and carrying it through to the end,[174] the form always in layered succession [as with fish scales]. The periods that begin the journey anticipate the concepts (*yi**) in the middle of the composition; the words used at the close go back to carry through the significance of the previous lines. In that way the external pattern interconnects like lacework, and the inner truth (*yi**) pours through the veins, as the calyx contains the flower, head and tail being one unified form.

This is Liu Hsieh's model of structural unity, and it is very much an organic model. Compared to the Aristotelian notion of poetic unity based on the mutual necessity of parts, Liu Hsieh stresses a less determinate linearity of the text. A stronger difference is Liu Hsieh's stress on intricacy, like the ducts and veins of a living thing; and we might note that such an intricate structure is spoken of in terms of vessels for the concepts, *yi**, to "pour through." Unity here is very much a unity of movement related to organic life. It is a version of the familiar "unity in multiplicity" of Western aesthetics, but a version closest to the organic theories of the Romantics. From the model of organism we move next to social relations as a model of relations between elements of a text.

若辭失其朋。則羇旅而無友。事乖其次。則飄寓而不安。是以搜句忌於顛倒。裁章貴於順序。斯固情趣之指歸。文筆之同致也。

If some period should lose its friends, it will have no companions on its journey; the event (*shih**) will stray from its proper sequence, and it will find no resting place, drifting and lodging only temporarily.[175] Thus, in seeking lines, one should reject inversions of the proper order; and in cutting paragraphs to shape, one should value sequence. This is indeed the natural direction of the impulse of the affections (*ch'ing*-ch'ü**), the shared accomplishment of rhymed and unrhymed writing (*wen*-pi*).

The remaining paragraphs of this chapter, on the qualities of different line lengths, different possibilities of rhythm in rhymed periods, and on the use of particles, have been omitted.

斷章有檢。積句不恆。理資配主。辭忌失朋。環情節調。宛轉相騰。離合同異。以盡厥能。

Supporting Verse

    There are standards in dividing paragraphs,
    But no constants in combining lines.
    The principle depends on matching the dominant [concept];
    Avoid letting language lose its companions.
    Let the affections revolve in time with the melody,
    Rolling around, each mounting up beyond the others.
    Dividing and joining likenesses and differences,
    Thus you will do all possible in this [*chang-chü*].

CHAPTER 35
Parallel Phrasing, Li-tz'u 麗辭

造化賦形。支體必雙。神理為用。事不孤立。夫心生文辭。運裁百慮。高下相須。自然成對。

When Creation (*Tsao-hua**) unfurled the shapes (*hsing**) [of things], the limbs of all bodies (*t'i**) were in pairs. In the functioning of spirit's principle (*shen*-li**), no event (*shih**) occurs alone. And when mind generated literary language (*wen*-tz'u**), giving thought to all manner of concerns and cutting them to pattern, by Nature (*Tzu-jan**) parallelism was formed, just as [the concepts of] high and low are necessary to one another.

In this chapter's opening paragraph, literary parallelism is justified on the analogy of the bilateral symmetry of nature. In lines 143–150 of "The Poetic Exposition on Literature," Lu Chi conceived the isolation of an element in a literary work as a problem. Liu Hsieh treats the issue as a positive principle: words and references (shih*, "events") require counterparts, like the mutually supporting limbs of a living organism. The model of the mutual necessity of "high" and "low" is of particular importance: a line in parallel construction takes on value and significance in relation to its companion line in the same way that relative qualities define one another. The rest of the chapter takes up classifications of parallelism; these classifications are relatively crude when compared to the classificatory systems for parallelism in the following centuries.

CHAPTER 36

Comparison and Affective Image, Pi*-hsing* 比興

Most of the theoretical chapters of *Wen-hsin tiao-lung* address questions of both poetry and prose. In discussing comparison (*pi**) and affective image (*hsing**), Liu Hsieh enters the exclusive realm of poetry in its lineage from the *Book of Songs* and draws heavily on the tradition of exegesis of that Classic.[176] His focus of interest in questions of "metaphor" (stretching the term even beyond the latitude of its modern usage) is subtly different from the concerns of Western theory of metaphor: for Liu Hsieh affective image is "concealed" from rational understanding, and it is this that radically separates it from comparison. Because the mechanism by which affective image functions is latent (*yin*), its operations are interior (*nei*) and thus it works on the affections (*ch'ing**) directly, unmediated by the understanding.

詩文宏奧。句輻六義。毛公述傳。獨標興體。豈不以風通而賦同。比顯而興隱哉。故比者。附也。興者。起也。附理者切類以指事。起情者依微以擬議。起情故興體以立。附理故比例以生。比則畜憤以斥言。興則環譬以記諷。蓋隨時之義不一。故詩人之志有二也。

The *Book of Songs* has breadth and profundity, and within it are contained the Six Principles. Yet in Mao's commentary, the only notice is given to the form (*t'i**) of affective image (*hsing**).[177] This is surely because *Feng** [an "Air"] communicates (*t'ung**) [clearly] and exposition (*fu*) does the same; comparison (*pi**) is overt; only *hsing** is covert (or "latent," *yin*).[178] *Pi** is based on contiguity; *hsing** rouses. That which has contiguity in some principle (*li**) cleaves to some shared category (*lei*) and thereby indicates some matter (*shih**). On the other hand, that which rouses the affections depends on something subtle for the sake of reflective consideration. The affections are roused, and thus the normative form of *hsing** is established. When there is contiguity in some principle, an exemplary case of *pi** appears. In *pi** the accumulation of strong feeling is expressed in a verbal complaint. In *hsing** there is a circling comparison[179] to record their criticisms (*feng*). This is probably because the conditions of the times were different, and thus the intent (*chih**) of the poets of the *Book of Songs* took two forms.

The terms *pi** and *hsing** cannot be separated from their provenance in the tradition of interpretation of the *Book of Songs*, and their usage there must be assumed to be paradigmatic for the historical development of the two terms. Because the poems of the *Feng** section of the *Book of Songs* were often taken as criticism of government, the swerve from direct language (*fu*) that occurs in both *pi** and *hsing** was taken as a response to social threat. *Pi** belonged to safer times; the more covert form of *hsing** was necessary when complaint could not be more openly expressed. Liu Hsieh is not suggesting that these original social circumstances will necessarily stand behind all subsequent uses of *pi** and *hsing**; rather he is simply explaining the historical motivations that generated the two different modes.

Liu Hsieh begins with a standard question in the exegesis of the *Book of Songs*: why does the Mao commentary note only *hsing**? To provide the answer, Liu lists the first four of the "Six Principles" in their traditional sequence of *feng**, *fu*, *pi**, *hsing** (*ya** and *sung* are unproblematic and do not need to be mentioned) and shows that of these only *hsing** is latent (*yin*) and hence in need of the commentator's explicit attention.

The set of distinctions made between *pi** and *hsing** is remarkably cryptic, and I have tried to translate it as "literally" as possible. *Pi** and *hsing** are differentiated on essentially two grounds: the distinction between overt and covert, and the distinction between natural principle (*li**) and the affections (*ch'ing**). Modern Western literary thought, with its stress on metaphor and substitution tropes, will have difficulty here; it is essential to note that because the Chinese tradition had largely abandoned a theory of signs in favor a notion of language that incorporated motive, circumstance, and state of mind, the tradition did not develop a theory of tropes and figures. In Western terms *pi** is a trope, but *hsing** is not; that is, *pi** uses one word to "refer" to something else; *hsing** uses words to stir a certain response. The grounds of comparison in a *pi** are based on common "principle" (*li**) and shared category (*lei*), the *tertium aliquid* of Western theory of metaphor. *Hsing**, on the other hand, is based on association, which occurs within mind rather than in the world, and thus it is covert. The statement that "*pi** is contiguity" is based on the etymological interpretation of the word; and its implication here is that, according to some principle (fierceness, courage), two phenomena (Achilles and a lion) can be "set side by side." Because this contiguity occurs in the external world rather than in the movements of the reflecting mind itself, it is overt.

While affective image (*hsing**) can often, on close reflection, be found to have some metaphorical basis, the issue of *hsing** in traditional literary thought lies outside the scope of Western theory of metaphor: *hsing** is not how a word is "carried over" from its "proper" sense to a new one, but rather how the presentation of some phenomenon (*wu**) in words is mysteriously able to "stir" (*hsing**) a response or evoke a mood. Such a response, as it occurs, is prereflective and hidden from the understanding. In amplifying the notion of *hsing**, Liu Hsieh does speak of it as "a circling comparison"; but this is a remarkably cryptic phrase which, if nothing else, suggests a swerve that keeps the relation covert.[180] Most classical explanations of *hsing** prefer terms like *t'o* 託, "to entrust" one's feelings to some object; being replete with the writer's feelings, the object reveals them when touched on in reading.[181] The other term used by exegetes of *hsing** is *yü* 喻 (or 諭), "to have an intended point." Liu Hsieh uses both of these terms in his discussion of *hsing** in the following passage. Stress should be placed on the covertness of *hsing**, the quality that makes it appropriate for strong feelings that must be kept hidden.

觀夫興之託諭。婉而成章。稱名也小。取類也大。關雎有別。故后妃方德。尸鳩貞一。故夫人象義。義取其貞。無從于夷禽。德貴其別。不嫌於鷙鳥。明而未融。故發注而後見也。

When we consider the intended points lodged (*t'o-yü*) in *hsing**, the work is completed by subtle indirectness.[182] "The words it uses are small, but their implications by categorical analogy are large."[183] "*Kuan* sing the ospreys" makes a distinction [between the sexes], and thus the Queen Consort is compared [to those birds] in virtue (*tê**); the dove is pure and true, thus the lady is likened to it in righteousness (*yi**).[184] In the latter case, the principle (*yi**) is to be found only in the dove's purity; do not pursue [the connection between the dove and the lady] as if it were an ordinary bird. In the former case, the virtue that is valued is distinction; do not disapprove of the osprey because it is a bird of prey. "It is getting brighter but not yet full sunlight":[185] thus they can be visible only after commentary has been given.

Liu Hsieh is put in difficulty because he is trying to make explicit a mode that is, by his own definition, implicit. Being explicit and "logical," he is compelled to use the inappropriate language of comparison here to describe the operations of *hsing**. And we can see him tripping over his own feet as he struggles to be explicit about the different operations of the explicit and implicit modes. His purpose is to prevent the reader from making a substantial comparison in reading *hsing**: "do not pursue [the connection between the dove and the lady] as if it were an ordinary bird." Comparison (*pi**) is to be understood by reflection; *hsing** is to be understood immediately. But because immediate understanding may become a problem in later ages, commentary is necessary. The paragraph is given to avert the danger of conflating the two modes, of reading *hsing** as if it were *pi**. The Queen Consort is not "like" an osprey; the osprey evokes a quality of relations between mates that informs the way we read about the Consort.

且何謂為比。蓋寫物以附意。颺言以切事者也。故金錫以喻明德。珪璋以譬秀民。螟蛉以類教誨。蜩螗以寫號呼。澣衣以擬心憂。席卷以方志固。凡斯切象。皆比義也。至於麻衣如雪。兩驂如舞。若斯之類。皆比類者也。

　楚襄信讒。而三閭忠烈。依詩製騷。諷兼比興。炎漢雖盛。而辭人夸毗。詩刺道喪。故興義銷亡。於是賦頌先鳴。比體雲構。紛紜雜遝。倍舊章矣。

What then is *pi**? It is to describe a thing (*wu**) in such a way as to attach (*fu*, "be contiguous") a concept (*yi**) to it, to let one's words sweep forth so as to cleave to some matter (*shih**). Thus gold and tin refer to illustrious virtue; jade tablets are used as comparisons with an outstanding person; the caterpillar of the moth is likened to the process of education; cicadas describe a lot of noise; washed robes imitate a melancholy in the heart; a mat rolled up is a simile for firmness of intent: in all these cases [the situation] cleaves to the image (*hsiang**), and every one has the principle (*yi**) of *pi**.[186] Lines like "Robes of hemp like the snow" or "The two trace horses seem to dance" are all *pi**.[187]

King Hsiang of Ch'u trusted slanderers, yet Ch'ü Yüan was fiercely loyal [even though banished by the king]. Ch'ü Yüan constructed his *Li Sao* along the lines of the *Book of Songs*; and in his indirect criticism (*feng*), he combines both *pi** and *hsing**. When the Han was in the heights of its glory, the rhetors were servile; the Way of criticism we find in the *Songs* perished, and as a result the principle of *hsing** was lost. Then poetic expositions (*fu*) and odes (*sung*) had primacy, and the form of *pi** constructed profuse and disorderly cloud-shapes, turning their back on the former statutes.

Because the same word is used, most critics filiated the "poetic expositions" (*fu*) of the Han court writers to the principle of direct exposition (*fu*) in the "Six Principles" of the *Book of Songs*. Liu Hsieh did so himself in an earlier chapter on the poetic exposition. In this chapter, however, only *pi** and *hsing** are under direct consideration, so that he reclassifies the poetic exposition under the comparatively overt mode, the "form of *pi**" (*pi**-*t'i**). Since he considers *pi** as inferior to *hsing**, Liu Hsieh uses the reclassification to express his sense of the devolution of Han literature from the heights of the *Book of Songs* and the *Li Sao*. The servility of the Han court writers makes *hsing** impossible because *hsing**, as a mode of criticism, would effectively touch the interior of the ruler, as well as coming from the interior, the

genuine feelings, of the writer. Yet another motive for Liu Hsieh's reclassification may have been the tendency to read many Han poetic expositions as
figural; thus "unfigured exposition," the meaning of the term *fu* when applied
to the *Book of Songs*, was inappropriate.

夫比之為義。取類不常。或喻於聲。或方於貌。或擬於心。或譬於事。宋玉高唐云。纖條
悲鳴。聲似竽籟。此比聲之類也。枚乘菟園云。焱焱紛紛。若塵埃之間白雲。此則比貌之
類也。賈生鵩賦云。禍之與福。何異糾纏。此以物比理者也。王襃洞簫云。優柔溫潤。如
慈父之畜子也。此以聲比心者也。馬融長笛云。繁縟絡繹。范蔡之說也。此以響比辯者
也。張衡南都云。起鄭舞。蟺曳曳緒。此以容比物者也。若斯之類。辭賦所先。日用乎
比。月忘乎興。習小而棄大。所以文謝於周人也。

The principle (*yi**) of *pi** has no constant in the way it makes categorical analogies (*lei**). Comparisons may be made by sound, by appearance, by [state
of] mind (*hsin**), or by event (*shih**). A comparison by category of sound
can be seen in Sung Yü's "Poetic Exposition on Kao-t'ang":

> The thin twigs sing sadly,
> Their sound like pipes and ocarinas.

A comparison by categories of appearance can be seen in Mei Sheng's "Rabbit
Garden":

> Fleeting and in profusion,
> [The birds] are like dust among the white clouds.

A comparison of things to principles (*li**) can be seen in Chia Yi's "The Owl":

> How different from the twining of a cord
> Is good fortune's relation to ill fortune.

Sound is compared to [a state of] mind in Wang Pao's "Transverse Flute" [in
which the music is described as]:

> Gentle and full of kindliness,
> Like a father caring for a son.

Resonance is compared to good argument in Ma Jung's "The Long Flute":

> Opulent and continuous [music]:
> The oratory of Fan [Chü] and Ts'ai [Tse].

Manner is compared to a thing in Chang Heng's "Southern Capital":

> Then arose the dancers from Cheng,
> Silkworms spinning their threads.

Cases like this are foremost in poetic expositions. But continual use of *pi** led to a forgetfulness of *hsing**; and habitual practice (*hsi*) of the lesser along with rejection of the greater makes their writing inferior to that of the Chou.

Note that Liu Hsieh first gives examples of similes, using a range of the many Chinese terms of similitude. At the end, he gives two metaphors, neither using the term of similitude ("like") but both close to simile in their immediate juxtaposition with their referents.

A subtle transformation has taken place here. Despite the fact that some of the most famous examples of *hsing** were supposed to be from society in its perfection (the first poem of the *Book of Songs*), Liu Hsieh accepts the conventional association of *hsing** with indirect criticism (*feng* 諷): its hiddenness follows from the repression of pain and indignation that implies a threat in the external world (as the "Great Preface" says of *feng**, "the one who speaks it has no culpability"). In purely literary terms, however, *hsing** is considered the more effective and "greater" mode. The writers of poetic expositions "rejected the greater" mode (*hsing**) and thus ended up producing works that were inferior to the *Book of Songs*. But in the age of the *Book of Songs*, the decision between *pi** and *hsing** came "probably because the conditions of the times were different, and thus the intent of the poets . . . took two forms." The Han writers of poetic expositions chose *pi** because of "habitual practice" (*hsi*)—theirs was a decision made on literary grounds and the conventions of contemporary literary practice. Here we find the beginnings of a distinction between the age of the Classics, when literature and society were a seamless unity, and a later age of literary history, governed by "habitual practice" and conscious decision.[188]

至於揚班之倫。曹劉以下。圖狀山川。影寫雲物。莫不纖綜比義。以敷其華。驚聽回視。資此効績。又安仁螢賦云流金在沙。季鷹雜詩云青條若總翠。皆其義者也。故比類雖繁。以切至為貴。若刻鵠類鶩。則無所取焉。

When we reach writers like Yang Hsiung and Pang Ku, and all those since Ts'ao Chih and Liu Chen, they depicted the mountains and streams, perfectly delineated clouds and creatures; we find that every one wove the principle of *pi** into his works in order to display the splendor of those things, startling the ears and dazzling the eyes; they depended on this for their success. We see this principle in P'an Yüeh's "Fireflies":

Drifting gold upon the sands

or in Chang Han's "Unclassified Poem":

Green branches like massed kingfisher feathers.

Though the category of *pi** is rich and various, perfect likeness is what is valued. If a person carves a snow goose in the resemblance of a duck, there is nothing to be gained from it.

詩人比興。觸物圓覽。物雖胡越。合則肝膽。擬容取心。斷辭必敢。攢雜詠歌。如川之渙。

Supporting Verse

> The *pi** and *hsing** of the poets of the *Songs*
> Observed perfectly whatever they encountered.
> Though things were as far apart as Hu [in the north] and Yüeh [in the south],
> When put together, they were as liver and gall.
> To imitate appearance and get the heart
> Decisive words must be used with daring.
> Then gathered into poetry and song,
> They will sweep along like a stream.

CHAPTER 40
Latent and Out-Standing, Yin-hsiu 隱秀

Although an opposition between "latent" (*yin* 隱) and "salient" or "out-standing" (*hsiu* 秀) had precedent in the century preceding *Wen-hsin tiao-lung*, Liu Hsieh's application of these concepts to literature was entirely his own. Because the concept of latency (*yin*) treats the question of subtext—whether we understand subtext as "meaning" in the Western sense or the Chinese notion of "reserve," *han-hsü* 含蓄—this is a very important chapter. Unfortunately it is also fragmentary, with a major lacuna right at the point where the suggestive remarks of the opening would normally be developed.[189]

The privilege accorded to depth in the tradition of Western literary thought would demand that an antithetical term such as *hsiu*, the "out-standing," be devalued as superficial. But the conceptual (or emotional) depth of "latency" is not given here as an independent value; rather, it requires the "out-standing" as an opposite or complementary virtue.[190] The "out-standing" is a positive quality without depth: its effect is immediate and "striking."

夫心術之動遠矣。文情之變深矣。源奧而派生。根盛而穎峻。是以文之英蕤。有秀有隱。隱也者。文外之重旨者也。秀也者。篇中之獨拔者也。隱以複意為工。秀以卓絕為巧。斯乃舊章之懿績。才情之嘉會也。

The ways of mind go far indeed; and the mutations of the affections in literature go deep. When the source is profound, branching streams grow from it;
when the root flourishes, the ear of grain stands lofty.[191] Thus, in the bright
flowering of literature, there are latent elements (*yin*) and elements that stand
out (*hsiu*). The latent is the layered significance that lies beyond the text (*wen**);
the out-standing is that which rises up uniquely within the piece. The latent is
fully accomplished in complex and multiple concepts. The out-standing shows
its craft in preeminent superiority. These are the splendid achievements of old
works, an excellent conjunction of talent and the affections.

As is often the case in Liu Hsieh's writing, the relation between antithetical
complements is remarkably indeterminate: we are never quite sure whether
yin and *hsiu* represent two different kinds of writing in two different kinds of
texts or two distinct aspects of the same text that are necessary to one
another (and if the latter, we are unsure whether they appear simultaneously
or sequentially). At moments Liu Hsieh clearly seems to have two different
kinds of writing in mind, but the opening passage strongly suggests an
organic relation between the two terms, suggesting their presence together
in the same text: the deep root produces the out-standing flower, and the
out-standing flower is the evidence of a deep root.

The notion of "layered significance" (*ch'ung-chih*) merits some comment.
The term *chih* here, translated as "significance," cuts across a number of
English concepts: it is often the "aims" or "intended meaning" in a text, but
in the restricted sense of the values held by the writer which are imparted in
the text. *Chih* is often associated with "distance," and is often less the
immediate impression of a text than its ultimate "import." Hence it is the
appropriate term for subtext.

Equally important in the concept of the latent are the notions of "layering" (*ch'ung*) and of "beyond the text" (*wen**-wai*). "Layering" suggests not
only multiplicity but also being covered over. The same ambiguity exists in
the ornamental variation later in the paragraph, "complex and multiple concepts" (*fu-yi**). We are uncertain whether Liu Hsieh is suggesting that there is
a single intended meaning that is beneath the surface (as one might presume
in the interpretation of Classics such as the *Book of Songs*) or that the text
is genuinely polysemous (as would follow from the model of the *Book of
Changes* invoked in the next paragraph).

The phrase "beyond the text" is the ancestor of a set of important "beyond
X" constrctions in later literary thought: "beyond words" (*yen-wai* 言外) and
"beyond images" (*hsiang**-wai* 象外). These "beyond" terms are strongly
associated with the later notion of "reserve" (*han-hsü* 含蓄), a plenitude of
intended meaning or feeling that is voluntarily or involuntarily withheld
from the surface of the text, but whose pressures are implicit within the surface of the text. A genuine fragment of the missing part of this chapter was

preserved in the twelfth-century *Sui-han-t'ang shih-hua* 歲寒堂詩話 by Chang Hsieh 張戒; this passage is even closer to the notion of "reserve" that developed in the Late T'ang and Sung: "The latent is present when the affections (*ch'ing**) lie beyond the wording; the out-standing is present when the manner wells up before one's eyes."[192] Thus the "latent" element, defined as being "beyond" the text, is variously given as "significance" (*chih*), "feeling" (*ch'ing**), and in the following section, "a truth" (*yi**). In the later transformations of a reserve that is "beyond the text," an organic model is usually not implicit; but in Liu Hsieh's formulation here, the organic model is important: not only are these qualities invisible on the surface of the text, they are the root from which the text grows. The "out-standing" is the opposite but related virtue, something that is not at all hidden but rather strikes the reader immediately.[193]

夫隱之為體。義主文外。秘響傍通。伏采潛發。譬爻象之變互體。川瀆之韞珠玉也。故互體變爻。而化成四象。珠玉潛水。而瀾表方圓。

When the latent is a normative form (*t'i**) [in itself], a truth (*yi**) is dominant beyond the text (*wen*-wai*); mysterious resonances get through (*t'ung**) all around, and hidden coloration (*ts'ai**) emerges from the sunkenness. One may compare it to the way in which the lines and images in a hexagram mutate to form another hexagram, or how rivers may contain pearls and jade. Thus when the individual lines mutate in the form of a hexagram, they transform into the Four Images [the four component digrams]. Pearls or jade sunken under the water will form round or square ripples.

The primary difference between the opening line here and the formulation in the preceding paragraph lies in the notion of "being a normative form in itself." It seems that the latent may be an aspect of any text, or it may be the "dominant" (*chu*) mode of one particular text. The presence of the latent is signaled by indirect evidence: "resonances" and "hidden coloration." The analogical model by which one can divine the source of these "resonances" is remarkable: the hermeneutics of the hexagrams of the *Book of Changes*.

The comparison of the operation of the "latent" mode to the transformations of the hexagrams was unique to Liu Hsieh and perhaps the most suggestive model for literary meaning in all *Wen-hsin tiao-lung*. This model would have provided a way to understand the operations of significance in a literary text apart from the state of mind of its author; but it was perhaps just such a dissociation of meaning from circumstance that kept the model from being developed later in the tradition.

The theory of the operation of the hexagrams in the *Book of Changes* is far too complicated to describe in detail here. Stated simply, a hexagram is the schematization of a phase of change based on the interpretation of six broken and unbroken lines, read from bottom to top. The nature of the hexagram is determined by the active interpenetration of two trigrams. Such interpenetration produces crucial lines that govern the transformation of one hexagram out of or into another (either the next hexagram in the sequence or an opposite or complementary one elsewhere in the sequence of the sixty-four hexagrams). Thus, not only is every hexagram a phase of change in its own right, that phase is schematically articulated by a relation to a complex set of antithetical, complementary, precedent, and succedent phases. Liu Hsieh here uses the technical terms for two of these sets of "transformations": the "mutation of the image" (*pien*-hsiang*) and the "alternation of form (*hu-t'i*).

Liu Hsieh clearly intended the application of such a model to "latent significance" only in a general way. It suggests that the surface of the text implies latent significance in the same way that one hexagram implicates another hexagram in a transformative relation. Thus, when we see the surface, we think of the latent state that produced the surface or to which the surface will inevitably lead through some orderly change. Thus the text signifies not by representation but by implicating a prior, future, antithetical, or complementary condition. In the same way, the folkloristic belief in pearls or jade producing different kinds of ripples (often described as *wen*) on the surface of the water is another way in which the latent become manifest on the surface. The major lacuna in the text occurs at this point. I have also omitted one authentic passage that goes with the lost section.

凡文集勝篇。不盈十一。篇章秀句。裁可百二。並思合而自逢。非研慮之所求也。

Excellent works usually do not make up even a tenth of a literary collection; and within a work, the out-standing lines are scarcely two in a hundred. In both cases [whole works and out-standing lines], we happen on them by a peculiar conjunction of thought; they are not to be sought by studious reflection.

"Latency" could be a property of an entire text or of a particular passage within a text, but the "out-standing" is very much a momentary effect that occurs in single lines or passages. As such, it bears some similarity to the "riding crop" described in "The Poetic Exposition on Literature," lines 123–132.

An important point about literary value flies past here, scarcely noticed: the acknowledgment that excellence is accidental (although Liu Hsieh would surely insist that much learning and skill are the necessary preconditions for having such happy accidents). Although he does so less often than Lu Chi, Liu Hsieh sometimes admits the limits of conscious effort in composition. But in the paragraph that follows, Liu sees what Lu Chi could not see: that conscious effort to achieve these two kinds of excellence—the latent and the out-standing—can produce grotesque counterparts in which each particular quality's virtues become vices. What separates the genuine forms of latent and out-standing from their flawed counterparts is precisely the fact that they are given "naturally" (*tzu-jan**) and are not within the scope of human effort.

或有晦塞為深。雖奧非隱。雕削取巧。雖美非秀矣。故自然會妙。譬卉木之耀英華。潤色取美。譬繪帛之染朱綠。朱綠染繪。深而繁鮮。英華曜樹。淺而煒燁。秀句所以照文苑。蓋以此也。

Sometimes mere obscurity and concealment are considered to be depth; though there may be some quality of mysterious profundity, it is not "the latent." Or intricate craftsmanship may aim at the artful; though it is lovely, it is not "the out-standing." Only Nature (*Tzu-jan**) can bring together these subtleties (*miao**), like plants and trees that are splendid in their flowering. A beauty obtained by added colors is like dying plain silk red and green. The silk dyed red and green is deeply colored, rich, and fresh. But the flowers that gleam on the trees have a shallow color, yet a glorious one—this is the way an out-standing line shines in the garden of letters.

Several central concerns in later literary thought are adumbrated in this chapter. Although the notion of significance or affections "beyond the words" may be the most important of these, the inobtrusive images of this closing passage are also significant. The praise of the natural and "shallow" color goes against our expectations developed in the earlier parts of the chapter: we would have expected the "out-standing" to dazzle us. But what is too brilliant is garish and cloys; the less extreme form strikes us more strongly. This is an important transformation of the aesthetics of incompletion and reserve that can be traced back to the "Record of Music" (see p. 53). In the oxymoronic gleaming paleness of the flowers, the distinction between the "latent" and the "out-standing" blurs somewhat; now in both modes something is withheld from the surface (though in the case of the "out-standing" it is not "something else" concealed but a degree of intensity of an overt quality). Such restraint, and its association with the natural, became a common theme in later aesthetics, particularly in Ssu-k'ung T'u's "Twenty-Four Categories of Poetry" (see especially the discussion of "Intricate Beauty," *ch'i-li*, pp. 321–323).

深文隱蔚。餘味曲包。辭生互體。有似變爻。言之秀矣。萬慮一交。動心驚耳。逸響笙匏。

Supporting Verse
　　Deep writing has latent richness,

Lingering flavor folded minutely within.
The words give rise to a change in form [as in a hexagram],
Something like the mutation of [a hexagram's] lines.
When language is out-standing,
All reflections join as one,
Stirring the mind, startling the ear,
Like the lofty resonance of a *sheng* or *pao* [two musical instruments].

CHAPTER 43
Fluency and Coherence, Fu-hui 附會

"Fluency and Coherence" treats essentially the same issues as "Paragraph and Period": organization and linear unity within the text. Since it does not need to address the question of the "divisions" of a text, however, it amplifies the question of unity more fully. An argument might be made that less fullness would have been preferable: Liu Hsieh gives us a wide array of incommensurate metaphors and models, each of which casts the question of unity in a slightly different perspective.

Fu is the term translated rather freely as "fluency." *Fu* is literally "adherence," the sequential contiguity that gives the text linear unity. That easy, unbroken movement is close to the English "fluency"; and when a text is not "choppy," we say it "flows." *Hui* is the paired term, an overall "coherence." Since later in the chapter Liu Hsieh speaks of "making the words flow (*fu*) and the truths cohere (*hui*)," commentators have usually interpreted *fu* and *hui* as an opposition between unity of language and conceptual unity.[194] This is not impossible, but there are other passages in the chapter that would argue against it. I would prefer to stress a more fundamental opposition between *fu* and *hui*: *fu* is linear unity realized in process, while *hui* is the unity of the piece grasped as a whole. It seems that one could have "fluency" without "coherence," and "coherence" without "fluency."

何謂附會。謂總文理。統首尾。定與奪。合涯際。彌綸一篇。使雜而不越者也。若築室之須基構。裁衣之待縫緝矣。

What is meant by fluency and coherence?—to bring together the principles of a literary work, to unite the beginning and the end, to determine what is to be added and what excluded, to have concord between the boundaries,[195] to fill out and organize the whole piece so that it will be varied without transgressing [the limits of variety into confusion]. It is like the necessary laying of the foundation and building the frame in constructing a house, or like the way in which making clothes depends on sewing and fine stitching.

The "principles of a literary work" (wen*-li*) may refer either to the essentially literary principles of composition or to the principles of the outer world that appear immanent in the work. Compounds such as wen-li* help to blur any distinctions we might want to make between the two: the li* that shapes a literary work is tacitly identified with the li* that works in the external world.

The opening models of building and sewing suggest that organization is done to some prior blueprint or plan, which the writer then executes. This plan gives "foundation and frame"; and as the writer fills in the spaces, all the seams meet perfectly. It is a delightfully simple, if not very inspiring, model for composition; but it is also a model that disappears immediately, never to return. In the next section, we discover that we are constructing neither house nor gown, but a human body.

夫才量學文。宜正體製。必以情志為神明。事義為骨髓。辭采為肌膚。宮商為聲氣。然後品藻玄黃。摛振金玉。獻可替否。以裁厥中。斯綴思之恆數也。

When a talented youth studies literature, he should have the proper model of form. He should take the affections and intent (ch'ing*-chih*) as the element of spiritual understanding (shen*-ming); take events (shih*) and truths (yi*) as the bone and marrow; take language and coloration (ts'ai*) as the skin and flesh; take musical qualities as the voice and ch'i*. Only then can he judge the categories of [Heaven's] purple and [Earth's] brown,[196] strike forth the tones of metal and jade, suggest the best course or come up with alternatives to a bad course, and in that way judge what is fitting. This is the constant order (shu*) of linking thoughts (ssu*) together.

"Fluency and Coherence" is more a didactic than a descriptive chapter; the interest in pedagogy and the scholastic tone were appropriate to a young man fresh out of the monastery school and quite different from the contemporary mode of discourse on literature carried on in the aristocratic salons. Liu Hsieh postulates a hierarchy of stages, beginning with the most basic elements and working outward. The most basic elements in writing are ch'ing* and chih*, corresponding to mind ("spiritual understanding," shen*-ming) in a human being. Following the generative hierarchy outward, the writer creates a living body with voice. Note that however physical the intermediate stages, the final stage of voice is the element that externalizes the primary stage, "spiritual understanding." This vision of unity, an organic and generative unity of inside and outside, is very different from having a blueprint or pattern and executing it. But no sooner does Liu Hsieh postulate a unity of inside and outside, than he turns to a new set of models unifying the many and the one.

凡大體文章。類多枝派。整派者依源。理枝者循幹。是以附辭會義。務總綱領。驅萬塗於
同歸。貞百慮於一致。使眾理雖繁。而無倒置之乖。羣言雖多。而無棼絲之亂。扶陽而出
條。順陰而藏跡。首尾周密。表裏一體。此附會之術也。

From a general point of view,[199] a literary work usually has many branchings
[like a tree] and divisions into multiple watercourses. Keeping these watercourses correct depends on the source; to organize (*li**) the branchings requires
following the trunk. So to make the words flow (*fu*) and the truths cohere
(*hui*), one must endeavor to keep the overview and main points together.
Travel swiftly down ten thousand paths, but come to the end together; formu-
late a hundred different concerns into a single unity.[198] Despite their complexity, one must keep a large number of principles from the error of being put in
the wrong order; and despite their multiplicity, one must avoid letting the
hosts of words fall into the confusion of tangled threads. Branches are put out
to take in the sunshine, while the traces are hidden where there is shade. Beginning and end are an integral whole; inside and outside are the same form (*t'i**).
This is the technique of fluency and coherence.

Here we have models of a tree with its branches and a river with its tributaries. This is one of the clearest statements of Liu Hsieh's idea of organic unity.
While the idea on "unity in multiplicity" must be familiar to Western readers, there is one aspect of the model of the tree that should be stressed: multiplicity is the external form, while the unifying "trunk" stands "within" or
"behind" multiplicity. Unity should always be implicit in multiplicity ("the
traces are hidden"); it should not be an explicit structure of organization, as
were the models with which Liu began the chapter. Since all particulars grow
organically from the primary unity, excessive attention to a detail can disorder the whole.

夫畫者謹髮而易貌。射者儀毫而失牆。銳精細巧。必疏體統。故宜詘寸以信尺。枉尺以直
尋。棄偏善之巧。學具美之績。此命篇之經略也。
　　夫文變無方。意見浮雜。約則義孤。博則辭叛。率故多尤。需為事賊。且才分不同。
思緒各異。或製首以通尾。或尺接以寸附。然通製者蓋寡。接附者甚眾。若統緒失宗。辭
味必亂。義脈不流。則偏枯文體。夫能懸識湊理。然後節文自會。如膠之粘木。豆之合黃
矣。是以駟牡異力。而六轡如琴。並駕齊驅。而一轂統輻。馭文之法。有似於此。去留隨
心。修短在手。齊其步驟。總轡而已。

A painter may be attentive to a hair and change the [overall] appearance [in a
portrait]; an archer may focus on a single strand and miss the wall. Too sharp
attention to some fine point of craft necessarily distances one from the gov-

erning unity of form. So we should bend the inch to make a reliable foot and twist the foot for the sake of the straight yard, reject craft in some one-sided excellence, and study the achievement of integral beauty. This is the enduring generality in producing a piece.

The mutations of literature have no bounds, and the points of view in concepts are various and unstable. If too terse, your truth will be solitary; if too extensive, the words may get out of control; insouciant haste brings many excesses; in hesitation the matter may get out of hand. Moreover, the measures of talent that people have are not the same; each differs in what his thoughts touch upon. Some work from the beginning straight through to the end; some join parts together by the inch and foot. I suspect, however, that those who work all the way through are few, while those who join [small sections] are many. In unifying sentiments, if you lose sight of what's important, the flavor of the words (tz'u*-wei*) will be confused; and if the veins through which a truth passes do not admit smooth flow, then the form of the work will become desiccated. Only after deep consideration of the whole pattern of pores in the skin will the sections naturally achieve coherence, as glue sticks to wood, as white tin mixes with yellow gold.[199] A team of four horses may differ in strength, but the six reins that guide them are like the strings of a lute;[200] they drive together on both sides of the carriage, one axle unifying all the spokes.[201] The method of guiding a work of literature resembles this. One goes off or lingers as the mind wishes;[202] keeping the reins tight or loose lies in the power of one's hand.[203] To make them prance together in an even pace is nothing more than gathering the reins together.

The cautious and well planned construction, suggested at the opening of the chapter, is acknowledged here ("some join parts together by the inch and foot"); but it is now devalued in comparison to yet another model ("working from the beginning straight through to the end"), composition as an ongoing process like driving a carriage. The work now seems to move under its own power, and the task of the writer is to control those forces, to guide and restrain.

故善附者異旨如肝膽。拙會者同音如胡越。改章難於造篇。易字艱於代句。此已然之驗也。昔張湯擬奏而再却。虞松草表而屢譴。並理事之不明。而詞旨之失調也。及倪寬更草。鍾會易字。而漢武歎奇。晉景稱善者。乃理得而事明。心敏而辭當也。以此而觀。則知附會巧拙。相去遠哉。

Those who are expert at contiguity can put different significances together as close as liver and gall, while those clumsy at coherence can take even the same tones and leave them as far apart as Hu [in the far north] and Yüeh [in the far south]. To revise a work is more difficult than producing one, and to change a word is harder than to redo the sentence. This has long been a proven fact. Long ago, Chang T'ang twice had to withdraw a memorial on which he had worked much; Yü Sung was often reprimanded for the position papers he drafted. In both cases the principle and the matter at hand were not clear; and the language and significance had lost the melody. But when Ni K'uan changed the draft [of Chang T'ang's memorial] and when Chung Hui altered some words [in Yü Sung's position papers], Han Wu-ti exclaimed at how marvelous the former was and Tsin Ching-ti praised the excellence of the latter. Then the principle was grasped, and the matter at hand was clear; the mind showed a quickness, and the language was appropriate. Considering these examples, we can realize how far apart are skill and clumsiness in contiguity and coherence.

Earlier the writer was advised not to pay too close attention to a detail; the detail should emerge from a sense of the whole. Here we find that the unity and success of the whole can depend on the detail, and that a slight change in the process of revision can constitute the difference between total failure and perfection.

若夫絕筆斷章。譬乘舟之振楫。會詞切理。如引轡以揮鞭。克終底績。寄深寫送。若首唱榮華。而膝句憔悴。則遺勢鬱湮。餘風不暢。此周易所謂臋無膚。其行次且也。惟首尾相援。則附會之體。固亦無以加於此矣。

When you stop your brush and end a work, it is like raising the oars when we ride in a boat. Making the words cohere and the principles be apposite is like drawing in the reins and shaking the whip. To end well and truly achieve something will send something off with it.[204] If you sing out splendidly in the beginning, but the lines in the bridal train [of the lovely opening] are dreary, the residual momentum will become bogged down and blocked, and the lingering wind (*feng**) will not spread. This is what the *Book of Changes* means by "no skin on the thighs—cannot proceed."[205] If only the beginning and end connect, there is nothing to add in the form (*t'i**) of fluency and coherence.

The beautiful metaphor comparing raising the writing brush to lifting oars suggests an important value, developed later in the tradition: after the words are done, there remains a residual momentum, and that momentum carries the text to its true conclusion. The significance of a work is often described as *kuei* 歸, "that to which the text comes home," the end of its journey. But such a return occurs after the words are finished, the last stage carried by the text's residual force.

篇統間關。情數稠疊。原始要終。疏條布葉。道味相附。懸緒自接。如樂之和。心聲克協。

Supporting Verse

> The piece's unity is stabilized,
> The numbers of the affections are in layers.
> Beginning with origins and properly ended,
> The sparse branches spread with leaves.
> The flavor of the Way lies in contiguity,
> Diverse sentiments joining together,
> As harmony in music,
> The mind's voice blends.[206]

CHAPTER 44
The General Technique

In "The General Technique," Liu Hsieh joins the contemporary debate regarding the question of what is and what is not *wen**.[207] This is not the question of "what is literature?" as it has been formulated in the West. The grand aetiology of *wen** in "Its Source in the Way" was one kind of "definition," but not a definition that could ever answer the question, what language or writing is **not** *wen**? In fifth century literary discussion, however, *wen** was considered in opposition to several other terms, including *yen*, the most general term for "language," and *pi*, literally "brush[work]." In broad terms *pi* was conceived as a plain, serviceable prose, in contrast to the more prestigious *wen**; but the precise distinction between the two was a matter of debate. As Liu Hsieh points out in the opening, there were many who made the distinction purely on the basis of rhyme (*wen** being rhymed, and *pi* unrhymed). However, far too many older unrhymed works had always been called *wen** to make such a distinction acceptable to a literary scholar like Liu Hsieh.

Liu Hsieh offers his own, rather confused argument for a proper set of distinctions, but soon wanders off into a series of assertions that there is some "general technique" for drawing together all particular aspects of a literary work. Despite his claims to the contrary, he never says anything more about such a technique than that it exists and is very important.

今之常言。有文有筆。以為無韻者筆也。有韻者文也。夫文以足言。理兼詩書。別目兩名。自近代耳。顏延年以為筆之為體。言之文也。經典則言而非筆。傳記則筆而非言。請奪彼矛。還攻其楯矣。何者？易之文言。豈非言文。若筆為言文。不得云經典非筆矣。將以立論。未見其論立也。

予以為發口為言。屬筆曰翰。常道曰經。述經曰傳。經傳之體。出言入筆。筆為言使。可強可弱。分經以典奧為不刊。非以言筆為優劣也。

In common parlance these days, a distinction is made between *wen** and *pi*, with *pi* as writing without rhyme and *wen** as writing with rhyme. Now the principle of having "pattern (*wen**) adequate for the words"[208] is present both in the [rhymed] *Book of Songs* and [unrhymed] *Book of Documents*; to view them as belonging to two separate categories is a recent phenomenon. Yen Yen-chih considers that *pi*, as a normative form (*t'i**), is language (*yen*) with pattern (*wen**) [but without rhyme]; thus the Classics are plain language (*yen*), but the "records and traditions"[209] are *pi* and not plain language. And how may I hoist Yen Yen-chih on his own petard?[210] The "Patterned Language" (*Wen**-*yen*) of the *Book of Changes* is obviously "language with pattern" (*yen wen**). If Yen Yen-chih would have it that *pi* is "language with pattern," then he can't say that the Classics are not *pi*. He wants this argument to stand, but I don't see how it can.

In my opinion, whatever comes from the mouth is [plain] "language" (*yen*); whatever is put to brush is called "writing" (*han*); the constant Way is called a "Classic"; and the transmission of a Classic is called a "tradition" (*chuan*). The form (*t'i**) of the Classics leaves [spoken] language and enters "writing" (*pi*); but since the writing is governed by the spoken language, it can be more or less [patterned]. The Six Classics are indispensable for their authority and their profundity; they cannot be evaluated on the grounds of spoken language versus writing.[211]

Liu Hsieh begins by stating two contemporary opinions on the distinction between *wen** and *pi*: first, the easy distinction of rhyme; second, Yeh Yen-chih's more interesting notion that the real distinction is between texts that were consciously "written" (*pi*) and simply "writing down" what was said (on the assumption that the early Classics were simply a "writing down" of the words or the Sages). In Yeh Yen-chih's distinction, *wen** becomes a quality that can inhere in writing and appears at a certain point in the historical evolution of the Classics. Thus for Yen Yen-chih, *wen**, corresponds to self-conscious literary "style," whose stylization asserts difference from the spoken language. Liu Hsieh attempts to refute this with an argument based on authority: the *Wen**-*yen*, one of the "Wings" of the *Book of Changes* attributed to Confucius, implicitly claims in its title to have *wen**, even though it lacks the stylization that is later called *wen**. Where Yen Yen-chih makes a subtle and cogent argument about the appearance of literary style, Liu Hsieh is hopelessly muddled. But Liu unwittingly accepts Yen's basic shift of the distinction from the question of rhyme to the question of spoken versus written style; in trying to exclude the Classics from the question altogether, his own position in the question seems to get away from him and is never fully explained.

昔陸氏文賦。號為曲盡。然汎論纖悉。而實體未該。故知九變之貫匪窮。知言之選難備矣。

It is claimed that Lu Chi's "Poetic Exposition on Literature" gave all the fine points;[212] but what he really provided was a careless discussion of small details, not something comprehensive in regard to the actual forms (*shih*-t'i**). Thus the understanding of the full range of transformations has not been exhausted, and the [power of] selection that comes from understanding language is hardly yet complete.

Liu Hsieh is attempting to stake his own claim to offer the definitive statement on *wen**. To do so seems to require that he discredit his predecessors. Lu Chi, whose "Poetic Exposition on Literature" was probably the most famous theoretical work on literature in Liu Hsieh's time, comes in for special criticism: the assertion here that Lu Chi concentrated too much on detail is outrageously unfair, but it is closely related to Liu Hsieh's criticism elsewhere that "The Poetic Exposition on Literature" lacks organization. Liu Hsieh's frequent return to criticism of Lu Chi is a good indication that he felt an uncomfortably strong influence from his great predecessor; and as we might expect, as he "corrects" Lu Chi's shortcomings in the following passage, he repeatedly echoes the formulations and draws on the points made in "The Poetic Exposition on Literature."

凡精慮造文。各競新麗。多欲練辭。莫肯研術。落落之玉。或亂乎石。碌碌之石。時似乎玉。精者要約。匱者亦鮮。博者該瞻。蕪者亦繁。辯者昭晢。淺者亦露。奧者複隱。詭者亦典。或義華而聲悴。或理拙而文澤。知夫調鐘未易。張琴實難。伶人告和。不必盡窕槬之中。動角揮羽。何必窮初終之韻。魏文比篇章於音樂。蓋有徵矣。夫不截盤根。無以驗利器。不剖文奧。無以辨通才。才之能通。必資曉術。自非圓鑒區域。大判條例。豈能控引情源。制勝文苑哉。

Those who give intense reflection to producing literary works try to outdo one another in novelty and beauty; most of them are inclined to polish their diction (*tz'u**); but are unwilling to study the art [as a whole]. Jade in vast quantities may be scattered among the rocks, while scarcest rocks may at times seem like jade. Someone who cares for the essentials insists on terseness—but then someone who cannot think of anything to say is equally sparing with his words. Someone who is broad [in interests] can be comprehensive and ample; but then abundance can be found equally among writers who are disorganized and verbose. A person who is good at argumentation makes things perfectly clear, but the shallow person is equally obvious. The strength of a profound writer may be in something latent and hidden, but the merely weird writer also has convolutions. Sometimes the principle (*yi**) is splendid, but the tones are dreary; sometimes the principle is clumsy, but the ornament (*wen**) is rich.[213] We realize that tuning a bell is not easy, and to string a zither is hard indeed. When the professional musician announces that [a bell] is in harmony, it is not always the case that it strikes a mean between the overly loud and the overly soft.[214] Stirring the note *chüeh* and lightly brushing the note *yü* [in tuning a zither] does not necessarily mean a command of the tones all the way from the beginning to the end.[215] There is much to substantiate Ts'ao P'i's comparison of a literary work to a musical piece. There is no way to prove the sharpness of a tool except by cutting the coiling roots of a tree; in the same way there is no way to distinguish a comprehensive talent (*t'ung**-*ts'ai*) unless he can analyze the mysteries of literature. The ability of a person of talent to be comprehensive depends on understanding the techniques of the art. Unless he has a perfect and clear view of this realm and can base his decisions securely on its norms, he cannot hold the reins of the fountainhead of the affections and contrive a victory in the garden of letters.

The reader of *Wen-hsin tiao-lung* is frequently struck by occasions of genuine insight, occasions which Liu Hsieh ultimately proves incapable of pursuing. The passage above is an excellent example. Liu Hsieh recognizes that all the qualities that were commonly observed by contemporary criticism made no distinction between very good and very bad writing; for example, "terseness" applies equally to a writer who expresses complex ideas with a wondrous economy and to someone who has very little to say. Liu grasps that there is something else in a work, something essential, that differentiates good *wen** from bad *wen**. He defines this as "understanding the techniques of the art"; but he cannot quite explain exactly what this might be.

是以執術馭篇。似善弈之窮數。棄術任心。如博塞之邀遇。故博塞之文。借巧儻來。雖前驅有功。而後援難繼。少既無以相接。多亦不知所刪。乃多少之並惑。何妍蚩之能制乎。若夫善弈之文。則術有恆數。按部整伍。以待情會。因時順機。動不失正。數逢其極。機入其巧。則義味騰躍而生。辭氣叢雜而至。視之則錦繪。聽之則絲簧。味之則甘腴。佩之則芬芳。斷章之功。於斯盛矣。

Thus to lay hold of these techniques and guide a piece is much like a master gambler's full understanding of the odds (*shu**). To abandon these techniques and follow one's own will (*hsin**, "mind") is like rolling the dice and hoping for good luck. Writing done by the roll of the dice may receive some fine points of art unexpectedly; but even though he may achieve something in speeding ahead, he cannot continue it later on. If it is too little, he has no way to add to it; if too much, he does not know how to trim it down. And left in uncertainty by any question of quantity, how then will he be able to manage the question of quality, whether it is good or bad? The writing of a good gambler is one in which there is a technique that recognizes constant odds. He arranges things by group and ranks, awaiting the proper conjunction of the affections [when he can use them]. He goes with the timely moment and takes his opportunities, and never misses what is proper (cheng*). If knowing the odds, he encounters the occasion, and the occasion joins with his sense of craft, then significance and flavor (yi*-wei*) will leap out, language (tz'u*) and ch'i* will come to him in abundance. When we look at it, it is a multicolored brocade; listen to it and it is strings and woodwinds; taste it and it is sweet and rich; wear it on your sash and it is the fragrance of flowers. The achievement of determining a literary work is at its height here.

This passage supplements and corrects the point made earlier in "Latent and Out-Standing," that the finest moments in writing come fortuitously. Here the writer must be ready with a mastery of all skills in order to be able to make best use of that fortuitous moment when it presents itself. The central metaphor of gambling, however, quietly confesses the powerful element of chance that is beyond the command of skill.

夫驥足雖駿。纆牽忌長。以萬分一累。且廢千里。況文體多術。共相彌綸。一物攜貳。莫不解體。所以列在一篇。備總情變。譬三十之輻。共成一轂。雖未足觀。亦鄙夫之見也。

Though the feet of your race horse be strong, avoid letting the rope be too long: even if it is only one problem among ten thousand possible problems, still it is enough to ruin a journey of a thousand leagues.[216] This is even more true in the many techniques involved in a literary form (wen*-t'i*), where all must be woven into a unity; if just one thing goes awry, then the form will always come apart. Therefore I have set them out in this one chapter[217] and unified all the mutations of circumstance (ch'ing*). Compare it to thirty spokes coming together at the hub. Although it may not be worth consideration, it is the way I see things.

As in the section on revision in "Fluency and Coherence," one error can destroy the whole work. The broader issue of some instinctive or lucky ability (possessed by the good gambler), which will ensure success, reverts to some particular lapse that the trained and cautious writer should be able to identify and control. There is a pedagogic claim embedded in Wen-hsin tiao-lung: understanding the principles announced in the work should enable a person to write well. Often when Liu Hsieh draws close to the intuition that good *wen** comes from some innate ability, he turns away and assures us that there is some "technique," the careful mastery of which will ensure success.[218]

文場筆苑。有術有門。務先大體。鑑必窮源。乘一總萬。舉要治繁。思無定契。理有恆存。

Supporting Verse

> In the field of letters and the garden of brushes,
> There are techniques and there are gates.
> First put your efforts into the overall form;
> Your reflections must reach all the way to the source.
> By going with one thing you comprehend all,
> Getting the essentials controls elaborations.
> Thought has no predetermined patterns,
> But natural principle is permanent.

CHAPTER 46
The Sensuous Colors of Physical Things, Wu*-se* 物色

"The Sensuous Colors of Physical Things" is an overelaborate translation for the common term *wu*-se**, which could be rendered simply the "appearances of things." The elaborate translation is intended to make us pause over the term, to consider the ways in which it implies more than simply "appearances," and to recognize that in this chapter Liu Hsieh has made the common compound lyrical. In addition to referring to surface appearance and manner, *wu*-se** was also the term for sketching a "likeness" by which a person could be recognized; and it may have been that association which lead Liu Hsieh to the issue of description later in the chapter. In "Spirit Thought" he had used the term *wu** in the broader philosophical sense of "object," meaning whatever might be encountered by mind in the spirit journey. Here *wu** are the preeminently physical things of the natural world, sensuous presences. "Color," *se**, is not only surface appearance, it also implies a sensuous, at times sensual allure. *Se** was the word chosen to translate the Sanskrit *rûpa*, appearances that cause delusion and desire. In human beings *se** is associated primarily with the face—bare skin and the possibility of recognition.

春秋代序。陰陽慘舒。物色之動。心亦搖焉。蓋陽氣萌而玄駒步。陰律凝而丹鳥羞。微蟲猶或入感。四時之動物深矣。若夫珪璋挺其惠心。英華秀其清氣。物色相召。人誰獲安。

Springs and autumns follow on in succession, with the brooding gloom of dark Yin and the easeful brightness of Yang. And as the sensuous colors of physical things are stirred into movement, so the mind, too, is shaken. When the Yang force sprouts [in the twelfth month], the black ant scurries to its hole; and when the Yin begins to coalesce [in the eighth month], the mantis feasts.[219] It touches the responses of even the tiniest insects: the four seasons stir things into movement deeply. Then there is the tablet of jade that draws forth the kindly mind, and the splendor of flowers that brings clear *ch'i** to stand out high (*hsiu*). All the sensuous colors of physical things call to one another, and how amid all this may man find stillness?

Here, toward the end of the book, Liu Hsieh finally develops the question first addressed in "Its Source in the Way," accounting for how and why writing can adequately manifest the world and a human being be "the mind of Heaven and Earth." The answer is simple, beautiful, and persuasive: "All the sensuous colors of physical things call to one another." It is a world of universal beckoning, stirring, and attraction; and the human being, as a physical part of that world, cannot remain "still" and aloof from the cosmic jostling. Thus there is an organic relation between the condition of the world around a writer and his state of mind (*ch'ing**). This is a significant revision of the position in the "Great Preface" to the *Book of Songs*, on how a poem is the "outcome" of a person's having been stirred by political circumstance. In *Wen-hsin tiao-lung*, the political circumstances that supposedly produced the *Songs* have been replaced by cyclical nature. The form of the relation, however, is identical: there is continuous stimulation from the external world, and such stimulation involuntarily provokes human response. This transfer of the human being from a social world into a natural world was consistent with the literature of Liu Hsieh's age, in which overt political reference played a less significant role than it had in previous centuries.

是以獻歲發春。悅豫之情暢。滔滔孟夏。鬱陶之心凝。天高氣清。陰沈之志遠。霰雪無垠。矜肅之慮深。歲有其物。物有其容。情以物遷。辭以情發。一葉且或迎意。蟲聲有足引心。況清風與明月同夜。白日與春林共朝哉。

When spring appears with the incoming year, feelings (*ch'ing**) of delight and ease infuse us; in the billowing luxuriance of early summer, the mind, too, becomes burdened. And when autumn skies are high and its air (*ch'i**) is clear and chill, our minds, sunken in the darkness of Yin, are intent upon far things; then frost and snow spread over limitless space, and our concerns deepen, serious and stern. The year "has its physical things, and these things have their appearances";[220] by these things our affections are shifted, and from our affections language comes. The fall of a single leaf may meet a concept (*yi**) [and we know that autumn is coming];[221] in the voices of insects, we find something capable of drawing forth our thoughts.[222] And how much stronger [than these merely partial evidences] are cool breezes and a bright moon together on the same night, or radiant sunlight and spring groves in the same morning.

Such a notion of seasonal moods is presently in great disfavor in modern Western literary thought (all empirical confirmation to the contrary); the reason is quite simply that to acknowledge their existence would be to restrict the writer's freedom; it would admit that he is a physical being who is, to some degree, determined by nature and natural circumstance. All the forces of a long and complex history of Western literary thought are mustered against such a possibility. However, the way in which Chinese theorists clung to and continually reaffirmed a determinate organic bond with nature casts the shadow of a different anxiety. The fear implicit in a claim such as Liu Hsieh makes here is that the literary work might be groundless, the product of mere convention or of play and whimsy, and thus capable of lies and deceit (a fear about which Liu Hsieh is quite explicit elsewhere).

Here and in the paragraph that follows, a distinction is drawn between the partial, which leads to the whole by "categorical association" (lei*), and the overwhelming totality of complete circumstance: "sunlight and spring groves in the same morning." The link between the two is of great importance to literature, because the literary text can offer only the "partial," a reduction of the manifold of experiential circumstance to a structure of "partial evidences." Nevertheless, we are able in literature, as in the world, to apprehend the overwhelming whole in the partial.

是以詩人感物。聯類不窮。流連萬象之際。沈吟視聽之區。寫氣圖貌。既隨物以宛轉。屬采附聲。亦與心而徘徊。

When poets were stirred by physical things, the categorical associations were endless.[223] They remained drifting through all the images (hsiang*) of the world, even to their limit, and brooded thoughtfully on each small realm of what they saw and heard. They sketched ch'i* and delineated outward appearance, as they themselves were rolled round and round in the course of things; they applied coloration (ts'ai*) and matched sounds, lingering on about things with their minds.

This is one of the most beautiful and important passages in Wen-hsin tiao-lung, describing the all-important relation between the human mind and the outer world. We should first note the difference between the statement here and earlier poetic theory, which is represented by the opening paragraphs of this chapter. There the human mind is thrown into the world of physical things, is stirred and shaken by that world because the human being, too, is part of the physical universe. But "the poets" seem to give themselves over to this universal process, both moving with things and "sketching" them.

Although the activity described seems intensely mimetic, we should note two important qualifications. First, the poets are "sketching the *ch'i**" of things, as well as outward appearance. The *mimêsis* of some impelling energy in things is, to say the least, a problematic notion. Poetry is, quite frankly, not very good at the description of appearances. Just as Aristotle evaded Plato's critique of the *mimêsis* of appearances by claiming that drama is the *mimêsis* of an "action" (a peculiar abstraction that becomes increasingly complex as one reflects on what it means), so Chinese theorists shifted the attention from descriptions of physical appearances to the promise that poetry can make manifest (or sometimes, as here, to represent) the interiors of things: the spirit, the affections, *ch'i**. Although in this passage Liu Hsieh accepts the representation of surface appearance as a legitimate complement of "sketching the *ch'i**," most later critics would place the highest value on the literary presentation of the inner "spirit" of a thing or some elusive quality of manner.

The second qualification of this statement of *mimêsis* is that the poets are not mere observers: their relation to the things represented in their poems is not one of subject and object. They can successfully present things in writing because they "linger" beside them and "roll round and round with them." This peculiar formulation mediates between a claim of "objective" observation and a claim of being themselves merely passive objects of nature's stirrings. The poets participate with things in nature, and their ability to perfectly present things in poetry is based on such sharing. The precise relation is being "with things," *yü wu**, a phrase weighted with associations of the Sage, who can share with nature without himself being nature's object.[224]

"Categorical associations" are *lien-lei**, linking things by category (*lei**). An example of this earlier in the chapter would be the single leaf that lets one know the year is coming to an end. But on a deeper level, it refers to the mysterious correspondences that underlie the physical world, including the mysterious bonds that make us respond to the seasonal changes and the changes in things.

故灼灼狀桃花之鮮。依依盡楊柳之貌。杲杲為出日之容。瀌瀌擬雨雪之狀。喈喈逐黃鳥之聲。喓喓學草蟲之韻。皎日嘒星。一言窮理。參差沃若。兩字窮形。並以少總多。情貌無遺矣。雖復思經千載。將何易奪。

Thus the phrase "glowing" (*cho-cho*) catches the quality of the freshness of peach blossoms; "waving lightly" (*yi-yi*) gives the fullness of the manner of willows; "shimmering" (*kao-kao*) is the way the sun looks when it just comes out; "billowing" (*piao-piao*) imitates the quality of snow falling; *chieh-chieh* catches the voice of the oriole; *yao-yao* emulates the tones of insects in the grasses. A "gleaming sun" (*chiao-jih*) or "faint stars" (*hui-hsing*) each gives, in a single phrase, the fullness of natural principle.[225] "Of varying lengths" (*ts'en-ts'e*) and "lush and moist" (*wo-jo*) say in two characters everything that can be said about shape (*hsing**). All of these use little to comprehend much, with nothing omitted of circumstance (*ch'ing**) or appearance. Even if one gave these lines a thousand more years of consideration, one could not change or alter anything in them.

The citation of a series of descriptive compounds from the *Book of Songs* may make this paragraph particularly difficult for the Western reader to appreciate; but the concerns addressed here are of great significance: we see here some of the highest values in literary language. Before considering the values themselves, we should first consider why these phrases from the *Book of Songs* seemed perfectly to embody such values: the *Book of Songs* was memorized from childhood; and each poem carried a wealth of associations, an exegetical tradition, and a context, all of which seemed to infuse certain usages in individual *Songs* with a quality of perfection (a quality that cannot be even approached in my lame translations of the descriptive compounds). These canonical passages fulfill a peculiar linguistic hope: that there be a special kind of language which does not name a thing but presents its essential "quality."[226] The categorical "names" of things may also be said to "use little to comprehend much"; but names only present "what" things are, not "how" they are. We have seen earlier in the tradition a desire for language to "give the full measure of" something, to be adequate for it. Liu Hsieh claims precisely this capacity for the descriptive phrases of the *Book of Songs* that they capture things as sensuous presences in all their fullness, hence "use little to comprehend much."[227]

及離騷代興。觸類而長。物貌難盡。故重沓舒狀。於是嵯峨之類聚。葳蕤之羣積矣。及長卿之徒。詭勢瓌聲。模山範水。字必魚貫。所謂詩人麗則而約言。辭人麗淫而繁句也。

When the *Li Sao* appeared in place [of the *Book of Songs*], it was more extensive in its treatment of things encountered. It is hard to give the full measure of the appearances of things, and thus extensive descriptions were piled one on top of another. At that point, descriptive phrases for qualities such as "towering heights" and "vegetative lushness" clustered in great numbers. By the time we get to Ssu-ma Hsiang-ju and those around him, the scope of mountains and waters was displayed with aberrant momentum (*shih**) and outlandish sounds, and the characters were strung together like fish. This is what Yang Hsiung meant when he said that the poets of the *Book of Songs* were terse in their language, using beauty to give a normative standard, while the rhetors were lush in their lines, using beauty to seduce us.

In both the *Ch'u-tz'u* 楚辭 and the closely related poetic expositions (*fu*) of the Han, description played an important role; and both made extensive use of the kind of binomial expressions found in the *Book of Songs*. Too many of even such individually acceptable phrases, however, seemed to Liu Hsieh to diminish the effectiveness of description. This belief is closely linked to his earlier interest in "partial evidence" and "using little to comprehend much": there is something in the concentration of the whole into a few details that sustains the impression of naturalness. In contrast, the very extensiveness of the *Ch'u-tz'u* and the Han poetic exposition seemed to call attention to the incapacity of language to exhaust the appearances of things. In addition, the lushly descriptive language of poetic expositions seemed almost a sensual indulgence, a pernicious intoxication with words.

至如雅詠棠華。或黃或白。騷述秋蘭。綠葉紫莖。凡摛表五色。貴在時見。若青黃屢出。
則繁而不珍。

　　自近代以來。文貴形似。窺情風景之上。鑽貌草木之中。吟詠所發。志惟深遠。體物
為妙。功在密附。故巧言切狀。如印之印泥。不加雕削。而曲寫毫芥。故能瞻言而見貌。
即字而知時也。

When they wrote on the wild plum blossoms in the Odes [of the *Book of Songs*], it was "some yellow, some white." When the *Li Sao* tells of the autumn orchid, it's "dark green leaves" and "purple stalks." Whenever describing colors, it's important to note what is seen in season: if green and yellow appear too often, then it is an excess not worth prizing.[228]

　　In recent times, a value has been placed on resemblance to external shape in literature.[229] They look to the circumstantial quality (*ch'ing**) in scene and atmosphere; they carve out appearances of the vegetation. What emerges in their chanting is the depth and far-reaching quality of that upon which their minds were intent. They consider the highest excellence to be getting the forms of things (*t'i*-wu**),[230] and the greatest accomplishment to reside in close adherence [to the original]. Their artful language catches the manner of things like a seal pressed in paste, minutely delineating the finest details, with no need of further embellishment. Thus by looking at the language we see the appearance; and through words, we know the moment (or "time," "season," *shih*).

Here Liu Hsieh seems to be caught between opposing impulses. On the one hand, there is an overtone of condemnation toward his contemporaries for excessive attention to craft (condemnation that he expresses more explicitly elsewhere). On the other hand, in the context of this chapter, descriptive detail can be a virtue, and he cannot help but acknowledge their accomplishments. Perhaps the most remarkable concession to their success is to be found in his reference to the "far-reaching quality of that upon which their minds were intent," to the personal concerns "lodged" in the description. This is a touchstone of positive value, a sign that they held to what is basic in writing. The image of description as a seal pressed in paste is a rich one: it presumes that language can receive an organic impression of the thing itself (and it recalls the mythic origin of the written word, in observation of the tracks of birds). Presuming such an organic relation between linguistic description and the natural world, the radical claim of the final sentence becomes reasonable: as with a snapshot (in contrast to photography as an "art"), we have in literature some direct access to absent things—persons, places, moments. "Through words, we know the moment."

然物有恆姿。而思無定檢。或率爾造極。或精思愈疏。且詩騷所標。並據要害。故後進銳筆。怯於爭鋒。莫不因方以借巧。即勢以會奇。善於適要。則雖舊彌新矣。

Things have constant postures, but thought (*ssu**) has no predetermined rule. Sometimes we reach the ultimate quite by chance and spontaneously; sometimes the more intensely we think about it, the more it eludes us. Moreover, the standard established by the *Book of Songs* and *Li Sao* has occupied all the essential ground, so that even sharp-witted writers of these later ages tremble to cross swords with them [their predecessors]. Every one of our modern writers follows their methods to borrow their artfulness and goes with their momentum (*shih**) to comprehend some excellence. Yet if one is a master at grasping the essentials, it will become completely fresh, though old.

This paragraph is an excellent example of exposition by a movement of compensation. It also illustrates how compensatory exposition can undermine any single proposition. In the previous paragraph Liu Hsieh had concluded that modern writers were able to take the perfect impression of the external world by close observation; moreover, he phrased his observation in such a way as to suggest that this was a distinctive trait of modern writers. By the end of this paragraph, Liu Hsieh has concluded that earlier poets had already expressed everything perfectly and that modern writers achieve all their novel effects by borrowing from and making variations on the work of their predecessors. We might consider the strange series of moves by which the critic performs this turn to the opposite direction.

The first corrective move occurs against the notion that language can give the organic impression of the things of the world. Things themselves may have the constancy to provide such a reliable impression, but human thought is ever-shifting and various and consequently cannot be relied upon to take a perfect impression. Sometimes a poet can describe something perfectly without any effort, but at other times he cannot find the proper words to describe the thing no matter how hard he tries (the discussion of description in the previous paragraph had implied great effort). The general unreliability of literary thought in trying to produce a perfect description leads Liu Hsieh to consider the *Book of Songs* and *Li Sao*, where the description of things is already perfect. And now it seems that the modern writer—whether in difficulty or not—need only work from the essentials embodied in the older poetry in order to produce fresh effects. This, he concludes, they do. At last the modern poets, who had previously worked from nature, are seen to work from earlier literature. Both positions are, of course, true; but Liu Hsieh does not say "both are true"; rather, he proposes one version, then corrects it and compensates for its one-sidedness by stating the alternative.

是以四序紛迴。而入興貴閑。物色雖繁。而析辭尚簡。使味飄飄而輕舉。情曄曄而更新。古來辭人。異代接武。莫不參伍以相變。因革以為功。物色盡而情有餘者。曉會通也。

The four seasons revolve in their profusion; but for them [the seasonal changes] to enter a writer's stirrings (*hsing**), calm is important. Though the sensuous colors of physical things are lush and dense, their exposition in language demands succinctness. This will make the flavor as if floating and rising above the world; it will make the circumstance (*ch'ing**) luminous and always renewed. Since ancient times, writers have followed in each others' footsteps from age to age; but all have brought about mutations, each in differing ways, and they have found that the greatest accomplishment lies in the capacity both to follow and to change radically. When the sensuous colors of physical things are finished, something of the affections (or "circumstance," *ch'ing**) lingers on—one who is capable of doing this has achieved perfect understanding.

If a set of quite distinct, even conflicting positions all seem to have some truth, the tendency in earlier Chinese writing is to state each one, without attempting to reconcile the conflicts. Such conflicting elements may appear in movements of compensation, as in the previous paragraph; or they can appear when the same question is posed in a new context, as occurs here.[231] The question here is the relation between the writer and the world: the chapter began with the human being caught up in the universal beckoning of the physical world; it shifted then to the poets who "rolled round and round with things," who were not so much the objects of nature's beckonings and stirrings as subjects sympathetically sharing the experiences of other things; now we are informed that in order to write successfully a person must achieve "calm" amid nature's turbulence. This is the venerable assertion of the necessity of some distance on the part of the writer, a demand made in "The Poetic Exposition on Literature" and in Liu Hsieh's own "Nature and Form." It is easy to reconcile these conflicting positions as stages in the writing process, but it is significant that Liu Hsieh does not do so; they are all "true." What is gained by the relative autonomy of contradictory positions is a clear sense of the resonance of each different position with other concerns; each answers the question properly in the context in which it is posed. In the paragraph above, we can see clearly the relation between calm and the notion of reserve, which is part of the structure of partialness discussed earlier. Against the lush multiplicity of the world, the writer must "hold back," must be "succinct." The world's multiplicity is to be concentrated in the partial. In such reserve is the energy that gives the literary text resonance. Liu Hsieh here uses the term "flavor" (*wei**) as a model: it is not just the concentrated and momentary "taste," but the unfolding and savoring of flavor after the initial moment of tasting. Such withholding, such restriction to the partial and essential imparts a lightness and freedom to a text, and allows it to un-fold in reading as if under its own power. This leads to one of the earliest explicit statements of a value central in later poetics, *han-hsü*, the quality of "reserve" from which associations linger on after the words.[232] Liu Hsieh does not use the term *han-hsü* here, but his formulation is interesting: "When the sensuous colors of physical things are finished, something of the affections (or "circumstance," *ch'ing**) lingers on." The external surfaces, the "sensuous colors" (*se**), of things and of things made manifest in words are momentary; what survives them is the *ch'ing**—something of their quality, their mood, the circumstances, the way we respond to them. In later poetics, such concepts as "reserve" were to become easy commonplaces; in *Wen-hsin tiao-lung*, we can see the roots of such concepts in some of the oldest con-cerns of Chinese literary thought: surface and subsurface, making something limited "last long," the part that leads back to the whole.

若乃山林皋壤。實文思之奧府。略語則闕。詳說則繁。然屈平所以能洞監風騷之情者。抑亦江山之助乎。

Mountain forests and the marshy banks of rivers are indeed the secret treasure houses of literary thought. Yet if the words are too brief, the description wants something; and if too detailed, it's overlush. Yet the reason Ch'ü Yüan was able to fully examine the mood (*ch'ing**) of the *Book of Songs* and *Li Sao* was, I am sure, the assistance of those rivers and mountains.

This is a peculiar and very beautiful closing to the chapter, reaffirming the part played by the external world in literature: the rivers and mountains "assist" the poet, join with him in the act of writing. We hesitate to point out that this is yet a fourth position in the presumed relation between the poet and the natural world.

山沓水匝。樹雜雲合。目既往還。心亦吐納。春日遲遲。秋風颯颯。情往似贈。興來如答。

The mountains in folds with rivers winding,
Mixed trees where the clouds merge:
When the eyes have roamed over them,
The mind expresses them.
The days of spring pass slowly,
The winds of autumn howl.
Our affections go out as a gift,
And stirring (*hsing**) comes back like an answer.

CHAPTER 48
The One Who Knows the Tone, Chih-yin 知音

Po-ya was a master of playing the zither, and Chung Tzu-ch'i was a master of listening. When Po-ya played his zither, his mind might be intent upon (*chih**) climbing a high mountain, and Chung Tzu-ch'i would say, Masterful! Uprearing, towering like Mount T'ai." Then Po-ya's mind might be intent upon the flowing water, and Chung Tzu-ch'i would say, "Masterful! Onrushing and roiling like the Yangtse and Yellow River." Whatever was in Po-ya's mind, Chung Tzu-ch'i knew it. Po-ya wandered to the dark north slope of Mount T'ai and suddenly encountered a terrible rainstorm. Stopping beneath the cliff, his heart full of melancholy, he took up his zither and played it, first a melody of the downpour, then the tone of the mountain itself collapsing. And every melody he played, Chung Tzu-ch'i followed the excitement to the utmost. Then Po-ya put down his zither and said with a sigh of admiration, "Masterful, masterful indeed—the way you listen. The images you see in your mind (*chih**) are just the same as the ones in mine. How can I keep any sound concealed from you?"

T'ang wen chapter of the *Lieh-tzu*

The story of Po-ya and Chung Tzu-ch'i is the source for the phrase *chih-yin*, "the one who knows the tone," someone who has the special talent to understand the nature and state of mind of another person manifest through some performance of an art, originally music but easily transferred to a literary text. The *chih-yin* is perhaps best understood in the context of the old Confucian value *chih-jen*, "to understand people." While *chih-jen* is a general capacity, *chih-yin* was, above all, a relation between two individuals. Liu Hsieh, in transferring the term to the role of the reader or critic, hoped to retain something of the term's original intimacy; but he also diminished its force by enjoining the reader to a general capacity of appreciation, the ability to recognize many different kinds of "tones." What had been a question of friendship becomes evaluative judgment.

"The One Who Knows the Tone" presents a miscellany of issues around the question of the capacity to appreciate and understand the works of others. For Liu Hsieh this capacity is everywhere threatened: by blind prejudices, by competitiveness and a lack of generosity, by the limitations of human nature that make each type respond most strongly to its own kind. If Liu gives up some of the intimacy of the term's original context and transforms "knowing the tone" into a trained ability, he does so to oppose forces that inhibit understanding, the premise with which Ts'ao P'i began his discourse on literature: "Literary men disparage one another."

As in many other traditions, Chinese writers on literature often took recourse to an analogy with music. One reason was, of course, that poetic texts were often sung and accompanied by instrumental music. The question of the lost music played a central role in the hermeneutic tradition of the *Book of Songs*, and it was the particular role assigned to music there that helped to shape the musical analogy for later critics of literature: in the *Book of Songs*, the lost music was supposed to have let every listener know at once how to understand the words of the *Song*. Music was a mediating ground of mood that would let listeners know whether the words were ironic, whether they carried undercurrents of unstated feelings held in reserve, and so forth. Hence the musical analogy became a way to refer to the overall quality of a statement apart from its obvious semantic "content." Since this quality is fortuitously called "tone" in English, the English reader may legitimately hear that usage in the title of this chapter. The primary difference in the two traditions is that in the Chinese version "tone" is a central rather than an adjunct quality. Whether tone is some typological category of mood or an immediate access to the individual's heart (Liu Hsieh speaks of it in both ways), the concept of "tone" radically mediates the reader's understanding of language. As in the hermeneutic tradition of the *Book of Songs*, one cannot fully understand the words without understanding the way in which they are delivered. What is ultimately understood from this process is some integral of "state of mind," rather than semantic "content" stripped of its circumstantiality.

The greatest difference between the role of music in the hermeneutic tradition of the *Book of Songs* and the role of tone in *Wen-hsin tiao-lung* is that in the *Book of Songs* the effect of the lost music was supposed to have been immediate and universal. Liu Hsieh's is a world that has fallen into division and a world in which such universality is a lost ideal. Since the Eastern Han, there had been a growing interest in the typological divisions between humans, and Liu Hsieh suspects we can have immediate appreciation only for those "tones" that correspond to our own "type." The chapter attacks such limitations and proposes a process of cultivation by which universal appreciation can be restored.

知音其難哉。音實難知。知實難逢。逢其知音。千載其一乎。夫古來知音。多賤同而思古。所謂日進前而不御。遙聞聲而相思也。昔儲說始出。子虛初成。秦皇漢武。恨不同時。既同時矣。則韓囚而馬輕。豈不明鑒同時之賤哉。至於班固傅毅。文在伯仲。而固嗤毅云下筆不能自休。及陳思論才。亦深排孔璋。敬禮請潤色。歎以為美談。季緒好詆訶。方之於田巴。意亦見矣。故魏文稱文人相輕。非虛談也。至如君卿脣舌。而謬欲論文。乃稱史遷著書。諸東方朔。於是桓譚之徒。相顧嗤笑。彼實博徒。輕言負誚。況乎文士。可妄談哉。

Hard it is to know the tone, for tones are truly hard to know; and such knowledge is truly hard to come upon—to come upon someone who knows the tone may occur once, perhaps, in a thousand years. Since ancient times those who have known the tone have often held their contemporaries in contempt and thought most of those of the past. This is what is meant by "not driving the horses that are brought to you every day, but instead longing for those whose reputation is known from afar." Long ago when the "Gathered Discourses" of Han Fei first appeared, the First Emperor of Ch'in expressed regret that he was not a contemporary; Han Wu-ti did the same when the "Master Emptiness" of Ssu-ma Hsiang-ju was just completed. When the writers were discovered to be, in fact, contemporaries, Han Fei was imprisoned and Ssu-ma Hsiang-ju treated with contempt. This is a clear example of how contemporaries are treated with disdain. In the case of Pan Ku and Fu Yi, their writing [showed qualitative similarity] like the relation of a younger brother to an elder brother. Yet Pan Ku mocked Fu Yi by saying that whenever he used his writing brush, he couldn't stop himself.[233] When Ts'ao Chih discussed talent, he made a deep attack on Ch'en Lin; but when [his friend] Ting Yi requested that Ts'ao Chih help him add some polish to his writing, Ts'ao Chih expressed admiration for the fitness of Ting's request; then Ts'ao Chih compared Liu Hsiu, who was fond of reviling others, to [the pre-Ch'in orator] T'ien Pa: in these examples Ts'ao Chih's point of view (yi*) can be seen. We can see that Ts'ao P'i's claim that "literary men disparage one another" was not groundless.[234] Lou Hu had a quick tongue, but he made terrible mistakes when he tried to discuss literature; he even claimed that when the Grand Historian Ssu-ma Ch'ien had written his *Historical Records*, he had asked the advice of Tung-fang So; when Huan T'an and his friends heard this, they looked on Lou Hu as an object of ridicule. If a person of little worth like Lou Hu must endure scorn for his disparaging remarks, is it acceptable for a literary man to speak rashly?

Liu Hsieh develops his premise of the difficulty of "knowing the tone" in an odd way: granting the fact that true understanding may occur only once in a thousand years, he takes that as a paradigm, with the implication that a writer will likely find someone who appreciates his worth only far in the future. He then twists the paradigm into a negative form in which the reader despises the present and honors the past. Therefore, when the First Emperor of Ch'in and Han Wu-ti appreciated the writings of men who happened to be contemporaries, they assumed that those works were, in fact, written long ago. Once the writers were shown to be contemporaries, both lost favor and came to bad ends. Obviously Liu Hsieh's point is directed against a blind reverence for the past simply because it is past; but the movement to that point from his opening remarks is an excellent example of a truly twisted argument. In the second set of examples (of professional jealousy), he takes the example used by Ts'ao P'i.

故鑒照洞明。而貴古賤今者。二主是也。才實鴻懿。而崇己抑人者。班曹是也。學不逮文。而信偽迷真者。樓護是也。醬瓿之議。豈多歎哉。

夫麟鳳與麏雉懸絕。珠玉與礫石超殊。白日垂其照。青眸寫其形。然魯臣以麟為麏。楚人以雉為鳳。魏氏以夜光為怪石。宋客以燕礫為寶珠。形器易徵。謬乃若是。文情難鑒。誰曰易分。

夫篇章雜沓。質文交加。知多偏好。人莫圓該。慷慨者逆聲而擊節。醞籍者見密而高蹈。浮慧者觀綺而躍心。愛奇者聞詭而驚聽。會己則嗟諷。異我則沮棄。各執一隅之解。欲擬萬端之變。所謂東向而望。不見西牆也。

There are cases of people with penetrating discernment, who nevertheless value the past while showing contempt for the present: such were the two rulers mentioned above. There are those who have great and excellent talent, but who honor themselves and disparage others: Pan Ku and Ts'ao Chih were examples of this. Then there are those whose learning does not come up to their [surface] eloquence (*wen**), who believe lies and err from the truth: such was Lou Hu. The theory that a great work might end up covering a jar was not an excessive anxiety.[235]

A unicorn is far different from a roebuck; a phoenix is just as different from a pheasant. Pearls and jade are not the least the same as ordinary pebbles and stones. Yet in full sunlight the pupils of men's eyes seemed to catch the [wrong] shapes. The officers of Lu thought a unicorn was a roebuck; someone from Ch'u thought a pheasant was a phoenix; a man of Wei took the shines-by-night jade as an unlucky magic stone; and the native of Sung thought that a piece of gravel from Mount Yen was a precious pearl.[236] Errors like these could still be made despite the fact that it was easy to show the difference in form; yet the affections in literature (*wen*-ch'ing**) are hard to see clearly, and who can claim they are easy to distinguish?

Works of literature are various, their substance and pattern are intertwined in many ways. What we [seem to] know usually involves some biased affection; in no one is judgment as perfect and comprehensive as it should be. Those with powerfully impulsive emotions will tap out the rhythm when they hear a voice singing. Those who feel more strongly than they outwardly show will be transported when they perceive a confidential manner. When they observe some intricacy, the minds of insubstantially clever persons will leap in delight. Those who love strangeness will listen in amazement when they hear something bizarre. People recite with admiration whatever corresponds to the way they themselves are, and they will reject whatever differs from themselves. Each person holds to a one-sided comprehension and through it hopes to estimate the ten thousand stages of mutation. This is what is meant by the saying, "not seeing the western wall because you are looking east."

Liu Hsieh envisions a world of ignorance and error, where misprision of truly valuable writing threatens it with obscurity and loss. He sees the ultimate source of error in a typological limitation that causes readers to appreciate only what corresponds to their own type. As in Ts'ao P'i, this leads to the call for a "comprehensive talent" (t'ung*-ts'ai*)—though Liu Hsieh does not use that term—someone capable of understanding all the variations ("mutations") of typological limitation.

凡操千曲而後曉聲。觀千劍而後識器。故圓照之象。務先博觀。閱喬岳以形培塿。酌滄波以喻畎澮。無私於輕重。不偏於憎愛。然後能平理若衡。照辭如鏡矣。是以將閱文情。先標六觀。一觀位體。二觀置辭。三觀通變。四觀奇正。五觀事義。六觀宮商。斯術既形。則優劣見矣。

　　夫綴文者情動而辭發。見文者披文以入情。沿波討源。雖幽必顯。世遠莫見其面。覘文輒見其心。

You can understand sound only after playing ten thousand tunes; you can recognize the capabilities of a sword only after examining a thousand. You must first endeavor to observe widely in order to have the impression (hsiang*) that comes from comprehensive understanding. Look to the loftiest mountain to know the shape of the little mound; consider the waves of the ocean to know the significance of the ditch. Only after escaping a purely private sense of what is worthwhile and what is of no importance, only after avoiding one-sidedness in loves and hates, can one see principles (li*) on an even balance; only then can one see words clearly as in a mirror. Thus to observe the affections in literature, first set forth these six points to be considered: consider how the normative form is given; consider how the words are arranged; consider continuity and mutation; consider whether it is normal or unusual; consider the events and principles [contained in it] (shih* yi*); consider the musical qualities. When these techniques are practiced, the relative values will be obvious.

In the case of composing literature, the affections are stirred and words come forth; but in the case of reading a work of literature, one opens the text and enters the affections [of the writer], goes against the current to find the source; and though it may [at first] be hidden, it will certainly become manifest. None may see the actual faces of a remote age, but by viewing their writing, one may immediately see their minds (hsin*).

This is one of the clearest traditional statements of the reading process in its most normative form: to read is an inversion of the process that produced the text, and what is finally known in that process is the mind of the writer.

豈成篇之足深。患識照之自淺耳。夫志在山水。琴表其情。況形之筆端。理將焉匿。故心之照理。譬目之照形。目瞭則形無不分。心敏則理無不達。

It is never that an accomplished work is too deep. Rather we should worry that our capacity for recognition is too shallow. If a person's mind is intent on the mountains and rivers, a zither can express his state of mind (ch'ing*). This is even more true when things are given form by the tip of a writing-brush; then it is not possible at all that the basic principles remain hidden. The way in which mind apprehends basic principle (li*) is like the way in which our eyes apprehend shape.[237] If the eyes are clear, every shape can be made out; if the mind is alert, every principle reaches it.

Here literature is privileged over music in its capacity to transmit what is interior. Liu Hsieh uses "state of mind" (ch'ing*) as the interior term transmitted by music and "natural principle" (li*) as the term transmitted by writing; but he has used ch'ing* often enough as the interior term transmitted by writing that it should not be excluded. Rather, the point seems to be that writing, in giving us access to mind (hsin*), encompasses both ch'ing* and li*, the integral of the circumstantial and the universal.

然而俗監之迷者。深廢淺售。此莊周所以笑折楊。宋玉所以傷白雪也。昔屈平有言。文質疏內。眾不知余之異采。見異唯知音耳。揚雄自稱心好沈博絕麗之文。不事浮淺。亦可知矣。

夫唯深識鑒奧。必歡然內懌。譬春臺之熙眾人。樂餌之止過客。蓋聞蘭為國香。服媚彌芬。書亦國華。翫澤方美。知音君子。其垂意焉。

In their erring estimation, however, ordinary people abandon what is deep and esteem the shallow. This was the reason Chuang-tzu mocked the [folksong] "Breaking the Willow Branch";[238] this was the reason Sung Yü was distressed at the song "White Snow."[239] Long ago Ch'ü Yüan said, "Both cultivation (wen*) and substance (chih*) pass within me, but the crowd does not understand my rare luster." Only one who knows the tone can perceive what is rare. Yang Hsiung claimed that in his heart (hsin*) he loved writing that had depth, breadth, and utter loveliness; one can see here, too, that he would have nothing to do with insubstantial shallowness.

Only those who recognize what lies deep and who see into the profound will always feel the thrill of an inner joy [when they read a great work], much in the way average people bask in the warmth of a terrace in spring, or the way in which music and food will stop the passing traveler. I have heard that the marsh-orchid, the most fragrant plant in the land, has an ever sweeter scent when worn. Writing is also the glory [or "flowering," *hua*] of the land, and it becomes most beautiful when appreciated. It is my hope that the superior person who knows the tone will think on this.

洪鍾萬鈞。夔曠所定。良書盈篋。妙鑒迺訂。流鄭淫人。無或失聽。獨有此律。不謬蹊徑。

Supporting Verse

> A great bell of thousands of pounds
> Must be tuned by music masters like K'uei and K'uang.
> When excellent works fill a bookchest,
> Only subtle discernment can correct them.
> The drifting music of Cheng seduces people,[240]
> Don't be misled by listening to it.
> Only by these regulations
> Can one avoid erring on the path.

CHAPTER 50
What I Had in Mind: Afterword, Hsü-chih 序志

The form of *Wen-hsin tiao-lung* is related to a tradition of essay collections, works such as the Han *Huai-nan-tzu* and the *Lun-heng* of Wang Ch'ung. Such works often included as their final chapter a statement of the author's background and intent in the composition of the work. This is roughly the function of the present chapter.

夫文心者。言為文之用心也。昔涓子琴心。王孫巧心。心哉美矣。故用之焉。古來文章。以雕縟成體。豈取騶奭之羣言雕龍也。

The patterned/literary mind (*wen*-hsin**) means the use of mind (or "intense effort") in writing (making *wen**). Once there was Chüan-tzu's "Mind of the Zither" (*Ch'in-hsin**)[241] and Wang-sun's "Artful Mind" (*Ch'iao-hsin**).[242] Mind (*hsin**) is a fine thing indeed, and thus I have used it here. Moreover, literary works (*wen*-chang**) have always achieved their form (*t'i**) by carving and rich ornamentation. Yet I do not mean what the group of people around Tsou Shih called "carving dragons" (*tiao-lung*).[243]

Liu Hsieh opens with a strong echo of the preface to Lu Chi's "Poetic Exposition on Literature": "Whenever I consider what is made by persons of talent (*ts'ai**), there is something within me that lets me grasp their strenuous efforts (or "use of mind," *yung-hsin**)." Like Lu Chi, he is playing on words here, referring to "mind" both as a term in the title and as a faculty (though we might observe that Lu Chi was thinking of the "strenuous effort" in literary writing, whereas Liu Hsieh considers it in the composition of his own critical work). Liu Hsieh, concerned always with the value of writing about literature and with asserting the superiority of his own work to that of his predecessors, begins with a false genealogy, implicitly setting the title of his work in a set with two other, largely unknown works, while avoiding mention of Lu Chi, to whom he owes so much.

In "The Poetic Exposition on Literature" Lu Chi developed an opposition between the speculative operations of mind and reading or tradition; here Liu Hsieh builds his title with a similar pair of terms: "carving and rich ornamentation" are associated here with tradition. Yet "carving dragons" is an activity that carries potentially pejorative connotations, connotations of delusory craft; and Liu Hsieh tries to take care to dissociate his own sense of craft from the pejorative sense.

夫宇宙綿邈。黎獻紛雜。拔萃出類。智術而已。歲月飄忽。性靈不居。騰聲飛實。制作而已。夫有肖貌天地。稟性五才。擬耳目於日月。方聲氣乎風雷。其超出萬物。亦已靈矣。形同草木之脆。名踰金石之堅。是以君子處世。樹德建言。豈好辯哉。不得已也。

予生七齡。乃夢彩雲若錦。則攀而採之。齒在踰立。則嘗夜夢執丹漆之禮器。隨仲尼而南行。旦而寤。迺怡然而喜。大哉聖人之難見哉。乃小子之垂夢歟。自生人以來。未有如夫子者也。敷讚聖旨。莫若注經。而馬鄭諸儒。宏之已精。就有深解。未足立家。唯文章之用。實經典枝條。五禮資之以成。六典因之致用。君臣所以炳煥。軍國所以昭明。詳其本源。莫非經典。

The universe goes on and on forever; and among the multitudes, worthy men have been many and various.[244] To rise above the crowd and emerge from the [common] categories can occur only through wisdom and skill. Yet the years and months fleet past, and the soul (*hsing*-ling*) does not stay here permanently. The only way to make one's reputation soar and one's accomplishments take flight is by [literary] composition. There is in man's outward appearance a likeness to Heaven and Earth, and his nature (*hsing**) is endowed with the five materials;[245] we may compare his eyes to the sun and the moon; we may liken his sound and breath to the wind and thunder. The way he passes beyond all the things of the world is truly the force of spirit (*ling*). His form (*hsing**) shares the frailty of the trees and plants, yet his name is more firm than metal or stone. Thus a superior person (*chün-tzu*) lives in his own age, founding his virtue (*tê*) and establishing words.[246] It is not simply a fondness for disputation; it is that he feels some basic unease.[247]

It was at the age of six that I dreamed of clouds of many colors like a brocade, then climbed up to them and culled them. When I had passed the age of thirty,[248] one night I dreamed that I was holding ritual vessels of red lacquer, going off southward with Confucius.[249] The next morning when I awoke, I was cheerful and happy. It is hard indeed to have a vision of the Sage, yet did he not send down a dream to me, a mere child?! There has never been anyone else like the master since the birth of the human race.[250] Classical commentary is the very best way to expound and elucidate the intent of the Sage; yet Ma Jung, Cheng Hsüan, and other Confucian scholars have expanded upon the Classics and gotten their essence.[251] Even if I had some profound interpretations, they would not be enough to found my own lineage [of scholarship].

The role of literary works (wen*-chang*) is, in fact, a branching out from the Classics: the Five Rites depend on them to be carried out, and the Six Bureaus function by their means.[252] Literary works are the way that the relation between the prince and his officers as well as the relation between army and state are made perfectly clear. If we carefully trace these back to their roots, they are always to be found in the Classics.

The association of a work of literary theory and criticism with the Confucian tradition of "establishing words," by which a person may hope for some cultural immortality, goes far beyond the modest intentions of earlier critical writing. Dispute over the fine points of literary art was already part of social practice in the salons of the southern courts. Liu Hsieh links himself to one of the parties in such disputes, the conservatives who saw their role as one of preserving Confucian values and the literary tradition. By placing himself in the tradition of Confucius and classical commentary (recalling that Confucius himself was supposed to have provided supplementary "commentaries" for the Book of Changes and described himself as one who "transmitted but did not make"), Liu Hsieh implicitly defends the notion that a work of literary criticism can be "establishing words." The Confucian scholar preserves, corrects, and passes judgments on texts; he is primarily a conservator. This essential Confucian labor has been performed fully for the Classics; but insofar as literature lies in the direct lineage of the Classics, it requires a similar care. The model of Sagely judgment was implicit in Ts'ao P'i's "Discourse on Literature" and Lu Chi's "Poetic Exposition on Literature"; it is quite explicit here, with Liu Hsieh dreaming of Confucius, as Confucius himself dreamed of the Duke of Chou. This grandiose claim for the role of literature and the critic is a measure of Liu Hsieh's anxiety, shared by many in his age, regarding the culture of the Southern Dynasties, as is explicit in the following paragraph.

而去聖久遠。文體解散。辭人愛奇。言貴浮詭。飾羽尚畫。文繡鞶帨。離本彌甚。將遂
訛濫。蓋周書論辭。貴乎體要。尼父陳訓。惡乎異端。辭訓之異。宜體於要。於是搦筆
和墨。乃始論文。

詳觀近代之論文者多矣。至於魏文述典。陳思序書。應瑒文論。陸機文賦。仲洽流別。宏
範翰林。各照隅隙。鮮觀衢路。或臧否當時之才。或銓品前修之文。或汎舉雅俗之旨。或
撮題篇章之意。魏典密而不周。陳書辯而無當。應論華而疏略。陸賦巧而碎亂。流別精而
少功。翰林淺而寡要。又君山公幹之徒。吉甫士龍之輩。汎議文意。往往間出。並未能振
葉以尋根。觀瀾而索源。不述先哲之誥。無益後生之慮。

Yet we have gone long and far from the Sage, and the normative forms of
literature have divided and scattered.[253] The rhapsodes (*tz'u*-*jen*)[254] fell in love
with whatever was unusual, and in language they valued what was insubstantial and deceptive. They enjoyed adding paint to decorate feathers[255] and wove
patterns (*wen**) into their leather belts and sashes.[256] Their departure from the
basics (*pen*) gets ever more extreme, as they pursue the erroneous and excessive. When the *Book of Documents* discusses language (*tz'u**), it values bringing
out the essentials.[257] When Confucius set forth his teaching, he expressed his
dislike for unusual principles.[258] Although the [statement on] language [in the
Book of Documents] and [Confucius'] teaching are different, it is proper to bring
out the essentials.[259] Thus I took my brush in hand and mixed my ink, beginning my discourse on literature.

Let us examine closely recent discourses on literature (and there are many
of these indeed): from Ts'ao P'i's "Exposition of the Authoritative" [i.e., the
"Discourse on Literature" in *Authoritative Discourses*] to Ts'ao Chih's letters
and prefaces, to Ying Ch'ang's "Discourse on Literature," to Lu Chi's "Poetic
Exposition on Literature," to Chih Yü's "Divisions," to Li Ch'ung's "Grove
of Brushes":[260] each shed light on some corner, but few examined the great
high road; some evaluated the talents of their own age, while others weighed
and ranked the writings of earlier masters; some vaguely pointed out the principles by which a gracious (*ya**) style could be distinguished from a low style,
while others made judicious choices to show the intent (*yi**) behind particular
works. Ts'ao P'i's "Discourse on Literature" is very suggestive but not
comprehensive;[261] Ts'ao Chih's letters are well argued but miss the mark;
Ying Ch'ang's discourse is splendid but cursory; Lu Chi's poetic exposition is
artful but a mishmash; Chih Yü's "Divisions" get to the essence but accomplish nothing; Li Ch'ung's "Grove of Brushes" is shallow and wanting in the
essentials. In addition, there have been Huan T'an, Liu Chen, Ying Chen, and
Lu Yün, and others, who have raised questions about the meaning of literature
(*wen**-*yi**) in general terms. Here and there, worthwhile things show up in
their works; but none of them began with the leaves to trace things back to the
root or observed the waves to search out the fountainhead. Since they did not

transmit the injunctions of the ancient Sages, they have been of little benefit to the concerns of the later-born.

Although Liu Hsieh claims not to be simply "fond of dispute," his was a disputatious age. To make a place for his own work, Liu feels it necessary to dismiss all predecessors writing on literature (over a thousand years later, in "The Origins of Poetry," Yeh Hsieh will do the same, rejecting all his predecessors for their lack of systematic order, and dismissing Liu Hsieh among the others; see p. 579 below). Despite his claims of originality, it is impossible to read *Wen-hsin tiao-lung* and not hear the words of Liu's critical predecessors echoing throughout.

蓋文心之作也。本乎道。師乎聖。體乎經。酌乎緯。變乎騷。文之樞紐。亦云極矣。若乃論文敘筆。則囿別區分。原始以表末。釋名以章義。選文以定篇。敷理以舉統。上篇以上。綱領明矣。至於割情析采。籠圈條貫。摛神性。圖風勢。苞會通。閱聲字。崇替於時序。褒貶於才略。怊悵於知音。耿介於程器。長懷序志。以馭羣篇。下篇以下。毛目顯矣。位理定名。彰乎大易之數。其為文用。四十九篇而已。

This work of mine on the literary mind (*wen*-hsin**) has its base in the Way [Chapter 1], takes the Sage as its teacher [Chapter 2], finds the normative forms (*t'i**) [of literature] in the Classics [Chapter 3], consults the Classical Apocrypha [Chapter 3], and shows the [initial] mutation in the Sao [i.e., the *Ch'u-tz'u* tradition, Chapter 4]. Here the pivotal point of literature has been followed through to its limit. In discussing rhymed (*wen**) and unrhymed (*pi*) writings [Chapters 6 to 25],[262] I have divided them into their various domains, explained the name [of each genre] to show their significance (*yi**) behind it, selected examples to establish the genre clearly, given an exposition of its principle (*li**) to bring out the continuity. Thus in the first part of the book, the unifying precepts are quite clear.

In my analysis of the "Affections and Bright Coloration" [*ch'ing*-ts'ai**, Chapter 31], I have delimited the scope and shown the internal structure. I have expounded "Spirit" [*Shen**, Chapter 26] and "Individuating Nature" [*Hsing**, Chapter 27]; I have sketched questions of "Wind" [*Feng**, Chapter 28] and of "Momentum" [*Shih**, Chapter 30]; I have incorporated questions of "Coherence" [*Hui*, Chapter 43] and "Continuity" [*T'ung**, Chapter 29]; I have examined the nature of "Euphony" [*Sheng*, literally "sounds," Chapter 33] and "Word Choice" [*Tzu**, Chapter 39]. Rise and fall are treated in "Temporal Sequence" [Chapter 45]; praise and criticism are offered in "An Overview of Talent" [Chapter 47]; "The One Who Knows the Tone" [Chapter 48] brings up matters that disturb us. In "Showing the Vessel's Capacity" [Chapter 49], I have been forthright and clear. My constant concerns are here in "What I Had in Mind: Afterword," by which I have organized all the various chapters. In the second half of the work, the organization is obvious. Showing the position of principle (*li**) and determining the names of things is made evident in the number given in the great *Changes* [i.e., *Yi ching*]; there are only forty-nine used for the discussion of literature.[263]

夫銓序一文為易。彌綸羣言為難。雖或輕采毛髮。深極骨髓。或有曲意密源。似近而遠。辭所不載。亦不勝數矣。及其品列成文。有同乎舊談者。非雷同也。勢自不可異也。有異乎前論者。非苟異也。理自不可同也。同之與異。不屑古今。擘肌分理。惟務折衷。按轡文雅之場。環絡藻繪之府。亦幾乎備矣。

但言不盡意。聖人所難。識在缾管。何能矩矱。茫茫往代。既洗予聞。眇眇來世。倘塵彼觀也。

To evaluate and classify a single work is easy, but to fully incorporate all that has been written is hard. Though as light and brightly colored as a pelt or hair, their depths may go all the way to the bone and marrow. There are some works that have subtle (*ch'ü*) ideas (*yi**) and secret fountainheads, apparently obvious but actually far-reaching; there are countless aspects that I have not been able to put into words.[264] In my rankings and categories here, I have sometimes agreed with comments made previously; this was not merely echoing: the force of the situation was such that I could not differ with them. On the other hand, there are cases where I differ from earlier discourses; this is not a rash inclination to be different, but simply that the principle (*li**) involved made it impossible for me to agree. In my agreements and disagreements I have disregarded whether opinions were recent or ancient. I have "split the flesh to discern the principle" [done a close analysis], making my sole endeavor to get to the heart of the matter. In grasping the reins on the meadows of literary graces and looping the halter in the treasure house of eloquence, I think this is virtually complete.

But the Sage recognized the problem in the way "what is said does not give the fullness of the concept in the mind."[265] How can a capacity no greater than that of a pitcher or a pipe grasp the fixed standards?[266] Ages past are remote and hazy, yet they have cleansed my hearing;[267] generations to come are indistinct in the distance, and this may only becloud their vision.

生也有涯。無涯惟智。逐物實難。憑性艮易。傲岸泉石。咀嚼文義。文果載心。余心有寄。

Supporting Verse
    Human life has its bounds,
    Only wisdom is unbounded.
    Investigating external things is hard indeed,

But going with one's nature is easy.
Proud and lofty, a boulder in a stream,
Chewing over the significance of literature.
If literature truly carries mind,
Then my mind has found a lodging.

The Twenty-Four Categories of Poetry

It is a measure of the strangeness and the problems of "The Twenty-Four Categories of Poetry" by Ssu-k'ung T'u 司空圖) (837–908) that if the title *Shih-p'in* 詩品 did not contain the word "poetry," there would be no way even to guess to what these elusive verses referred. They could just as easily be "characters" in traditional psychology or more transient "moods," or they could refer to qualities of painting, calligraphy, or music, or any other activity in which categories of manner played an important role. They employ a vocabulary applicable equally to personality and to the arts. It was a vocabulary that had been in the process of formation and refinement for centuries.

Not all Chinese aesthetic vocabulary is as vague and tenuous as it often seems in translation; but there is a subclass of traditional aesthetic vocabulary that holds a hazy imprecision as its highest value, and it was precisely to this genuinely "impressionistic" mode that Ssu-k'ung T'u was attracted.

Elusiveness is more than a value for Ssu-k'ung T'u; it is an obsession; and as such, it plays counterpoint to the generic purpose of "The Twenty-Four Categories," which is to characterize a set of discrete qualities, together constituting a complete range of modal variation. A genre that promises to makes distinctions is being employed by a writer whose inclination is to blur all distinctions.[1] For this reason, some of Ssu-k'ung T'u's critics have claimed that the categories are the exposition of a single point of view. Although this is clearly not the case, it is true that a single point of view shades and twists everything he writes, more or less reconciling each distinct quality with his own values. Perhaps the best example of these conflicting forces is the eighteenth category, "Solid World": in this case a critic, for whom the elusive is the highest value, tries to describe a solid, direct, and highly defined mode; by the end of the verse, definiteness has somehow reversed itself into the elusive.

Despite its uniqueness, "The Twenty-Four Categories of Poetry," is a work with deep roots in earlier poetics and in critical comment on personality, painting, and calligraphy.[2] Perhaps of first importance here are the categories of personality that arose with the tradition of "personality appraisal" in the Eastern Han. Out of this there developed a rich vocabulary of manner, with fine distinctions and gradations. Critics of personality often went beyond such general terms to describe manner by means of some image drawn from nature. Both qualitative and imagistic characterizations were soon transferred into the growing discourse of critical comment (*p'ing* 評) on calligraphy, painting, and literary style.

From the Southern Dynasties through the T'ang, such descriptions grew in size and complexity; and taxonomies began to appear, in which lists of qualities were given independent of their association with particular individuals. As in "Nature and Form" in *Wen-hsin tiao-lung*, the common practice in prose taxonomies was to give the list, then to amplify each term with explanation or examples. This practice can be seen in some of the taxonomies of the T'ang *Wen-ching mi-fu-lun* 文鏡秘府論 (*Bunkyō hifuron*), where the amplification of each category is given either by the primary critic or by a later critic in the form of a commentary. "The Twenty-Four Categories" is a late and intensely idiosyncratic version of such a taxonomy.

Characterizations of manner often used four-character phrases or pairs of four-character phrases. Ssu-k'ung T'u extends this into tetrasyllabic verse; and in doing so, he enters the strong generic traditions of that form; this, too, exerts a powerful influence on the peculiarities of "The Twenty-Four Categories." One useful parallel here can be found in the "supporting verses" (*tsan* 贊) at the end of the chapters of *Wen-hsin tiao-lung*: like Ssu-k'ung T'u's verses, the "supporting verses" are extremely terse and elliptical, to the point that they are often comprehensible only as "headlines" for the prose that they follow. If we lost the prose chapters of *Wen-hsin tiao-lung* and had only the "supporting verses," we would be presented with problems of interpretation similar to those presented by "The Twenty-Four Categories." Ssu-k'ung T'u's own collected works contains a long *tsan* on "Poetry and Poetic Expositions," in a style very similar to that of "The Twenty-four Categories of Poetry." Tetrasyllabic verse was also the favored form of Taoist philosophical poetry, finding its first full development in the largely lost *hsüan-yen* 玄言 poetry of the Eastern Tsin. Although after the Eastern Tsin such verse was no longer considered literary and "poetry," it continued to be written voluminously in Taoist works (and in some Buddhist works) during the T'ang. There are good reasons why such verse was disregarded by literary men: it was jargon-ridden and often no more than a collection of resonant slogans. Such verse strives to give the impression of profundity by the illusion of making propositions (though propositions can and often have been drawn out of it by exegetes who define the terms and the logical relations in the lines). Unfortunately, Ssu-k'ung T'u was immensely attracted to this superficial Taoist rhetoric of mystery and profundity, and it compromises all the best aspects of his work: at its worst it is the "poetics of Oz."

Ssu-k'ung T'u concerns himself with qualities that are on the margins of our apprehension, and his willful mystifications can be in some degree justified as a manner of presentation that corresponds to the poetic values restated throughout the verses. The "form of proposition" gives the reader the impression that there is some definite message in the words; at the same time, mystification conceals the putative proposition and compels the reader to construct the "message" out of the fragmentary words. For this reason "The Twenty-Four Categories" are more happily read without commentary; one need not confront the disconcerting variety in their exegesis. Unfortunately, this is true only when reading them in the Chinese.

Like "The Poetic Exposition on Literature" and the *Wen-hsin tiao-lung*, "The Twenty-Four Categories of Poetry" has accumulated a substantial body of commentary: in his *Erh-shih-ssu shih-p'in t'an-wei*, Ch'iao Li offers three full pages on the first four lines of the first category. There are numerous points of disagreement in the interpretation of "The Poetic Exposition on Literature," but these disagreements pale before the wildly varying interpretations of lines in "The Twenty-Four Categories of Poetry. " Commentators guess what Ssu-k'ung T'u ought to be saying, then construe the words to obey the putative intention. In most texts, language imposes certain restrictions that chasten the willful exegete; in "The Twenty-Four Categories of Poetry" the language is so elastic that contradictory and even incommensurate interpretations all flow with equal ease from the same lines.[3] Imagistic lines usually present no difficulties; the real problems lie in lines that present themselves as propositional (see comments on the first four lines of the first mode). The simple truth is that we have no way of determining what such problematic lines mean; nor, we suspect, were the lines meant to "signify" in any conventional sense: they are the headlines of an unwritten poetics that the reader himself must infer.

Despite the deep disagreements in what the text says in any of its parts, there is remarkable agreement about the general point being made for each category. The parts are incomprehensible, but the impression of the whole is clear. This fact merits some reflection. In the title of each category, what we have is a term that is loaded with resonance for most readers familiar with Chinese literary thought. Images and bits and pieces of statements in each of Ssu-k'ung T'u's verses contribute to (or perhaps stated more precisely, "are assimilated to") the central term. What we would consider the most basic lexical and grammatical determinations are called for only when the scholar chooses to undertake the work of exegesis, either in expanded classical Chinese or in the vernacular. When one reads these poems in Chinese, they make perfectly good sense in their own way; but when one tries to translate them, that good sense falls to pieces.

The practice of suggesting alternative interpretations was fruitful in commenting on "The Poetic Exposition on Literature"; but this is less certain in the case of "The Twenty-Four Categories of Poetry." What I will offer below is *an* interpretation, one of the valid possibilities that will lead to the generally agreed upon quality described. In treating individual passages, I will also discuss a few of the more important alternative interpretations offered by primarily modern commentators. As was the case in my commentary on "The Poetic Exposition on Literature," for the sake of convenience I will refer to the major commentaries by the names of their authors. These commentaries are given in Section I.F.1 of the bibliography.

One of the greatest difficulties of commenting on "The Twenty-Four Categories of Poetry" is the difficulty of maintaining a mediating position. One can remain quite sensible when discussing the larger issues of Ssu-k'ung T'u's poetics and the poems as a whole;[4] but when one begins to examine the poems in detail, which is to say, discussing how the lines establish the identity of each category and its differences from others, one has entered Ssu-k'ung T'u's world. English readers will often legitimately wonder to what in poetry itself the qualities might refer. They may wonder on what level statements are made. For instance, when Ssu-k'ung T'u speaks of force, there is almost always an element of storing up and an element of actualization of stored force: is this what a poet does before he writes? or is it something immanent in the text as a whole (the actualized force in the text implying reserve behind it)? or does it describe the movement of the text (from reserve to actualization)? or does it describe the affect of the text (stored force in the text that is actualized in the savoring that follows reading)? It is perhaps wisest to understand the qualities described on a high level of generality, as applicable to any of the frames of reference suggested above. The translations can be deceptive here: English demands that I choose between the imperative and the indicative, between the subject "he" and the subject "it" (the text), between the coordinate and the conditional. The Chinese drifts happily between all these decisions, which are, as so often in classical Chinese, truly irrelevant.

"The Twenty-Four Categories of Poetry" will probably appeal to poets, but will irritate academic critics and literary theorists beyond all measure. Both will be justified in their responses. Ssu-k'ung T'u is not only grasping for elusive distinctions, he is willfully mystifying them. Yet if one juxtaposes the descriptive passages in the various categories, one can indeed see subtle distinctions of quality that are both an essential part of the experience of poetry and are exceedingly difficult to describe in any language, Chinese or English. The poems teach attention to such subtle differences, how the quality of one scene or tone of voice is unlike another. And it is precisely in that aspect, rather than in the ideology of elusiveness in its own right, that the work represents an important aspect of Chinese literary "thought."

Apart from one ambiguous reference by Su Shih (1037–1101), who lamented that the work was not sufficiently appreciated, there is no mention of "The Twenty-Four Categories of Poetry" until the first half of the seventeenth century.[5] In this the work suffered the general fate of works on T'ang poetics during the Sung, Yüan, and early Ming. In "Ts'ang-lang's Remarks on Poetry," Yen Yü was probably influenced by Ssu-k'ung T'u's letters about the value of elusive "poetic" scenes, but there is no evidence that he was familiar with "The Twenty-Four Categories of Poetry." During the Ch'ing, "The Twenty-Four Categories of Poetry" became extremely popular, generating numerous commentaries and imitations, and was referred to often in critical writing. Since the seventeenth century, it has been generally considered the most important example of T'ang poetics.

THE TWENTY-FOUR CATEGORIES OF POETRY

CATEGORY 1
Potent, Undifferentiated, Hsiung-hun 雄渾

大用外腓。真體內充。返虛入渾。積健為雄。備具萬物。橫絕太空。荒荒油雲。寥寥
長風。超以象外。得其環中。持之非強。來之無窮。

The greatest functioning extends outward;
The genuine form is inwardly full.
Reverting to the empty brings one into the undifferentiated;
Accumulating sturdiness produces the potent.
5   It contains the full complement of all things
Stretching all the way across the void:
Pale and billowing rainclouds;
Long winds in the empty vastness.
It passes over beyond the images
10   And attains the center of the ring.
Maintaining it is not forcing;
Bringing it never ends.

Lines 1–2: The couplet is based on the standard philosophical opposition between "form" or "body" (*t'i**) and "function" or "operation" (*yung* 用). The first lines here are willfully hermetic, even in the context of the "Twenty-Four Categories." Most of the problems arise from the first line's use of *fei*, originally the "calf" of the leg. In one usage in the *Book of Songs*, *fei* is a loan for another graph meaning "to shrivel." This became the most common later usage of *fei*. Read in this sense, the line would be rendered "The greatest functioning outwardly shrivels"; that is, in this mode all outward activity withdraws so that unrealized, potential power can be accumulated within. The other meaning of *fei* is to "ward," as in the actions taken by sheep and cattle to protect the abandoned infant Hou Chi 后稷 in the *Sheng-min* 生民 ode of the *Book of Songs*. This sense is roughly followed by Ch'iao Li. If we accept this sense of *fei*, the line would mean "Its primary functioning is to protect externally, while . . . " or (reading the first hemistich as the direct object) "On the outside it wards off functioning, while . . . " Lü Hsing-ch'ang and Tsu Pao-ch'üan take *fei* as "extend" or "flex": "Its great functioning extends externally, while . . . " Chao Fu-t'an is close to this interpretation, glossing *fei* as "transforms," while paraphrasing the hemistich as "manifests itself externally." I have followed Lü because his reading makes the clearest sense; but it requires considerable stretching of the meaning of *fei*.

An additional complication occurs in the phrase "great[est] function": this may be the ultimate realization of potential action, or it may be used, as in the *Chuang-tzu*, as an inverted kenning for "The Useless," that which has no function. Such an interpretation would, of course, require drastic reinterpretation of the other hemistich. Whatever happens on the outside, the second line is clear: this condition of unlimited potential force depends on fullness within. The phrase *chen-t'i** may either be, as I have taken it, the "genuine form" of the "potent, undifferentiated" mode; or with Chao and Ch'iao, as having true feelings or experience within; or with Tsu Pao-ch'üan, "to take the genuine [Way] as one's form."

Lines 3–4: The two terms of the category are here each amplified in a single line. Each line of the couplet consists of two clauses that may be taken as a single predicate, as I have done, or as separate—in a coordinate, conditional, or successive relation. Ch'iao Li interprets *fan* ("reverts") as "replaces," producing a sense of the line opposite to the interpretations of other commentators; that is, the form moves from emptiness to solidity and actualized force. There is also some uncertainty about whether the "emptiness" is a condition of mind or an external quality, the character of the Way.

Lines 5–6: The "void," *T'ai-k'ung*, is both in the primordial space of cosmology and the "sky," preparing for the cloud image in the following couplet.

Line 9: "Beyond the images," *hsiang*-wai*, is considered a key term in Ssu-k'ung T'u's poetics and refers to something that lies "outside" definite form; it is something that produces determinate and changing forms but is itself formless. One may understand this condition either as an abstract (*hsing-erh-shang* 形而上) potentiality or as a sensuous formlessness like the billowing clouds.[6]

Line 10: "The center of the ring" is a phrase from the *Chuang-tzu* referring to the still unrealized power for transformation. The condition of *hsiung-hun* ("undifferentiated, potent") is in many ways analogous to *Ch'ien* 乾, which is the first hexagram in the *Book of Changes*. *Hsiung-hun* is a primordial condition of active force and as yet unrealized possibilities of mutation and differentiation. To achieve this condition is to be, in the words of Chuang-tzu and Ssu-k'ung T'u, "in the center of the ring": the empty space around which a wheel turns. *Hsiung-hun* is ceaseless activity following from pure potentiality.

The opening lines set outer and inner in opposition, with their counterparts "functioning," *yung*, and "form," *t'i**. Function, of course, is an active movement outward—even though the problems with the use of *fei* leave us uncertain precisely what happens outwardly: the outward is an extension of the inner (as is presumed universally true in the theory of manifestation), or the outward transforms while the inner stays the same (as in the image of the clouds), or the outward must "wither away" so that the inward can be nurtured and made replete, in preparation for a return to the outward (as in the demand for stillness before action made in Lu Chi and Liu Hsieh).

The second couplet takes up the two terms of the category. *Hun*, the "undifferentiated," is the primordial state of chaos, before distinctions have been formed; this term holds all possibilities of determinate realization within itself. *Hun* is more sensuous than our translation, "undifferentiated": as in the image of the billowing clouds, it is a visible chaos with temporal and spatial extension; but in it, all emergent shapes are constantly changing and blurring into all others. There is some question whether *hsü**, the "empty," is to be identified with the condition of *hun*, (since the plasticity of *hsü** works well with "undifferentiation") or whether it is the condition that precedes *hun* (or in Ch'iao Li's interpretation, the condition that must be supplanted for *hun* to be realized). The term *chien*, "sturdy," is applied to the operations of Heaven in the discussion of the hexagram *Ch'ien* in the *Book of Changes*. It is a force that cannot be stopped; and it is identified with *hsiung*, the "potent," by which individual transformations are realized in the potentiality of *hun*.

Since the condition *hsiung-hun* is one prior to stable differentiation, all things are contained within it. And this in turn leads to the notion of transformation, the favorite image for which in the Chinese tradition is a cloud formation, which we see rolling upon us in the fourth couplet. The clouds are an appropriate sensuous figure for *hun*, while the steady gale that drives them will be associated with *hsiung*.

In the fifth couplet, "beyond the images" refers to a scene in which there are no distinct shapes ("images"); every form blurs into every other form (as in the scene of gale-driven clouds). This is the "center of the ring," the "emptiness" (or complete fluidity, *hsü**) that is prior to all particularization and from which all particulars are generated.[7]

The closing injunction is one of Ssu-k'ung T'u's favorite motifs. One cannot grasp the *hsiung-hun* condition forcefully; it cannot be achieved by an act of will. One must somehow "be" the condition, and then it will operate permanently.

In many of Ssu-k'ung T'u's categories, it is relatively easy to see what sort of text would be characterized by the qualities described. Because "potent, undifferentiated" (in Ssu-k'ung T'u's version) is not a truly determinate quality in its own right, but rather a capacity to produce all determinate qualities, it can be manifest only in the impression of energy, in an ability constantly to produce new forms and transformations of old ones.[8] In his "Letter to Mr. Li Discussing Poetry" (p. 352) Ssu-k'ung T'u speaks strongly in favor of a poet's ability to work in many different modes and subtle variations (citing couplets from his own poems as examples); while the "potent, undifferentiated" is not simply such variation in its own right, it would be the generative force from which such variation came.

CATEGORY 2

Limpid and Calm, Ch'ung-tan 沖淡

素處以默。妙機其微。飲之太和。獨鶴與飛。猶之惠風。荏苒在衣。閱音修篁。美曰載歸。遇之匪深。即之愈稀。脫有形似。握手已違。

> Reside in plainness and quiet:
> How faint, the subtle impulses (*chi**).
> Infusing with perfect harmony,
> Join the solitary crane in flight.
> 5   Like that balmy breeze of spring,
> Pliantly changing in one's robes.
> Consider the tones in fine bamboo—
> Lovely indeed, return with them.
> One encounters this not hidden deeply away;
> 10 Approach it and it grows more elusive.
> If there is some resemblance of shape,
> The grasping hand has already missed it.

Line 1: We do not know whether the phrase *so ch'u* is "reside in plainness" or "everyday life" or "remain at rest": in any case the *ch'u*, "reside," is opposed to the potent activity of the preceding category. It is a stillness that lets one apprehend the subtle operations of nature. Forcefulness shapes the world; this is the opposite condition that is receptive and pays attention.

Line 2: The capacity to apprehend the "subtle impulses" seems to follow from the stillness of the first line. *Chi** are the subtle, initial movements of natural process that are blotted out when the subject asserts itself through intensity, activity, or desire. Tsu Pao-ch'üan takes the *chi* as the faint movements of mind responding to the outer world.

Line 3: Perfect harmony is the balanced interaction of Yin and Yang by which natural processes operate. This line appears to be based on a passage describing the Sage in the *Tse-yang* 則陽 chapter of the *Chuang-tzu*: "Thus, without speaking, he [the Sage] infuses others with harmony, standing together with them and bringing about their transformation." "Infuse," *yin* 飲, is literally "give to drink." The question in this line is who or what is doing the "infusing" and what is being "infused." It may be that the poet, by attaining the condition in the first couplet, is himself infused; but the source passage in the *Chuang-tzu* suggests that the poet, like the Sage, imparts harmony to his surroundings. Such "influence" would be conceptualized as *feng**, which is echoed in the way in which the spring "breeze" (*feng**) acts on things in lines 5 and 6. Such harmony may be the precondition of moving off with the crane in the next line.

Line 4: The crane is associated with immortal beings, suggesting that in this mode one can transcend the everyday world. The reference to immortal beings is much stronger in other categories: here the primary association seems to be some unhindered motion, a freedom of relation to the world that comes from the absence of intensity.

Line 6: *Jen-jan*, translated as "pliantly changing," describes a quality of softness or pliancy that is easily set into gentle motion; here it seems to refer to both the changing shapes of robes in a light breeze and the breeze itself. To apprehend the delicate motions of the breeze depends on the softness and stillness of the robes, and the wearer's attention. One should not overlook the implicit analogy between the "breeze," the "influence" imparted by one thing to another, and the poet's "song": all are *feng**.

Line 8: This line is specially problematic: Lü Hsing-ch'ang takes it as the beauty coming to (colloquial English "coming home to") the person who observes; Ch'iao Li and Chao Fu-t'an have the poet or person in the "limpid and calm" mode experiencing the sounds of the bamboo and going back with their lovely tones in mind—presumably producing the "tone" of a "limpid and calm" poetic mode.

Lines 9–10: "Limpid and calm" is found in the encounter with surfaces, not in willfully penetrating to the depths of things; intense reflection or observation is considered much like aggressive action. The line might also be taken in the conditional, interpreting deep as "hard to find": "If one comes on such things by chance, they will not be deep [i.e., hidden away]." *Hsi*, "elusive" or "rare" in the tenth line may be interpreted either that such a scene grows subtle and wonderful as one draws near, or that it eludes the person who comes too near. This last indecision can be taken as a touchstone of the peculiar difficulties of "The Twenty-Four Categories of Poetry": we have two exactly opposite interpretations, but both can be easily assimilated to the "limpid and calm" mode.

Line 11: The line may be understood as translated above, that the "limpid and calm" has no shape; and thus if one tries to bind it to fixed shapes, it is lost. This is the most common sense of *hsing*-ssu*, "semblance of shape," a technical term for sensuously descriptive language. With a slight twist we might also interpret *hsing*-ssu* in a broader mimetic sense as "the semblance of a limpid and calm scene": in this case, we would render the lines, "One may have some vague semblance of its form, but . . . "

Line 12: The injunction against trying to take hold of these qualities and make them definite is a motif that recurs throughout "The Twenty-Four Categories."

Ch'ung-tan, "limpid and calm," was already a well established term in the appraisal of personality, suggesting a gentleness without ambition or aggression. Later this quality was often used to describe the poetry of T'ao Ch'ien 陶潛 (ca. 365–427). Yang Chen-kang's 楊振綱 *Shih-p'in chieh* 詩品解 (quoted in Kuo Shao-yü's *Shih-p'in chi-chieh*) tries to explain the order of the categories on the model of the structure of the hexagrams in the *Book of Changes*. Each category, carried to its extreme, produces a deficiency that is remedied by the following category. While this principle of sequencing is not convincing for every relation between adjacent categories, in some sets of two or more categories such a principle of opposition is clear. There is no doubt that the receptivity of "Limpid and Calm" is in some way set in contrast to the active strength of "Potent, Undifferentiated." Here it is easy to recall the beginning of the *Book of Changes*, with the passivity of the hexagram *K'un* following the activity of the primary hexagram *Ch'ien*.

The productive energy of the "potent, undifferentiated" encompasses everything. The primary difference in the "limpid and calm" mode is the appearance of the separate human subject, attempting to apprehend things external to himself and to enter into a harmonious relation with his surroundings. The poet and/or poem grows calm and becomes receptive. On its blankness, all the most delicate qualities of the world are able to appear.

CATEGORY 3
Delicate-Fresh and Rich-Lush, Hsien-nung 纖穠

采采流水。蓬蓬遠春。窈窕深谷。時見美人。碧桃滿樹。風日水濱。柳蔭路曲。流鶯比鄰。乘之愈往。識之愈真。如將不盡。與古為新。

Brimming full, the flowing waters;
Lush and leafy, springtime stretching far.
Secluded in a deep valley
At times see a lovely lady.

<pre>
5   Emerald fills the peach trees,
         Breeze and sunlight on waters' banks.
         Willows shade the curves in the path,
         Gliding orioles are close neighbors.
         The more you go forward along with it,
10   The more you understand it truly.
         If you hold to it without ceasing,
         You join with the old and produce the new.
</pre>

"Rich-lush," *nung*, is one possible antithesis of *hsien* ("delicate-fresh"). *Nung* may refer to the "darkness" or the "richness" of a color, the "density" of shade, or the "strength" of wine or passion.

Lines 1–2: Like *p'eng-p'eng*, "lush and leafy," *ts'ai-ts'ai* originally described a density of vegetation, but it was commonly extended to be descriptive of any fullness or quantity: hence "brimming over." Lü Hsing-ch'ang and Tsu Pao-ch'üan take *ts'ai-ts'ai* as "fresh and bright," and Ch'iao Li somehow extends "fullness" to arrive at a similar interpretation. This interpretation is probably based on a different definition of the character when used singly and in other compounds. Lü Hsing-ch'ang associates the *ts'ai-ts'ai* with ripples, whose patterns, catching the light, would be a good example of *hsien*. Lü also associates the scene of the second line with red flowers, another *hsien* element. Ch'iao Li is probably correct, however, that the primary association of the second line is with foliage, producing a *nung* scene that contrasts with the *hsien* scene of the first line.

Lines 3–4: *Yao-t'iao*, translated as "secluded," may also mean "beautiful," as Ch'iao Li takes it. The Mao commentary on the *Book of Songs* had, however, fixed the meaning as "secluded," and it is in this sense that it is used here, suggesting the density of vegetation and the obstructions of the hills around the valley. Lü Hsing-ch'ang takes the fourth line as referring to many lovely ladies, seen "now and again" in the valley. This is not impossible, but the passage seems to stress the unique occurrence. One may avoid the implied subject of "see," *chien*, by reading it *hsien*, "appear."

Line 5: In this context "emerald peaches," *pi-t'ao*, are a special, fruitless variety; hence the reference seems to be to the foliage.

Line 8: Chao Fu-t'an interprets "neighbors" as the orioles being crowded together with one another.

Line 9: Ch'iao Li reads *ch'eng* as *ch'eng-hsing**, "to follow one's whim," thus stressing giving oneself over to the mood. Lü Hsing-ch'ang twists the sense of *ch'eng* to the more voluntary "pursue."

Line 10: "Truly" is *chen*, a heavily loaded philosophical term, implying what is "genuine" about the mode.

Line 11: *Chiang*, translated as "hold to," can either be to "take hold of" or to "accompany." In "The Twenty-Four Categories" willful "holding" usually results in the loss of the mode.

Line 12: "Old" here implies what is constant and permanent rather than what simply comes from the past.

Hsien and *nung* are antithetical qualities; and as Lü Hsing-ch'ang points out, they are both complementary and mutually compensatory. They are terms for a sensuousness that verges on sensuality, and were commonly used together to describe lovely women. We should note that Ssu-k'ung T'u draws no categorical distinction between modes that would seem to be primarily interior (such as "limpid and calm") and modes that seem primarily to describe external scenes, such as this one. The interior mode has a corresponding quality of scene; and the sensuous, external mode has a corresponding state of mind. Throughout "The Twenty-Four Categories" distinctions between inner and outer blur.

The commentators differ greatly as to which lines correspond to *hsien* and which to *nung*, but they generally agree that the structure of the first eight lines somehow balances one quality against the other. These first eight lines present a "world" (*ching**) of *hsien-nung*, and the last eight lines instruct the connoisseur how to apprehend that "world."[9]

The first two lines seem to be a delicate-fresh scene followed by a rich-heavy-lush scene, establishing the pattern of opposition. In the three couplets that follow, however, the rich-heavy-lush scene is given in the first line of the couplet; these *nung* scenes are in danger of being oppressively heavy and unvaried. That unvaried ground, usually of vegetation, is articulated by the second line of the couplet, in which the delicate-fresh element appears upon the ground: the woman, the light sparking on the water, the orioles flying past. In their opposition, each component draws attention to the other, but it is usually the *hsien* element that "appears" (associated with bounded time, light, and motion) and draws our attention to it. See Category 14, Lines 11–12, for how a dense, monochrome scene can succeed without the introduction of an antithetical quality. As he so often does in the concluding lines, Ssu-k'ung T'u enjoins the connoisseur to give himself over to the appreciation of such qualitative relations. He assumes that these qualities are not immediately apparent. As an aesthetician, his role is to point toward them, to call attention to their existence; but understanding the quality requires a duration of savoring, confronting such a scene (in a text or in the world) and "going along with it." The validation of the mode appears only in such a process.

"Join with the old and produce the new" is a refiguring of the *hsien-nung* opposition itself. *Nung* has no association with the old or constant (except perhaps the visual continuity of the foliage scenes); but the element of freshness in *hsien* can be linked to the new and is reinforced by the *hsien* images in the descriptive couplets, where something altogether different appears against the constant ground. The phrasing of line 12 echoes a critical commonplace about balancing old and new, normative and unique; but the context of the *hsien-nung* opposition gives the commonplace a new twist, rediscovering it in the sensuous qualities of the scene.

CATEGORY 4
Firm and Self-Possessed, Ch'en-cho 沈著

綠林野屋。落日氣清。脫巾獨步。時聞鳥聲。鴻雁不來。之子遠行。所思不遠。若為平生。海風碧雲。夜渚月明。如有佳語。大河前橫。

A rude dwelling in green forests,
As the sun sets, the air is clear.
He takes off his headband, walks alone,
At times hearing voices of birds.
5   The wild geese do not come,
And the person travels far away.
But the one longed for is not far—
It is as it always was.
A breeze from the sea, emerald clouds,
10   Moonlight brightens the isles by night.
If there are fine words,
The great river stretches out before him.

Line 5: Wild geese were conventional figures of messengers; thus "the wild geese do not come" refers to the absence of messages from a friend.

Line 6: "The person," *chih-tzu*, is a *Book of Songs* tag phrase; *so-ssu*, "the one longed for," in the following line is a *yüeh-fu* (early song lyric) phrase. Both terms lend an archaic and archetypical tone to the lines, as if speaking of "the beloved" in English.

Line 8: Ch'iao Li interprets "it is as," *jo-wei*, as "achieves the condition of." In either case the *ch'en-cho* state overcomes the possibility of loneliness by a deeper contentment that recalls a permanence of friendship in which distance does not matter. It is this confidence and not physical proximity that makes "the one longed for . . . not far."[10] Chao Fu-t'an takes the line rather differently: "yet how can it be as it used to be?"

Lines 9–10: Ch'iao Li suggests that this scene is correlative for the relaxation of the speaker's spirit, following the confident recollection of the friendship in the preceding lines. Kuo Shao-yü takes these as more general correlatives for *ch'en-cho*, the former being a kinetic manifestation and the latter being a static manifestation.

Lines 11–12: There is great disagreement about these lines, and the various explanations are only suppositions. Most commentators see in the river an image of the security, ubiquitousness, or openness of either the condition *ch'en-cho* or of words uttered in such a condition. Sun Lien-k'uei's *Shih-p'in yi-shuo* alone sets the flux of the river against the *ch'en-cho* condition, and says that *ch'en-cho* is present when the words do not drift or sink, in other words, are secure.

Ch'en-cho refers to some quality of security, stability, and self-confidence that may be manifest in an actual person's personality, in the personality of a poetic style, or in a scene of the natural word presented in a poem. Lü Hsing-ch'ang is perhaps overinterpreting (though doing so entirely within the lexicographical tradition) when reading this compound as the fusion of an antithetical pair—*ch'en* being an element of literal "sunkenness," and *cho* being an element of clarity—but she is correct insofar as the condition is predicated on a certain tension, a self-assurance that proves itself by overcoming the threat of depression. Here is a good example of a case where Yang Chen-kang's principle of a sequence through oppositions breaks down; Yang tries valiantly to explain the transition from *hsien-nung* as an antithetical supplement: "The 'delicate' easily passes into the frivolous; the 'rich-lush' may be damaged by fatness [complacency]; this is how it becomes tinged by the shortcoming of instability and lightness; thus he progresses to the quality of the 'firm and self-possessed.'"[11]

The opening scene is one of isolation; but it is a far from gloomy isolation, and the gesture of removing one's headband (in English "letting one's hair down") suggests a positive freedom from restraints. Despite the commentators' assurance that this is, indeed, specifically a *ch'en-cho* scene, the qualities of mood in the description of scenes in the various categories do overlap; the scene of the opening four lines could legitimately be characterized in a variety of ways. What is important is that it is presumed to embody the mood in question; and the reader pays close attention to the gestures, the juxtaposition of forms, and received associations to apprehend such a mood.

A threat to the good cheer of the opening four lines arises in the thought of a companion from whom one is separated and from whom one has no news. A shift in mood could easily occur at this point, and Lü Hsing-ch'ang is correct in suggesting that such a situation has the repressed potential to become dark. *Ch'en-cho* asserts itself against such a possibility, with a self-assurance that makes it as if the friend were present.

The real difficulties of the poem are in the last four lines, and Ch'iao Li is probably correct in associating the scene, opening into light, with a corresponding "opening" of the feelings (as might be said in Chinese)—a restoration of confident cheer. The "fine words" must be *ch'en-cho* words, which play counterpoint to the absence of news from the friend. Words seem necessary to actualize this mood; but when they are present, the mood finds its counterpart in the scene.

Lofty and Ancient, Kao-ku 高古

畸人乘真。手把芙蓉。汎彼浩劫。窅然空蹤。月出東斗。好風相從。太華夜碧。人閒
清鐘。虛佇神素。脫然畦封。黃唐在獨。落落玄宗。

     The man of wonder rides the pure,
     In his hand he holds a lotus;
     He drifts on through unfathomed aeons,
     In murky expanses, bare of his traces.
5   The moon emerges in the eastern Dipper,
     And a good wind follows it.
     T'ai-hua Mountain is emerald green this night,
     And he hears the sound of a clear bell.
     In air he stands long in spiritual simplicity,
10   All limits and boundaries lightly passed.
     The Yellow Emperor and Sage-King Yao are in his solitude:
     Noble and unique—those mysterious principles he reveres.

Line 1: The "man of wonders" is a term drawn from the *Chuang-tzu*, referring to a *hsien* 仙, an "immortal being," or simply one who rises above the ordinary world. The "pure" ridden here probably refers to the pure ether (*ch'i**) and suggests a neo-Taoist spirit-flight.

Line 2: This line is a shortened version of a line in Li Po's nineteenth "Old Mode" (*Ku-feng** 古風), beginning:

    Westward I climbed Lotus Blossom Peak
    And far in the distance saw Bright Star:
    In her hand she held a lotus,
    Walking in air, striding the Utterly Clear.

The goddess Bright Star was said to reside in the Hua Mountain cluster, one of whose peaks was "Lotus Blossom" (*lien-hua* 蓮花, a term for lotus different from the *fu-jung* of the third line). This cluster is also the "T'ai-hua Mountain" referred to in line 7.

Line 3: "Aeons" (*chieh*) refer to Buddhist *kalpas*. Since the passage of *kalpas* involves a scouring of the earth, Tsu Pao-ch'üan takes this as referring primarily to passing unconcerned through human catastrophes. This seems unnecessary. On no clear authority, Chao Fu-t'an spatializes *chieh* and has the immortal passing over vast spaces. This also seems unlikely, especially considering that the mode involves the style of the past reappearing in the present.

Line 5: This refers to one of the five divisions of the heavens in Taoist cosmology.

Line 9: This line presents serious difficulties. I have taken *hsü-chu* as "in air he stands long," in parallel with the *hsü-pu*, "walking in air," of the Li Po lines. The character *chu* 佇, meaning "stand long," is often extended to mean "await" or "expect" (see the commentary to 1.1 of "The Poetic Exposition on Literature"; furthermore it can be exchanged with another *chu* 貯, meaning "amass" or "store up," hence "nurture." It is in the latter sense that both Lü Hsing-ch'ang and Chao Fu-t'an interpret *chu* (though they try to make it an extension of "await"). Lü and Chao differ in the way they handle *hsü**: Lü takes it as "void," the manner in which the immortal "nourishes spiritual simplicity." Chao understands it as "the empty place," a Taoist kenning for mind. Ch'iao Li reads *hsü-chu* close to the way in which I have interpreted the phrase, but he makes the scene even less concrete: the spirit-thought (spiritual simplicity) of the poet stands long in a realm of formlessness (*hsü**). One suspects that Ch'iao Li has the opening of "The Poetic Exposition on Literature" in mind here.

Lines 11–12: Chao Fu-t'an interprets these lines to mean:

> Like the Yellow Emperor and Yao, he is alone:
> Noble and unique, he becomes the mysterious exemplar.

Lü Hsing-ch'ang reads "are his sole concern" instead of "in his solitude," and suggests an interpretation similar to Chao's as an alternate explanation for the last line.

Kao, "lofty," and *ku*, "ancient," often compounded as here, were very common categories of critical judgment. Among T'ang taxonomies *kao-ku* was listed as a category of mood in Chiao-jan's 皎然 "Models of Poetry" (*Shih-shih* 詩式, late eighth century) and in Ch'i-chi's 齊己 "Exemplary Forms of the *Feng* and *Sao*" (*Feng*-Sao chih-ko*, 風騷旨格, late ninth century). However, Ssu-k'ung T'u's strong association of these qualities with a Taoist vision of ethereal purity is idiosyncratic. In some cases Ssu-k'ung T'u speaks from a general consensus regarding the use of these categorical terms of manner; but in other cases, as here, he gives his own version. The Yellow Emperor and Yao, who appear at the end, are properly "ancient"; but the Confucian would not recognize his Yao here.

After the first couplet, the immortal being becomes formless and ethereal, leaving the dominant motif of emptiness, unbounded space and time. One means by which qualities are articulated in "The Twenty-Four Categories of Poetry" is through the recurrence of common elements in very different scenes. In such scenes the distinctions between the modes become much clearer. One might note the metamorphoses of sky scenes: In "Potent, Undifferentiated," we have

Pale and billowing rainclouds;
Long winds in the empty vastness.

In "Firm and Self-Possessed" we have

A breeze from the sea, emerald clouds,
Moonlight brightens the isles by night.

Clearly "firm and self-possessed" clouds are a different kind of clouds, a few massy cumulus clouds "in" the sky rather than "potent, undifferentiated" clouds that cover the sky or some portion of it; and the relative stability of their form is strengthened by their visual association with the isles, bright in the moonlight. The "lofty and ancient" mode requires void, space unfilled or filled with intangibles such as moonlight or the sound of a bell: thus the clouds are removed:

The moon emerges in the eastern Dipper,
And a good wind follows it.
T'ai-hua Mountain is emerald green this night,
And he hears the sound of a clear bell.

All is wind, light, and sound, with the only shape in the void being the mysterious and dark mass of Mount T'ai-hua, around which immortal beings from the past play unseen.

CATEGORY 6

Decorous and Dignified, Tien-ya* 典雅

玉壺買春。賞雨茆屋。坐中佳士。左右修竹。白雲初晴。幽鳥相逐。眠琴綠陰。上有飛瀑。落花無言。人淡如菊。書之歲華。其曰可讀。

With a jade pot he purchases spring [wine],
Appreciates rain under a roof of thatch.
Fine scholars are his guests,
All around him, fine bamboo.
5   White clouds in newly cleared skies,
Birds from hidden places follow one another.
A reclining lute in the green shade,
And above is a waterfall in flight.
The falling flowers say nothing:
10   The man, as limpid as the chrysanthemum.
He writes down the seasons' splendors—
May it be, he hopes, worth the reading.

Line 1: Lü Hsing-ch'ang objects to the flatness of the standard interpretation of "spring" here as a kenning for spring wine. She prefers to have the person taking in the spring scene. This has precedent in Yang T'ing-chih, who suggests that the line refers to an excursion; but as Chao Fu-t'an points out, the next three lines seem distinctly sedentary.

Line 4: Sun Lien-k'uei suggests that the bamboo here are metaphors for the scholars. While bamboo were conventionally associated with scholars, here they would seem to form part of the scene, "echoing" in the natural world the party of scholars, rather than being metaphors for them.

Line 7: Lu Hsing-ch'ang and Chao Fu-t'an note that the lute is not being played; rather than playing, the human is absorbed in listening to the sound of the waterfall.

Line 10: "Limpid," *tan*, is a quiet, unruffled manner with no strong feelings to block or influence one's appreciation of the scene. That same quality, as a "paleness" of color, characterizes the chrysanthemum.

Line 12: Commentators all stress the element of appreciation and enjoyment in "read," *tu*.

We should note that "decorous and dignified" is given as the first of the eight normative forms (*t'i**) in "Nature and Form" in *Wen-hsin tiao-lung*. Ch'iao Li interprets the first four lines here as an alternation between *tien* ("decorous") and *ya** ("dignified"): he characterizes the first line as *tien-mei* 典美, "decorously beautiful"; the second line as *feng*-ya** 風雅, a "'poetic' dignity"; the third line as *tien-tse* 典則, "decorously normative"; and the fourth line as *ya*-jun* 雅潤, "gentle and generous dignity." These fine modal discriminations are far too tenuous to sustain, at least in English; but they offer an excellent example of the traditional form of modal analysis. Even a contemporary scholar such as Ch'iao Li looks for the distribution of binary terms within couplets, assuming traditional rhetorical amplification (that the poem is constructed by breaking compounds down into their component parts). *Tien-ya** is considered the general compound, within which *tien* and *ya** are more highly determined (restricted) elements. Each of these then combines into other compounds, which are still more precise and determined. Lü Hsing-ch'ang, the more Western-influenced scholar, also retains something of this traditional analytical procedure, observing that the first line is comparatively *tien* and the second line comparatively *ya**.

   Tien, translated as "decorous," is the term applied to the early Classics and has been translated elsewhere in this volume as "canonical" and "authoritative." Ssu-k'ung T'u's usage no longer necessarily refers to the quality of the early Classics. Like many other modal terms here, *tien* is a translator's despair: it contains elements of "gravity" (with no implication of somberness), a natural "politeness" (with no sense of artificial social restraints); it is plain and simple, and it is associated with antiquity as what is basic and enduring.

Note that *tien-ya**, unlike the preceding modes, is treated as a sociable quality. The gathering, however, is a quiet one, a shared appreciation of the scene, along with a mirroring pleasure in the fact that the appreciation is indeed shared. The guests are together looking out rather than interacting with one another; that quiet unity is echoed in the bamboo all around. Such appreciative silence recurs in the silence of the lute, whose music is foregone to appreciate the sound of the waterfall. The objects of such silent appreciation form a natural progression, from the rain to clearing skies, to the rain water now spilling over the falls. The same silence returns in the falling flowers, paired with the chrysanthemum, the last flower of the year, associated with the dignity of old age and calm acceptance.

T'ang poets and their readers were intensely aware of the seasonal markers of scenes. Ssu-k'ung T'u's seasonal mixing contributes in no small measure to the strange sense of indeterminacy in these poems, that they are "worlds of the mind" (*yi**-*ching**), constructed by the recombination of various elements from sensuous experience, rather than being tied to some particular scene of the empirical world. The first line strongly suggests spring (though some explanations of "spring wine" would allow for a late autumn scene). The "green shade" of line 7 is conventionally a summer scene, though it could be extended to late spring or early autumn. The falling flowers are almost always a mark of late spring, though in their close juxtaposition with chrysanthemums, they could conceivably refer to late autumn. In their contrary indications the seasonal markers in this verse cancel one another out; and though we would be inclined to read *sui-hua* in line 11 as "the season's flowering" (i.e., a spring"), the general confluence of seasons in the poem leads to a more abstract interpretation as the "seasons' splendors."

CATEGORY 7
Washed and Refined, Hsi-lien 洗鍊

如鑛出金。如鉛出銀。超心鍊冶。絕愛緇磷。空潭瀉春。古鏡照神。體素儲潔。乘月
返真。載瞻星氣。載歌幽人。流水今日。明月前身。

As the ore gives forth gold,
As the lode gives forth its silver,
The mind, perfected, smelts and refines,
Rejects love of all that is stained and worn.
5   An empty pool infuses springtime,
An ancient mirror reflects the spirit.
They embody plainness, store up the pristine,

And in moonlight turn back to what is pure.
He gazes on the *ch'i** of the stars
10   And sings of the recluse.
The flowing water is right now;
The bright moon, its former self.

Lines 1–2: "Lode" here translates *ch'ien*, "lead," given here (impossibly) as a silver ore. Both lines are, of course, figures of a poetic precision that gives only the "refined essence." The presumption is that in the formation of the poetic mind, or the formulation of "poetic ideas," or poetic language, there is much dross, within which a smaller element of "essence" must be derived.

Line 3: Although "perfected" is *ch'ao*, "transcend," "go beyond," Western notions of "transcendent mind" should be avoided; this is a mind that is "perfected," able to go beyond the sensuous imperfections to essence. If the first couplet were taken as referring to the formation of the poetic mind, then this line would be "The mind, perfected, is smelted and refined."

Line 4: This refers to the "hard and white" of *Analects* XVII.7: "May we not call that 'hard' which can be polished without wearing down. And may we not call that 'white' which can be dirtied without being stained." *Chüeh-ai*, usually interpreted as "rejects love of" or "ceases begrudging [giving up] what is . . . ," has been understood by a few as "loves intensely" (*chüeh* can work either way). Such an interpretation, of course, requires considerable exegetical ingenuity to reconcile it with the rest of the poem; for instance, he loves the stained and worn because it presents an opportunity for washing and refining. Chao Fu-t'an accepts this interpretation of *chüeh-ai*; Ch'iao Li gives it as a possibility; Lü Hsing-ch'ang rejects it out of hand.

Line 5: This line of liquid purity refers to the "washed" (*hsi*) element of the title. The pool's "emptiness" refers to a clear, uncovered surface. *Hsieh*, translated as "infuses," basically means "to pour out," as of water, and is commonly extended to refer to the flowing of water (note that by Chinese literary convention the water of a pool, *t'an*, should be still). The commentators all know that the line should somehow refer to reflections or spring light in the clear water, and they work on *hsieh* to make it perform its anticipated task. The two basic resolutions are either to make *hsieh* active (the pool carries spring light or reflections in its currents) or passive (spring scenes or light are "poured into" the pool). A far better explanation (and one consistent with T'ang usage) would be to emend this *hsieh* to another *hsieh* 寫, without the water radical; this *hsieh* means "delineate," and was a common poetic usage to refer to water's reflective capacities, hence parallel to the "reflection" in the following line (cf. Cat. 20, l. 3).

Line 6: This line refers to the "refined" (*lien*) element of the title. Recall that the reference here is to a bronze mirror. A dull mirror will reflect only a rough outline, but a good mirror captures the animate liveliness of human appearance: the mirror's capacity to "reflect spirit (*shen**)" should be understood primarily in this sense. Nevertheless, the more numinous interpretation of "spirit," often spoken of in terms of glowing light, should be held in reserve as the counterpart of the "moonlight in water" motif.

Lines 7–8: At this point the commentators go off in many different directions. The central question seems to be whether the subjects of these lines are the reflective media of the preceding couplet or the poet, who "washes and refines" in the following couplet. Since similar activities of self-purification are enjoined in other of the categories, it is quite reasonable to take these lines as referring to the poet, as many commentators do. But since these twelve line verses often break into three four-line units, and since it makes even better sense, I prefer to read this couplet in connection with the preceding couplet: hence the translation "they." Pool and mirror are not only pure and polished, they capture the luminous purity in outer things, thus purifying them. As figures for the poem or poetic mind (the clear pool being a traditional Buddhist metaphor for mind), pool and mirror not only reflect the outer world, they etherealize it, purifying it of all that is dross and material. Kuo Shao-yü takes *t'i**, "embody," as I have done; Ch'iao Li takes it as "adhere closely to"; Lü Hsing-ch'ang and Tsu Pao-ch'üan take it as "intuitively grasp." In line 8, Chao Fu-t'an, reading the poet as the subject, argues strenuously (and incorrectly, I think) for interpreting "pure," *chen*, as a scene of the "immortals'" world, to which the poet returns in the moonlight.

Lines 9–10: The stars are constituted of the essence of *ch'i**. That luminous halo of *ch'i** around the stars plays counterpoint to the "recluse," *yu-jen*, literally "person hidden in darkness." Some commentators want to make the recluse do the singing; this makes good sense and is grammatically possible (taking the *ko* transitively as "sets to singing"), but it is not the most natural reading of the line.

Lines 11–12: The reference here is clearly to the figure of moonlight in the water, whose strong Buddhist associations are reinforced by the terminology of reincarnation in the last line. The actual moon is the previous incarnation; the reflection in the water is the present incarnation. This works well with our interpretation of lines 5–8, with the reflections in pool and mirror serving to refine away the dross, something that should also occur in transmigration. "Right now" is literally "today"; clearly Ssu-k'ung T'u intends this only in the loosest sense of "present"; but the reference to "day" is unfortunate, considering the image of moonlight (all commentators ignore the "day" aspect, presumably taking it in its abstract Buddhist sense rather than in its more precise sense as required by good literary Chinese).

Though one of the most beautiful and characteristic of Ssu-k'ung T'u's categories, this is also one of the most difficult. There is considerable disagreement among the commentators as to the precise interpretation of many lines and phrases (though, as is often the case, general agreement on the overall effect). The poem seems to move between two notions of "washed and refined." The first version is the "hard and white" of the *Analects* passage, which leads to a fairly conventional notion of purity and refining something to its essence. This first refinement moves to reflective surfaces, however, producing the second vision of "washed and refined" in reflection itself. This revised version is elusive and ethereal, and seems to be the product of the poetic mirror-mind that catches "spirit," while removing all that is dross and material. In this process, the quasi-concrete thing becomes etherealized; and reflected poetic image is compared to the process of reincarnation, in which the soul may be perfected toward Buddhahood in realizing the "emptiness" of the world (emptiness being also associated with the reflected light and the flowing water). The poem is exceedingly cryptic, both in its elliptical expression and in its mixture of many different images.

CATEGORY 8
Strong and Sturdy, Ching-chien 勁健

行神如空。行氣如虹。巫峽千尋。走雲連風。飲真茹強。蓄素守中。喻彼行健。是謂
存雄。天地與立。神化攸同。期之以實。御之以終。

Set spirit in motion as through the void,
Set *ch'i** in motion as though in a rainbow:
A thousand yards down in the Wu Gorges
Are speeding clouds and continuous winds.
5   He drinks of the pure, feeds on the forceful,
Stores up plainness, and holds to the center.
It is figured by the sturdiness of Heaven's motions:
This is known as "retaining the potent."
He stands together with Heaven and Earth,
10   Sharing spirit's transformations (*shen*-hua**).
He looks to make it actual (*shih**),
And guide it on all the way to the end.

Lines 1–2: "Spirit," *shen**, in this case seems very close to "spirit thought," *shen*-ssu**, which is always said to move without obstructions. *Shen** is insubstantial, while *ch'i** is substantial, a vaporous force: courageous soldiers are said to produce rainbow manifestations from their *ch'i** (in a similar way Tsu Pao-ch'üan takes the *ch'i** as emitted by an immortal being flying through the void). Thus the insubstantial *shen** goes with "void," and *ch'i** goes with the relatively substantial "rainbow."

Lines 3–4: The Wu Gorges were proverbial for their danger, violence, darkness, and their powerful forces of current, wind, and fog.

Line 6: Kuo Shao-yü and Ch'iao Li interpret *su*, "plainness," as "regularly," and *chung*, "center," as "within the self": thus the poet attains this state by that often described process of continuous nurturing within. The phrasing is so close to Category 7, line 7, that such an interpretation of *su* would seem unlikely. *Chung*, "center," could be either "within the self" or the more abstract "center" where one stands prior to action in any particular direction, like the "center of the ring" in Category 1, line 10.

Line 7: "Heaven's" is interpolated in the translation because it is implicit, owing to its use in the *Ch'ien* hexagram of the *Book of Changes*: "Heaven's motions are sturdy: the superior person drives himself without resting." The balanced ratio of reserved strength and its forceful expenditure make this category close to "Potent, Undifferentiated," which also is linked to the hexagram *Ch'ien*. *Yü*, translated as "figured by," is the term in literary Chinese that most closely corresponds to metaphorical and allegorical operations of meaning. One might translate it in the other direction as "It refers to . . . "; that is, this mode is the surface expression of which the sturdiness of Heaven's motions is the significance. Ch'iao Li takes *yü* as "understands"; this is a legitimate extended use of the term, but weak.

Line 8: "The potent" is *hsiung*, one of the terms of the first category.

Line 10: The "spirit's transformations," *shen*-hua**, must refer to the the mysterious forces of transformation in ongoing creation (*Tsao-hua**).

This is one of the easier categories and very closely related to "Potent, Undifferentiated." Like all categories of forceful action, it lays stress on the process of storing up energy. It differs, however, from "Potent, Undifferentiated" by being force that is determinate, actual, and with direction. The touchstone couplets for comparison are "Potent, Undifferentiated," Lines 7–8:

> Pale and billowing rainclouds;
> Long winds in the empty vastness.

In contrast, in the present category we have the more directed force of the clouds blowing down the Wu Gorges. Both possibilities are contained in the hexagram *Ch'ien*: the potential for all action or a single realized action, carried through to the end.

CATEGORY 9
Intricate Beauty, Ch'i-li* 綺麗

神存富貴。始輕黃金。濃盡必枯。淡者屢深。霧餘水畔。紅杏在林。月明華屋。畫橋碧陰。金罇酒滿。伴客彈琴。取之自足。良殫美襟。

If spirit (*shen**) preserves wealth and honor,
One cares little for yellow gold.
When the rich-and-lush (*nung*) reaches its limit, it will wither and dry up,
But the pale will always grow deeper.

5   In the last of the fog by the water's edge,
There are red apricot blossoms in a grove.
The moon shining bright in a splendid chamber,
A painted bridge in the emerald shade.
Golden goblets full of wine,

10   A companion strumming a lute.
If this is accepted, sufficient in itself,
It will express all the loveliest sensations.

Lines 3–4: Lü Hsing-ch'ang understands this couplet as implying that the condition of line 3 will occur if *ch'i-li** is absent, while the condition of line 4 will occur if "intricate beauty," *ch'i-li**, is present. The reason for such an interpretation is the common association of *ch'i-li**'s luxuriance with *nung*, and its dissociation from *tan*, "pale." However, it seems that throughout the verse Ssu-k'ung T'u is offering a more radical reinterpretation of the category, suggesting that a *nung ch'i-li** will destroy itself and lose it allure, while a *tan ch'i-li**, as characterized by the scenes in the lines that follow, sustains the quality by keeping it perpetually emergent.

Line 5: Lü Hsing-ch'ang prefers an alternate text, which reads the line as *lu-yü shan ch'ing* 露餘山青, "In the remaining dew the mountains are green."

Line 7: "Splendid" here is *hua*, "flowery": it implies not only grandeur but also a rich decoration that takes on a quality of veiledness or tasteful dimness when seen in the moonlight.

Line 11: "Sufficient in itself" may also be understood personally as "and one is satisfied with it."

*Ch'i-li** was a well-established category of manner that was as often condemned in the T'ang as approved. It is a particular "fanciness"; to its detractors it was associated with wealth, frivolity, and dissipation. Probably because of the potentially pejorative aspects of the quality, Ssu-k'ung T'u tries to shift the definition of the authentic manifestation of the quality away from material and surfaces to a quality of spirit: hence the rejection of "yellow gold" (though one might note that the poem returns to gold in the ninth line). This is one solution to the conflict, arising in several of the categories, between Ssu-k'ung T'u's own values and the received associations of a particular mode; without fundamentally altering the understanding of the quality, he "withdraws" it from the surface. Modes of force are made legitimate by being understood as force in potential; modes of sensuous surface are made legitimate by being veiled.

Although *ch'i-li** is reinterpreted as an "inner" quality, Ssu-k'ung T'u must find sensuous scenes that embody it; and as he often does, he resolves the problem of representing the "inner" by scenes of spatial or temporal "depth." In the second couplet he appeals to the the venerable principle of cyclical reversal: the fully manifest or external quality moves into desiccation; if veiled, the quality will exist in a perpetual condition of "coming out." The "rich and lush," *nung*, always hangs on the edge of overripeness; Ssu-k'ung T'u was able to defend the quality in Category 3 only because it was stabilized by the presence of an antithetical quality, "delicacy," *hsien*. If an overwrought, *nung* version of *ch'i-li** withers like autumn foliage in the process of appreciation, a *tan*, "pale," *ch'i-li** (however oxymoronic that combination will seem) endures. *Tan* often refers to a visual surface that is misted over or in which the colors are not too strong. This unusual combination of *tan* with *ch'i-li** is realized visually in the image that follows: in the dissipating fog that slightly veils the intricacy and bright colors of the flowering grove. But *ch'i-li** is often associated with human artifacts, and in the following couplet Ssu-k'ung T'u finds other ways to veil ornamental glitter: by moonlight and deep shade. Finally, in the scene of restrained conviviality of the last descriptive couplet, the luxury implicit in the category returns with the golden goblet—not overwhelming the scene but as a single element, an attractive adjunct to a situation (drinking and sharing music with friends) whose center lies elsewhere.

The notion of "sufficient in itself" is important to Ssu-k'ung T'u's revision of *ch'i-li**. *Ch'i-li** is always in danger of moving to excess, and it can be successfully realized only if we are content with a *ch'i-li** in which that tendency is blocked, veiled, or somehow limited.

CATEGORY 10
The Natural, Tzu-jan* 自然

俯拾即是。不取諸鄰。俱道適往。著手成春。如逢花開。如瞻歲新。真與不奪。強得易貧。幽人空山。過水採蘋。薄言情悟。悠悠天鈞。

It's what you can bend down and pick up—
It's not to be taken from any of your neighbors.
Go off, together with the Way,
And with a touch of the hand, springtime forms.
5   It is as if coming upon the flowers blossoming,
As if looking upon the renewal of the year.
One does not take by force what the genuine provides,

What is attained willfully easily becomes bankrupt.
A recluse in the deserted mountains
10   Stops by a stream and picks waterplants.
As it may, his heart will be enlightened—
The Potter's Wheel of Heaven goes on and on forever.

Line 1: That is, what is available immediately and everywhere.

Line 2: *Neighbors* here does not necessarily refer to people; Ch'iao Li reasonably interprets the line as primarily referring to borrowing from the ancients (which usually means simply other literary texts). The point here is that the natural is precisely what is "at hand"; and whenever one feels that what is wanted is "somewhere else," a disjunctive relation of alienation and the displacement that occurs in desire are produced, doing violence to the natural.

Line 3: The "Way" here does not refer to any particular religio-philosophical system, but rather to the basic sense of "Way" on which all philosophical claims to the term are founded: that their particular tenets are the "Way" things are "naturally" (*Tzu-jan* *).

Line 4: The "touch of the hand" almost certainly refers to writing (although if one believed that these poems were mistitled, it could just as easily refer to calligraphy or the brushwork of painting). Ch'iao Li stresses that "springtime" here is primarily renewed life and vitality, which follows from his interpretation of "neighbors" as the ancients; that is, in the "natural" mode one is always, like Nature itself, beginning anew.

Lines 5–6: There are two distinct possibilities of interpretation here. One may take these lines as following "the springtime" produced by the touch of the writing hand, an organic bounty that accompanies successful participation in the "natural" mode. Or one may take the lines as stressing the accidental aspect of the natural mode: whatever comes is given by its own natural process and is not subject to human will. This second interpretation, favored by most commentators, leads into the rest of the poem.

Line 7: Ch'iao Li and Tsu Pao-ch'üan interpret *to*, translated as "take by force," as "change," that is, to willfully interfere. Again this line has two distinct possibilities of interpretation: either what is offered by the "genuine," *chen* (an attribute of natural process), can only come on its own accord and cannot be taken by force; or one should not willfully interfere with what the genuine has already given.

Lines 9–10: The image of the recluse picking waterplants is a figure of what is provided by chance, easily, abundantly, and naturally. See also "The Poetic Exposition on Literature," lines 208–212, where there is a bounty, supposedly easily available, that is somehow unattainable.

Lines 11–12: The "Potter's Wheel" is from the *Chuang-tzu*, a figure of the continuous generative processes of creation. Chao Fu-t'an takes line 11 as conditional: "If his heart becomes enlightened, . . ." This and the following categories are the most famous and influential of the twenty-four; the first couplets of both were frequently quoted. While the values of the natural and spontaneous are very old ones in the tradition, Ssu-k'ung T'u offers a radicalization of those values that was to become dangerously influential: both in this poem and elsewhere in "The Twenty-Four Categories" there is an explicit rejection of conscious effort. Nowhere is Ssu-k'ung Tu's spiritual allegiance to philosophical Taoism clearer. An open rejection of self-conscious action is, however, an extremely problematic event in a tradition of literary thought.

Unlike the earlier texts of Western poetics such as Longinus' "On the Sublime," which required only the appearance of spontaneity (often with the proviso that such appearance was the result of supremely self-conscious craft), Ssu-k'ung T'u's demand here is that the poem actually come naturally: the poet need only learn how to let it happen. Like the Sage, the poet moves "with" the Way, and takes what is given as it is given. He transmits it to his work whenever he sets his hand to paper and is not allowed to brood on his writing or to revise: it comes "right out" and "comes out right." This intimidating demand, with its alluring resonance in both Confucian and Taoist values, is even more difficult in poetry than in moral action: the real human poems that resulted from attempts to achieve this mode survive as evidence of how dull, awkward, and unreadable the "poetry" given by nature can be. An interesting resolution to this problem was given by the late Ming critic Yüan Hung-tao, writing on the literary works of his brother: there he judged the awkward places in his brother's poetry to be the best because they were the true signature of his brother's spontaneity.[12]

One mark of the problematic aspects of this category is the poem's abstractness. It is remarkable that in this category of "The Natural, " we have one of the few cases where there are no descriptions of "natural" scenes that illustrate the category. In the two couplets presenting scenes, both use natural imagery to make a conceptual point rather than to offer an example or embodiment of the mode. In the case of the third couplet, the stress is on the chanceness of the encounter with natural process rather than on the scene encountered (even here the "renewal of the year" is abstract, and the "flowers blossoming" general). Exactly the same point could have been made by substituting autumn clouds, the migrations of birds, or any scene of natural process. In the same way, in the scene of the recluse stopping by a stream and picking water plants, the force is not in the specific sensuous relations of this particular scene but in the idea of taking what nature freely offers close at hand. In contrast, the natural scenes presented in the majority of the categories embody the mode under discussion. It is significant that the most "natural" aspect of the poem is the unpoetic phrasing of the first line: it is language, seeming to embody an unreflective movement of mind, that carries the weight of the "natural," *tzu-jan**, rather than any particular aspect of the outer world.

CATEGORY 11

Reserve/Accumulation Within, Han-hsü 含蓄

不著一字。盡得風流。語不涉己。若不堪憂。是有真宰。與之沉浮。如淥滿酒。花時返秋。悠悠空塵。忽忽海漚。淺深聚散。萬取一收。

> It does not inhere in any single word
> Yet the utmost flair is attained.
> Though the words do not touch on oneself,
> It is as if there were unbearable melancholy.
> In this there is that "someone in control,"
> Floating or sinking along with them.
> It is like straining the thickest wine,
> Or the season of flowers reverting to autumn.
> Far, far away, specks of dust in the sky;
> Passing in a flash, bubbles on the ocean.
> Shallow and deep, clustering, scattering,
> Thousands of grains are gathered into one.

5

10

Han-hsü implies both "reserve" in the English sense, as applied to personality, and to a reserve of unexpressed significance or emotion that lies implicit behind or beneath the words and unfolds after the words of the text are over.

Line 1: Or "By not getting stuck in single words . . . " Some older commentators want to take *chu* in its common meaning as "write," thus: "without putting a single word to paper." This interpretation misses the point.

Line 2: "Flair" is here an attempt to translate the term *feng**-*liu*, usually an intensely emotional quality of personality, easily stirred to love or battle, a sensibility that responds strongly to people, natural scenes, or traces of the past. Here it is a more general panache, for which "flair" will have to serve. The important point is that *feng**-*liu* is an extremely outward and outgoing quality; consonant with his treatment of other positive outward qualities, Ssu-k'ung T'u claims that it finds its ultimate expression when it is implicit, in "reserve."

Lines 3–4: Some commentators here prefer the alternate textual reading *nan* 難 for *chi*, "oneself," yielding the translation: "Though the words do not touch on hardships." In such cases the *jo*, "as if," in the fourth line, is replaced by *yi* 已, "already" that is, even before any mention of hardship is made.

Line 5: "Someone in control": This term is from the "Treating Things as Equal" (*Ch'i-wu lun*) chapter of the *Chuang-tzu*:

> Rage and delight, sorrow and joy, anxieties, misgivings, uncertainties, and all manner of faint-heartedness, frivolity, and recklessness, openness and posturing—all are music from the empty spaces, mushrooms forming in ground mist. Day and night one follows another, but no one knows where they sprout from. That's all there is! They come upon us from dawn to dusk, but how they came to be—who knows? Without them there is no me, and without me they have nothing to hold on to. That's pretty much how it is. But I don't understand how they are set in operation. It may be that there is someone in control, but he leaves no trace for me to find. No doubt that he can act, but I don't see his form; he is there in the circumstance but has no form.

The "someone in control" is the identity that unifies the flux of human consciousness.

Line 6: "Floating or sinking along with them": that is, coming into and disappearing from sight along with the words. Ch'iao Li interprets this as "[someone in control] who causes it to be manifest or hidden." Such an interpretation is consistent with the *Chuang-tzu* passage alluded to in the preceding line, but it depends on forcing the sense of *yü* "with," to mean "cause." The notion of "floating and sinking with" something was a common one and is the most natural reading. In this case the *Chuang-tzu* source passage is twisted slightly to make the point that the "someone in control," intuited behind the words, appears elusively and intermittently. The "someone in control" could just as easily be "something in control"; and Lü Hsing-ch'ang interprets it not as the person but the quality *feng*-liu*, "flair," hidden in control and governing the words. This is possible, though it runs against the implications from the *Chuang-tzu* source passage. Lü furthermore interprets the *chih* as "it" (the something in control) rather than "them" (the words), thus having the words sinking and floating along with the "something in control," the quality *feng*-liu*.

Line 7: "Straining the thickest wine": As one continues straining, one finds more and more lees; in the same way, *han-hsü* reveals ever greater depths of the person or the quality. Because of the *Chuang-tzu* passage, I would prefer to take the human "state of mind" (or a modal scene mediating mind) as the ground of this infinite fertility; I do not believe, as some commentators do, that such fertility is produced by the categorical quality itself. The primary point here is that the text does not reveal itself immediately, but rather in the course of time the reader apprehends more and more turnings and complexities.

Line 8: The main modern commentators (Kuo Shao-yü, Ch'iao Li, Tsu Pao-ch'üan, Chao Fu-t'an, and Lü Hsing-ch'ang) all take this as referring to a sudden appearance of chilly autumn weather in a spring scene that causes the blossoms to close up and withhold their color and scent; that "closing up and holding within" is the analogue of *han-hsü*. Sun Lien-k'uei's *Shih-p'in yi-shuo* of the Ch'ing is similar, having the blossoms slow to open in an early spring chill. Such readings seem even more forced than is usual for commentary on "The Twenty-Four Categories." *Han-hsü* is a mode of inverse expression, in which a strong feeling is effectively conveyed precisely by being withheld. Furthermore, "conveying" is understood as a process, in which the text "unfolds" as it is savored. Thus I would prefer to take this line on the model of the preceding line, referring to the process of the text's unfolding in which one mode (spring) may revert to its opposite (autumn).

Line 9: Some of the commentators take *yu-yu* ("far, far away") as "many"; I prefer to keep it in a rough approximation of its usual sense as "the quality of what is vast, far-reaching, and going on and on forever" (often applied to the heavens and rivers).

Line 10: *Hu-hu*, "passing in a flash," is the quality of something appearing and disappearing or passing by so quickly that it seems illusory, hard to see, and hard to grasp.

Many critics have taken *han-hsü* to be the essence of Ssu-k'ung T'u's poetics; and it was certainly the category most fully developed in later literary thought, always recalling its treatment here.[13] For many later critics, *han-hsü* was the dominant value for all poetry. In this context we should, on the one hand, keep in mind that *han-hsü* is only one quality in Ssu-k'ung T'u's twenty-four. It is even, in many ways, the exact opposite of the "natural," the preceding category, a category in which Ssu-k'ung T'u shows just as much interest. On the other hand, we should recognize that values which are most fully developed in *han-hsü* play an important role in his treatment of many other categories: the problems of *ch'i-li**, for example, are resolved by withdrawing "intricate beauty" from the surface, keeping it in "reserve." Thus it is fair to say that besides being a particular category *han-hsü* is a general value. Nevertheless, in some categories *han-hsü* would be inappropriate or destructive: the "natural," for instance, a category of immediacy and surfaces, cannot permit it. Therefore, to say it is a general value is not to say it is universal.

The central question in *han-hsü* is the difference between surface and subsurface. The surface text is evidence of subsurface, but it is not a sign of the subsurface. The words are signs, but *han-hsü* operates on a different level, not getting "stuck" in the words. In this sense the category is a late avatar of some of the oldest concerns in Chinese literary thought, such as Mencius' "understanding language," which reveals how the speaker "is" rather than what he wants to "say." The most obvious example of this lineage is in the second couplet: one may make no reference to a feeling of unhappiness, but unhappiness is revealed as the ground on which one speaks of something else. The withholding (holding in "reserve") of feeling—the fact that one does not or cannot talk about something—becomes itself part of the code of the intensity of feeling.

In the fifth line a new question arises, that of unity and multiplicity, following from the *Chuang-tzu* passage, which is the most famous discussion of emotion in Chinese. As often in Chinese exposition, there is a structural unity in which several different terms are tried out in different versions of the same relation. One version is a unified "someone in control" set against the multiplicity of feelings or words or both. Whether one takes that "someone/something in control" as the unity of the author's psyche (as I do, following the *Chuang-tzu*) or as the unity of the mode itself (as does Lü Hsing-ch'ang), this unifying presence is intuited in and behind the multiplicity of words or the changing states of mind evoked. The second version of the structure is the limited unity of the text and the multiplicity of affects or significance that follows from it. Such multiplicity emerging from unity appears in the image of straining wine: as the text unfolds in being appreciated, countless changes and variations continue to appear—bubbles and dust motes, appearing for a moment and then gone. These two versions of unity versus multiplicity can be roughly reconciled. For example, we may postulate a process in which the unified and limited text unfolds into constantly changing affects; behind those affects the reader will have an intuition of "someone in control" in the unity of the authorial psyche. Thus we could read the last line as the variety of change apprehended in savoring the text; such a multiplicity is "gathered into one" either in the verbal unity of text or in the intuition of a person (the author), who is the ground on which those changing affects occur.

CATEGORY 12
Swaggering Abandon, Hao-fang 豪放

觀花匪禁。吞吐大荒。由道返氣。處得以狂。天風浪浪。海山蒼蒼。真力彌滿。萬象在旁。前招三辰。後引鳳凰。曉策六鼇。濯足扶桑。

Viewing the flowers can't be forbidden—
He swallows in all the great wilderness.
Arising from the Way, bringing back *ch'i**,
Residing in the attainment, he becomes wildly free.
5 A wind streams down from the heavens,
Mountains over the ocean, a vast blue-grey.
When the pure force is full,
The thousands of images are right around him.
He summons sun, moon, and stars to go before him,
10 He leads on phoenixes behind,
And at dawn whips on the great turtles,
Bathes his feet at the *fu-sang* tree.

Line 1: This line presents serious problems of interpretation, and a remarkable variety of versions have been offered. Kuo Shao-yü gives the most straightforward interpretation of the line, that there is no prohibition against enjoying the flowers when they bloom, being given freely by nature. As Lü Hsing-ch'ang, reviewing the various interpretations, wisely notes, this makes good sense but has little to do with the category *hao-fang*. I might add that it also has little to do with the rest of the poem. Lü Hsing-ch'ang's interpretation is a slight variation on this, roughly followed in my translation above: that no one can stop a person from enjoying the flowers. This preserves at least some sense of the willfulness of the category. One way to fit the line into the poem is to make it a metaphor for the ease with which a character of "swaggering abandon" has access to the whole world; thus "he swallows in the great wilderness (the ends of the earth) with no more sense of limitation than a person viewing the flowers."

Another way to solve a serious problem of interpretation is by emendation; and an interesting emendation appears in the version of the poem given by Sun Lien-k'uei and followed by Ch'iao Li: this version reads 化 ("transformation") instead of 花 ("flowers"), producing the rough translation: "Observing that nothing is prohibited in the process of transformation," or a more natural interpretation using this variant, "Observing transformation is not forbidden." Both interpretations using "transformation" make good sense, but the reading is not supported by earlier texts. Tsu Pao-ch'üan offers, "Viewing flowers in the palace grounds," taking "forbidden" to refer to the Forbidden City. This interpretation both forces the sequence of the argument and does violence to the negative *fei*.

Line 2: *T'un-t'u* means literally "swallows and spits out." This is a hyperbolic statement of mastery that is a signature of the swaggering personality. If we take the "great wilderness," the *terra incognita* surrounding the civilized world, as the place where such flowers blossom, then we might consider this to be a *hao-fang* flower-viewing, as opposed to a more enclosed viewing of flowers in a garden. A collateral passage cited in Chao Fu-t'an offers a suggestive precedent in the "Discourse on Ch'in's Excesses" (*Kuo-Ch'in lun* 過秦論) by Chia Yi 賈誼 (200–168 B.C.), in which the overreaching First Emperor of Ch'in is described as having "a mind that would swallow up the wilderness in all eight directions" (i.e., a desire to conquer the universe). Considering how well known the "Discourse on Ch'in's Excesses" was, and that the First Emperor's nature could well be described as *hao-fang*, this may well the source passage of the line.

Line 3: "Arising from the Way" suggests that such aggressive energy follows from the course of nature, but the phrase can also be taken as an injunction to "follow the Way" in order to avail oneself of such energy. "Bringing back," *fan*, is the same word translated as "reverting to" in Poem (or Category) 11, line 8. A phrase like "bring back *ch'i**" or "reverting to *ch'i**" manages to be sonorous without meaning very much. Lü Hsing-ch'ang says that *ch'i** is the same as the Way, and that the phrase means "return to the Way." Ch'iao Li says that the *ch'i** is the "primal *ch'i**," and that if one follows the Way, one will bring back the primal *ch'i** into one's breast. Tsu Pao-ch'üan simply elides it in his translation. Chao Fu-t'an interprets *ch'i** as the *hao-fang* mode and twists the interpretation of *fan*, taking the line to mean "the *ch'i** of swaggering abandon evolved out of the Way."

Line 4: This line is almost as sonorously enigmatic as the preceding one. "Attainment," *tê*, is cognate with *Tê*, "inner power." Lü Hsing-ch'ang takes it as "attaining the Way." "Attainment" may also be taken in the sense of *tê-yi**, "satisfaction," a self-contained delight in oneself and one's situation. My interpretation above roughly follows that of Kuo Shao-yü. Ch'iao Li takes the variant reading 易, "easy," for 以; and he takes the line as the negative variation on *hao-fang*: the kind of *hao-fang* one attains by keeping still (or gets by chance) too easily leads to mere bluster. Tsu Pao-ch'üan reads *ch'u*, as "everywhere," hence "If the conditions of line three are met, everywhere he achieves wild freedom."

Line 6: These may refer to the isles of the immortals in the ocean.

Lines 7–8: This couplet suggests that when the mode of "swaggering abandon" is perfected and replete in the self, then all things of the world are available to be grasped and presented through the poem.

Line 11: These are immense turtles of myth that dwell in the ocean. Sometimes they are said to bear up the immortal isles suggested in line 6.

Line 12: The *fu-sang* tree is where the sun rises. The last four lines are a common type of description of the "great man," *ta-jen* 大人, one mode of Taoist adept (also applied to a conquering emperor) whose mastery of universal process is symbolized by his movement through the cosmos with an entourage of mythical creatures doing his bidding.

As a category of manner, *hao-fang* is no more subtle than its poem: it is an aggressive extravagance. It belongs to the same family as "potent, undifferentiated" and "strong and sturdy" but is a more clearly human quality, perhaps deriving from nature's force, but not identified with it. The *hao-fang* figure seems to be a blend of a Taoist sorcerer and Ch'in's First Emperor; it is force that compels rather than force that impels.

Unlike *han-hsü*, the preceding category, *hao-fang* is a quintessentially outward quality. It is hard to justify the sequences described in Yang Chenkang's *Shih-p'in chieh* in every case; but throughout "The Twenty-Four Categories" there are clusters where such serial oppositions do seem to play an important role in the sequencing. "Reserve" does compensate for the sublime shallowness of the "natural"; and the grotesquely extroverted *hao-fang* does compensate for the reticence of "reserve." In the same way the following category, "essence and spirit," compensates for the crudeness of *hao-fang*.

Hao-fang is an important category in Chinese aesthetics, far more interesting than Ssu-k'ung T'u's treatment of it suggests. Indeed, someone who wanted to parody the category could scarcely have done a more effective job (though works in this mode sometimes hang at the edge of self-parody). In the second and fourth couplets Ssu-k'ung T'u's Taoist jargon approaches mumbo-jumbo: all the categories of external action require some form of nurturing or storing of power, and power can be exerted only by working in and through natural process. The third couplet is merely a scene of natural force, and the last four lines are a conventional icon of the cosmic fulfillment of human will, appropriate to a conquering emperor.

CATEGORY 13

Essence and Spirit, Ching-shen* 精神

欲返不盡。相期與來。明漪絕底。奇花初胎。青春鸚鵡。楊柳樓臺。碧山人來。清酒深杯。生氣遠出。不著死灰。妙造自然。伊誰為裁。

> Seek to bring back the unending,
> Intending to meet and go together.
> Bright ripples on the very bottom.
> Wondrous flowers beginning their gestation.
> 5   A parrot in the green springtime,
> Tower and terrace among the willows.
> Someone comes to the emerald hills—
> Clear wine, a deep goblet.
> The *ch'i** of life goes out far,
> 10   Not remaining in the dead ashes.
> It subtly produces the So-of-itself (*Tzu-jan**)—
> Who could have cut it to plan?

Lines 1–2: The first line could also be translated as, "In wanting (or "planning") to revert, [one finds] the inexhaustible." The meaning of this couplet remains entirely in the domain of fanciful speculation. As an example of how it has been handled by the older commentators, I translate the paraphrase by Yang T'ing-chih: "Essence arises from a drawing together; and should a person turn back [inward] and seek it, then he will have an inexhaustible store, and spirit will attain the means to be nurtured. Mind, determining that [i.e., the inexhaustible store] as what it would meet with, will consequently come together with it." This interpretation invokes the process of nurturing of one's forces that appears in so many of the categories. Lü Hsing-ch'ang takes the elusive direct object of the second line as a *ching-shen**, "scene-world," and makes the second line the condition from which the first line follows as a consequence. Thus, if one can meet an "essence and spirit" scene and express it, one will attain what is inexhaustible. Tsu Pao-ch'üan confesses the obscurity of the line and guesses, "The movement of human spirit will be ceaseless if one gathers it in and stores it up inside." I do not think these lines were ever conceived by Ssu-k'ung T'u as a clear proposition, even though they, like other lines in "The Twenty-Four Categories," follow the Taoist "spiritual recipe" formula. Such "spiritual recipes" have the structure of a necessary series of conditions that will lead to a given end. Such a structure in itself carried a certain mystique of authority. Yet the particular content of the stages—the definition of each condition and its relation to others—often remained deliberately obscure. Such obscurity contributed to the mystique. Each component of these lines represents a version of Ssu-k'ung T'u's favorite ideological slogans: "bringing back" or "reversion," turning back inward and to essences and origins; "inexhaustible," the plenitude that follows from reversion; "date to meet," anticipating the relation of "being with" some quality or kind of scene.

Lines 3–4: "Ripples" will be associated with outward pattern (*wen**); their appearance here, reflected on the bottom of a pond or stream, may suggest some correspondence between outer and inner. Most commentators simply take the phrase "very bottom" to refer to the clarity of the water. While this is implied, I think that the phrasing suggests the phenomenon of light patterns that form on the bottom of rippling shallow waters. The "gestation" of flowers suggests the unfolding of pattern from inside to outside. Clearly the ripples are the "essence and spirit" of the water scene, the animate and visible pattern of water's transparency and formlessness. The buds bear the same relation of "essence and spirit" to the flowers.

Lines 5–6: The implication in the sixth line is that bits of the building, conventionally painted red, appear through the dense leafage of the willows. I think the same relation is implied by the appearance of the parrot in the foliage, but Kuo Shao-yü takes the mention of the parrot to refer to sounds. Chao Fu-t'an takes the variant reading *ch'ih-t'ai* 池臺, "pool and terrace," in line 6.

Line 7: This line can also be read, "A person from the emerald hills [i.e., a recluse] comes."

Line 8: Ch'iao Li takes the variant reading *man-pei* 滿杯, "fills the goblet."

Lines 9–10: Tsu Pao-ch'üan takes these as qualities that a poem should have, though it is perhaps preferable to consider them simply qualities of this mode. "Dead ash" (whose "deadness" is no dead metaphor in Chinese) is a phrase originally from the *Chuang-tzu*, but in later usage it commonly referred to utter unconcern: in the Taoist version, this was generally considered a positive condition (cf. Cat. 19, l. 6); but here it is clearly negative.

Lines 11–12: Or, with Chao Fu-t'an, "Who can reckon the measure of [i.e., discuss reflectively] a subtly produced natural scene?"

*Ching-shen** is the animating essence that gives vitality to things. The images of the second couplet and the more general description in the fifth couplet suggest the way in which that center of vitality extends and unfolds. The images in the rest of the poem, however, are simply a pleasant springtime scene that adds nothing.

CATEGORY 14

Close-Woven and Dense, Chen-mi 縝密

是有真迹。如不可知。意象欲出。造化已奇。水流花開。清露未晞。要路愈遠。幽行
為遲。語不欲犯。思不欲癡。猶春於綠。明月雪時。

This does possess genuine traces,
But it is as though they cannot be known.
As the concept–image is about to emerge,
The process of creation is already wondrous.
5 Water flowing, flowers opening,
The clear dew not yet dried away,
The strategic road getting ever farther,
The slowness of passage through secluded places.
The words should not come to redundancy,
10 The thought should not tend to naïveté.
It is like the spring in greenness,
Or bright moonlight where there is snow.

Lines 1–2: "Genuine traces," *chen-chi*, are the marks by which something can be authenticated. A colophon authenticating a painter's work, for instance, will often refer to the painting as a whole as *chen-chi*, the "genuine traces" of that particular painter. The implicit opposition in the couplet is between constituent components and the whole. We might like to take the lines as referring to any "close-woven and dense," *chen-mi*, scene, whether in nature or in poetry; in such a case, the point would be that the component parts disappear into the whole. It seems more likely, however, that the question is specifically the production of an art work, in which the *chi* are the "traces" of productive craft. Thus the couplet suggests that such traces exist and are perhaps visible to one who looks closely and skillfully enough; but at the same time it stresses the fact that when viewed without close scrutiny, the "traces" of the production seem to disappear and the work appears seamless.

Lines 3–4: "Concept-image" is *yi*-hsiang**, the envisagement of the poetic scene in mind, which is communicated to the reader through the text.[14] What is singular about *yi*-hsiang** in Ssu-k'ung T'u's usage here is qualifying it as *yü-ch'u*, "about to emerge": it is not distinct and fully realized within the text, but rather hangs on the edge of our apprehension. That state of "coming into being" is the "process of creation," *Tsao-hua**, which in this case is "wondrous" without needing to be fully realized. Such marginalized pattern on a solid ground is illustrated in the closing images.

Lines 7–8: There is little agreement among the commentators on how to take these lines. Kuo Shao-yü explains the "strategic road," *yao-lu*, as a strategic military road: the farther it extends into a border region, the more important it becomes. This seems somewhat fanciful, though in keeping with the ordinary usage of the term *yao-lu*. Ch'iao Li makes the "strategic road" a metaphor for the "essential way," referring to the experience of this mode by the figure of passing through dense vegetation. It could be, more concretely, the path through the vegetation, in whose winding density the traveler seems to go on and on slowly. Chao Fu-t'an, elaborating on the interpretation in the *Shih-p'in chien-chieh*, takes the couplet as referring to two complementary aspects of poetic structure: there is a "main road" that is broad and takes one far; and there are also small, winding side paths, meant for slower passage and appreciation. This interpretation works well with the following couplet, in which the problem raised in the ninth line would correspond to the dense side paths, and the problem raised in the tenth line would correspond to the main road.

Line 9: Here Ssu-k'ung T'u uses the term of technical poetics for redundancy, *fan*, literally "trespassing" or "overlapping." Such a danger is strong in this mode, whose density (weaving too closely) threatens to cause elements to overlap. Tsu Pao-ch'üan takes it as excessive density of detail.

Lines 11–12: These lines are the perfect figures for *chen-mi*: both are complex scenes whose patterns are in a single color. The monochrome ground removes the sharp color contrasts that dominate many scenes (cf. Cat. 13, ll. 5–6) or the articulation of qualities by contrast (cf. Cat. 3, ll. 3–8); instead the attention is directed to the more subtle complexity of pattern and shading in such scenes: this accounts both for the quality of density and of pattern which hangs at the edge of apprehension.

Chen-mi, "close-woven and dense," is a particularly obscure category that has generated more than the usual amount of exegetical fantasy. The primary reference is to weaving, "texture," and this quality suggests work so fine and careful that the traces of craftsmanship disappear unless one looks very closely. Commentators generally agree that the verse stresses some kind of organic unity (e.g., a monochrome ground) that makes the work seem all of one piece.

Each of these modes requires a device of articulation, sometimes internal contrast and sometimes, as here, withdrawing the mode or one of its aspects to the margins of our apprehension. "Delicate-fresh and rich-lush" (Cat. 3) and "intricate beauty" (Cat. 9) are two categories against which this category can be understood. The "rich-lush" (*nung*) aspect of Category 3 is particularly close to the monochrome ground of *chen-mi* (although *chen-mi* also encompasses the snow scene of line 11, which would not be *nung*); but in Category 3, the figure of dense vegetation becomes an undifferentiated ground against which the "delicate" (*hsien*) can appear. In the case of *chen-mi*, there is no contrasting "delicate"; and as a result, the monochrome density of the vegetation reveals in itself intricate pattern on the margins of our apprehension. "Intricate beauty" (*ch'i-li*) has some similarities, but there the pattern withdrawn to the margins of apprehension is bright and delicate, "misted over." Note, however, that all three belong to the family of static modes, as opposed to the active, aggressive modes.

CATEGORY 15

Disengagement and Rusticity, Shu-yeh 疏野

惟性所宅。真取弗羈。控物自富。與率為期。築屋松下。脫帽看詩。但知旦暮。不辨何時。倘然適意。豈必有為。若其天放。如是得之。

He lodges according to his nature (*hsing**),
Takes spontaneously, without being bound up;
He grows wealthy gathering things in,
Anticipating joining with directness.
5   He builds his cottage beneath the pines,
Removes his cap, looks at poems;
He knows only of dawn and sunset,
Makes no further distinctions of time.
By chance something suits his mood—
10 Why need he act purposefully?
If he lets himself go according to nature (*t'ien*),
In this way he attains it.

Line 1: Ch'iao Li extends "take lodging" to "be at rest in," "go along with." One could translate the line: "It is his nature in which he is at rest," or "Wherever his nature is at rest, . . ." In either case, the lines describe someone who follows his inclination. The identification of "rusticity" (*yeh*), opposed to what is cultivated or civilized, with following one's true nature is a characteristically Taoist point of view.

Line 2: Lü Hsing-ch'ang understands "takes" as to get a "disengaged and rustic" world (*ching**). Chao Fu-t'an is close to this, understanding the object of "takes" to be the "materials" for a poem. Ch'iao Li and Lü differ on the quality of the "spontaneously," (*chen*, "authentic"): Ch'iao (and I agree) interprets this as the quality of the poet's relation to the world, a natural reception that is close to the notion of the "spontaneous." Lü Hsing-ch'ang suggests, on the contrary, that what the person apprehends must be "genuine" (i.e., having a ground in nature), and therefore the person who would attain it cannot be "offhand" or act according to his whims.

Line 3: Ch'iao Li and Chao Fu-t'an understand this "wealth" of outer things as the material for poetry, which is roughly the same as Lü Hsing-ch'ang's "taking" a "disengaged and rustic" world. Lu and Tsu Pao-ch'üan prefer the reading *shih* 拾, "to pick up," rather than *k'ung*, "to rein in," "to gather in."

Line 6: Removing one's cap is a gesture of ease and freedom from social restraint.

Lines 7–8: This is one of the conventional characteristics of the recluse: the observation of limited and natural markers of time, rather than socially marked time or longer spans that would imply remembrance or expectation. Most commentators take "distinctions of time" as referring to markers of historical time such as dynasties. Following Kuo Shao-yü, Ch'iao Li and Chao Fu-t'an associate this with T'ao Ch'ien's description of the denizens of "Peach Blossom Spring," who, having fled the world's troubles into the mountains centuries earlier, did not even know of the existence of the intervening dynasties.

Line 9: Sun Lien-k'uei interprets *t'ang*, "if by chance," as *ch'ang* 徜, "to roam freely."

Shu, translated as "disengagement," is literally a "separation," and often implies "carelessness" or "remissness." This is a fairly straightforward mode, with few real difficulties: acting according to the dictates of one's nature and disregarding social convention. One, perhaps unexpected way to locate this category might be to place it between the "natural" (Cat. 10) and "swaggering abandon" (Cat. 12). The word "lets himself go" in line 11 above is *fang*, translated as "abandon" in Poem 12. Both "disengagement and rusticity" and "swaggering abandon" involve letting oneself go, being freed of all restraints; but the quality of the countermotion against restraint is quite different in the two modes: "swaggering abandon" produces self-assertion against repression, and mastery against being mastered (note the use of the term "forbidden" in Cat. 12, l. 1); in contrast, the antithesis here would be between "being bothered" and "being left alone," or "refusing to be bothered."

From the other side, the "natural" proposes an identity between external and internal nature: it is a condition in which one goes along with what is accidentally encountered; there is no "doing as one pleases" (as there is in "disengagement and rusticity") because one has transcended any notion of pleasure that proposes action. In the "natural," there is no element of restraint to articulate freedom. "Disengagement and rusticity" seeks a direct expression of will (l. 4), and will is precisely what is transcended in the "natural." I should add that such contrasts are tentative and merely for convenience: in actual practice they would overlap considerably. One might, for example, argue whether the poetry of T'ao Ch'ien represented "limpid and calm," the "natural," or "disengagement and rusticity"; but to choose one of these modes rather than another would imply a particular interpretation of T'ao's poetry.

CATEGORY 16
Lucid and Wondrous, Ch'ing-ch'i 清奇

娟娟群松。下有漪流。晴雪滿汀。隔溪漁舟。可人如玉。步屐尋幽。載瞻載止。空碧悠悠。神出古異。澹不可收。如月之曙。如氣之秋。

    Charming in their beauty, a stand of pines,
    And beneath is a rippling stream.
    Sunlit snow fills the sandbars,
    A fishing boat across the creek.
5   An agreeable person, like jade,
    Pacing clogs seek in secluded places.
    Now peering, now stopping,
    Emerald skies stretching on and on.
    The spirit gives forth ancient marvels,
10   So limpid it cannot be held back,
    Like dawn's moon-brightness,
    Like autumn in the weather (ch'i*).

Lines 1–2: Sun Lien-k'uei associates the pine scene with the "wondrous" aspect of this mode and the water scene with the "lucid." Lü Hsing-ch'ang suggests the reflections of the pines are rippling in the stream.

Line 3: Lü Hsing-ch'ang points out the change from the darkness of the snowfall to the sudden brightness with a clearing sky, a quality that could be easily described as "lucid," ch'ing (or "fresh"). Lü is less convincing when she tries to argue that the fishing boats (which she sees as plural) are examples of the "wondrous."

Line 9: This line can also be read, "The spirit [of this mode] is produced from ancient marvelousness." Chao Fu-t'an plausibly interprets "spirit" here as "spirit thought" (shen*-ssu*), which will lead to composing a poem. Tsu Paoch'üan takes "marvels," yi, simply as the "differences" between antiquity and now.

Line 10: Lü Hsing-ch'ang interprets the "limpidity" as referring to "ancient marvels," and "drawn back" as "grasped": "This couplet explains a 'lucid and wondrous' world (ching*), the expression of whose spirit naturally transcends the common and ordinary, and has the particular quality of antiquity's uncanny marvels. Yet these 'ancient marvels' are natural manifestations and utterly lack the marks of such ancient marvels as might be produced by intense reflective thought: thus it says, 'in their limpidity they cannot be grasped.'" This reading associates limpidity with Ssu-k'ung T'u's favorite motif of the elusive.

Lines 11–12: As in the tenth line, it is not clear whether these similes describe the marvel-producing spirit (i.e., the person) or the marvels produced. Kuo Shao-yü takes the "dawning" term of line 11 as "the brightness of the moon just rising."

Ch'ing-ch'i was a fairly common model category, listed as a normative form (*t'i**) in Ch'i-chi's 齊己 "Exemplary Forms of the *Feng* and *Sao*" (*Feng*-Sao chih-ko* 風騷旨格, late ninth century). Here it seems associated with a surprising freshness, a "sparkling."[15] The first eight lines are devoted entirely to producing a *ch'ing-ch'i* scene. We might contrast the third line here, "Sunlit snow fills the sandbars," with the closing scene of "close-woven and dense" (Cat. 14, l. 12): "Or bright moonlight where there is snow." Both are scenes of white on white; but in the case of "close-woven and dense," the brightness is withheld so that we will notice the subtlety of shading and pattern (thus making the snow scene more like the foliage scenes that dominate Ssu-k'ung T'u's treatment of that mode). The *ch'ing-ch'i* scene is a sudden radiance after the snow clears, with a fishing boat included to articulate the scene. Also shading contrasts are produced by lines of darkness and shadow (ll. 1, 6).

Ssu-k'ung T'u does not favor such sharp luminosity, and he mitigates it with the "limpidity" (*tan*) of the tenth line, a quality that would apply to the paleness of the dawn moon in the eleventh line.

CATEGORY 17
Twisting and Turning, Wei-ch'ü 委曲

登彼太行。翠繞羊腸。杳靄流玉。悠悠花香。力之于時。聲之于羌。似往已迴。如幽匪藏。水理漩洑。鵬風翶翔。道不自器。與之圓方。

Climbing the T'ai-hang Mountains,
Azure winding, hairpin curves:
Obscure, misted over, flowing jade;
From far, far away, the scent of flowers.
As action is to its own season,
As notes [of music] to the Tibetan flute,
Seeming to have gone, it has already returned;
As if secluded, then no longer concealed.
Water's patterns swirl endlessly;

5

10   P'eng winds hover around and around.

The Way is not bound to a vessel-shape—

He joins it becoming round or square [according to circumstances].

Lines 1–2: "Hairpin curves" are literally "sheepguts," a kenning for narrow and winding mountain paths. The T'ai-hang mountain range was famous for such paths. The "azure" can refer either to bluish mountain mists or to dense vegetation. Such constant turning, without a direct path to obvious ends, is the quality of the mode.

Line 3: Most commentators agree that the "flowing jade" refers to streams. In Chao Fu-t'an's commentary his collaborator, Huang Neng-sheng, offers the anomalous but attractive explanation that it refers to wisps of the mist. Lü Hsing-ch'ang takes it as real jade, the kind that gives off mist, suggesting the famous metaphor for a poetic scene that Ssu-k'ung T'u quotes in his "Letter to Chi P'u on Poetry" (see p. 357). "Obscure" also implies "in the distance": the figure is probably the glint of streams through the fog in the distance, though it may simply refer to the general fogginess of the mountain scene.

Line 4: Lü Hsing-ch'ang takes *yu-yu* as "continuous" rather than "far far away."

Lines 5–6: These lines are obscure. The similes of seasonal labor and music seem to refer to recurrence, and turning back (reprise), which is the consequence of the "winding" in this mode. "Action in its season" (*li chih yü shih*) may be simply "the application of force as the occasion demands." If we take *li chih yü shih* in this sense, then the element of circuitousness is equally implicit: aggressive force will be conceptualized as pushing "straight" through, while the timely application of force where it is most advantageous will follow a less direct course. Tsu Pao-ch'üan takes *li chih yü shih* as referring to the name of an ancient bow (Timely Force, *Shih-li*), whose bending Tsu supposes to correspond to the winding quality of the mode; this seems extreme. The *ch'iang* translated here as "Tibetan [flute]" is also a poetic particle; and some commentators have produced other interpretations following that sense of the word, seeing in the lines, for instance, how the particle *ch'iang* imparts a subtlety to the recitation. The interpretation "Tibetan flute," whose music is often desribed as "winding," seems preferable.

Lines 7–8: These lines could refer to seasonal labor and the notes of the nomad flute, or to the mountain paths, or to the mode in general. In a broader sense, we see here the pattern of alternation between opposites that follows from "twisting and turning."

Lines 9–10: I have followed Ch'iao Li, Tsu Pao-ch'üan, and Lü Hsing-ch'ang in interpreting *shui-li** as "water's patterns" (i.e., ripples); but there is also much to be said for Kuo Shao-yü's interpretation as "the inherent principle of water is to..." The interpretation of *li** as "patterns" maintains the parallelism of the couplet; but Kuo's interpretation would be the most natural way to take the phrase *shui-li** if considered independently. "P'eng winds" refer to the P'eng, a legendary bird in the *Chuang-tzu*, so large that its wingspan touched both edges of the horizon. It required a mighty "whirlwind" to carry it to its proper height. Both are figures of circling, one sinking down and the other soaring up.

Line 11: This line may be read, "The Way cannot be treated as a vessel for some use." Or in Chao Fu-t'an's paraphrase: "The Way of poetry is like the way of all skills, in that one should not let oneself be restricted by the physical forms of things."

Wei-ch'ü was an old and very common descriptive category, always used positively. It implies constant and subtle twists in the movement of thought, theme, style, and mood. The opening description of traveling on narrow mountain paths is an excellent metaphor for the quality. The path provides interest by offering ever new perspectives, without achieving any single "prospect" that gives a sense of the whole. Always responding to changing and unforeseen circumstances, this is a mode of sequential unity rather than unity given from a single overview. The images of glinting streams and flowers in the second couplet are elements of the whole that appear indirectly and in the distance. The fragmented scene gives way to figures of circling, in which there is both movement to opposites (l. 8) and recurrence (l. 7). This is further related to the Way, which, like water, takes the shape of whatever it encounters.

If the "strong and sturdy" (Cat. 8) developed the aspect of force in "potent, undifferentiated" (Cat. 1). "twisting and turning" develops the aspect of constant transformation, which recurs again, in a slightly different mode in "flow and movement" (Cat. 24). Neither "twisting and turning" nor "flow and movement" is determinate mode in itself, but rather a shifting ground on which many determinate modes may appear and disappear; the affective result, however, is the quality of constant change itself. The supreme instability of the *wen-ch'ü* mode gives way to its opposite in the concreteness of the following mode.

CATEGORY 18

Solid World, Shih*-ching* 實境

取語甚直。計思匪深。忽逢幽人。如見道心。清澗之曲。碧松之陰。一客荷樵。一客
聽琴。情性所至。妙不自尋。遇之自天。泠然希音。

The words employed are extremely direct,
The formulation of thought does not go deep:

Suddenly one meets a recluse—
It is as if seeing the mind of the Way.
5   The bends of clear torrents,
The shade of emerald pines:
One fellow carries firewood.
Another fellow listens to a zither.
The perfection of nature and the affections
10   Is so subtle it cannot be sought.
One chances on it as Heaven wills—
Delicate, the faint and rare tones.

Line 2: The point here is that *shih*-ching** is a mode of surfaces, in which there is no sense of hiddenness. Ch'iao Li expresses it nicely: "In your diction and lines there is nothing but what is visible right before your eyes, audible in your ears, or stirred in the mind; your hand writes it out and it's complete, without any intense reflection or complex considerations or purposeful search for depth."

Line 3: Since recluses are not often encountered, we have a hint that such directness does not reveal a commonplace world.

Line 4: "The mind of the Way" (*Tao*-hsin**) may be an abstraction, the quality of such a scene; or it may be "a mind that has attained the Way," referring to the recluse.

Lines 5–8: This is a scene of reclusion. Ch'iao Li interprets *ch'ü*, "bends," as "melodies," the "music of nature."

Line 9: Ch'iao Li interprets this line to mean "that to which one reaches by following one's own affections and nature."

Line 10: "Cannot be sought"; that is, it cannot be sought willfully. Lü Hsing-ch'ang interprets this as "sought within oneself"; that is, it must be found in the external world. While such an interpretation is not impossible, there is nothing in the text to warrant it.

Line 12: "Faint and rare tones," *hsi-yin*, echoes *Lao-tzu* XIV: "What can be listened to but not heard is called the 'faint and rare.'" Kuo Shao-yü makes the point that out of the "solid," *shih**, emerges the elusive.

Ssu-k'ung T'u's categories often seem to be differentiated from one another by recurrent antitheses, one of which is that between surface and depth. Categories of concealment and depth often are described in terms of depths emerging to the surface, whereas categories of surface, such as this one, often begin in the direct and obvious, then become elusive.

There is some similarity between this mode and that other mode of surfaces, the "natural" (Cat. 10). In both cases one attains the subtle by not seeking it, by remaining on the surfaces of things. As in one strain of modern poetics a poem should "not mean but be," there is in the Chinese tradition a pleasure in the description of concrete empirical scenes. Often poets use the scenes of the world to refer to some intelligible pattern or as correlatives for their emotions; both practices privilege "depth," and run counter to the value of a "solid world." However, as Ssu-k'ung T'u suggests, in letting the world be itself, genuine subtlety will arise.

CATEGORY 19
Melancholy and Depression, Pei–k'ai 悲慨

大風捲水。林木為摧。適苦欲死。招憩不來。百歲如流。富貴冷灰。大道日喪。若為雄才。壯士拂劍。浩然彌哀。蕭蕭落葉。漏雨蒼苔。

A great wind rolls up the waters,
The trees of the forest are shattered.
He suffers to the point of death,
Calls for respite, but it does not come.
5   Lifetime's hundred years seem to flow on,
Riches and honor leave him cold as ash.
The great Way declines more and more each day—
Who nowadays is bold and talented?
The knight in his prime pats his sword,
10   His boundless lament increasing.
The winds moan through the falling leaves,
Rain drips on the grey moss.

Lines 1–2: Lü Hsing-ch'ang says such scenes are examples of a pervasive destructive force that produces the *pei-k'ai* mode.

Line 4: Lü Hsing-ch'ang interprets, "He seeks the only person who could offer comfort, but he does not come."

Line 6: Realizing his mortality, a person in the *pei-k'ai* mode is indifferent to worldly lures. Tsu Pao-ch'üan interprets it slightly differently, that "riches and honor" will ultimately turn to ashes.

Line 8: The rhetorical question seems to lament the lack of someone to oppose the decline of the Way.

Pei-k'ai is one of the clearest of all the categories, a series of correlative scenes and situations that give rise to feelings of despair. Ssu-k'ung T'u is rarely at his best in these purely subjective modes, of which "Swaggering Abandon" is another.

Description, Hsing-jung 形容

絕佇靈素。少廻清真。如覓水影。如寫陽春。風雲變態。花草精神。海之波瀾。山之嶙峋。俱似大道。妙契同塵。離形得似。庶幾斯人。

> One awaits the ultimate spiritual purity,
> Soon brings back what is pure and genuine.
> Like seeking reflections in the water,
> Like delineating bright spring.
> 5　The changing appearance of wind-blown clouds,
> The spirit and essence of flowering plants,
> The waves of the ocean,
> The jaggedness of mountains—
> All are like the great Way,
> 10　Match their subtle beauty, share their dust.
> Whoever attains resemblance by diverging from external shape
> Approximates such a person.

Line 1: In the first line, we have the same problem with the usage of *chu* that we find in Poem 5, line 8. *Chu* basically means to "stand long," commonly extended to mean "await." There is another, related *chu*, 貯 that means "amass." Most modern commentators take *chu* in this latter sense, but I would prefer to interpret *chu* as earlier in the sense of "await" or "expect." "Spiritual purity," *ling-so*, is one of those supremely vague phrases in which Ssu-k'ung T'u delights: we are uncertain whether it is a Taoist abstraction, a quality of things in the outer world, or something within the poet.

Line 2: Ch'iao Li, Chao Fu-t'an, Tsu Pao-ch'üan, and Lü Hsing-ch'ang interpret *hui* as "put in operation" or "make manifest" rather than "bring back"; moreover, Ch'iao relates that "operation" to the process of description. Ch'iao also puts stress on the *shao*, more like "only a little" than "gradually." Hence he takes the couplet as the negative consequence of intensity: "If one expects spiritual substance too intensely, one will put the pure and genuine into circulation only a little." The difference between the interpretation given in the translation and Ch'iao's is an excellent example of how lines in these poems can produce opposite interpretations depending on one's presuppositions. I have followed Yang T'ing-chih, Chao Fu-t'an, Tsu Pao-ch'üan, and Lü Hsing-ch'ang in interpreting *shao* as "in no time," "soon."

Lines 3–4: These lines clearly refer to the mimetic problems in description. According to Ch'iao Li's interpretation, this couplet refers to the difficulty of description; according to the interpretation in the translation, the lines refer to the necessity of attending to the "spirit" of what is described (whatever that may be). In the third line, Kuo Shao-yü interpolates waves and speaks of the difficulty of seeing reflections in them. One difficulty here is in the interpretation of *ying*, which may refer either to "reflections" in the water or "light" shining on the water. Lü Hsing-ch'ang rejects the interpretation as "reflections," though it would seem the most obvious.

Lines 5–8: These lines name natural phenomena whose essential qualities, because of constant change, are hard to capture in description. The "jaggedness" of the mountains is, of course, not in change, but it is a complexity that is equally hard to describe.

Lines 9–10: The general point of these lines is that the essence of such things (ll. 3–8) cannot be captured simply and on the surface, either because of their changes, their elusiveness, or their complexity. In all these aspects, such phenomena are like the Way itself, which is just as variable. The only resolution for someone who would describe such things is a kind of union with them, suggested in the phrase from *Lao-tzu*, to "share their dust"; to achieve some kind of primordial identification with what they "are," rather than trying to catch how they "appear."

Line 11: Here I follow Kuo Shao-yü and Chao Fu-t'an in interpreting *li-hsing** as "diverge from external shape"; Ch'iao Li take the two hemistiches as coordinate, interpreting *li-hsing** as to "make manifest external shape." One might also reasonably interpret the phrase as "cleave to external shape," producing an interpretation similar to Ch'iao Li's but philologically more likely. Neither of these interpretations of *li*, however, is as natural as the one given above. Most commentators take "resemblance," *ssu*, as "spiritual resemblance," *shen*-ssu*. The line seems to play on the common compound *hsing*-ssu*, the technical term for "description that gives the semblance of external form." The line breaks up the compound to indicate a kind of "resemblance" (*ssu*) different from that of "external form" (*hsing**).

Line 12: That is, approximates a master of description.

This category, which addresses the problem of *mimêsis* rather than describing some particular quality of scene or state of mind, differs from the other twenty-three categories; but it is significant because of the importance the later tradition attached to *shen*-ssu*, "spiritual resemblance" and the rejection of the *mimêsis* of surfaces. Although it was undecided whether the "spiritual resemblance" was to the external object represented or to the artist, "spiritual resemblance" developed into a virtual ideology in later aesthetics.[16] One reason to reject the *mimêsis* of surfaces is quite clear in the middle couplets here: an intense awareness that things are always in transformation. (From such a point of view, the Western artist's "still life" or even the model who has to sit "still" would be strongly anti-mimetic.) Because it is the "spirit," *shen**, of a thing that unifies its transformations, the poet or painter would try to catch that animate identity. Unfortunately, unlike surfaces, *shen** is exceedingly hard to locate; and we must recognize what a problematic value this is. Again we note that Ssu-k'ung T'u takes a concern conventionally associated with surfaces and reinterprets it in terms of elusiveness, change, and depth.

CATEGORY 21

Transcendence, Ch'ao-yi 超詣

匪神之靈。匪機之微。如將白雲。清風與歸。遠引若至。臨之已非。少有道氣。終與
俗違。亂山喬木。碧苔芳暉。誦之思之。其聲愈希。

    It comes not from the magic spark of spirit,
    It comes not from the subtlety of [Nature's] impulses (*chi**).
    It is as if joining the white clouds,
    Going off with a clear wind.
5   Drawn from afar, one seems to reach it;
    Approach it, it is already gone.
    If for a moment you have the *ch'i** of the Way,
    You will ultimately escape the ordinary.
    Tall trees in tangled mountains,
10   Emerald moss, sweet-scented radiance:
    Sing of it, brood on it,
    And the sounds grow ever rarer.

Lines 1–2: There are many problems here. "The magic spark of spirit" (*shen** *chih ling*) probably refers to the intuitive capacity of mind, implying that the transcendent mode is not attained through any sharpness of apprehension. "The subtlety of [Nature's] impulses" are the secret and faint workings by which nature's processes are initiated and sustained. The second line may deny that "transcendence" is related to how well the human mind apprehends these workings in Nature; then again it may deny that the mind can attain the transcendent mode from the natural impulses within mind itself. Lü Hsing-ch'ang points out that all these interpretations create more problems than they solve. Her solution is to reinterpret *fei* (normally meaning "is not") as "that," a very archaic usage. This interpretation produces exactly the opposite interpretation of the lines: "It is in the magic spark of spirit; it is in the subtlety of [Nature's] impulses." While such an interpretation more comfortably answers our expectations, it is exceedingly unlikely that Ssu-k'ung T'u would have used *fei* in that sense, or that any T'ang reader would have understood it in that sense. Ch'iao Li locates "transcendence" as a third condition, belonging neither to the spiritually mysterious nor to the natural: hence he takes "the magic spark of spirit" as referring not to the human mind but to incomprehensible operations of spiritual divinity in the world. At the same time, stressing the pragmatic quality of the second line, he interprets chi* as "occasions," so that transcendence is not part of what happens in Nature's cyclical time. I would suggest that the negations of these two lines should be read in the context of the preceding poems, many of which do hold "the magic spark of spirit" and the "subtlety of [Nature's] impulses" as values. The negations strenuously attempt to distinguish this mode from preceding modes (many of which seem to involve some quality of "transcendence" in the Chinese sense), and thus they reveal just how close many of these lines are to lines in other categories.

Lines 3–4: Chao Fu-t'an does not presume the presence of the human subject and interprets this as the clear wind accompanying the white clouds.

Lines 5–6: Kuo Shao-yü takes these lines as referring to the elusiveness of the mode, that it cannot be achieved willfully. Lü Hsing-ch'ang, following roughly the same line of thought, makes the point that the condition of "transcendence" is one of constant movement, a continual "going beyond," in which any stasis falls back into the ordinary world; hence the condition is like the constant motion of wind and clouds. As soon as one "approaches it" (lin, with the implication of standing still nearby), it evaporates in being reduced to a distinct object of consciousness. Ch'iao Li has the "approaching" being the time when one tries to capture it in poetry.

Lines 7–8: As in the preceding category, much depends on how we understand shao, translated as "for a moment." Line 7 could also be rendered, "If one has even the least ch'i* of the Way." Unfortunately, it can also quite naturally be rendered, "There is little ch'i* of the Way in it" (thus producing a radical interpretation that would follow from the negations in ll. 1–2). To complicate matters, Ch'iao Li, Chao Fu-t'an, and Tsu Pao-ch'üan read shao as "youth": "If as a youth one matches the Way." Although this is by no means an impossible reading for shao, it is difficult to see how it can be justified here, except perhaps as a balance for chung, "ultimately." Ch'iao Li and Tsu Pao-ch'üan both take the variant ch'i 契 instead of ch'i*: hence, "match the Way."

Line 10: In another version, "sweet-scented radiance" is "square radiance," probably referring to light through a door; however, the fragrance of sunlight striking the moss makes perfectly good sense.

Line 12: "The sounds grow ever rarer" may mean that the more one understands this mode, the more subtle one's poetry grows (as in the hsi-yin 希音 of the Lao-tzu). Or it may mean that if a poet broods on it too much, the "sounds" appropriate to it increasingly escape him (see comments on Cat. 2, ll. 9–10). Tsu Pao-ch'üan understands this line in yet a third sense, in terms of the notion in the Chuang-tzu of "when one attains the meaning, one forgets words"; that is, the more it is understood, the more words disappear altogether.

Ch'ao means to pass beyond the limits, concerns, and ties of this world; though conventionally rendered "transcendence," it should not be confused with more precise religious and philosophical uses of that term in Western languages. *Yi* means to "reach" or "arrive." Lü Hsing-ch'ang takes the compound as "the attainment of transcendence."

CATEGORY 22
Drifting Aloof, P'iao-yi 飄逸

落落欲往。矯矯不群。緱山之鶴。華頂之雲。高人惠中。令色絪縕。御風蓬葉。汎彼無垠。如不可執。如將有聞。識者期之。欲得愈分。

Set apart, on the point of departing,
Rising loftily, not of the crowd:
The crane of Hou Mountain,
A cloud of Mount Hua's peak.
5   The lofty person acquiesces to what lies within,
His fine countenance amid the coiling vapors.
A tumbleweed that rides the winds,
Drifting on in the boundless.
It is as though it cannot be grasped,
10   But yet as if he might hear something.
Those who understand hope for this,
But if you want to have it, it grows ever more apart.

Lines 1–2: Each line opens with a reduplicative compound: *lo-lo* and *chiao-chiao*. Both describe a quality of personality that is high-minded, free, and holds apart from others.

Lines 3–4: "The crane of Hou Mountain" was the bird on which the immortal Wang-tzu Ch'iao was said to have ascended to Heaven. Both clouds and cranes were common figures for someone who felt free of ties to the social world and could drift back and forth without constraints.

Lines 5–6: The interpretation of *hui* as "acquiesces" roughly follows Kuo Shao-yü. Ch'iao Li interprets *hui* as "to be intelligent." Lü Hsing-ch'ang and Tsu Pao-ch'üan take the variant *hua* 畫 instead of *hui*: hence "the lofty person in the painting." *Yin-yün* is more precisely the "intercoiling manner of the primordial *ch'i**," the interaction of Yin and Yang through which natural process occurs. It is uncertain whether this radiant face riding through the mists is among such vapors or generates them.

Lines 7–8: The "tumbleweed," *p'eng* (actually a rather different plant whose upper part is blown loose from its roots and carried around by the wind), was a conventional figure for someone who wandered free of ties to family or place. Tsu Pao-ch'üan, taking the "drifting on" literally, suggests that it is a figure for a boat; considering that this line has the same pattern as Category 5, line 3 (where the interpolation of a boat would be ridiculous), this seems rather unlikely.

Lines 11–12: Ch'iao Li, Tsu Pao-ch'üan, and Lü Hsing-ch'ang read *ling* 領, "gain an intuitive grasp of," for *ch'i*, "hope for" or "expect." In line 12 they read *ch'i chih* 期之, "hope for it," instead of *yü-te*, "want to have." I have followed Kuo Shao-yü's readings.

There were elements of the "drifting aloof" mode in several earlier categories, but here it is a mode unto itself. Its primary characteristics need little comment: it moves with things but has no attachments, no signs of care.

CATEGORY 23

Expansive Contentment, Kuang-ta 曠達

生者百歲。相去幾何。歡樂苦短。憂愁實多。何如尊酒。日往烟蘿。花覆茆簷。疎雨相過。倒酒既盡。杖藜行歌。孰不有古。南山峨峨。

Life can be only a hundred years—
How far from that are we now?
Pleasure and joy are terribly brief;
Far greater is sorrow and melancholy.
5   Better, with a goblet of wine,
To go off every day into misty vines;
Or where flowers shade a roof of thatch
With a light rain passing by.
When the upturned cup is emptied,
10   He leans on his staff and goes singing.
To whom does it not occur?—
South Mountain towering high.

Lines 1–4: These lines are a free recreation of lyric formulae used in many anonymous Han poems and songs.

Line 5: Lü Hsing-ch'ang offers an alternative interpretation for *ho ju*, "better," as "why not?"

Line 11: The reference here is death.

Line 12: South Mountain was the traditional emblem of the permanent, in contrast to human mortality.

This is one of the most direct and most appealing of the categories. While it lacks the intellectual complexity of some, it also avoids the pretentiousness and willful obfuscation that haunts many of the poems. More than any of the other categories, it fuses the circumstances of the mode and a performance of the mode itself, sustained by rich echoes from the poetic tradition.

"Expansive contentment" seems to be quite consciously set against "melancholy and depression" (Cat. 19). Both begin with a sense of human mortality; but while "melancholy and depression" is a simple, univocal mode, "expansive contentment" sets an inebriate and fragile satisfaction against the background of despair. That background radically changes the quality of the joys in the landscape, which are described in lines that alone could have found a place in any of a dozen categories. An excellent earlier example of the application of this category can be found in the biography of Chang Han in the *Tsin History*: "Someone once said to him, 'Why is it that you are so willing to suit your whims of the moment and, alone of us all, not work for posthumous fame?' Chang answered, 'It's better to have a cup of wine here and now than to bring myself posthumous fame.' Everyone honored his expansive contentment."[17]

CATEGORY 24
Flowing Movement, Liu-tung 流動

若納水輨。若轉丸珠。夫豈可道。假體如愚。荒荒坤軸。悠悠天樞。載要其端。載聞其符。超超神明。返返冥無。來往千載。是之謂乎。

Like a waterwheel drawing in,
Like rolling the sphere of a pearl—
No!—how *can* it be spoken of?
Such borrowed forms are clumsy.
5 Earth rolls boundlessly on its axis;
Heaven turns forever on its pivot.
First inquire of their origins,
Then hear of their correspondences.
Passing beyond and beyond into divine light,
10 Then back and back further to dark nothingness.
Coming and going, a thousand years—
Might this be what it means?

Lines 3–4: This protest may echo *Lao-tzu* I: "The Way that can be spoken of is not the constant Way." The oblique language of metaphor and parable was the continual recourse of early Taoists, distrustful of the capacity of words to present the truth directly and preferring "borrowed forms" (t'i*) that were overtly distinct from the truth they indicated.

Line 8: "Correspondences," *fu*, is interpreted by Lü Hsing-ch'ang as the empirical operation of Heaven and Earth, "corresponding" or "responding" to their inner structure, their "origins." Tsu Pao-ch'üan interprets the couplet to mean that if one investigates the origins, one's poetry will correspond to the operations of Heaven and Earth.

Line 9: *Shen*-*ming*, "divine light" or "spiritual illumination" is the spiritual core of a person or external divinity.

Ssu-k'ung T'u had a genuinely Taoist distrust of anything that could be easily grasped, a conviction that everything important was necessarily elusive: the family line of his thought can be traced directly back to Chuang-tzu's Wheel-wright Pien. Like his Taoist forebears, he often has recourse to simile. Any tentative understanding we may reach he cancels, pointing to something still further beyond. That general impulse in his work becomes explicit in this final poem of the series, in which he rejects his own metaphors for the continuous cyclical operation of the Way. This is not so much a particular mode of poetry as a poem on the operations of the universe, and how its subtle motions of change, intuitively apprehended, should be the ground for poetry.

SELECTIONS FROM OTHER WORKS

In addition to "The Twenty-Four Categories of Poetry," which was preserved independently, Ssu-k'ung T'u's collected works contain various other discussions of poetry and aesthetics. The two following letters are the most famous.

Letter to Mr. Li Discussing Poetry 與李生論詩書

文之難而詩尤難。古今之喻多矣。愚以為辨於味而後可以言詩也。江嶺之南。凡足資於適口者。若醯非不酸也。止於酸而已。若醝。非不鹹也。止於鹹而已。華之人所以充飢而遽輟者。知其鹹酸之外。醇美者有所乏耳。彼江嶺之人。習之而不辨也宜哉。

Compared to the difficulties of prose, the difficulties of poetry are extreme.[18] There have been illustrative examples in both ancient and modern times; but in my opinion we can adequately speak of poetry only in terms of making distinctions in flavors (*wei**).

In everything that suits the palate in the region south of Chiang-ling, if it is a pickled dish, then it is indeed sour—but it is nothing more than sour. If it is a briny dish, then it is quite salty—but nothing more than salty. The reason people from the north, when eating such food, simply satisfy their hunger and then stop eating is that they recognize it somehow falls short of perfect excellence and lacks something beyond the distinction between "the merely sour" and "the merely salty." And as one might expect, the people of Chiang-ling, because they are used to such food, are incapable of making any finer distinctions.

The vocabulary of "flavor" (wei*) in Chinese poetics has an importance far beyond the use that Ssu-k'ung T'u makes of it here, which is in terms of distinctions and gradations; but even here the master metaphor of "flavor" is suggestive.[19] The opposition is between gross categories that have names, and fine judgments for which there are no names. Furthermore, those finer gradations are learned by experience: one who knows only the gross categories can apprehend only the gross categories; to be able to recognize the finer distinctions requires the education of a sensibility.

詩貫六義。則諷諭抑揚渟滀淵雅皆在其中矣。然直致所得。以格自奇。

Poetry encompasses the Six Principles; moreover, indirect criticism and metaphorical illustration, modulations, purity and reserve, gentleness and grace (ya*) are all encompassed within them. However, what is achieved by directness becomes wondrousness by its character (ko*).

Most of the elements that Ssu-k'ung T'u mentions as being within the range of the "Six Principles" are particular qualities. Ko*, on the other hand, which Tsu Pao-ch'üan identifies with feng*-ko*, "style," is a category (like "flavor") that admits further differentiation; that is, not everyone will necessarily have "style" or "character," but for those who do, "character" is only a category within which individual differences appear. The following passage shows that ko* is very much like "normative form" (t'i*, as in Liu Hsieh's usage, "normative styles").

前輩諸集。亦不專工於此。矧其下者耶。王右丞韋蘇州。澄澹精緻。格在其中。豈妨於遒舉哉。賈閬仙誠有警句。然視其全篇。意思殊餒。大抵附於蹇澁。方可致才。亦為體之不備也。噫。近而不浮。遠而不盡。然後可以言韵外之致耳。

In the literary collections of the previous generation, we can find no one who really concentrates on this [i.e., ko*]; and we find it even less in the writers since. In the supreme limpidity and delicacy of Wang Wei and Wei Ying-wu, we do find such "character" (ko*); and this certainly did no harm to their capacity for a forceful mode. But in the poetry of Chia Tao we may indeed find startling lines; but if you consider his works as wholes, the thought and power of conception (yi*-ssu*) are rather feeble. In general, he shows his talent only in a rugged obscurity; and this indicates a want of comprehensiveness in his [mastery of] forms (*t'i**). Indeed, one can speak of affect beyond the rhymes only when it is close at hand without being frivolous or far-reaching without escaping one altogether.

When Ssu-k'ung T'u speaks of poets having a "character," *ko**, it is easy to think of it as one determinate character that manifests their personality. Like Liu Hsieh in the chapter "Nature and Form," however, Ssu-k'ung T'u believes that a poet should be able to comprehend a range of styles. Wang Wei (699–761) and Wei Ying-wu (ca. 737–ca. 792) mastered *ko**, and thus were able to write in different modes, the forceful as well as the limpid and delicate. Chia Tao (779–843), a poet of the "previous generation," is faulted because he is limited to one particular mode, a rugged obscurity. Chia's problem is limitation rather than the lack of suggestiveness, as Tsu Pao-ch'üan suggests. Particularly interesting is the implied relation between *ko** and poetic unity: if one attains a *ko**, that holds the poem together; in contrast, the masters of the craft of the couplet such as Chia Tao always risk failure of overall unity. It should be observed, however, that Ssu-k'ung T'u himself goes on to quote a long series of his own couplets.

Kuo Shao-yü reads *tao*-hsüeh* 道學, "study of the way," for *ch'iu-chü*, "forceful manner."

愚幼嘗自負。既久而愈覺缺然。然得於早春。則有「草嫩侵沙短。冰輕著雨銷」又「人家寒食月。花影午時天」又「雨微吟足思。花落夢無憀」。得於山中。則有「坡暖冬生筍。松涼夏健人。」又「川明虹照雨。樹密鳥衝人。」得於江南。則有「戍鼓和潮暗。船燈照鳥幽。」又「曲塘春盡雨。方響夜深船」又「夜短猿悲減。風和鵲喜靈。」得於塞下。則有「馬色經寒慘。鵰聲帶晚飢。」得於喪亂。則有「驊騮思故第。鸚鵡失佳人。」

I used to have great confidence in myself when I was young; but with the passage of time, I have gradually come to realize how much is lacking in my work. Still I achieved the following couplets on "early spring";

> The grass was tender, getting shorter as they encroach the sands;
> The ice is light, melting as the rain touches it.

And:

> Someone else's house: the moon on Cold Food Festival;
> Shadows of flowers: the sky at noontime.

And

> The rain is faint, my poems full of brooding;
> Flowers fall, dreams of helpless misery.

I got the following couplets on "being in the mountains":

As the slopes warm up, shoots grow in winter;
A chill under pines, summer invigorates the man.

And:

The stream is bright, a rainbow shines in the shower;
The trees are dense, birds fly against the person.

I got the following on "South of the Yangtze":

The fortress drums blend with the dark high waters;
Lanterns on boats light up the hidden birds.

And:

A bend in the pond, the rain as spring ends;
Sound from one direction: a boat deep in the night.

And:

As the nights grow short, sad cries of gibbons diminish;
Breezes turn balmy, magic in the joy of magpies [who announce good
  fortune].

I got this on the topic of "the frontiers":

The colors of horses pass through winter's gloom;
Sounds of hawks carry with the evening hunger.

I got these on the "civil wars":

The noble steed longs for its former mansion,
And the parrot has lost its fair mistress.

又「鯨鯢入海涸。魑魅棘林幽。」得於道宮。則有「碁聲花院閉。幡影石壇高。」得於夏
景。則有「地涼清鶴夢。林靜蕭僧儀。」得於佛寺。則有「松日明金像。苔龕響木魚。」
又「解吟僧亦俗。愛舞鶴終卑。」得於郊原。則有「遠陂春早滲。猶有水禽飛。」得於樂
府。則有「晚妝留拜月。春睡更生香。」得於寂寥。則有「孤螢出荒池。落葉穿跛屋」。
得於恬適。則有「客來當意愜。花發遇歌成」。雖庶幾不濱於淺涸。亦未廢作者之譏訶
也。又七言云。「逃難人多分隙地。放生鹿大出寒林」。又「得劍乍如添健僕。亡書久似
憶良朋」。又「孤嶼池痕春漲滿。小欄花韻午晴初」。又「五更惆悵回孤枕。猶自殘燈夢
落花」。又「殷勤元旦日。歌舞又明年」。皆不拘於一概也。

And:

For the leviathan the human sea dries up,
And trolls are in the high hawthorn groves.

This I got on a "Taoist temple":

> The sound of chimes: the flowering gardens are closed;
> Shadows of streamers, the stone altar set high.

Among the couplets I got on "summer scenes," there is:

> The earth is cool, clearing the dreams of cranes;
> Woods grow still, the deportment of monks more strict.

I got these on the topic of "a Buddhist temple":

> Sun through pines brightens the gilded statues,
> Moss-filled niches resound with wooden fish clappers.

And:

> In understanding poetry the monk still shows secular concerns;
> In its love of dancing the crane finally shows itself a low creature.

On the topic of "the meadows":

> On far embankments spring is somber early.
> Yet still there are the waterfowl in flight.

From the [themes of] the old ballads (*yüeh-fu*) I got:

> After evening make-up she lingers to pay her respects to the moon,
> Her sleep in spring produces even more fragrance.

On the topic of "isolation and melancholy":

> A solitary firefly emerges from the overgrown pool;
> Falling leaves come through the broken roof.

On the topic on "contentment":

> A guest's arrival: occasion for feeling pleased;
> Flowers come out: a chance to complete the song.

Although it is hoped that that these do not border on a shallow dryness, still they will not escape earning the scorn of writers. Among couplets in seven-character lines I got:

> Many are the men fleeing the troubles, unused lands are divided up;
> The deer, set free, grow large and come out of the winter woods.

And:

> Getting a sword suddenly seems like getting an extra tough servant;
> My lost books have long resembled good friends still remembered.

And:

> The solitary isle is but a scratch on the pond as spring floods fill it;
> By a tiny railing the tones of flowers, first in noon's clear skies.[20]

And:

> Depressed in the last watch of night, I return to my lonely pillow;
> While still the dying lamp dreams its falling flowers/sparks.

And:

> The sun of New Year's morning does its best,
> With songs and dances, another year again.[21]

These are not limited to any single measure.

What Ssu-k'ung T'u has done in this letter bears very close similarity to the couplet taxonomies in technical manuals of poetics, in which large groups of couplets are quoted to illustrate different categories. In this list, the kind of category (the topics given in quotation marks in the translation) would be *yi**, "concepts," or often in technical poetics, "themes." Although Ssu-k'ung T'u has offered these to show his own versatility, historical perspective lends a certain irony to the attempt: in these lines, the later reader cannot help hearing the essential sameness of the Late T'ang couplet style. Some of the couplets are finer than others; but through all the diversity of "characters" (*ko**) offered as examples, the later reader notices only the unity of a period style.

蓋絕句之作。本於詣極。此外千變萬狀。不知所以神而自神也。豈容易哉。今足下之詩。時輩固有難色。倘復以全美為上。即如味外之旨矣。勉旃。司空表聖再拜。

[The composition of quatrains depends on attaining the highest perfection.][22] Beyond this [variety], there are a thousand mutations and ten thousand appearances; we cannot understand how they achieve this quality of spirit (*shen**), and yet that quality is attained of itself—this is truly not easy.

People of this generation will surely find fault with your poetry; but if you take a complete beauty as your highest goal, you will realize those implications beyond flavor. Work at it!

Respectfully,
Ssu-k'ung T'u

"Implications beyond flavor" (wei*-wai chih chih) is considered one of the key concepts of Ssu-k'ung T'u's poetics: it is precisely that subtle and animate variety that transcends the common categorical limitations.

Selection from "A Letter to Chi P'u on Poetry" 與極浦書

戴容州云。詩家之景。如藍田日暖。戾玉生煙。可望而不可置於眉睫之前也。象外之象。景外之景。豈容易可談哉。然題紀之作。目擊可圖。體勢自別。不可廢也。愚近作虞鄉縣樓及柏梯二篇誠非平生所得者。然「官路好禽聲。軒車駐晚程」即虞鄉入境可見也。又「南樓山最秀。北路邑偏清假。」令作者復生。亦當以著題見許。

Tai Shu-lun once said: "The scene (ching*) given by a poet is like the sun being warm on Indigo Fields and the fine jade there giving off a mist—you can gaze on it but you can't fix it in your eyes." Such image beyond image (hsiang*), such scene beyond scene—how can it be discussed easily? Still, works that recount an experience can delineate what strikes the eye; and though the normative forms (t'i*) and momentum (shih*) of such works differ [from the perfection of "image beyond image, scene beyond scene"], they are not to be dismissed.

Recently I wrote "The County Building in Yü-hsiang" and "The Cypress Ladder." I certainly would not claim that these are the best things I've ever done, but still in

> Sweet voices of birds on the official highway:
> I halt my coach on its evening journey

the vista on entering Yü-hsiang can be seen. Or consider:

> From the south tower the hills stand out grandly,
> From the north highway the town is especially clear.

If the great writers of the past were born again, I'm certain they would grant my success with this topic.

There is some irony in the fact that this famous quotation attributed to Tai Shu-lun (ca. 732–789) and the statement of Ssu-k'ung T'u's own poetic values are merely a preface to more modest poetic aspirations: to present actual experience with clarity. We are never presented with "image beyond image" and "scene beyond scene" (some spiritual presence that transcends empirical images and scenes); instead we are given solid couplets of a lower order, but still more easily attained. The greatest difficulty of holding the elusive as a value is that any particular presentation of it falls out of the elusive and into a poetry that can indeed be grasped by mortal human beings.

"Remarks on Poetry": *Shih-hua*

Before the eleventh century, Chinese literary theory and criticism had appeared primarily in the genres of "high" literature—letters, essays, prefaces, and poems—or in distinctly "low" forms such as technical manuals.[1] Many of the works that are now taken as the best representatives of Chinese literary thought (e.g., *Wen-hsin tiao-lung* and Chung Jung's *Shih-p'in*, "Gradations of Poets," from the second decade of the sixth century) lay outside the usual genres of critical discourse.

In the eleventh century a new critical genre appeared, the *shih-hua* 詩話 or "remarks on poetry." *Shih-hua* belonged to a group of genres that can be characterized as "informal prose," considered neither as "low" as manuals of technical poetics nor as "high" as the formal prose genres.[2] Although such informal prose and its use in literary discussion grew out of a rich lineage of T'ang and pre-T'ang anecdotal writing, in the hands of Sung stylists it became a distinctive form, with a studied ease that had its own unique appeal and authority.

The first *shih-hua*, by Ou-yang Hsiu 歐陽修 (1007–1072), was probably originally entitled simply *Shih-hua* (later known as *Liu-yi shih-hua* 六一詩話, Liu-yi being one of Ou-yang Hsiu's pseudonyms). This work consists of twenty-eight short entries: anecdotes, opinions on poetry, and reminiscences of discussions with friends. Ou-yang Hsiu was the first master of several genres of informal prose, but he was also the dominant literary figure of his age in the "higher" prose genres. His prestige combined with the inherent charm of "Remarks on Poetry" to initiate a series of similar works, leading ultimately to the establishment of *shih-hua* as a genre. The next work modeled on Ou-yang Hsiu's "Remarks" was a "Continuation of the Remarks on Poetry," *Hsü shih-hua* 續詩話, by Ssu-ma Kuang (司馬光; 1019–1086), after which the form passed into common usage. In addition to works bearing the generic title *shih-hua*, comments similar to *shih-hua* are found throughout the numerous collections of random notes (*pi-chi*) and anecdotal collections of the Sung.

Like many genres, *shih-hua* began as a form of oral and social discourse that finally took on written form, either recording an oral and social situation or attempting to recreate the impression of such a situation. Although discussion of poetry had always accompanied the practice of the art, by the late eighth century it was something of an established social occasion for literary men to sit together and discuss the fine points of poetry, to tell literary anecdotes, and to offer opinions of poets and descriptions of their styles. This practice was continued and extended in the much wider literary society of the Sung. Ou-yang Hsiu's "Remarks on Poetry" presents itself as recalling and recording just such an oral world of discourse on poetry; and in counterpoint with comic anecdotes, there is often a subdued, elegiac tone that contributes to its appeal. A similar basis in anecdote and oral discussion of poetry characterizes many of the early *shih-hua* and some of the best later *shih-hua*. The *ad hominem* literary polemics of many later "remarks on poetry" is a darker outgrowth of that same tradition, a stylized attempt to convey immediacy.

As the genre became firmly established, the oral and social roots of the form diminished in importance: writers would record their opinions on various literary questions, at some point editing and publishing them. Sometimes the form of this "gathering" would be apparently random, attempting to preserve the appearance of casualness from the genre's origins; but from the Southern Sung on, we find more and more *shih-hua* organized in a loose chronological or generic order or both.[3] The more systematic the genre became, the more the original aesthetic values and the *pen-se** 本色, the "original color," of the genre was lost. "Ts'ang-lang's Remarks on Poetry" of the thirteenth century may be the most influential work that bears the name *shih-hua*, but so much of the "original color" is lost that it scarcely deserves the title *shih-hua*: it is a mixed form made up of several critical genres and rising to *shih-hua* only in its last two chapters.

"Ts'ang-lang's Remarks on Poetry" and the trend toward systematization in some Southern Sung *shih-hua* should be understood in the context of the popularization of literary studies in the later Southern Sung and early Yüan. The Northern Sung intellectuals cultivated an appearance of ease; sophisticated discussion of poetry was supposed to be a pastime. In the Southern Sung, we find the beginnings of a mass audience, seeking advice on composition from the masters and guidance in judgment. The printing industry of Hang-chou fed the desires of the urban bourgeoisie to participate in elite culture by the transformation of *shih-hua* into a poetic education. There were systematically organized anthologies of *shih-hua* (*Jade Chips of the Poets, Shih-jen yü-hsieh* 詩人玉屑);[4] anthologies of poems with famous *shih-hua* comments appended (the *Shih-lin kuang-chi* 詩林廣記 and *Chu-chuang shih-hua* 竹莊詩話), and anthologies to teach composition (such as *Poetry in Three Forms, San-t'i shih* 三體詩, and *Ying-k'uei lü-sui* 瀛奎律髓).

Although it is not universally true, a tendency to organizational randomness in *shih-hua* often appears in direct proportion to the sophistication and eminence of the writer (there are some striking exceptions such as Chao Yi's 趙翼 [1727–1814] *Ou-pei shih-hua* 甌北詩話). The motives behind such a preference are essential to understanding the form. When the *shih-hua* first appeared in the Sung, one of its closest generic counterparts was the *yü-lu* 語錄, "recorded sayings," of the philosophers. Although the Sung Neo-Confucian *yü-lu* are often filiated to the "sayings" of the Ch'an masters, both Ch'an and Neo-Confucian "sayings," along with the *shih-hua*, derive their form, their appeal, and their particular authority in large measure from the *Analects* of Confucius. By understanding the generic constitution of the authority and appeal of the *Analects*, one can begin to understand why the *shih-hua* came to occupy such an important position in Chinese literary thought.

In the Western system of generic contracts, a writer does not need to be a good person to write an important treatise on ethics. As a genre the "treatise" promises only to be about the good. The designation "treatise" leads us to assume only that the writer has thought seriously and systematically "about" the subject, has made certain premises and followed them to their conclusions, has been rigorous and consistent. In short, the generic contract of a "treatise" on ethics implicates the author's capacity for thought rather than his virtue.

Such genres of thought do exist in the Chinese tradition, but often they have been tacitly found wanting.[5] The only adequate model for writing on ethics is a genre like the *Analects*, which presents the words of a "good person" responding immediately to the demands of circumstance, either from instinct or from a reserve of wisdom attained through self-cultivation. Such a form functions by revealing rather than writing about; it does not address the question of "What is the good," but rather presents the record of someone who *is* good. Given these values, the ethical treatise in the Western sense will be *a priori* a tainted and misguided project: in thinking about the good (without necessarily being good at the same time), the writer admits a fundamental disjunction between the quality of the thinking and the object of thought.

In contrast, a work like the *Analects* gives an adequate and authentic presentation of the good as the circumstantial evidence of a truly good person: it is, of necessity, a fragmentary and discontinuous surface, whose unity is discovered only in the depths of the person from whom circumstantial responses are elicited. A canonical text like the *Analects* enters into a reciprocal relation with such values, reinforcing them by its purely conventional authority (i.e., merely by the cultural assumption that it is an important text); and its own importance is reconfirmed by those very values it helps to create.[6]

Such values, embodied in and promulgated by the *Analects*, should clarify why Ou-yang Hsiu's "Remarks on Poetry," and not *Wen-hsin tiao-lung*, became the dominant model for Chinese discourse on literature. Liu Hsieh was no one: he was an invisible thinker writing a "treatise." His opinions were not elicited from a reserve of experience and understanding, but rather were presented as demanded by the logic of his exposition. His claim to speak authoritatively about literature was supported only by the *Wen-hsin tiao-lung* itself.

In contrast, Ou-yang Hsiu's "Remarks on Poetry" are the words of the great Ou-yang Hsiu, someone who had thought much on literature all his life, and someone who possessed a wealth of experience, anecdote, and wisdom. In the English tradition, Dr. Johnson offers a reasonably close analogy. The text of Ou-yang Hsiu's *shih-hua* is only what the master happened to write down: it is the fragmentary evidence of a person greater than the evidence itself. The randomness (and often a stylized crankiness) in the best *shih-hua* appeals to values in which words have worth because they are elicited by chance from an interesting person.

The cultural resonance of such a genre makes the *shih-hua*, at its best, a peculiar art form in its own right. Writers are more often aggressive or playful or witty in *shih-hua* than in more formal genres because the intellectual force of the form is inseparable from its aesthetic force, and both depend upon the projection of a personality. Wang An-shih (1021–1086) and Su Tung-p'o, the two dominant literary intellectuals of the generation after Ou-yang Hsiu, wrote no *shih-hua* of their own, but *shih-hua*–style comments, both genuine and fabricated, gathered around them; and in those comments they became the *dramatis personae* of their own legendary personalities. The strident ranting of Yen Yü at the end of the Southern Sung—"if you don't agree with me, you don't know anything about poetry"—was a vulgarized attempt to project the strong personality of the *shih-hua* writer.

The following selections from Ou-yang Hsiu's "Remarks on Poetry" give the flavor of the genre at its inception. The beauty, profundity, and continuity of these casual reminiscences is not obvious; but if the reader attends to them with the thoughtfulness they deserve, they gradually reveal Chinese literary thought at its most characteristic.

It would be extravagant to suggest that the "Remarks on Poetry" has a conscious internal design. Yet the subtle echoes, the reversals, the complications, and the questions left in suspension are equally characteristic of Ou-yang Hsiu's critical writing in the "high" genres. What we find in his "Remarks on Poetry" is not studied artistry but a style of thought. And a "style of thought" is exactly what the *shih-hua*, conceived as a literary genre, promises.

SELECTIONS FROM "REMARKS ON POETRY" OF OU-YANG HSIU

VII

鄭谷詩名盛於唐末。號雲臺編。而世俗但稱其官為鄭都官詩。其詩極有意思。亦多佳句。但其格不甚高。以其易曉。人家多以教小兒。余為兒時猶誦之。今其集不行於世矣。梅聖俞晚年官亦至都官。一日會飲余家。劉原父戲之曰。聖俞官必止於此。坐客皆驚。原父曰。昔有鄭都官。今有梅都官也。聖俞頗不樂。未幾。聖俞卒。余為序其詩為宛陵集。而今人但謂之梅都官詩。一言之謔。後遂果然。斯可歎也。

The fame of Cheng Ku's poetry was at its height at the end of the T'ang. His collected works were called the "Cloud Terrace Collection," but it was commonly referred to by Cheng's office title as "The Poems of Cheng of the Prison Board." His poetry was very thought-provoking and contained many excellent lines, but the style was not really elevated. Because it was so easy to understand, people used his poetry for teaching children—even when I was a child, we still chanted his poems. Nowadays his works are not in circulation. Late in his life Mei Yao-ch'en also reached a position on the Prison Board. One day we were having a drinking party at my house, and Liu Ch'ang teased him, telling him he would never get any higher than his present position. The guests were all shocked at this, but Liu Ch'ang went on: "Well, just as there used to be a Cheng of the Prison Board, now we have a Mei of the Prison Board." This made Mei Yao-ch'en quite depressed. Soon afterwards Mei died. I wrote a preface to his poems as the "Wan-ling Collection," but now people refer to it only as "The Poems of Mei of the Prison Board." It is a sad thing that one word spoken in jest can determine the way things are ever thereafter.

This modest anecdote is filled with echoes of Ou-yang Hsiu's abiding concerns in regard to literature, concerns to which he returned time and again throughout his long career. Foremost among these concerns were the fragility of reputation, failures of understanding, and the loss of literary works along with all memory of their authors. Ts'ao P'i had made a grand promise in the "Discourse on Literature," that by his own efforts a writer could transmit his name to posterity, even without having achieved important deeds in the service of the state (see pp. 68–69). Ou-yang Hsiu, a reader of old bibliographies, was intensely aware of how deceptive that promise could be, how easily a collection of literary works could be lost in the longer spans of history. In a prose epistle on parting from Hsü Wu-tang, he had written:

> I have read the "Bibliography" in Pan Ku's *History of the Han* and the "Catalogue" of the T'ang Imperial Library, and I have seen listed there the writers since the Ch'in and the founding of the Han, prolific writers with over a hundred works and the less prolific still with thirty or forty works. There were countless such, yet their works have been scattered and lost so that scarcely one or two in a hundred have survived. And I felt sorry for these men: the literary qualities of their works were beautiful indeed and their language was carefully wrought, yet what happened to them was no different from the flowers of plants and trees being whirled away in the breeze, or the pleasant sounds of animals and birds passing our ears. When I consider how strenuously they used their minds (*yung-hsin**) and all their hard efforts, what difference is there from the way in which ordinary people are constantly busy and striving. All of a sudden they were dead; although some lasted longer than others, in the long run they passed into oblivion like the other three—like the plants and trees, like the animals and birds, and like ordinary people. Such indeed is the unreliability of words. Virtually every educated man in modern times aspires to the immortality of the Sages and for all his lifetime devotes his whole heart to writing—they are all to be pitied.

Recognizing how easily writing may be lost and the writer forgotten, Ou-yang Hsiu often reflected on how this came to happen, what caused some poetry to survive and other poetry to be disregarded and slip out of circulation. Against this general tendency to forgetfulness, he set for himself the task of remembering and recording, correcting misjudgments and preserving fragments.

To explain for us the sting of Liu Ch'ang's quip, Ou-yang Hsiu must lay out the history of Cheng Ku's reputation—once much admired, later thought too simple and fit only for teaching children, finally no longer available. Cheng's reputation had fallen in the common estimation, and now he is candidate for oblivion—the metamorphosis into a mere bibliographical entry. Ou-yang Hsiu gives us the background by which we can understand the analogy: not only did both Cheng and Mei rise no higher than an office on the Prison Board, both were known for their simplicity—perhaps good poetry for children. Yet in clarifying the analogy, Ou-yang Hsiu tries to suggest the unfairness in the common judgment of Cheng Ku, how there is much in his poetry that is worthwhile.

Not only did the quip hurt Mei Yao-ch'en, it lives on still. Despite Ou-yang Hsiu's best efforts in his preface to show the importance of Mei's poetry, people have taken to calling the collection "The Poems of Mei of the Prison Board." If we follow the analogy, the threat is that Mei's works too will be misprized, treated with contempt, and gradually pass out of circulation. The power of the sharp word of slander or contempt was an old motif in the Chinese literary tradition: the cruel word, even spoken in jest, can destroy its victim and live on as the only thing people remember.

It is a simple anecdote about losses and the failure to appreciate simplicity; it concerns the mockery of poets, of which there is much in "Remarks on Poetry." It is a pained memory of the pain felt by a dear friend, now dead—he died "soon afterward," as if the wound inflicted by the cruel word never healed. And now Mei seems in danger of a second death in having his poems misprized, a misprision based on comparison with another poet whose own works have been long misprized. The critic's responsibility is to correct such raise judgments and to save reputations.

IV

梅聖俞嘗於范希文席上賦河豚魚詩云。「春洲生荻芽。春岸飛楊花。河豚當是時。貴不數魚鰕」。河豚常出於春暮。羣遊水上。食絮而肥。南人多與荻芽為羹。云最美。故知詩者。謂祗破題兩句。已道盡河豚好處。聖俞平生苦於吟詠。以閑遠古淡為意。故其構思極艱。此詩作於罇俎之間。筆力雄瞻。頃刻而成。遂為絕唱。

At a party given by Fan Chung-yen, Mei Yao-ch'en wrote a poem on the blowfish that began,

> On springtime sandbars sprouts of reeds appear,
> Springtime shores fly with willow blossoms.
> It is at this time the blowfish
> Is valued beyond all other fish and shrimp. . .

The blowfish always appear toward the end of spring and swim in schools at the top of the water, getting fat by eating drifting willow floss. Southerners often make a soup of blowfish and reed sprouts, which is supposed to be delicious. Those who truly understand poetry will realize that the opening two lines have made all the right points in regard to blowfish. Mei Yao-ch'en worked hard at poetry for his entire life, his intention being a leisurely distance and primordial plainness. His conceptual structure is extremely strenuous. This poem was composed among the cups and platters of a party, but the force of his brush is potent and rich. It was completed in just a short time, yet afterwards became a famous piece.

It is all too easy to overlook and misjudge a subtle simplicity in poetry. Of course, Ou-yang Hsiu tells us, "those who truly understand poetry" will not do so. We will not readily acknowledge our obtuseness and insensitivity; if the lines sound utterly offhand, we discern how appropriate that is for a piece composed extempore at a banquet, an ease that embodies the eager anticipation of eating blowfish in blowfish season. And now, looking back on the lines, we begin to detect the peculiar and subtle quality of this lyric voice: how, when the eyes of the southern poet see reed sprouts and willow floss on the water, he will inevitably think of the blowfish, just invisible beneath the surface of the water. But most of all, the beauty of the lines lies in a wry victory of simplicity and an ordinary human, rather than a "poetic" response. What appeared to be a conventional "poetic" scene in the opening couplet is revealed to be a recipe and anticipation of soup. Basic pleasures, at once local and seasonal, emerge out of poetic convention. This voice belongs to someone hungry for something more immediate than literary fame. Now when we read the second couplet, we smile. Suspecting we had missed this fineness, Ou-yang Hsiu annotates for us the cuisinary connection between the ingredients of the literary landscape and the ingredients for blowfish soup.

A poetry that is simple and basic is not necessarily simple to achieve. Ou-yang Hsiu tells us that the ease of Mei's lines came from a lifetime of serious effort at perfecting his poetry; his "spontaneity" came from longstanding "intention" (yi*) to achieve "leisurely distance and primordial plainness" (hsien-yüan ku-tan). Casually and gently we are reminded that poetic casualness may be the mark of high art. Could the same be true perhaps of other casual writing, such as "remarks on poetry"?

V

蘇子瞻學士。蜀人也。嘗於淯井監得西南夷人所賣蠻布弓衣。其文織成梅聖俞春雪詩。此詩在聖俞集中。未為絕唱。蓋其名重天下。一篇一詠。傳落夷狄。而異域之人貴重之如此耳。子瞻以余尤知聖俞者。得之因以見遺。余家舊蓄琴一張。乃寶曆三年雷會所斲。距今二百五十年矣。其聲清越。如擊金石。遂以此布更為琴囊。二物真余家之寶玩也。

The scholar Su Shih is a native of Szechwan. Once he purchased a bow-wrapping of aboriginal textiles sold by the southwestern barbarians. Into this cloth had been woven Mei Yao-ch'en's poem "Spring Snow." This poem is not considered an important piece in Mei Yao-ch'en's collected poems. It seems to me that Mei's fame was so great throughout the world that every single piece was passed on until it fell among the barbarians, and it is remarkable how those foreigners valued it. Knowing how close I was to Mei Yao-ch'en, Su Shih made a present of it to me when he got hold of it. My family has long had in its possession a zither, carved in 827 by Lei Hui, two hundred and fifty years ago. Its tone is as sharp and clear as if one were striking a piece of metal or stone. I used this piece of textile as the zither bag. These two objects are truly the family treasures.

Ou-yang Hsiu's "Remarks on Poetry" is the paradigm of the shih-hua tradition not only because of its historical priority, but also because, in its quiet way, it offers so many perspectives on the act of valuing. The most common antithesis in describing literature's influence was "going far" and "lasting long" (cf. Lu Chi's "Poetic Exposition on Literature," ll. 251–258). Here one of Mei Yao-ch'en's poems, not originally thought important, acquires value by a strange history of appreciation. Indeed, so that we can fully appreciate its metamorphosis into a treasure, Ou-yang Hsiu informs us that the poem was not considered exceptional. It is a measure of the admiration for Mei's poems that they "go far," and here they go far indeed, even beyond the boundaries of Chinese civilization. "Spring Snow" has been trapped in its migrations and worked into the textile of an aboriginal bowcase—for reasons no one can guess.

The second layer of appreciation that adds value to the poem-object comes from Su Shih. When he sees the textile, he thinks of Ou-yang Hsiu's friendship with Mei and imagines how much Ou-yang Hsiu would enjoy this strange proof of how "far" Mei's poetry had gone. Thus the poem returns to China, and now is valued by Ou-yang Hsiu not only for its connection with Mei Yao-ch'en, but also as a reminder of Su Shih's generosity and thoughtfulness. As a wrapping for one of Ou-yang Hsiu's family treasures, an old zither, the embroidery will be cherished and preserved: it will "last long" with the zither. They belong together: great poetry, with the power to "last long," is often said to have the tones of "metal and stone," just like the zither.

To "value" a poet or a poem is purely an act of mind; it is hard to show. The transformation of the text into textile (a tangible object, strangely reminiscent of the transformation of a "poetic" scene into a recipe for soup) makes the event of valuing substantial and more easily demonstrable. Yet what gives the poem-object value is neither its intrinsic literary worth nor its commercial worth as commodity: it acquires value because it has gathered a particular history of affection. (For the contrary case, see entry XX.)

The sequencing of entries in the "Remarks on Poetry," while apparently random, often reinforces the themes taken up in the entries themselves. The sequence of the translation has been somewhat rearranged, but we should note that this and the preceding entry establish Mei Yao-ch'en's reputation. Mei's next appearance is in the seventh entry (translated previously), where Mei's reputation is undermined. Thus the theme of that entry, the rise and fall of a reputation, is echoed in the sequence of entries on Mei.

VI

The capping line of the couplet in the following entry makes reference to one of the most infamous acts of Ch'in Shih-huang, the unifier of China, a mass burial of Confucian scholars.

吳僧贊寧。國初為僧錄。頗讀儒書。博覽強記。亦自能撰述。而辭辯縱橫。人莫能屈。時有安鴻漸者。文辭雋敏。尤好嘲詠。嘗街行遇贊寧與數僧相隨。鴻漸指而嘲曰。「鄭都官不愛之徒。時時作隊。」贊寧應聲答曰。「秦始皇未坑之輩。往往成羣。」時皆善其捷對。鴻漸所道。乃鄭谷詩云。「愛僧不愛紫衣僧」也。

The Wu monk Tsan-ning was the Registrar of Monks early in the dynasty. He had studied Confucian writings extensively, was widely read and had a good memory; moreover, he was himself a skilled writer whose discourses and arguments were such that no one was able to humble him. At that time there was a certain An Hung-chien, a bright and witty stylist, who was particularly good at mocking verses. He once met Tsan-ning on the street with several monks following him; An Hung-chien made a gesture towards Tsan-ning and produced the following mocking verse:[7]

> Fellows of the sort that Cheng Ku didn't like, ones who often come in squads.

Tsan-ning answered him as quick as an echo:

> That class yet uninterred by Ch'in Shih-huang, ones that form flocks everywhere.

At the time everyone admired the cleverness of Tsan-ning's response. An Hung-chien had been referring to a line in a poem by Cheng Ku that went: "I like monks, but not the sort that wear the purple robes" [purple robes being the prerogative of monks who served in court].

A number of the entries in "Remarks on Poetry" are nothing more than good jokes (and Tsan-ning's capping lines are indeed deliciously amusing in Chinese); but the triviality of such an anecdote is an essential, rather than a superfluous part of the work. The good joke disarms us, convinces us that here we are reading simply for our own amusement, that there is no secret motive on the part of the critic to instruct us. When we encounter such an entry, we readily believe that the "Remarks on Poetry" is simply a series of random jottings. In short, the inclusion of the trivial anecdote is the structural form of memory's chance workings: it carries the tacit message that these entries are simply "what happened to come to mind."

However attractive the possibility, the human mind no more works by random chance than the natural universe. In this apparently gratuitous display of wit we immediately note motifs from earlier entries and adumbrations of later ones. The second entry in "Remarks on Poetry" had been another joke of mocking.

仁宗朝有數達官以詩知名。常慕白樂天體。故其語多得於容易。嘗有一聯云。「有祿肥妻子。無恩及吏民。」有戲之者云。「昨日通衢遇一輜軿車。載極重。而羸牛甚苦。豈非足下肥妻子乎。」聞者傳以為笑。

During the reign of Jen-tsung [1023–1063] there were a number of successful officials famous for their poetry. They admired the style of Po Chü-yi, and thus their diction achieved its effects by simplicity. One of them had a couplet that went,

> A salary that goes to fatten my wife and children,
> No generosity extending to clerks and commoners.

Someone teased the writer: "Yesterday, as I was going along the avenue, I chanced upon a woman's curtained coach. Its load was extremely heavy, and the poor oxen pulling it were having a terribly hard time. I take it this was your 'fattened wife and children'?" The story was passed on as a good joke.

The fourth and fifth entries had concerned questions of proper valuation. In the sixth entry we return to mockery, in this case with a retort that turns the mockery back on the original mocker—for these lines Tsan-ning was admired. This prepares us for the more extensive anecdote on mockery and proper valuing in the seventh entry (which appears as my first selection), in which Liu Ch'ang's quip damages Mei Yao-ch'en's reputation. In the sixth entry the poet Cheng Ku appears with a line expressing contempt for a certain type of monk; he reappears in VII, himself the object of scorn. In the seventh entry we learn that Cheng Ku's poetry is generally forgotten; but like Liu Ch'ang's quip, the verse of scorn quoted in this entry is remembered. Or is it remembered?—Ou-yang Hsiu feels it necessary to annotate the reference and quote the line.

"Remarks on Poetry" alternates between praise and blame, liking and disliking, friendship and enmity. These variations on value become intertwined with questions of preservation and loss, first in VII with the disappearance of Cheng Ku's poems from general circulation, and then again in the eighth entry.

VIII

陳舍人從易。當時文方盛之際。獨以醇儒古學見稱。其詩多類白樂天。蓋自楊劉唱和。西崑集行。後進學者爭效之。風雅一變。謂之「崑體」。由是唐賢諸詩集幾廢而不行。陳公時偶得杜集舊本。文多脫誤。至送蔡都尉詩云。「身輕一鳥」。其下脫一字。陳公因與數客各用一字補之。或云「疾」。或云「落」。或云「起」。或云「下」。莫能定。其後得一善本。乃是「身輕一鳥過」。陳公歎服。以為。「雖一字。諸君亦不能到也。」

In these days when literature is in full flower, Secretary Ch'en Ts'ung-yi is uniquely praised for his old-style learning. His poems are very much like those of Po Chü-yi. After Yang Yi and Liu Yün wrote their series of group compositions and the "Hsi-k'un Collection" became current, aspiring writers did their best to imitate that style. Poetry underwent a complete change, and the new fashion was called the "Hsi-k'un style." Because of this, the poetry collections of the great T'ang masters were virtually abandoned and not in common circulation. At one point Ch'en chanced to obtain an old edition of Tu Fu's poetry, the text of which was full of errors and lacunae. In Tu Fu's poem sending off Waterworks Commissioner Ts'ai, there was the line,

His body light: a single bird . . .

One character had been lost. Thereupon Ch'en and several of his friends tried to fill in the missing space with a word. One tried,

[His body light: a single bird] goes swiftly.

Another tried,

[His body light: a single bird] sinks.

And another,

[His body light: a single bird] rises.

And another,

[His body light: a single bird] descends.

No one could get it just right. Later Ch'en got hold of a good edition, and found that the line was, in fact,

His body light: a single bird in passage.

Ch'en accepted his defeat with a sigh: as he saw it, even though it was a question of only one word, neither he nor any of his friends could equal Tu Fu's choice.

Again we find an anecdote concerned with the vagaries of fashion and what is in danger of being lost. The fashionable admiration for a group of contemporary poets results in the neglect of the great T'ang poets; textual corruption and losses seem to follow from neglect. Ou-yang Hsiu is unquestionably mythologizing the neglect here: T'ang masters were not forgotten, especially by the Hsi-k'un poets themselves. But Ou-yang Hsiu is telling a story of what happens when we cease to study and conserve the tradition: gaps appear and those gaps are a vanished excellence that no modern poet can repair.

In our own time we accept the irreparability of a textual lacuna: conjecture is always marked as such. Not so in the Sung: there survived then some basic courage and self-confidence that by trial and error one might discover the missing word. The missing word would be the word that everyone recognized was perfect for the line, and in its perfection everyone would know that the word was Tu Fu's word. Courage, however, does not necessarily ensure success; and in their failure to find the perfect word on their own, Ch'en

Ts'ung-yi and his friends discover something about what can be lost by changes of fashion and failures of proper appreciation. In this anecdote there is none of the modern sense of the sanctity of the text, but there is a sense of past genius that makes a textual loss potentially irrecoverable. Such convivial rewriting of lines (usually the lines of contemporary poets) was a standard type of *shih-hua* anecdote—poetry remained, at its best, a form of social play—but Ou-yang Hsiu suggests a poetry beyond social play, poetry whose genius reveals the limited competence of ordinary persons.

The demonstration is effective: Tu Fu's line *is* vastly superior to the attempts of Ch'en Ts'ung-yi and his friends. "In passage" (literally "passes by") is the verb that makes the metaphor perfect for a parting poem, implicating a stable point (for Tu Fu, the person saying farewell) that defines the bird's motion. The word also leaves movement open on both sides of the passage and conveys the brevity of the present moment.[8]

In *shih-hua* (and presumably in the oral discussions that the written genre recalled) a new stylistics was developing, focusing attention on the use of particular words. Readers were learning to stop and savor the aptness of certain choices. At its most characteristic, Chinese poetry did not depend on striking metaphors and bold images; rather there was great pleasure in the precise qualities of simple words and how their implications gave shape to a scene. This is precisely the case with Tu Fu's "in passage," *kuo*.[9]

Again Ou-yang Hsiu returns to the question of learning to value what is both perfect and simple. A less reflective reader, caught up in the fashion of the times, might prefer the more obvious effects of the Hsi-k'un poets, who did use striking metaphors, bold images, and erudite allusions. Under the dominance of such a fashion, a choice of words like Tu Fu's can be overlooked, forgotten, perhaps even disappear from the text altogether. It is the tacit responsibility of the writer of the "Remarks on Poetry" to teach the proper attention and to preserve what is in danger of vanishing.

IX

國朝浮圖以詩名於世者九人。故時有集號九僧詩。今不復傳矣。余少時。聞人多稱之。其一曰惠崇。餘八人者。忘其名字也。余亦略記其詩有云。「馬放降來地。鵰盤戰後雲」。又云。「春生桂嶺外。人在海門西」。其佳句多類此。其集已亡。今人多不知有所謂九僧者矣。是可歎也。

The Buddhist monks who were famous for poetry in the present dynasty were nine; thus the collection of their works was called "The Poems of the Nine Monks." It is no longer in circulation. When I was young, I heard people praising them highly. One was named Hui-ch'ung, but I've forgotten the names of the other eight. I even remember a bit of their poetry. There was a couplet that went,

Horses set to graze on the land since the surrender,
A hawk wheels through clouds after the battle.

And another,

Spring appears beyond Cassia Ridge,
But the person lies west of Seagate Mountain.

Most of their best lines were of this sort. Their collected works have been lost, and people nowadays don't even know there were any "Nine Monks." This is very sad . . .

There are degrees of loss. One conserves what one can, namely, the fact, unknown to many contemporaries, that the Nine Monks existed; the fact that they were once popular; and the two couplets Ou-yang Hsiu can remember. Yet he adds, as if unaware how this casual information relates to his topic: "One was named Hui-ch'ung, but I've forgotten the names of the other eight."

To place this gesture of conservation in context, we might cite a passage from Ou-yang Hsiu's great collection of old inscriptions, the "Records of Gathering Ancient Things," *Chi-ku lu* 集古綠. Among more considerable inscriptions, Ou-yang Hsiu records the following fragments of a commemorative stele from which has been lost the name of the man whose life was there commemorated.

> This is the stele of someone unknown, from the Han. Characters have been worn away, and I was able to make out neither his family name nor his given name. All that we can make out is "Ranked foremost in the district examination for merit and set off for the capital"; and again "the deepest sorrow in his mourning, comparable to that of Min Sun . . . [fragments of office titles omitted]"; and again "showed a strict, unswerving authority, like a roaring tiger displayed a soldier's courage"; and again "in his sixty-third year, during the intercalary month of 181, he grew sick and died." Some of the strokes of the remaining characters are still complete, but they are not enough to make any sense of them. Pieces like this, preserved by those of us who love old things, need not all be of use to this age. And these remnants that have been worn away and in part lost are especially to be regretted. This is merely an odd passion on the part of those of us who love old things. Dated the fifth day of the sixth month of 1064.

This is a minor note preserving utterly useless information—of no use to that age when all knowledge was supposed to be put to practical use. Its preservation is a mere passion on the part of someone who loves old things, an antiquarian and collector. Yet Ou-yang's Hsiu's "odd passion" is deeply revealing: there is something in him that cannot permit the loss to memory of this unknown man—his early success, the sincerity of his mourning, his character. Ou-yang Hsiu is aware of the gratuitousness of the gesture: he explains that such acts of conservation "need not all be of use to this age"—he is almost puzzled by this impulse that serves neither state nor kin nor obvious personal pleasure—it is an "odd passion," *p'i.* The same "odd passion" is at work in the "Remarks on Poetry."

X

孟郊賈島皆以詩窮至死。而平生尤自喜為窮苦之句。孟有移居詩云。「借車載家具。家具少於車」。乃是都無一物耳。又謝人惠炭云。「暖得曲身成直身。」人謂非其身備嘗之不能道此句也。賈云。「鬢邊雖有絲。不堪織寒衣。」就令織得能得幾何。又其朝飢詩云。「坐聞西床琴。凍折兩三絃。」人謂其不止忍飢而已。其寒亦何可忍也。

Both Meng Chiao and Chia Tao were impoverished by poetry until their deaths, but all their lives they took special delight in lines on suffering and poverty. In Meng Chiao's poem "Moving House" we read,

> Let me borrow your wagon to move my household goods—
> My household goods are less than a wagonload.

This is complete destitution. In another poem, "Thanking Someone For a Gift of Charcoal," he writes,

> It has warmed a twisted body into a straight body.

People have said that a line like this could be written only by someone who had lived through such an experience. Chia Tao wrote,

> Though threads of white silk now hang in my locks,
> I cannot weave of them clothes against the cold.

Even if he had tried that sort of weaving, he wouldn't have gotten much cloth. In another poem, "Hungry at Dawn," we read,

> Just now I hear the zither by the west bed,
> Two or three strings snap, made brittle by the cold.

People have said that this is not only suffering from hunger—the cold is also unbearable.

A link between poetic mastery and lack of success in public life was a favorite theme of Ou-yang Hsiu's criticism.[10] With this theory he had consoled Mei Yao-ch'en for his failure to achieve high office—at least until Liu Ch'ang offered the alternative model of Cheng Ku, who had failed in public life and was also held in contempt as a poet. There may, however, be satisfactions in poetry quite different from fame, either literary or political. Absorption in poetry can bring about a paradoxical delight in framing the perfect poetic expression of one's misery. This entry modulates from the question of being valued to a series of entries on poetic craft.

Reading these lines of Meng Chiao and Chia Tao, others ("people have said") sigh in commiseration with the hardships referred to in their poetry; they read not the art itself but the conditions of life that could have produced such poetry. Yet the only word of pleasure in the entry is the artistic pleasure of the two poets in producing the very lines that so disturbed others. For Ou-yang Hsiu, however, there is something too finely wrought in the craft of Chia Tao's first couplet, something that causes Ou-yang Hsiu to depart from his usual practice of reading the person in the poem. He makes fun of Chia's extravagant couplet on weaving clothes of his white hair: "Even if he had tried that sort of weaving, he wouldn't have gotten much cloth." The art that reveals its art inspires distrust; better the art like Mei Yao-ch'en's poem on the blowfish, an art in which long practice produces what seems extempore and natural.

XI

唐之晚年。詩人無復李杜豪放之格。然亦務以精意相高。如周朴者。構思尤艱。每有所得。必極其雕琢。故時人稱朴詩。月鍛季煉。未及成篇。已播人口。其名重當時如此。而今不復傳矣。余少時猶見其集。其句有云。「風暖鳥聲碎。日高花影重。」又云。「曉來山鳥鬧。雨過杏花稀。」誠佳句也。

In the last years of the T'ang, poets no longer had the grand, expansive style (*ko****) of Li Po and Tu Fu; but they did devote themselves to achieving excellence in refined concepts (*ching- yi****). Poets like Chou P'u worked very hard to develop thoughts in poetry; and in everything they did, we always find an intense craftsmanship. People of the time praised Chou P'u's poetry saying: "He smelts it for a month, refines it for a season, and even before the poem is finished, it is already on everyone's lips"—such was his fame in his own age; and nowadays his work is no longer transmitted. When I was young, one could still find his collected poems. Among his couplets was one:

> The wind is warm, the voices of birds shatter,
> The sun high, the shadows of flowers heavy.

And another:

> As daybreak comes, birds of the hills make commotion,
> A rain passes, and apricot blossoms grow fewer.

These are truly fine lines.

Ou-yang Hsiu was a great historian and scholar of epigraphy, the critic who set for himself the task of conserving damaged poetic reputations and forgotten poets.[11] Yet he was himself in part responsible for the great changes of poetic taste that occurred in the eleventh century, changes that led his contemporaries to neglect the poets that had been famous in his own youth. With his immense prestige, he had taught an entire generation to value the "primordial plainness" and the casual naturalism of Mei Yao-ch'en. This shift in poetic taste undermined the overriding interest in the craft of the regulated couplet that had dominated poetics since the early decades of the ninth century. Here in his old age he looks back to remind his contemporaries of those poets now no longer fashionable.

Ou-yang Hsiu had claimed that there was indeed a reserve of craft in Mei Yao-ch'en's easy, extempore lines on the blowfish: Mei had worked at poetry all his life and could therefore produce perfect lines on the spot at a banquet. Chou P'u here represents another version of craft, a process of gradually refining lines. Chou P'u spent so long on his poems that versions of them were widely known even before he finished perfecting them. They may have been widely and immediately circulated in Chou P'u's own time, but now they are forgotten; even the most intense craftsmanship is no guarantee of survival. There are fine couplets here, worth recording and remembering. It is an occasion for considering what there might be, apart from reputations that change with fashion, that gives a poem value, as in the next entry.

XII

聖俞嘗語余曰。詩家雖率意而造語亦難。若意新語工得前人所未道者。斯為善也。必能狀難寫之景。如在目前。含不盡之意。見於言外。然後為至矣。賈島云。「竹籠拾山果。瓦缾擔石泉。」姚合云。「馬隨山鹿放。雞逐野禽栖。」等是山邑荒僻。官況蕭條。不如「縣古槐根出。官清馬骨高」為工也。余曰。語之工者固如是。狀難寫之景。含不盡之意。何詩為然。聖俞曰。作者得於心。覽者會以意。殆難指陳以言也。雖然亦可略道其髣髴。若嚴維。「柳塘春水慢。花塢夕陽遲」。則天容時態。融和駘蕩。豈不如在目前乎。又若溫庭筠。「雞聲茅店月。人迹板橋霜。」賈島。「怪禽啼曠野。落日恐行人」。則道路辛苦。羈愁旅思。豈不見于言外乎。

Mei Yao-ch'en once said to me, "Even if a poet follows the bent of his thoughts (*yi**), the formation of wording [for those thoughts] is still difficult. The very best thing is to have new thoughts and well-crafted diction, to achieve what no one has ever said before. You have to be able to give the manner of a scene (*ching**) that is hard to describe, to bring it as if before your eyes; it must hold inexhaustible thought in reserve (*han*), thought that appears beyond the words. Only then is it perfect. Chia Tao has a couplet:

A bamboo basket gathers the mountain fruit,
A pottery jug carries the rocky stream.

Yao Ho writes,

His horse goes off with the mountain deer to graze,
And his chickens follow wild birds to their roosts.

Both of these convey the dreariness of life in an official post in some wild and remote mountain town. But these are not so well-wrought as

The county residence is old: an ash tree's roots come out of the ground,
The official is pure: his horse's bones jut high."

And I said to him, "These are indeed good examples of well-wrought diction. But what poems give the manner of a scene that is hard to describe and hold inexhaustible thought in reserve?"

Mei Yao-ch'en answered, "When a writer has attained it in his own mind (*hsin**), then the reader will comprehend it through the concept (*yi**). It may be almost impossible to indicate or present in words, but nevertheless he can roughly articulate its vague outline. For example, there is Yen Wei's

In the willow pond, spring's waters spread,
On the flowered slope, the evening sun goes slowly.

Here the appearance of the sky [or weather] and the quality of the season are relaxing, balmy, carefree. Isn't it just as if before your eyes? We find another example in Wen T'ing-yün:

A cock crows: moonlight on the thatched inn,
A person's footprints in the frost on the plank bridge.

Or Chia Tao:

Strange birds cry out in the broad wilderness,
And the setting sun puts fear in the traveler.

Here we have the hardships of the road, the sorrow of travel, the thoughts that come on journeys. And don't you see how they appear 'beyond the words'?"

Ou-yang Hsiu has made this, the longest theoretical passage in "Remarks on Poetry," appear more natural by turning it into an anecdotal reminiscence and putting most of it in the mouth of Mei Yao-ch'en (thus preserving his own role as observer, commentator, and recorder). Ou-yang's question in the middle serves to break Mei's exposition and to remind the reader of its putative site in past occasion. In the same way, the informal style makes the passage seem less a theoretical disquisition than Mei's telling his friend his thoughts on what makes a great poetic scene.

Mei Yao-ch'en begins his statement by picking up the opposition between spontaneous composition and careful craftsmanship developed in the earlier entries. Mei was the foremost figure of the easy, "natural" style that gave the impression of "following the bent of one's thoughts," *shuai-yi** 率意. Yet here he speaks for values we might not have realized he held: the difficulty of perfectly phrasing those spontaneous thoughts (using the technical term of the couplet craft, *tsao-yü* 造語, the "formation of wording"). Throughout the "Remarks on Poetry" we learn that in poetry things are not as they seem (except for "those who truly understand poetry," who see through illusions to the truth). Mei Yao-ch'en, the representative of the leisurely discursive style of the Northern Sung, pays close attention to the phrasing of descriptions of scene like any ninth-century master of regulated veres. What seems an offhand piece on the blowfish is in fact the fruit of a lifetime of poetic craft.

However important Mei Yao-ch'en may have been in the formation of the Northern Sung poetic style against the last remnants of the regulated-verse styles of the late T'ang and Five Dynasties, his comments here belong very much to the older tradition of poetics by which the regulated-verse styles were perpetuated.[12] The influence of Ssu-k'ung T'u's letters is unmistakable here. In contrast, Ou-yang Hsiu's "Remarks on Poetry" is a mode of critical discourse that is congruent with the emerging Northern Sung poetic taste, incorporating and naturalizing issues of T'ang technical poetics within its wider scope and less pedagogic voice.

When Mei Yao-ch'en speaks of combining "following the bent of one's thoughts" with the "formation of wording," he (or Ou-yang Hsiu recreating the dialogue) varies the phrasing in a significant way. There is no question that "well-crafted diction" is the proper consequence of the "formation of wording"; but we should not overlook the parallel phrase, the presumed consequence of "following the bent of one's thoughts": here the term used is "new concepts" (*yi**). As in Western pre-Romantic texts, spontaneous composition is presumed to produce "originality," in the sense of both what is new and what comes uniquely from the self. The aim is stated quite plainly: "to achieve what no one has said before." Novelty as a value had a long history in Chinese literary thought (see Lu Chi, "The Poetic Exposition on Literature," ll. 27–30); but in its early stages it was mere novelty, discovered by learned reflection on what had previously been omitted, rather than following spontaneously from the self. During the Sung, variations on the formulation here—"to achieve what no one has said before"—became commonplace.

The focus of attention and the site of originality is the descriptive couplet. For Mei, the difficulty lies in the translation of the quality of a circumstantial mood and individual perception into the ten words of a pentasyllabic couplet, leaving the quality immanent "beyond the words." The basic terms of the problem, as Mei understands it, are among the oldest in the tradition: the limitation of language and the fullness of what is to be conveyed through language. For a scene to achieve presence ("to bring it as if before your eyes"), it must be fully circumstantial; yet full circumstantiality is impossible in ten words. The solution is that the ten words be chosen and arranged so that full circumstantiality is implied "in reserve."

The presumptions of such a solution are not untenable: the way in which a circumstantial mood appears in perceptual experience is through the relations between a few determinate elements (a theory not unfamiliar in the modern visual arts). In contrast, the attempt to achieve circumstantiality through extensive description ("within the words") deprives the reader of freedom: by the sheer multiplication of relations among elements, it thwarts attention to any particular relation. Only by limiting the determinate elements of a scene can the poet allow the reader to reflect on the implied relations and internalize them. One can never know if the reader perceives the same implicit relations in a scene that the poet intended; but because such a representation of the scene engages the reader, he necessarily understands it as a scene in which the poet was similarly engaged.

Following what was apparently a standard practice of social discussion of poetry, Mei Yao-ch'en then quotes three touchstone couplets on "the dreariness of life in an official post in some wild and remote mountain town."[13] Such multiple quotations often served the purpose, as here, of establishing a hierarchy of value. All three couplets are clever, but the cleverness of the third couplet is more subtle in its comparison between the roots of an old tree, rising out of the earth, and the bones of a lean horse: the juxtaposition links ruggedness, age, and incorruptibility (an official who accepted bribes would ride a well-fed horse).

These three couplets are very much "conceptual" (yi*, in the sense of being based on a clever idea). Ou-yang Hsiu will allow that the language is "well wrought," but not that they place a scene before one's eyes and convey inexhaustible yi*; that is, he implies by his question that there is a single point to the couplets which, once grasped, conveys a sense that there is not further meaning. To answer Ou-yang Hsiu's objections, Mei Yao-ch'en tries again; and his second triad of couplets is more remarkable, less "conceptual," and closer to the common sense of a poetic effect that lies "beyond words." Mei Yao-ch'en's prefatory remarks on how this occurs are of interest: the writer "attains it in his own mind," and the reader "comprehends it through concept." We note that there is no indication whether the writer is standing before the scene, recollects it, or invents it; but we do know that the poetic scene is an event in mind (much like the notion of aesthetic or poetic "ideas" for Kant and Romantic theorists). It is probably the emphasis on some unitary whole in the mind that leads Mei Yao-ch'en to use the term yi*. Yi* was a broad term, ranging here from something like the Baroque sense of "concept" or "conceit" (which would characterize the first triad of couplets) to the notion of an "aesthetic idea" (which would be appropriate for the second triad of couplets). The term for the reader's understanding is hui, literally to "meet": the assumption is that the poet's yi* and the reader's yi* will correspond.[14]

The difficulty in this process of transference lies in the mediating words, which are incapable of determining the yi*: what they can do is, literally: "to articulate its appearing vaguely"; that is, the words can make the yi* appear, but only in a blurred form, as if seen in the distance through some obstructing veil. The attentive reader can transcend the mediating distortion and grasp the yi*—its haziness is a guarantee of its authenticity.

The Western reader may well wonder why the second triad of couplets is so superior to the first. This difficulty lies partially in the second veiling distortion of translation and partially in the aesthetic values of the art of the couplet. Consider the couplet by Wen T'ing-yün. First, a couplet has what we may call a "ground," a basis of linguistic antitheses that defines its scope.[15] Abstract class concepts in Chinese are usually antithetical compounds; for example, horizontal distance is "far-near" and vertical extension is "high-low." The two lines of a couplet are often arranged around such "ground" antitheses. In Wen T'ing-yün's couplet we have an up-down antithesis, which gives us a scene of vertical extension without depth—appropriate to the traveler, whose vision of what lies ahead is blocked. Moreover, "to look up and down"—a paired event that is implied in the movement of attention in the couplet—also happens to be a compound meaning "instantly," conveying the momentary quality of the scene. The "senses" are usually presented by a "sound-sight" compound, and here we have an aural line set against a visual line. A "journey" is constituted of "stopping for the night and moving on," which is also implicated in the antithesis between the two lines. This is the "ground," which by no means guarantees a great couplet, but which defines a stable order and the scope on which a great couplet might appear—here a "moment," just before dawn, between resting for the night and setting out, the senses sharpened by the solitude of the scene, the vertical movement of attention in the two lines balanced by the horizontal vector of the bridge, which announces the prospect of setting out.

The genius of this couplet lies first in the juxtaposition of the moonlight on the thatch and the frost on the planks of the bridge, both cold and filmy layers of white over the visible strips of some human fabrication, a layer that is marked and penetrated by passage in the second line of the couplet. The juxtaposition is also a sequence of events: the sound of some unseen fowl is heard; and as the poet looks up, he sees only moonlight in the thatch. The sound, of course, makes no mark on the moonlight; and the other presence, that of the bird, is momentary and invisible. He then looks down and sees prints in the moonlit frost on the bridge—the startling evidence of another human presence, someone who has preceded him. The call of the rooster will waken other travelers. In the solitude of the first line, the poet is shown a lovely privacy; he has this scene to himself and will take a path which others will follow. The second line of the couplet, with its evidence that someone has preceded him, undoes the mood of "being first," of having the scene to himself. The words of the couplet simply name what is present; the interest of the couplet lies in the implicit relations between the elements of the scene and how those relations implicate a state of mind "beyond the words."[16]

XIII

聖俞子美。齊名於一時。而二家詩體特異。子美筆力毫雋。以超邁橫絕為奇。聖俞覃思精微。以深遠閑淡為意。各極其長。雖善論者不能優劣也。余嘗於水谷夜行詩略道其一二云。「子美氣尤雄。萬竅號一噫。有時肆顛狂。醉墨灑滂霈。譬如千里馬。已發不可殺。盈前盡珠璣。一一難揀汰。梅翁事清切。石齒漱寒瀨。作詩三十年。視我猶後輩。文辭愈精新。心意雖老大。有如妖韶女。老自有餘態。近詩尤古硬。咀嚼苦難嘬。又如食橄欖。真味久愈在。蘇豪以氣轢。舉世徒驚駭。梅窮獨我知。古貨今難賣。」語雖非工。謂粗得其髣髴。然不能優劣之也。

Mei Yao-ch'en and Su Shun-ch'in were both equally famous, but the styles (t'i*) of the two poets were quite different. There was a grandness and bravura in the force of Su Shun-ch'in's brush, and his work was remarkable for its overreaching and fierce energy. Mei Yao-ch'en thought deeply and went to the subtle essences of things; his [poetic] thoughts (yi*) were deep and far-reaching, yet calm and plain. Each poet made the most of his own strong points, and even the best critics could not rate one above the other. I once compared several aspects of their work in my poem "Going Out at Night at Shui-ku":

> Su Shun-ch'in's ch'i* is extremely strong:
> Thousands of caves call out in a single howl.
> Sometimes he lets himself go in a wild madness,
> And his drunken brush streams with ink.
> Compare him to a horse that runs a thousand leagues—
> Once he gets moving, he can't be stopped.
> Pearls [of poetry] fill the spaces before him,
> Hard to prefer one of them.
> Old Mei Yao-ch'en labors at the pure and precise:
> Teeth of stone scoured by cold rapids.
> He has been writing poetry for thirty years
> And looks on me as the younger generation.
> Yet his writing grows increasingly honed and fresh
> Though his mind and thoughts (hsin*- yi*) grow older.
> Compare him to a woman of entrancing beauty
> Whose charms are still ample, even in age.
> His recent poems are extremely ancient and blunt;
> One chews on them, and they're hard to swallow down:
> It's like eating kan-lan fruit—
> The true flavor gets stronger with time.
> Su's bravura surges with ch'i*—
> All the world is startled by it.
> But Mei, in his poverty, is understood by me alone—
> The ancient ways are hard to sell these days.

Even though my words here are not well wrought, I still think I've gotten the vague outline. Still, it is impossible to rate one above the other.

In entry XII, Mei Yao-ch'en delivered a discourse on the well-wrought couplet in the familiar style of ninth-century regulated verse, presenting a scene of which the reader could grasp the "vague outline." In counterpoint, Ou-yang Hsiu gives us an exuberant, discursive poem in the new Northern Sung style: its wording, he tells us, is not at all well wrought, and it gives the "vague outline" of the different qualities of two poets rather than a poetic scene (recall how, in the lines on the blowfish, Mei Yao-ch'en transformed a conventional poetic scene into an expression of personality). Most striking is the difference between the poetic values identified *by* Mei Yao-ch'en in entry XII and the poetic values *in* Mei Yao-ch'en's work here as identified by Ou-yang Hsiu.[17]

There is no difficulty in appreciating the well-crafted descriptive couplet; however elusive the mood of the scene may be, its beauty is immediately apparent. In contrast, Mei Yao-ch'en's poetry is described as an acquired taste, like the exotic *kan-lan* fruit, initially unappealing but increasingly pleasurable in the savoring. This returns us to the theme of valuing, developed earlier in "Remarks on Poetry." In contrast to the more obvious virtues of Su Shun-ch'in that win the admiration of many, there is a subtle plainness in Mei Yao-ch'en that is in danger of being misunderstood and undervalued. The critic is the *chih-yin** 知音, "the one who knows the tone": it is his role to call attention to virtues that are overlooked—not at the expense of Su Shun-ch'in's more obvious virtues, but complementing them.[18]

XV

聖俞嘗云。詩句義理雖通。語涉淺俗而可笑者。亦其病也。如有贈漁父一聯云。「眼前不見市朝事。耳畔惟聞風水聲。」說者云。患肝腎風。又有詠詩者云。「盡日覓不得。有時還自來。」本謂詩之好句難得耳。而說者云。此是人家失却貓兒詩。人皆以為笑也。

Mei Yao-ch'en once said, "Even though the idea (*yi**-*li**) may be communicated, a couplet is flawed if the language is too common and laughable. For example, there was a couplet in a poem entitled "To a Fisherman" that went,

> Before his eyes he does not see what happens in market and court,
> His ears hear only the sound of water and the wind.

Someone commented that this showed the symptoms of a liver ailment and an infection of the kidneys. Another person wrote a couplet on [composing] poetry:

All day I seek but do not find,
Then at times it comes to me on its own.

He was referring to the difficulty of achieving good couplets in writing poetry, but someone commented, "This is a poem on a family losing its cat." Everyone thought this was funny.

In the "Remarks on Poetry," there are many willful and mocking misinterpretations of poems. In the second entry (translated in the commentary to entry VI), the clumsy couplet of a successful official was turned into the butt of mockery; Ou-yang Hsiu himself had made fun of a couplet by Chia Tao; and here Mei Yao-ch'en makes jokes on a pair of couplets. Ostensibly the problem is poor phrasing which, though the reader knows well what was intended, leaves the poem vulnerable to the twist of comic interpretation.

There is something basic to the Northern Sung sensibility here: in each case, a "poetic" situation is mocked by being taken literally or made to refer to some "low," everyday circumstance. We recall that the poet offering these joking interpretations had himself begun a poem with a lovely spring river scene of reed sprouts and willow floss, only to bring it down to earth as the ingredients of blowfish soup. One could not say that Mei was being comic in those lines, but the interplay between the "poetic" and the everyday is the same form used to make jokes out of these couplets of others.

Previously, in entry XII, Mei described the perfect poetic scene, a conjunction of concept and diction. The least lapse from perfection threatens to turn the response into mockery. And we note that the second of these failed couplets itself concerns precisely the question of laborious craftsmanship and the spontaneous line, treated earlier in entry XII.

XVIII

詩人貪求好句而理有不通。亦語病也。如「袖中諫草朝天去。頭上宮花侍宴歸。」誠為佳句矣。但進諫必以章疏。無直用藁草之理。唐人有云。「姑蘇臺下寒山寺。半夜鐘聲到客船。」說者亦云句則佳矣。其如三更不是打鐘時。如賈島哭僧云。「寫留行道影。焚却坐禪身。」時謂燒殺活和尚。此尤可笑也。若「步隨青山影。坐學白塔骨。」又「獨行潭底影。數息樹邊身。」皆島詩。何精麤頓異也。

It is also a flaw in language when a poet, trying hard to get a good line, fails to communicate (*t'ung**) the principle (*li**). For example,

The draft of a remonstrance in my sleeve, I go off to the dawn court,
With palace blossoms over my head, I return having served at a feast.

This is really an excellent couplet; but when one submits a remonstrance, it must be written out formally—to present only a draft is simply not the way things work [literally, "no such principle"]. A T'ang poet wrote,

> Beneath Ku-su Terrace, the Cold Mountain Temple—
> The sound of whose bell at midnight reaches the traveler's boat.

Someone commented on this that the lines were excellent but ignored the fact that midnight was not a time when the temple bell was rung. Or take, as a further example, Chia Tao's "Lament For a Monk" with the lines

> They sketched and preserved his outline as he practiced the Way,
> But burned away the body that sat in meditation.

What is ludicrous here is that sometimes a reader thinks they burned a live monk. Couplets like

> I walked on, pursuing the green mountain's shadow,
> Sat and studied the bones in the white pagoda

and

> Alone I walked, a reflection at pool's bottom,
> And often rested a body beside the trees

are both from Chia Tao's poetry. Whatever their texture, they become suddenly strange.

Mei Yao-ch'en used willful misinterpretations to make fun of awkward phrasing; Ou-yang Hsiu begins with cases of misinformation (with a typical Ou-yang Hsiu twist: in the untranslated entry XVI, he had just praised poetry for providing a reliable source for historical information not otherwise available).[19] Referring a line of poetry to everyday reality may make it comic; in a more serious vein, Ou-yang Hsiu here measures the lines against the everyday facts and finds the couplets wanting: one simply does not bring drafts of documents to court; the temple bell does not ring at midnight (though later *shih-hua* writers will tell us Ou-yang Hsiu was himself mistaken here). Immediately, however, the prohibition against poetic license modulates in another direction, to a daring couplet by Chiao Tao in which the burden of failed understanding is placed on the foolishness of the reader (the couplet refers to a deceased monk, whose body was cremated and of whom a portrait survives).

Beneath all the variations in these entries lies the problem of understanding. There are misprisions that can destroy a reputation and lead to a poet's work falling out of circulation; there are comic misunderstandings, intentional and unintentional; there is misinformation; there is the labor of finding the perfect words to communicate the envisioned scene. Always the verbal poem mediates, sometimes blocking understanding, and sometimes, as in the final Chia Tao couplets quoted, communicating a sudden strangeness within the words.

XIX

松江新作長橋。制度宏麗。前世所未有。蘇子美新橋對月詩所謂。「雲頭灩灩開金餅。水面沉沉臥彩虹」者是也。時謂此橋非此句雄偉不能稱也。子美兄舜元。字才翁。詩亦遒勁。多佳句。而世獨罕傳。其與子美紫閣寺聯句。無媿韓孟也。恨不得盡見之耳。

A long bridge had recently been built over the Sung River, the grandeur and beauty of whose construction had never been seen before. Su Shun-ch'in wrote of it in "Facing the Moon on the New Bridge":

> In the undulating current of clouds a golden cake appears,
> Sunken below the water's surface, a brightly colored rainbow rests.

At the time people said that the bold magnificence of this couplet made it the only thing that could do justice to the bridge. Su Shun-ch'in had an elder brother Su Shun-yüan, whose poetry was also forceful and filled with excellent couplets. But unlike [those of] his brother, his poems are rarely seen. The linked verse he wrote with his brother, "On Purple Tower Temple," can stand without embarrassment beside the linked verses of Meng Chiao and Han Yü. Unfortunately I haven't been able to see the entire piece.

Su Shun-ch'in's couplet, with its daring metaphor drawn from everyday life, is typical of the new Northern Sung style: a "cake" (*ping*) drops an edible moon amid a gorgeously "poetic" description—just as Mei Yao-ch'en's mouth had watered contemplating the spring river scene.

Su Shun-ch'in's widely known and admired couplet characteristically leads Ou-yang Hsiu to thoughts of Su's brother, whose poetry was no less remarkable, but is forgotten now, no longer easy to find. As with the broken Han stele and the Nine Monks, of whose names he can remember only one, Ou-yang Hsiu calls attention to what is fragmentary and incomplete (in his mind at least), a vanished excellence—the linked verse that could "stand without embarrassment beside the linked verses of Meng Chiao and Han Yü," but which Ou-yang Hsiu has not seen in its entirety.

XX

晏元獻公文章擅天下。尤善為詩。而多稱引後進。一時名士往往出其門。聖俞平生所作詩多矣。然公獨愛其兩聯云。「寒魚猶著底。白鷺已飛前。」又「絮暖鮆魚繁。豉添純菜

紫。」余嘗於聖俞家見公自書手簡。再三稱賞此二聯。余疑而問之。聖俞曰。此非我之極
致豈公偶自得意於其間乎。乃知自古文士。不獨知已難得。而知人亦難也。

Yen Shu's literary works dominated his age, and he was especially good at
poetry. Yet he often promoted younger writers, and famous scholars of the
time often found a place under his wing. Mei Yao-ch'en wrote a great many
poems in his life, but Yen Shu had a special fondness for two of Mei's couplets:

> The cold fish still cleave to the bottom,
> The white egret already flies on ahead.

And:

> Willow floss grows warm, the pickerel are dense,
> Water-spiders increase, the ch'un plants turn purple.

In Mei Yao-ch'en's house I saw a calligraphy piece in Yen Shu's own hand
praising these couplets over and over again. Dubious [of Yen Shu's judgment],
I asked Mei about it; and he said, "This is not my work at its best; I'm sure it's
just that Yen Shu happened to find some personal satisfaction in them." This
teaches us that not only is it hard for a literary man to find someone who truly
understands him, knowing others is also hard.

In this entry, the closely related issues of understanding and valuing are
drawn together, leaving us with a problem rather than a solution. Here we
should recall entry V in which Mei Yao-ch'en's "Spring Snow" acquired value
for Ou-yang Hsiu precisely because of its personal associations. We should
also recall the difference between Mei's exposition of poetic values in entry
XII and Ou-yang Hsiu's quite different description of the virtues of Mei's own
poetry in entry XIII. Must the qualities appreciated in a poem coincide with
the poet's self-understanding? Or can a poet judge his own poems? (See *Mencius* on *chih-yen*, "understanding language," for the possibility of a negative
answer: p. 22.) If we accept Mei Yao-ch'en's earlier description, understanding occurs only when the reader's mind "meets" the poet's mind. How
then can Yen Shu prize these couplets for which Mei himself has such little
regard? Mei Yao-ch'en concludes that Yen must have appreciated these
verses only for some "personal satisfaction." There may be appreciation without understanding—at least from Mei's point of view.[20]

XXI

楊大年與錢劉數公唱和。自西崑集出。時人爭效之。詩體一變。而先生老輩。患其多用故
事。至於語僻難曉。殊不知自是學者之弊。如子儀新蟬云。「風來玉宇烏先轉。露下金莖
鶴未知。」雖用故事。何害為佳句也。又如「峭帆橫渡官橋柳。疊鼓驚飛海岸鷗。」其不
用故事。又豈不佳乎。蓋其雄文博學。筆力有餘。故無施而不可。非如前世號詩人者。區
區於風雲草木之類。為許洞所困者也。

Yang Yi [974–1055] wrote group compositions on shared themes with Ch'ien Wei-yen, Liu Yün, and others. Out of this came the "Hsi-k'un Collection," which everyone at the time imitated, with the result that the poetic style of the age was entirely transformed. Gentlemen of the older generation objected to their excessive use of allusions, to the point that the words were obscure and incomprehensible. I wonder if this isn't simply a scholar's failing. Take, for example, these lines by Liu Yün on the "New Cicadas":

> The wind will come to the marble dome: beforehand the raven [weather vane] turns;
> The dew descends on the columns of gold, and the crane does not know.

The fact that this uses allusions does not prevent it from being a fine couplet. On the other hand:

> The high sail crosses past the willows of the post-road bridge,
> A roll of drums startles to flight the gulls beside the lake.

Here no allusions are used, but it also is a fine couplet. In my opinion their forceful writing and broad learning provided them ample power of style [*pi-li*, "force of brush"]; thus they could do anything. This is not what the preceding generation had given the name "poet" to, the sort of writer who trifled around with winds, clouds, grasses, and trees—the things we find wrong with Hsü Tung's work.

In a world of general misunderstanding and often destructive misunderstanding, the critic has the responsibility to be cautious, balanced, and generous. In entry X, Ou-yang Hsiu could not restrain himself from making fun of an extravagant couplet by Chia Tao; in entry XVIII, he makes fun of a reader who misunderstands an extravagant couplet by the same Chia, and then proceeds to give Chia Tao's strangeness its due. In his younger years, Ou-yang Hsiu had objected to the influence of the Hsi-k'un group; in entry VIII, he commented how the Hsi-k'un style had been so much in vogue that people no longer paid any attention to the T'ang masters (an exaggeration, probably considering the Hsi-k'un group from the point of view of one of those "gentlemen of the older generation," Ch'en Ts'ung-yi). Here he balances his previous censure with generosity and gives the Hsi-k'un masters their due. If they sometimes used allusions excessively, he understands this as the natural disposition of scholars. Then he shows allusions well used and a couplet without allusion.

But praise is somehow always coupled with dispraise. To reflect on the values that make Yang Yi's verses good is to accept criteria by which other kinds of verses become poor. Hsü Tung, the object of Ou-yang Hsiu's criticism, was a poet of sufficient insignificance that no one would question Ou-yang Hsiu's judgment. But Hsiu's work was not unlike that of Cheng

Ku, which Ou-yang Hsiu had defended early in the "Remarks on Poetry." It is the nature of the act of valuing that every positive judgment makes possible a negative judgment somewhere else. It is inescapable, as in the following entry.

XXII

西洛故都。荒臺廢沼。遺迹依然。見於詩者多矣。惟錢文僖公一聯最為警絕。云「日上故陵煙漠漠。春歸空苑水潺潺。」裴晉公綠野堂在午橋南。往時嘗屬張僕射齊賢家。僕射罷相歸洛。日與賓客吟宴於其間。惟鄭工部文寶一聯最為警絕。云「水暖鳧鷖行哺子。溪深桃李臥開花。」人謂不減王維杜甫也。錢詩好句尤多。而鄭句不惟當時人莫及。雖其集中自及此者亦少。

The relics and ruins of the old capital at Lo-yang, terraces overgrown with vegetation and abandoned pools, offer melancholy reflection; they appear in poetry often. One of the most striking examples is a couplet by Ch'ien Wei-yen [d. ca. 1033]:

> The sun rises over the ancient highlands, through mist billowing;
> Spring returns to the empty parks, where waters still burble on.

Greenwilds Hall of P'ei Tu, Lord of Tsin [765–839], lay south of Wu Bridge, and later came into the possession of the household of Chang Ch'i-hsien [943–1014]. When Chang Ch'i-hsien gave up his ministerial post and returned to Lo-yang, every day he would hold poetry banquets for his guests there. One couplet from such poetry banquets, a couplet by Cheng Wen-pao [953–1013] is striking:

> In the warmth of these waters the ducks and gulls move to feed their young;
> Where the creek valley's deepest, peaches and plums blossom, lying horizontal.

People said this was in no way inferior to Wang Wei or Tu Fu. There are a great many good lines in Ch'ien Wei-yen's poems; but as for Cheng Wen-pao's couplet, not only could none of his contemporaries equal it, very little in his own collected poems could equal it.

XXIV

石曼卿自少以詩酒豪放自得。其氣貌偉然。詩格奇峭。又工於書。筆力遒勁。體兼顏柳。為世所珍。余家嘗得南唐後主澄心堂紙。曼卿為余以此紙書其籌筆驛詩。詩曼卿平生所自愛者。至今藏之。號為三絕。真余家寶也。曼卿卒後。其故人有見之者。云恍惚如夢中。言我今為鬼仙也。所主芙蓉城。欲呼故人往遊。不得。忽然騎一素騾。去如飛。其後又云。降於亳州一舉子家。又呼舉子去。不得。因留詩一篇與之。余亦略記其一聯云。「鶯聲不逐春光老。花影長隨日腳流。」神仙事怪不可知。其詩頗類曼卿平生。舉子不能道也。

Ever since he was a youth, Shih Man-ch'ing [994–1041] found satisfaction in a brash expansiveness, both in poetry and drinking. His spirit (ch'i*) and appearance were exceptional, and the manner (ko*) of his poetry was daring and unusual. He was also good at calligraphy; and the force of his brushwork was strong, much prized in the age, its style (t'i*) uniting the styles of Yen Chench'ing and Liu Kung-ch'üan. Once I got hold of some of the famous "Pure Heart Hall" paper, produced for the Last Emperor of the Southern T'ang [Li Yü]. Using this paper, Shih Man-ch'ing wrote out for me his poem on Ch'ou-pi Post Station [from which Chu-ko Liang (181–234) had dispatched the Shu-Han armies]. This poem had always been Shih's favorite. I still have this copy and call it my greatest prize, the real family treasure. After Shih died, one of his old friends saw him, all in a blur as if in a dream; and Shih said: "I've now become an immortal and have been placed in charge of Lotus City." He wanted to invite his old friend to go off wandering with him; and when the friend was unwilling, Man-ch'ing rode off in a fury on a white mule, as if flying. After that I also heard it said that he descended to the house of a provincial candidate for the examination and asked him to go away with him. When the man was unwilling, Man-ch'ing left a poem for him. I even roughly remember one of the couplets:

> The voices of orioles do not grow old with the light of spring;
> The shadows of flowers always follow the sunbeams drifting on.

The question of gods and immortals is not something we can know anything about; but the poem is indeed very much like what Man-ch'ing wrote when he was alive, and it is beyond the capacities of that provincial candidate.

Along with Mei Yao-ch'en and Su Shun-ch'in, Shih Man-ch'ing had been one of the contemporary poets much admired by Ou-yang Hsiu. Very little of Shih's work is extant, but he was clearly part of the revolution in poetic taste occurring, under Ou-yang Hsiu's sponsorship, in the first half of the eleventh century. In this entry we see the familiar motifs of "Remarks on Poetry": valuing, preservation, and finally a most peculiar case of recognizing the person in the poem. In the first part of the anecdote, we see Ou-yang Hsiu in his familiar role: recognizing what is valuable and preserving it against loss. Ou-yang Hsiu had kept Mei Yao-ch'en's "Spring Snow" in textile for some "personal satisfaction," while acknowledging it was not one of Mei's more important poems. In this case, however, Shih Man-ch'ing's self-understanding of what is valuable in his own poetry wins out: it is his favorite poem in his best calligraphy written on rare paper; it is a treasure to preserve against the attrition that time works on the collections of poets.

But then the dead poet comes back—or at least so they say—and is still producing poetry (of course, Ou-yang Hsiu has lost most of Shih's "posthumous" poem and can "roughly remember" only one of the couplets). Ou-yang Hsiu is a sophisticated Sung intellectual; he does not want to believe this; but he cannot help recognizing Shih Man-ch'ing in the lines. The logical extension of one who truly understands the poet and knows how to value his works is the connoisseur, capable of authenticating an attribution. Ou-yang Hsiu smiles: it does indeed sound like Shih Man-ch'ing—and it could not possibly have been written by that young man who received the poem in a dream!

Ts'ang-lang's
Remarks
on
Poetry

"Ts'ang-lang's Remarks on Poetry," *Ts'ang-lang shih-hua* 滄浪詩話 (early to mid thirteenth century), by Yen Yü 嚴羽, is the most famous and most influential work in the genre of "remarks on poetry," *shih-hua*.[1] Although it contains sections of true *shih-hua*, it is essentially a mixed critical form: both its structure and its tone served as models for the subsequent development of Yüan and Ming poetry manuals (*shih-fa** 詩法, "rules of poetry"). In ways both obvious and subtle, the influence of "Ts'ang-lang's Remarks on Poetry" was immense. Passages from the first chapter, "On Making the Right Distinctions in Poetry," were among the most widely circulated statements of poetic theory during the centuries that followed, while variations on Yen's positions were treated as virtual truisms. Yen Yü would have felt this was only his due: he himself modestly claimed that his was the ultimate formulation of the nature of poetry for all time, and that by his work all earlier dispute and error were resolved.[2] Soon after its appearance, a version of the first chapter was reprinted in the thirteenth-century critical anthology *Jade Chips of the Poets* (*Shih-jen yü-hsieh* 詩人玉屑).[3] By the fourteenth century, bits and pieces of "Ts'ang-lang's Remarks on Poetry"—terms, sentences, and paraphrased opinions—were already commonplace. The range of Yen Yü's influence was at first seen primarily in informal criticism and in the popular pedagogy of poetry; but we soon find "Ts'ang-lang's Remarks on Poetry" beginning to make substantial inroads in the more authoritative critical genres such as the preface and the discourse.

Perhaps the single most powerful consequence of the popularity of "Ts'ang-lang's Remarks on Poetry" was the canonization of the High T'ang as the immutable standard for poetry, at the expense of mid- and late-T'ang writers.[4] The belief that the High T'ang represented the culmination of poetry had roots reaching all the way back into the High T'ang itself. But Yen Yü granted the period a special quality of authority, a literary historical orthodoxy on the model of Ch'an orthodoxy.[5] Such a notion of absolute poetic values embodied in a past historical moment remained, for better or worse, an integral part of the way in which later readers understood poetry.[6] At times this orthodoxy of High T'ang poetry was cautiously qualified or vigorously opposed, but it remained the conventional wisdom against which all other opinions were articulated. Yen Yü's "poetic curriculum," based on the study of High T'ang and earlier models, was codified and elaborated by Ming archaist writers.[7] Even more important, Yen Yü established the very notion of a "poetic curriculum": the "study of poetry," hsüeh-shih 學詩, became a strict discipline, based on literary history and explicitly modeled on the study of the Confucian Classics.

A tradition of literary thought is not so much an aggregate of positions as a form of understanding and a structure of discourse within which positions are situated. The significance of a position comes from the way it is used and its relation to other parts of the discourse, parts that may seem less important in themselves. If we consider the way in which Yen Yü uses concepts, we may find that the most profound legacy of "Ts'ang-lang's Remarks on Poetry" was its negativity. For Yen Yü value and authority could be sustained only by vigorous opposition to and denunciation of alternatives: the authority of the High T'ang was maintained by discrediting all subsequent changes that had occurred in poetry, while the authority of Yen Yü's own statements was supported by heaping scorn on imagined opponents. The allegiance of his readers is commanded not only by sweet promises of success, but also by threats of contempt for any deviation. What had previously been a range of available stylistic choices was now, for the believer, reduced to one correct choice. This ideology of restriction reappears most strongly in the work of the Ming archaists; and Yen Yü's rhetoric of contempt became a permanent feature of Chinese discourse on literature, even among later critics like Yeh Hsieh, who pleaded for a historical relativism of value.[8]

Yen Yü's influence remained powerful in both popular and erudite poetics (although more consistently influential in the former than in the latter). "Ts'ang-lang's Remarks on Poetry" exerted great influence on the critical opinions of the supremely sophisticated Wang Shih-chen 王士禎 (1634–1711). In this case, attention was given not to Yen Yü's orthodoxy of poetic pedagogy, but to his comments on the ineffable and elusive perfection of High T'ang poetry, a quality that Wang Shih-chen himself struggled to attain.

"Ts'ang-lang's Remarks on Poetry" is divided into five chapters, the first and third of which are translated here. The first chapter, "Making the Right Distinctions in Poetry" (Shih-pien 詩辨), is a series of essays on pedagogy and values, with some typical shih-fa* material embedded in the middle. The following chapter, "Poetry's Normative Forms" (Shih-t'i* 詩體), is a long list of everything that might be considered a t'i*, but subdivided into genres, period styles, individual styles, and so on (showing a new awareness of the importance of these distinctions). Such lists would fall roughly within the scope of shih-fa* material. The third chapter is entitled "Rules of Poetry" (Shih-fa* 詩法) and contains the lists of virtues and dangers and general pragmatic advice typical of the shih-fa* form. The fourth chapter, "Critical Comments on Poetry" (Shih-p'ing 詩評), gathers random judgments on particular periods, poets, and poems; although shih-fa* also often contain such sections, this is typical shih-hua material. The final section, "Philological Notes" (K'ao-cheng 考證), treats particular philological questions along with problems of attribution; such material is more appropriate to shih-hua than to shih-fa*.

The jargon, the tone of voice, and the mannered vernacular style of Ch'an Buddhist writings dominate the first chapter. For many centuries critics of Yen Yü have been fond of pointing out his misunderstanding of Ch'an Buddhism (while defenders maintain his deeper understanding). His analogy between poetry and the discipline of Ch'an was already commonplace in his day, but remains to the present the most commonly discussed and most agonizingly uninteresting aspect of "Ts'ang-lang's Remarks on Poetry."[9] Far more interesting is Yen Yü's peculiar extension of the Ch'an analogy in the attempt to arrogate to himself the authoritative voice of a Ch'an master. The resulting style is a matter of taste: the closest English analogy might be the stylized "tough guy" talk of detective fiction; and if the American reader can conceive of a literary essayist adopting the voice of a Raymond Chandler hero, while at the same time larding his speech with the poorly understood jargon of German metaphysics, something of the quality of Yen Yü's style can be grasped: as I said, it is a matter of taste.

"Ts'ang-lang's Remarks on Poetry" is very much a product of the last century of the Sung, and the magnitude of its influence suggests that the sense of crisis and loss tacitly permeating the work touched a deep chord in late classical poetics. In the early centuries of the tradition poetry had made grand promises: to make the true inner condition of the human heart known to others, to grant cultural immortality, to make manifest the latent principles of the universe. Throughout the Sung Dynasty, we can see a developing sense that something had gone terribly wrong; behind an often shrill mask of optimism, we read a powerful anxiety that poets were slipping ever further from the heights of their T'ang predecessors.[10]

T'ang poetics had largely been concerned with complacent restatements of received truths, tricks of the trade (one passage in Bunkyō hifuron profoundly advises a poet to get plenty of sleep and not to try to write when he is tired), and technical advice on how to avoid embarrassing blunders. Sung poetics became increasingly concerned with how to write great poetry. The loss of confidence implicit in such a shift of interest should be obvious. Beneath the stylized self-assurance and stridency of "Ts'ang-lang's Remarks on Poetry," there is a retrospective melancholy similar to that of "Longinus" in *On the Sublime*, at the end of which an unnamed philosopher is quoted as saying: "To such a degree has some universal barrenness of words taken hold of life." Both texts share a yearning for some lost and ineffable magic of affect in earlier poetry; both texts promise a "technique" for recovering it, and both belong to the category of a *technologia* [a "how-to" manual]. Both make the peculiar claim that by strenuously following its prescriptions a student can attain some quality that transcends conscious effort. Yen Yü offers a course of reading and study that will lead to *ju-shen** 入神, "divinity," a condition that is beyond self-conscious control and analytic explanation. Such a promise may account for the attraction "Ts'ang-lang's Remarks on Poetry" held for later readers: Yen Yü forthrightly faced the truth of a vanished greatness in poetry and at the same time declared that in his work the aspiring poet could find the means to recapture some small part of it.

Of Yen Yü himself we know very little. A collection of approximately one hundred and fifty poems survives, which seems to have originally circulated together with "Ts'ang-lang's Remarks on Poetry." We may credit the last shreds of good literary taste in the thirteenth century with the separation of Yen's poems from "Ts'ang-lang's Remarks on Poetry." In the restrained judgment of the modern scholar Chang Chien: "Looking at Yen Yü's poetry, [we see that] he was not really able to follow his own theories."[11]

CHAPTER 1
Making the Right Distinctions in Poetry[12]

I.

夫學詩者以識為主。入門須正。立志須高。以漢魏晉盛唐為師。不作開元天寶以下人物。若自退屈。即有下劣詩魔入其肺腑之間。由立志之不高也。行有未至。可加工力。路頭一差。愈騖愈遠。由入門之不正也。故曰。學其上。僅得其中。學其中。斯為下矣。又曰。見過於師。僅堪傳授。見與師齊。減師半德也。工夫須從上做下。不可從下做上。先須熟讀楚詞。朝夕諷詠以為本。及讀古詩十九首。樂府四篇。李陵蘇武漢魏五言皆須熟讀。即以李杜二集枕藉觀之。如今人之治經。然後博取盛唐名家。醞釀胸中。久之自然悟入。雖學之不至。亦不失正路。此乃是從頂𩕳上做來。謂之向上一路。謂之直截根源。謂之頓門。謂之單刀直入也。

Judgment (*shih**) is the dominant factor (*chu*) in the study of poetry. The beginning must be correct (*cheng**), and your mind must be set on (*chih**) the highest goals. Take for your teacher the poetry of the Han, Wei, and High T'ang; don't act the part of those after the K'ai-yüan [713–741] and T'ien-pao [742–755] reigns. If you retreat from this in the least, the vilest poetry demon will enter your breast—and this will be because your mind was not set on the highest goals.[13] If you haven't yet reached your goals, you can always try harder; but if you err in your direction at the beginning, the more you rush on, the farther you will get off course. This will be because your beginnings were not correct. If you study the very best, you will reach only the middle level; but if you study the middle level, then you will come out on the bottom. Furthermore, you can get instruction only from a teacher whose perception surpasses your own; if your perception equals that of your teacher, it reduces the teacher's value by half. You have to work from the beginning to the end; you can't work back from the end to the beginning.[14] First of all, you should read the *Songs of Ch'u* (i.e., *Ch'u-tz'u*) until you are thoroughly familiar with them and chant them day and night to have them as your basis (*pen**). Next read the "Nineteen Old Poems," the four principal "Ballads" (*yüeh-fu*), Li Ling, Su Wu, and the pentasyllabic poems of the Han and Wei—you should read these until you are thoroughly familiar with them.[15] Then consider these works piled side by side with the collected poems of Li Po and Tu Fu—just as people study the classics nowadays. Only after that should you pick and choose widely among the other famous writers of the High T'ang, letting them ferment in your breast. Finally, after a long time, you will spontaneously (*tzu-jan**) achieve enlightened insight (*wu-ju*).[16] Even though you may not yet have reached the full fruition of your studies, at least you won't have lost the proper road. This is what I mean by "working from the very top." This is called the "highest road"; this is called "entering directly to the source"; this is called "the gate of sudden [enlightenment]"; this is called "going straight in with a single blade."[17]

"Judgment (*shih**) is the dominant factor in the study of poetry." The determination of some "dominant factor" (*chu* 主, literally a "host" or "master") was one of the normative acts in Chinese discourse on literature.[18] A fixed hierarchy of relations is assumed between the various aspects of a literary work, and the perfect attainment of the "dominant factor" will result in all other aspects spontaneously performing their proper roles. It is significant that Yen Yü here identifies *shih* 識, "judgment" or "recognizing," as the "dominant factor." In so doing, he shifts the locus of poetry's "dominant factor" from some internal aspect of the work (such as *ch'i** or "concept," *yi**) to a capacity that resides solely in the writer; moreover, it is a capacity that treats the writer primarily as a reader, first of others' poems and then of his own. Although later in the chapter Yen Yü will condemn the bookishness of Sung poetry, in his first sentence this Sung critic presumes that the reading of poetry is the essential basis of poetic composition. The requisite capacity for judgment should be clearly distinguished from a more general "knowing," *chih* 知. Judgment involves the application of some prior knowledge to making the correct distinctions in a given set of circumstances. Yen Yü does not recommend knowing what poetry should be in an abstract theoretical sense;

rather he recommends recognizing or judging what is best through reading a historical sequence of poems. There is, in fact, no explicit theoretical ground for such judgments: Yen Yü presumes that, if such a sequence of reading is followed, the proper judgments will become self-evident and eventually proper judgment in poetic praxis ("knowing how to") will follow spontaneously.[19]

"The beginning must be correct (*cheng**), and your mind must be set on (*chih**) the highest goals." The "course" of study of poetry is conceptualized as a journey, a journey through the history of poetry. Such a journey has two imperatives: to choose the proper destination (the "highest goals," the High T'ang) and to work toward that destination from the right beginning. Poetic history is given as a predetermined sequence, growing to perfection and passing immediately thereafter into decline. Writing from his own late age of decline, Yen Yü recommends that the reader follow that sequence to its fruition, then stop. While such a program might seem to hold the aspiring poet forever in the glow of perfection, Yen Yü recognizes that having reached this moment, the student-reader is already dwelling in the afterglow: "If you study the very best, you will reach only the middle level."

In some ways Yen Yü was the forerunner of the true historicist poetics of Yeh Hsieh in the seventeenth century. At that later period, as in the historicist poetics of German Romanticism, the possibility was raised that a knowledge of literary history could redeem the writer from the determinations of history: by understanding the historical variations of poetry, the historicist poet can hope either to incorporate all historical possibilities within himself or to go beyond them.[20] Yen Yü, too, believes in the necessity of knowing the history of poetry; but instead of a historical relativism of value (as in Yeh Hsieh), he believes that there is only one moment of perfection, a goal that always threatens to elude recapture. His initial formulation is deeply pessimistic, warning the aspiring poet that studying even the very best will bring him only to the middle level. Later he holds up the possibility of a poetic enlightenment as if it were still within reach.

Despite his pessimism, Yen Yü resists the thought that great poetry can no longer be written in the thirteenth century. He faces the sorry state of the poetry of his age and tries to analyze its ills. As he sees it, initially at least, the problem is not one of absolute incapacity, but rather of a lack of judgment: people no longer "know how to" write good poetry, and "knowing how" is predicated on recognizing what great poetry is. What Yen Yü offers his readers is not basic principles but a complete poetic education. If from the very beginning a student of poetry—and in the thirteenth century we can begin to speak of "students of poetry" as we could not earlier—reads only the best poetry, that student will have only the best models. The hope is that if an aspiring poet never encounters the failed, fallen poetry of the Sung, he will not be "infected" by it.

In aspiring to write poetry "like" the poetry of the High T'ang, Yen Yü swerves radically from the old Confucian assumption that poetry manifests the historical moment of the world outside itself (a problem that did not escape the notice of Yen Yü's critics). "Ts'ang-lang's Remarks on Poetry" is an anti-Confucian poetics not because it uses the Ch'an metaphor for poetry; rather it turns to the Ch'an metaphor and the heterodox jargon of Ch'an to find some authority for a poetics that is already anti-Confucian. Yen Yü would like poetry to be a closed world: it has its own history independent of the larger phases of human history. Without such a presumption of the historical autonomy of the art, his course of poetic education would be futile: a late-Sung poet who stopped his reading at the High T'ang would still be a late-Sung poet. And yet, ironically, the very desire to assert poetry's autonomy from some integral history of the civilization is recognizable as belonging to the intellectual world of the Southern Sung. The growing specialization of disciplines in the period would have disposed most readers to acknowledge the necessity of expertise confined to a single area of study.

The poetry of the Han, Wei, and High T'ang is *cheng* 正, "proper" or "orthodox." In a peculiarly elliptical version of the history of poetry (a lineage, described as though continuous, leaving a gap of four centuries between the Wei or Tsin and the High T'ang), Yen Yü announces a literary historical orthodoxy based on the model of orthodox transmission in Buddhism and Neo-Confucianism. This poetic orthodoxy, however, unlike its Buddhist and Neo-Confucian antecedents, presumes that there is one moment in poetic history that embodies the "perfection" of poetry (in the sense of something gradually attaining fulfillment, then falling away).[21] If we reflect on it, this is a most peculiar model, positing something like an Aristotelian entelechy for literary genres, or a biological model in which one stage of life is one's "prime." Nevertheless, this model of literary history is still taken for granted by most Chinese literary historians and many Western literary historians. As a "natural" descriptive model it is utterly untenable, but as a historical structure of valuing, it has immense consequences. That is, although there is no inherent or "natural" set of poetic values that make Sung poetry inferior to T'ang poetry, the establishment of a High T'ang orthodoxy reinforced a matrix of poetic values based on High T'ang poetry, values according to which Sung poetry could not but be inferior to T'ang poetry.[22]

The desire for a literary historical orthodoxy grew out of a fear of rampant change and the historical relativity of poetic values. In its desire to impose a single, permanent set of values on poetry, such orthodoxy was a doomed but immensely attractive project. Facing a similar grandeur of past poetry, Friedrich Schiller developed a set of double standards, "naive" and "sentimental." Schiller's concept of the "sentimental," despite his attempts to make it ahistorical, was essentially a new set of values by which the later-born poet, such as the poet born after the High T'ang, could be as great or greater than his predecessors. Yen Yü did not admit a second standard: there was no way the moderns could equal the old poets. Yen Yü did not promise that by an orthodox course of poetic study we could become Li Po or Tu Fu; he promised only that we could thereby avoid the humiliating worst. Our only power is to limit the degree of our fallenness. We can always strive with all our might and do somewhat better; but the High T'ang teacher, whose very superiority makes it possible for us to learn and improve, will always be just out of reach. It is a melancholy and deeply pessimistic opening, for all the bravura of its exhortation.

Yen's poetic curriculum is not simply the High T'ang apogee of poetry, but rather the *history* of the best poetry up to that point. We should note how the concept of *cheng**, "proper" or "orthodox," has changed: in the "Great Preface" to the *Book of Songs cheng** was the beginning, after which occurred *pien**, "mutation." In "Ts'ang-lang's Remarks on Poetry" *cheng** is a long lineage of maturation, reaching fruition in the High T'ang, then lapsing into *pien**, "mutation," or "devolution." Furthermore, *cheng** and *pien** have lost their cultural and ethical dimensions: they now belong purely to the history of poetry.[23]

As Yen Yü changes the concept of *cheng**, the ultimate *cheng** of poetry, the *Book of Songs*, has been excluded from the curriculum. In "Revering the Classics" in the *Wen-hsin tiao-lung* and elsewhere, all forms of secular literature derived their authority from the ability to trace each back to one or another Confucian Classic. Yen Yü begins his curriculum with the *Songs of Ch'u*: a barrier has been erected between the Classics and "secular" poetry. The study of poetry should be "just like" study of the Classics; but the analogy is predicated on the assumption that the two belong to discontinuous realms.[24]

The student is to read the old poetry, let it settle, and then at some point there is a leap of understanding. The terms Yen Yü uses link this leap of understanding to Ch'an enlightenment. But this is a Ch'an variation on the oldest Chinese model of learning, with roots in ethics, statecraft, and Classical studies. Knowledge is to be assimilated until at some point it becomes "second nature." Early Confucian and Taoist thinkers were deeply concerned with the gap between "knowing" and "being," or between "knowing what is good" (or even "doing good") and "being good." This opposition between self-conscious knowledge and spontaneous, unself-conscious knowledge was a major concern in Chinese intellectual history. Out of it grew one Confucian version of learning in which a long process of study and self-cultivation gradually led to spontaneous performance. The most famous example was Confucius at seventy, who "followed his desires and still did not trangress" (*Analects* II.4)—the reunification of instinct and rightness.

The Ch'an Buddhist transformation of this structure of learning involved a long and rigorous discipline, terminated by a breaking point of enlightenment, a sudden rupture after which one was beyond discipline. That notion of a gap, a radical discontinuity, was a formal embodiment of the absolute discontinuity recognized between merely knowing and being. It is on this Ch'an model that Yen Yü's poetic education is founded: its end is not imitating or recovering earlier poetry, but passing through earlier poetry to an assimilated understanding of the essence of poetry.

There is a structural identity between Yen Yü's description of literary history and this traditional model of learning. Literary history is described in terms that are the reverse image of the learning process. Learning's gap between knowing and being has been transformed into a literary historical discontinuity between a self-conscious "now" of study and an unself-conscious "then," the High T'ang. Poetic history moves from the perfection of enlightened unself-consciousness to the flawed self-consciousness of later poetry; the student reverses the course, first recognizing the goal through study, assimilating it, then leaping back across the barrier of history in a moment of enlightenment. As in the *Chuang-tzu*, where the natural human is often the historically primordial human, Yen Yü would have the novice poet learn to be what poets once were long ago.

The event is "spontaneous enlightenment," *tzu-jan* wu-ju* 自然悟入. It is not an act of will, nor can it be willed: it can only be prepared for. Enlightenment means many things, but in Yen Yü's case it is primarily a unity of knowing and being; and it is a means going beyond a rhetoric of parts and stages (as in a *shih-fa**) back into unity. "Spontaneous enlightenment" is the end of a course of study, just as the single term "divinity," *ju-shen** 入神 (literally "entering the spiritual") concludes the subsequent list of enumerated rules and categories. From multiplicity and division, the later poet hopes to return to unity; from language he returns to the ineffable; from the pragmatic, magistral, and tendentious, he moves to the elusive and visionary. Yen Yü's blend of the technical and the almost mystical recalls another critical work that was troubled by literature's decline and sought to return to the greatness of ancient writers, *On the Sublime*.

II.

詩之法有五。曰體製。曰格力。曰氣象。曰興趣。曰音節。

III.

詩之品有九。曰高。曰古。曰深。曰遠。曰長。曰雄渾。曰飄逸。曰悲壯。曰淒婉。其用工有三。曰起結。曰句法。曰字眼。其大槩有二。曰優游不迫。曰沉著痛快。詩之極致有一。曰入神。詩而入神。至矣。盡矣。蔑以加矣。惟李杜得之。他人得之蓋寡也。

II. Poetry has five rules (*fa**): 1) construction of form (*t'i*-chih*); 2) force of structure (*ko*-li*); 3) atmosphere (*ch'i*-hsiang**, literally *ch'i*-image); 4) stirring and excitement (*hsing*-ch'u**); 5) tone and rhythm (*yin-chieh*).

III. Poetry has nine categories: 1) lofty; 2) ancient; 3) deep; 4) far; 5) long; 6) potent, undifferentiated; 7) drifting aloof; 8) noble grief; 9) gentle melancholy.

There are three areas that demand care: 1) the opening and closing; 2) the rules for constructing lines (*chü-fa**); 3) the "eye" of the line [a position in a line usually occupied by a verb or descriptive, which bears special stylistic force].

There are two overall situations: 1) straightforward and carefree; 2) firm, self-possessed, and at ease.

There is only one supreme accomplishment: divinity (*ju-shen**).

Where poetry has "divinity" it is perfect and has reached its limit; there is nothing to add to it. Only Li Po and Tu Fu attained this; the others achieve it only imperfectly.

Interposed between the first discursive section on the course of study in poetry and the following section building an analogy between poetry and Ch'an, we find this series of lists, characteristic of manuals of popular poetics from the T'ang on. Such lists belong to the genre known as "rules for poetry" (*shih-fa**), or "structural frames for poetry" (*shih-ko**), or "models for poetry" (*shih-shih* 詩式). In modern studies of "Ts'ang-lang's Remarks on Poetry," there is a fondness for comparing the contents of such lists, but such comparisons reveal very little. The impulse to list is itself interesting: such lists pretend to be an authoritative and comprehensive map of some aspect of literature, but in fact they are neither authoritative nor comprehensive. Yen Yü's "nine categories" is clearly an attempt to fill out the number nine; he could just as easily have given seven, twelve, or even twenty-four categories. The actual numbers are less significant than the sequence of lists, focusing down from the "nine categories" to three, two, and then one. This is a structural embodiment of moving toward what is essential—the unity that comprehends all difference.

The "five rules" are not so much "rules," *fa**, in themselves as they are a division of the poem into aspects through which *fa** can be discussed.[25] *T'i**-chih*, "construction of form," is roughly the thematic and structural formulation of a text according to generic and subgeneric norms (the subgeneric norms being roughly associated with thematic convention). To offer a Western example, a work of detective fiction has a determinate sequence of normative events and a complement of agents who are functions of those events. The emphasis in *t'i**-chih* is on the interdependency and wholeness of the work in regard to a given norm. *Ko**-li*, "force of structure," is the linear integrity of the structure; again to use the example of detective fiction, a work requires a certain complement of interrelated agents and events to be a work of detective fiction, but such completeness does not guarantee the forceful integrity of the plot; this latter aspect of structure, how the plot "moves" is *ko**-li*.

*Ch'i**-hsiang**,* "atmosphere," is an integral of quality, with reference to the whole or to some part; it is the impression that the text makes apart from the linearity of structure. In Western criticism impressionistic comments on quality are usually *ch'i**'-hsiang**:* to continue our example of detective fiction, a work may be witty and parodic, or grittily naturalistic, or somber, suggesting some submerged and pervasive evil. There is an analytic asceticism in Western literary criticism that deeply distrusts comment on *ch'i**-*

*hsiang**; yet however much scholastic criticism struggles to ignore it, the apprehension of *ch'i**-*hsiang** remains an essential part of literary reading.

*Hsing**-*ch'ü**, "stirring and excitement," is the quality of the text in reference to to the reader: it is an affective force, both animating the text and catching the reader up in relation to it. In our example of detective fiction, "suspense" would be a subcategory of *hsing**-*ch'ü**: a work may be structured for suspense (its *ko**-*li*) and have an "atmosphere" (*ch'i**-*hsiang**) conducive to suspense, but neither in itself guarantees true suspense. By catching a reader up in a living relation to the text, *hsing**-*ch'u** animates the text, makes it seem less of an artifact; thus traditional theorists often compared *hsing**-*ch'ü** to the spirit or soul.

*Yin**-*chieh*, "tone and rhythm," is the auditory aspect of a poem, combining the purely phonic (*yin**) with the rhythms of movement (*chieh*) in the grouping of syntactic units. For example, a seven-character line with a single predicate has a very different rhythm from a seven-character line made up primarily of paratactic two-character compounds. Note that in these groupings traditional criticism makes clear distinctions between the first and second "rules" and between the third and fourth "rules," as Western criticism usually would not.

The styles or manners that constitute the "nine categories" are particularly poorly conceived. Two very common stylistic categories, "lofty and ancient" (*kao-ku*, combined in Ssu-k'ung T'u's "Twenty-Four Categories of Poetry") and "deep and far" (*shen-yüan*) are divided into four separate categories. "Long" (*ch'ang*) might be understood as something like "far" or as "long-winded": alone it has no place in such a list. The final compound categories are all common ones, the sixth and seventh having been included in Ssu-k'ung T'u's "Twenty-Four Categories of Poetry."

The "three areas that demand care" are all common topics in technical criticism, whereas the "two overall situations" are modal elaborations of the common opposition between *tung* 動 and *ching* 靜, activity and quiescence. The numeration focuses down to the unitary quality of "divinity," *ju-shen**, already a common term of praise that is here raised to the highest value in poetry.[26] The perfect attainment of this highest value in poetry is limited to the two greatest poets of that brief period of poetic perfection, the High T'ang.

IV.

禪家者流乘。有小大。宗有南北。道有邪正。學者須從最上乘。具正法眼。悟第一義。若小乘禪。聲聞辟支果。皆非正也。論詩如論禪。漢魏晉與盛唐之詩。則第一義也。大曆以還之詩。則小乘禪也。已落第二義矣。晚唐之詩。則聲聞辟支果也。學漢魏晉與盛唐詩者。臨濟下也。學大曆以還之詩者。曹洞下也。大抵禪道惟在妙悟。詩道亦在妙悟。且孟襄陽學力下韓退之遠甚。而其詩獨出退之之上者。一味妙悟而已。惟悟乃為當行。乃為本色。然悟有淺深。有分限。有透徹之悟。有但得一知半解之悟。漢魏尚矣。不假悟也。謝靈運至盛唐諸公。透徹之悟也他。雖有悟者。皆非第一義也。吾評之非僭也。辯之非妄也。天下有可廢之人。無可廢之言。詩道如是也。若以為不然。則是見詩之不廣。參詩之不熟耳。試取漢魏之詩而熟參之。次取晉宋之詩而熟參之。次取南北朝之詩而熟參之。次取沈宋王楊盧駱陳拾遺之詩而熟參之。次取開元天寶諸家之詩而熟參之。次獨取李杜二公之詩而熟參之。又取大曆十才子之詩而熟參之。又取元和之詩而熟參之。又盡取晚唐諸家之詩而熟參之。又取本朝蘇黃以下諸家之詩而熟參之。其真是非自有不能隱者。儻猶於此而無見焉。則是野狐外道。蒙蔽其真識。不可救藥。終不悟也。

In the tradition of Ch'an Buddhism there are the Greater and Lesser Disciplines; there is a northern patriarchate and a southern patriarchate; there is the orthodox (cheng*) Way and a heterodox Way. The student must follow the very highest discipline, perfect the orthodox "eye of the Law" (fa*-yen) and become enlightened to the primary Truth.[27] Neither the lesser vehicle of Ch'an's enlightenment by "merely hearing the Word" nor enlightenment by "self-realization" are orthodox.

Considering poetry is just like considering Ch'an. The poetry of the Han, Wei, Tsin, and High T'ang is the "primary truth." The poetry since the Ta-li reign [766–779] is the lesser discipline of Ch'an and has fallen into the "secondary truth." The poetry of the late T'ang is enlightenment by "merely hearing the Word" or by "self-realization." To study the poetry of the Han, Wei, Tsin, and High T'ang is to be under the Lin-chi School; but to study the poetry since the Ta-li reign is to be under the Ts'ao-tung School.

Speaking generally, the Way of Ch'an is concerned only with enlightenment. The strength of Meng Hao-jan's learning is far below that of Han Yü; but the reason that his poetry stands singularly above Han Yü's is simply the fact that Meng's poetry is consistently enlightened. Enlightenment is, indeed, the necessary procedure, it is the "original color" (pen*-se*).[28]

Still, there are distinctions of depth in enlightenment: there is limited enlightenment and a fully penetrating enlightenment; there is enlightenment that achieves knowledge of only one thing and partial comprehension. The Han and Wei are superior—they did not need enlightenment. From Hsieh Ling-yün to the High T'ang masters there is fully penetrating enlightenment. Although there is some enlightenment among the others, in no case is it the "primary truth." My criticism here is not excessive, and my analysis is not in error. There are those in the world who can be disregarded as persons but whose words cannot be disregarded. Such is the Way of Poetry; and if you think it is not so, you do not have broad experience of poetry, and you have not reflected fully on poetry.

Try taking the poems of the Han and Wei and reflecting on them fully; then do the same with the poetry of the Tsin and Liu-Sung; then again with the poetry of the Northern and Southern Dynasties. Then take and do the same with Shen Ch'üan-ch'i, Sung Chih-wen, Wang Po, Yang Chiung, Lu Chao-lin, Lo Pin-wang, and Ch'en Tzu-ang [early T'ang poets]; then take the masters of the K'ai-yüan and T'ien-pao reigns; then take Li Po and Tu Fu; then take the Ten Masters of the Ta-li reign; then take the poetry of the Yüan-ho reign [the mid T'ang], then take all the masters of the late T'ang; and then take the various writers of our own dynasty from Su Shih and Huang T'ing-chien on. In doing so, it is impossible to conceal what is truly right and what is not. And if, by some chance, you still cannot see it from this, then some weird, outlandish Way has obscured your capacity for genuine judgment: there is no saving you, for you will never be enlightened.

As stated earlier, the analogy between poetry and Ch'an was already commonplace in the thirteenth century; but there was already in that tradition a certain ambiguity as to whether poetry was like Ch'an in its essence or whether the study of poetry functioned in a way similar to the discipline of Ch'an (i.e., the process that leads to enlightenment). This ambiguity is implicit in the concept of enlightenment itself, which is both a momentary event, anticipated and occurring in an unenlightened world, and also a condition that subsists without reference to the unenlightened world. As Yen Yü amplifies the analogy, the contradictions between the condition and the event, with its preliminary discipline, become apparent. There is no question that Yen Yü's initial point is that both the discipline of Ch'an training and the study of poetry are concerned with a moment of enlightenment, when discipline is transcended, when knowing and being are a unity. A question does remain, however, regarding the condition of enlightenment attained—whether poetic enlightenment is like or is the same as Ch'an enlightenment.

It has been properly pointed out by Richard Lynn that the Ch'an analogy is precisely an analogy rather than a statement of identity.[29] However, the analogy is concerned with the means, the discipline, and leaves unresolved the question as to whether the ends to which those means work are or are not identical. The question is simply, can there be two distinct conditions of enlightenment, a poetic enlightenment and a Ch'an enlightenment? A distinction in means might be quite proper in an unenlightened world of difference, but from a Ch'an point of view a distinct "poetic enlightenment" would be absurd, except as referring to a distinct sphere of activity in which the unitary condition of enlightenment might manifest itself to the unenlightened.

We may therefore distinguish three possible levels on which Yen Yü might be asserting the relation between poetry and Ch'an. On the lowest level, he might be restricting himself purely to procedures: both Ch'an discipline and the study of poetry work towards a moment when each, in its own way, achieves a level of intuitive, prereflective understanding. Yen Yü's comment that the poets of the Han and Wei "did not need enlightenment" supports the procedural interpretation. Since these poets were unself-conscious (like Schiller's "naive" poets they "were" nature), they were spared the process of a pre-enlightenment discipline that leads to enlightenment.[30]

The second level builds on the procedural analogy but goes further. This level would be an analogy between the condition of Ch'an enlightenment and poetic "enlightenment" (enlightenment placed in quotation marks because it is not really enlightenment in the religious sense, but some unique state that can only be described through the simile of Ch'an enlightenment). In this case the scene presented by an "enlightened" poet would have a quality of elusive and prereflective "rightness" to it, as one presumably would understand the world following Buddhist enlightenment.

On the third level, Yen Yü would be asserting an essential identity between the condition of poetic enlightenment and Ch'an enlightenment: there is only one condition of enlightenment, which may be attained through poetry and is manifest in it. The disciplines are similar, and the end is the same. Although Chinese critics have often pointed out the incompatibility between Ch'an wordlessness and the poet's world of words, for Yen Yü the essential quality of poetry was precisely what lay "beyond the words." The choice of Meng Hao-jan as the enlightened poet, as a contrast to the learnéd poetry of Han Yü, strongly suggests that Yen Yü intended a more basic connection between poetry and Ch'an than simply the procedures of attaining enlightenment (a contrast between Li Po and Han Yü would have been very different). But it is uncertain whether he intended the conditions of poetic and Ch'an enlightenment to be identical or merely analogical.

The core of the Ch'an analogy—that poetic enlightenment is in some degree or way "like" Ch'an enlightenment—may be ambiguous, but it does have some content, however minimal. Yen Yü takes the received analogy ("poetry is like Ch'an") and amplifies it to find new points of correspondence, extending it into partisan sectarian lore. If attaining poetic enlightenment is in some way like Ch'an enlightenment, then the ways of studying poetry must in some way be like the hierarchical array of Ch'an sects.

We might well wonder why Yen Yü could not just as easily have built this part of his analogy on cooking—major and minor traditions, a northern and southern school, one who wants to cook well should study the "best" way, and so on. At this level, he is simply decorating the claim that poetry is one of those disciplines whose various schools show a (presumably) self-evident hierarchy of value. Nevertheless, we might consider why the choice of the Ch'an sectarian analogy is unwittingly apt. In both Ch'an Buddhism and Yen Yü's poetics, there is a profound contradiction between competing means or "ways" and the unitary end, beyond all means, to which they all promise access. Trapped between contentious multiplicity and unity, the assertion of one orthodox way is the representation of unity and truth within a world of choice and division.

From the point of view of critical voice, the most interesting aspect of the passage is its petulance, which leads to a strident tirade. He anticipates being attacked for what he is saying (and despite the fact that there were those in the thirteenth century who admired the poetry of the mid and late T'ang, the supremacy of the High T'ang was already so generally conceded that violent disagreement would have been highly unlikely); Yen Yü even anticipates being dismissed as a person of no importance. He counters his imaginary detractors with a paraphrase of *Analects* XV.22: "He said. 'The best do not advance another merely on account of what he says, nor do they disregard what he says merely on account of the person.'" Yen Yü can almost sense the sneers of his readers.

Under the threat of being disbelieved and the threat of personal attack, Yen Yü changes his poetic curriculum: again he tells us to read the history of Chinese poetry, but our putative lack of faith in him has made us no longer worthy of his magistral solicitude to protect us from the infection of inferior poetry. Now he tells us to continue reading, on after the High T'ang. If we do so, he tells us, the decline of poetry will be self-evident. Previously, judgment had meant to know only the good; now judgment means to know both the good and the bad by their self-evident differences.

But suppose, after following this course of reading, it is *not* self-evident to us: the very possibility infuriates him, and he concludes the section with a stridency rare in Chinese writing—if you don't believe me, you are a hopeless fool. The mannered magistral tone of the opening gives way to a shouting demand that he be granted authority; disagreement must be punished with humiliation. Yen Yü is often spoken of as the parent of poetic orthodoxy. There *had* been a quiet orthodoxy of consensus long before him; his is the voice of a new and unpleasant form of orthodoxy, uncertain of itself and demanding absolute conformity, an orthodoxy in which unbelievers are threatened with punishments of scorn and insults. And strangely, this intensely personal relation that he would establish with us—master and unswervingly obedient disciples—is counterbalanced by an elusively impersonal notion of the nature of poetic vision.[31]

V.

夫詩有別材。非關書也。詩有別趣。非關理也。然非多讀書。多窮理。則不能極其至。所謂不涉理路。不落言筌者。上也。詩者。吟詠情性也。盛唐諸人惟在興趣。羚羊掛角。無跡可求。故其妙處透徹玲瓏。不可湊泊。如空中之音。相中之色。水中之月。鏡中之象。言有盡而意無窮。近代諸公乃作奇特解會。遂以文字為詩。以才學為詩。以議論為詩。夫豈不工。終非古人之詩也。蓋於一唱三歎之音。有所歉焉。且其作多務使事。不問興致。用字必有來歷。押韻必有出處。讀之反覆終篇。不知着到何。在其末流甚者。叫噪怒張。殊乖忠厚之風。殆以罵詈為詩。詩而至此。可謂一厄也。然則近代之詩無取乎。曰有之。吾取其合於古人者而已。國初之詩尚沿襲唐人。王黃州學白樂。天楊文公劉中山學李商隱。盛文肅學韋蘇州。歐陽公學韓退之古詩。梅聖俞學唐人平澹處。至東坡山谷始自出己意以為詩。唐人之風變矣。山谷用工尤為深刻。其後法席盛行。海內稱江西宗派。近世趙紫芝翁靈舒輩。獨喜賈島姚合之詩。稍稍復就清苦之風。江湖詩人多效其體。一時自謂之唐宗。不知止入聲聞辟支之果。豈盛唐諸公大乘正法眼者哉。嗟乎。正法眼之無傳久矣。

唐詩之說未唱。唐詩之道或有時而明也。今既唱其體曰唐詩矣。則學者謂唐詩誠止於是耳。得非詩道之重不幸邪。故予不自量度。輒定詩之宗旨。且借禪以為喻。推原漢魏以來。而截然謂當以盛唐為法。雖獲罪於世之君子。不辭也。

Poetry involves a distinct material (ts'ai*) that has nothing to do with books. Poetry involves a distinct interest (ch'ü) that has nothing to do with natural principle (li*). Still, if you don't read extensively and learn all there is to know about natural principle, you can't reach the highest level. But the very best involves what is known as "not getting onto the road of natural principle" and "not falling into the trap of words."[32]

Poetry is "to sing what is in the heart."[33] In the stirring and excitement (hsing*-ch'ü*) of their poetry, the High T'ang writers were those antelopes that hang by their horns, leaving no tracks to be followed. Where they are subtle (miao*), there is a limpid and sparkling quality that can never be quite fixed and determined—like tones in the empty air, or color in a face, or moonlight in the water, or an image (hsiang*) in a mirror—the words are exhausted, but the meaning is never exhausted.

The writers of recent times show a forced cleverness in their understanding; they make poetry out of mere writing, they make poetry out of mere learning, they make poetry out of discursive argument. Of course, such poetry is good in the sense of being well-wrought, but it is not the poetry of the older writers. It may well be that there is something lacking in the tones (yin) of their work, that quality which, "when one person sings, three join in harmony."[34] In their writing, they often feel obliged to make references (shih*) with no regard to stirring and excitement (hsing*-ch'ü*); they feel that whatever words they use must have a tradition of previous usage and that the rhymes they choose must have a source in some earlier text. When you read such poems and reflect on them as a whole, you have no idea what they are getting at. The last and least of such poets rant and rave extravagantly, completely at odds with the poetic tradition (feng*) of courtesy and generosity, even to the point where they make poetry out of snarling insults. When poetry reaches this level, we may consider it to be in grave danger. If this is true, should we then learn nothing from recent poetry? No, there are things worth learning, but only those things which coincide with the older writers.

The poets at the beginning of our dynasty still followed in the footsteps of the T'ang writers: Wang Yü-ch'eng learned from the poetry of Po Chü-yi; Yang Yi and Liu Yün learned from Li Shang-yin, Sheng Tu learned from Wei Ying-wu; Ou-yang Hsiu learned from the old-style poetry of Han Yü; Mei Yao-ch'en learned from the moments of serene limpidity (p'ing-tan) in the T'ang writers.[35]

When we come to Su Shih and Huang T'ing-chien, we begin to have poets who first form their own conceptions (yi*) and then make a poem out of them. At this point the influence (*feng**) of the T'ang writers underwent a mutation (*pien**). By dint of great efforts, Huang T'ing-chien achieved some really striking effects, so that afterwards his evangelical methods drew a spate of followers, who were called by everyone in the world the "Chiang-hsi School." In more recent times writers such as Chao Shih-hsiu and Weng Chüan have found unique enjoyment in the poetry of Chia Tao and Yao Ho, and to a certain extent brought back the "clear and bitter" manner (*feng**) practiced by some T'ang writers. Poets of the Chiang-hu School generally imitate this form, and these days they call themselves the "T'ang tradition"! They don't realize that they are doing nothing more than tasting the fruits of "merely hearing the word" and "self-realization"—it is certainly not the "greater discipline," the orthodox "eye of the law" of the High T'ang masters.

For a long time now the orthodox "eye of the law" has not been transmitted. Though the true explanation of T'ang poetry has not been proclaimed, it may be that someday the Way of T'ang poetry will become manifest. Since they [the Chiang-hu School] now proclaim their version of T'ang poetry as [the true] T'ang poetry, those who study poetry may think that T'ang poetry goes no farther than this. For this reason, I have not been deterred by my own [limited] capacity and have hastily set out the true values of poetry; moreover, I have used Ch'an as an illustration, tracing the origins of poetry back to the Han and Wei and claiming decisively that one should take the High T'ang as one's rule (*fa**). Even though I may be blamed by the gentlemen of this age, I retract nothing.

The opening passages of this section are very famous, often quoted and commented on. And these opening passages indeed raise many questions. First, do the two beginning sentences mean that *part of* what is essential to poetry has nothing to do with books and natural principle? Or is this a more radical statement, that the essential stuff and excitement of poetry is *entirely* distinct from learning and reflective thought (the *yu* 有 is ambiguous and can be construed either way). In the first case, we might translate: "In poetry there is a distinct material . . . "; in the second case: "Poetry has its own distinct material . . ." The translation above attempts to' leave these important alternatives in suspension. Clearly Yen Yü considers this "distinct material" to be the most important thing in poetry, what is essentially "poetic."

A second question is the precise reference of *ts'ai**, translated as "material." *Ts'ai** is the innate "stuff" of something in regard to its capacity for use or being put into practice. When written as 才, *ts'ai** is often applied in reference to human beings and means something like "talent," an innate capacity for accomplishment; when written 材, *ts'ai* is the useful "material" of objects. However, the two graphs are frequently exchanged, being essentially the same word. *Ts'ai** had previously been used mainly (though not exclusively) in a quantitative sense: one spoke of it in terms of "how much" there was.

Ts'ai as "talent" had often been associated with a store of learning, which was the "material" used in composition (in the Western tradition we should not forget the parable of the "talents" in Matthew 25:14–30, by which a degree of monetary endowment became a permanent figure for spiritual endowment).[36] If one has much, one can spend much; and in popular usage *ts'ai** was often associated with the capacity to write readily and voluminously. In English usage poetic "talent" is an abstract ability, but *ts'ai** was never entirely dissociated from the "material" (whether learning or something else) that the poet had in his mind and was able to use in making a poem (cf. the discussion of the use of "material" in Yeh Hsieh's metaphor of building a house, pp. 562–568).

By using the phrase "a distinct *ts'ai**," Yen Yü transforms this primarily quantitative term into a primarily qualitative term; and by dissociating it from learning, he destroys the easy identification between "talent" as pure capacity and a capital of poetic "material." Most commentators and translators take *ts'ai** as talent ("poetry involves a distinct talent . . ."), and "talent" is certainly implicit in the passage. However, I have here rendered it "material" because, even though it was in the poet, here it is primarily something perceived in the poem (as *ch'ü**, "interest" or "*élan*", is present in both but perceived primarily in the poem). What is at issue here is not so much the enabling capacity ("talent") but the visionary percepts that become true poetry's "material."

An interesting event occurred in regard to Yen Yü's statement about "books," *shu*. In his commentary Kuo Shao-yü gives a long discussion of the common misquotation of this line as "has nothing to do with learning" (reading *hsüeh* 學 instead of *shu* 書). Not only does this substitution indicate how the line was understood; it is a rhetorical radicalization of Yen Yü's statement, adding the thrill of heresy in directly dismissing the sacrosanct concept of *hsüeh*, "learning." It would be attractive and fully consonant with the stress on the "poetic" as lying "beyond the words," to read *shu* as "what is written," leading to the translation: "has nothing to do with what is written in the text." But Yen Yü's clear use of "learning," *hsüeh*, in the amplification of this opening forbids such a reading. We must understand *shu*, "books," as referring to earlier literature.

A survey of the numerous comments on these opening passages reveals how profoundly later readers were disturbed by what Yen Yü had said here. Some agreed with him enthusiastically; others bitterly attacked him; but no one could take these propositions entirely for granted. We might well have expected the responses to be strong: Yen Yü is claiming autonomy, not simply for the history of poetry, but for what is essentially "poetic" in any particular poem. The "talent" that was manifest in the truly poetic "material" of a poem was not simply manifesting the natural principle (*li**) of the world, nor was that genuine poetic "material" defined by its participation in a poetic tradition, however autonomous from general history.[37] Such a claim for something uniquely poetic ran counter to the entire tradition of Chinese literary thought. And if Yen Yü was often brash and polemical, in this respect at least we must concede the necessity of such a stance in order to make his claim heard.

During the Sung, major changes had taken place both in the conception of *li*** and in the role of literary learning. A degree of dissatisfaction with these transformations made it possible for at least some readers to welcome Yen Yü's heretical declarations (a welcome that would have been much less likely in an earlier era). Prior to the Sung *li*** simply meant "how the world works": to dissociate poetry from *li*** would have been to deny its truth, its basis in the natural and human universe.[38] Without considering the complex changes in the interpretation of *li*** in the Sung (changes that are irrelevant to Yen Yü's position here), it can be said that by Yen Yü's time *li*** had acquired strong associations of theoretical philosophical speculation, with close ties to those discursive aspects of Sung poetry to which he strongly objected. Unable to dissociate the older notion of "the way the world works" from acts of discursive interpretation within the poem, Yen Yü rejected altogether the essentiality of *li*** to poetry. Whereas the High T'ang poet might have understood his own poem as the perfect embodiment of "how it was then" (the older notion of *li***), Yen Yü would have found in the same poem some luminous quality of the "poetic," entirely distinct from *li***, both in the older sense and in the Sung sense.

In the separation of *li*** from poetry, the category *ch'ü***, "interest," is carefully chosen. Of all the non-formal aspects of poetry, *ch'ü*** is the one most easily dissociated from *li***. Yen Yü reminds us that what is offered in the best poetry is not understanding but engagement, a peculiar excitement in art that is *sui generis*.[39]

Yen Yü's dissociation of the quintessentially "poetic" from a basis in the poetic tradition is at once both more complicated than and inseparable from the commonplace notion of "the study of poetry," *hsüieh-shih*, as it was conceived in his time. In the T'ang, a young person read poetry, perhaps studied some technical prescriptions, and then wrote poems. No T'ang poet would have conceived of poetry apart from learning and reading earlier poems: the necessary relation between reading and composition was unproblematic and self-evident. But by the thirteenth century, the "study of poetry" had become an intense, formalized, and self-conscious program, one that would have been altogether alien to the T'ang experience.

By the thirteenth century, traditions of informal critical discourse on poetry (as embodied in the *shih-hua*, the "remarks on poetry") and a growing commentary tradition had contributed to a situation in which the first thing any educated reader would notice in a poem would be its literary sources and its intertextual play with earlier poetry. In this regard, commentaries to "Ts'ang-lang's Remarks on Poetry" inevitably mention the powerful Chiang-hsi school of poetry, which made intertextual play one of its main tenets.

Although the Chiang-hsi school's cult of sources was certainly a primary object of Yen Yü's attack here, the obsession with intertextuality was a universal phenomenon in poetic circles of the twelfth and thirteenth centuries.

In his own program for the "study of poetry," Yen Yü cannot entirely abandon Sung bookishness; but he transforms it, intensifies it, and then transcends it. For him, earlier poetry and its books are both loved and resented, necessary and unnecessary. Yen Yü's student is to begin with an intensive course of reading (and in contrast to the Chiang-hsi school's ahistorical sense of the poetic past, Yen Yü's is a historical course of reading); but this is a course of study that is ultimately supposed to take the student beyond study—the moment of enlightenment in which the possibility of true poetry first appears. As was the case with li*, Yen Yü's dissociation of the essence of poetry from intertextuality may have been occasioned by a rejection of the Sung transformation of the "study of poetry"; but he articulated the separation in a radical way.

No sooner had Yen Yü made these two radical pronouncements than he backed off and qualified their heretical implications: of course one must understand li* thoroughly; of course one must read widely. Even as he acknowledges the importance of li* and the poetic tradition, we know that he means to say: "They are necessary for writing a poem, but they have nothing to do with what is 'poetic' in the poem." Yen Yü's audience understood what he meant quite clearly: the radical opening comments were remembered and repeatedly cited, not his reasonable retreat from heresy (except by those defenders who wanted to show that Yen was really more moderate that he seemed). It was for the heresy that he was attacked, and it was for the heresy that he was praised: he had raised something like the possibility of "pure poetry" in his work. In the context of the tradition of literary thought, such a possibility was truly heretical, and Yen Yü ostentatiously wrapped himself in the mantle of cheng*, "orthodoxy."

As Yen Yü drew back from his heterodox position, again making a place for poetic learning and understanding li*, he tried to reestablish the canonical authority of his position by quoting a commonplace from the "Great Preface": "Poetry is to sing what is in the heart." Though later critics always remember that Yen Yü cited this, it was not what he meant at all—it is an evasion, a hiding of his tracks.[40] Nowhere else in this chapter does he speak of anything remotely associated with "singing what is in the heart," the ch'ing*-hsing* ("affections and nature") of poets. Rather, he is interested in an elusive poetic beauty that is experienced in reading poems and the way that beauty is achieved. This rare moment is radically distinct from the universal and eternal ground of poetry described in the "Great Preface."

Yen Yü then gives us the famous and striking image of the antelope, hanging by its horns in a tree to escape discovery by hiding its tracks. In his commentary to "Ts'ang-lang's Remarks on Poetry," Kuo Shao-yü cites several passages in the Ch'an Ch'uan-teng lu to show the Ch'an use of the image. It is certainly such Ch'an usage of the image that Yen Yü has in mind; but one cannot help noticing how utterly inappropriate the image is at this point, and how, with its Ch'an overtones, it cannot be easily reconciled with the preceding reference to the phrase from the "Great Preface," "singing what is in the heart." It *should* be assimilated to the critical cliché of the "absence of traces": no obvious marks of conscious crafting. But the image of the antelope is one of concealment, of desiring not to be found: what is hidden is the creature, or in the analogy, the poet with his living circumstances and concerns—precisely the contents of the "heart" (ch'ing*-hsing*) that he is supposed to be singing. Ch'an and Yen Yü seek an ineffable presence of truth; recognition of such a truth may admit varying degrees of perfection (anything short of perfection being a mediation that shows "traces"), but the truth itself does not admit particularity and individuation. This is quite the opposite of the traditional concept of poetry, "singing what is in the heart," which is inseparable from the individuality of the poet and the particularity of the poet's circumstances. We have here two sets of values that lead readers in opposite directions.

The images that follow make clear what really interests Yen Yü: each image—"tones in the empty air, color in a face, moonlight in the water, an image in a mirror"—is something intangible, something that eludes definition. Yen Yü is searching for something like the pure and elusive "poetic image"; it is not something that forcefully transmits human thought and feeling, but something indefinite and always just out of reach. As in Western traditions of reflection on the sublime and the beautiful, the focus here is entirely on a quality of the reader's experience: productive poetics is reduced to the question of how to produce such an effect. But the quality of the experience which concerns Yen Yü differs sharply from both the sublime and the beautiful. The sublime involves some index of the transcendent; the beautiful is bound up with the experience of definite form. The experience that lures Yen Yü is rather one of elusive presences, *miao**, the "wondrously subtle." The famous string of metaphors for this quality follow in the tradition of Tai Shu-lun's description of the poetic scene, "you can gaze on it but you cannot fix it in your eyes" (see p. 357).

There is some ground—empty space, face, water, mirror (loosely corresponding to the verbal text of the poem)—but that ground is not the poetry itself. True poetry is an elusive presence that hovers tenuously in or on that ground. The ground, the words of the poem or the definite scene represented, is necessary; but it is not the poetry any more than the mirror is the reflection. One thing, the verbal poem, is finite; it can be grasped and it ends. The other thing, the poetry, eludes the finite.[41]

After giving a glimpse of the ultimate in poetry, Yen Yü engages in the most virulent attack on Sung poetry that had yet appeared. Indeed, it was so virulent and (*if* one accepts Yen Yü's values) so true, that it was largely responsible for killing the taste for Sung poetry for almost four centuries. There is some irony in the fact that Sung poetry was despised on account of values that are deeply rooted in Sung literary thought, culminating in this mortal blow that was delivered itself in the Sung.

The nature of Yen Yü's charges reinforces his theoretical point: Sung writers take something that is not poetry and try to make poetry out of it. The assumption is that there is something quintessentially proper to poetry: "the poetic." Anything that is not "the poetic" is alien to poetry. The tradition of poetic values that followed from the "Great Preface" had sufficient latitude to embrace the full range of changes in Chinese poetic history, including Sung poetry; Yen Yü's poetics did not. Despite his citation of the "Great Preface," Yen Yü did not accept that poetry is "what is in the heart," *ch'ing*-hsing**, "affections and nature." Such a formulation made poetry the mere medium for the appearance of something that existed independent of poetry. From Yen Yü's point of view, the witty, discursive manner of Su Shih's poetry was simply not "poetic." Yet that manner was precisely Su's *ch'ing*-hsing**, and for Su to "make poetry out of discursive argument" was indeed "singing what was in his heart": it was that which made Su Shih's poetry great and much loved. Yen Yü proposed new values: though Su Shih's poetry might be authentic, it was not poetic.

CHAPTER 3
The Rules of Poetry

I.

學詩先除五俗。一曰俗體。二曰俗意。三曰俗句。四曰俗字。五曰俗韻。

In the study of poetry you must first eliminate five kinds of uncouthness (*su*): 1) uncouth form (*t'i**), 2) uncouth concepts (*yi**), 3) uncouth lines (*chü**), 4) uncouth words, 5) uncouth rhymes.

It is a common error to believe that during the T'ang the language of poetry was close to the spoken language; it is true, however, that in the Sung there was a far greater tension between the classical and vernacular styles. There are various reasons for this: first, the development of a semi-vernacular written language used by literary men (which characterizes parts of "Ts'ang-lang's Remarks on Poetry" itself); second, changes in literary pedagogy involving the widespread use of books; third, the prevalent influence of mixed poetic styles, particularly those of Huang T'ing-chien and later of Yang Wan-li, which use sharply marked differences, by alternation, between the "high" or "poetic" and the "low" or "vernacular" (*su*, translated above as "uncouth").

Yen Yü's initial move to eliminate what is *su* is the way in which writing must be learned by any group that is linguistically displaced by history or locale from what is conceived as a norm of writing. This is no less true of the way in which American students learn written English. The teaching process depends largely on continually correcting solecisms and "vernacular" expressions. Teaching composition in such a historical situation inevitably becomes a negative pedagogy, a process of censure that inculcates discomfort with whatever comes easily but is recognized as *su*.[42]

The five categories of potential uncouthness are simply a way of saying "avoid the uncouth in all aspects of poetry." It is unclear exactly how Yen Yü conceived the problems in these categories—if, as seems unlikely, he gave the matter any thought at all. "Uncouth form" may mean that certain subgenres were inherently "uncouth" and thus should be avoided; it may mean that a poet should avoid emulating certain poets, such as Huang T'ing-chien (who himself inveighed against "uncouthness"); it may be that certain ways of structuring a poem would be considered "uncouth." Are "uncouth rhymes" Hudibrastic rhymes or clichéd rhymes ("moon" "June," the Chinese equivalent being *jen*, "person," and *ch'un*, "spring"), or are they rhymes that would have been perfect rhymes in the Sung but imperfect and not allowed in the T'ang (though earlier Yen Yü objects to those who insist on having T'ang sources for every rhyme)? The generality of Yen Yü's cautions allows the serious student of poetry to be anxious about slipping into *su* in any part of the poem.

II.

有語忌。有語病。語病易除。語忌難除。語病古人亦有之。惟語忌則不可有。

Poetry has offenses in language and errors in language. Errors in language are easy to eliminate, but offenses in language are very difficult to eliminate. Even the ancients made errors in language, but offenses in language they would not allow.

It is not at all clear exactly what constitutes an error, *ping*, and what constitutes an "offense," *chi*. Technical faults were usually called "errors," while "offenses" is a term often used to describe some lapse into "uncouthness," *su*. The force of the passage would seem to be that there are potential failings far worse than formal incorrectness.

III.

須是本色。須是當行。

It must be the original color; it must show expertise.

Both *pen**-*se**, "original color," and *tang-hsing*, "expertise," were established parts of the jargon of thirteenth-century poetics. "Original color" was the older term, originating in the metaphor of the literary work as a fabric. "Expertise" was applied almost exclusively to the question of generic specialty—work in prose, poetry, or song lyric (*tz'u*). In different ways, both terms point to the notion that each form of literature has qualities that are "proper" to it; those qualities are also what are seen as historically its "original" qualities. Success in a given genre means the mastery of such qualities, which is the work of an "expert" who has read and reflected upon the history of a genre.

IV.

對句好可得。結句好難得。發句好尤難得。

Its easy to get good parallel couplets [in a regulated verse], but hard to get a good closing couplet. But a good opening couplet is the hardest of all.

V.

發端忌作舉止。收拾貴在出場。

It is an offense to overdo it in the opening; at the conclusion, it is important to leave space for the exit.

Kuo Shao-yü cites Sung precedents for this use of what appears to be the metaphor of a Sung variety play (*tsa-chü* 雜劇) to describe the movement of a poem. The precise meaning of *chü- chih*, translated as "overdo it," is uncertain: its usual meaning is simply "behavior" or "action"; but in the context of the dramatic metaphor, it suggests the stylized motions that were part of the semiotic repertoire of Chinese theater. Here Yen Yü seems to be advising a leisurely opening, without rushing into the matter of the poem. The second clause admonishes against abrupt closure; one must leave a space for suggestiveness at the end.

VI.

不必太著題。不必多使事。

One need not stick to the topic too closely. One need not use many references (*shih**).

T'i, translated as "topic," is also the title of the poem. Adhering too strictly to the title will make the poem seem like an exercise, the kind of rhetorical amplification of the components of a title by which a student learns to write; a certain liberty of association gives a sense of individuality and authenticity. Kuo Shao-yü cites a passage from Chu Hsi's "Sayings" (*Yü-lei* 語類): "When older writers composed a poem, they didn't stick to the topic one hundred percent and it turned out fine; nowadays when people compose a poem, the more they stick closely to the topic, the worse it is." The avoidance of references was, ironically, a prescription for one kind of mid- and late-T'ang pentasyllabic regulated verse, a style much imitated in Yen Yü's day and to which he objected strongly.

VII.

押韻不必有出處。用字不必拘來歷。

One need not have textual sources for the rhymes one uses. One need not be confined to particular precedents in using words.

As Kuo Shao-yü indicates, this injunction can be traced directly back to a commonplace first articulated by Huang T'ing-chien, that in Tu Fu's poetry and in Han Yü's prose every word had a textual antecedent. This commonplace was closely linked to a style of commentary on literature, growing in the Southern Sung and ultimately derived from Li Shan's commentary to the *Wen hsüan*, which confined itself largely to citation of the sources used for the phrases in a line. In Sung poetry, this close attention to precedent usages (and precedents in rhymes—only T'ang and pre-T'ang precedents were acceptable) was closely associated with the Chiang-hsi school of poetry. We might note that by not confining himself to usages and rhymes with precedents, the poet was immediately in greater danger of lapsing into *su*, "uncouthness."

VIII.

下字貴響。造語貴圓。

Euphony is important in the choice of words; "roundness" is important in diction.

Chinese discourse on literature was, at this stage, blessed not to distinguish perfectly between the semantic aspect of language and the purely formal (phonic, syntactic—though exceptions exist in rhyme and tonal balance).

Thus a category such as "resonance," *hsiang*, translated as "euphony," combines the phonic with the semantic to produce an all-around sense of "harmony": it "sounds good." Ever since sound and sense were put asunder in Western literary thought, wise critics have been trying to reunite them; but the assumption persists that there is a purely phonic level of poetry. One can easily imagine an analysis of an English poem in which the word "dung" is phonically attractive, but remains semantically jarring; such a word would not be *hsiang*, "resonant." "Roundness," *yüan*, suggesting "perfection," is a quality of stylistic smoothness and polish: Valéry is "round"; Donne is distinctly "not round."

IX.

意貴透徹。不可隔靴搔痒。語貴脫洒。不可拖泥帶水。

In concept (*yi**) value the pellucid—you can't scratch what itches through boots. In diction (*yü*), value the brisk and aloof—don't drag it through water and mud.

One of the attractions of "Ts'ang-lang's Remarks on Poetry" is the occasional flash of a homey and down-to-earth image, often deriving, as here, from a Ch'an saying. The first sentence is directed against obscurity and excessive ornamentation: there is a dimension of "classicism" in Yen Yü, though it is expressed more with the roughness of Ben Jonson than the polish of Corneille.

X.

最忌骨董。最忌趁貼。

The greatest offense of all is to be arcane; the greatest offense of all is preciousness.

XI.

語忌直。意忌淺。脉忌露。味忌短。音韻忌散緩。亦忌迫促。

Directness is an offense in diction (*yü*). Shallowness is an offense in concept (*yi**). It is an offense to leave the veins of a poem exposed. Shortness is an offense in flavor. Languor is an offense in tone and rhyme (*yin-yün*); here, a nervous haste is also an offense.

Although concept should be "pellucid," the diction should not be too direct. Indirection was also part of roughly contemporary injunctions in the diction of song lyric (*tz'u*) (as in the contemporary manual of song lyric, the *Yüeh-fu chih-mi* 樂府指迷). The "veins" of a poem are what carry the *ch'i**, and they should be infused with the whole, not exposed on the surface. Exposing the "veins" is what one finds in a novice's essay: "having treated X, I will now go on to Y."

XII.

詩難處在結裹。譬如番刀。須用北人結裹。若南人便非本色。

The hardest thing in poetry is the successful tempering. Take a Manchurian knife as an example: it must be a northerner who tempers; if it's a southerner, it is not the "original color" (*pen**-se**).

XIII.

須參活句。勿參死句。

One must practice vital lines (*huo-chü*), not dead lines (*ssu-chü**).

"Vital lines" and "dead lines" were originally Ch'an Buddhist terms which were commonly applied to poetry in the Southern Sung. The antithesis quickly outgrew its Ch'an origins and developed into a linguistic and literary interest in "vital word" (*huo-tzu* 活字) versus "dead words" (*ssu-tzu* 死字), "vital method" (*huo-fa** 活法) versus "dead method" (*ssu-fa** 死法).[43] Here Yen Yü is clearly harking back to the Ch'an provenance of these categories, "vital" and "dead"; but he cannot block out the rich associations the categories had acquired in literary discourse. Most discussions of them treat them as if they could be defined; in fact, they are essentially categories of affect, and the various attempts to explain them do nothing more than identify various means to achieve a certain affect. In Ch'an, it may be the living discourse of the master as opposed to the "dead letter" of scripture. In poetry, it consists of various techniques to convey vitality, such as humor, the use of particles to suggest spoken discourse, and images drawn from everyday life. Unfortunately these techniques and the Sung poets most strongly associated with the "vital method" were both objects of Yen Yü's disapproval.

XIV.

詞氣可頡頏。不可乖戾。

In phrasing (*tz'u**), *ch'i** can have vigorous flexibility, but [it should] not [reach the extreme of] arrogant and swaggering willfulness.

Chieh-hang ("vigorous flexibility") and *kuai-li* ("arrogant and swaggering willfulness") are compounds describing manner, put together to form a progression from a positive quality to its negative extreme.

XV.

律詩難於古詩。絕句難於八句。七言律詩難於五言律詩。五言絕句難於七言絕句。

Regulated verse is more difficult than old-style verse. Quatrains are more difficult than octaves [i.e., eight-line regulated verse]. Heptasyllabic regulated verse is more difficult than pentasyllabic. Pentasyllabic line quatrains are more difficult than quatrains in heptasyllabic lines.

Such magistral comparisons and relative judgments, strung together to create hierarchies, were the very stuff of poetic pedagogy.

XVI.

學詩有三節。其初不識好惡。連篇累牘。肆筆而成。既識羞愧。始生畏縮。成之極難。及其透徹。則七縱八橫。信手拈來。頭頭是道矣。

Studying poetry has three stages. At first one doesn't recognize what's good and bad: one lets the brush go, filling up whole stacks of paper. Once the capacity of recognizing quality is attained, one becomes embarrassed and, for the first time, draws back in anxiety: at this stage it's really hard to finish anything. At last when everything becomes pellucid, one acts with bold independence, trusting to whatever the hand touches, and yet follows the Way [of poetry] every time.

More than any other passage in "Ts'ang-lang's Remarks on Poetry," this entry embodies the late-classical poetic education, reconciling self-consciousness and unself-consciousness in a concept of "second nature." First, there is a stage of spontaneity with no regard to standards of judgment. The embarrassment that follows from learning standards represents the capacity to see oneself from the outside, to judge self as other, to recognize self as "limited." At this moment the self contracts in anxiety, no longer willing to let itself be seen lest it be judged and found wanting. It is in this period that the "study of poetry" really occurs: norms are practiced and assimilated until there occurs the leap of enlightenment, when standards that were previously external to the self become "second nature."

XVII.

看詩須着金剛眼睛。庶不眩于旁門小法。

In observing a poem, one must fix upon it "metal-hard eyes," so that you may not be dazzled by secondary sects and lesser rules.

Yen Yü offers his own note that "metal-hard eyes" come from Ch'an discourse. "Metal-hard eyes" are like "eyes of the law," a dispassionate discernment in which the true nature of things becomes apparent.

XVIII.

辯家數如辯蒼白。方可言詩。

When one can distinguish the masters in the same way that one can distinguish grey from white, then one can speak of poetry.

This passage is more effective when one realizes that "white," *pai*, is also the "silvery" quality of polished metal. A note here, probably by Yen Yü himself, gives a judgment attributed to Wang An-shih: when Wang criticized literary works, he considered formal construction (*t'i**-*chih* 體製) first, and only then did he decide whether the poem was successful or clumsy. This note seems to qualify the point of the entry: that formal correctness is a judgment that should be made prior to the finer discrimination between the shining and the dull.

XIX.

詩之是非不之爭。試以己詩置之古人詩中。與識者觀之而不能辨。則真古人矣。

One need not engage in disputes about what is right and wrong in poetry. Just place your poems among the poems of the older writers. If someone with a capacity for judgment can't tell the difference, then you yourself are a genuine "older writer."

Yen Yü's project of eternal poetic norms, erected against the acceptance of historicity in Confucian poetics from the "Great Preface" on, proved immensely alluring; but it was a project doomed to failure. In this passage, as earlier, Yen Yü, appeals to what seems self-evident in the reading process. It eventually became obvious, however, that while contemporary readers might not be able to distinguish a new poem from a poem by older writers, later readers *would* be able to make such a distinction all too easily: a Ming reader could see clearly the difference between a genuine High T'ang poem and a Sung poem trying to use High T'ang standards; at the same time, the Ming poet felt that his own "High T'ang" poem effaced its historicity. However, the Ch'ing reader would later perceive clearly the difference between an authentic High T'ang poem and a Ming attempt to keep to the High T'ang norm.

Yen Yü hoped for a poetic language that would remain in an eternal springtime, when the works of the modern poet would be confused with works of the old poets, when there would be poetry without the history of poetry. He also knew that spring had not yet come and that the language of all existing poetry was marked by historical change. The very next passage in "Ts'ang-lang's Remarks on Poetry," the first of the subsequent chapter of "Critical Comments on Poetry," begins in counterpoint to the passage above.

大曆以前。分明別是一副言語。晚唐。分明別是一副言語。本朝諸公分明別是一副言語。如此見。方許具一集眼。

Before the Ta-li reign [i.e., in the High T'ang], there is clearly one kind of language; in the late T'ang, it is clear that there is another kind of language; and in the various masters of our own dynasty, it is clear that there is yet another kind of language. When you see things this way, then we can allow that you have perfected the "Dharma-eye" [capable of making proper judgments].

This counterpoint embodies the tension that runs throughout "Ts'ang-lang's Remarks on Poetry": a peremptory orthodoxy will somehow become an intuitive sense of what is right; the deepest immersion in the history of poetry and a perfect judgment of all its distinctions will somehow lead us out of history and its distinctions to that moment when you place your poetry among the poems of the older writers and "someone with the capacity for judgment can't tell the difference."

C   N
H   I
A   N
P   E
T
E
R

Popular Poetics: Southern Sung and Yüan

In *"Ts'ang-lang's* Remarks on Poetry" Yen Yü set up the model of the High T'ang as the immutable standard for poetic composition. He subsequently noted that some poets of his age took a T'ang model not from the High T'ang but from the mid and late T'ang. The influence of this latter group of Southern Sung poets and critics, interested in the fastidious craftsmanship of regulated verse, can be seen in Chou Pi's 周弼 *Poetry in Three Forms* (*San-t'i shih* 三體詩).[1]

CHOU PI'S POETRY IN THREE FORMS

Poetry in Three Forms (compiled ca. 1250) is an anthology of four hundred and ninety-four T'ang poems in three genres: quatrains in heptasyllabic lines and eight-line regulated verses in both pentasyllabic and heptasyllabic lines. Each of the three main generic divisions is further grouped under various structural patterns and topics of poetics. To each of these subdivisions Chou Pi attached explanatory introductions. Below are translated the section introductions for heptasyllabic quatrains and pentasyllabic regulated verse.

The later twelfth and thirteenth centuries saw the rise of the great urban centers of the lower Yangtze region, particularly of Hang-chou, the Southern

Sung capital. During this age commercial publication flourished, literacy spread, and poetic composition became a favorite pastime among the lower gentry and urban bourgeoisie. Poetry clubs and song clubs appeared; competitions were held, sometimes of a broad scope, with invitations issued to other clubs throughout the region. The record of one such competition survives: early in 1287, the "Society of the Moonlit Spring" (*Yüeh-ch'üan yin-she* 月泉吟社) distributed to all the poetry clubs in the area the topic "Miscellaneous Responses to Fields and Gardens in the Days of Spring." According to the record of the competition, entitled *Yüeh-ch'üan yin-she* after the name of the club, two thousand seven hundred and thirty-five responses were received, of which seventy-four poems by sixty different poets were selected; these were published with critiques by the judges, praiseworthy couplets from other poems, the charter of the club, the rules of the contest, letters exchanged with participants discussing interesting points of poetics, and the prizes awarded. It was to this world that *Poetry in Three Forms* belonged.

Poetry was supposed to be the involuntary manifestation of a state of mind. Given this assumption as canonical orthodoxy, there was always something faintly illegitimate about a prescriptive poetics, a technical manual on composition. On the other hand, there really were prescriptions and norms of propriety in poetic composition, the violation of which would lead to failure and social humiliation. Thus, among novice poets, there was a hunger for method, for teachers and manuals of composition that could teach the uninitiate to write well. From the early T'ang on, there had developed a large literature of technical poetics to satisfy such a need (and as in the West, an increasingly clear distinction was drawn between technical competence and higher values). The spreading interest in poetic composition in the late twelfth and thirteenth centuries, combined with the savvy of the publishing industry, produced a spate of such works. *Poetry in Three Forms* is an anthology of T'ang poetry to teach composition: by reading Chou Pi's notes and the examples given, the sophisticated son of a Hang-chou merchant could learn to construct a poem properly.

The great intellectuals from the Southern Sung through the Ch'ing were understandably uncomfortable about the promise of detailed formulae that would assure success in poetic composition. When such sophisticated writers were prescriptive, they tended to be pithy and general. But the writers of popular poetics, who were often speaking to an audience with a far lower degree of literary education, felt no such reservations; they offered systematic expositions filled with examples and analyses (just as the modern critical genre of the "Reader's Guide to Poet X" often does not hesitate to tell the reader what a particular poem "means"). Such works of popular poetics compensate for their lack of subtlety by revealing some of the most basic assumptions of traditional poetics, making explicit what better critics were wise enough to leave implicit.

In the section introductions to his anthology, Chou Pi focuses on a question of poetics often touched but never before treated systematically: the assumption that a poem is composed of balances between "solids," *shih**, and "emptinesses," *hsü**. In his anthology, he sets out to systematize those ratios, to show the affective consequences of certain sequences and how to dispose them to produce a successful poem.

I. The Quatrain in the Heptasyllabic Line

A. *Solid Continuation*, Shih*-chieh 實接

絕句之法。大抵以第三句為主。首尾率直。而無婉曲者。此異時所以不及唐也。其法非惟久失其傳。人亦鮮能知之。之實事寓意而接。則轉換有力。若斷而續。外振起而內不失於平妥。前後相應。雖止四句。而涵蓄不盡之意焉。此其略爾。詳而求之。玩味之久。自當有所得。

In general we may say that the third line is dominant in the technique (*fa**) of the quatrain. Later ages have not been able to match the T'ang in the ability to go straight from the beginning to the end with no subtle turns. Not only has this technique (*fa**) not been transmitted for a long time, few people even know of it. There will be force in the shift (*chuan-huan*) if one continues [the movement of the poem] with some solid event (*shih*-shih**) in which one's concepts (*yi**) can lodge. It seems to break but still continues. The outside is lively and the inside does not get lost in immobility: beginning and end respond to one another. Though there are only four lines, inexhaustible concepts (*yi**) are stored up within them. This is the rough outline. If you go into it in more detail and savor it for a long time, you will grasp it quite naturally.

Chuan 轉 (appearing above as *chuan-huan* 轉換 and translated as "shift") was the technical term for the third line of a regulated quatrain and the third couplet of a regulated verse. The third line is the "dominant" (*chu*, "host" or "master"), the focus of attention and skill on which the formal success of the poem depends. Critics often sought a hierarchy of importance, some "dominant" [factor], the attainment of which would bring all other aspects of a piece to perform their roles properly. Among theorists of literature, the "dominant" was usually some general principle: *chu* is the term Ts'ao P'i uses when he says that *ch'i** is the "dominant factor" in literature; later critics claimed that the "dominant factor" was "concept" (*yi**), "natural principle" (*li**), or Tao*. Here, in the pragmatic world of technical poetics, it is a line or a couplet that serves as the animating pivot of the form.

In a "solid continuation," a couplet of concrete images (i.e., a "solid" first couplet) is continued by another "solid" scene in the beginning of the second couplet. This form is contrasted with the more common "empty continuation," in which a concrete scene is followed by some explicit statement or manifestation of the affections. The "solid continuation" goes "straight," focusing on the given facts of externals, with none of the "subtle turns" associated with the movement of the affections. In sustaining such an external focus, however, there is something that stirs the affections ("in which one's concepts can lodge"). Thus the "solid continuation" may still serve the function of response, implicitly "answering" the opening couplet, while seeming simply to extend its descriptive realm. "It seems to break but still continues" may refer to the conclusion of the quatrain where, with no response articulated, the poem is apparently "left hanging"; but that very force of incompletion leads the reader to feel the subjective implications of the external description ("still continues"). While this is the interpretation of "breaks but still continues" that is most in keeping with the tradition of poetics, many of Chou Pi's examples involve a break in continuity at the third line: here, too, we have an apparent "break" that "still continues." By bridging that apparent discontinuity the reader finds that "beginning and end respond to one another."

From Chou Pi's various examples it is clear that the third line of the quatrain is the focal point of the "solid continuation." In many cases, the third line simply names a place, object, or day; such a line serves as the topic on which the fourth line offers a comment that indirectly relates to the first couplet. For example, Chou includes the famous "Mooring by Night at Maple Bridge" by the late-eighth-century poet Chang Chi 張繼 (I here break the long heptasyllabic line into two hemistiches):

> The moon is setting, crows cry out,
>   and frost fills the sky,
> River maples and fishermen's fires
>   face someone who lies here melancholy.
> Beyond the walls of Ku-Su,
>   Cold Mountain Temple:
> At midnight the sounds of its bell
>   reach the traveler's boat.[2]

The first couplet, moving from the surrounding scene to the perceiver in the center, creates an evocative nightscape for the poet. Even before explicitly stating that he is lying awake in melancholy, the poet implies wakefulness by the very fact that he is making such late-night observations, and implies distress by his wakefulness. The associations of such a scene would be loneliness on a journey.

The third line or "shift" is the "solid continuation." In many cases such a "shift" line or couplet involves a real change in tone or point of view. In this form, however, Chou Pi advocates a straightforward, linear exposition: a slight change in topic that ultimately serves to amplify rather than alter the momentum of the poem. The third line seems to leave the immediate scene by naming and locating a temple; but the fourth line, with the sound of the midnight bell reaching the boat, brings the temple back to the situation at hand. It is a "solid" couplet, given without explicitly subjective intrusion (in contrast to "lying in melancholy" of the second line). But though it seems to be the mere statement of an event, this particular occurrence is weighted with associations that are played off against the opening couplet ("it seems to break but still continues"): the resonance of the temple bell, pervasive yet invisible, reminds the listener of the illusion of experience and emotion, the Buddhist sense of the insubstantiality of "life afloat," a reminder particularly forceful for one who is literally afloat. The very "solidity" of the second couplet seems to turn away from the subjectivity of the opening, but such refusal to subjectively qualify the presentation of the "solid" scene in the second couplet only makes it more forceful.

B. Empty Continuation, Hsü-chieh 虛接

謂第三句。以虛語接前二句也。亦有語雖實而意虛者。於承接之閒。略加轉換。反與正相依。順與逆相應。一呼一喚。宮商自諧。如用千鈞之力。而不見形迹。繹而尋之。有餘味矣。

An "empty continuation" refers to a case in which the third line continues the preceding two lines with "empty words." There are also cases when the concepts are "empty" (hsü*) even though the words are "solid" (shih*). In the space between receiving (ch'eng) and continuing, this somewhat strengthens the shift (chuan): the result is that forward movement and reversal depend on one another; sequential movement and retrograde movement respond to one another; one calls out and the other shouts back; the notes kung and shang are in harmony. It is as if using enough force to bear a thousand pounds, yet no traces [of artistic manipulation] are to be seen. If you look into it thoroughly, you will find plenty to savor.

"Empty words," hsü*-yü (along with the more common term hsü*-tzu 虛字) was a category in traditional linguistics to refer to words now called "particles." In the context of the concerns of traditional language theory, however, these words are distinguished not in their grammatical role as a "part of speech," but rather for the quality of subjective relation they imparted to an utterance. As Chou Pi says, a line that is technically "solid" (i.e., lacking "empty words") may still be "empty" because the "concept" (yi*) that informs it imparts to that scene a strong subjective coloring. Not all the couplets in Chou Pi's examples contain "particles," but all are "empty" in articulating a feeling or opinion. Ch'eng, "receiving," is the technical term for the second line of a regulated quatrain and the second couplet of a regulated verse.

The assumption in this passage is that "empty" follows "solid" in the two couplets of a quatrain, thus creating the antithetical balances described. The strong sense of a countermovement in the second couplet "response" is close to the buried semantic force in the English term "reaction," as if the movement of response were in some way "against" the momentum of the initial stimulus. The fact that this form shows no "traces" of conscious manipulation attests to the very commonness of the form: its structure is so expected that it seems natural.

One of the poems anthologized under this heading is the following playful verse by the late-eighth-century poet Ch'in Hsi 秦系, "Written on the Cell of the Monk Ming-hui":

> From dawn to dusk before the eaves
>   rain increases the flowers,
> Here eighty monks of the southland
>   sup on parboiled sesame:
> Now fixed in meditation, when
>   will they emerge again,
> Unaware that nesting swallows have
>   crapped on their cassocks?

The first couplet is purely descriptive, setting in opposition the worlds outside and inside the temple: the former is the lush spring world of fertility and growth, of eating, and defecating; the latter is the austere world of the monastery, whose inhabitants seek to overcome the demands of all that is bodily (though here discovered eating, a concession to their bodily natures). By its speculative act of wondering how the meditating monks can remain so indifferent to what lies outside them, the third line becomes "empty," implicating an act of mind on the part of the poet. Even though it makes reference to something external, it is explicitly a private point of view. As Chou Pi suggests, the "empty continuation" makes the two couplets of the quatrain mutually dependent (in contrast, in the Chang Chi quatrain quoted earlier the two couplets supplement one another, but they do not so radically qualify one another that the understanding of each is dependent on the other).

C. Use of Reference, Yung-shih* 用事

詩中用事。既易窒塞。況於二十八字之間。尤難堆疊。若不融化。以事為意。更加以輕率。則鄰於里謠巷歌。可擊竹而謠矣。凡此皆用事之妙者也。

In any poem, the use of references can cause obstructions; and this problem is all the greater when you have only twenty-eight words. It is especially difficult to use multiple references. If one does not blend the reference into the poem, and if one makes the references the main point, and further if the references are light and direct, then you will have something close to village ballads and street songs, sung to the tapped rhythm of bamboo sticks. Cases like this represent the most perfect use of references.

The point here seems to be that quatrains are too short to use allusions to old stories to support some contemporary topic; rather, if the poet is going to use a reference, it should itself be the topic of the poem. The "village ballads" referred to were often political doggerel in which the references were obvious.

D. *First Couplet Parallel*, Ch'ien-tui 前對

接句兼備虛實兩體。但前句作對。而其接亦微有異焉。相去僅一閒。特在乎稱停之閒耳。

We have given a comprehensive treatment of the two forms that differ regarding the "solidity" or "emptiness" of the third [literally "continuing"] line. When the first couplet is parallel, there is a slight difference in the quality of the third line. Though that difference is small, perfect balance depends on recognizing that difference.

The following translation has been left somewhat wooden to preserve the parallelism of the first couplet. The poem is "Evening on a Journey," by the ninth-century poet Kao Ch'an 高蟾:

> Wind scatters over the ancient slopes,
>   startling up night-lodging geese;
> The moon looks down on the grass-grown fortress,
>   causing to rise the cawing crows.
> Done reciting my poem, I cannot bear
>   how there's no one around to be seen;
> Now and again the cold lamp
>   lets fall a single spark.

When Chou Pi speaks of "a slight difference in the quality of the third line," he is probably referring to the disjunctive contrast that occurs when a discursive third line follows immediately upon a highly "artful" opening couplet. The poem above makes thematic use of such a contrast: when Kao Ch'an refers to "reciting [his] poem," we might easily associate it with the preceding, very "poetic" couplet. The final image, least stylized, plays off against the opening couplet.

E. *Second Couplet Parallel*, Hou-tui 後對

此體唐人用亦少。必使末句。雖對而詞足意盡。若未嘗對。不然則如半截長律。皚皚齊整。略無結合。此荊公所以見誚於徐師川也。

T'ang writers use this form very rarely. Even though the final couplet is parallel, carrying a sense of completion both in the words and the concept, one must make it as if it were not parallel. Otherwise it would be like an eight-line regulated verse cut in half, but with hardly any sense of conclusion [literally "tying together and uniting"]. It was for an error like this that Hsü Fu (d. 1140) made fun of Wang An-shih.

The parallel couplet has a sense of internal completeness. Chou Pi says here *tz'u tsu yi chin* 詞是意盡, "the language is adequate and the concept exhausted." But because the conclusion of a poem should convey a sense of openness and lingering associations, and because (after the middle of the seventh century) parallel couplets were rarely used in closure of any poetry, a final parallel couplet, by its very internal completeness, conveyed the impression of a fragmentary longer poem.[3]

One of the poems anthologized by Chou Pi is Wang Wei's 王維 famous "Cold Food Festival by the River Ssu":

Beside the walls of Kuang-wu
  I encountered the end of spring,
A traveler returning to Wen-yang
  whose tears wet his kerchief.
Falling flowers so silent,
  birds crying out in the hills;
Willows and poplars so green,
  a person crossing the water.

In this poem Wang Wei has achieved a precarious perfection, but it is not at all the self-effacing parallelism advocated by Chou Pi ("as though it were not parallel"). Although the figure of a person crossing a river was an appropriate closing image, the Chinese syntax of the couplet is poetically stylized and appropriate only for the middle couplets of an eight-line poem; that is, it calls attention to itself as a parallel couplet. Such masterful balance between signatures of completion and incompletion was only for major poets; Chou Pi's other examples show an unambitious competence that was more appropriate for his pedagogic purposes. For example, the late-eighth-century poet Han Hung's 韓翃 "Spending the Night on Stone Burgh Mountain":

The floating clouds do not reach
  level with this mountain;
The mountain fogs are bluish grey,
  and my gaze grows more uncertain.
The dawn moon for a moment flies
  among its thousand trees,
And autumn's star river beyond it lies,
  west of its several peaks.

The final two categories, on tonal balance, have been omitted.

II. Regulated Verse in the Five-Syllable Line

A. Middle Couplets Solid, Ssu-shih* 四實

謂中四句皆景物而實。開元大曆多此體。華麗典重之間。有雍容寬厚之態。此其妙也。稍
變然後入於虛。閒以情思。故此體當為眾體之首。昧者為之。則堆積窒塞。寡於意味矣。

This means that the four middle lines are all things of the scene (*ching*-*wu**),
thus "solid." This form is often found in the poetry of the K'ai-yüan reign
[713–741] and Ta-li reign [766–779]. It is at its most perfect when there is a
relaxed and open manner, while at the same time retaining lushness and canonical gravity. The slightest mutation (*pien**) will bring you into the "empty,"
mixing in thoughts and the affections (*ching*-*ssu**). Consequently this form
should be given first of all. When someone ignorant uses it, it becomes all piled
up and obstructed, and is deficient in the flavor of concept (*yi*-*wei**)

The association of "middle couplets solid" with the High T'ang (the K'ai-
yüan and T'ien-pao reigns) implies that this structure is "normative" (or
"orthodox," *cheng**) for regulated verse in the five-syllable line. Such a structure is *cheng** in the sense that the term is used in the "Great Preface": it is
conceived as "primary" (both historically and in authority) in an ideal history
of the genre, and other forms "mutate" (*pien**) out of it. This structure is
given as the first section in regulated verse in the five-syllable line and presumably should be learned first. There is a peculiar instability in its perfection, on the one side in danger of falling into excessive density and becoming
"clogged," on the other side tending naturally to mutate toward the "empty."

One of Chou Pi's examples is "Passing Abandoned Pao-ch'ing Temple" by
Ssu-k'ung shu 司空曙, a poet of the second half of the eighth century:

> Among yellow leaves a temple from an earlier reign,
> Monkless now, its chilly halls appear.
> Its pools in sunshine, turtles emerge to bask,
> Its pines shadowed, cranes fly turning back.
> By ancient pavements a stele lies flat in the grass,
> In verandas' shade paintings are mixed with moss.
> Its sites of meditation are lost and gone,
> And this world of dust grows ever more mournful.

B. Middle Couplets Empty, ssu-hsü 四虛

謂中四句皆情思而虛也。不以虛為虛。以實為虛。自首至尾。如行雲流水。此其難也。元
和已後用此體者。骨格雖存。氣象頓殊。向後則偏於枯瘠。流於輕俗。不足采矣。

This means that the four middle lines all involve affections and thoughts
(*ch'ing*-*ssu**) and thus are "empty." The real difficulty here lies in making your

"empty" lines not simply "empty"; instead you should make solid lines "empty," so that from beginning to end they are like drifting clouds or flowing water. Among those who used this form since the Yüan-ho reign [806–820], even though the basic manner [literally "bone structure," *ku*-ko**] survived, the atmosphere (*ch'i*-hsiang**) suddenly was altered. As time passed, the form tended to a bare dryness on the one side, and on the other side, drifted in to a lightness and low manner. Nothing of this sort is worth anthologizing.

Implicit in Chou Pi's descriptions of "middle couplets solid" and "middle couplets empty" is an ideal sequence of generic changes, devolving from the "proper," *cheng**, which is an animate solidity, to an acceptable mutation (*pien**), in which "solid lines are made empty." Once this process of mutation is begun, however, it leads inevitably to mere emptiness, a poetry that simply describes how the poet feels. Empty couplets tend to be discursive, and the two dangers into which later manifestations of this form sink are a discursive "dryness" (writing *about* thoughts and feelings without a sense of their relation to the sensuous world) or an equally discursive "lightness and low manner" (a mode combining wit and chattiness with vernacular particles). Both the initial, acceptable mutation and the degenerate devolution of the form share the same "bone structure," *ku*-ko**: in them the formal description of the ratio of solid and empty will be identical. However, the mood or "atmosphere" (*ch'i*-hsiang**) created by the two variations will be entirely different.

Tai Shu-lun's 戴叔倫 (late eighth century) "New Year's Eve at the Way Station called 'The Rock'" is a good example of obviously "empty" middle couplets, directly implicating subjectivity.

> In this inn none concern themselves with me,
> The cold lantern is my only friend.
> The night when soon a whole year will be done,
> The person's thousand mile return not yet made.
> In dreariness I grieve at what happened before,
> In separation I laugh at this body of mine,
> Whose melancholy face and aging hair
> Tomorrow morning meet spring once again.

Under this rubric, Chou Pi also anthologizes the famous "Written on the Rear Garden of Broken Mountain Temple" by the mid-eighth-century poet Ch'ang Chien 常建. This poem is perhaps a good example of "making solid lines empty." Though technically solid, the straightforward middle couplets of this poem imply a movement and engagement on the poet's part that give them a tone quite different from the fragmented observations in the middle couplets of Ssu-k'ung Shu's poem on Pao-ch'ing Temple above.

In the clear dawn I entered the ancient temple,
As first sunlight shone high in the forest.
A winding path led to a hidden spot,
Meditation chamber deep in the flowering trees.
Mountain light cheers the hearts of its birds,
The pool's reflections void the human heart.
Nature's million sounds all grow silent here,
I only hear the tones of the temple bell.

(Ch'ang Chien's second couplet is not perfectly parallel.)

C. Second Couplet Empty, Third Couplet Solid, Ch'ien-hsü hou-shih 前虛後實

謂前聯情而虛。後聯景而實。實則氣勢雄健。虛則態度諧婉。輕前重後。劑量適均。無窒塞輕俗之患。大中以後多此體。至今宗唐詩者尙之。然終未及前兩體渾厚。故以其法居三。善者不拘也。

This means that the second couplet concerns the affections (*ch'ing**) and thus is empty; the third couplet concerns the scene (*ching**) and thus is solid. Where it is solid, the momentum (*shih**) of the *ch'i** is vigorous and sturdy. Where it is empty, the manner is flexible and harmonious. First the light, then the heavy—a perfect balance that gives none of the problems either of obstruction or of lightness and a low manner. This form has been found often in poetry since the Ta-chung reign [847–859], and even now it is esteemed by those who take the T'ang as their model. But in the final analysis, it cannot match the two preceding forms in richness and undifferentiation; thus I have placed it third. True masters will not be confined to it.

The position that Chou Pi gives this form in the history of T'ang poetry suggests that it is the late-T'ang model that many of his contemporaries were following. The challenge in each of these modes is to achieve the proper balance between "solid" and "empty." The first two forms pose the greater challenge: giving fluidity to the "solid" and giving a sense of concreteness to the "empty." The present form solves the problem of balance, but the solution is formulaic; though a poet may achieve some success using it, such a success yields a lesser accomplishment than does mastery of the two preceding modes.

D. Second Couplet Solid, Third Couplet Empty, Ch'ien-shih hou-hsü 前實後虛

謂前聯景而實。後聯情而虛。前重後輕。多流於弱。唐人此體最少。必得妙句不可易。乃就其格。蓋發興盡。則難於繼。後聯稍閒以實。其庶乎。

This means that the second couplet is of the scene, thus solid; the third couplet is of the affections, thus empty. When you have first the heavy, then the light, you often drift into weakness. This form appears rarely among the T'ang writers. Turn to this structure (*ko**) only when you have perfect couplets that cannot be changed. When the initial stirring (*hsing**) is ended, it is hard to keep going. It works best when something of the solid is mixed into the third couplet.

It is simply not true that this form is rare among T'ang writers. There is something of an ideological aversion in Chou Pi's comments, a sense of some essential flaccidity in the movement from solid to empty. Since the fourth and last couplet of a regulated verse is almost always empty, albeit in the mode of response rather than exposition, this argument (that empty should not follow solid) is untenable.

E. Unity of Concept, Yi-yi* 一意

唯守格律。揣摩聲病。詩家之常。若時出度外。縱橫於肆。外如不整。中實應節時。又非造次所能也。

The constant principle for a poet is simply to observe the set patterns and pay heed to tonal faults. If, however, from time to time he exceeds the measure, going wherever he pleases, the exterior may seem improper, but the inner substance (*shih**) responds to the rhythm. This cannot be done haphazardly.

This passage does not mean that formally perfect regulated verses need not have a unity of concept, but rather that the "concept" may, in its unfolding, give an internal unity to the piece even when the formal requirements are violated. The category is essentially a way to acknowledge poetic greatness achieved outside formal means, and it is no accident that the first two of the four poems anthologized are by major High T'ang poets.

The first poem included under this heading, Wang Wei's famous "Villa in the Chung-nan Mountains," violates both parallelism (in the second couplet) and tonal patterns to such a degree that it is usually considered "old-style" verse rather than regulated verse. Chou Pi's inclusion of the poem in the pentasyllabic regulated-verse section suggests something of his sense of latitude in the form—a vague sense that the poem "sounds like" regulated verse in some way.

> In my middle years I grew very fond of the Way,
> And late made my home by South Mountain's edge.

When the mood came upon me, I'd always go off alone;
I experienced scenic splendors for myself alone;
I walked on to the place where the waters ended,
Sat and looked on the moments when clouds rose.
By chance I would meet an old man of the woods;
We'd chat and laugh, delaying my time of return.

F. The Opening Lines, Ch'i-chü 起句

發首兩句。平穩者多。奇健者。予所見惟兩篇。然聲大重。後聯難稱。後兩篇發句亦佳。
聲稍輕。終篇均停。然奇健不及前兩篇遠矣。故著此為法。使識者自擇焉。

The two lines that begin a poem are usually even and steady. I have seen only two pieces in which the beginning was remarkably forceful. Nevertheless, when the [initial] sound is too strong, the later couplets have difficulty maintaining balance. In the second pair of poems [of the four included in this section in the anthology], the opening lines are also excellent, but their tone is somewhat muted; and these poems, as wholes, are in perfect balance. But in remarkable forcefulness they come nowhere near the first pair of poems. Thus in following this model (*fa**, "rule"), I suggest that those who understand choose for themselves.

G. The Closing Lines, Chieh-chü 結句

結句以意盡而寬緩。能躍出拘攣之外。前輩謂如截奔馬。予所得。獨此四首足見。四十
字。字字不可放過也。

In the closing lines, the concept (*yi**) is used up and the poem relaxes; but still the lines are able to leap beyond all boundaries and constraints. Someone of an earlier generation said this was like abruptly halting the movement of a galloping horse. Of the poems I know, only the four following [in the anthology] are worth showing. In each there are forty words, but of those forty words not a single one can be overlooked.

Chou Pi's poetic taste is often questionable, but rarely as misguided as in the eight poems selected under this and the preceding headings, poems that, despite Chou Pi's superlatives, are remarkably ordinary. All are by minor poets; and there are many poems in the anthology whose opening and closing couplets are far more distinguished. However, the values announced in the section headings are significant. A strong opening does risk unbalancing the poem as a whole. And the ideal for poetic closure was a relaxation in the tempo of the poem, a sense of resolution that was at the same time suggestive in a way that lingered in the reader's mind.

H. Poems on Things, Yung-wu* 詠物

隨寓感興而為詩者易。驗物切近而為詩者難。太近則陋。太遠則疎。此皆於和易寬緩之中
精切者也。

It is easy to write a poem responding to one's stirrings (*kan*-hsing*), and following the thing in which those stirrings find a lodging. But, it is hard to write
a poem examining the things themselves and keeping close to them. If too
close to the thing, the work is crude; if too far, then the work is too aloof. The
following poems all get to the essence in a relaxed and easy manner.

This comment reflects the Sung interest in the "thingliness" of the things of
the world: it is difficult to write about a thing as thing. The easy alternative is
the more traditional mode in which the thing is worthy of attention only
insofar as it becomes the occasion of or vehicle for human feeling. The relation between the thing and the response it stirs is often spoken of as "lodging" one's affections in things, that is, speaking about *ch'ing** through some
object.

Among the poems anthologized is the High T'ang poet Ch'u Kuang-hsi's
儲光羲 "A Stream in the Mountains," which exemplifies well the problems
indicated by Chou Pi.

> There is a stream that flows in the mountain;
> One may ask, but I don't know its name.
> Shining on ground, it gives the sky's color;
> Falling through sky, it makes rain's sound.
> It comes bending, more full from a deep brook,
> Branches off, level in a small pool.
> Limpid and unruffled, seen by none,
> Every year it is always pure.

The poem concerns a stream, but one to which such qualities are ascribed
that it may be taken as an emblem of a recluse's life. Indeed the Japanese
commentary by the monk Soin of 1637 takes the stream as a figure (*yu**) of
wisdom.[4] Perhaps it is best to say that Chou Pi advises a kind of *yung-wu* that
hangs ambiguously between the "thingliness" of the thing and reference to a
human situation.

In the third of the three forms, regulated verse in seven-syllable lines,
Chou Pi treats essentially the same categories as he treated in regulated verse
in five-syllable lines. In each case he refers the reader back to the discussion
in the five-syllable line and adds comments on the differences of treatment
appropriate for the seven-syllable line, whose length prohibits either absolute
solidity or absolute emptiness.

YANG TSAI'S "POETIC RULES OF THE MASTERS"

Manuals of poetic composition, to which we may give the general name *shih-fa** ("rules of poetry"), were a popular form of discourse on literature and a genuinely "low" critical genre: their texts are often corrupt, suggesting hasty commercial publication; attributions of authorship are often questionable; the contents are often amalgams of practical commonplaces or of unacknowledged borrowings or of both. Such works are often structured so as to create the illusion of systematic exposition.

Despite their innumerable faults, such poetic manuals teach us much about how poetry was studied; reading and composition were inseparable, and the lessons in composition offered are usually based on interpretations of technique in earlier poetry. Writers of *shih-fa** often speak with an authoritative, magistral voice, one that knows all the "tricks of the trade"—values, prohibitions, categories of variation, and techniques. Moreover, the poetic manuals teach us the jargon of late classical poetics. The following *shih-fa** of the fourteenth century is attributed on reasonably sound authority to Yang Tsai 楊載 (1271–1323), who was an important classical poet of the Yüan: it can be taken as representative of the form.

Remarks on Poetry through the Ages, Li-tai shih-hua 歷代詩話, includes two other Yüan technical works in addition to Yang Tsai's "Poetic Rules of the Masters" (*Shih-fa chia-shu* 詩法家數). Both of these are by Fan Peng 范梈 (also known as Fan Te-chi 范德機; 1272–1330): one, *Mu-t'ien chin-yü*, 木天禁語 is made up largely of technical terms with examples; the other, *Shih-hsüeh chin-luan* 詩學禁臠, consists of exemplary poems with discussions of their structure.

[Introduction]

夫詩之為法也。有其說焉。賦比興者。皆詩製作之法也。然有賦起。有比起。有興起。有主意在上一句。下則貼承一句。而後方發出其意者。有雙起兩句。而分作兩股以發其意者。有一意作出者。有前六句俱若散緩。而收拾在後兩句者。

There are various theories about rules (*fa**) in poetry: exposition (*fu*), comparison (*pi**), and affective image (*hsing**) are all rules in the construction of poetry. There may be an expository beginning, a beginning with a comparison, and a beginning with *hsing**. There are cases when the dominant concept (*yi**) is in the first line; next will come a line that keeps closely to the first line; and only thereafter does one develop the concept. In other cases, there is a double beginning with a matched pair of lines that divide into two legs which develop the concept. In still other cases, a single concept is developed all the way through. And in still other cases, the first six lines will seem wandering and disparate, but they will be drawn together in the last two lines.

This is a discussion of *taxis*. For exposition, comparison, and stirring, see pages 45–46. The first case described above seems to be one in which the topic, fully laid out in the first line, is further qualified in the second line, then the formal development of the topic begins in the third line. The second category of structure is interesting as the oldest form of amplification in both poetry and prose: if elements A and B form the binary concept AB (e.g., *shan-shui* 山水, "mountains-and-water," a landscape), then the poem may develop AB, AA, BB . . . or AB, AB, AB . . .

詩之為體有六。曰雄渾。曰悲壯。曰平淡。曰蒼古。曰沉著痛快。曰優游不迫。

Poetry has six normative forms (*t'i**): 1) potent and undifferentiated; 2) resolute melancholy (*pei-chuang*); 3) limpidity (*p'ing-tan*); 4) hoary antiquity (*ts'ang-ku*); 5) firm, self-possessed, and utterly comfortable; 6) straightforward and carefree.

The first of these is the first category in Ssu-k'ung T'u's "Twenty-Four Categories of Poetry." The last two are the two "overall situations" in "Ts'ang-lang's Remarks on Poetry."

詩之忌有四。曰俗意。曰俗字。曰俗語。曰俗韻。

The things to be shunned in poetry are four: 1) uncouth concepts, 2) uncouth words, 3) uncouth diction, 4) uncouth rhymes.

See "Ts'ang-lang's Remarks on Poetry," chapter 3, part I.

詩之戒有十。曰不可硬礙人口。曰陳爛不新。曰差錯不貫串。曰直置不宛轉。曰妄誕事不實。曰綺靡不典重。曰蹈襲不識使。曰穢濁不清新。曰砌合不純粹。曰徘徊而劣弱。詩之為難有十。曰造理。曰精神。曰高古。曰風流。曰典麗。曰質幹。曰體裁。曰勁健。曰耿介。曰淒切。

Ten things are to be warned against in poetry. One may not 1) block up the mouth [i.e., cacophony ?]; 2) be overripe and lack freshness; 3) be all topsy-turvy with no continuity; 4) proceed on too straight a course with no graceful swerves; 5) talk wildly about matters that are not factual (*shih**); 6) write with a sensual delicacy that lacks classical gravity; 7) imitate without knowing how to make good use [of an earlier work]; 8) be all murky with no clarity; 9) pile things up, missing the true essence; 10) be weak, uncertain, and full of hesitation.

Poetry has ten areas of difficulty: 1) informing principle (*li**); 2) spirit (*ching-shen**); 3) lofty antiquity; 4) gallantry [*feng*-liu**, a quality combining sensibility, amorousness, and hot-headed belligerence]; 5) canonical richness (*tien-li**); 6) a substantial trunk (*chih*-kan*); 7) constructing normative form (*t'i*-tsai*); 8) sturdiness; 9) resoluteness and magnanimity; 10) piercing desolation.

Note how such lists indiscriminately mix questions from completely different categories: here we find universal questions (1–2), modes (3–5, 8–10), and purely technical issues (6–7).

大抵詩之作法有八。曰起句要高遠。曰結句要不著迹。曰承句要穩健。曰下字要有金石聲。曰上下相生。曰首尾相應。曰轉摺要不著力。曰占地步。蓋首兩句先須闊占地步。然後六句若有本之泉。源源而來矣。地步一狹。譬猶無根之潦。可立而竭也。今之學者。倘有志乎詩。須先將漢魏盛唐諸詩。日夕沈潛諷詠。熟其詞。究其旨。則又訪諸善詩之士。以講明之。若今人之治經。日就月將。而自然有得。則取之左右逢其源。苟為不然。我見其能詩者鮮矣。是猶孩提之童。未能行者而欲行。鮮不仆也。

There are eight general rules to consider in composition: 1) the beginning lines should be lofty and far-reaching; 2) the closing lines should not get stuck in their tracks [i.e., should allow for continuing associations]; 3) the second couplet (*ch'eng*) should be stable and sturdy; 4) you should have the sound of metal and stone in your use of words; 5) what precedes must generate what follows; 6) head and tail should respond to one another; 7) the turning [*chuan*, the third couplet] should not show effort; 8) you should have secure mastery of the area through which you move. We may say that the first two lines should first secure a broad area through which to move, and only then will the next six lines be like a spring with a source, pouring from its fountainhead. If the area through which you move is too narrow, it will be like a trickle without any origin; it can dry up in a moment.

Should some modern student set his mind (*chih**) on poetry, he should first take all the poetry of the Han, Wei, and High T'ang, then chant those poems thoughtfully both day and night. When he is thoroughly familiar with their words and has thought seriously about their implications, he may seek out experts in poetry with whom to discuss and elucidate the poems, just as today people study the Classics. As he progresses from day to day and from month to month, if something comes to him naturally then he should use it. He will encounter the sources of poetry all around him. If he does not do this, then rarely, I think, will he succeed in becoming adept at poetry. Such a person is just like a babe in arms who wants to walk but is not yet able: rarely will that babe avoid falling flat on his face.

The first part of the second paragraph is a rephrasing of the program of study in "Ts'ang-lang's Remarks on Poetry".

余于詩之一事。用工凡二十餘年。乃能會諸法。而得其一二。然於盛唐大家數。抑亦未敢
望其有所似焉。

For more than twenty years I have devoted my single-minded efforts to poetry, and now I comprehend all the rules and succeed in one or two. Nevertheless, I still dare not even hope to reach anything even close to the masters of the High T'ang.

The True Source of the Study of Poetry, Shih-hsüeh cheng-yüan 詩學正源

風雅頌賦比興

詩之六義。而實則三體。風雅頌者。詩之體。賦比興者。詩之法。故賦比興者。又所以製
作乎風雅頌者也。凡詩中有賦起。有比起。有興起。然風之中有賦比興。雅頌之中亦有賦
比興。此詩學之正源。法度之準則。凡有所作。而能備盡其義。則古人不難到矣。若真賦
其事。而無優游不迫之趣。沉著痛快之功。首尾率直而已。夫何取焉。

Airs (*Feng**) Odes (*Ya**) Hymns (*Sung*) Exposition (*Fu*) Comparison (*Pi**) Stirring (*Hsing** affective image).

These are the "Six Principles," but in fact three are normative forms (*t'i**) of poems: Airs, Odes, and Hymns are the normative forms of poetry; exposition, comparison, and *hsing** are the [compositional] rules (*fa**) of poetry. Thus exposition, comparison, and *hsing** are also means by which one can compose in the forms Airs, Odes, and Hymns. In all poems, there can be an opening with exposition, an opening with comparison, or an opening with *hsing**. All three occur in the Airs; all three occur likewise in the Odes and Hymns. This is the true source for the study of poetry and the standard for all rules and regulations. If you can fulfill these principles (*yi**) anywhere in your writing, then the ancients are not hard to reach. If you just give straight exposition of some matter, you will lack the excitement (*ch'ü**) of being "straightforward and carefree" or the accomplishment of being "firm, self-possessed, and utterly comfortable"—if all it does is go straight through from beginning to end, what is worth considering in it?

The sections that follow should give something of the true flavor of a popular poetic manual. This is neither literary theory nor criticism, but literary pedagogy. There is a series of headings that raise conventional areas of discussion in composition. Under these headings, we have a very loose mix of categories, precepts, and warnings, with offhand comments added where it seems appropriate. However rough, the translation is smoother than the original, in which full sentences are mixed in with mere lists of topics. One imagines a teacher listing things for his students to remember and occasionally adding, "Now pay special attention to this!"

The Measuring Tape for Writing Poetry, Tso-shih chun-sheng
作詩準繩

立意
要高古渾厚。有氣概。要沉著。忌卑弱淺陋。

Establishing the Concept (yi*)
It must be lofty and ancient, rich and undifferentiated, with a standard of *ch'i**; it must be firm and self-possessed, shunning weakness, shallowness, and baseness.

鍊句
要雄偉清健。有金石聲。

Refining Lines
It must be potent and grand, clear and sturdy, having the sound of metal and stone.

琢對
要寧精毋弱。寧拙毋巧。寧樸毋華。忌俗野。

Polishing Parallelism
It is better coarse than weak, better [honestly] clumsy than artful, better plain than flowery; but shun uncouthness and rusticity.

寫景
景中含意。事中瞰景。要細密清淡。忌庸腐雕巧。

Describing Scene (ching*)
Concept held in reserve within the scene; peering at the scene through some event (*shih**). It must be fine and dense, clear and limpid; shun the commonplace and overwrought.

寫意
要意中帶景。議論發明。

Describing Concept (yi*)
It must be so that concept bears the scene (*ching**) within it; discursiveness clarifies.

書事

大而國事。小而家事。身事。心事。

*Writing of an Event (*shih**)*

On a large scale, there are national affairs (*shih**); on a small scale, there are family affairs, affairs pertaining to oneself, affairs pertaining to the heart/mind.

用事

陳古諷今。因彼證此。不可著迹。只使影子可也。雖死事亦當活用。

*Use of References (*shih**)*[5]

Set forth antiquity to criticize (*feng**) the present; use one thing to prove another; don't show your tracks—it's all right if you give a shadow; though it be a dead reference, it can be used in a lively way.

押韻

押韻穩健。則一句有精神。如柱礎欲其堅牢也。

Choice of Rhymes

If the choice of rhyme is stable and sturdy, the whole line will have spirit (*ching-shen**)—like the base of a column, you want it to be firm.

下字

或在腰。或在膝。在足。最要精思。宜的當。

Placing Words

It may be in the waist, in the knee, or in the foot [positions within a single line]; most of all think carefully here; it must be just right.

The Essential Rules of Regulated Verse, Lü-shih yao-fa 律詩要法

起承轉合

Opening (*ch'i*) Continuing (*ch'eng*), Turning (*chuan*), Drawing Together (*ho*).

These are the function-names of the four couplets of a regulated verse and the four lines of a quatrain.

破題

或對景興起。或比起。或引事起。或就題起。要突兀高遠。如狂風捲浪。勢欲滔天。

*Broaching the Topic (*p'o-t'i, first couplet*)*

It may begin with a *hsing** facing a scene; it may begin with a comparison (*pi**); it may begin with a reference (*shih**, or "an event," something happening); it may begin by taking up the title. It must heave up high and far, like a hurricane rolling up the waves, its momentum (*shih**) ready to sweep over the heavens.

頷聯
或寫意。或寫景。或書事。用事引證。此聯要接破題。要如驪龍之珠。抱而不脫。

Jaw Couplet (han-lien, the second couplet)
It may describe a concept (*yi**), or a scene (*ching**), or an event (*shih**), or make a reference (*shih**), or prove something. This couplet should connect to broaching the topic [i.e., the first couplet]. It should be like the pearl of a black dragon, held tight and not allowed to slip away.

頸聯
或寫意。寫景。書事。用事引證。與前聯之意相應相避。要變化如疾雷破山。觀者驚愕。

Neck Couplet (ching-lien, third couplet)
It may describe a concept, or a scene, or an event, or make a reference, or prove something. It responds to but swerves away from the concept of the preceding couplet. It should be a transformation, like a sudden peal of thunder breaking over the mountains—all onlookers are startled and terrified.

結句
或就題結。或開一步。或繳前聯之意。或用事。必放一句作散場。如剡溪之棹。自去自回。言有盡而意無窮。

Concluding Lines (chieh-chü)
It may tie up the topic, may step off in a new direction, may shoot like a stringed arrow back into the concepts of the preceding couplets, or may make a reference. One must set at least one line free as a place for dispersal: like a rowboat on Yen Creek, going off on its own or turning around on its own—the words are over, but the meaning (*yi**) is endless.

七言
聲響。雄渾。鏗鏘。偉健。高遠。

The Seven-Character Line
Resonance potent, undifferentiated, ringing, grand and sturdy, lofty and far-reaching.

五言
沉靜。深遠。細嫩。

The Five-Character Line
Brooding and still, deep and far-reaching, delicate and tender.

Under the two most common line lengths, in seven and five characters, Yang Tsai simply lists qualities conventionally associated with each. Some are complementary; some are mutually exclusive. These are presumably the qualities a student should aim for. He follows these lists with a brief discussion of general questions of poetic structure.

五言七言。句語雖殊。法律則一。起句尤難。起句先須闊占地步。要高遠。不可苟且。中間兩聯。句法或四字截。或兩字截。須要血脈貫通。音韻相應。對偶相停。上下勻稱。有兩句共一意者。有各意者。若上聯已共意。則下聯須各意。前聯既詠狀。後聯須說人事。兩聯最忌同律。頸聯轉意要變化。須多下實字。字實則自然響亮。而句法健。其尾聯要能開一步。別運生意結之。然亦有合起意者。亦妙。

詩句中有字眼。兩眼者妙。三眼者非。且二聯用連綿字。不可一般。中腰虛活字。亦須迴避。五言字眼多在第三。或第二字。或第四字。或第五字。

Although lines of five and seven characters have different numbers of words in a line, the same rules apply to both. The opening lines are the hardest, for in the opening lines one must secure a broad area through which to move: it must be lofty and far-reaching, and one cannot achieve this improperly. As for the two middle couplets, one may group the characters in twos or fours, but what is essential is that the blood vessels run through them [i.e., it should have animate continuity], that the sounds respond to one another [i.e., it should achieve tonal balancing and general euphony], that parallel constructions hold one another steady, and that what precedes and what follows be in balance. Sometimes two lines share a single concept (*yi**); sometimes each line has its own concept. But if the first of the middle two couplets shares a concept between its two lines, then the second of the middle two couplets must allot a separate concept for each of its lines. If the first of the middle couplets sings of the manner of things, then the second of the middle couplets must speak of some matter (*shih**) involving humanity. What should most be shunned is both of the middle couplets' being of the same mold. When the "neck couplet" [third couplet] turns the concept (*chuan-yi**) and brings about a metamorphosis (*pien*-hua**), one should use many solid (*shih**) words: if the words are solid, it will be naturally resonant, and the line construction (*chü-fa**) will be sturdy. The final couplet ought to set off in another direction and conclude the piece by infusing it with another life. If this is done and at the same time it is able to draw together with the opening couplet, then this is finesse (*miao**).

In a line of poetry there are "eye words" (*tzu-yen*) [strong words, usually verbs, that carry a special stylistic force]. To have a pair of eye words is finesse; but three eye words won't do. And one cannot use binomes in the same way in two couplets; there one should also avoid empty words (*hsü-tzu*) [i.e., particles] and "active" words (*huo-tzu*). In a five-syllable line, the eye is usually in the third position, but it may also occur in the second, fourth, and fifth positions.

Series of examples of the eye word in different positions in the line has been omitted.

杜詩法多在首聯兩句。上句為頷聯之主。下句為頸聯之主。

The rule (*fa**) in Tu Fu's poetry is that the first line of the first couplet governs the second couplet, while the second line of the first couplet governs the third couplet.

In the context of T'ang poetry before him, this is a mark of Tu Fu's formal training and conservatism. This is formal amplification: AB, AA, BB . . .

七言律難于五言律。七言下字較粗實。五言下字較細嫩。七言若可截作五言。便不成詩。須字字去不得方是。所以句要藏字。字要藏意。如聯珠不斷。方妙。

Regulated verse in the seven-character line is more difficult than regulated verse in the five-character line. In the seven-character line, the choice of words tends to the rough and substantial (*shih**); in the five-character line, the choice of words tends to be fine and delicate. If a part of a seven-character line can be cut out to make a five-character line, then the poem is imperfect. A poem is just right only when no word can be deleted. Thus a line should hide its words, and the words should hide their concept (*yi**). It has the greatest finesse (*miao**) when it is like an unbroken string of pearls.

The Essential Rules of Old-Style Verse 古詩要法

凡作古詩。體格句法俱要蒼古。且先立大意。鋪敘既定。然後下筆。則文脈貫通。意無斷續。整然可觀。

Whenever one writes old-style verse, both the structure of the form (*t'i*-ko**) and the construction of lines (*chü*-fa**) must be in the ancient manner. First of all, one establishes the overall concept (*t'ai-yi**); then, only after one has determined how it should be developed, should one set one's brush to paper: then the veins of the writing will be unified (*kuan-t'ung**), there will be no discontinuities in the concept; and in its correctness, it will be worth consideration.

Old-Style Poetry in the Five-Character Line 五言古詩

五言古詩。或興起。或比起。或賦起。須要寓意深遠。託詞溫厚。反復優游。雍容不迫。或感古懷今。或懷人傷己。或瀟洒閒適。寫景要雅淡。推人心之至情。寫感慨之微意。悲懽含蓄而不傷。美刺婉曲而不露。要有三百篇之遺意方是。觀漢魏古詩。藹然有感動人處。如古詩十九首。皆當熟讀玩味。自見其趣。

Old-style poetry in the five-character line may begin with a *hsing**, a comparison (*pi**), or with straight exposition (*fu*). It is necessary that the concepts be lodged deep and far, and that the diction (*tz'u**) be gentle and gracious; it moves back and forth with ease, stately and never pressed. One may be stirred by antiquity and thus think on the present; one may think on others and feel pain for oneself; one may be cool, aloof, and self-content. Description of the scene must be graceful (*ya**) and limpid; one investigates the ultimate affections (*ch'ing**) of the human mind; one describes the subtle thought (*yi**) in strong emotions. Sorrow and grief are held in reserve (*han-hsü*) and no pain is expressed; praise and attack are indirect and not obvious; it is correct when one has the concepts that have come down to us from the *Book of Songs*. Consider those places in the old-style poems of the Han and Wei that stir people to swelling emotion. Works like the "Nineteen Old Poems" [a group of anonymous works probably dating from the second century] should be read thoroughly and their flavor enjoyed—you will perceive the flair (*ch'ü**) in them quite naturally.

Old-Style Poetry in the Seven-Character Line 七言古詩

七言古詩。要鋪叙。要有開合。有風度。要迢遞險怪。雄俊鏗鏘。忌庸俗軟腐。須是波瀾開合。如江海之波。一波未平。一波復起。又如兵家之陣。方以為正。又復為奇。方以為奇。忽復是正。出入變化。不可紀極。備此法者。惟李杜也。

Old-style poetry in the seven-character line should unroll [a term for linear exposition related to *fu*]; it should have its opening and its drawing together; it should have style; it should pass far into the distance, be daring and strange, potent and grand in its ringing. Shun the commonplace, weak, and worn out. It should have wavelike openings and comings together, just like the waves of the rivers and the sea: before one wave is stilled, another rises. Also it is like military formations: first it is normal (*cheng**), then unconventional; and no sooner has it become unconventional than it is normal again. Emerging from and entering again into transformation (*pien**-hua**), its limits cannot be reckoned. Only Li Po and Tu Fu have achieved the fullness of this rule. [The opening and drawing together are dazzling; the tones and rhymes are ringing;

the rules are dark and mysterious; spirit-thought goes far; learning is full; the argument is transcendent.][6]

Quatrains 絕句

絕句之法。要婉曲回環。刪蕪就簡。句絕而意不絕。多以第三句為主。而第四句發之。有實接。有虛接。承接之間。開與合相關。反與正相依。順與逆相應。一呼一吸。宮商自諧。大抵起承二句固難。然不過平直敘起為佳。從容承之為是。至如宛轉變化工夫。全在第三句。若于此轉變得好。則第四句如順流之舟矣。

The rules of the quatrain demand sinuousness and circling, cutting away all unnecessary growth for the sake of concision, with the result that the lines break off [*chü chüeh*, inverting the generic name *chüeh-chü*], but the meaning (*yi**) does not break off. Usually the third line is the dominant, and the fourth line develops it. There is a distinction between the "solid continuation" (*shih**-chieh*) and the "empty continuation (*hsü**-chieh*); and in the relation between the second line (*ch'eng*) and the third line (*chieh*), openings are balanced with drawings together, forward motions and reversals depend on one another, sequential movement and retrograde movement respond to one another, one calls out while another draws in, the notes *kung* and *shang* are in harmony. Generally speaking, the first and second lines are the hardest; nevertheless, excellence may be attained by nothing more than opening with a straightforward exposition, after which a relaxed second line is correct. The skill of sinuousness and transformation resides entirely in the third line. If the turn or transformation (*chuan-pien**) is well executed, then the fourth line will be like a boat following the current.

See Chou Pi's discussion of the "empty continuation" in quatrains, p. 425.

After the discussion of quatrains, there is a long section discussing the norms of treatment for various occasions for poetry. The following passage is one example.

Climbing a High Place and Looking Out, Teng-lin 登臨

登臨之詩。不過感今懷古。寫景歎時。思國懷鄉。蕭灑遊適。或譏刺歸美。有一定之法律也。中間宜寫四面所見山川之景。庶幾移不動。第一聯指所題之處。宜敘說起。第二聯合用景物實說。第三聯合說人事。或感歎古今。或議論。却不可用硬事。或前聯先說事感歎。則此聯寫景亦可。但不可兩聯相同。第四聯就題主意發感慨。繳前二句。或說何時再來。

Poems on climbing high places and looking out confine themselves to being stirred by the present while thinking on the past, describing the scene and reacting to the season, thinking of the state and longing for one's home, the dispassionate contentment of rambling, or perhaps criticism to reform a person's behavior—this form has determinate rules (*fa*-lü*). In such a poem, the poet should describe the scene (*ching**) of the mountains and rivers all around him, virtually to the point that nothing in the scene could be moved. The first couplet makes reference to the places stated in the title, and one should begin by saying something about that. The second couplet uses the things of the scene (*ching*-wu**), drawing them together in solid (*shih**) discourse. The third couplet draws the above together with discourse on human affairs, or with an emotional reaction to past and present, or with some discursive proposition; one cannot, however, get into strident moralizing. If the second couplet has already treated the emotional reaction to events, then it is all right to describe the scene in the third couplet; but the two middle couplets must not be the same. The fourth couplet gives an emotional response to the dominant concept (*chu-yi**) of the title, at the same time shooting a connection back into the two preceding lines—or you can say simply "When will I come again?"

This is a remarkably unembarrassed exposition of the conventional components of one poetic subgenre. Such a discussion answered the novice's need to know what to say next (and what not to say next) on a particular occasion.

The concluding "General Discussion" is a miscellaneous gathering of observations, many of which were in wide circulation.

General Discussion [selections]

詩要有天趣。不可鑿空強作。待境而生自工。或感古懷今。或傷今思古。或因事說景。或因物寄意。一篇之中。先立大意。起承轉結。三致意焉。則工緻矣。結體命意鍊句用字。此作者之四事也。體者。如作一題。須自斟酌。或騷或選或唐或江西。騷不可雜以選。選不可雜以唐。唐不可雜以江西。須要首尾渾全。不可一句似騷。一句似選。

Poetry [should have a natural excitement (*ch'ü**). It] cannot be forced out of pure speculation: it becomes spontaneously well-wrought if one waits for it to arise out of the world at hand (*ching**).[7] One may be stirred by the past and think on the present; one may be distressed by the present and long for the past; one may speak of a scene (*ching**) through some event (*shih**); one may lodge one's concepts (*yi**) in some thing (*wu**). In a single work, first establish the general idea (*yi**), and bring in the concept again and again through all four couplets; if you do this, the work will be finely done. The four tasks of a writer are: 1) constructing form, 2) commissioning concept, 3) refining lines, and 4) choosing words. As for form (*t'i**), when you take a topic, you must determine whether it is to be in the Sao mode, or in the *Wen hsüan* mode, or in the T'ang mode, or in the Chiang-hsi mode. But the Sao mode cannot be mixed with the *Wen hsüan* mode; the *Wen hsüan* mode cannot be mixed with the T'ang; and the T'ang cannot be mixed with the Chiang-hsi. It must be fused as a whole from beginning to end: you cannot have one line here like the Sao and another line there like the *Wen hsüan*.

The "Sao" style refers to the manner of the *Ch'u tz'u;* the *Wen-hsüan* was the most famous anthology of pre-T'ang poetry. The Chiang-hsi school was the most important group of poets of the twelfth century, poets who based their practice loosely on Huang T'ing-chien. Ironically, Huang T'ing-chien's work itself is characterized by clever mixing of modes, precisely what is prohibited here.

詩要鋪敘正。波瀾闊。用意深。琢句雅。使字當。下字響。觀詩之法。亦當如此求之。

In poetry it is necessary that the exposition be normative [*cheng**, straight as opposed to inverse], the waves must stretch broadly, the concept must be deep, the refinement of lines must have dignity (*ya**), the use of words must be apt, and the positioning of words must be resonant. In this manner the rules of poetry should be sought.

凡作詩。氣象欲其渾厚。體面欲其宏闊。血脈欲其貫串。風度欲其飄逸。音韻欲其鏗鏘。若琱刻傷氣。敷演露骨。此涵養之未至也。當益以學。

In all writing of poetry, the atmosphere (*ch'i*-hsiang**) should be rich and undifferentiated, the face of the form should be vast, the veins and arteries should be continuous all the way through, the style (*feng*-tu*) should drift along calmly without anxiety, the tones and rhymes should ring. If you harm the *ch'i** by excessive craft or expose the bone (*ku**) by blatant exposition, this is because you have not reached the final stage of careful nurturing—it must be ameliorated by study.

詩要首尾相應。多見人中間一聯。儘有奇特。全篇湊合。如出二手。便不成家數。此一句一字。必須著意聯合也。大概要沉著通快優游不迫而已。

In poetry the beginning and end must respond to one another. One will often see an absolutely marvelous couplet being circulated; but if we consider the coherence of the work as a whole, it seems to come from two different hands. This will not make a master. In every word and in every line, one must pay close attention to unifying—that overall principle that one must be either "firm, self-possessed, and utterly comfortable" or "straightforward and carefree."

語貴含蓄。言有盡而意無窮者。天下之至言也。如清廟之瑟。一倡三歎。而有遺音者也。

In diction value "holding in reserve" (*han-hsü*). "The words are used up, but the concept never ends" is the most perfect saying in the world. Like the zither in the "Pure Temple" [of the *Book of Songs*], "one person sings, and three sigh in response—there are tones that are omitted."

The former saying was a poetic commonplace whose most famous source was "Ts'ang-lang's Remarks on Poetry"; the latter quotation is from the "Record of Music."

詩有意格。意出於格。先得格也。格出於意。先得意也。意格欲高。句法欲響。只求句字末矣。

Poetry has concept (*yi**) and manner (*ko**, or "fixed form"). When the concept emerges from *ko**, one first of all attains the *ko**. When *ko** emerges from concept, then first of all one attains the concept. Both concept and *ko** should be lofty; the construction of lines (*chü-fa**) should be resonant; the least important thing to do is to seek the words for the line.[8]

詩有內外意。內意欲盡其理。外意欲盡其象。內外意含蓄。方妙。

Poetry has internal and external meaning (*yi**, concepts). The internal meaning should exhaust principle (*li**); the external meaning should exhaust image (*hsiang**). The greatest finesse (*miao**) is shown when both inner and outer meaning are kept in reserve (*han-hsü*).

The internal *yi** seems to refer to conceptual coherence; external *yi**, to the coherence of the empirical scene.

詩結尤難。無好結句。可見其人終無成也。詩中用事。僻事實用。熟事虛用。說理要簡易。說意要圓活。說景要微妙。議人不可露。使人不覺。

The closing of a poem is particularly hard: if the closing is not good, then we see that the person has accomplished nothing. In using references in poetry, recondite references may be used "solidly" (*shih**), but familiar references should be used "emptily" [*hsü**; i.e., touched on lightly and related to a person's thoughts]. When principle (*li**) is presented, it should be done simply; concepts (*yi**) should be presented in a round [i.e., perfect] and lively manner;

scene (*ching**) should be presented subtly. Mockery of someone should not be obvious, so that the person will not be aware of it.

人所多言。我寡言之。人所難言。我易言之。則自不俗。

What others say in many words, I should say in few words; what others find hard to say, I find easy to say—if this is the case then I will avoid uncouthness (*su*).

詩有三多。讀多。記多。作多。

Three aspects of poetry should be "much": read much, remember much, write much.

句中要有字眼。或腰。或膝。或足。無一定之處。

In a line, one word should be the eye: it may be in the waist, in the knee, or in the foot of the line [positions within the line]—there is no fixed place.

詩要苦思。詩之不工。只是不精思耳。不思而作。雖多亦奚以為。古人苦心終身。日鍊月煅。不曰「語不驚人死不休」。則曰「一生精力盡於詩」。今人未嘗學詩。往往便稱能詩。詩豈不學而能哉。

Poetry demands painstaking reflection: if a poem is no good, it's only because the writer didn't give it enough reflection. If you write without reflection, what good does it do to write in quantity? The older poets spent their whole lives in such painstaking reflection, honing and refining their poems for days and months. If it wasn't,

> If my lines don't startle others, I'll find no peace in death,

then it was,

> For a lifetime the core of my strength has been used up in poetry.

The moderns never study poetry, yet they are always claiming to know about poetry. How can a person be good at poetry without studying it?

The "Discussions to While Away the Days at Evening Hall" and "Interpretations of Poetry" of Wang Fu-chih

The critical writing of Wang Fu-chih 王夫之 (1619–1692) is remarkably rich and varied, ranging from comments in formal prose genres such as prefaces and letters, to commentaries on the *Book of Songs* and *Ch'u-tz'u*, to critical anthologies, to *shih-hua* such as "Interpretations of Poetry" (*Shih-yi* 詩譯) and "Discussions to While Away the Days at Evening Hall" (*Hsi-t'ang yung-jih hsü-lun* 夕堂永日緒論), the preface of which is dated 1690. This large corpus of literary theory and criticism should be set in the context of Wang Fu-chih's voluminous work in other fields, as a classical scholar, historian, and philosopher. Although his work was unappreciated and virtually unknown until the late Ch'ing, Wang Fu-chih was one of the most talented, learned, and prolific figures in a century notable for its talent, learning, and productiveness.

Much of Wang Fu-chih's sharpest critical and theoretical writing is to be found in his *Broad Commentary on the Book of Songs* (*Shih kuang-chuan*

詩廣傳〕and in his three anthologies, *A Critical Anthology of Old Poetry* (*Ku-shih p'ing-hsüan* 古詩評選, on pre-T'ang poems), *A Critical Anthology of T'ang Poetry* (*T'ang-shih p'ing-hsüan* 唐詩評選), and *A Critical Anthology of Ming Poetry* (*Ming-shih p'ing-hsüan* 明詩評選). There are, unfortunately, serious difficulties in presenting these works to the English reader. The *Shih kuang-chuan* has deep roots in the long and complex tradition of scholarship on the *Book of Songs*, and the issues it addresses are often comprehensible only within that tradition (the reader can see something of the complexity of that tradition in my discussion of the first entry below). On the other hand, Wang's critical and theoretical comments in the anthologies respond *ad hoc* to particular poems, and their value is often apparent only by close familiarity with the poems to which they are attached.[1] Although the "Discussions" are in many ways less intellectually supple than the preceding works, this *shih-hua* remains one of the finest in the tradition.

As a passionate loyalist to the fallen Ming, Wang Fu-chih worked largely in isolation from the scholarship of his day; he was a cantankerous figure, given to extreme judgments. He was an excellent thinker, but he was also a tendentious one. He was a solitary revisionist, seeking to reunite the values of secular poetry to his own understanding of the values embodied in the *Book of Songs*; and like all solitary revisionists, his solitude gave him the license to articulate positions that would have been more difficult to maintain in the more sociable world of most Ch'ing scholarship.

Although the "Discussions" are no more unified than most "remarks on poetry," the same values and concerns recur throughout. Wang begins by distinguishing the indeterminacy of affect and significance in the *Book of Songs* from the later poetic tradition (allowing a few privileged moments in the later tradition to preserve something of the ancient poetry). As the poems of the *Book of Songs* are valued for the absence of any single determinate intent, poetry in the later tradition is valued for precisely the opposite, for its historical authenticity: a single, empirically determined unity of state of mind, situation, and moment. In the best later poetry we should see "what it was really like then." In a less subtle way than his contemporary Yeh Hsieh, Wang Fu-chih is here taking up arms against the aesthetic values that grew out of the lineage of "Ts'ang-lang's Remarks on Poetry," against the claim that poetry is a speculative art divorced from the direct presentation of lived experience. Throughout the "Discussions," Wang returns repeatedly to the proposition that aesthetic effect cannot be separated from an empirical event, what the poet really perceived and what the poet really felt.

DISCUSSIONS TO WHILE AWAY THE DAYS AT EVENING HALL

子曰。小子。何莫學夫詩。詩可以興。可以觀。可以群。可以怨。

He said, "My little ones, why don't you study the *Book of Songs*? By the *Songs* you can stir, you can consider, you can express fellowship, you can show resentment."

Analects XVII.9

I

興。觀。羣。怨。詩盡於是矣。經生家析鹿鳴嘉魚為羣。柏舟小弁為怨。小人一往之喜怒耳。何足以言詩。可以云者。隨所以而皆可也。詩三百篇而下。唯十九首能然。李杜亦髣髴遇之。然其能俾人隨觸而皆可。亦不數數也。又下或一可焉。或無一可者。故許渾允為惡詩。王僧孺庾肩吾及宋人皆爾。

"Stir," "consider," "express fellowship," "show resentment": this says everything there is to say in regard to poetry. Classical scholars interpret "The Deer Cry Out" [of the *Book of Songs*] as expressing fellowship; they take "Cypress Boat" and "The Small Cap" [of the *Songs*] as showing resentment—as if these were nothing more than some small-minded person losing himself in joy or rage. How can you talk about the *Songs* with such a person? In saying "can by" [Confucius means that] "by" any one [of the *Songs*] all [four functions] "can" be realized. After the *Book of Songs* only the "Nineteen Old Poems" were able to achieve this.[2] Li Po and Tu Fu will also hit upon something vaguely like this, but it is not all that common that one of their poems is able to produce any of the four [functions] depending on what [situation] a person encounters. On the level beneath Li Po and Tu Fu, sometimes one [of the four] can occur; sometimes none can occur. Thus Hsü Hun must be considered a dreadful poet; Wang Seng-ju and Yü Chien-wu [Southern dynasties poets] and the Sung writers are all the same.

This passage with its claims that every poem in the *Book of Songs* can be seen to have any of the four canonical functions of poetry should be read in the context of a very similar passage, the second entry in Wang's "Interpretations of Poetry," *Shih-yi*:

> "By the Songs you can stir, you can consider, you can express fellowship, you can show resentment." That says everything there is to say. According to this criterion you can judge the grace and success of Han, Wei, T'ang, and Sung [poetry]. And you *must* use this criterion to read the *Book of Songs*. In saying "can by" [Confucius means that] "by" whichever [of the *Songs*] all [four functions] "can" be realized. By what "stirred" [the writer of the *Song*] you can "consider," and the stirring becomes deeper. By what was "considered," you yourself can be "stirred," and the consideration becomes more reflective. By the *Song's* "expression of fellowship," you may feel "resentment," and the resentment is intensified and not to be forgotten. By the *Song's* "show of resentment," you can "express fellowship" and the expression of fellowship is all the more warm and cordial. One goes beyond [any single one of] the four

affections (ch'ing*), and thus gives rise to the four affections. One wanders within the four affections, and the affections are obstructed by nothing. The writer [of the Song] engages a single, unified thought; but each reader grasps it according to his own state of mind (ch'ing*). [Here Wang includes two complicated historical examples in which the original mode of a Song was transformed into a different mode by a new context]. The wanderings of human affections are unbounded, and what is valued in having the Songs is that each person meet it with his own state of mind. [The passage closes with this as a criterion for judging poets, periods, and critics.][3]

Like so many critics before him, Wang Fu-chih here attempted to assume the authority of Confucius' voice. Confucius commented that the Book of Songs could be "summed up in one phrase—no warped thoughts" (Analects II.2). Wang Fu-chih made the same essentialist gesture, though in different words: "That says everything there is to say in regard to poetry." Several times Confucius expressed his approval of a disciple by saying he could now "talk about the Songs (yen Shih 言詩)" with that person; Wang uses the same phrase negatively, finding run-of-the-mill classicists unworthy of dialogue ("How can you talk about the Songs with such a person?").

Such echoes of Confucius' voice may have helped lend authority to a position that was radical in its implications. Confucius acknowledged four possible functions in any one of the Songs (the capacities to stir, consider, express fellowship, show resentment).[4] Wang Fu-chih accepted that each Song did have some original inherent affective quality (this is clear from the two examples omitted in the passage from "Interpretations of Poetry" above); but when placed in relation to the present circumstances of a reader, the original quality might be transformed into any of the other four. Such a capacity for the transformation of affective quality was taken by Wang to be the essential characteristic of the Songs.

Wang's hermeneutic was not without some basis in the long history of interpretation of the Book of Songs: a contradiction in the interpretation of a Song was often explained as due to varying circumstances in its application. For example, if the exegetes could not decide whether a Song was criticism or praise, they might say that it was composed in praise of King X, but when recited in the decadent age of King Y, was intended as criticism (by the contrast between the state of affairs in King Y's reign and the days of King X).

Wang's position here represents a penultimate stage in the evolution of the hermeneutics of the Book of Songs.[5] From the Han through the T'ang, every poem of the Book of Songs was presumed to have an authorial or editorial (i.e., from Confucius) intention that would necessarily generate a specific response in the reader. That is, if the poem expressed resentment (either directly or ironically, by assumed context), the reader's affections would be shaped or imprinted with the normative feeling of resentment and the kind of circumstances in which such a response would be appropriate.[6] It was on such a presumption that the notion of the Book of Songs as a moral education of the sentiments was founded. Such confident assumptions about the determinate affect of the *Songs* was crumbling in the Sung, and finally collapsed in Chu Hsi's attempt to reconcile the dubious morality of certain of the *Songs* with Confucius' dictum that the *Songs* have "no warped thoughts" (*Analects* II.2). Chu Hsi's dangerous resolution was that the virtue embodied in an individual *Song* resided in the virtue of the reader (thus a virtuous reader would recognize immorality in certain of the *Songs* and have his moral sense sharpened by the experience). The reader is no longer "imprinted" by the *Song*; and there is a balanced, reflective relation between the inherent quality of the *Song* and the nature of the reader.

Wang Fu-chih goes several steps further: the functional quality of each *Song* becomes an event in reading—not an original quality to be contemplated, but a relation between the original quality and the present circumstances of the reader. This is remarkably similar to Gadamer's acceptance of readerly "prejudice" in *Truth and Method* and his rejection of Schleiermacher's hermeneutic project to recover a text's original intent. In Wang Fu-chih's view, we are not essentially interested in the past world embedded in the *Book of Songs* or in the normative moral project of the Classic per se; rather, that past world is always framed by and leads back into the circumstantial situation of the present. The *Song* does have inherent qualities, but these qualities "appear" to us only in relation to the present. Moreover, as Wang develops this position in the "Interpretations of Poetry," one kind of response in reading resolves into another: contemplation becomes stirring; stirring becomes contemplation; resentment and the expression of fellowship alternate. In the latter part of the passage from "Interpretations of Poetry" above, the poem becomes a play of the moral affections (*ch'ing**).

In the final part of the first entry in the "Discussions," Wang addresses the serious problem of how these ultimate values, embodied in the *Book of Songs*, relate to the later, "secular" poetic tradition.[7] The question is whether the significance of the poetic text is finally determined by the writer's circumstances (or some other originating circumstance) or by the reader's circumstances. The truism that significance comes, in fact, from both is less interesting than how the reader perceives his role—as listening to Other or as immediately applying the words to himself. The tradition of literary interpretation (as opposed to the interpretation of the *Book of Songs* after Chu Hsi) had always stressed that the writer was of central importance, that the reader's primary function was to listen, to understand the other, and to share. Thus if a T'ang poem "expresses resentment," the Ch'ing reader should understand it purely in those terms. Even the revision of that project in Yen Yü's notion of "poetic image" still did not shift the center of the reading experience to the reader's appropriation of the poem for his own situation. To have placed the center of significance in the reader's own circumstantially determined response would have seriously undermined the very basis of post-Classical poetry; and Wang Fu-chih avoids that threat by asserting that the reader-centered mode of poetry scarcely survives after the "Nineteen Old Poems." Thus the reader-centered text is retained as the highest value in poetry, but kept securely on the reservation of antiquity, allowing Wang Fu-chih to go on to discuss "secular" poetry in familiar terms—as in the next passage, where he tells us that in poetry authorial concept (*yi**) is the "dominant factor."

I said above that the position described is the "penultimate" phase in the interpretation of the *Book of Songs*. The final move, which Wang makes in his *Broad Commentary on the Book of Songs*, is truly radical and distinctly modern. Wang takes the notion that the particular quality of a *Song* is a relation between its original quality and present circumstance, that the affect shifts through alternatives in the process of reading; in the *Broad Commentary on the Book of Songs*, he claims that such shifting qualities do not occur merely in the process of reading, but rather are inherent in the original poem. Antithetical qualities of affect inhere in each of the *Songs*: a *Song* may both express fellowship and show resentment, with each contradictory quality necessary to the other. One occupies the center, while the other is "lodged to the side," latent as an implicit alternative that strengthens the primary quality. Of course, this multiplicity of qualities, shadowed by their alternatives, is restricted to the ancient poetry of the *Book of Songs*.

> If in the expression of fellowship [the writer] does not forget resentment, yet the resentment is lodged to the side and does not obviously conflict, then one can have resentment and not be in any danger of failing to express fellowship. Thus the expression of fellowship is securely planted and not blind. Only the poets of the ancient dynasties could feel resentment and still be able to express fellowship, or to feel fellowship and still be able to show resentment.[8]

The modern reader may be somewhat put off by the fact that this sophisticated theoretical position must be put in terms of the paradigmatic examples, "expressing fellowship" and "showing resentment." In part, this is due to the richness those terms had acquired in the exegetical tradition of the *Book of Songs*; in part, it is because literary Chinese refers to the variations within a class concept by one privileged antithesis. If we were to translate Wang's argument above into the conceptual forms of English argument, we would get something like this:

> If, in presenting one emotion, the writer does not forget other contradictory emotions and, further, if those contradictory emotions are submerged and not set in conflict with the first, then they can be present without disrupting the presentation of the primary emotion. (In contrast, if both are overt, then one has a state of conflict rather than one emotion shadowed by latent alternatives.) In this way the primary emotion has a firm ground in not suppressing the contradictions that attend it.

This is still not quite a Western argument, but it is a persuasive statement on the credible presentation of emotion or mood: no emotion is unitary, but rather it is a complex balance of alternatives, desired or feared. These alternatives are not necessarily in open conflict with the primary emotion, but rather stand off "to the side."

II

無論詩歌與長行文字。俱以意為主。意猶帥也。無帥之兵。謂之烏合。李杜所以稱大家者。無意之詩十不得一二也。煙雲泉石。花鳥苔林。金鋪錦帳。寓意則靈。若齊梁綺語。宋人搏合成句之出處。役心向彼掇索。而不恤己情之所自發。此之謂小家數。總在圈繢中求活計也。

No matter whether it is in poetry, song, or writing in long lines [prose], concept (*yi**) is always the dominant factor. Concept is like a leader, and troops without a leader are called a mob. The reason Li Po and Tu Fu are acclaimed as great masters is that such [governing] concept is absent in less than ten or twenty percent of their poems. If such concept is lodged in mists, clouds, streams, stones, flowers, birds, mosses, forests, gilded spreads or tents of brocade, then any of these can become numinous (*ling*). But when it comes to the florid diction of the Ch'i and Liang poets or to the "source texts" [from earlier poets] which Sung writers compounded to make their own poetic lines— when Sung writers discuss poems they always look for "sources" for every word—then one's mind (*hsin**) is made a servant in the task of gathering from others and no heed is paid to what one's own affections (*ch'ing**) bring forth spontaneously. This makes a person a "minor master"—something like trying to make your living while a prisoner in the stocks.

Ever since Ts'ao P'i, in his "Discourse on Literature," had claimed that *ch'i** was the "dominant factor" (*chu*) in poetry, various other claimants to the role had arisen, each with its own lineage of supporters. The dominance of *yi**, some "concept" or "conceptual intent," had first been proposed by the historian Fan Hua 范曄 (398–445); but it was the poet Tu Mu 杜牧 (803–853), author of a commentary on the military classic *Sun-tzu* 孫子, who had introduced the military metaphor used here by Wang Fu-chih in his opening lines, and Tu who had first warned of disarray if hierarchical order was not maintained.

Such a model of command and subordination is itself more significant than any particular decision about which element is "in command" (or serves as "host," another meaning of *chu* which comes into play in Wang's sixth entry below). Instead of seeing elements of the text in hierarchies, Chinese literary thought tended to see them as organically related, the aspects or stages in a process: it favored models of the text as organism. As we have seen, however, such an organic model (associated with "natural," involuntary self-manifestation) tends to surrender authorial control; and the contrary desire to assert control generated this alternative model of command and subordination. A command structure was, in fact, only one variation on a whole range of essentialist or originary descriptions of the writing process, defining some root from which the rest of a poem grows. Each claims that if the writer masters one dominant factor, all other elements will fall into their proper place (as Wang does in the next entry); and it is this belief in spontaneous conformity to proper authority that separates such theories from "low," how-to poetics and from Western rhetorical theories, both of which are models of perfect authorial control.

As Wang Fu-chih is using it here, *yi** is some intended meaning or purpose. "Mists, clouds, streams, stones" and other non-human things are not valuable simply in themselves, but should carry a sense of the poet's own concerns. Without being metaphorical, their presentation should be infused with the poet's interests. Here, too, is subordination: their presence in the poem is revealed as a function of mind. The "numinous," *ling*, quality that they achieve is precisely what is said to distinguish human beings from other things of the world ("mankind is the most numinous of beings," *wei jen tsui ling* 惟人最靈): thus imbuing the things of the scene with *ling* is a humanization of the landscape.

Wang Fu-chih clearly sees these values in opposition to the sensuously ornamental poetry of the later Southern Dynasties (Ch'i and Liang) and to the intertextual play of Sung poetry. But in the polemical impulses beneath the passage, Wang has overstated his case and drawn close to a totalitarian vision of composition ruled by overt conceptual intent; and he will attempt to escape from this in the subsequent entry. That he does not entirely mean what he says is attested by several passages in his critical anthologies, in which he attacks the idea that *yi** is the "dominant factor" in poetry. For example, in commenting on a poem by the fifth-century poet, Pao Chao, he attacks Sung poetry for precisely the position he advocates here:

> Here sensuous beauty arises from sound and sentiment (*sheng-ch'ing** 聲情). In contrast, when Sung writers discussed poetry, they took *yi** as the dominant factor. In this sort of stuff, where *yi** is used like a public declaration, there is little difference from [the words of] a village Taoist priest or a blind girl singing moral ballads.[9]

More radically in his anthology of Ming poetry Wang writes:

> Poetry's far-reaching breadth and depth, along with its setting aside the old and pursuing novelty, do not reside in *yi** [acts of willful intention]. The T'ang poets wrote old-style poems with *yi**; Sung writers wrote regulated verses and quatrains with *yi**; and [in both cases] poetry perished. *Yi** is fine for supplementing the *Book of Changes* or expounding on the *Book of Documents*, but it has nothing to do with the *Book of Songs* [or "poetry" in general].[10]

把定一題一人一事一物。於其上求形模。求比似。求詞采。求故實。如鈍斧子劈櫟柞。皮屑紛霏。何嘗動得一絲紋理。以意為主。勢次之。勢者。意中之神理也。唯謝康樂為能取勢。宛轉屈伸以求盡其意。意已盡則止。殆無剩語。夭矯連蜷。煙雲繚繞。乃真龍。非畫龍也。

If a person decides on a certain topic, or person, or event, and then first of all seeks to describe its appearance, or seeks some similitude, or seeks flashy rhetoric, or anecdotes and relevant facts, it resembles nothing so much as hacking at an oak tree with a blunt ax—fragments of the bark scatter all over the place, but you never get even the least sliver of the grain. As concept (*yi**) is the dominant factor, momentum (*shih**) follows from it. Momentum is the principle of spirit (*shen**-li**) within concept. Only Hsieh Ling-yün [385–433] was able to grasp momentum so that it wound sinuously, contracting and stretching in such a way that the concept was completely fulfilled. When concept was completely fulfilled, it stopped without any excess of words. It winds and coils, like clouds and vapors intertwining—a true dragon this, and no painted dragon.

Chopping hardwood with a blunt ax goes no farther than the bark: it touches only externals and never reaches the "heart" (*hsin**, also the "heartwood" of a tree, its "core") of the matter. In addition to the implicit double reference of *hsin**, another play on words is involved in "grain," *wen**-li** 紋理, which is essentially no different from *wen**-li** 文理, the "principle of writing." The metaphor both continues the second entry in its focus on inner *yi** and at the same time modulates toward a more organic description of the unfolding text in the rest of the passage. One looks not for surfaces but what lies in *hsin** ("heartwood"/"mind"); and even though the metaphor seems to locate the *hsin** in the topic of the poem, it soon becomes apparent that it is the authentic *hsin** of the writer.

In *Wen-hsin tiao-lung** "momentum", *shih**, followed organically from "normative form," *t'i**. Here momentum follows naturally from the more particular and interior *yi**. Every *yi** has its own momentum, in which the textual presentation of the *yi** unfolds until it is completely fulfilled. In the inner force that emerges naturally from *yi**, the text seems to have vital, organic life, a "principle of spirit," *shen**-li**. The image of command and control in the second entry of "Discussions" here becomes an organic center that carries all externals along with it. *Yi** is a hypostatized whole; through *shih**, "momentum," it takes on extension in space and time in the temporality of the text.

A "painted dragon" is the result of focus on mere externals, as described in the opening metaphor: it does not move organically. The true dragon is an image of transformation and inner power; moreover, as the true dragon draws the changing configurations of the clouds along with its movements, so the determining factors (*yi** with its *shih**) of a poem pull external, easily determinable elements of a text in changing configurations around their movement.

The metaphor of the dragon was given a famous elaboration by Chao Chih-hsin 趙執信 (1662–1744) in the first entry of his *shih-hua*, "On Dragons," *T'an-lung lu* 談龍錄 (preface 1709, but recalling an earlier discussion). It is very unlikely that Chao knew of Wang Fu-chih's comment:

> Hung Sheng [1646?–1704, poet and dramatist] had long been a follower of Wang Shih-chen [the most prominent poet of the latter part of the seventeenth century] and was also a friend of mine. One day we were all discussing poetry at Wang Shih-chen's house; and Hung Sheng, despising the lack of order in contemporary poetry said, "A poem is like a dragon, with head, tail, claws, horns, scales, and fins—if any one of these is missing, it's no dragon." Wang Shih-chen scoffed at this: "A poem is indeed like the divine being which is the dragon: you may see its head without seeing its tail. In the clouds nothing more may be revealed than a claw or a scale—no one ever gets to see the whole form. What you are talking about is nothing more than the sculpture or painting of a dragon." At that point I said, "The divine being which is the dragon contracts and stretches in its transformations and has no fixed form (*t'i**) whatsoever. One who gazes at it sees only a blur, and at best may point out a scale or a claw; but of course the dragon, complete from head to tail, is right there."[11]

This series of metaphors comprehends three increasingly sophisticated senses of form and its relation to "what is presented" in a poem. Hung Sheng offers the view most often seen in popular poetics (a view scorned by sophisticated literary men such as Wang Shih-chen and Chao Chih-hsin), that there is a fixed form made up of component parts, corresponding to the whole of what is presented. A good poem, then, gives an orderly presentation of these "parts." The problem seen in such a conception of poetry is that it is essentially incomplete by being inanimate, hence the reference to sculpture and "painting" (here *hui* 繪 rather than the more elevated term *hua* 畫, *hui* carrying something of the quality of "illustration"). Wang Shih-chen's response to the incompleteness of static presentation—the inability to write animate spirit into the surface of the text—is a willful incompleteness of presentation on the part of the poet: revealed form becomes synecdoche, constantly pointing beyond the surface to a greater whole. Chao Chih-hsin takes this a step further to a notion of transformational form, in which what appears on the surface of the text is always in flux, pointing beyond the surface to the animate metamorphoses of "what is presented." These values become clearer if we recall that classical poetry is concerned with the animate motions of mind/heart (*hsin**) or with the apprehension of the world by mind. Wang

Fu-chih would probably have taken the part of Chao Chih-hsin, while reminding him that the poem-dragon is not simply transformation but some center (*yi**) from which transformations follow.

IV

「池塘生春草」。「蝴蝶飛南園」。「明月照積雪」。皆心中目中與相融浹。一出語時。即得珠圓玉潤。要亦各視其所懷來。而與景相迎者也。「日暮天無雲。春風散微和」。想見陶令當時胸次。豈夾雜鉛汞水。能作此語。程子謂見濂溪一月坐春風中。非程子不能知濂溪如此。非陶令不能自知如此也。

> Pool and pond grow with springtime plants
>
> [Hsieh Ling-yün]
>
> Butterflies flutter in the southern gardens
>
> [Chang Hsieh (d. ca. 307)]
>
> The bright moon shines on drifts of snow
>
> [Hsieh Ling-yün]

In each of these, what is in the mind and what is in the eye are fused together. Once they come out in language, we get a perfect sphere of pearl and the moist sensation of jade: what is essential is that in each case the poet looks to what comes from his own heart and to what meets the scene (*ching**) at hand.

> At the evening of the day no clouds are in the sky,
> And springtime breezes spread faint balminess.

In your imagination you can see T'ao Ch'ien's state of mind at that moment. One of those alchemists, with his concoctions of mercury and lead, could never write lines like these. Ch'eng Hao [1032–1085, Neo-Confucian philosopher] claimed to have seen Chou Tun-yi [1017–1073, also a Neo-Confucian philosopher] "sit a whole month in the spring breeze." No one but Ch'eng Hao could have understood Chou Tun-yi so well; no one but T'ao Ch'ien could have understood himself so well.

As Tai Hung-sen points out, Wang Fu-chih has misremembered the story of Chun Kuang-t'ing seeing Ch'eng Hao as a story of Ch'eng Hao seeing Chou Tun-yi.[12] Tai further suggests that Wang Fu-chih's contemptuous reference to "alchemists" is to affirm T'ao Ch'ien's Confucian values, rather than the Taoist values conventionally attributed to him; but it seems more likely that the term refers to the poetry of T'ao Ch'ien's Eastern Tsin contemporaries, in which Neo-Taoist alchemical and spiritualist themes played an important role.

This is the first passage in the *shih-hua* treating one of Wang Fu-chih's central concerns, the perfect fusion of scene (*ching**) and the affections or "state of mind" (*ch'ing**). The three examples with which he opens are as simple as they are famous (the two Hsieh Ling-yün lines being much more well known than the line by Chang Hsieh). For Wang such simplicity is an essential part of their naturalness: a more ingenious line would implicate a reflective twisting of perception. More elusive is the way in which *ch'ing** participates at all in the articulation of the scenes: this requires a certain disposition on the part of the reader to see in the lines something deeper than neutral description; it is perhaps the way the beauty of these scenes engages us, making us recognize that the poetic formulation of the scene must have involved a corresponding engagement on the poet's part. That engagement on the part of the poet is implicit and muted, therefore, as if "fused" with the scene itself. In the same way, T'ao Ch'ien's couplet presents not simply the scene as it was in itself, but T'ao Ch'ien's "state of mind" (*ch'ing**) at that moment; the state of mind found some corresponding quality in the scene at hand, and that perfect match of inner and outer becomes the couplet we have.

The fifth entry in Wang Fu-chih's "Discussions," given next, depends on the story that the T'ang poet Chia Tao was trying to decide whether to use the verb "pushes" or "knocks at" in a line "The monk . . . the gate beneath the moon." While he was wandering through the streets of the capital, reciting the verse in both ways to weigh the choice, he got in the way of the magistrate, who just happened to be the famous writer Han Yü. Chia Tao explained what he was doing, to which Han Yü answered "Use 'knock.'" Eventually the compound "push-knock," *t'ui-ch'iao* 推敲 became the standard term to describe careful stylistic judgments.

V

「僧敲月下門」。祇是妄想揣摩。如說他人夢。縱令形容酷似。何嘗毫髮關心。知然者。以其沈吟「推」「敲」二字。就他作想也。若即景會心。則或推或敲。必居其一。因景因情。自然靈妙。何勞擬議哉。「長河落日圓」。初無定景。「隔水問樵夫」。初非想得。則禪家所謂現量也。

"The monk knocks at the gate beneath the moon" is nothing more than mere guessing, false speculation (*hsiang*), as if trying to describe someone else's dream. Even if the description seems very lifelike, it doesn't truly touch the heart in the least. Those who understand this will recognize that brooding over the choice between "push" and "knock" is mere speculation on behalf of some other. But if the scene (*ching**) meets mind (*hsin**), then it may be "push" or it may be "knock," but it will have to be one or the other: since it will follow from scene and follow from state of mind (*ch'ing**), the line will be naturally (*tzu-jan**) numinous and subtle (*ling-miao**). There will be none of the bother of debating the right choice.

"Over the long rivers sinks the circle of sun" [a line by Wang Wei] did not start out as a predetermined scene. "Ask the woodcutter on the other side of the river" [Wang Wei] did not start out as something thought up (*hsiang-tê*). This is what the Ch'an masters call "Presence."

Here and in the seventh entry of the "Discussions," we see the full force of a non-fictional poetic tradition. Many earlier critics had expressed dissatisfaction with the poetics of "push-knock," craftsmanship based on careful stylistic choices; but Wang Fu-chih was the first to grasp why the story was repugnant to one strain in traditional literary thought. To ponder such a choice meant that Chia Tao had never actually experienced that scene; or if he had experienced such a scene, that he allowed willful distortion in its presentation. This choice admits inauthentic and purely "literary" criteria. Such a stylistic indecision meant that the scene that would appear in a poem was invented. The next assumption made by Wang Fu-chih was that such a scene could never be poetically effective because good poetry arises only when one's state of mind happens on its counterpart in the external world. This not only excludes traditional Western fictionality, in which the poet invents circumstances for states of mind he does not feel, it also excludes the Romantic revision of such fictionality in which the poet is allowed to invent circumstances for authentic states of mind. According to Wang Fu-chih, if Chia Tao had been there, he would have known whether the monk "pushed" or "knocked"—and whatever action the monk (probably Chia Tao himself, who had been a monk before he came to the capital) took, that action would have appeared effectively in poetry only if it had genuinely mattered to him. That demand for empirical truth, both internal and external, yields the poetic sense of "Presence," *hsien-liang*.

VI

詩文俱有主賓。無主之賓。謂之烏合。俗論以比為賓。以賦為主。以反為賓。以正為主。皆塾師賺童子死法耳。立一主以待賓。賓無非主之賓者。乃俱有情而相浹洽。若夫「秋風吹渭水。落葉滿長安」。於賈島何與。「湘潭雲盡暮煙出。巴蜀雪消春水來」。於許渾奚涉。皆烏合也。「影靜千官裏。心蘇七挍前」。得主矣。尚有痕迹。「花迎劍佩星初落」。則賓主歷然。鎔合一片。

In both poetry and prose there is a host [*chu*, translated earlier as "dominant factor"] and there are guests. Guests without a host are known as a "mob." In popular poetics, writers may take comparison (*pi**) as the guest and unfigured exposition (*fu*) as the host; or they may take movements of reversal as the guest and straightforward movement as the host. All of these are "dead rules" (*ssu-fa**) by which village schoolmasters hoodwink little boys. When there is a host to attend to the guests, and when all the guests are indeed guests of that host, then for everyone the states of mind (*ch'ing**) [proper to each member in the relation] are fused together [i.e., the state of mind of being a guest or host exists only in that reciprocal relation].

Consider a couplet like [Chia Tao's]

Autumn winds blow over the Wei,
And falling leaves fill Ch'ang-an.

What does that have to do with Chia Tao?! Or [Hsü Hun's]

The clouds are gone from the pools of the Hsiang, the evening mists emerge,
When the snow melts to the west in Szechwan, springs floods come down.

How is that involved with Hsü Hun? Both couplets are "mobs." But [Tu Fu's]

This shadow calms among the thousand officers,
The heart revives before the seven ranks.

There is indeed a host here, but it still shows the traces [of conscious craftsmanship]. [Consider Ts'en Shen's]

Flowers greet the sword-hung sash just as the stars are setting.

Here the relation between guest and host is perfectly clear, fused into a single piece.

Wang Fu-chih probably recognized the potential for abuse in his earlier discussion of *yi** as equated with the "dominant factor" or "host" (*chu*). In the passage on momentum, he attempted to modulate his discussion toward a more organic view of the elements in a poem. Here he develops a model of *chu* very different from the "command" of a military officer. *Chu*, the "host," acts on behalf of the guests, as the guests defer to the intentions of the host: the two roles exist only through their mutual relation, or as Wang Fu-chih says, they are "fused together." In the examples he gives, it is clear that in the proper host-guest relation the "host," *yi**, is not abstract "concept," but rather what is on the poet's mind. *Yi** not only guarantees authenticity, it also lets us know "who the poet is," gives a sense of identity, as in the following passage from Wang's *Critical Anthology of T'ang Poetry*:

The Way of poetry must set up a host to take care of the guests, and following from that, to describe the scene before you (*hsien-ching** 現景). If you have one statement of affections and one of scene and there is a clear boundary between them, then the relation of host and guest will break down into confusion, and in neither will you have any sense of who the writer is. A scene established outside of what is on a person's mind (*yi**) or something coming to mind outside of a [particular] scene is very much like eyes and a nose appearing on a cyst: weird, not normal.[13]

The couplets which lack a "host" are those that do not implicate the poet. Obviously a great deal depends on how much one reads into a line of poetry: the opening examples in the fourth entry of the "Discussions," held up as the perfect fusion of ching* and ch'ing*, on the surface no more directly concern their poets than does Chia Tao's famous couplet cited here—indeed many traditional critics found the Chia Tao couplet very beautiful and intensely personal.

The only criterion that would discredit the couplets of Chia Tao and Hsü Hun is that both speak of things beyond the perceptual experience of the moment (cf. "Discussions," entries V, VII, and VIII). The "lie" of fictionality (even the mild extrapolation of Chia Tao's inner vision to encompass all Ch'ang-an) makes a couplet or a line an "art product" and thus inauthentic. What *is* strange is that a line so mannered as Ts'en Shen's above is given as an example of perfect authenticity. Wang Fu-chih's judgment and his examples are often questionable, but at the same time he shows a courageous and intelligent radicalism in carrying some of the central assumptions of traditional poetics to their inevitable conclusion. Nowhere is that clearer than in the next passage.

VII

身之所歷。目之所見。是鐵門限。即極寫大景。如「陰晴眾壑殊」。「乾坤日夜浮」。亦必不踰此限。非按輿地圖便可云「平野入青徐」也。抑登樓所得見者耳。隔垣聽演雜劇。可聞其歌。不見其舞。更遠則但聞鼓聲。而可云所演何齣乎。前有齊梁。後有晚唐及宋人。皆欺心以炫巧。

What one has passed through with one's own body, what one has seen with one's own eyes—these are iron-gated limits. Even when describing scenes of the greatest magnitude, such as [Wang Wei's description of the vista of a mountain range], "Some in shadow, some in sun—its many valleys differ," or [Tu Fu looking over the vastness of Lake Tung-t'ing], "Heaven and Earth float day and night," one still must not transgress these limits. It was not by examining some map that Tu Fu could write, "The level wilderness goes off into Ching and Hsü"; rather, this is simply what he saw when climbing high in a building. If one listens to an opera being performed on the other side of a wall, one can hear the songs but cannot see the dances. If one is still further away, one can hear the sound of the drums, but can't even tell what play is being performed. The first case describes the poetry of the Ch'i and Liang; the second case describes the late-T'ang and Sung poets. But both deceive the mind with their dazzling cleverness.

If it is true that a genuine "state of mind," ch'ing*, and a genuine "scene," ching*, come into being through one another, if, in other words, it is true that they are a mutually defining relation, then the radical claim made in this passage becomes necessary. An invented scene will be entirely contingent on the poet's "state of mind": it will not have the autonomous subsistence that makes it possible to generate that "state of mind" (see "Discussions" entry XVII). Such an invented scene will expose itself to the reader as an intentional construct rather than as an encounter. In this we see most clearly the claim that lies at the heart of classical Chinese poetry: its capacity to make us care for it is grounded in the poet's accidental encounters in empirical, historical experience. Though the presumption differs strongly from deep and unstated presumptions in the Western tradition about emotion or "state of mind," it is a presumption that may have some truth to it: one cannot have genuine *ch'ing* without genuine *ching**; authentic inner reality and encountering the outer world are bound together.

We should first note that this is a theoretical exposition of values in poetry and not a description of the way poetry always is; moreover, the explicitness of the claim as it is made here (as opposed to its status as implicit assumption in early theory) is an indication that poetry was indeed turning to a different course, one in which the demand of "art" might indeed overwhelm empirical, historical experience. The explicit demand for this kind of authenticity can be made only when surrounded by the danger of inauthenticity. Although this appears in a world where poetry is becoming inauthentic "art," it retains great importance as a value.

One indication of these new directions is Wang Fu-chih's singularly inappropriate choice of drama as a metaphor for direct and indirect experience. As in the West, Chinese drama feigns emotion and feigns experience; and the arias of Chinese operatic drama were dangerously close to being the inauthentic fictional counterparts of classical poetry, in which a character in the play sings a lyric response to some circumstance that is not real. Hearing a dramatic performance across a wall and from a distance may be a credible metaphor for speculative and indirect experience; but if we complete the analogy with someone directly observing the performance, we would have "the direct experience of and authentic response to something feigned"— which is precisely what Wang Fu-chih says is not possible. Drama's early importance in the Western literary tradition established a literary theory based on fictionality; drama's much later appearance in China, its popularity and undeniable emotional effectiveness, posed a serious challenge to traditional poetic theory and its non-fictional values. Fictionality was probably the primary reason neither drama nor prose fiction was admitted to the category of "literature."

Wang Fu-chih's enemy here is the late-T'ang poet who writes a good couplet, then waits to construct a poem in which to place it (cf. Ou-yang Hsiu's "Remarks on Poetry," XI, p. 374). His fear is that such poetry will be effective and alluring, just as drama is alluring; but unlike drama, where we know the emotion is feigned, the false line in lyric poetry may be mistakenly taken as genuine. Against that fear Wang Fu-chih essentially repeats the claim made in *Mencius* II.A.2: "When someone's words are one-sided, I understand how his mind is clouded." That is, if one knows how to read well, inauthentic poetry (such as that of Chia Tao or Hsü Hun) will reveal itself as inauthentic; and when it is revealed as inauthentic, it cannot be genuinely moving.

VIII

一詩止於一時一事。自十九首至陶謝皆然。「夔府孤城落日斜」。繼以「月映荻花」。亦自日斜至月出詩乃成耳。若杜陵長篇。有歷數月日事者。合為一章。大雅有此體。後唯焦仲卿。木蘭二詩為然。要以從旁追敘。非言情之章也。為歌行則合。五言固不宜爾。

A single poem is limited to one time and to one event (*shih**). From the "Nine-teen Old Poems" to T'ao Ch'ien, it was always that way. When Tu Fu wrote, "On K'uei-chou's solitary walls the setting sun slants," and followed it by the line "The moon shines on the reed blossoms," the poem was completed be-tween the time that the sun set and the time when the moon came out. But in Tu Fu's longer poems, there are some events (*shih**) that occur within the space of several days or months, joined within a single work. Such a form can also be found in the "Greater Odes" [of the *Book of Songs*]. Thereafter only "Southeast Flies the Peacock" and the "Ballad of Mu-lan" are in this mode. It is essential that such poems be related from the outside; they are not works which articulate the affections (*ch'ing**). This works well in songs, but it is not at all acceptable in poetry in pentasyllabic lines.

Wang Fu-chih continues to struggle with the problem of "presence" and au-thenticity, turning now to narrative poems which, by their nature, extend beyond a unified moment in time. It is the desire for authenticity rather than for verisimilitude that leads him to this quasi-Aristotelian requirement of the unity of time and event. However, there is a mode of narrative poetry that goes beyond a unified moment. A brief linear span of time, as in the lines quoted from the second of Tu Fu's "Autumn Meditations" can be assimilated to the demand for "one time" by the notion of the time of composition or the time of a unified experience (from sunset to moonrise). Poems that treat longer spans of time force Wang to appeal to the authority of precedents in the "Greater Odes" of the *Book of Songs*. This leads him to a notion of generic contracts, that in some forms of poetry the speaker may bear a re-lation to what is said that is not immediate: "related from the outside," or literally "reflectively told in sequence from the sideline," *ts'ung-p'ang chui-hsü* 從旁追敘. Note that he speaks of this generic contract as a restric-tion: such a mode of presentation is acceptable in one form, but it should never transgress its boundaries into other forms. Wang Fu-chih's real interests lie in the poetry of immediacy, which he wants to protect from the potential inauthenticity of distance.

IX

古詩無定體。似可任筆為之。不知自有天然不可越之榘矱。故李于鱗謂唐無五古詩。言亦
近是。無即不無。但百不得一二而已。所謂榘矱者。意不枝。詞不蕩。曲折而無痕。戌削
而不競之謂。若于鱗所云無古詩。又唯無其形埒字句與其粗豪之氣耳。不爾。則「子房未
虎嘯」及玉華宮二詩。乃李杜集中霸氣滅盡和平溫厚之意者。何以獨入其選中。

Since old-style poetry has no predetermined form [*t'i**; i.e., no tonal restrictions, no demands for parallelism, and no set length], it seems that it is something one can write however one pleases. Such an attitude fails to understand
that the form has its own restrictions which are natural to it and cannot be
transgressed. It was for this reason that Li P'an-lung [1514–1570] said that
there were no [true] old-style poems written in the T'ang—and what he said is
close to the truth. It is not that there weren't any at all but rather that scarcely
one or two in a hundred [were worthy of the category "old-style"]. The restrictions that I referred to are as follows: that [the development of] the concept
(*yi**) not divide into branches, that the diction (*tz'u**) not get swept away, that
the twists show no traces [of conscious craftsmanship], and that there be no
struggle in the construction. When Li P'an-lung said that the T'ang lacked
old-style poetry, he was referring only to its not having the form and line
construction [of earlier old-style poetry] and to its lack of the rough and bold
ch'i*. If this were not the case, why would Li P'an-lung have included in his
anthology [of T'ang poetry] only Li Po's [poem with the line] "Tzu-fang has
not yet given his tiger's roar" and Tu Fu's "Yü-hua Palace"—poems which, in
the collected works of both poets, have an attitude (*yi**) that involves over-
weening *ch'i**, obliterating all harmonious calm and gentleness.

Even though old-style poetry (*ku-shih* 古詩) had fixed line length, a caesura in
a fixed position in the line, and couplet rhyme, comparison to the greater
restrictions of regulated verse forms made it seem the very image of freedom.
Wang Fu-chih does not consider the remaining formal restrictions of old-style
verse, but he does feel that the form has certain inner standards that should
not be transgressed. Here, as is often the case, the critic derives a sense of
generic norms from the best early writings in a particular form. In this case
the norms of old-style poetry seem to have been set by pre-T'ang old-style
poems; thus T'ang old-style verse, inescapably embodying the immense
changes that had occurred in the T'ang, always seemed to miss those generic
"norms."

One of Wang's characterizations of old-style verse is of particular interest
in the way in which it touches on the T'ang sense of poetic craft: this is the
requirement that "the concept not divide into branches." The formal structure of T'ang regulated verse permitted a mode of "division" (in the technical

rhetorical sense) in which a given topic could be broken into component parts, and those antithetical components be simultaneously amplified in the lines of parallel couplets: such division of the topic is "branching." Partially because of its greater length and partially because of the early norms of the genre, old-style verse was more linear. But the rhetorical training of T'ang poets was such that they often followed antithetical "branching" when they wrote in old-style verse. Such branching would be a division of the poem's energy or *ch'i**, and true old-style verse should have a unitary and linear momentum.

XI

以神理相取。在遠近之間。纔着手便煞。一放手又飄忽去。如「物在人亡無見期」。捉煞了也。如宋人咏河魨云。「春洲生荻芽。春岸飛楊花。」饒他有理。終是於河魨沒交涉。「青青河畔草」與「綿綿思遠道」。何以相因依。相含吐。神理湊合時。自然恰得。

When something is achieved with the principle of spirit (*shen* li**), it lies in the space between what is remote and what is close at hand. No sooner does one put one's hand to it than it is finished; but if one lets it loose, it fleets away. For example, the line "The things remain, the person has perished, never to be seen again" [Li Ch'i (690–751)] has tried to grasp [the topic] too tightly. In contrast, when the Sung poet [Mei Yao-ch'en] writes of the blowfish,

> On springtime sandbars the sprouts of reeds appear,
> The springtime shores fly with willow blossoms,

the couplet touches natural principle (*li**) abundantly, but ultimately has nothing to do with blowfish. When [in the folk ballad "Watering My Horse by the Great Wall," the opening line] "Green, green the grass by the river" is joined with "Continuing on and on, I think of the one on a far road," how is it that they so depend on one another, each holding the other within and producing the other? When they are fused by the principle of spirit (*shen*-li**), then the poet has it just right naturally (*tzu-jan**).

In the first two examples Wang Fu-chih is concerned with the relation between the words and what one is writing "about." In the third example, the first two lines of the folk lyric "Watering My Horse by the Great Wall," he is essentially concerned with the relation between the two lines. As is so often the case in Chinese literary theory, the frames of reference shift freely: the center of interest is the quality of the relation itself, conceived on a relatively abstract level. In this case, a good relation is one that lies between "remoteness" (by which Wang means that no relation is immediately apparent) and obviousness (the "close at hand"). Echoing Ssu-k'ung T'u's category of "limpid and calm" (see pp. 306–308 above), "The grasping hand has already missed it," here when a poet tries to give a circumstance too determinate an expression, he loses it altogether. The remarkably wooden line by the T'ang poet Li Ch'i 李頎 for once serves Wang Fu-chih as an excellent example. Wang's counter-example, the opening lines of Mei Yao-ch'en's poem on the blowfish, is a less apt example of lines that have nothing to do with the topic; obviously Wang Fu-chih had not read or did not recall Ou-yang Hsiu's "Remarks on Poetry" (see pp. 365–366 above); otherwise he would have known that these lines do indeed relate to the blowfish. However, Wang Fu-chih would still have objected to Mei's lines, because their relation to the topic is one of local cuisine rather than of shen*-li*.

Wang Fu-chih is seeking a quality of relation that seems natural and necessary, but which eludes a too-determinate definition. One might assert various relations between the opening lines of "Watering My Horse by the Great Wall": for example, the grass keeps on going like the speaker's longing, or the eye moves over the meadows into the distance towards the unseen traveler far away, or nature's vital renewal is set in opposition to the barrenness of the speaker's isolation from her beloved—but no single interpretation exhausts the potential relations. A relation that is necessary but indeterminate has the quality of "spirit," shen*, because the apparent necessity transcends human understanding: it is to be discovered as if inhering in the situation, not intentionally given by the poet.

XII

太白胸中浩渺之致。漢人皆有之。特以微言點出。包舉自宏。太白樂府歌行。則傾囊而出耳。如射者引弓極滿。或即發矢。或遲審久之。能忍不能忍。其力之大小可知已。要至於太白止矣。一失而為白樂天。本無浩渺之才。如決池水。旋踵而涸。再失而為蘇子瞻。萎花敗葉。隨流而漾。胸次局促。亂節狂興。所必然也。

All the Han poets had the kind of vast and far-reaching sentiments that we find in Li Po's breast; what is remarkable in their work is the way in which they indicate those sentiments with subtle words, thus making them grand and all-encompassing. In Li Po's yüeh-fu [imitation folk ballads] and songs, the words pour forth as if emptied out of a bag. For example, when an archer draws his bow to the fullest extent, he may either shoot at once or he may wait a long time, giving [the shot] slow consideration: by his ability to hold back and maintain his position, one can tell whether he has great strength or not. That capacity reached its ultimate with Li Po. It then fell a level and became Po Chü-yi [772–846], who showed an essential lack of that vast and far-reaching talent: just as when you block water to form a pool, you find that in a short space it dries up. It then fell another level and became Su Tung-p'o [1037–1101], fallen flowers and broken leaves rippling in the current: his feelings were so constrained that it was inevitable [he would become a person of] erratic principles and mad excitements (*hsing**).

A sense of the poet's concerns held in reserve remained an important value throughout the tradition. In this case, however, such reserve is a mark of neither repression due to an excess of pain, nor of dignity, nor of shyness; rather it is a gesture of power, holding back the force, letting it build in order to release it at the most appropriate and effective moment. The metaphor of the archer (a popular analogy in poetics, used by the Sung poet and critic Huang T'ing-chien 黃庭堅 [1045–1105] and and the Ch'ing critic Chin Sheng-t'an 金聖歎 [1608–1661] among others) is here one of great tension easily maintained, a tension that is not apparent in the words, but rather inferred from the disparity between assumed tension and ease. In the case of Po Chü-yi, the strength gives out; in the case of Su Tung-p'o, the bowman's arm begins to tremble from the strain.

XIII

> You made no objection to this far southern post:
> In your high hall you have aged kin.
> Its towers and terraces, layered vapors, mirages
> In its towns and hamlets mermen mix with men.
> The ocean is dark with rain from Triple Mountain,
> But blossoms are bright when spring comes to the Five Ridges.
> This land is rich in precious jade,
> So take care not to resent your pure poverty.
>
> > Ts'en Shen, "Sending Master Chang on his
> > Way to the Post of Chief Clerk in
> > South Seas County"

「海暗三山雨」接「此鄉多寶玉」不得。迤邐說到「花明五嶺春」。然後彼句可來。又豈嘗無法哉。非皎然高樣之法耳。若果足為法。烏容破之。非法之法。則破之不盡。終不得法。詩之有皎然虞伯生。經義之有茅鹿門湯賓尹袁了凡。皆畫地成牢以陷人者。有死法也。死法之立。總緣識量狹小。如演雜劇。在方丈臺上。故有花樣步位。稍移一步則錯亂。若馳騁康莊。取塗千里。而用此步法。雖至愚者不為也。

"The ocean is dark with rain from Triple Mountain" could not be succeeded directly by "This land is rich in precious jade." Only after bending away by saying "But blossoms are bright when spring comes to the Five Ridges," can he bring in the latter line. Of course there is a rule (*fa**) here, but it is not at all "rule" in the sense that the term is used by Chiao-jan [late-eighth-century critic] or by Kao Ping [fifteenth-century anthologist of T'ang poetry]. If we took such things as our "rules," they would not allow us to freely develop a poem. A rule of no rules lets us develop a poem inexhaustibly, and finally we can find no rule. Chiao-jan and Yü Chin in poetry, Mao K'un, T'ang Pin-yin, and Yüan Huang in classical studies—all these men mark off a space as a corral in which to trap people: these are "dead rules" (ssu-fa*). The establishment of dead rules generally derives from narrow capacity for understanding. As when a play is performed, since one is on a small stage, there are all kinds of [formalized] foot movements; if a foot movement is just a little off, everything is thrown into confusion. But for hurrying along a busy highway on a journey of a thousand leagues, not even the biggest fool in the world would use [stage] rules of foot movement.

Although the literary elite often propounded general principles of composition and ruthlessly criticized lapses in poetic judgment (much like their English counterparts in the late seventeenth and eighteenth centuries), sophisticated critics commonly scorned the "rules" of popular poetic pedagogy. Wang Fu-chih began with the Ts'en Shen example, pointing out the necessity of modulating from the ocean storm to a bright spring scene before turning to the consolation of the final lines. Because Wang perceived necessity in this case, he recognized that the move was in some sense governed by "rule." Such a "rule," however, grew out of the particular situation of the poem and could not be generalized as a pedagogic law of composition. Wang Fu-chih's contemporary, Yeh Hsieh, developed some of his finest critical insights at precisely this juncture between a generalized "rule" and a particular determination of what was necessary in a particular poem. Wang's primary aim, however, was merely to attack the popular pedagogic sense of "the rules," and he fell away from his first intuition—of some ad hoc concept of "rule" different in kind from "the rules" of popular pedagogy. Instead he contradicted himself, dismissing the issue with the commonplace abrogation of all rules, "a rule of no rules."

XIV

情景名為二。而實不可離。神於詩者。妙合無垠。巧者則有情中景。景中情。景中情者。如「長安一片月」。自然是孤棲憶遠之情。「影靜千官裏」。自然是喜達行在之情。情中景尤難曲寫。如「詩成珠玉在揮毫」。寫出才人翰墨淋漓。自心欣賞之景。凡此類。知者遇之。非然。亦鶻突看過。作等閒語耳。

Affections (ch'ing*) and scene (ching*) have two distinct names, but in substance they cannot be separated. Spirit (shen*) in poetry compounds them limitlessly and with wondrous subtlety (miao*). At the most artful there is scene-within-affections and affections-within-scene. An example of affections-within-scene is [Li Po's] "A sheet of moonlight in Ch'ang-an." This is naturally (*tzu-jan**) the sentiment (*ch'ing**) of lodging alone and recalling someone far away. [Tu Fu's] "My shadow calms among the thousand officers" is naturally the sentiment of delight on reaching the provisional capital [after escaping the territory held by the rebel forces of An Lu-shan]. Scene-within-affections is particularly hard to describe precisely; for example [Tu Fu's] "The poem completed, pearls and jade lie in the flourished brush" describes the scene of a free-flowing manner in the brushwork of a person of talent and the poet's appreciation of it. All cases of this sort will be encountered only by those who truly understand; otherwise a person will read over [such passages] carelessly, taking the words as if written unthinkingly.

The fullest and best exposition of the unity of *ching** and *ch'ing** is given in "Discussions," entry XVII. Although Wang Fu-chih would like to maintain the inseparable unity of the two concepts (and makes a good argument for doing so in "Discussions," entry XVII), here their unity is given as a goal and not as an accomplished fact. Even the goal, as stated here, preserves the distinction between the two—as affections-within-scene and scene-within-affections, compound terms that already had a long history.[14] Affections-within-scene was often noted in traditional criticism, and the quality appears in most of the couplets and lines that Wang cites with admiration in earlier passages. Here the particular verbal description of the scene seems perfectly to embody the poet's state of mind (*ch'ing**) as he faces that scene. For most Western readers the lines quoted do not, in themselves, embody such a mood; but in the Chinese reading tradition, such lines could not be conceived apart from expectations of qualities of mood, apart from the received associations of the images, and apart from the poems in which such lines were embedded and the circumstances surrounding those poems. Thus the line by Li Po is heard in the context of Li's version of an old folk song, the "Tzu-yeh Song":

> A sheet of moonlight in Ch'ang-an,
> From thousands of doors the sound of pounding clothes for winter.
> Autumn winds blow without stopping,
> And through them all, the mood of Jade Pass.
> When will the nomads be conquered at last
> And my true love leave these far campaigns?

Unfortunately symmetry demands that Wang produce scene-within-affections to match affections-within-scene. Others had attempted to explain what scene-within-affections might be, but Wang Fu-chih's solution is particularly ingenious, even though it forces him in the direction of approving the fictional imagination, of which he so passionately disapproves elsewhere. Scene-within-affections becomes a metaphorical scene, generated from the poet's authentic mood. This is, however, dangerously close to violating

Wang's earlier dictum: "What one has passed through with one's own body, what one has seen with one's own eyes." The only thing that might redeem a line like the one by Tu Fu is the occasional poem surrounding it, which could sustain the metaphorical deviation by its circumstantial presence. Another element that keeps the line from violating the rules of empirical truth is that it does not pretend to give an actual scene: indeed these metaphors, "pearls and jade," are so conventional in their reference to composition that Wang must warn his audience not to "read over" them, but rather to attempt to conceive of them visually as a scene. It should be noted, however, that in entry XVI Wang gives a non-metaphorical example of scene-within-affections, Tu Fu's

> From friends and kin not a single word,
> Old now and sick, I have this lonely boat.

"This is, by its very nature (*tzu-jan**) a poem on climbing Yüeh-yang Tower. Just try and put yourself in Tu Fu's place: lean on a railing and gaze off into the distance, and these two lines—of what is in the mind and what is in the eye—will spontaneously emerge. This is also scene-within-affections."

In his critical anthologies Wang makes frequent reference to the relation between scene and the affections. For example:

> There are cases when the words never touch [explicitly] on the affections, and yet the affections are limitless: this is because the eye of the mind governs and it does not depend on external things.

> At Heaven's edge I recognize a boat returning,
> Among the clouds I make out trees by the river.

> Secretly it is a person gazing fixedly, with feelings held within, who calls this forth. When you describe a scene in this way, it is a lively scene. If they didn't have "hills and ravines in the breast" or natural feelings (*hsing*-ch'ing**) in their eyes, even the older writers could not have delivered a line—even if they had read all the books in the world. Ssu-ma Hsiang-ju once said that a person could write a poetic exposition if he read a thousand poetic expositions: this is a great man deceiving others.[15]

The phrase "eye of the mind" (*hsin*-mu* 心目) is usually used like English "the mind's eye," an essentially imaginative envisagement. But in this context, Wang is clearly using it as the structure of attention: both what a person sees and the way he sees are governed by circumstantial interests.

XVII

近體中二聯。一情一景。一法也。「雲霞出海曙。梅柳渡江春。淑氣催黃鳥。晴光轉綠蘋」。「雲飛北闕輕陰散。雨歇南山積翠來。御柳已爭梅信發。林花不待曉風開」。皆景也。何者為情。若四句俱情。而無景語者。尤不可勝數。其得謂之非法乎。夫景以情合。情以景生。初不相離。唯意所適。截分兩橛。則情不足興。而景非其景。且如「九月寒砧催木葉」。二句之中。情景作對。「片石孤雲窺色相」四句。情景雙收。更從何處分析。陋人標陋格。乃謂「吳楚東南坼」四句。上景下情。為律詩憲典。不顧杜陵九原大笑。愚不可瘳。亦孰與療之。

To have one couplet of the affections (*ch'ing**) and one couplet of scene (*ching**) in the middle couplets of a regulated verse is one rule (*fa**). [But consider middle couplets such as Tu Shen-yen's:]

> Dawn with white and rose clouds emerging from the lake,
> Spring with plums and willows crossing the river.
> The pristine air hastens the orioles,
> And the clear light makes the green duckweed coil.

Or [Li T'eng's heptasyllabic quatrain]:

> Clouds fly from the northern palace gates, their pale shadows dispersing,
> And the rain ends on South Mountain, a mass of foliage comes forth.
> Already willows by the royal moat race the first plums to come forth,
> And flowers in groves do not wait on the wind of dawn to blossom.

All of these are lines of scene (*ching**); not one of them could be called a line of the affections (*ch'ing**). And other cases in which the middle four lines are all lines of the affections with no scene phrases are particularly numerous. Yet can any of these be called contrary to the rules?

Scene is put together (*ho*) by the affections, and the affections are generated by the scene. Initially they are not distinguished and are nothing more than what coincides (*shih*) with one's thoughts (*yi**). If you separate them into two independent categories, then the affections will not be adequate to stir (*hsing**), and the scene will not be one's own scene. Take, for example, the two lines [of Shen Ch'üan-chi, beginning]:

> The cold pounding blocks of late autumn hasten the leaves on the trees,
> [Ten years of campaign and garrison—she remembers the man in Liao-tung.]

In these lines [the statement of] the affections (*ch'ing**) and the scene are set in opposition. Or the four lines [of Li Ch'i, beginning:]

> In the single stone, in the lone cloud, glimpse the color of his face,
> [Moon gleaming on the clear pool reflects his heart of Ch'an.
> At the commanding wave of his monk's staff, flowers fall from Heaven;
> He sits and reclines in his peaceful cell, as springtime plants grow deep.]

Here the affections and the scene each gather the other in. And at what point could they be analyzed separately? If a dolt wanted to set up a doltish structural model (*ko**) as his standard, then he would claim that the four lines [of Tu Fu],

> Wu and Ch'u split to the southeast,
> [Ch'ien and K'un float day and night.
> From friends and kin not a single word,
> Old and sick now, I have this lonely boat,]

with their first couplet of scene and with their second couplet [stating] the affections set the canonical standard for all regulated verse;[16] and such a person would not pay attention to the gales of laughter that would come from the grave of Tu-ling [i.e., Tu Fu]. Such stupidity cannot be cured, and no one would even try to cure it.

Some Chinese critics develop subtle arguments in the sequence of their examples; Wang Fu-chih would perhaps have been wise to avoid them altogether. His examples often cast doubt on his theoretical points, or at best, as here, blunt the subtlety of his point. Nevertheless, buried at the center of this entry is a theoretical statement that perfectly articulates the relation between *ching** and *ch'ing**.

We have here a critique of the subject-object dichotomy in its occasional and circumstantial mode. Subject and object are determined by their reciprocal relation: my state of mind (*ch'ing**) comes into being through the determining agency of scene (*ching**), and at the same time the configuration of the scene that I perceive is a product of my state of mind. This is not to say that self and world lack subsistence, determinations, and given dispositions independent of the encounter. But self and world are always realized *in* the circumstantial encounter.

According to Wang, *ching** is "put together" (*ho* 合) by *ch'ing**. *Ho* implies integration, even fusion: "scene" is the outer world as "composed" by one's state of mind. Or, as he said in the comment cited earlier, "the eye of the mind governs": perception organizes external things according to the dictates of a particular state of mind. As is usually the case in Chinese criticism, Wang does not distinguish *ching** in a poem and *ching** as part of the experience of the world, thus implicitly asserting an essential identity between them. *Ching**, "scene," implies a standpoint, both internal and external: it is some particularly configured aspect of the world as known by a particular someone. Thus the particular integration of a scene is a product of a given person's "circumstance" or "state of mind" (both *ch'ing**).

At the same time, a particular "state of mind" is generated by what one perceives in the world; it comes into being as a result of the very scene it "composes." The two mutually defining terms, *ching** and *ch'ing** occur simultaneously. In tracing the origins of this event, Wang does grant a degree of priority to mind: the two terms are "nothing more than what coincides with one's thoughts"—*yi**, "thoughts" or "concepts," being, we may remember, "the dominant factor." In Wang Fu-chih's scheme of things, *yi** functions very much as *chih** did in the "Great Preface." *Yi** combines a sense of "concerns" with "the way one conceives of things"; but most important here is the fact that *yi** is given as something that transcends the occasional and circumstantial aspect of *ch'ing** and the momentary coincidence that is the "*ching*-ch'ing** event." Hidden in Wang Fu-chih's formulation is the common compound *shih-yi** 適意, "to coincide with one's thoughts/intentions" in the sense of "to suit one." Therefore the coincidence of *ching** and *ch'ing** is nothing more than what "suits" a person's concerns, a vector of attention arising from a predisposition of *yi** that transcends the moment.

Were the two terms *ching** and *ch'ing** entirely autonomous, then the *ch'ing** "would not be adequate to stir (*hsing**)." Wang Fu-chih's formulation here is surprising: we might expect him to say that given the dissociation of the two, the "scene," *ching**, would no longer be able to stir the response of the reader. What he in fact says is more interesting. A statement of mood, state of mind, or the affections that lacks a reciprocal definition in exterior circumstance would be *ch'ing** as pure object.[17] Wang Fu-chih is touching here on an essential question of reading (since *hsing** here is what the poem is supposed to do to the reader). *Ch'ing** is necessary in the self, and authentic *ch'ing** "are always one's own." If given as pure object, *ch'ing** are not themselves; they can exist only in the domain proper to them, the "interior," *nei*. Thus the *ch'ing** of another person (the poet) can exist in poetry only in a special mode that involves equally "having as one's own" and also "recognizing as other": that mode is sharing. This interior ground in which one can have *ch'ing** "as one's own" as well as recognizing them as another's can occur only in the regeneration of *ch'ing**; and that regeneration can occur only bound to a particular *ching**, "scene." Thus the only way adequately to share the *ch'ing** of another is in experiencing the same *ching**, "scene," presented in the poem. The poetic *ching** is the fixed form of a mutually defining relation; encountering it, the reader is made to "stand" where the poet stood. Thus Wang Fu-chih's statement is quite precise: only in being bound to "scene" will the *ch'ing** of another person be able to stir me.

The second consequence of the division between *ching** and *ch'ing** is less difficult. The phrase translated as "one's own scene" is *ch'i ching**, *ch'i* being the third person possessive pronoun, often with the force of a demonstrative. *Ching** without *ch'ing**, scene without an adequate individual state of mind participating in its composition, becomes detached from the particularity of experience: it becomes an inauthentic simulacrum of scene which fails to manifest the world as it is/was because it fails to manifest the world as known by anyone in particular.

Modern theorists of poetry would fault Wang Fu-chih for failing to give due consideration to the mediation of a normative and received language, to the idea that poetry is a revision of private experience within the common words of the tribe. Moreover, Chinese poets did not usually try, as Western poets did, to mark the privacy of experience by radically twisting the words of the tribe. Wang Fu-chih would have understood this critique in terms of the problem of the force of past poetry and the capacity to "say what no one before had said." Without engaging too deeply in the dubious enterprise of responding to hypothetical Western literary theorists of the twentieth century on behalf of a seventeenth-century Chinese theorist, I would suggest that Wang Fu-chih would probably share the common and quixotic belief of one tradition of Chinese literary theorists: that a strong and authentic personal vision would indelibly stamp the shared language with a particular identity, just as personality stamps the spoken language.

Wang Fu-chih's examples, which lead him off the central theoretical issue and do not illustrate it, are concerned with the presentation of *ching** and *ch'ing** as modes of discourse in poetry. One need not mechanically alternate the two modes because, when authentically presented, they are an organic unity. No matter whether the line is conventionally classed as *ching** or *ch'ing**, in authentic poetry both will be present in either.

XVIII

起承轉收。一法也。試取初盛唐律驗之。誰必株守此法者。法莫要於成章。立此四法。則不成章矣。且道「盧家少婦」一詩作何解。是何章法。又如「火樹銀花合」。渾然一氣。「亦知戍不返」。曲折無端。其他或平鋪六句。以二語括之。或六七句意已無餘。末句用飛白法颺開。義趣超遠。起不必起。收不必收。仍使生氣靈通。成章而達。至若「故國平居有所思」。「有所」二字虛籠喝起。以下曲江。蓬萊。昆明。紫閣。皆所思者。此自大雅來。謝客五言長篇。用為章法。杜更藏鋒不露。搏合無垠。何起何收。何承何轉。陋人之法。烏足展騏驥之足哉。近世唯楊用修辨之甚悉。用修工於用法。唯其能破陋人之法也。

Opening (*ch'i*), continuing (*ch'eng*), turning (*chuan*), and closing (*shou*)—that is one rule (*fa**) [see Yang Tsai, pp. 440–441]. But if you try testing this out against the regulated verse of the early T'ang and High T'ang, you won't find any poet who feels he must adhere rigidly to this rule.

Nothing is more important in rules than giving a complete [structure to the] unit (*chang**). If you set up this rule of four-part structure, you won't have a complete unit. How are we to understand a poem like [Shen Ch'üan-ch'i's "Alone Not Seeing," which begins] "Young wife of the house of Lu"? What is the "rule of unit composition" (*chang**-*fa**) here? A poem like [Su Wei-tao's "On the Fifteenth Day of the First Month," which begins] "On firetrees [fireworks] silver blossom/sparks merge" is a single, undifferentiated breath (*ch'i**). [Tu Fu's "Preparing Winter Clothes," which begins] "I understand that the man on frontier duty does not turn home" has fine turnings with no definite origin or end. In other poems there may be straightforward exposition for six lines, with everything drawn together in the last two lines; or in the sixth or seventh line the concept (*yi**) may be [finished] with nothing remaining, but then the last line or lines may use the "flying white" rule [of calligraphy] to soar off again, so that the principle (*li**) and interest (*ch'ü**) in the lines are carried afar.

When the opening does not necessarily open and the conclusion does not necessarily conclude, then the *ch'i** of life will get through magically (*ling-t'ung**); the unit (*chang**) will be complete and attain its ends. [When in the fourth of his "Autumn Meditations" Tu Fu writes,] "There is something on my mind, of homeland and the life I knew," those words "there is something" speculatively [*hsü**, literally "emptily"] encompasses things and calls them up, so that reference later [in the sequence] to the Twisting River, to P'eng-lai Palace, to K'un-ming Pool, and to Purple Tower Mountain are all "what was on his mind." This comes from the "Greater Odes" [of the *Book of Songs*]. In his longer poems, Hsieh Ling-yün had used this same form as his "rule for unit composition" (*chang**-*fa**), but Tu Fu hid the sharp point even more effectively [than Hsieh] and did not let it become obvious, gathering things together limitlessly.[18] Where is the "opening"? where the "closing"? where does it "continue"? where does it "turn"? The notion of "rules" held by jackasses will never permit a famous steed like Ch'i-chi to let his hooves run free. In recent times only Yang Shen [1488–1559] has given a thorough analysis of this, and his skill in the use of the rules lay entirely in his ability to break free of "rules" as they have been conceived by jackasses.

This represents the standard reaction on the part of the better critics of the seventeenth century to the strictures of popular poetics, taught in local schools and circulated in poetic manuals. Popular anthologies often chose examples that conformed to this sense of the "rules," thus perpetuating the illusion that T'ang poets adhered to those rules rigidly. Wang carefully makes a judicious selection from such anthology pieces to attack the notion of rigid rules.

XXIII

王子敬作一筆草書。遂欲跨右軍而上。字各有形埒。不相因仍。尚以一筆為妙境。何況詩文本相承遞邪。一時一事一意。約之止一兩句。長言永歎。以寫纏綿悱惻之情。詩本敎也。十九首及上山采蘼蕪等篇。止以一筆入聖證。自潘岳以凌雜之心作蕪亂之調。而後元聲幾熄。唐以後間有能此者。多得之絕句耳。一意中但取一句。「松下問童子」是已。如「怪來妝閣閉」。又止半句。愈入化境。近世郭奎「多病文園渴未消」一絕。髣髴得之。劉伯溫。楊用修。湯義仍。徐文長有純淨者。亦無歇筆。至若晚唐餖湊。宋人支離。俱令生氣頓絕。「承恩不在貌。敎妾若為容。風暖鳥聲碎。日高花影重。」醫家名為關格。死不治。

Wang Hsien-chih [344–386] wrote calligraphic pieces in "grass script" without ever lifting his brush from the paper (yi-pi), thus hoping to excel [his father] Wang Hsi-chih [generally considered the greatest calligrapher of all time]. Every character had its proper form and its own boundaries, and none pressed on any of the others; yet still he was able to make a wondrously subtle world (miao*-ching*) without ever lifting his brush from the paper—to be able to do this is even more applicable to the basic processes of continuation and succession in poetry and prose. A single moment, a single event, or a single idea (yi*) should be kept within no more than one or two lines; yet the essential lession of poetry is to make words last long and extend sighs in order to describe brooding feelings (ch'ing*) all wound up inside a person. Poems like the "Nineteen Old Poems," "I Climbed the Mountain to Pick Greens," and some others manage to show perfection precisely by "never lifting the brush from the paper." Those primordial sounds have become virtually extinct ever since P'an Yüeh [247–300] produced his turbulent melodies out of the tumult of his heart. Since the beginning of the T'ang, there have occasionally been poets capable of this, and they usually achieve it in quatrains. [Chia Tao's]

> Beneath the pines I asked his servant boy;
> [He said the master's gone off to pick herbs.
> He's right here on this mountain,
> But the clouds are so deep I can't tell where]

is an example of using only one line for each idea (yi*). [In a quatrain on the cast-off consort P'an Chieh-yü,]

> Strange—how her dressing chamber is closed
> [When the women leave court, they don't greet her,
> But all go off to within the spring gardens—
> Among the flowers, sounds of talk and laughter],

[Wang Wei] manages it in half lines, and moves into a world of transformation (hua*-ching*), even more than in the preceding poem.

In more recent ages Kuo K'uei's [fourteenth-century] quatrain that begins, "So sick now in the Wen Garden, my thirst not yet gone" catches some semblance of it. There are some pure moments of it in the work of Liu Chi [1311–1375], Yang Shen [1488–1559], T'ang Hsien-tsu [1550–1616], and Hsü Wei [1473–1548]; the brush does not stop on the paper. But when it comes to something like the decorative glitter of the late T'ang or the incoherence of the Sung writers, both cause the breath of life to stop instantly. [Consider Tu Hsün-ho's "Resentment in the Spring Palace":]

Royal favor is not on the face,
Which makes me unable to adorn myself.
The wind is warm, voices of birds shatter,
The sun is high, the shadows of flowers heavy.

Doctors call this a "closed case"—death beyond cure.

The phrase translated as "never lift the brush from the paper," *yi-pi*, 一筆, means literally in "one brush [movement]." What attracts Wang here is a sense of kinetic and organic unity, a unified movement in which all the components (the characters in calligraphy, the single moment, single event, or single idea in poetry) are kept distinct. In the criticism of poetry and prose this is often referred to as *yi-ch'i**, "in one breath." As Wang Fu-chih so often observed in his criticism, this ideal is seen to have existed in the earliest poetry, but to have survived only imperfectly thereafter.

XXIV

不能作景語。又何能作情語邪。古人絕唱句多景語。如「高臺多悲風」。「胡蝶飛南園」。「池塘生春草」。「亭皋木葉下」。「芙蓉露下落」。皆是也。而情寓其中矣。以寫景之心理言情。則身心中獨喻之微。輕安拈出。謝太傅於毛詩取「訏謨定命。遠猷辰告」。以此八字如一串珠。將大臣經營國事之心曲。寫出次第。故與「昔我往矣。楊柳依依。今我來思。雨雪霏霏」。同一達情之妙。

If one cannot write the language of scene, how then can one write the language of the affections? The finest lines of the older poets are the lovely language of scene. For example,

On high terraces the melancholy winds are strong

[Ts'ao Chih (192–232)]

Butterflies flutter in the southern gardens

[Chang Hsieh]

Pool and pond grow with springtime plants

[Hsieh Ling-yün]

On the flood plain, leaves fall from the trees

[Liu Yün (465–517)]

The lotus collapses beneath the dew

[Hsiao Ch'üeh]

are all examples of this, and the affections are lodged within them. When one articulates the affections through the principle [*hsin**-li**, literally "mind-principle"] of describing scenes, then the most elusive and singular figurings of what lies in mind and body are lightly drawn out. The Grand Tutor Hsieh An chose these lines from the *Book of Songs* [256]:

> With grand counsels he makes mandates fixed,
> With far-reaching plans, makes propitious declarations.

He considered these eight words to be a string of pearls, describing the fine turns of mind (*hsin*-ch'ü*) of a great officer managing state affairs. For this reason it was the same in communicating the affections as *Book of Songs* [157]:

> Long ago when we left
> The willows were light and waving;
> Now when we return
> The snow is thickly falling.

Wang Fu-chih is referring to a famous story in *A New Account of Tales of the Word* (*Shih-shuo hsin-yü*) in which Hsieh An asked his nephew Hsieh Hsüan what he thought were the best lines of the *Book of Songs*. Hsüan offered the passage "Long ago when I left . . . " and Hsieh An countered with "With grand counsels . . . "[19]

XXV

有大景。有小景。有大景中小景。「柳葉開時任好風」。「花覆千官淑景移」。及「風正一帆懸」。「青靄入看無」。皆以小景傳大景之神。若「江流天地外。山色有無中」。「江山如有待。花柳更無私」。張皇使大。反令落拓不親。宋人所喜。偏在此而不在彼。近唯文徵仲齋宿等詩。能解此妙。

There are scenes on a large scale; there are scenes on a small scale; and these are scenes on a small scale within scenes on a large scale. [The lines]

> As willow leaves open, they give themselves to the fine breeze
>
> [Tu Shen-yen]

> Flowers cover the thousand officers, the pure light shifts
>
> [Tu Fu]

> The wind bears straight on, a single sail hung far
>
> [Wang Wan]

and

> Blue haze—look in and [the mountain is] not there
>
> [Wang Wei]

are all scenes on a small scale that convey the spirit of a scene on a large scale.

The river flows out beyond Heaven and Earth,
The color of the mountain between presence and absence

[Wang Wei]

Mountains and rivers as if awaiting someone,
But flowers and willows show no private favors.

[Tu Fu]

Couplets like these are grandiose; and in contrast [to the previously cited examples] their unrestrained self-sufficiency is achieved at the cost of intimacy. Sung writers were particularly fond of the latter type rather than the former, whose subtleties (miao*) have been understood in recent times only by Wen Cheng-ming [1470–1559] in "Spending the Night in My Library" and other poems.

XXVI

情語能以轉折為含蓄者。唯杜陵居勝。「清渭無情極。愁時獨向東」。「柔櫓輕鷗外。含悽覺汝賢」之類是也。此又與「忽聞歌古調。歸思欲霑巾」更進一格。益使風力遒上。

Tu Fu alone holds supreme mastery in his ability to have the language of the affections (ch'ing*) twist into a reserve of feeling (han-hsü). Examples of this kind of writing are

The clear Wei lacks any feeling at all—
It heads east on its own, in spite of my sorrow

and

The agile prows lie beyond the light gulls,
Restraining my gloom, I recognize their nobility.

A couplet like

Suddenly I hear an old tune sung,
Longing for home makes me want to soak my kerchief with tears

takes this mode (ko*) one level further, making its affective force (feng*-li) even stronger.

XXVII

含情而能達。會景而生心。體物而得神。則自有靈通之句。參化工之妙。若但於句求巧。則性情先為外蕩。生意索然矣。松陵體永墮小乘者。以無句不巧也。然皮陸二子差有興會。猶堪諷咏。若韓退之以險韻。奇字。古句。方言。矜其餖飣之巧。巧誠巧矣。而於心情興會一無所涉。適可為酒令而已。黃魯直。米元章益墮此障中。近則王謔菴承其下游。不恤才情。別尋蹊徑。艮可惜也。

If the affections kept in reserve (*han-ch'ing**) can be effectively communicated; if one meets the scene [*hui-ching**; i.e., if one discovers in the scene the counterpart of one's own concerns] and this gives rise to mind [*sheng-hsin**; i.e., generates thoughts and feelings]; and if further one embodies things (*t'i*-wu**) and attains their spirit (*shen**)—then there will be lines that communicate magically (*ling*-t'ung**) and that participate in the wondrous subtlety (*miao**) of the work of transformation (*hua**). But if one seeks only artfulness (*ch'iao*) in a line, then one's nature and affections (*hsing*-ch'ing**) will be swept along beforehand [i.e., before they can emerge spontaneously] by [mere] externals, and the concepts (*yi**) generated will be dull and lifeless. The Sung-ling style (*t'i**) [of the late-T'ang poets P'i Jih-hsiu (ca. 834–883) and Lu Kuei-meng (d. ca. 881)] always falls into the secondary tradition [literally the "lesser Vehicle" of Buddhism] because every line is artful. Nevertheless P'i Jih-hsiu and Lu Kuei-meng have occasions of [genuine] stirring (*hsing*-hui* 興會) and one can still chant their works. But in cases like that of Han Yü, who vaunts his artfulness with a flashy variety of difficult rhymes, strange words, archaic lines, and regional expressions—artful it may be, but it does not have the least thing to do with the human affections (*hsin*-ch'ing**) and occasions of being stirred (*hsing*-hui*). Such writing is appropriate only for compositions at drinking bouts. Huang T'ing-chien and Mi Fu [1052–1107] succumbed to this failing even more, and in recent times Wang Ssu-jen [1574–1646] has continued its worst aspects. It is truly a pity that such writers care nothing for talent and feeling (*ts'ai*-ch'ing**) and seek an entirely separate path.

XXXV

「落日照大旗。馬鳴風蕭蕭」。豈以「蕭蕭馬鳴。悠悠旆旌」為出處邪。用意別。則悲愉之景原不相貸。出語時偶然湊合耳。必求出處。宋人之陋也。其尤酸迂不通者。既於詩求出處。抑以詩為出處考證事理。杜詩「我欲相就沽斗酒。恰有三百青銅錢。」遂據以為唐時酒價。崔國輔詩「與沽一斗酒。恰用十千錢。」就杜陵沽處販酒。向崔國輔賣。豈不三十倍獲息錢邪。求出處者。其可笑類如此。

Setting sunlight shines on the great banners,
Horses whinny in the shrill wind.

[Tu Fu]

The source for this should not be sought in the lines [from the *Book of Songs*]:

Horses cry out, shrill,
Far, far go the pennons and standards.

Since the concepts (*yi**) operating in these two cases are distinct, these two scenes—one of sorrow and one of exultation—do not involve any borrowing whatsoever; Tu Fu's lines represent only a chance coincidence of phrasing. The need to find a source for everything is the stupidity of Sung writers. But the most painfully absurd and incomprehensible situations are when, having looked for sources in a poem, one then uses the poem itself as a historical source to investigate the way things really were [shih*-li*, "the principle behind events"]. There is Tu Fu's couplet:

> I want to go there to buy a gallon of wine:
> I have just three hundred coins of green bronze.

Then one takes that as evidence of the cost of wine in the T'ang. Next we read Ts'ui Kuo-fu's poem:

> I want to buy a gallon of wine,
> And use exactly ten thousand coins.

If we went to Tu Fu's wineshop to buy wine, then sold it to Ts'ui Kuo-fu, we could make a three thousand percent profit. This is a good example of how ridiculous it is to go hunting sources.

Wang Fu-chih here takes a stand against what was considered a standard move of intertextual borrowing: to use the words of an old text in a new sense. What is remarkable about this passage is the way it contradicts one of Wang's most unique and firmly held positions: that the same lines can be used to express different, even opposite feelings.

SELECTIONS FROM "INTERPRETATIONS OF POETRY"

III

「采采苯苢」。意在言先。亦在言後。從容涵泳。自然生其氣象。即五言中。十九首猶有得此意者。陶令差能彷彿。下此絕矣。「采菊東籬下。悠然見南山」。「眾鳥欣有託。吾亦愛吾廬」。非韋應物「兵衞森畫戟。燕寢凝清香」所得而問津也。

[In the poem from the *Book of Songs* that begins] "We keep gathering the plantain," the concept (*yi**) is there before the words, and it is there after the words; it moves leisurely and soaks through the words, so that it naturally (*tzu-jan**) generates the atmosphere (*ch'i*-hsiang**) of the poem. Among poems in five-character lines, the "Nineteen Old Poems" still were able to use concept this way; and T'ao Ch'ien catches a bit of the semblance; but afterwards it is gone. [Couplets by T'ao Ch'ien like]

I pick chrysanthemums beneath the eastern hedge,
Then, far in the distance, catch sight of South Mountain

or

The flock of birds rejoice in having a place to lodge,
And I, too, love my own cottage

—these are not lines that a poet like Wei Ying-wu, with lines like

The guards, a dark mass of painted pikes,
As we feast reclining, a clear scent hangs in air,

could ever grasp and ask the way to proceed.

It is not exactly clear what Wang means by "the concept is there before the words, and it is there after the words." It seems to suggest some state of mind out of which the poem emerged naturally and which continues on in the reader after having recited the poem; the text becomes simply the connection between the two and the means of communication. The craftsmanship of Wei Ying-wu's famous couplet is intrusive and disrupts the sense of the poem's spontaneous generation from a state of mind. Because the lines do not seem naturally produced, they cannot have a natural effect on a reader.

IV

「昔我往矣。楊柳依依。今我來思。雨雪霏霏。」以樂景寫哀。以哀景寫樂。一倍增其哀樂。知此。則「影靜千官裏。心蘇心挼前」。與「唯有終南山色在。晴明依舊滿長安」情之深淺宏隘見矣。況孟郊之乍笑而心迷。乍啼而魂喪者乎。

Long ago when we left,
The willows were light and waving;
Now when we return,
The snow is thickly falling.

[Book of Songs, 157]

To write of one's misery in a scene of joy, or to write of one's joy in a scene of misery doubles the misery and doubles the joy. [Tu Fu's]

This shadow calms among the thousand officers,
The heart revives before the seven ranks

and [Li Cheng's]

All that remains is the color of Chung-nan Mountain,
As ever clear brightness fills Ch'ang-an

—here the depth or shallowness of feeling (*ch'ing**), the expansiveness or narrowness of feeling is obvious. Even more consider Meng Chiao who at one moment laughed, his heart led astray, and at another moment cried out, his spirit vanishing.

The lines from the *Book of Songs* describe a military campaign, the troops recalling the pain of departure in the presumably joyous springtime scene and experiencing the joy of return in the gloom of winter. The Tu Fu lines speak of his feelings on reaching the temporary headquarters of the Emperor, after a desperate escape from the capital, then held by the An Lu-shan rebels. The lines by Li Cheng 李拯 describe the scene around the capital after the sack of Ch'ang-an in Huang Ch'ao's rebellion. In both of these cases the circumstances surrounding the poems heighten the force of the lines. This poetry of contrasting opposites is set against the work of Meng Chiao, whose failures in the civil service examination produced desperately unhappy poems, and whose final success produced a poem of exultation. Wang Fu-chih's interest in the tension between opposites is closely related to his theories about "expressing fellowship" and "showing resentment": see the final part of the commentary to "Discussions," entry I.

V

唐人少年行云。「白馬金鞍從武皇。旌旗十萬獵長楊。樓頭少婦鳴箏坐。遙見飛塵入建章。」想知少婦遙望之情。以自矜得意。此善於取影者也。「春日遲遲。卉木萋萋。倉庚喈喈。采蘩祁祁。執訊獲醜。薄言還歸。赫赫南仲。玁狁于夷。」其妙正在此。訓詁家不能領悟。謂婦方采蘩而見歸師。旨趣索然矣。建旌旗。舉矛戟。車馬喧闐。凱樂競奏之下。倉庚何能不驚飛。而尚聞其喈喈。六師在道。雖曰勿擾。采蘩之婦亦何事暴面于三軍之側邪。征人歸矣。度其婦方采蘩。而聞歸師之凱旋。故遲遲之日。萋萋之草。鳥鳴之和。皆為助喜。而南仲之功。震于閨閣。室家之欣幸。遙想其然。而征人之意得可知矣。乃以此而稱「南仲」。又影中取影。曲盡人情之極至者也。

A "Ballad of Youth" by the T'ang poet [Wang Ch'ang-ling (ca. 698–756)] goes:

> On white horse with gilded saddle, he's gone off with Emperor Wu,
> Banners and flags in the tens of thousands, they hunt at Ch'ang-yang.
> High in the building his youthful wife sits playing her zither,
> She sees the dust flying far away, entering Chien-chang.

We can imagine the feelings (*ch'ing**) of the youthful wife as she gazes into the distance, and this shows mastery in catching the shadow of her pride and satisfaction. The subtlety of the following [stanza from the *Book of Songs*] lies in exactly the same thing:

The days of spring are lengthening,
The grass and the trees flourish,
The orioles are warbling,
Women pick artemisia in crowds.
With captive warbands to be tried,
We make our way homeward.
Glorious is Lord Nan-chung—
The Hsien-yün tribes are quelled.

The exegetes of the Classics could not fully understand these lines, claiming that the wives saw the returning army as they were picking artemisia: this makes the import and interest (*chih-ch'ü** 旨趣) of the lines dreary. With pennons and banners flying, with halberds and pikes raised, with the din of horses and chariots, and with the victory music being played everywhere, how is it that the orioles don't fly up and away, and much less how could one still hear their warbling? When the grand army is on the march—and let us grant that they were not causing trouble—why would these women picking artemisia boldly show their faces right next to the columns? The troops are on their way home, and they guess that their wives will be picking artemisia and will hear the victory songs of the returning army; thus the lengthening daylight, the flourishing of the grasses, and the harmony of the birds singing all add to their delight; and the achievements of Lord Nan-chung will resound in the women's chambers. From afar they imagine how it will be, with delight in good fortune in the houses. And we can understand the satisfaction of the troops on the march. Then, in all this, to [imagine the women] praising Lord Nan-ching is to catch a shadow in a shadow and treat in the finest detail the limits of the human affections.

The term "shadow" (or "reflection") suggests something whose presence is recognized by indirect evidence. Wang Ch'ang-ling does not have to speak of the young wife's pride in her husband's presence in the imperial entourage: it is implicit in the way the distant scene is described. She cannot see the entourage in the distance, but she can see the dust from the horses' hooves, which is a shadow not only of their movement towards Chien-chang Palace, but also of her close attention to the scene. That same implication of a state of mind in describing a scene is applied even more radically to the lines from the *Book of Songs*: the lines are taken as describing a speculative scene, the troops imagining their return home. Note how the standard interpretation is rejected on empirical grounds: that the tumult of the returning army would disturb the peaceful scene in the opening. Having located the poem in the minds of the returning soldiers, Wang Fu-chih goes a step further: it would be reasonable to have the soldiers themselves singing the praises of Lord Nan-chung, but Wang is so caught up in the soldiers imagining the putative response of their wives that he attributes the praise of Lord Nan-chung to the unseen women, the soldiers thinking of how their wives will honor their commander.

It is interesting to contrast these two examples of "good" speculation with the "bad" speculation in "Discussions," entry V. There speculation is a purely poetic act; here it rises from genuine feeling, and the relation between scene and the affections is real, even if the scene itself is "empty" and imaginary. To use the example Wang gives in the fifth entry of the "Discussions," Chia Tao, in poetic speculation, does not know whether the monk should "knock" or "push"; one way to know which act was performed would be to be present in the physical scene; another way to know would be to have the scene rise up spontaneously in the mind, as here. Such a speculative scene still has a claim to natural reality, but in this case the natural reality is an interior one. Unlike the examples given in "Discussions," entry XIV, this kind of speculative scene could properly be called "scene-within-affections."

VII

「庭燎有煇」。鄉晨之景。莫妙於此。晨色漸明。赤光雜煙而饢饢。但以「有煇」二字寫之。唐人除夕詩「殿庭銀燭上熏天」之句。寫除夜之景。與此彷彿。而簡至不逮遠矣。「花迎劍佩」四字。差為曉色朦朧傳神。而又云「星初落」。則痕迹露盡。益歎三百篇之不可及也。

There is no more subtle description of the scene before dawn than the line [from the *Book of Songs*], "From torches in courtyard there is a glow." The colors of the dawn sky are gradually brightening, and the reddish light mixes with smoke and darkens in flashes; but it is described with no more than the words, "there is a glow."

The line from a New Year's Eve poem by a T'ang poet [Tu Shen-yen], "In the palace courtyard the silver candles scent the heavens above," describes the scene of New Year's Eve somewhat like the line from the *Book of Songs*, but it falls far short in the perfection of simplicity. The first four characters of Ts'en Shen's line, "Flowers greet the sword-hung sash," pretty much convey the spirit (*shen**) of the first pale glimmering of dawn; but when he finishes that line with "the stars begin to set," the traces [of his craftsmanship] are completely exposed. This makes us reflect all the more on the fact that the *Book of Songs* cannot be equaled.

XIV

謝靈運一意回旋往復。以盡思理。吟之使人卞躁之意消。小宛抑不僅此。情相若。理尤居勝也。王敬美謂「詩有妙悟。非關理也」。非理抑將何悟。

In the poetry of Hsieh Ling-yün one idea (*yi**) will circle around and go back and forth until his train of thought (*ssu*-li**) is exhausted. Chanting it will cause all nervous and reckless notions (*yi**) to melt away. But not only is the "Small Dove" [from the *Book of Songs*] the same in this respect, the feeling (*ch'ing**) in it is also comparable, and natural principle (*li**) resides in it particularly strongly. Wang Shih-mou [1536–1588] said that poetry involves a perfect enlightenment (*miao*-wu*) that has nothing to do with natural principle (*li**). If there's no natural principle, what's there to become enlightened of?

The statement attributed to Wang Shih-mou is a rephrasing of Yen Yü's words in "Ts'ang-lang's Remarks on Poetry"; as Tai Hung-sen points out, they were actually cited by Wang Shih-mou's brother, Wang Shih-chen. Wang Fu-chih will have none of such aesthetic mysteries: for him poetry is founded in natural principle, not in any wooden, philosophical way, but rather in the complex empirical truths by which the world works.

XVI

興在有意無意之間。比亦不容雕刻。關情者景。自與情相為珀芥也。情景雖有在心在物之分。而景生情。情生景。哀樂之觸。榮悴之迎。互藏其宅。天情物理。可哀而可樂。用之無窮。流而不滯。窮且滯者不知爾。「吳楚東南坼。乾坤日夜浮。」乍讀之若雄豪。然而適與「親朋無一字。老病有孤舟」相為融浹。當知「倬彼雲漢」。頌作人者增其輝光。憂旱甚者益其炎赫。無適而無不適也。唐末人不能及此。為玉合底蓋之說。孟郊。溫庭筠分為二壘。天與物其能為爾壘分乎。

Affective image (*hsing**) lies between the intended and the unintended; comparison (*pi**) also does not permit minute [intentionally artistic] craft. What concerns the affections (*ch'ing**) is scene, which forms "amber and seed" [fusion?] together with the affections. Even though the affections are distinguished from scene by the one's belonging to the self, and the other's belonging in things (*wu**), still with scene giving rise to the affections and affections giving rise to scene, with the conflict of misery and joy, with the encounter of splendor and despair, they take secret lodging in one another. The natural affections (*t'ien-ch'ing**) and the principles in things can bring misery and can bring joy; and their functioning is endless, moving in their courses without getting bogged down. One who is exhausted and bogged down cannot understand them. [When Tu Fu writes],

> Wu and Ch'u split to the southeast,
> Heaven and Earth float day and night,

all at once we read a daring grandeur in the lines; but they happen to become fused with

From friends and kin not a single word,
Old now and sick, I have this lonely boat.

Note that "Great is the River of Stars" is used [in one of the *Songs*] to praise [the Chou king's] influence on the people, and the line magnifies the king's glory; but the same line is used [in another of the *Songs*] to express anxiety about a severe drought and magnifies the sense of blazing heat [by suggesting that there were no clouds in the sky]: it applies to no particular situation, and yet there is no situation to which it may not apply. That man from the end of the T'ang [Liu Chao-yü] did not reach this level of understanding when he put forward his theory about a jade box's needing a base and a lid [that fit together perfectly, a metaphor for parallel couplets]; Meng Chiao and Wen T'ing-yün divided things into two piles. Can Heaven and the things of the world be divided up by drawing lots as in distributing household property?

The Origins of Poetry

"The Origins of Poetry," *Yüan-shih* 原詩, completed by Yeh Hsieh 葉燮 (1627–1703) in 1686, was the first serious attempt at a comprehensive and organized poetics since *Wen-hsin tiao-lung*.[1] Indeed, the pervasive concern with the theoretical grounds of poetry gives "The Origins of Poetry" an even stronger claim on the genre of a "poetics" than *Wen-hsin tiao-lung*. In contrast to the Western and Indian traditions, the composition of such a poetics was not the realization of a value already well established in the Chinese tradition. To investigate the grounds ("origins") of poetry was a response to a sense of crisis: it was not the disinterested exposition of knowledge for its own sake, but rather a hope to redeem poetry from decline.

> The reason poetry has been unable to rouse itself to some lasting vitality is that the criticism of poetry, for its entire history, has been disorganized and lacking in unity.
>
> "The Origins of Poetry," Outer Section

In the context of traditional Chinese literary theory, this is a most startling proposition. Critics had often hoped to guide the art and to restore it to former glories by precepts and particular judgments; many had accused their opponents of leading poetry astray by wrong-headed notions; but no one had placed the blame on his predecessor's conceptual disorganization. For Yeh Hsieh, this is indeed the heart of the problem; its solution, a comprehensive and unified exposition of the basic principles of the art, an exposition whose very form will guarantee freedom from the error and one-sidedness that follow from ad hoc judgments.

Accordingly, Yeh Hsieh does something remarkable in the continuation of the passage above: he reviews the tradition of earlier literary theory, not merely to agree or disagree with positions taken, but also to judge the methodological quality and thoroughness of previous criticism. Yeh accuses Liu Hsieh, his chief rival in the attempt to write a comprehensive poetics, of an inability to "sustain an argument (ch'ih-lun 持論).[2] Yen Yü is charged with not adequately developing the proposition that judgment is the essential prerequisite for the study of poetry.[3] Yeh Hsieh's criticism of his predecessors is largely valid: they did not, as Yeh Hsieh does, develop and defend a theory. Yet this impulse to create a unifying system made Yeh Hsieh's treatise something of an anomaly in the tradition; and, though read and admired, it was ultimately less influential than the more fragmentary insights of some of Yeh Hsieh's contemporaries.

As in the case of the *Wen-hsin tiao-lung*, there has been a renewal of interest in "The Origins of Poetry" in this century, following the introduction of Western poetics, whose values give a special place to the comprehensive treatise as a critical genre. Although these imported values have distorted our understanding of Chinese literary thought as a whole, the intrinsic merits of "The Origins of Poetry" are such that a revival of interest in Yeh Hsieh's work can only be welcomed. For Western readers, it offers a useful introduction to traditional Chinese poetics in its last and most sophisticated phase, showing how the central concerns and terms of the tradition might have worked together if investigation of the theoretical basis of poetry had been of primary interest.

"The Origins of Poetry" is divided into an "Inner Section" and an "Outer Section," each consisting of two chapters. The most systematic exposition of poetic theory occurs in the "Inner Section." The first chapter of the "Outer Section" treats miscellaneous theoretical points, while the second chapter gives a loosely chronological discussion of the history of poetry. The main selection below is a translation of the greater part of the "Inner Section," omitting the discussion of literary historical issues that begin and conclude it. The remainder of the "Inner Section" and selections from the "Outer Section" are given in the supplement to this chapter.

From the thirteenth century on, there had been an increasing willingness to consider poetry as a relatively autonomous activity: this is evident in the interest in technical poetics, in the questions of models and precursors among the earlier poets, and in the developing discourse on some quality that was quintessentially "poetic." Such a concern with some mysterious quality of poetic effect was primarily the legacy of Yen Yü's "Ts'ang-lang's Remarks on Poetry," which had gradually risen from its role as the foremost text in popular poetics and poetic pedagogy to become a strong force in high poetics. Beginning as a powerful countertradition, by the mid seventeenth century Yen Yü's poetics had reached the stage where it could genuinely be characterized as "orthodox," the position to which it had so stridently aspired. There remained some critics who were primarily interested in poetry as a social document or as a document of subjective history; but, on the whole, these concerns were weaker than various forms of interest in the art and the quality of impression it made.[4] In many ways Yeh Hsieh's "Origins of Poetry" was an attempt to break down that sense of poetry's mysterious autonomy and to show how it participated in the workings of the universe. In an age when poetry and philosophy were conceived as quite distinct disciplines, Yeh Hsieh asserted the unity of poetic and philosophical concerns, insisting that the essential questions of poetry were shared by the human and natural world. Yeh used the same terms as philosophical discourse and often reminded his readers that what he was saying did not apply to poetry alone. To many of his contemporaries his use of philosophical terminology would have been repulsive; yet his was a heroic (if futile) effort, in the best traditions of Chinese thought, to reintegrate poetry with first principles. In this, even more than in the genre of the "treatise," Yeh Hsieh recalls Liu Hsieh.

In the first part of the section translated below, Yeh Hsieh describes the way in which things come-to-be in poetry in terms of the way in which things come-to-be in the world. The three levels of "coming-to-be" are "natural principle" (li^*), "event" ($shih^*$), and "circumstance" or "feeling"/"mood"/"the affections" ($ch'ing^*$). The force that sustains the process of their coming-to-be is $ch'i^*$; and the necessity of the way in which something comes-to-be, understood retrospectively, is "rule" (fa^*). Implicit here is the notion that what constitutes a poem and what is understood in reading a poem are *identical* to the constitution of the world and what is known through an experience of the world. What *may* distinguish poetry (what distinguishes the best poetry) is clarified in the last part of the section translated: this is the capacity to communicate perceptions of the most elusive operations of principle, event, and circumstance, perceptions that would be inaccessible to ordinary humanity. These most elusive operations of principle, event, and experience correspond to the mysterious "poetic" quality that was the highest value in "Ts'ang-lang's Remarks on Poetry." Thus Yeh Hsieh removes Yen Yü's "poetic image" from the autonomous realm of poetry and gives it back a place in the empirical world outside poetry, though perceptible to only a privileged few. Poetry differs from other language in its ability to transmit a consciousness of the world that differs in intensive degree from other kinds of consciousness.

After the section on the world's coming-to-be, Yeh Hsieh shifts to a long discussion of epistemology, grounded in *shih* 識, "[the capacity for] judgment [of how things are]." Although Yeh Hsieh probably takes this term from "Ts'ang-lang's Remarks on Poetry," he uses it in an entirely different way. Yen Yü was concerned with the novice poet's "recognizing" true values in earlier poetry; Yeh Hsieh requires that a poet judge or recognize the operation of principle, event, and circumstance in a general sense, encompassing equally the judgment of earlier poetry, judgment in the act of composition, and judgment of the world. Following "judgment" there are three other enabling categories that make possible the communication of what is recognized to others: talent, courage, and force. Of these "courage" is the most interesting, treating how present writers may be intimidated by past masters and the "rules."

Although he argues vigorously against Ming archaist theorists, Yeh Hsieh is in their lineage, focusing on many of the same concerns and attempting to redefine many of their central terms. Nowhere is this more apparent than in his treatment of "rule" (fa*), a term central both to Ming archaist poetics and to the popular poetics of Yeh Hsieh's own day (although by the time Yeh Hsieh is finished redefining it, it would no longer be recognizable to either). In these concerns, Yeh Hsieh touches marginally on a group of contemporary theorists and writers known as the "Formal School," *Ko-tiao p'ai* 格調派, who radically modified Ming archaist theory by vigorously attacking it while remaining very much under the compelling influence of many aspects of Ming archaist poetics.

FROM THE "INNER SECTION" OF "THE ORIGINS OF POETRY"

"INNER SECTION"
Chapter 1 (Main Selection)

或曰。「今之稱詩者。高言法矣。作詩者果有法乎哉。且無法乎哉。」余曰。「法者虛名也。非所論於有也。又法者定位也。非所論於無也。

Someone said to me: Those who claim to know about poetry nowadays make much of "rules" (*fa**). Are there really rules in writing poetry, or is poetry something without rules?

I answered: Rules are an empty name and thus not to be considered as if existing actually. On the other hand, rules are determinate positions and thus not to be considered as non-existent.

To clarify Yeh Hsieh's distinction between "empty name," *hsü*-ming*, and "determinate position," *ting-wei*, we might use the example of driving a car. There is no actual way or "rule for driving"; there are many driving manuals (as there were many poetry manuals in Yeh Hsieh's time), but anyone who drives knows that a driving manual does not contain the "way to drive a car." Thus "rules" in this case are an "empty name"; the phrase "the way to drive a car" names something that cannot be fully determined or fully described before the actual performance. Yet when one is driving, one must do certain things at one moment and other things at another moment: that "must" is the "way" or "rule" as a determinate position. Since rules are virtual, they do exist, but no particular determination of rule occurs until it is called forth in the particular. As elsewhere in "The Origins of Poetry," Yeh Hsieh takes a conventional opposition (in this case, between those who believe in the decisive importance of *fa** and the opponents of *fa**) and rises above it; in doing so, he demonstrates that the concept is far more complex than it appears in the crude positions, both pro and con, taken by conventional literary polemicists.

子無以余言為惝恍河漢。當細子晰之。自開闢以來。天地之大。古今之變。萬彙之賾。日星河嶽。賦物象形。兵刑禮樂。飲食男女。於以發為文章。形為詩賦。其道萬千。余得以三語蔽之。曰理。曰事。曰情。不出乎此而已。然則詩文一道。豈有定法哉。先揆乎其理。揆之於理而不謬。則理得。次徵諸事。徵之於事而不悖。則事得。終絜諸情。絜之於情而可通。則情得。三者得而不可易。則自然之法立。故法者當乎理。確乎事。酌乎情。為三者之平準。而無所自為法也。故謂之曰虛名。

So that you won't think what I have just said is as vague and hazy as the Milky Way, I should clarify the fine points for you. Since the beginning of the universe, the magnitude of Heaven and Earth, the mutations of past and present, all the mysteries of the millions of things, the sun and stars, the rivers and mountains, the images and forms (*hsiang*-hsing**) in which things unfold, war and punishments, rites and music, food and drink, the relations between men and women—all of these have come forth as literary works (*wen*-chang**) and have taken shape (*hsing**) as poems and poetic expositions (*fu*). The Way is infinitely varied, but I can cover it in three words: "natural principle" (*li**), "event" (*shih**), and "circumstance" (*ch'ing**, the affections, a "state of mind"). Nothing lies outside of the scope of the three words. If this is the case, then how can there be determinate rules covering the entire Way of poetry and prose? First, reflect on natural principle in something; and if your reflection in regard to natural principle is not in error, then you have grasped the natural principle. Then find evidence of that principle in an event; and if the evidence found in event does not contradict the principle, then you have grasped event. Finally assess it in regard to circumstance (*ch'ing**); if, assessed according to circumstance, it still comes through (*t'ung**), then you have grasped circumstance. When all three have been grasped and cannot be altered, then natural (*tzu-jan**, or "so-of-themselves") rules are established. Thus rules are the even balance of what is right according to principle, what is made actual in event, and what is infused in circumstance; but there is nothing by which rules can have subsistence in their own right. For this reason I have said that rules are an empty name.

The chief characteristic of good literary theory is to show the depth of important questions that initially can be posed very simply. In this case, the question is "How 'should' a poem be written?" or "Are there any 'shoulds' in the writing of poetry?" Yeh Hsieh sets out to investigate the nature of that "should" (*fa**) on a theoretical level. If his investigation is not easy in Chinese, it is doubly difficult in English translation, forced into a conceptual vocabulary that has neither the resonance nor the precision of the original.

Although Yeh Hsieh makes precise discriminations in some areas, he avoids drawing a distinction between 1) the operations of nature, 2) the process of composing a poem, and 3) the judgment of a poem by another person. Sometimes he refers specifically to one of these; at other times he refers to another. The tacit ideology seems to be that since the operations of nature are the "matter" of the poem, the observation of nature is in fact identical to the act of composition. The same would hold true in reflection on the successful poem of a predecessor. In the chapter "Its Origins in the Way," Liu Hsieh grounded the act of literary composition within the larger principle of nature's self-manifestation in "pattern." Yeh Hsieh does not even make the argument that literature reenacts natural process; he simply assumes they are the same.

The particular model for nature used by Yeh is the orthodox Neo-Confucianism of Chu Hsi: natural process begins with "natural principle" (*li**) and works outward, unfolding into the phenomenal world. This movement from universal natural principle to the particular phenomenon, not unfamiliar in Western philosophy, is both the way the world works (from the inside out) and the way philosophical reflection should work. One begins by reflecting on some particular object (*ko**-*wu**), later given by Yeh Hsieh as the explicit model for reflecting on the poem of a predecessor); within the particular one understands the universal natural principle; then one follows the unfolding of that principle back into the particular. As this applies to nature, so it applies to the compositional process and judging the work of another poet.

Yeh Hsieh's contemporaries who "make much of rules" are speaking of the "rules of poetry" in a limited sense. Not only does Yeh Hsieh provide a larger philosophical model that subsumes the notion of "rules" (*fa**), his model also integrates the operations of poetry with the operations of the natural world outside of poetry.

One potential confusion should be addressed here. Long habits of Western theology and philosophy lead to a notion of natural principle as "law"; and "law" is also one of the meanings of *fa**, "rules." The illusion of terminological overlap can lead to a misunderstanding of this passage, which might seem to say that a poem comes to be out of natural principles as laws (*li**) but has no predetermined laws (*fa**). Although both *fa** and *li** involve necessity, they are clearly distinguished. In its pure form *li** occurs on such a high level of generality that it contains no particular determinations; for example, "being a pine tree" in the most general sense is *li**. *Li** admits incongruous, even apparently contradictory manifestations within the particular according to the circumstance; for example, many things can happen to a pine tree, but all occur through its being a pine tree. The underlying unity of these various manifestations becomes apparent only through careful observation of how *li** unfolds into the particularities of event and circumstance. *Fa**, "rule" or "law," is the necessity or rightness by which natural principle unfolds into a particular circumstance. For example, we see a pine tree at a particular moment and perceive how its present condition is a particular conjunction of topography, light, weather; we recognize that it had to be the way it is through its being a pine tree; that sense of necessity or rightness is *fa**.

As this is true for the coming-to-be of the "matter" of poetry, so it is also true of the poem: the poem's coming-to-be (encompassing the "matter" of the poem, its composition, and its unfolding as a text) is the organic unfolding of *li**. "Rules" are what must be done (or had to have been done) at a particular point, and thus are the "even balances" between its stages. But "rules" name nothing: they do not exist as general categories apart from the particular determinations of the moment and cannot be given beforehand.

Next Yeh Hsieh turns to "determinate position," the mode in which "rules" properly occur.

又法者國家之所謂律也。自古之五刑宅就以至於今。法亦密矣。然豈無所憑而為法哉。不過揆度於事理情三者之輕重大小上下。以為五服五章。刑賞生殺之等威差別。於是事理情當於法之中。人見法而適愜其事理情之用。故又謂之曰定位。

Furthermore, rules are what the state calls "law" (*lü*, or "regulation"). Since that time in antiquity when the conditions for the five punishments were set, on up to the present, such rules have been very comprehensive. But how could there be rules without anything to base them on? In fact these "rules" are nothing more than an evaluation of the gravity, magnitude, and elevation of the event, the principle, and the circumstance. Out of this are ascertained distinctions of degree in regard to the various kinds of official uniforms, punishments and rewards, life and death. Thus event, principle, and circumstance are present in these rules. When someone looks upon the rules, he may feel satisfaction in the functioning of the particular event, principle, and circumstance. Thus we may say that rules are a determinate position.

Here Yeh Hsieh uses the example of "rules" (*fa**) in regard to rewards, punishments, and the sumptuary laws of the civil service. The key statement is "When someone looks upon the rules, he may feel satisfaction . . . " In the case of the state, external determinations have evolved out of categorical adjudications of event, principle, and circumstance. But the essence of such rules is not any autonomous existence of the categorical norm, but rather in a particular moment when someone perceives a situation and says to himself "*that* is how it must be." The point here is the necessity of "rules" (*fa**) can properly be known only after the fact, in the judgment of the particular case. Yeh Hsieh is working out here a Chinese version of the Kantian "free conformity to law."

及稱詩者。不能言法所以然之故。而曉曉曰法。吾不知其離一切以為法乎。將有所緣以為法乎。離一切以為法。則法不能憑虛而立。有所緣以為法。則法仍託他物以見矣。

In fact, those who claim to know about poetry are unable to say why rules are established the way they are; and as they babble on about the "rules," I cannot tell whether they conceive of rules as something separate from the whole or whether they conceive of rules as contingent on a particular something. If one conceives of rules as something separate from the whole, then one should reflect on the fact that rules cannot be established on emptiness (*hsü**). If one conceives of rules as contingent on a particular something, then rules would be dependent on some alien entity inorder to be manifest.

Yeh Hsieh believes that rules are ongoing determinations, arising in the relations between the stages of a poem's coming-to-be. Thus he is forced to dismiss any notion that rules have an autonomous existence apart from the particular whole of the text. More interesting is the fact that he must also dismiss the contingency of rules. Rules occur in particulars but are not bound to them; that is, no particular rule is bound to any particular moment in the text: to say "every time X occurs, you must do Y" is a misuse of "rules." When something correct does occur in the text, however, we say "that is how it must be." Rule occurs in the organic relation between empty and solid, general and particular.

吾不知統提法者之於何屬也。彼曰。「凡事凡物皆有法。何獨於詩而不然。」是也。然法有死法。有活法。若以死法論。今譽一人之美。當問之曰。「若固眉在眼上乎。鼻口居中乎。若固手操作而足循履乎。」夫妍媸萬態。而此數者必不渝。此死法也。彼美之絕世獨立。不在是也。又朝廟享燕。以及士庶宴會。揖讓升降。紋坐獻酬。無不然者。此亦死法也。而格鬼神。通愛敬。不在是也。然則彼美之絕世獨立。果有法乎。不過即耳目口鼻之常而神明之。而神明之法。果可言乎。彼享宴之格鬼神。合愛敬。果有法乎。不過即揖讓獻酬而感通之。而感通之法。又可言乎。死法則執塗之人能言之。若曰活法。法既活而不可執矣。又焉得泥於法。

And I do not know in which class to put those who bring up rules in a general way; these are the ones who say "Every event and every thing (*wu**) has its rules. Why should poetry alone be different?" This may be so, but there are "dead rules" and "animate rules." If I were going to praise a person's beauty according to dead rules, I would ask, "Are there brows over the eyes? Are a nose and a mouth located in the middle? Do the hands take hold of things and do the feet walk along?" There are countless postures (*t'ai*) conveying grace or ugliness, yet I would never be able to get beyond the scope of questions such as those—these are "dead rules." Such beauty as stands unique, preeminent in all the world, is not to be found through them. Or take the case of sacrificial banquets at court ceremonies and the parties of scholars and commoners—all the bowing and yielding place, the precedences and deferences, the order of seating, the toasts and answering toasts—all are the same: dead rules. Contact with the gods and ghosts, the communication of love and respect are not to be found in them.

If this is so, then are there any rules at all in such beauty as stands unique, preeminent in ail the world? Such rules are nothing less than some spirit (*shen**) that illuminates (*ming*) precisely those same constants: ears, eyes, mouth, and nose. And, finally, can rules for the way spirit illuminates things be spoken of? Are there any rules at all for contacting the gods and ghosts or for the union of love and respect at a party? They are nothing less than what is felt and conveyed (*kan**-t'ung**) in those bowings and yieldings, toasts and answering toasts. And can one speak of the rules for what is felt and conveyed? Dead rules can be spoken of by the sort of person who takes a firm grasp of things. But if we are considering animate rules, then the rules are truly animated and absolutely cannot be "grasped" firmly. And in that case how could a person become bogged down in the rules?

The distinction between "animate rules," *huo-fa**, and "dead rules," *ssu-fa**, was an old one in poetics (and before that, in Ch'an Buddhist discipline, though by Yeh Hsieh's time the Buddhist origins of the term were in the background), and never so clearly illustrated as in the examples here. "Dead rules" are those that govern any hypostatized norm or "constant," *ch'ang* 常. Animate rules, on the other hand, occur only in the particularity of process (it should be pointed out that even though Yeh admits "dead rules" here, only "animate rules" conform to his earlier description of what rules are) . The term *huo*, set in opposition to *ssu*, "dead," is more than simply being "alive": it is "lively," "vital," or "animate," charged with energy and activity. One cannot become "bogged down' in such rules because they are the form of movement itself rather than a code against which a movement may measure itself. Obviously "animate rules" must be prereflective. They can be legitimately spoken of in a theoretical way before enactment, as Yeh Hsieh does here (although the way in which animate rules are integrated into particularity makes such theoretical discourse a mode alien to the level on which such rules become actual); they can also be considered after they have been enacted, as Yeh Hsieh later does in his analysis of several Tu Fu couplets. But in the time of their coming-to-be, animate rules are only immanent in the particularity of action.

In short, as in the philosophical aesthetics of the eighteenth century in Europe, Yeh Hsieh is forced to metadiscourse. Kant knew well that no rule could be given whereby a particular thing could be judged beautiful or not beautiful; what he could do was to describe the ground upon which such judgments could be made and the form of such a judgment. Yeh Hsieh, concerned with processes, knows that no rule or set of rules can predetermine the totality of a natural process or action in all its contingency, precisely because what distinguishes a truly natural process or action is its freedom to respond to unforeseen contingencies. But as with Kant, the grounds of such a process or action can be described. Yeh Hsieh's is a genuine, but very peculiar "metaphysical" position, peculiar because it is constituted so as to exclude the possibility of any "physics"—that is, of any adequate description of fixed and repeatable (or "constant") rules immanent in nature, except on the lowest level, "dead rules."

而所謂詩之法。得毋平平仄仄之拈乎。村塾曾讀千家詩者。亦不屑言之。若更有進。必將曰。律詩必首句如何起。三四如何承。五六如何接。末句如何結。古詩要照應。要起伏。析之為句法。總之為章法。此三家村詞伯相傳久矣。不可謂稱詩者獨得之秘也。

Can what we call the "rules of poetry" do without choices of level and deflected tones [the basis of versification in classical poetry]? Even those who have read the *Poems of a Thousand Poets* at some village school don't think it worth the effort to mention tonal regulations. When a person reaches a more advanced level, the teacher will have to tell him how the opening couplet must begin a regulated poem, how the third and fourth lines must carry it on, how the fifth and sixth lines must connect, and how the last couplet must bring things to a conclusion. He will be told that "reflecting and responding" (*chao-ying*) is essential in old-style poetry, how such poems must "rise up" and "sink down." He will analyze a poem in terms of the rules of couplet construction (*chü-fa**) and bring it all together in "rules of the piece as a whole" (*chang*-fa**). This sort of thing has long been taught by old schoolmasters in little villages; we can hardly claim that these are the unique mysteries of those who claim to know about poetry.

Here Yeh Hsieh locates the version of *fa** that he has just been criticizing in popular poetic pedagogy. The categories satirized here were precisely what most of Yeh Hsieh's contemporaries considered *fa**. We might note that the unifying trait of these "dead rules" is that they are all prescriptions given prior to an act of writing. Yeh Hsieh next goes on to dispute another, less technical notion of *fa**.

若舍此兩端。而謂作詩另有法。法在神明之中。巧力之外。是謂變化生心。變化生心之法。又何若乎。則死法為定位。活法為虛名。虛名不可以為有。定位不可以為無。不可為無者。初學能言之。可可為有者。作者之匠心變化。不可言也。夫識辨不精。揮霍無具。徒倚法之一語。以牢籠一切。譬之國家有法。所以儆愚夫愚婦之不肖。而使之不犯。未聞與道德仁義之人講論習肄。而時以五刑五罰之法恐懼之而迫脅之者也。

Setting aside the two cases above [rules as separate from the whole and rules as contingent upon particulars], we find the claim that there is yet another kind of rule in writing poetry. Here rule is to be found in spiritual illumination (*shen*-ming**) and is beyond the power of mere craft. This is what is called "transformation (*pien*-hua**) giving rise to mind." What is it like—this rule of "transformation giving rise to mind"? In this case, dead rules are the determinate position and animate rules are the empty name. Whatever is empty name cannot be considered to exist actually, and whatever is determinate position cannot be considered non-existent. Any beginning student can talk about what cannot be considered non-existent. And since it cannot be considered to exist actually, no one can talk about the artistic mind of the writer amid its transformations. In this case, the powers of judgment and discrimination are not getting what is essential; things are left vague, fuzzy, and incomplete; such people pointlessly depend on the word "rule" to embrace everything. This can be compared to the state's having rules [or "laws"] by which they warn against misconduct on the part of foolish men and women to keep them from committing crimes, all the while these people have never heard of the discourses or practices of people of virtue, kindness, and righteousness; nevertheless the five punishments are used to terrify them and to intimidate them.

After dismissing the commonplace technical prescriptions of *fa** in popular poetics, Yeh Hsieh turns to attack a more sophisticated version of *fa**, in which the transformations that occur in the functioning of "animate rules" are an ineffable mystery. Such a view might be associated with the theories of the contemporary poet Wang Shih-chen 王士禎 (1634–1711), growing out of the fascination with the ineffably "poetic" in "Ts'ang-lang's Remarks on Poetry." Insofar as such theorists retain the concept of *fa**, they retain a concept of determinacy: a successful poem had to be written the way it was. But they refuse to allow any reflection on precisely what it was in the poem that made it successful, because that quality for them is a mystery.

In the previous section, Yeh Hsieh had rejected the possibility of an adequate "physics" for poetry, the possibility that a prior rule can be given which determines a particular move in a poem. Here he rejects a pseudo-metaphysics that refuses to describe even the ground upon which a particular move can be determined. In such a case, dead rules would be permitted as prior determinations, but they would not be what is essentially "poetic" in the text: thus they would be given as determinate positions. On the one hand, Yeh Hsieh cannot accept this acquiescence to dead rules because he insists that every particular move or determination must be discovered in process, not given beforehand. On the other hand, in such a theory animate rules would be placed beyond the realm of discourse. Since the ineffability of trans-formations was an accepted commonplace in contemporary poetics, it would have been easy for Yeh Hsieh's readers to misunderstand his previous discussion in this way: his description of animate and dead rules in a woman's beauty and banqueting would easily lead to an interpretation that he was speaking of something ineffable. What Yeh Hsieh finds particularly pernicious about this second interpretation of *fa** is the disjunction it allows between a particular move or determination and what is truly essential. What is beautiful occurs in and through the particular words, not "beyond" them. For him the essential rules of why a particular move was made are obvious—once the move is completed. He wants to unify the metaphysical and the empirical, to show the grounds on which a particular move can be understood.

Yeh Hsieh's analogy to law (*fa**) is rhetorically effective, even if it proves nothing: in the analogy to "dead rules," a person would be held liable to legal strictures without being given the possibility of knowing why the law is the way it is, that is, without understanding the ethical principles that are the basis of law. The dead rules of popular poetics are "the letter of the law," producing behavior that is "law-abiding" but not necessarily "good." The contrasting ineffable "animate rules" would be like a mystic notion of the good that has no connection with the strictures of law and allows for no particular determinations. The alternative analogy on the legal model is to "hear of the discourses and practices of people of virtue, kindness, and right-eousness." In this way of looking at things, a code of statutes is not adequate to learn moral action, but moral action can be learned by observing its embodiment. Moral education spontaneously produces law-abiding acts, and the larger principle of morality is immanent in those acts. Thus in poetry "animate rules" also show their manifest determinacy ("determinate positions"): one can observe a text and know why a certain move was made.

惟理事情三語。無處不然。三者得。則胸中通達無阻。出而數為辭。則夫子所云辭達。達者通也。通乎理。通乎事。通乎情之謂。而必泥乎法。則反有所不通矣。辭且不通。法更於何有乎。

These three words—principle, event, circumstance—are the same everywhere. If these three can be grasped, then what is in one's heart can be communicated (*t'ung*-ta*) without obstruction. If, as they emerge, they unfold in words (*tz'u**), then we have what Confucius meant by "language attaining its ends (*ta*)." "Attaining ends" is communicating, which is to say communication in principle, communication in event, and communication in circumstance. But if one is bogged down in the rules, then on the contrary there will be something not communicated. And if the language does not communicate, what point is there to rule?

This paragraph is based on the concept of *t'ung**, translated as "communicate" and meaning "to go all the way through," or, from the point of view of the listener, "to understand." *Ta*, "to attain ends," is the term of completion in "passage through." Here is the most telling critique of those who believe that "animate rules" are an ineffable mystery: in such cases, nothing is "communicated" but a sense of what is beyond the reader. In the proper functioning of animate rules, according to Yeh Hsieh's conception of them, "principle, event, and circumstance" are immanent and knowable. "Rule" itself is only the organic order of their emergence; and if, as in popular poetics, rule becomes opaque, then the *t'ung**, "passage through," is obstructed.

曰理。曰事。曰情三語。大而乾坤以之定位。日月以之運行。以至一草一木一飛一走。三者缺一。則不成物。文章者。所以表天地萬物之情狀也。然具是三者。又有總而持之。條而貫之者。曰氣。事理情之所為用。氣為之用也。譬之一木一草。其能發生者。理也。其既發生。則事也。既發生之後。夭喬滋植。情狀萬千。咸有自得之趣。則情也。苟無氣以行之。能若是乎。又如合抱之木。百尺干霄。纖葉微柯以萬計。同時而發。無有絲毫異同。是氣之為也。苟斷其根。則氣盡而立萎。此時理事情俱無從施矣。吾故曰。三者藉氣而行者也。得是三者。而氣鼓行於其間。絪縕磅礴。隨其自然。所至即為法。此天地萬象之至文也。豈先有法以馭是氣者哉。不然。天地之生萬物。舍其自然流行之氣。一切以法繩之。夭喬飛走。紛紛於形體之萬殊。不敢過於法。不敢不及於法。將不勝其勞。乾坤亦幾乎息矣。

In their largest sense, these three terms—principle, event, and circumstance—are how the positions of *Ch'ien* and *K'un* are determined, how the sun and moon move in their courses. Even down to every plant, tree, bird, and beast, if even one of these is missing, then the thing (*wu**) is not complete. Literary works (*wen*-chang**) are the means by which the circumstances and the manner (*ch'ing*-chuang*) of Heaven and Earth, and all things are manifested (*piao*, "externalized").

To complete these three, however, there is something else which unites and sustains, which orders and threads through them: this is *ch'i**. Insofar as principle, event, and circumstance function, it is *ch'i** that makes them function. Take as an example a plant or tree. Its potential for coming to life is principle (*li**). That it comes to life is "event" (*shih**) . Having once come to life, it burgeons and twines, is nurtured and takes root in countless manners (*ch'ing**-chuang*), in all of which there is the delight (*ch'ü**) of the thing being itself—this is "circumstance" (*ch'ing**, "mood"). But this cannot happen unless there is *ch'i** to carry it along.

Or consider some tree an armspan in girth, rising a hundred feet into the upper air, with delicate leaves and slender branches to be counted in the tens of thousands; all came forth at the same time, but none are identical to any of the others—this is the action of *ch'i**. But if you should cut its roots, the *ch'i** will be exhausted, and it will immediately begin to wither. In such a case, neither principle, nor event, nor circumstance would have any way to carry through. For this reason we say that all three depend upon *ch'i** to be carried along. When all three are present with *ch'i** driving along through them, the thing swells out in profusion; the way in which it follows its natural course (*tzu-jan**) wherever it leads is "rule." This is the supreme pattern (*wen**) in Heaven and Earth and all things. How could anyone think that "rule" comes first and drives this *ch'i**? If it were otherwise, then when Heaven and Earth generated all things, they would set aside their naturally (*tzu-jan**) flowing *ch'i** and the whole would be regulated according to rules; the burgeoning plants, the birds and beasts in their dazzling multitude of forms (*hsing**-t'i**) would never dare transgress the rules and would likewise never fail to live up to the rules. This would be unbearably oppressive; and Heaven and Earth would probably be ready simply to cease.

Many questions arise in regard to this, one of the central theoretical sections of "The Origins of Poetry." First, one must wonder exactly how this eloquent description of the natural cosmos relates to poetry. In the preceding section, principle, event, and circumstance were what was "communicated" (*t'ung**) in poetry; and this section opens by speaking of poetry as the means by which the circumstances and manner of Heaven, Earth, and all things are externalized. Yeh Hsieh stresses poetry as a means of manifestation. Yet here, he seems to make *fa** or "rule" in literature only analogous to *fa** in the workings of the world. He shifts from a notion of *fa** in reference to the process by which literature manifests the world to one of *fa** in the internal processes of the world itself. The blurring of this distinction is significant. As we have said, Yeh Hsieh does not want to discriminate between these cases; he would like to see poetry both as an extension and repetition of the process of nature's coming-to-be. The principle, event, and circumstance "in" a poem are also the principle, event, and circumstance "of" that poem *qua* poem.

"Principle" (*li**) and "event" (*shih**) are categories that are relatively easy to understand. *Ch'ing** is more difficult, and our translation as "circumstance" captures only part of it. *Ch'ing** is the quality of manner of something at a given moment; *ch'ing** are also the "emotions" or "affections," and thus this circumstantial quality of the thing conveys or seems to embody a mood, a mood that is ultimately communicated to the observer or reader. *Ch'ing** is the final term in the triadic process of manifestation, the form in which the world presents itself before us. By stressing *ch'i**, Yeh Hsieh stresses the animate, self-impelled quality of this process.

In contrasting process governed by *ch'i** with process governed by *fa**, Yeh Hsieh reveals his central objection to the common notion of *fa**: "How could anyone think that rule comes first (*hsien*)?" When *fa** first became a central concern in the Southern Sung, the original interest had been in it as a productive "method." This implication of productive, prior method remained central to discussions of *fa** through Yeh Hsieh's time: one studied the *fa** of Tu Fu's poetry in order to write like Tu Fu. In Yeh Hsieh's radically revised interpretation, the aspect of productive method is no longer legitimate. For him, *fa** has its existence and is accessible to reflection only after the completion of a process. If given as complete beforehand, *fa** becomes external to the process and corrupts it.

In Yeh Hsieh's discussion of the unacceptable notion that *fa** is something given prior to the composition of a text, the language of tyranny and coercion predominate, echoing the ancient question of voluntarism versus involuntarism in composition. In contrast, when he speaks of how the text aspires to reenact the spontaneous self-production of nature, the phrase he uses is "the delight of the thing being itself," *tzu-tê chih ch'ü**. *Ch'ü** here is "interest," "flair," a joyous panache; *tzu-tê* is literally "attaining self," the achievement of being what one is. In this notion of composition, *fa** retains its essential element of determinacy; but Yeh Hsieh believes that such determinacy, though present and accessible to reflection, must be *discovered* by the poem itself, in the process of its coming-to-be. This distinction between prior, coercive *fa** and *fa** discovered through unfolding is not simply a difference in means: it becomes a quality manifest in the thing itself, in its manner, and thus it is communicated immediately to any reader or observer.

草木氣斷則立萎。理事情俱隨之而盡。固也。雖然。氣斷則氣無矣。而理事情依然在也。
何也。草木氣斷則立萎。是理也。萎則成枯木。其事也。枯木豈無形狀。向背。高低。上
下。則其情也。由是言之。氣有時而或離。理事情。無之而不在。向枯木而言法。法於何
施。心將曰。法將析之以為薪。法將斲之而為器。若果將以為薪為器。吾恐仍屬之事理情
矣。而法又將遁而之他矣。

It is certainly true that when the *ch'i** of a plant or tree is cut off, it instantly begins to wither: principle, event, and circumstance are exhausted along with the *ch'i**. Nevertheless, when the *ch'i** is cut off, the *ch'i** no longer exists; but principle, event, and circumstance are still present. Why do I say this? The fact that a plant or tree begins to wither when its *ch'i** is cut off is itself a principle. When it withers, it turns into a bare, dried-up tree, and that is an event. And who would claim that there is no special manner in a bare, dried-up tree— front and back, high and low—this is its circumstantial quality.

Considered from this point of view, we may say that *ch'i** may sometimes be separated from a thing; but if principle, event, and circumstance are lacking, then the thing is not there. And if someone should want to speak of rules in regard to a bare, dried-up tree, how would rules be applied? The answer is that rules would cut it up and make firewood out of it; rules would carve it up and make a vessel out of it. Even when it is finally transformed into firewood or a vessel, I believe that event, principle, and circumstance would still inhere in it. But rules would have hidden these away and made it into something else.

Here Yeh Hsieh shifts to the common sense of *fa** as "productive method" or "instrumentality." The rhetorical game is to emphasize that the application of a prior *fa** presumes the inanimate deadness of the thing to which it is applied, its *ch'i** having been cut off. The essential distinction is between the poem as an organic growth and the poem as artifact. Even in the artifact, principle, event, and circumstance are present (in this context Yeh Hsieh seems to be speaking of the categories as residual from some first, natural state of the thing from which *ch'i** has been cut off rather than as reconstituted in the artifact). In regard to poetry, this opposition would work itself out as follows: an authentic, "natural" poem would be, as in the "Great Preface," a poem that comes into being spontaneously, from the particular nature of the poet and from the poet's circumstantial encounter with the world. The moment one begins to understand that process as "using" experience or knowledge to write a poem, a gap of intentionality is created, and the text becomes an inanimate artifact, always revealing its alienation from the living world. Yeh Hsieh's distinction is problematic; but it does speak to basic values in reading and writing poetry, values that were as old as the tradition itself.

天地之大文。風雲雨雷是也。風雲雨雷變化不測。不可端倪。天地之至神也。即至文也。試以一端論。泰山之雲。起於膚寸。不崇朝而徧天下。吾嘗居泰山之下者半載。熟悉雲之情狀。或起於膚寸。瀰淪六合。或諸峯競出。升頂即滅。或連陰數月。或食時即散。或黑如漆。或白如雪。或大如鵬翼。或亂如散髮。或塊然垂天。後無繼者。或聯綿纖微。相續不絕。又忽而黑雲興。土人以法占之曰將雨。竟不雨。又晴雲出。法占者曰將晴。乃竟雨。雲之態以萬計。無一同也。以至雲之色相。雲之性情。無一同也。雲或有時歸。或有時竟一去不歸。或有時全歸。或有時半歸。無一同也。此天地自然之文。至工也。若以法繩天地之文。則泰山之將出雲也。必先聚雲族而謀之曰。吾將出雲。而為天地之文矣。先之以某雲。繼之以某雲。以某雲為起。以某雲為伏。以某雲為照應。為波瀾。以某雲為逆入。以某雲為空翻。以某雲為開。以某雲為闔。以某雲為掉尾。如是以出之。如是以歸

之。——使無爽。而天地之文成焉。無乃天地之勞於有泰山。泰山且勞於有是雲。而出雲且無日矣。蘇軾有言。「我文如萬斛源泉。隨地而出。」亦可與此相發明也。

The greatest patterns (*wen**) of Heaven and Earth are the winds and clouds, rain and thunder. Their transformations cannot be fathomed, their origins and ends cannot be known. They are the supreme divinity of Heaven and Earth, the supreme pattern. But if I may treat them from one point of view, then consider the clouds of Mount T'ai. I spent half a year by Mount T'ai, and I am thoroughly familiar with the manner of its clouds. They rise from the tiniest sliver and spread flooding over the ends of the earth. Sometimes peaks will struggle to emerge, and the clouds will rise up over the summits and obliterate them. Sometimes they will bring several months of continuous darkness; sometimes they will disperse in a brief interval. Sometimes they are as black as lacquer, sometimes white as snow, sometimes as huge as the wings of the P'eng bird [whose wingspan stretches across the whole sky to both horizons], sometimes as disorderly as tangled tresses. At times, they hang lumplike in the heavens with nothing following upon them; at other times, they are continuous, delicate, faint—moving on and never ceasing.

Black clouds may suddenly arise, and the natives of the region will make predictions according to the rules: "It's going to rain." And it never does rain. Or sunlit clouds may come out and they predict, "It's going to be a nice day." And it rains. The forms of the clouds are countless: no two are the same. And likewise in their colors and countenances, in their natures and circumstantial manners, no two are the same. Sometimes the clouds turn back; sometimes they go off and do not turn back; sometimes they turn back completely; sometimes only half turn back—it is never the same. This is the pattern of Heaven and Earth, the supreme achievement.

But let us suppose that the pattern of Heaven and Earth were to be regulated by rules. Then when Mount T'ai was going to send out its clouds, it would first muster the tribes of clouds and give them their orders: "I am now going to send you clouds out to make 'the pattern of Heaven and Earth.' You, go first; you, follow; you, go up; and you, you there, lie low. You, cloud, shine; you, make ripples like waves; you, double back in; you, spread out in the sky; you, open up wide; and you, lock your gates fast. And you over there, you shake your tail." If Mount T'ai sent them out like this and brought them back like this, then there wouldn't be the least vitality in any of them. And this would be the formation of the pattern of Heaven and Earth!? The result of such a situation would be that Heaven and Earth would feel that the presence of Mount T'ai was a burden; and Mount T'ai in turn would feel that having clouds was a burden. And those clouds would still have to be sent out every single day!

Su Tung-p'o had a saying: "My writing is like a million-gallon stream: it pours forth according to the lay of the land." This can illustrate what I mean.

Although it does not really advance Yeh Hsieh's argument, this beautiful and comic passage on the clouds of Mount T'ai is an eloquent statement of deep values in the tradition: one of the highest goals is a poetry in which the *ch'ing** (affections, mood, circumstantial manner) would be as animate and changing as the clouds of Mount T'ai, always unpredictable. We can see quite clearly here why the concept of "intentionality" can have no place among positive literary values: the poet who would "intend" meaning or order into a text becomes like the cloud-master of Mount T'ai, an oppressor who robs vitality from the motions of mind.

或曰。「先生言作詩。法非所先。言固辨矣。然古帝王治天下。必曰大經大法。然則法且後乎哉。」余曰。帝王之法。即政也。夫子言。「文武之政。布在方策。」此一定章程。後人守之。苟有毫髮出入。則失之矣。修德貴日新。而法者舊章。斷不可使有毫髮之新。法一新。此王安石之所以亡宋也。若夫詩。古人作之。我亦作之。自我作詩。而非述詩也。故凡有詩。謂之新詩。若有法。如敎條政令而遵之。必如李攀龍之擬古樂府然後可。詩末技耳。必言前人所未言。發前人所未發。而後為我之詩。若徒以效顰效步為能事。曰此法也。不但詩亡。而法亦且亡矣。余之後法。非廢法也。正所以存法也。夫古今時會不同。即政令尚有因時而變通之。若膠固不變。則新莽之行周禮矣。奈何風雅一道。而踵其謬戾哉。

Someone then said, What you have just said about rules not being given as prior in composition is lucidly argued. But the way in which the ancient emperors and kings managed the world must be called the greatest canon and the greatest rules—in this case, can one say that the rules are posterior?

I answered, The rules of the emperors and kings were their governance. And Confucius said, "The governance of Kings Wen and Wu is set forth in documents." This is indeed a set program, and people of later times hold to it. If they diverge from it by the least measure, then they fail it altogether. "In the cultivation of virtue, it is important to make it new every day"; but these rules, set forth in earlier writing, do not permit even the least measure of "making new." By making new rules (*fa**, "laws"), Wang An-shih destroyed the Sung dynasty.

On the other hand, when it comes to poetry, the ancients wrote it, and I also write it. We are speaking here of poems written of the self and not the transmission of the Poems [i.e., the *Book of Songs*, where there is a responsibility to maintain the old unchanged]. Whatever poems we have can be considered new poems. If we are speaking here of rules that must be followed like instructions and government edicts, it will only work if we end up writing something like Li P'an-lung's [1514–1570] "Imitations of the Old Ballads."

Poetry is a "final" art: it must say what no one before has ever said and bring out what no one before has ever brought out. Only then can it be "my" poem. If a person thinks it is real mastery to ape the expressions and gait of others and call this "rules," then not only will poetry be destroyed, [a legitimate concept of] rules will also be destroyed. If I have made rules into something posterior, it does not mean that I have abandoned rules; rather this is the way to preserve rules.

The situations of ancient and modern times are not the same. Even government edicts are promulgated and changed according to the times. If a person is rigid and will not change, then we end up with something like the use of the *Rites of Chou* in Wang Mang's New [*Hsin*] dynasty [A.D. 8–23, a brief period of usurpation in the Han dynasty]. Why should the Way of Poetry (*feng*-ya**) follow in the footsteps of such folly?

"Final art" is a clumsy translation of *mo-chi*: *mo* is the "branch-tip," the antithesis of *pen**, the "root." *Mo* is the final stage of a process, often the "consequence" or "outcome" of what has gone before; thus it is also "of the present." Although Yeh Hsieh is giving the term a positive twist here, *mo* often implies "minor" or "lesser," echoing earlier critics from Ts'ao Chih on who spoke of literature as the "minor Way," *hsiao-Tao** 小道. Perhaps most important here in Yeh Hsieh's usage is that *mo* is differentiated and individuated, as opposed to *pen**, which comprehends and unifies distinction. Therefore to fulfill its *mo* nature, poetry must be original, both in the sense of "unique" and in the sense of being "one's own." We might note here that the commonplace assumptions of Western thought since at least the mid eighteenth century are exactly the inverse of this: Western "originality" locates individuation in the *pen**, root or "origin," while the comprehensive norm is *mo*, the result of a process of socialization.

Yeh Hsieh's notion of poetry as a "final art" (or "minor art") had long been a common critique leveled against poetry by some Confucian philosophers and the proponents of state service and political morality; Yeh Hsieh accepts the term *mo* but, as he does with *fa**, reinterprets it and gives it new meaning.

Poetry here emerges out of the present and the self: it is essentially immediate and individuated. This position has, in fact, canonical authority in the "Great Preface: "The affairs of a single state, rooted in [the experience of] a single person, are called *Feng**." This is not to say that the universal and normative cannot appear in poetry, but they are given as mediated by the experience of a particular person at a particular moment.

We might add here that even though conventional Confucian piety requires that Yeh Hsieh acknowledge the authority of the *fa** of the ancient Sages, Yeh Hsieh's ingenious attempt to distinguish between originary (*pen**) *fa** and the *fa** of "final," present circumstances does not redeem originary *fa** from the implicit charge of oppressiveness that robs action of spontaneity. Modern poets, like the ancient Sages, "give the rule" in their writings; but the poets exact no greater obedience than our sigh: "Ah, that is precisely how it should have been done."

"INNER SECTION"
Chapter 2 (Opening)

曰理。曰事。曰情。此三言者足以窮盡萬有之變態。凡形形色色。音聲狀貌。舉不能越乎此。此舉在物者而為言。而無一物之或能去此者也。曰才。曰膽。曰識。曰力。此四言者所以窮盡此心之神明。凡形形色色。音聲狀貌。無不待於此而為之發宣昭著。此舉在我者而為言。而無一不如此心以出之者也。

Our three terms—principle, event, and circumstance—are adequate to encompass the changing manners (*pien**-t'ai*) of everything that exists. There is no shape (*hsing**), color, sound (*yin-sheng*), or appearance (*chuang-mao*) that lies beyond their scope. All of these are spoken of as being present in a thing, and there is not a single thing that can do without them.

There are four other terms—talent, courage (*tan*, "gall"), judgment, and force—these are adequate to encompass the spiritual illumination (*shen**-ming**)* of a particular mind. Each shape and color, sound and appearance depends on these four qualities to become bright and manifest. All four of these are spoken of as being present in the self, and there is not a one that comes forth except through the particular mind.

From an anatomy of the coming-to-be of the outer world, Yeh Hsieh turns to an anatomy of consciousness, the preconditions of mind that make good poetry possible. In the context of traditional literary thought, perhaps the greatest weakness of Yeh Hsieh's poetics is his discussion of the role of mind in writing: for him the quality of the individual mind of the writer is *not* what is known through reading poetry; rather mind is valued purely in its capacity for knowing and conveying knowledge of the outer world. Later, when he discusses Tu Fu, he values Tu Fu's lines not because they let us know Tu Fu, but rather because they make manifest for us subtle principles in the outer world, principles that no one but Tu Fu could perceive.

"Talent," *ts'ai**, is pure capacity, a limited, quantitative measure that exists in a person in potential. "Judgment," *shih**, is an old category in such lists, figuring prominently in "Ts'ang-lang's Remarks on Poetry." "Force," *li* 力, is the secret counterpart of *ch'i**, an energy that gives the work extension and endurance.

"Courage," *tan*, is the most interesting and unexpected addition to this matrix of the poetic consciousness. Its appearance here is a tacit acknowledgement of intimidation: in writing, the self is somehow put at risk by comparison to others, particularly by comparison to predecessors. To try to write well is to assert one's identity within a community, and that act is fraught with anxieties. "Courage" implies danger, putting oneself at risk; yet the ultimate hope, as we will see, is a freedom from anxiety, a pure joy in the doing.

以在我之四衡。在物之三合。而為作者之文章。大之經緯天地。細而一動一植。詠歎謳吟。俱不能離是而為言者矣。在物者前已論悉之。在我者雖有天分之不齊。要無不可以人力充之。其優於天者。四者具足。而才獨外見。則羣稱其才。而不知其才之不能無所憑而獨見也。其歉乎天者。才見不足。人皆曰才之歉也。不可勉強也。不知有識以居乎才之先。識為體而才為用。若不足於才。當先研精推求乎其識。人惟中藏無識。則理事情錯陳於前。而渾然茫然。是非可否。妍媸黑白。悉眩惑而不能辨。安望其敷而出之為才乎。文章之能事。實始乎此。

If one has these four considerations in the self and the three combined aspects of outer things, and thereby produces an innovative [*tso-che*, "by a maker"] work of literature, then nothing in song, effusion, or ballad can be articulated apart from these [constituent elements]—whether it is in the largest scope of the warp and woof in the loom of Heaven and Earth, or in the more minute sense that involves every moving thing and growing thing. I have already discussed in great detail the three which are in outer things (*wu**). As for the four that are in the self, even though there are disparities in natural endowment, there is not a one of them whose shortcomings cannot be compensated for by human effort. When someone is given excellence by Nature (*T'ien*), all four are ample within him; but only talent is outwardly visible. Then everyone will praise that person's talent, without realizing that talent cannot be visible by itself, without being dependent on something. In those who have been left deficient by Nature, it is talent that appears insufficient, and everyone says "Deficient in talent—can't be made up for by effort." Such people do not understand that judgment occupies a position prior to talent: judgment is the form (*t'i**), and talent is only its functioning (*yung*). If someone has insufficient talent, he must first investigate thoroughly and search in his [capacity for] judgment. If a person lacks [the capacity for] judgment within himself, then principle, event, and circumstance are set forth in confusion before him: they are all mixed together and indistinct—true and false, acceptable and unacceptable, beauty and ugliness, black and white are all in a blur and cannot be discriminated. In such a situation, how can a person hope that everything will unfold and emerge in such a way that shows talent? It is in this that the mastery of literature truly begins.

今夫詩。彼無識者既不能知古來作者之意。并不自知其何所興感觸發而為詩。或亦聞古今詩家之論。所謂體裁格力。聲調興會等語。不過影響於耳。含糊於心。附會於口。而眼光從無着處。腕力從無措處。即歷代之詩陳於前。何所決擇。何所適從。人言是則是之。人言非則非之。夫非必謂人言之不可憑也。而彼先不能得我心之是非而是非之。又安能知人言之是非而是非之也。有人曰。詩必學漢魏。學盛唐。彼亦曰學漢魏。學盛唐。從而然之。而學漢魏與盛唐所以然之故。彼不能知。不能言也。即能效而言之。而終不能知也。又有人曰。詩當學晚唐。學宋。學元。彼亦曰學晚唐。學宋。學元。又從而然之。而置漢魏與盛唐所以然之故。彼又終不能知也。或聞詩家有宗劉長卿者矣。於是矗然而稱劉隨州矣。又或聞有崇尚陸游者矣。於是人人案頭無不有劍南集以為秘本。而遂不敢他及矣。如此等類不可枚舉一槩。人云亦云。人否亦否。何為者耶。夫人以著作自命。將進退古人。次第前哲。必具有隻眼。而後泰然有自居之地。倘議論是非。聾瞀於中心。而隨世人之影響而附會之。終日以其言語筆墨為人使令驅役。不亦愚乎。且有不自以為愚。旋愚成妄。妄以生驕。而愚益甚焉。原其患。始於無識不能取舍之故也。是即吟咏不輟。累牘連章。任其塗抹。全無生氣。其為才耶。為不才耶。

In poetry a person who lacks judgment cannot know what was on the mind (*yi**) of writers of ancient times, nor can he even know what touched and stirred such writers to make poems. On the other hand, that sort of person may well have heard the discussions of past and present poets. But concepts such as "formal construction" (*t'i*-tsai*), "force of structure" (*ko*-li*), "musicality" (*sheng*-tiao*), "occasioning stimulus" (*hsing*-hui*) and other such terms, are nothing more than an echo in the ear, a blur in the mind, something that hung by chance once in the mouth; his clarity of vision still has nothing to see, and the strength of his wrist [essential in calligraphy] still has nothing to which to apply itself. If you set the poems of all ages before him, how will he make a choice among them? What will suit him? If someone tells him it's good, then it's good; if someone tells him it's not good, then it's not good. This is not to say that what the other tells him is necessarily unreliable—only that such a person is incapable of first judging the work for himself, in his own mind. How then can he judge the judgment of others?

Someone tells him, "In poetry you must study the Han, Wei, and High T'ang." Then that sort of person obligingly agrees and says, "Study the Han, Wei, and High T'ang." But that sort of person can never know or tell you why he should agree about the Han, Wei, and High T'ang. Or he may copy someone else and tell you why, but he can never know why. Then somebody tells him that in poetry he should study the late T'ang or the Sung or the Yüan. He will again agree and say, "Study the late T'ang, Sung, and Yüan." But he will never know why he should set aside his previous agreement about the Han, Wei, and High T'ang.[5] Persons of this sort may have heard that there are poets who particularly revere Liu Ch'ang-ch'ing [d. ca. 785], whereupon they will all sing the praises of Liu Ch'ang-ch'ing with one voice. Or they may have heard that there are those who hold Lu Yu [1125–1210] in the highest honor;

whereupon Lu Yu's *Chien-nan Collection* will sit on everyone's desk as a secret treasure, nor will they dare concern themselves with any other poet. Examples of this are too numerous to mention. What others assert, they, too, assert; what others deny, they, too, deny. Why does this happen? A person who would be self-reliant in his writing, who would elevate the status of some of the older writers while lowering the status of others, who would give some sort of ranking to the masters of the past, must have achieved a fresh and discerning eye; only then can he have a secure place to stand. Supposing one debates the value of something but is deaf and blind in the heart, simply adhering to the general opinion of the age and being driven along all day by the words and writings of others—is that not foolish? But it so happens that such people do not consider themselves foolish at all, whereupon their foolishness becomes error, and their error breeds arrogance, and their folly gets even worse.

If we consider the source of this problem, it originates in the inability to make choices because of a lack of [the capacity for] judgment. Yet they recite their poems ceaselessly, page upon page, work upon work, scribbling whatever they please, with no life in it at all—should we call this talent or lack of talent?[6]

Even though Yeh Hsieh is primarily concerned with the autonomy of poetic creation, the deeply ingrained habits of the critical tradition lead him to associate autonomous judgment in composition with autonomous judgment of earlier poetry. The courage (*tan*) necessary to oppose intimidation when writing merges with the courage to go against contemporary fashion in judging works in the poetic tradition.

Yeh attacks literary fashion for the same reason that he attacks the older notion of *fa**: it is a series of prior determinations, and not something produced spontaneously out of the self on universal grounds. Like Yen Yü before him, Yeh Hsieh uses a rhetoric of embarrassment, fine flourishes of scorn to wrest assent to positions that are elsewhere argued persuasively. Unfortunately, in Yeh Hsieh's case, the force of his rhetoric contradicts the position itself: his rhetoric demands assent to the position that people should not assent to a position out of social pressure, but rather should discover it in themselves.

惟有識則是非明。是非明則取舍定。不但不隨世人腳跟。并亦不隨古人腳跟。非薄古人為不足學也。蓋天地有自然之文章。隨我之所觸而發宣之。必有克肖其自然者。為至文以立極。我之命意發言。自當求其至極者。

Only when there is [the capacity for] judgment are the values of things clear; and when the values of things are clear, choices can be made decisively. Not only does one avoid following on the heels of the opinion of the age, one also avoids following on the heels of the older writers—nor is this denigrating the older writers as not being worth study. In Heaven and Earth there are Nature's (*Tzu-jan**) literary works (*wen**-chang**) which appear according to what I myself encounter. One must be able to catch the semblance of that naturalness (*tzu-jan**) to make the perfection of pattern (*wen**, "writing") as one's ultimate value. In the concepts (*yi**) that I form and in the words (*yen*) that I utter, I must seek that ultimate value.

This is a remarkable passage on taking Nature, *Tzu-jan**, the "So-of-Itself," as the ultimate standard in writing, setting it up as the sole goal to which a writer aspires. As so often in literary Chinese, there are fruitful ambiguities here: the phrase *Tzu-jan** chih wen**-chang** may mean "Nature's literary works," texts that already exist latent in the world (Heaven and Earth), which are made manifest by our chance encounters with them; or the phrase may mean "spontaneously produced literary works," in which *Tzu-jan** refers to the process of composition rather than to the process of Nature, and which does not necessarily presume the prior existence of the text, virtual in the world. However deeply Yeh Hsieh's version of "Nature" belongs to the Chinese tradition, at least part of the notion of literary art presented here leads inescapably to a version of *mimêsis*. *Mimêsis* is hidden in the seemingly innocuous phrase "catch the semblance of," *k'o-hsiao*, which also carries implications of "doing justice to."

Against the capacity to judge things "as they are," Yeh Hsieh sets the intimidation of fashion, values imposed by others. We should note how easily Yeh shifts between critical judgment ("following on the heels of the opinion of the age") and creative judgment ("following on the heels of the older writers"). Like Yen Yü, Yeh Hsieh believes that critical judgment should be self-evident; but he does not always seem to believe, as Yen Yü did, that creative judgment is necessarily mediated by critical judgment (i.e., that one must read and recognize the great poetry of predecessors in order to write well oneself). For Yeh Hsieh, clear judgment is a fundamental capacity that permits a direct encounter between the poet and the world he makes manifest in writing. It should be added, however, that elsewhere Yeh Hsieh speaks of the necessary mediation of reading earlier poetry much as Yen Yü did.

In this and the following passage, Yeh Hsieh's use of the terminology of self and his willingness to reject the necessary mediation of poetic tradition suggest the influence of the late-Ming vitalist poetics of the Yüan brothers. As he does with other strains of the theoretical tradition, Yeh Hsieh transforms these received elements and reconciles them with other positions to which they once might have seemed opposed. For Yüan Hung-tao, the rejection of tradition was the pure means to assert self; for Yeh Hsieh, freedom from the prejudices of tradition and fashion not only asserts self, it is inextricable from a clarity of judgment that allows the poet to "do justice to" the world in his poetry.

昔人有言。「不恨我不見古人。恨古人不見我。」又云。「不恨臣無二王法。但恨二王無臣法。」斯言特論書法耳。而其人自命如此。等而上之。可以推矣。譬之學射者。盡其目力臂力。審而後發。苟能百發百中。即不必學古人。而古有后羿養由基其人者。自然來合我矣。我能是。古人先我而能是。未知我合古人歟。古人合我歟。高適有云。「乃知古時人。亦有如我者。」豈不然哉。故我之著作與古人同。所謂其揆之一。即有與古人異。乃補古人之所未足。亦可言古人補我之所未足。而後我與古人交為知己也。惟如是。我之命意發言。一一皆從識見中流布。識明則膽張。任其發宜而無所於怯。橫說豎說。左宜而右有。直造化在手。無有一之不肖乎物也。

There is an old saying, "I don't regret that I cannot see the people of former times; I regret that the people of former times could not see me." Another goes, "I don't regret that I lack the [calligraphic] method (*fa**) of Wang Hsi-chih and Wang Hsien-chih; I regret rather that they lacked my method." Even though this saying refers specifically to calligraphy, it shows remarkable self-confidence, and it can be extended to other levels.

Let me make a comparison to archery: if I exercise the full force of my eye and arm, shooting only after due consideration; and if then I hit the center a hundred times in a hundred shots, I need not study former masters. But in former times there were archers, such as Hou Yi and Yang Yu-chi, who quite naturally matched my accomplishments. I am capable of this; there were people of former times before me who were also capable of this. And I can't say whether I match the people of former times or the people of former times matched me. Kao Shih [706–765] once wrote, "Now I understand that among the people of former times there were those who were as I am." Of course this is true. So when what I write is the same as what a former master wrote, it means that we were one in our reflections. And when I write something different from former masters, I may be filling in something missing in their work; or it is possible that the former masters will be filling in something missing in my work. Only then can I form a bond of close and understanding friendship [*chih-chi*, one who "knows the self"] with the people of former times.

If it goes on like this, then every single concept I form and every word I utter will flow out from judgment and perception. When judgment is clear [*ming*, or "bright"], one's courage expands: I let it manifest itself with no trembling anxieties. You can say things however you please, and whatever you do turns out just right. The process of creation (*Tsao-hua**) is in my hands, and there is nothing that fails to do justice to the things of the world (*wu**).

Yeh Hsieh's exhortations to self-confidence are a measure of the degree of intimidation felt by late-classical writers when confronting the achievements of earlier literature. Here one cannot resist quoting Edward Young's "Conjectures on Original Composition" from 1759, encouraging a similar confidence and outlining the dangers of abject admiration for precursors.

> But why are *Originals* so few? not because the writer's harvest is over, the great reapers of antiquity having left nothing to be gleaned after them; nor because the human mind's teeming time is past, or because it is incapable of putting forth unprecedented births; but because illustrious examples *engross*, *prejudice*, and *intimidate*. They *engross* our attention, and so prevent a due inspection of ourselves; they *prejudice* our judgment in favor of their abilities, and so lessen the sense of our own; and they *intimidate* us with the splendor of their renown, and thus under diffidence bury our strength. Nature's impossibilities and those of diffidence lie wide asunder.[7]

Yeh Hsieh's appeal to a standard of value independent of any historical embodiment is a way to escape intimidation by the great writers of antiquity.

It is important to stress that the core of Yeh Hsieh's concern is the autonomy of artistic creation, not mere difference from predecessors. If the poet, acting on his own, produces something similar to an earlier master, it is a happy coincidence; and because both were autonomously produced, the later work will presumably have a value equal to the earlier. Difference from the work of a predecessor, when it arises autonomously, becomes a complement that is neither more nor less valuable than the predecessor's work.[8]

且夫胸中無識之人。即終日勤於學。而亦無益。俗諺謂為兩腳書櫥。記誦日多。多益為累。及伸紙落筆時。胸如亂絲。頭緒既紛。無從割擇。中且餒而膽愈怯。欲言而不能言。或能言而不敢言。矜持於銖兩尺矱之中。既恐不合於古人。又恐貽譏於今人。如三日新婦。動恐失體。又如跛者登臨。舉恐失足。文章一道。本攄寫揮灑樂事。反若有物焉以桎梏之。無處非礙矣。於是強者必曰。古人某某之作如是。非我則不能得其法也。弱者亦曰。古人某某之作如是。今之聞人某某傳其法如是。而我亦如是也。其黠者心則然而秘而不言。愚者心不能知其然。徒夸而張於人。以為我自有所本也。更或謀篇時。有言已盡本無可贅矣。恐方幅不足而不合於格。於是多方拖沓以擴之。是蛇添足也。又有言尚未盡。正堪抒寫。恐逾於格而失矩度。亟闔而已焉。是生割活剝也。

Those with no capacity for judgment in their hearts may be diligent in study the whole day through and still derive no benefit from it. In the words of the popular phrase, they are "two-footed bookcases." Every day they memorize and recite more; and the more they do this, the more they become entangled in it. Then when it comes to spreading out their paper and setting their brushes to it, their hearts are as if filled with tangled threads; what comes to their minds is in such confusion that they have no way to choose. Midway they lose heart, and their courage steadily fails them. Either they want to speak and cannot, or they can speak but dare not. They take pride in spending time in the most careful adjudications, fearful lest what they write not be in accord with former masters and also fearful lest they be mocked by their contemporaries. They are just like new brides, constantly afraid of committing some breach of etiquette; or like climbers to some high prospect, at every moment afraid of losing their footing.

The Way of literature (wen*-chang*) is based on the free, unfettered joy of expressing oneself. If instead there is something in it that puts a person in shackles, then obstacles appear everywhere. In such a case the stronger writer will say, "The work of such and such an older writer was thus and so, and I am the only one who has grasped his method (fa*)." The weaker writer will say, "The work of such and such an older writer was thus and so, and I have heard that such and such a contemporary writer transmits his method thus and so, and I, too, do it thus and so." The crafty types agree in their hearts but keep it secret and say nothing; the ignorant types don't understand how it is, but make hollow boasts to others, thinking they have some true basis in themselves. Moreover, it sometimes happens that when organizing a whole work, a person will have said everything he could and can't come up with anything else; but afraid that the piece won't be long enough and that it won't fit the formal structure (ko*), he extends it haphazardly in many directions: this is called "adding feet to a snake." In other cases, there is still more to say and the person could easily keep on writing, but in his fear of transgressing the formal structure (ko*) and missing the measure, he brings it abruptly to a conclusion: this is "cutting something off in the bloom of life."

之數者。因無識。故無膽。使筆墨不能自由。是為操觚家之苦趣。不可不察也。昔賢有言。「成事在膽。」文章千古事。苟無膽。何以能千古乎。吾故曰。無膽則筆墨畏縮。膽既詘矣。才何由而得伸乎。惟膽能生才。但知才受於天。而抑知必待擴充於膽耶。吾見世有稱人之才。而歸美之曰。能斂才就法。斯言也。非能知才之所由然者也。夫才者。諸法之蘊隆發現處也。若有所斂而為就。則未斂未就以前之才。尚未有法也。其所為才。皆不從理事情而得。為拂道悖德之言。與才之義相背而馳者。尚得謂之才乎。

Cases of this sort come from a lack of courage which follows from a lack of the capacity for judgment; this causes the brush to be unable to act freely. One cannot help but observe that this is a tribulation for writers. Long ago a wise man [Han Ch'i] said, "Completion depends on courage." Another [Tu Fu] said, "Literature is a deed of eternity"; but if one lacks courage, it is impossible to attain eternity. For this reason I assert that if courage is lacking, brush and ink will shrivel up [in fear]. And if a person's courage is humiliated, how can talent extend itself? Only courage can engender talent. It is commonly understood that talent is only received from Heaven, but do people realize that talent also depends on being extended and made full by courage?

I have seen how popular opinion praises a man's talent, making the point of its approbation the fact that such a person can restrain his talent and make it conform to the rules (*fa**). To say this is to misunderstand how talent develops as it does. Talent is that point from which all the rules emerge in abundance.

If there is something that restrains talent and makes it conform, then there can have been no rules [already inherent] in the talent before it was restrained and made to conform. "Talent" of this sort is not something achieved through principle, event, and circumstance: its words run counter to morality and the Way, since it rushes off in the opposite direction from the true significance (*yi**) of talent. Therefore, how can we still even call it talent?

Having made "rules" posterior to a particular composition, Yeh Hsieh is brought to the Kantian position that "genius" (*ingenium*, that which is innate; cf. *ts'ai**, "endowment") is that which *gives* the rule rather than that which obeys the rules.[9] For Yeh Hsieh the only valid rules are those produced out of talent and therefore virtual in talent. He cleverly develops this by saying that conformity to external rules shows that there are no rules already virtual in such a person; presumably such internally generated rules, inherent in the very operation of talent, would take precedence over external rules. Although both Kant and Yeh Hsieh sound abstract in this, the point made is empirically valid and elegantly simple: a work of talent or genius, which successfully goes beyond the norms, by its very success creates a new sense of how one "ought to" write; it makes the unanticipated seem (or "reveals the unanticipated as") natural and necessary.

Although Yeh Hsieh has earlier allowed for a happy coincidence between the expression of a modern writer and his predecessors, the primary value of the autonomy of artistic production easily shifts to "originality" as a value in its own right: we suppose that whatever comes spontaneously from the self will be unique precisely because of the uniqueness of self. There is, however, in the Chinese tradition another current of thought that presumes that mind, acting spontaneously and with clarity, will perceive what is paradigmatic and normative. The Western notion of genius reconciles this apparent contradiction: it is both unique and "natural" or normative. In the first paragraph of the following passage Yeh Hsieh also seems to unify the unique and the normative.

夫於人之所不能知。而惟我有才能知之。於人之所不能言。而惟我有才能言之。縱其心思之氤氳磅礴。上下縱橫。凡六合以內外。皆不得而囿之。以是措而為文辭。而至理存焉。萬事準焉。深情托焉。是之謂有才。若欲其斂以就法。彼固掉臂遊行於法中久矣。不知其所就者又何物也。必將曰。所就者乃一定不遷之規矩。此千萬庸眾人皆可共趨之而由之。又何待於才之斂耶。故文章家止有以才御法而驅使之。決無就法而為法之所役。而猶欲詡

其才者也。吾故曰。無才則心思不出。亦可曰。無心思則才不出。而所謂規矩者。即心思
之肆應各當之所為也。蓋言心思。則主乎內以言才。言法。則主乎外以言才。主乎內。心
思無處不可通。吐而為辭。無物不可通也。夫孰得而範圍其心。又孰得而範圍其言乎。主
乎外。則囿於物而反有所不得於我心。心思不靈。而才銷鑠矣。吾嘗觀古之才人。合詩與
文而論之。如左邱明。司馬遷。賈誼。李白。杜甫。韓愈。蘇軾之徒。天地萬物皆遞開闢
於其筆端。無有不可舉。無有不能勝。前不必有所承。後不必有所繼。而各有其愉快。如
是之才。必有其力以載之。惟力大而才能堅。故至堅而不可摧也。歷千百代而不朽者以
此。昔人有云。擲地須作金石聲。六朝人非能知此義者。而言金石。喻其堅也。此可以見
文家之力。力之分量。即一句一言。如植之則不可仆。橫之則不可斷。行則不可遏。住則
不可遷。易曰。「獨立不懼。」此言其人。而其人之文當亦如是也。譬之兩人焉。共適於
途。而值羊腸蠶叢。峻棧危梁之險。其一弱者。精疲於中。形戰於外。將裹足而不前。又
必不可已而進焉。於是步步有所憑藉。以為依傍。或藉人之推之挽之。或手有所持而捫。
或足有所緣而踐。即能前達。皆非其人自有之力。僅愈於木偶為人舁之而行耳。其一為有
力者。神旺而氣足。徑往直前。不待有所攀援假借。奮然投足。反趨弱者扶掖之前。此直
以神行而形隨之。豈待外求而能者。故有境必能造。有造必能成。

What others cannot know, only the self, in possessing talent, can know. What others cannot say, only the self, in possessing talent, can say. Let one's thoughts (*hsin*-ssu**) generate and swell boundlessly, high and low in every direction, and not one of the six limits of the universe, inside or out, can confine it. Put this down in writing (*wen*-tz'u**) and the perfection of principle will reside therein, thousands of events will be balanced therein, deep affections (*ch'ing**, "circumstance") will be lodged therein—this can be called "having talent."

But if a person would restrain talent and make it conform to rules, that person will certainly wander blissfully for a long time within those rules without knowing exactly what it is he is conforming to. [If asked,] such a person will, of course, say "I am conforming to a determinate, immutable standard." But since millions of utterly ordinary people can all follow the same course, why should doing so depend upon restraining one's talent? Therefore only through talent may a man of letters harness rule and make it gallop to his will; there is absolutely no case where someone conforms to rules and makes himself a servant of the rules yet still is able to boast of his talent.

For this reason I say that without talent one's thoughts (*hsin*-ssu**) cannot emerge. But one can also say that if there are no thoughts, talent cannot emerge. What are called the "standards" are simply what thoughts do in responding immediately and in each case appropriately.

In speaking of talent, when we treat it in terms of thought (*hsin*-ssu**), we make what is interior (*nei*) dominant; when we treat it in terms of "rules," we make what is exterior (*wai*) dominant. If we make what is interior dominant, there is no place to which thought cannot communicate (*t'ung**) [i.e., thought can conceive of anything]; brought forth in words (*tz'u**), there is nothing it cannot communicate [playing here on the double sense of *t'ung** both as to "understand" and to "make understood"]. In these circumstances who could put an encircling boundary around mind (*hsin**); and in such circumstances who could put an encircling boundary around the words (*yen*)? But if one makes what is external dominant, then one will be circumscribed by things [*wu**; i.e., the external rules] and there will be something in one's own mind that cannot be attained. One's thoughts (*hsin**-*ssu**) will lack the spark of magic (*ling*) and one's talent will dissolve.

I have considered men of talent in the past—men like Tso Ch'iu-ming, Ssu-ma Ch'ien, Chia Yi, Li Po, Tu Fu, Han Yü, and Su Shih—and regardless of whether they worked in poetry or prose, all the things of Heaven and Earth were brought into being in succession on the tips of their brushes: there was nothing they could not bring up; there was nothing they could not master; there need have been no antecedents before them for them to carry on, nor did there need to be anyone after them to continue what they did; each had his own delight. For talent like this there must be force (*li*) to carry it. Only when the force is great can talent be firm, and a perfect firmness cannot be broken. This is the way they have managed to pass through a thousand ages without decay. Someone [Sun Ch'o] said long ago: "When cast to the ground, it must have the sound of metal and stone." In the period of the Six Dynasties, they were unable fully to comprehend this truth (*yi**), yet they spoke of metal and stone as a metaphor for such firmness. In this, one can see force in prose writers.

The measure of force can be seen in a line or in a word: planted upright, it cannot be laid flat; stretched horizontally, it cannot be broken; in motion, it cannot be halted; stopping in one place, it cannot be shifted. The *Book of Changes* says, "Stand alone without fear." Though this applies to persons, a person's writing also ought to be like this.

Take the example of two men, both proceeding along a road when they come upon the kind of dangerous, winding mountain paths one finds in Szech-wan, with plank walkways along mountainsides and perilous bridges. The weaker one's spirit flags within him and his form trembles, to the point where he is almost unwilling to proceed; but compelled by the necessity of con-tinuing, he leans on something for support at every step. He may depend on the other to push and drag him along, or he may grasp something in his hand and hold tight, or he may carefully walk along following the course of some-one else. He may eventually reach the place that lies ahead of him, but it is never because of the force he himself possesses: he is worse than a wooden statue that moves by being carried by others.

The other one is a person with force: his spirit is vigorous and his *ch'i** ample. He goes straight off ahead, placing his feet boldly and decisively, without depending on anything to hang onto or make use of, but instead hurries to help the weaker one forward. This is having the spirit (*shen**) go and the body (*hsing**) follow it. It is not a capability that depends on looking for something external. Thus if there is a world [*ching**, a "mind-world"], one is necessarily able to create (*tsao*) it; and if the creation occurs, one is necessarily able to complete it.

Yeh Hsieh's frequent calls for decisive, self-reliant action indicate a deep anxiety about the intimidating power of past poetry. "Making what is interior dominant," *chu yü nei*, is a radical exhortation to cut off all consideration of other poetry and other formal imperatives in composition. The radicalness of the demand is a measure of his desire to be free of the "burden of the past," or at least free of the burden of contemporary opinion, and to be self-authorizing. In spirit (*shen**) he hopes to discover both a "freedom from" and a "freedom to," assuring us that the merely verbal manifestation will follow naturally and spontaneously from such free action of the spirit.

This quality of "force"—whether it appears in a single word or a line or a scene—is not a blustering aggressiveness of manner. Rather it is a sense of the unalterable rightness of the words, the writer's decisiveness in saying things a certain way, and the compelling power of that articulation. Most important, force is not something simply "deposited" in the words; it involves a relation between the poet and his words. Thus the same words, stolen by another, lose their force.

吾故曰。文言者。無力則不能自成一家。夫家者。吾固有之家也。人各自有家。在己力而成之耳。豈有依傍想象他人之家以為我之家乎。是猶不能自求家珍。穿窬鄰人之物以為己有。即使盡竊其連城之璧。終是鄰人之寶。不可為我家珍。而識者窺見其裏。適供其啞然一笑而已。故本其所自有者而益充而廣大之以成家。非其力之所自致乎。

In my opinion, the man who lacks force in "establishing words" (*li-yen**) cannot found his own household [i.e., become a distinct master]. My "household" is one I have absolutely as my own. Each person may have his own household, and its establishment depends upon his own force. He cannot simply indulge in a fantasy of someone else's household and consider it his own. This would be like being unable to get treasures for your household on your own and therefore stealing a neighbor's possessions and considering them yours; but even if a man steals all his neighbor's jade disks worth a string of cities [i.e., his most precious possessions], they are still the valuables of his neighbor and cannot be considered his own household's possessions. And when someone with the capacity for judgment looks into the matter thoroughly, it will appropriately provide him with a good laugh. To take what one has oneself as the basis, to amplify and extend that in order to establish one's own household—is that not something that can be accomplished by one's own force?

Clearly the humor is to be found more in the tenor of the metaphor than in the vehicle (owners and the authorities who maintain the rights of property are notoriously lacking in humor when it comes to theft): one opens oneself to mockery by stealing the poetic style of another and claiming it for one's own. Yeh Hsieh here is amplifying the phrase for mastery of an art or school of thought, "to found one's own household"; but the metaphor to which it leads him is not altogether apt. One problem of particular interest is that the literary application of the conventional phrase "to found one's own household," usually implies a circle of dependents and imitators, precisely the situation Yeh Hsieh is attacking.

然力有大小。家有巨細。吾又觀古之才人。力足以蓋一鄉。則為一鄉之才。力足以蓋一國。則為一國之才。力足以蓋天下。則為天下之才。更進乎此。其力足以十世。足以百世。足以終古。則其立言不朽之業。亦垂十世。垂百世。垂終古。悉如其力以報之。

Nevertheless there are varying degrees of force, as there are grand and minor households. Consider the talented men of former times: those whose force was adequate to cover an entire county became the talents of the county; those whose force was adequate to cover a region became the talents of the region; those whose force was adequate to cover the whole world became talents of the world. And when we go beyond this to those whose force was adequate for ten generations or for a hundred generations or for all time, then their establishment of words (li-yen*) was an undecaying patrimony that lasted ten generations or a hundred generations or for all time—in each case their capacity to endure depended on their force.

This passage echoes *Mencius* V.B.8.2 and Ts'ao P'i's "Discourse on Literature." Note that although Yeh Hsieh denies that talent is an innate capacity, force is treated as if it were and as if no effort can alter the amount of it each person has. It is an enabling power, playing here much the same role that ch'i* played in the triad of principle, event, and circumstance. Force is what gives a work extension and duration.

試合古今之才。——較其所就。視其力之大小遠近。如分寸銖兩之悉稱焉。又觀近代著作之家。其詩文初出。一時非不紙貴。後生小子。以耳為目。互相傳誦。取為模楷。及身沒之後。聲問即泯。漸有起而議之者。或間能及其身後。而一世再世漸遠而無聞焉。甚且詆

毀叢生。是非競起。昔日所稱其人之長。即為今日所指之短。可勝歎哉。即如明三百年
間。王世貞。李攀龍輩盛鳴於嘉隆時。終不如明初之高楊張徐。猶得無毀於今日人之口
也。鍾惺譚元春之矯異於末季。又不如王李之猶可及於再世之餘也。是皆其力所至遠近之
分量也。

Try placing side by side the talents of ancient and modern times: compare each
one in regard to his accomplishments and then consider the magnitude and
extent of each person's force: you will find that these two considerations correspond in the tiniest measure. Then again reflect on the writers of recent
times: when their poetry or prose first appears, their work is extremely popular in the age, and their younger followers and disciples think of the ear as the
eye; they recite it to one another and transmit it, taking it as their model. But
after such a writer dies, his reputation fades away, and critics of his work
gradually appear. Among such, there are a few whose works endure after
them, but after one or two generations, they become increasingly remote and
are no longer heard of. In the worst cases, harsh attacks spring up everywhere;
everyone wants to discuss their merits and failings; and those very points once
praised as their strengths are now pointed out as their weaknesses. What a pity.
Consider how in the three centuries of the Ming the group around Wang
Shih-chen [1526–1590] and Li P'an-lung [1514–1570] were so famous in the
Chia-ch'ing and Lung-ch'ing reigns; ultimately, however, they have not
escaped being attacked by our modern writers as much as have [early Ming
writers such as] Kao Ch'i [1336–1374], Yang Chi [1334–ca.1383], Chang Yü
[1333–1385], and Hsü Pen [1335–1380]. The extravagance of Chung Hsing
[1574–1624] and T'an Yüan-ch'un [1585–1637] at the end of the Ming did
not succeed in matching even Wang Shih-chen's and the Li P'an-lung's survival for over two generations. Each of these cases shows the measure and
extent of their force.

The vagaries of fashion and the inability of any of recent poets to achieve the
status of classics were matters of profound concern in the Ming and Ch'ing.
Although elsewhere Yeh Hsieh attacks the notion that the very possibility of
great writing is diminishing through history, the examples he gives here
secretly support that fear: fourteenth-century poets (though certainly far
short of the status of classics) have still not been entirely rejected; sixteenth-
century poets maintained their reputations for only two generations; early-
seventeenth-century poets were attacked immediately. What Yeh Hsieh does
not note is the ironic justice of this diminishing span of reputation: the
archaist poets of the sixteenth century built their reputations on attacking
earlier poets and began the very fashion of vilifying predecessors to which
they themselves soon fell victim.

統百代而論詩。自三百篇而後。惟杜甫之詩。其力能與天地相終始。與三百篇等。自此以外。後世不能無入者主之。出者奴之。諸說之異同。操戈之不一矣。其間又有力可以百世。而百世之內。互有興衰者。或中湮而復興。或昔非而今是。又似世會使之然。生前或未有推重之。而後世忽崇尚之。如韓愈之文。當愈之時。舉世未有深知而尚之者。二百餘年後。歐陽修方大表章之。天下遂翕然宗韓愈之文。以至於今不衰。信乎文章之力有大小遠近。而又盛衰乘時之不同如是。欲成一家言。斷宜奮其力矣。夫內得之於識而出之而為才。惟膽以張其才。惟力以克荷之。得全者其才見全。得半者其才見半。而又非可矯揉蹴至之者也。蓋有自然之候焉。千古才力之大者。莫有及於神禹。神禹平成天地之功。此何等事。而孟子以為行所無事。不過順水流行坎止自然之理。而行疏瀹排決之事。豈別有治水之法。有所矯揉以行之者乎。不然者。是行其所有事矣。大禹之神力。遠及萬萬世。以文辭立言者。雖不敢幾此。然異道同歸。勿以篇章為細務自遜。處於沒世無聞已也。

Considering the poetry of all the ages since the *Book of Songs*, only the poetry of Tu Fu has the force to last the full span of Heaven and Earth and thus is equal to the *Book of Songs*. Beyond these there have always been some in later generations who will give precedence to some particular work, while others will place that work's status lower: opinions differ, and people will take up arms in different causes. There are some works whose force is adequate to let them last a hundred generations, but within those hundred generations there are different periods of flourishing and decline: sometimes a reputation will be buried midway and rise again; sometimes what was rejected earlier is valued now; and it seems that the conditions of the moment are responsible for this. Sometimes a person will not be highly thought of in his own lifetime, but later generations will all at once begin to honor him. Consider Han Yü's prose: in Han Yü's own time there was no one in the world who understood him profoundly and esteemed him; but over two centuries later, after Ou-yang Hsiu made him widely known, all the world came unanimously to honor Han Yü's prose, honor which has never diminished up until the present. Truly force in literature has different degrees of magnitude and extent, but also it may rise and fall along with the differences of the times. If one wants to establish oneself as a master, one must exert force decisively.

What is attained within as judgment is brought out as talent; only courage can spread that talent; and only force can sustain it. Those who attain it completely will reveal their talent completely; those who attain only half will reveal only half their talent. Moreover, it is not something that can be pretended or forced: it can be anticipated only in the natural course of things.

No example of force and talent in all time equals that of Holy Yü [the Sage-King who controlled the floods by dredging the rivers of China]. What effort can equal that of Holy Yü in making the world secure? Yet Mencius considered that he did what he did without effort, simply following the natural (*tzu-jan**) principle (*li**) of the way water flows and collects in depressions. Of course, there is no other method (*fa**) for managing water to carry out this task of dredging channels and redirecting currents. Do you think this could have been carried out by pretending? Were it otherwise than the way it was, he would have encountered every sort of problem.

The holy force of Great Yü has reached afar to millions of generations; even though no establishment of words (*li-yen*) in writing (*wen**-*tz'u**) can hope to equal this. Still, different ways may go to the same end, and one should not resign oneself to the notion that composition is a minor vocation that will leave a person unknown in future ages.

The analogy between the magnitude of poetic achievement and the deeds of Sage-King Yü in cutting the watercourses of China was an old one, used by Han Yü to praise the greatness of Li Po and Tu Fu. Yeh Hsieh gives the old analogy a new twist by insisting that the greatest force, because it must be natural, comes with the greatest ease. If the least willful striving or straining occurs, the writer has failed.

大約才識膽力。四者交相為濟。苟一有所歉。則不可登作者之壇。四者無緩急。而要在先之以識。使無識。則三者俱無所託。無識而有膽。則為妄。為鹵莽。為無知。其言背理叛道。蔑如也。無識而有才。雖議論縱橫。思致揮霍。而是非淆亂。黑白顛倒。才反為累矣。無識而有力。則堅僻妄誕之辭。足以誤人而惑世。為害甚烈。若在騷壇。均為風雅之罪人。惟有識則能知所從。知所奮。知所決。而後才與膽力。皆確然有以自信。舉世非之。舉世譽之。而不為其所搖。安有隨人之是非以為是非者哉。其胸中之愉快自足。寧獨在詩文一道已也。然人安能盡生而具絕人之姿。何得易言有識。其道宜如大學之始於格物。誦讀古人詩書。一一以理事情格之。則前後中邊。左右向背。形形色色。殊類萬態。無不可得。不使有毫髮之罅。而物得以乘我焉。如以文為戰。而進無堅城。退無橫陣矣。若舍其在我者。而徒日勞於章句誦讀。不過勦襲依傍。摹擬窺伺之術。以自躋於作者之林。則吾不得而知之矣。

In short, talent, judgment, courage, and force support one another: if one is lacking, a person cannot achieve the status of a major writer. None of the four is more urgent than any of the others, but it is essential to begin with judgment. If a person lacks [the capacity for] judgment, then none of the other three will have anything to rely on. Courage without judgment leads to error, rashness, and ignorance: such words turn their back on principle, rebel against the Way, and are worthless. Talent without the power of judgment may yield a deftness and skill in dispute and a quickness of thought, but values will be all mixed up, black and white inverted, and one's talent will catch a person up in problems. Force without the power of judgment leads to writing that is opinionated and misleading—writing that can mislead people and deceive the people of the age—the harm it can do is extensive. These are all equally criminals in the world of poetry.

Only the man who possesses the capacity for judgment will know which course to follow, where to exert energy, what must be decided: thereafter talent, courage, and force all have something on which they can depend with confidence. Whether criticized or praised by the entire world, such a person is not swayed from his course; neither do his judgments depend on the judgments of others. The joy and satisfaction that come from this do not apply only to the Way of poetry and prose.

Nevertheless how can a person fully achieve such a manner above all others for his whole life? To say it another way, how can a person attain the power of judgment? The way to do so should be just as the *Great Learning* would have us begin—in the "investigation of things" (*ko*-wu**).

When one reads the poems and books of former masters, investigate [*ko**, "take the measure of," "look into the informing structure of"] each one in regard to principle, event, and circumstance. If you do so, then there is nothing you will fail to grasp—what lies ahead and what lies behind, what is in the center and what is on the sides, right and left, what the poet faces and what he turns his back to, every shape (*hsing**) and every color (*se**), the thousands of stances of all the different categories of things. By not allowing the most minute aspect to be missing, the thing (*wu**) is grasped, whereby the self is carried. If we take battle as a metaphor, there is no firm wall in the line of advance, and no blocking formations in the withdrawal.

Among those who rose to a place among the great writers, I have never known anyone who set aside what is in the self and spent days in pointless labor on philology and reading, who went no further than the techniques of plagiarism and dependence on others, imitation and surveying things with the intention to plunder them.

This passage shows Yeh Hsieh's allegiance to the orthodox Confucianism of Chu Hsi. *Ko*-wu** an essential concept in Chu Hsi's philosophy, a concept whose complexities go beyond the scope of this commentary. Put briefly, it involves the discovery of universal principle through directed empirical observation. Earlier Yeh Hsieh strongly suggested that the poet worked through a direct encounter with the world, unmediated by the poetic tradition; here Yeh, considering how to nurture judgment, returns to a position very close to the poetic pedagogy advocated by Yen Yü: we have the peculiar injunction to apply the Confucian principle of *ko*-wu** to reading.

Yeh Hsieh is making to the reader of poetry the promise of Chu Hsi's Neo-Confucianism, that by educated and directed reflection one can come to an integral understanding of principle (*li**), from which all the circumstantial relations of the thing can be known: origins, consequences, negations, and centerings. The text is a nexus of attitudes and relations, all of which are implicit; when "investigated" in regard to principle, event, and circumstance, they become apparent. The most mysterious aspect of this process in which "the self is carried," *ch'eng wo yen*, is "grasping the thing," *te wu**. This, too, has deep Neo-Confucian echoes: in understanding "how things are," the self can be authentically itself and in conformity with the natural order. What the self does naturally and spontaneously in such an authentic state is also universal. Although Yeh Hsieh's rhetoric often shows the influence of sixteenth- and seventeenth-century writers who define the self in opposition to the rest of the world, Yeh Hsieh's theoretical position is predicated on the notion that the spontaneous and "natural" movements of mind in writing participate in what is universally "natural," and not merely particular. The self's grasp of the world may be unique, but there is some real aspect of the external world to be grasped.

或曰。「先生發揮理事情三言。可謂詳且至矣。然此三言。固文家之切要關鍵。而語於詩。則情之一言。義固不易，而理與事。似於詩之義未為切要也。先儒云。天下之物。莫不有理。若夫詩似未可以物物也。詩之至處。妙在含蓄無垠。思致微渺。其寄托在可言不可言之間。其指歸在可解不可解之會。言在此而意在彼。泯端倪而離形象。絕議論而窮思維。引人於冥漠恍惚之境。所以為至也。若一切以理概之。理者。一定之衡。則能實而不能虛。為執而不為化。非板則腐。如學究之說書。閭師之讀律。又如禪家之參死句。不參活句。竊恐有乖於風人之旨。以言乎事。天下固有有其理而不可見諸事者。若夫詩。則理尚不可執。又焉能一一徵之實事者乎。而先生斷斷焉必以理事二者與情同律乎詩。不使有毫髮之或離。愚竊惑焉。此何也。」

Someone answered, "It may well be said that your exposition of these three terms—principle, event, and circumstance—is detailed and complete. But even though these three terms are unquestionably the essential keys for prose masters, if we are speaking of poetry, only the term 'circumstance' [*ch'ing**, "mood," "emotion"] has an unalterable significance (*yi**), while 'principle' and 'event' would seem not to be essential to the real significance (*yi**) of poetry. Long ago a Confucian scholar said that all the things of the world have natural principle. And yet it would seem that poetry is a thing not like other things. Where poetry is at its most perfect, its subtlety (*miao**) lies in a boundless reserve of the implicit (*han-hsü*) and in the thought reaching what is faint and indistinct; what is implicit in poetry lies between what can be said and what cannot be said; what it refers to lies at the conjunction between the explicable and the inexplicable; the words seem to be about one thing, while the meaning (*yi**) lies in something else. All points of reference are blotted out, and it takes leave of visible form (*hsing**-hsiang**); linear argument and discursiveness are broken, and the process of reflection reaches its limit, leading a person into a murky and hazy realm (*ching**)—and this is how it attains perfection. Natural principle (*li**) is a determinate balance; and if we try to frame the totality [of poetry] with natural principle, then it will be capable only of the concrete (*shih**), and it will not be capable of the empty/plastic (*hsü**); it will be something that holds fast, but not something that undergoes transformations (*hua**); at the least it would be inflexible, and at the worst it would have a conventional rigidity [*fu*, literally "rotten"]—just like a student's paraphrase of what he has read, like a village schoolmaster's rules of recitation, like a Ch'an master's using dead lines and not lively lines. I suspect that this sort of thing would be contrary to the precepts of true poets.

"Now in regard to 'event,' certainly there are cases in this world where there is a principle that does not become manifest in event. If in poetry even principle cannot be held fast, how can every single case be realized in a concrete event (*shih**-shih**)? Yet you maintain insistently that principle and event have the same normative authority as circumstance (mood) in poetry, and you will not allow even the least distinction [in relative importance] between them. I confess that I have my doubts. What do you say to this?"

The interlocutor's objections are a particularly eloquent version of a set of commonplace values in poetry, privileging *ch'ing** as the central concept. Although we have retained the translation "circumstance" for the sake of consistency, it is clear here that the interlocutor is shifting the semantic center of *ch'ing** closer to its more common use in poetics as "mood" or "state of mind." Previously Yeh Hsieh had been speaking of *ch'ing** as a category "in things," *tsai wu** 在物; the interlocutor is using the term to refer to the affective quality of poetry and what is apprehended in reading poetry—"mood" more than "circumstance." The privilege which the interlocutor accords to *ch'ing** is in the lineage of "Ts'ang-lang's Remarks on Poetry," which asserts that poetry has its own qualities distinct from other categories of discourse, knowledge, and experience. That lineage is particularly obvious in the interlocutor's emphasis on the subtle and elusive in poetry. Even by Yen Yü's time, *li**, natural principle, was taking on distinctly unpoetic associations with philosophical discourse (cf. "Ts'ang-lang's Remarks on Poetry": "Poetry has a distinct interest that has nothing to do with natural principle"). The supposed determinacy of *li** is here set in contrast with a conventional poetic value of indeterminacy, derived from Yen Yü's aesthetics. For these reasons the interlocutor cannot accept *li** as an essential part of poetry. This is a crucial point in the text, at which Yeh Hsieh attempts to break down the barrier Yen Yü had erected between poetic and extrapoetic experience. In the section that follows, Yeh Hsieh accepts those poetic values of subtlety and elusiveness, but he attempts to reintegrate them with principle and event, giving poetry a special place *within* universal processes.

We might here give some consideration to those values that Yeh Hsieh accepts and redefines. The interlocutor offers a commonplace: "Where poetry is at its most perfect, its subtlety lies in a boundless reserve of the implicit." "Points of perfection" *chih-ch'u*, may refer to those cases in poetry when the inherent values of the form are fulfilled; but, more importantly, they may also refer to those moments in reading when poetry fulfills its aesthetic potential—those moments when one says "Ah, now *that's* poetry." The category *miao**, translated as "subtlety," had, by Yeh Hsieh's time, become one general term for "excellence," though a mode of excellence that had not entirely forgotten its roots in the perception of a fineness on the very margins of understanding, something that is both essential and elusive. "Reserve of the implicit," *han-hsü*, was the eleventh of Ssu-k'ung T'u's "Twenty-Four Categories." *Han-hsü* was a very important aesthetic category, implicating not only an intensive depth, a sense that there is more than the surface value of the words, but also extensive affect: it is *han-hsü* that makes a text continue in the reader's mind after the words are over. That movement is not a linear movement toward "understanding," but an unfolding of elusive qualities that constitute a complete realm, *ching**.

Thus for the interlocutor what is essential to poetry does not lie in the fixed aspects that can be "understood" in the conventional sense; neither does it lie beyond what is definite and physical; rather the moments of true poetry lie in the intuition of something beyond the definite and the movement of the reader's attention toward that "beyond." When he says that "the words lie in one matter while the meaning lies in something else," he is not referring to a metaphorical operation, but rather to the fact that the words are the words of a concrete reality, but still aggregate to create a mood (*ch'ing**) or vision that lies beyond concrete reality and is somehow independent of the words. The poetic vision must be *hsü**, "empty" or "plastic," and irreducible to the determinate and concrete, which would be *shih**, "solid," and thus would embody a particular principle, *li**.

Yeh Hsieh and the interlocutor would agree that a "bad" concrete description would give us a sense of the physical presence of the scene in its simple, sensuous determinateness; a description in a nineteenth-century "realistic" novel often provides just this impression of tangible reality. A poetic, "plastic" description will catch the elusive qualities of "being-in-a-scene," in which a particular mood or state of mind is integrated into the concrete reality that surrounds mind; here a photographic determinacy of relations dissolves, and the scene remains sensuous without clearly defining forms and their relations . Yeh Hsieh will accept this notion of the "poetic," while qualifying it by the claim that such a "poetic" world is really grounded in natural principle, *li**. This he illustrates with examples from Tu Fu's poetry.

予曰。「子之言誠是也。子所以稱詩者。深有得乎詩之旨者也。然子但知可言。可執之理之為理。而抑知名言所絕之理之為至理乎。子但知有是事之為事。而抑知無是事之為凡事之所出乎。可言之理。人人能言之。又安在詩人之言之。可徵之事。人人能述之。又安在

詩人之述之。必有不可言之理。不可述之事。遇之於默會意象之表。而理與事無不燦然於前者也。

I answered: What you have said is quite correct, and what you claim shows you have a deep understanding of the precepts of poetry. But by natural principle you understand only that which can be firmly taken hold of and articulated as natural principle; I think you fail to understand that the ultimate natural principle is cut off from definite, denotative language (*ming-yen*). You understand event only in the sense of "there was that event," but I think you fail to understand "there was no such event" as something from which ordinary events emerge. Everyone can speak of natural principle that can be spoken of, so why should the poet speak of it? Everyone can relate an event that has verifiably occurred, so why should a poet relate it? There must be principle that cannot be articulated and events that cannot be related; one encounters them beyond a silent comprehension of the image in the mind (*yi*-hsiang**); and never do principle and event fail to gleam before it.

In his response, Yeh Hsieh is essentially asserting the "reality" of poetic vision, thus recovering the interlocutor's sense of the "poetic" as part of a unified interpretation of the world outside poetry. The elusive poetic vision is not pure fantasy or a mere effect of art; rather it is an access to the most elusive aspects of "what is." Not all principle can be named directly; there is an entire domain of principle that can be reached only through the "poetic," leaving behind the area of the definite and concrete. One first grasps the poet's "image in the mind," *yi*-hsiang**, and through that has an intuition of such principle. As is the case with the novice in the terminology of Western poetics, it takes some time and reflection before the initial impression of jargon resolves itself into a valid description of a work of art or our understanding of such.

今試舉杜甫集中一二名句。為子晰而剖之。以見其概。可乎。如玄云皇帝廟作「碧瓦初寒外」句。逐字論之。言乎外。與內為界也。初寒何物。可以內外界乎。將碧瓦之外。無初寒乎。寒者。天地之氣也。是氣也。盡宇宙之內。無處不充塞。而碧瓦獨居其外。寒氣獨盤踞於碧瓦之內乎。寒而曰初。將嚴寒或不如是乎。初寒無象無形。碧瓦有物有質。合虛實而分內外。吾不知其寫碧瓦乎。寫初寒乎。寫近乎。寫遠乎。使必以理而實諸事以解之。雖稷下談天之辨。恐至此亦窮矣。然設身而處當時之境會。覺此五字之情景。恍如天造地設。呈於象。感於目。會於心。意中之言。而口不能言。口能言之。而意又不可解。劃然示我以默會相象之表。竟若有內有外。有寒有初寒。特借碧瓦一實相發之。有中間。有邊際。虛實相成。有無互立。取之當前而自得。其理昭然。其事的然也。昔人云。王維詩中有畫。凡詩可入畫者。為詩家能事。如風雲雨雪景象之至虛者。畫家無不可繪之於筆。若初寒。內外之景色。即董巨復生。恐亦束手擱筆矣。天下惟理事之入神境者。固非庸凡人可摹擬而得也。

Now would it be all right if I took a few famous lines from Tu Fu's works to shed some light on the question for you, so that you can see the general outline? Let's take as an example the line in "The Temple of the Primal Mysterious Emperor": "The first chill, outside of its emerald [roof] tiles." If we consider the exact wording, it speaks of an "outside," which in turn makes a boundary with an "inside." What sort of thing is the "first chill" that there can be a boundary of inside and outside with it? Is it that outside the emerald tiles there is no first chill?[10] Chill is a form of the *ch'i** of Heaven and Earth. And this *ch'i** covers all the cosmos, leaving no place unfilled. Yet do these emerald tiles alone reside outside of it? Does the chill *ch'i** coil up and concentrate within those emerald tiles alone?[11] Does speaking of the "first" of the chill imply that this might not be the case in a severe chill? "First chill" is without image (*hsiang**) or form (*hsing**); in "emerald tiles" there is a thing (*wu**), and there is material (*chih**). Here he joins the empty and solid, yet makes a distinction between inside and outside; and we cannot tell whether he is describing the emerald tiles or the first chill, whether he is describing what is close at hand or what is far away. If one had to explain it in terms of natural principle and make it solid (*shih**) in event, then I fear that even the finely argued discussions of heaven by the Chi-hsia scholars [famous in antiquity] would reach their limits before they could treat something like this. However, putting oneself right there in the world of that moment (*ching**-hui*, the "scene-occasion"), we realize that the mood (*ch'ing**) and scene (*ching**) of these five words are as indistinct as if created by Heaven or given by Earth; yet they are manifest in image (*hsiang**), are stirring to the eyes, and are understood by the mind. The mouth cannot put into words those words that are in the concept (*yi**); or the mouth can put them into words, but then concept cannot explain them. There, delineated clearly, it shows us what lies beyond a silent comprehension of image in the mind; finally it is as if there *is* an inside and an outside, as if there *is* a chill and a first chill, all depending on this one solid thing, "emerald tiles," to be brought out. A space within is defined; there are boundaries; solid and empty complete one another; presence and absence are mutually established. There it is, right before you and self-subsistent, its natural principle shining out, its event pellucid. Long ago someone said that in Wang Wei's poetry there is painting. Any poem that "enters a painting," as they say, shows that the poet is considered a master. And there is scarcely a painter unable to depict with his brush the most plastic (*hsü**) images of a scene (*ching**-hsiang**), such as wind and clouds or rain and snow. But facing a scene like this, a scene of the first chill's inside and outside, even a Tung Yüan or a Chü-jan reborn would, I suspect, fold his hands and lay aside his brush. In all the world, it is only the movement of natural principle and event into a divine realm (*shen**-ching**) that absolutely no ordinary person can achieve by imitation.

Yeh Hsieh's task is to show that an elusive "poetic" scene is not some completely ineffable quality or impression, but rather that it can be understood as a unique perception of real categories and relations. Furthermore, that perception must be irreducible to commonplace categories and explanations ("Everyone can speak of the natural principle that can be spoken of, so why should the poet speak of it"). Yeh declares that the principle within the scene is self-evident, but that it cannot be spoken of in the reasonable words of prose. How then can his own critical prose point to that clear, self-evident manifestation of principle? His solution is a strange, frustrating, and intriguing piece of practical criticism, a series of questions that mark the difference between Tu Fu's vision and prose understanding. However awkward the result, Yeh's aim is to account for the uniqueness of a piece of poetry—not to reduce it to a commonplace paraphrase, as much contemporary criticism did.

Unfortunately Yeh Hsieh's "explanations" themselves require explanation, placing this commentator in the uncomfortable role of the Chi-hsia scholars mentioned above, attempting to draw marginal language a little closer to our world of prose understanding. It should be pointed out that Tu Fu's poem is a winter poem, though the phrase "first chill" seems to promise more severe cold yet to come. Yeh Hsieh observes how the spatial term "outside" creates a peculiar barrier to the chill, as if the tiles occupied a special space immune to winter's weather. We have no fixed point of observation in the poem: as Yeh Hsieh says, we do not know if it is near or far. We may be within the courtyard of the temple complex, with the tiles "outside" the cold within; we may be viewing the temple from afar, with the distant roof tiles somehow "outside" the cold we feel around us. Together the various alternatives create a sense of the tiles surrounded by the chill; but even surrounded by the cold, the tiles are somehow "outside," rather than "within" it. But most remarkable of all, we are seeing as a spatial relation an invisible difference in temperature.

As Yeh notes the cold is *hsü*, "plastic" like liquid, filling everything equally, boundariless. But these solid shapes of the tiles that lie "outside" the chill give it shape and boundary by limiting it. Even if the cold reaches everywhere in the whole world apart from them, the tiles, by remaining "outside" of the cold, give it boundaries like a solid thing.

As Yeh observes, this resistance of the temple tiles to universal weather may be restricted to this moment; the tiles may force a shape upon the cold only for the "first chill"; later, when the severe cold comes, this boundary between inside and outside may disappear. Therefore it is not only a privileged space the poet witnesses, it is also a privileged moment.

Tu Fu's line creates a peculiar sensuous reality, one that is comprehensible in terms of principle and event, but also a reality quite alien to either ordinary apprehension or description of sensuous experience. In Western poetics, one might say that the line creates a new perception of relations, shaping the way we envision such a scene; for Yeh Hsieh, Tu Fu discovers relations that were already present but which lay outside the normal limits of perception.

又宿左省作「月傍九霄多」句。從來言月者。祇有言圓缺。言明暗。言升沉。言高下。未有言多少者。若俗儒不曰「月傍九霄明」。則曰「月傍九霄高」。以為景象真而使字切矣。今曰多。不知月本來多乎。抑傍九霄而始多乎。不知月多乎。月所照之境多乎。有不可名言者。試想當時之情景。非言明。言高。言升可得。而惟此多字可以盡括此夜宮殿當前之景象。他人共見之。而不能知。不能言。惟甫見而知之。而能言之。其事如是。其理不能不如是也。又夔州雨濕不得上岸作「晨鐘雲外濕」句。以晨鐘為物而濕乎。雲外之物。何啻以萬萬計。且鐘必於寺觀。即寺觀中。鐘之外。物亦無算。何獨濕鐘乎。然為此語者。因聞鐘聲有觸而云然也。聲無形。安能濕。鐘聲入耳而有聞。聞在耳。止能辨其聲。安能辨其濕。曰雲外。是又以目始見雲。不見鐘。故云雲外。然此詩為雨濕而作。有雲然後有雨。鐘為雨濕。則鐘在雲內。不應云外也。斯語也。吾不知其為耳聞耶。為目見耶。為意揣耶。俗儒於此。必曰「晨鐘雲外度」。又必曰「晨鐘雲外發」。決無下濕字者。不知其於隔雲見鐘。聲中聞濕。妙悟天開。從至理實事中領悟。乃得此境界也。又摩訶池泛舟作「高城秋自落」句。夫秋何物。若何而落乎。時序有代謝。未聞云落也。即秋能落。何繫之以高城乎。而曰高城落。則秋實自高城而落。理與事俱不可易也。以上偶舉杜集四語。若以俗儒之眼觀之。以言乎理。理於何通。以言乎事。事於何有。所謂言語道斷。思維路絕。然其中之理。至虛而實。至渺而近。灼然心目之間。殆如鳶飛魚躍之昭著也。理既昭矣。尚得無其事乎。古人妙於事理之句。如此極多。姑舉此四語以例其餘耳。其更有事所必無者。偶舉唐人一二語。如「蜀道之難難於上青天」。「似將海水添宮漏」。「春風不度玉門關」。「天若有情天亦老」。「玉顏不及寒鴉色」等句。如此者。何止盈千累萬。決不能有其事。實為情至之語。夫情必依乎理。情得然後理真。情理交至。事尚不得耶。

Another case is the line in "Written While Spending the Night at the Ministry": "Much moon beside the highest wisps of clouds."[12] Those who had written of the moon in the past had written of it only as full or waxing and waning, as dark or bright, as ascending or sinking, as high in the sky or low. No one had ever written of it in terms of "much" or "little." Some ordinary scholar might have written, "Bright, the moon beside the highest wisps of clouds"; if not that, then, "Lofty, the moon beside the highest wisps of clouds." He would have considered that to be the true image of the scene (*ching**-*hsiang**) and his own words to have been used so as to get it just right. But Tu Fu says "much," and we don't know whether the moon is always "much" in its own right, or becomes so only by being beside the highest wisps of cloud. We don't know whether the moon itself is "much," or the realm illuminated by the moonlight is "much." There is something that cannot be put into definite, denotative language. But if you try to imagine the scene and the mood of that moment, then [you realize] it cannot be grasped by "bright" or "lofty" or "ascending." And only this word "much" can completely encompass the image of the scene (*ching*-hsiang**), this night in front of the halls of the palace. Others saw it, but they could neither understand it nor put it into words. Only Tu Fu saw and understood it and was able to put it into words. The event [what really happened] was like this, and thus its natural principle could not help being like this.

Another example can be found in the line from "Written in K'uei-chou, When It Was So Wet from Rain that I Could Not Climb the Bank": "The early morning bell is wet beyond the clouds." Is he taking the early morning bell as a physical object [rather than a sound] and thus "wet"? At a modest estimate the objects that then lay beyond the clouds could be counted in the millions; furthermore, the bell must have been in a temple, and in that temple apart from the bell, there would have been innumerable objects, so why is it only the bell that is "wet"? When he wrote these words, however, he wrote as he did because he was struck by something unique and singular on hearing the sound of the bell. Yet sound has no form, so how can it be "wet"? The sound of the bell entered his ears and he heard something; hearing is a faculty of the ear and can only distinguish sound, so how could the ear distinguish wetness" And he wrote "beyond the clouds": because his eyes at first saw clouds and not the bell, he said, "beyond the clouds." This poem, however, was written on the wetness of a rain; there is rain only after there are clouds. If the bell is being made wet by the rain, then the bell is "within" the clouds, and he should not say "beyond" [i.e., by saying "beyond" he implies that the rain has already passed the temple he does not see]. I cannot tell whether this is an account of what his ears heard, or what his eyes saw, or what his mind (*yi**) conceived. In this situation, a common scholar would surely have written "The early morning bell passes beyond the clouds," or "The early morning bell comes out beyond the clouds"; but under no circumstances would he have used the word "wet." They could not have understood that he saw the bell on the other side of the clouds and heard wetness in its sound: one can attain a visionary world (*ching*-chieh**) like this only with full enlightenment from Heaven and an understanding that comes from the ultimate in principle and concrete event.

Another example is the line in "Boating on Mo-ho Pond": "The high wall, autumn sinks down." What sort of thing is this "autumn" that it can "sink down"? The seasons do alternate in succession, but I have never heard that they "sink down." And even if autumn were able to "sink down," why link it to a high wall? Yet when one says "high wall . . . sinking down," then autumn truly does "sink down" [or "fall"] from the high wall. Here neither principle nor event can be altered.

Considering the four preceding examples from Tu Fu's works with the eyes of a common scholar, if we were speaking of them in terms of principle, wherein does principle get through (*t'ung**) here? If we are speaking of them in terms of event, in what does the event reside? Here one might say "the Way of language breaks off," the path of thought comes to an end. Nevertheless, the principle contained in these lines is something that becomes solid (*shih**) in the extreme of emptiness (*hsü**), something that becomes close at hand in the extreme of being remote and indistinct. They are fresh and radiant in the mind and eye, just as luminously present to us as the kite on the wing or a fish jumping. And when the principle is so manifest, can the event be lacking?

There are very many lines of the ancients which, like these, are subtle (*miao**) in event and principle; but I have taken these four lines of Tu Fu as examples of the rest. Among those in which event has even less reality, I might give a few lines of T'ang poets as examples:

The hardships of the road to Shu are more difficult than climbing the blue sky.

[Li Po]

It seems all the sea's water fills the palace waterclock.

[Li Yi]

The spring wind does not pass Yü-men barrier fort.

[Wang Chih-huan]

If Heaven had feelings, Heaven, too, would grow old.

[Li Ho]

Her face, white as jade, is not so lovely as winter's crows.

[Wang Ch'ang-ling]

Lines like these can be counted in the thousands: and even though there is no possibility that such things occurred as "events," they are truly lines in which the affections (*ch'ing**) are at their most intense.

The affections/circumstance (*ch'ing**) must depend on natural principle; and only when the affections/circumstance are fully attained is natural principle genuine.

And when the affections/circumstance and natural principle reach perfection jointly, is it possible that event will not be attained as well?

Even though natural principle (*li**) is prior to the affections/circumstance, perfection in the poetic manifestation of *ch'ing** is evidence of the perfect grasp of *li**, which is then immanent in the lines.

要之。作詩者。實寫理事情。可以言。言可以解。解即為俗儒之作。惟不可名言之理。不可施見之事。不可逕達之情。則幽渺以為理。想象以為事。惝恍以為情。方為理至事至情至之語。此豈俗儒耳目心思界分中所有哉。則余之為此三語者。非腐也。非僻也。非錮也。得此意而通之。甯獨學詩。無適而不可矣。

In essence, when the writer of a poem describes actual (*shih**) principle, event, and circumstance which can be put into words, and those words can be fully understood, then we fully understand that this is the work of an ordinary scholar. But if it is that natural principle which cannot be given in definite, denotative language, if it is the kind of event that cannot be set out before the physical eye, if it is the kind of affections/circumstance that cannot be instantly communicated, then the principle under consideration is hidden and elusive, the event is an image in the fantasy (*hsiang-hsiang**), and the affection/circumstance is vague and indistinct. Only then do you have words that are the perfection of principle, the perfection of event, and the perfection of affection/circumstance. Qualities such as these are not contained within the boundaries of ears, eyes, and thoughts of common scholars. If this is the case, then these terms I have used are not dead letter, not one-sided shackles. To understand these concepts (*yi**) and put them into action (*t'ung**) goes beyond the study of poetry alone. There is nothing for which they are inappropriate.

SUPPLEMENT FROM "THE ORIGINS OF POETRY"

The first two supplementary translations below complete the "Inner Section." The first passage, from "Inner Section," chapter 1, goes from the beginning of the work to the point where the main selection above begins. The passage from "Inner Section," chapter 2, continues where the main selection above breaks off. Finally, there are translations of some passages in the "Outer Section."

Many parts of "The Origins of Poetry" involve heated discussion of essentially "local" issues, reminiscent of modern academic criticism. From the perspective of three centuries, Yeh Hsieh appears as an intensely polemical writer, heaping scorn on his opponents with homely comparisons and numerous rhetorical questions. Because less commentary will be provided with these supplementary sections, I have taken greater liberties with the translation in order to make it as readable as possible.

"INNER SECTION"
Chapter 1 (Opening)

詩始於三百篇。而規模體具於漢。自是而魏。而六朝。三唐歷宋元明以至昭代。上下三千餘年間。詩之質文體裁格律聲調辭句。遞嬗升降不同。而要之詩有源必有流。有本必達末。又有因流而溯源。循末以返本。其學無窮。其理日出。乃知詩之為道。未有一日不相續相禪而或息者也。

Poetry began with the three hundred poems of the *Book of Songs*, and its forms were structurally complete by the end of the Han. During the more than three millennia from that time until the present (passing through the Wei to the Six Dynasties, to the T'ang, on through the Sung, Yüan, Ming, and into our present dynasty), there have been alternations and variations in all aspects of poetry: in the ratios of plainness and ornament (*chih*-wen**), generic structures (*t'i*-ts'ai*), formal rules (*ko*-lü*), sound patterns, and diction. What is essential in such variation is this: insofar as poetry has a source, it must also have streams that flow from it; insofar as it has roots, it must develop into branches. Furthermore, it is possible to follow the streams back to their source or to revert to the roots by following back along the branches: the material for study here is infinite and the natural principles (*li**) involved constantly emerge. From this we realize that the course of poetry has never ceased in its continuity even for a single day.

While Yeh Hsieh builds freely on the metaphorical paradigms of the river (source and stream) and the tree (root and branch-tip), it should be understood that in Chinese these are far closer to abstractions than they are in English: they are roughly origin and organic unfolding. Yeh's stress on the continuous organic historicity of poetry responds to theorists of poetry who believe that the history of poetry was concluded, that poetry had developed to certain unchanging norms which were thereafter available to anyone who understood them. Note that when Yeh Hsieh says "material for study," he means learning to write poetry well, not the academic study of poetry.

但就一時而論。有盛必有衰。綜千古而論。則盛而必至於衰。又必自衰而復盛。非在前者之必居於盛。後者之必居於衰也。乃近代論詩者。則曰。三百篇尚矣。五言必建安黃初。其餘諸體。必唐之「初」「盛」而後可。非是者必斥焉。如明李夢陽不讀唐以後書。李攀龍謂唐無古詩。又謂陳子昂以其古詩為古詩。弗取也。

If we consider it from the perspective of only a single period, then whenever there is a time of flourishing, there must also be decline. When we consider it from the perspective of all literary history, then we see that a period of flourishing must pass into decline, but at the same time it must go from decline to flourishing again. It is not true that the earlier writer is always in the position of a time of flourishing and that the later writer is always in a position of decline.

But there are recent theorists of poetry who have declared that while the *Book of Songs* is the noblest [poetic creation], poetry in the five-character line must follow the style of the Chien-an [196–220] and Huang-ch'u [220–227] reigns; other forms are all right only if they follow the early T'ang and High

T'ang. They feel it necessary to attack anyone who disagrees. Examples of this are Li Meng-yang's [1475–1529] injunction not to read anything after the T'ang and Li P'an-lung's [1514–1570] claim that there was no true old-style verse in the T'ang, or his further claim that there is nothing worthwhile in Ch'en Tzu-ang's [661–702] old-style verse considered purely as old-style verse.

Yeh Hsieh cites here some of the most famous catch-phrases of Ming archaist poetics. The argument is essentially that "old-style verse" (of indeterminate length without tonal balancing) reached its formal perfection in the first decades of the third century and that any stylistic evolution of the form is a falling away from perfection. The question of old-style verse in the T'ang is, in fact, a theoretical touchstone. The early T'ang and the High T'ang provide the generic models for regulated verse, but their old-style verse, as represented by Ch'en Tzu-ang here, is unacceptable. Were literary history bound strictly to historical period, then early-T'ang and High T'ang poetry should be good irrespective of genre. But for the Ming archaists all value is mediated through generic form. Therefore it is not the T'ang per se that flourishes; rather regulated poetry, by its own internal history, happened to reach its perfection in the T'ang.

自若輩之論出。天下從而和之。推為詩家正宗。家絃而戶習。習之既久。乃有起而掊之。矯而反之者。誠是也。然又往往溺於偏畸之私說。其說勝。則出乎陳腐而入乎頗僻。不勝。則兩敝。而詩道遂淪而不可救。

Once these positions had been taken, it seemed that everyone in the world went along with them and set them up as an orthodoxy (cheng*-tsung) for poets. As they say, everyone in the household has to practice the family songs. When this practice had continued for a long time, it was right and even inevitable that some would rise and attack the old positions, and the attackers would go to extremes in opposing them. Yet they, too, became everywhere immersed in one-sided and private theories. Whenever one of these theories of the antagonists of the old positions gained the upper hand, we passed over from conformist commonplaces into outlandishness. When neither gained the upper hand, we had a pair of bad theories. In this way, the course of poetry seemed to be going downhill without hope of being saved.

Here Yeh Hsieh is referring to the various opponents of archaism that arose in the late Ming, such as the Yüan brothers with their theories of vitalism. Yeh Hsieh is intensely aware of the way in which literary factionalism polarizes theoretical positions, how the social circumstances of discourse on poetry infect judgment.

由稱詩之人。才短力弱。識又矇焉而不知所衷。既不能知詩之源流。本末。正變。盛衰互為循環。並不能辨古今作者之心思。才力。深淺。高下。長短。孰為沿為革。孰為創為因。孰為流弊而衰。孰為救衰而盛。——剖析而縷分之。兼綜而條貫之。徒自詡矜張。為郛廓隔膜之談。以欺人而自欺也。於是百喙爭鳴。互自標榜。膠固一偏。勦獵成說。後生小子。耳食者多。是非淆而性情泪。不能不三歎於風雅之日衰也。

Because those who claim to know about poetry are short on talent and lack energy, their judgment is also blinded and they lack intuitive sense. Since they are incapable of understanding how the source and streams, the roots and branches, the normative (cheng*) and mutated (pien*), and flourishing and decline all operate in cycles, they are further incapable of discerning the thought (hsin*-ssu*) of either ancient or modern authors—not their thought, nor the energy of their talents, nor the relative depth of their work, nor their relative levels, nor their strengths and weaknesses. They cannot tell which ones were followers and which ones made a break with the past; they can't tell which were innovators and which were derivative; they can't tell which ones sank into decline and which ones saved literature from decline and made it flourish again. They make analyses in minute detail and combine them with unifying syntheses, followed by vain boasts about what they have achieved: their discourses are a barrier to understanding; and in deceiving others, they are themselves deceived. Thus we have a hundred voices all talking at once, each setting up its catch-phrases against the others, each stuck in some one-sided position which is rounded out by plundering others. Their younger followers have swallowed most of it, with the result that their sense of what is right is confused and their natural responses (hsing*-ch'ing*) are hampered. And we cannot help feeling discouraged at how the art of poetry (feng*-ya*) continually sinks lower and lower.

Beneath Yeh Hsieh's fierce denunciation of the poetic theory of his contemporaries is a remarkable faith that a clear understanding of literary history would be a way to redeem poetry from decline. Like Yen Yü and the archaists, all of whom he strongly rejects, Yeh Hsieh believes that successful poetry follows from knowledge, a knowledge of change and transformation that can be discovered in the history of poetry.

蓋自有天地以來。古今世運氣數。遞變遷以相禪。古云。「天道十年一變。」此理也。亦勢也。無事無物不然。寧獨詩之一道膠固而不變乎。

Since the beginning of the universe, the qualities of *ch'i** in the operations of history have moved through transformations and shifts, each quality yielding to the next. An old saying goes, "In the natural course of things, one mutation occurs each decade": this is natural principle (*li**), and this is also the inherent momentum (*shih**). Since this is true for every event (*shih**) and every thing (*wu**), it is most unlikely that the way of poetry alone be hard and fast, and never undergo mutation.

Note that the theory of change here is not one of gradual evolution, but rather of sharp changes in direction that occur at particular historical moments. Furthermore, Yeh Hsieh does not ground literary history in political and social history, but rather sees it as an independent process whose decade-changes follow the same laws of transformation that operate in the rest of the world.

今就三百篇言之。風有正風。有變風。雅有正雅。有變雅。風雅已不能不由正而變。吾夫子亦不能存正而刪變也。則後此為風雅之流者。其不能伸正而詘變也明矣。

If we look at the case of the *Book of Songs*, we note that the "Airs" section contains *both* "normative" (*cheng**) and "mutated" (*pien**) "Airs"; in the same way the section of "Odes" (*Ya**) consists of both normative and mutated "Odes." Since even the "Airs" and "Odes" necessarily passed from norm into mutation, and since Confucius [in editing the *Book of Songs*] could not permit himself to retain only the norm while taking out the mutated phases, it should be obvious that it is impossible to sustain the normative and suppress mutation in the later poetic (*Feng*-ya**) tradition.

For the discussion of norm and mutation in "Great Preface," see pp. 47–48. The question of whether "mutation," *pien**, was simply change or a falling away was an ancient one. Yeh Hsieh stands firmly on the side of those who believe that change is not necessarily devolution, and uses the inclusion of "mutated" genres in the *Book of Songs* to support his point. In doing so, of course, he evades the real issues of traditional interpretation of the *Book of Songs*, where "good poetry" is not so much an issue as a poetry that is "good" by revealing the changes in social and moral conditions. Later he takes up this issue directly, separating the history of the *Book of Songs*, which passes from norm to mutation according to the times, from subsequent literary history, which passes from norm to mutation according to poetry's own internal laws.

漢蘇李始創為五言。其時又有亡名氏之十九首。皆因乎三百篇者也。然不可謂即無異於三百篇。而實蘇李創之也。建安黃初之詩。因於蘇李與十九首者也。然十九首止自言其情。建安黃初之詩。乃有獻酬。紀行。頌德諸體。遂開後世種種應酬等類。則因而實為創。此變之始也。三百篇一變而為蘇李。再變而為建安黃初。建安黃初之詩。大約敦厚而渾樸。中正而達情。一變而為晉。如陸機之纏綿鋪麗。左思之卓犖磅礴。各不同也。其間屢變而為鮑照之逸俊。謝靈運之警秀。陶潛之澹遠。又如顏延之之藻繢。謝朓之高華。江淹之韶嫵。庾信之清新。此數子者。各不相師。咸矯然自成一家。不肯沿襲前人以為依傍。蓋自六朝而已然矣。其間健者。如何遜。如陰鏗。如沈烱。如薛道衡。差能自立。此外繁辭縟節。隨波日下。歷梁陳隋以迄唐之垂拱。踵其習而益甚。勢不能不變。

During the Han Dynasty, Su Wu and Li Ling originated poetry in the five-character line, and their work, along with the anonymous "Nineteen Old Poems," all follows from the *Book of Songs*. Despite the continuity, one cannot say that there are no differences between the Han poets and the *Book of Songs*: Su Wu and Li Ling really did originate it. In the same way, the poetry of the Chien-an and Huang-ch'u periods follows from Li Ling, Su Wu, and the "Nineteen Old Poems." In the "Nineteen Old Poems," however, the poet simply states what he feels (*ch'ing**), whereas in Chien-an and Huang-ch'u poetry, there are already a whole variety of forms (*t'i**), including dedications, answering poems, travel poems, praises of virtue, and the like. These opened the way for all kinds of social exchanges in the poetry of later ages. Thus we can see that the poetry of the Chien-an and Huang-ch'u followed from earlier poetry but truly originated, and this is the beginning of mutation. The tradition of the *Book of Songs* underwent a mutation and became the poetry of Li Ling and Su Wu; there was a second mutation and it became the poetry of the Chien-an and Huang-ch'u. The poetry of the Chien-an and Huang-ch'u is, as a whole, naive and genuine, balanced and expressive. There was another mutation in the poetry of the Tsin, whose authors differ from one another; for example, the continuous ornamental amplification in the poetry of Lu Chi [261–303], and the splendid unity in variety of Tso Ssu's [ca. 253–ca. 307] poetry. Then, in the course of time, there were frequent mutations—the noble aloofness of Pao Chao [ca. 414–466], the salient and surprising qualities of Hsieh Ling-yün [385–443], and the calm remoteness of T'ao Ch'ien [365–427]. In addition there was the floridity of Yen Yen-chih [384–456], the lofty splendor of Hsieh T'iao [464–499], the seductive allure of Chiang Yen [444–505], and the clear freshness of Yü Hsin [513–581]. Already, here in the Six Dynasties, we have reached the stage where none of these various poets took any of the others as a teacher, and every single one of them stood out as an independent figure in his own right (*tzu ch'eng yi-chia*), unwilling to be merely a follower by close imitation of some predecessor. Even some of the other stronger poets of the period, such as Ho Hsün, Yin Keng, Shen Chiung, and Hsüeh

Tao-heng, were almost able to establish their independence. Apart from these writers, the fashion of elaborate diction and stylistic lushness produced continually poorer work through the Liang, Ch'en, Sui, and on until the Ch'ui-kung reign [685–688] of the T'ang. Poets followed established practice ever more closely until the momentum (*shih**) was such that change was inevitable.

Yeh Hsieh's admiration for the variety of Six Dynasties poetry is remarkable for his age. Perhaps the most interesting theoretical point in this survey of poetic history up to the early eighth century is the way in which the concept of mutation (*pien**) shifts from the difference in period style to differences in individual style. Mutation occurs not through some mysterious force of literary history but through individuals voluntarily differentiating themselves from predecessors. In the early stages mutation is collective: the writers of the Chien-an and Huang-ch'u choose to differentiate themselves from their Han predecessors, but their work is treated as a collective move, reflected in the strong unity of the period style. Beginning in the Tsin, mutation becomes an individual act, with each poet differentiating himself (and in so doing, carrying the course of poetry further) from predecessors and contemporaries. Unlike in the Han, Chien-an, and Huang-ch'u, now any collective period style is seen as a conjunction of an independent figure and a group of weaker adherents.

小變於沈宋。雲龍之間。而大變於開元天寶高岑王孟李。此數人者。雖各有所因。而實一一能為創。而集大成如杜甫。傑出如韓愈。專家如柳宗元。如劉禹錫。如李賀。如李商隱。如杜牧。如陸龜蒙諸子。——皆特立興起。其他弱者。則因循世運。隨乎波流。不能振拔。所謂唐人本色也。

宋初詩襲唐人之舊。如徐鉉王禹偁輩。純是唐音。蘇舜欽梅堯臣出。始一大變。歐陽修亟稱二人不置。自後諸大家迭興。所造各有至極。今人一槩稱為宋詩者也。自是南宋金元作者不一。大家如陸游范成大元好問為最。各能自見其才。有明之初。高啟為冠。兼唐宋元人之長。初不於唐宋元人之詩有所為軒輊也。

There was a lesser mutation in the Ching-lung and Ching-yün reigns [708–712], which can be seen in the poetry of Sung Chih-wen and Shen Ch'üan-ch'i. Then a major mutation occurred in the K'ai-yüan [713–742] and T'ien-pao [712–756] reigns in the poetry of Kao Shih, Ts'en Shen, Wang Wei, Meng Hao-jan, and Li Po. Although the work of each of these poets had aspects that were developed from earlier poetry, every one of them was able to originate something in his own right. In the succeeding generations, there were a number of poets who established some distinct quality of affect: foremost among these were Tu Fu, who achieved the supreme synthesis, and Han Yü, the most striking; in addition there were those who were masters of some single quality, such as Liu Tsung-yüan [773–819], Liu Yü-hsi [772–842], Li Ho [791–817], Li

Shang-yin [813–858], Tu Mu [803–852], and Lu Kuei–meng [d. ca. 881]. Weaker poets simply went along with the historical forces of the age and followed what was current, unable to lift themselves above it: these constitute what is known as the "basic color" (pen*-se*) of T'ang poetry.

At the beginning of the Sung, poets followed closely the former T'ang manner, and the generation of Hsü Hsüan [916–991] and Wang Yü-ch'eng [954–1001] represented pure music of the T'ang. A major mutation did not occur until the appearance of Su Shun-ch'in [1008–1048] and Mei Yao-ch'en [1002–1060], both of whom Ou-yang Hsiu [1007–1072] tirelessly praised in the highest terms. Afterwards various authors appeared in succession, each of whom achieved supremacy in some particular quality. Modern critics simply lump them all together as "Sung poetry." Nor is there uniformity in the poetry of the Southern Sung, Chin, and Yüan writers. Each of the major poets, such as Lu Yu [1125–1210], Fan Ch'eng-ta [1126–1193], and Yüan Hao-wen [1190–1257], was able to show his own distinct talent. Of the early Ming writers, Kao Ch'i [1336–1374] was the most outstanding; his work integrated the various strengths of T'ang, Sung, and Yüan poetry, and cannot be ranked at a disadvantage in comparison to T'ang, Sung, and Yüan poetry simply on the grounds that he is a Ming poet.

Yeh Hsieh here sums up the history of Chinese poetry, bringing it up to the mid Ming, where discussion of the history of poetic theory supplants the history of poetry. Although by his time most sophisticated lovers of poetry were no longer entirely comfortable with the Ming archaist demand for exclusive devotion to the High T'ang, there was still a strong inclination to describe the history of poetry in terms of a relative ranking of periods. Yeh Hsieh displays shocking liberalism in completely denying any inherent value in a period (at least before the mid Ming): his point of view is still that of literary history, but it is a literary history comprised entirely of individual poets.

自不讀唐以後書之論出。於是稱詩者必曰唐詩。苟稱其人之詩為宋詩。無異於唾罵。謂唐無古詩。并謂唐「中」「晚」且無詩也。噫。亦可怪矣。今之人豈無有能知其非者。然建安盛唐之說。錮習沁入於中心。而時發於口吻。弊流而不可挽。則其說之為害烈也。原夫作詩者之肇端。而有事乎此也。必先有所觸以興起其意。而後措諸辭。屬為句。敷之而成章。當其有所觸而興起也。其意其辭其句劈空而起。皆自無而有。隨在取之於心。出而為情為景為事。人未嘗言之。而自我始言之。故言者與聞其言者。誠可悅而永也。使即此意此辭此句雖有小異。再見焉。諷咏者已不擊節。數見則益不鮮。陳陳踵見。齒牙餘唾。有掩鼻而過耳。譬之上古之世。飯土簋。啜土鉶。當飲食未具時。進以一臠。必為驚喜。逮後世膻騰炰瀹之法興。羅珍搜錯。無所不至。而猶以土簋土鉶之庖進。可乎。

Ever since the appearance of Li Meng-yang's position—that a person shouldn't read anything after the T'ang—whoever is good at poetry will inevitably have his work described as "T'ang poetry"; and if someone's poetry is described as being "Sung poetry," it's just like spitting on him. They [the Ming archaists] claimed that there was no true old-style verse written in the T'ang, and further claimed that there was no poetry worth mentioning from the mid T'ang and late T'ang. This should not be allowed to go unchallenged. It is impossible that our contemporaries are incapable of understanding how wrong this is; rather I think that the theory of the exclusive preeminence of Chien-an and High T'ang poetry has become so habitual and firmly entrenched that people simply take it for granted. People repeat it without thinking and cannot be rescued from sinking into such mindless commonplaces, the result being that the harm done by such theories is very severe.

Basically, when a person sets out to write poetry seriously, it is necessary that there first be some experience that stirs his thoughts (*yi**); only then does he find words for them, join those words into lines, and allow those lines to unfold into a complete poem. When it does happen that he experiences something and is stirred, then his thoughts, his words, and his lines appear out of thin air; and every one of them moves from non-existence into existence, and he takes them from his mind as he finds them there. These emerge as statements of the affections (*ch'ing**), of scene (*ching**), and of event (*shih**). What no one else has ever said before, I can say for the first time from my own self. For this reason both the person who speaks such words and the person who hears such words can truly delight in them and preserve them. But if you bring out the same thoughts, words, and lines a second time—even if there are minor differences in the new version—then the person who recites them will not be caught up enthusiastically by the poetry. As they are brought out again and again, they increasingly lose their freshness until they become commonplaces that are "overripe," leading others to hold their noses as they pass by.

We may compare the situation to the culinary arts: in earliest antiquity people ate from earthenware plates and drank from earthenware jugs; and since at this time the full range of cuisine had not yet been developed, people would always be delighted whenever a single dish of meat was served. But in later ages, the various techniques of dry-roasting, braising, and broiling fillets developed; delicacies were varied and different combinations were tried until all the possibilities had been explored. Would it still be all right to serve them from the kitchen on earthenware plates and in earthenware jugs?

This and the following analogies are close to, but differ in significant ways from, Western notions of progress. Furthermore, they do not at all adequately illustrate Yeh Hsieh's previous statements of how literary history operates, which is by constant mutations that are neither teleological nor cumulative and by mutations that are governed by only one rule—the avoidance of repeating what has been done before (although accidental recurrence remains a legitimate possibility). The analogy of cuisine turns instead to another common model of traditional literary history: the development from simple forms to a complete range of possibilities. Unlike theories of progress (and indeed unlike Yeh Hsieh's own concept of linear mutation offered earlier), this is not a series of discrete points that supplant one another but a gradual accumulation of variations. In the analogy between archaist poetics and the continuing use of earthenware utensils, original forms ("containers") are retained when history has produced a great variety of "contents" and forms to correspond to them. The appeal to culinary snobbishness is less significant here than the valid point of the critique: Ming archaist poetics could not accept the burden of history, and the falseness of their archaic forms was always obvious.

上古之音樂。擊土鼓而歌「康衢」。其後乃有絲竹匏革之制。流至於今。極於九宮南譜。擊律之妙。日異月新。若必返古而聽「擊壤」之歌。斯為樂乎。古者穴居而巢處。乃制為宮室。不過衛風雨耳。後世遂有璇題瑤室。土文繡而木梯錦。古者儷皮為禮。後世易之以玉帛。遂有千純百璧之侈。使今日告人居以巢穴。行禮以儷皮。孰不嗤之者乎。大凡物之踵事增華。以漸而進。以至於極。故人之智慧心思。在古人始用之。又漸出之。而未窮未盡者。得後人精求之而益用之出之。乾坤一日不息。則人之智慧心思。必無盡與窮之日。惟叛於道。戾於經。乖於事理。則為反古之愚賤耳。苟於此數者無尤焉。此如治器然。切磋琢磨。屢治而益精。不可謂後此者不有加乎其前也。彼虞廷喜起之歌。詩之土簋擊壤穴居儷皮耳。一增華於三百篇。再增華於漢。又增於魏。自後盡態極妍。爭新競異。千狀萬態。差別井然。苟於情於事於景於理。隨在有得。而不戾乎風人永言之旨。則就其詩論工拙可耳。何得以一定之程格之。而抗言風雅哉。如人適千里者。唐虞之詩如第一步。三代之詩如第二步。彼漢魏之詩。以漸而及。如第三第四步耳。作詩者知此數步為道途發始之所必經。而不可謂行路者之必於此數步焉為歸宿。遂棄前途而弗邁也。

In the music of early antiquity, people beat on earthenware drums and sang "The Crossroads." But later there developed musical instruments using silk, bamboo, gourds, and leather, which have continued in use down to the present, reaching the ultimate sophistication in the repertoire of southern melodies. Every musical subtlety has been explored, with new and different things appearing constantly. If now we had to return to antiquity and listen to the ancient "Stick-toss Song," would we even consider it music?

In antiquity people lived in caves and in trees. When they built any kind of shelter, it was only to protect themselves against storms. Later ages developed porphyry capitals for their columns and chambers of malachite, stucco walls with intricate decoration and brocaded timbers. In antiquity folded deerhide was used in ceremonies; later ages replaced this with silks and jade, until finally there were extravagant displays of silk work and jade disks by the thousands.

If you announced to someone in modern times that a person should live in caves or in the trees and should carry out ceremonies with deerhide, everyone would laugh at you.

There is a general tendency in things to become increasingly elaborate, always going a little bit farther until they reach an extreme. The wisest and most brilliant thoughts of human beings were first put into practice and gradually developed by the ancients; but some thoughts were not followed to their fullest extent, so that these remained available for later people to give them careful examination and to use and develop more fully. As the processes of the universe never rest, not even for a single day, so wise and brilliant human thoughts are never exhausted. [When we speak of how human thought always discovers something new, we do not mean] opposition to the Way, violence to constant truths, or running contrary to the principles behind how things operate (*shih*-li**): these are nothing more than the base stupidity of merely negating the past. If one can avoid making these mistakes, then one's thought becomes like the fashioning of a vessel: cutting, grinding, polishing, so that the more you work on it the finer it becomes. Nor can we claim that after us there will be nothing more to add to what we ourselves have done.

That song of earliest antiquity in which Yü expressed his happiness is the poetic equivalent of the earthenware plate, the music called "Stick-toss Song," living in a cave, or using double folds of deerhide in ceremonies. One level of elaboration was added to it in the *Book of Songs*, and another level of elaboration was added in the Han; then another level was added in the Wei, and after that every stance and beauty was explored, each person trying to be more novel than the rest, with a clear structure of differences in all those thousands of stances and manners. It is perfectly all right to consider the relative qualities of a person's poem, so long as that consideration focuses on whether the person achieved what he achieved by the disposition of his affections (*ch'ing**), events (*shih**), the scene (*ching**), and natural principle (*li**), and in doing so did not do violence to the precept of the poets of the *Book of Songs*, to "make words last long" (*yung-yen*); but the poem cannot be properly measured by some fixed and determinate form, with the "Airs" and "Odes" used as weapons against it.

To use the comparison of a person going on a journey of a thousand leagues, the poems of earliest antiquity by Kings T'ang and Yü are like the very first step; the poems of the Hsia, Shang, and Chou dynasties are like the second step. And with the poems of the Han and the Wei we are getting farther along, as with the third and fourth steps. Someone who writes poetry understands that these few steps must be passed through at the outset of the journey. But it is not right to claim that these few steps are the final destination of the traveler, that he should abandon the road ahead and go no farther.

The presumption behind this analogy to a journey lies at the heart of Yeh Hsieh's literary thought: like Yen Yü he believes that the ability to write poetry well comes from following poetry's history; but for Yeh Hsieh, the end of that history is deferred indefinitely, or at least not yet reached. Yen Yü believed that the study of the history of poetry would reveal self-evident norms, norms beset by dangers of corruption and decay; thus the history should be stopped at a certain point. The Ming archaists agreed with this position and radicalized it. For Yeh Hsieh, the values of poetry transcend a particular historical embodiment; history is merely change and difference, or accumulation and elaboration. If we read Yeh Hsieh carefully, however, we realize that even though there may be no moment of perfection, there was a Fall, a point after which poetic history unfortunately stopped: this point was the mid Ming, when archaist theory came to dominate the world of poetry, a moment of reversal. In his several recitations of the history of poetry, Yeh Hsieh does not take his descriptions of constant change beyond the early Ming; he does not bring the history of poetry up to the present day. In his own way, Yeh confronts the paradox of pluralism and relativism, that both are undermined by including their own negations. Yeh, of course, chooses to exclude the negation, not to admit the Ming rejection of change as one possibility of change; thus we have the uncomfortable stridency of his intolerant rejections of all intolerance.

且今之稱詩者。祧唐虞而禘兩周。宗祀漢魏於明堂是也。何以漢魏以後之詩。遂皆為不得入廟之主。此大不可解也。譬之井田封建。未嘗非治天下之大經。今時必欲復古而行之。不亦天下之大愚也哉。且蘇李五言與亡名氏十九首。至建安黃初。作者既已增華矣。如必取法乎初。當以蘇李與十九首為宗。則亦吐棄建安黃初之詩可也。

Those who claim mastery of poetry these days take the ancient Kings T'ang and Yü as their earliest ancestors and do obeisance to the Shang and Chou dynasties as the next level of their ancestry. The sacrifices to their immediate ancestors are performed in the temples of Han and Wei. But why is it that none of the poems after the Han and the Wei ever get to be the objects of worship in their chapels? It is utterly incomprehensible. Take the analogy of the ancient feudal liege system and the well-field system [by which land was divided into nine parts, farmed by eight peasant families, the ninth part going to the state]: these have always been the permanent principle for good government of the whole world; but at the same time if one had to return to ancient ways and tried to put them into practice, it would also be the biggest stupidity in the world.

When we reach the Chien-an and Huang-ch'u reigns, we find that the writers have added a new level of elaboration to the five-character-line poems of Li Ling, Su Wu, and the anonymous "Nineteen Old Poems." If we must always take our rule (*fa**) from the earliest examples, then we should make Li

Ling, Su Wu, and the "Nineteen Old Poems" the ancestor of our lineage—in which case, it is quite proper to reject the poetry of the Chien-an and Huang-ch'u.

The target here is archaist admiration for the poetry of the Chien-an and Huang-ch'u. As is usually the case with polemicists, Yeh Hsieh is misunderstanding and simplifying his adversaries here: the archaists did not generally hold to the simple notion that earlier was better; rather they believed that each form developed to a point of perfection, then declined. Although he mentions various forms, Yeh Hsieh tends to think of poetry as a single whole.

詩盛於鄴下。然蘇李十九首之意。則寖衰矣。使鄴中諸子。欲其一一摹倣蘇李。尚且不能。且亦不欲。乃於數千載之後。胥天下而盡倣曹劉之口吻。得乎哉。或曰。「溫柔敦厚。詩教也。漢魏去古未遠。此意猶存。後此者不及也。」不知溫柔敦厚。其意也。所以為體也。措之於用則不同。辭者。其文也。所以為用也。返之於體則不異。漢魏之辭。有漢魏之溫柔敦厚。唐宋元之辭。有唐宋元之溫柔敦厚。譬之一草一木。無不得天地之陽春以發生。草木以億萬計。其發生之情狀。亦以億萬計。而未嘗有相同一定之形。無不盎然皆具陽春之意。豈得曰。若者得天地之陽春。而若者為不得者哉。且溫柔敦厚之旨。亦在作者神而明之。如必執而泥之。則巷伯「投畀」之章。亦難合於斯言矣。

Poetry flourished in Yeh [the capital of the Ts'ao's during the Chien-an], but at the same time the mode of thought (*yi**) found in the poetry of Li Ling, Su Wu, and the "Nineteen Old Poems" sank into decline. Had the writers of Yeh been forced to imitate Li Ling and Su Wu in every detail, not only would they have been unable to do so, they furthermore would not have wanted to do so. Now, several thousand years later, can we get everyone in the whole world to imitate every one of the accents of the Ts'ao's and Liu Chen [d. 217] [Chien-an poets]?

Some say that what is to be learned through poetry is "gentleness and genuineness" and that since the Han and Wei were still not far from antiquity, this intent (*yi**) still endured then in ways that no later period could match. What they fail to understand is that "gentleness and genuineness" is the intent (*yi**)—that is, how the embodiment (*t'i**) is constituted—and that the realization (*yung*) of this intent will not be always the same. Wording (*tz'u**) is the patterning (*wen**), which is the way in which it [the intent or embodiment] is realized; [and though the wording may differ,] if we go back to the embodiment, there is no difference. The wording of Han and Wei poetry contains the Han and Wei version of gentleness and genuineness, but the wording of T'ang, Sung, or Yüan poetry has the T'ang, Sung, or Yüan version of gentleness and genuineness.

Take, for example, every single plant and tree, all of which are brought to life by receiving the bright forces of the spring. These plants and trees can be reckoned in the billions, and the circumstantial manners (ch'ing*-chuang) in which they come to life can also be reckoned in the billions. Never among all these is there a single predetermined, identical shape (hsing*), yet all alike are replete with the will (intent, yi*) of the bright forces of spring. No one can say that some of these have received the bright springtime forces of the world, while others have not.

In the same way, this principle of genuineness and gentleness is to be found in the writer's spirit (shen*) and is made manifest there. If you try to grasp it too tightly and tie it down, then a case like the stanza of "The Officer of the Inner Palace" [Book of Songs 200] which speaks of "throwing them [slanderers] to the wolves and tigers" will be rather hard to reconcile with the statement on "gentleness and genuineness."

For a similar critique of literalist versus "free" interpretation of the *Book of Songs*, see the passage from *Mencius*, pp. 24–26. Yeh Hsieh accepts the Confucian dogma, enunciated in the *Book of Rites*, that the *Book of Songs* imparts a lesson of "gentleness and genuineness" (wen-jou tun-hou), and that this remains a value for all subsequent poetry. But the analogy of the infinite circumstantial variety of nature, Yeh Hsieh's favorite analogy, allows for the manifestation of the principle in a wide variety of ways. Even the overt hostility of the "Officer of the Inner Palace" is simply one manifestation of "gentleness and genuineness" (although Yeh Hsieh does not attempt an explicit reconciliation of the principle and the tone of the passage). One falters in attempting to translate a phrase such as wen-jou tun-hou, loaded by tradition with a richness of association: it suggests a depth of honesty and goodness, a genuineness of feeling, a generosity.

從來豪傑之士。未嘗不隨風會而出。而其力則嘗能轉風會。人見其隨乎風會也。則曰其所作者。真古人也。見能轉風會者。以其不襲古人也。則曰今人不及古人也。無論居古人千年之後。即如左思去魏未遠。其才豈不能為建安詩耶。觀其縱橫踔踔。睥睨千古。絕無絲毫節曹劉餘習。鮑照之才。迥出儕偶。而杜甫稱其俊逸。夫俊逸則非建安本色矣。千載後無不擊節此兩人之詩者。正以其不襲建安也。奈何去古益遠。翻以此繩人耶。且夫風雅之有正有變。其正變係乎時。謂政治風俗之由得而失。由隆而污。此以時言詩。時有變而詩因之。時變而失正。詩變而仍不失其正。故有盛無衰。詩之源也。

In the past, bold and outstanding men have always emerged, moving along with the currents of the times [feng*-hui; lit., "the conjunction of feng*"], and their force has been capable of bending those currents (feng*-hui). When people see that such men move with the currents of the time, then they say that their writings are the authentic work of the ancients. But when they see that such men are capable of bending the currents, they will say that the modern writer is unequal to the ancients because he does not follow them closely. We don't have to go a thousand years after the ancients in order to observe this phenomenon. Take the case of Tso Ssu [ca. 250–ca. 305], who was not far removed from the Wei period. Of course his talent was capable of producing poetry in the Chien-an manner. But when we observe both his grand sweep and his anxious falterings, his proud gaze that looked down on all the past, we find not the least trace of the lingering poetic habits of writers like Ts'ao Chih [192–232] and Liu Chen. The talent of Pao Chao [ca. 414–466] rose far above his contemporaries, and Tu Fu praised Pao's "dashing aloofness." A quality like "dashing aloofness" is hardly the basic color (*pen-se**) of Chien-an poetry. The reason why a thousand years after these poets everyone still responds instinctively to their work is that they did not follow the Chien-an closely. Why is it then that the farther we go from antiquity, the more we find this kind of criterion used to restrict writers?

In the "Airs" and the "Odes" of the *Book of Songs* there is both norm (*cheng**) and mutation (*pien**). When they speak of norm and mutation as being contingent on the times, they are referring to the way in which government and customs pass from success to failure, from splendor to corruption. This is speaking of poetry in terms of the times: there are [social and political] mutations in the times, and poetry goes along with these. When the times undergo a mutation and fall from the norm, poetry undergoes a mutation and yet does not fall from its norm. Thus flourishing without decline is the source of poetry.

Yeh Hsieh here takes up the canonical position articulated in the "Great Preface" to the *Book of Songs*, that poetry manifests the changes in the society around it. If the proper "norm" (*cheng**) of poetry is to express the conditions of the age, then when the age undergoes a mutation, poetry must change along with it in order to preserve its "norm." This is close to Platonic and Aristotelian mimetic theory, that the "good" of an imitation is indifferent to the "goodness" of the thing imitated (though Yeh Hsieh, like the Mao exegetes of the *Book of Songs*, would probably insist that the response to bad times would be lament—that is, the response of a good person—rather than simply a mirroring of bad times). Thus in its essence or origins, poetry remains normative in undergoing mutations and therefore can remain in a state of flourishing even amid social decline. The alternative would be a poetry that refuses to change with the times, and thus falls away from its norm. Having discussed the "source," Yeh Hsieh next discusses the *liu* 流, the "currents" or multiple "streams" that follow from the source.

吾言後代之詩。有正有變。其正變係乎詩。謂體格聲調命意措辭新故升降之不同。此以詩言時。詩遞變而時隨之。故有漢魏六朝唐宋元明之互為盛衰。惟變以救正之衰。故遞衰遞盛。詩之流也。

I would say that in the poetry of later ages there is both norm and mutation; but in this case, the way in which norm and mutation are linked to poetry is in differences in formal models (*t'i*-ko**), in tone (*sheng-tiao*), in the ways in which concepts are formed (*ming-yi**), in diction (*tz'u**), in novelty versus archaism, in movements upward and downward. Here we are discussing the times in terms of their poetry: poetry undergoes a mutation and the times follow along with it. Thus we have had alternations of flourishing and decline in the Han, Wei, Six Dynasties, T'ang, Sung, Yüan, and Ming; and only by a mutation were people able to redeem the decline of the norm. Thus an alternation of flourishing and decline occurs in the streams (*liu*) of poetry.

Part of the difficulty here is due to the fact that Yeh Hsieh has shifted the meaning of "the times" from cultural and political history to literary history. The changes between flourishing and decline that occur in this case refer not to large cultural processes but to "T'ang poetry" or "Sung poetry." Hence he can say that when poetry changes, the times follow: this seems to be a statement about period style, rather than a grandiose claim regarding poetry's capacity to reform the world. The claim is essentially that poetry has acquired its own history and, at least in the aspects he mentions, is no longer tied to social history as the *Book of Songs* was.

In its "source" or "root" aspect (associated with early poetry), poetry is set in the context of the civilization as a whole: here, because it perfectly manifests the condition of the civilization as it passes through phases of norm and mutation, poetry is a continual flourishing that knows no decline. In poetry's "stream" or "branch" aspect (associated with later poetry), there is both flourishing and decline: some purely external aspect of poetry (formal models, tone, diction, etc.—the "stream" or "branch" aspects) passes into decline and needs to be redeemed by a mutation that announces a new period and restores poetry to a flourishing condition.

從其源而論。如百川之發源。各異其所從出。雖萬派而皆朝宗於海。無弗同也。從其流而論。如河流之經行天下。而忽播為九河。河分九而俱朝宗於海。則亦無弗同也。

To consider poetry in terms of its source, it resembles the way in which all rivers spring from their source; and though each differs in the way it goes, even branching into thousands of tributaries, still all make their way together to the sea. In this aspect they are all the same. But if we consider poetry in terms of its streams, it is like the way in which the stream of Yellow River passes through the whole world and then suddenly divides into the Nine Courses; and yet, though the Yellow River divides into nine parts, all make their way together to the sea. And in this case, too, all are the same.

Yeh Hsieh's analogies sometimes obfuscate more than they clarity. In this case, his rhetorical desire to stress the ultimate unity that underlies surface differences in poetry overcomes his attempt to make a contrast, so that both analogies are pretty much alike. Poetry is presumed to have a unified source and a unified "end" (all streams *kuei*, "return," to the sea) but are manifest in human history and human space by difference.

歷考漢魏以來之詩。循其源流升降。不得謂正為源而長盛。變為流而始衰。惟正有漸衰。故變能啟盛。如建安之詩。正矣盛矣。相沿久而流於衰。後之人力大者大變。力小者小變。

If we make a historical survey of poetry since the Han and Wei, tracing the movement from source to stream, along with poetry's periods of rise and fall, we cannot correlate the two antithetical movements, claiming that norm is the source and always flourishing, while mutation is the stream and the point where poetry passes into decline. Rather there are times when the norm suffers a gradual decline, at which point a mutation is able to reinitiate flourishing. Take for an example the poetry of the Chien-an, which was both normative and flourishing in the highest degree: after following along its course for a long time, its streams passed into decline. Afterward, those with great power produced great mutations, while those with less power produced lesser mutations.

Yeh Hsieh seems to understand the collective forces of history as essentially entropic. Against historical entropy are great individuals whose literary historical value is measured by the quantity of force their work exerts against entropy. In literature all change follows from such individuals.

六朝諸詩人。間能小變。而不能獨開生面。唐初沿其卑靡浮豔之習。句櫛字比。非古非律。詩之極衰也。而陋者必曰。此詩之相沿至正也。不知實正之積弊而衰也。迨開寶諸詩人。始一大變。彼陋者亦曰。此詩之至正也。不知因正之至衰。變而為至盛也。盛唐諸詩人。惟能不為建安之古詩。吾乃謂唐有古詩。若必摹漢魏之聲調字句。此漢魏有詩。而唐無古詩矣。且彼所謂陳子昂以其古詩為古詩。正惟子昂能自為古詩。所以為子昂之詩耳。然吾猶謂子昂古詩。尚蹈襲漢魏蹊徑。竟有全似阮籍詠懷之作者。失自家體段。猶譽

子昂不能以其古詩為古詩。乃翻勿取其自為古詩。不亦異乎。杜甫之詩。包源流。綜正變。自甫以前。如漢魏之渾朴古雅。六朝之藻麗穠織。瀟遠韶秀。甫詩無一不備。然出於甫。皆甫之詩。無一字句為前人之詩也。自甫以後。在唐如韓愈李賀之奇譎。劉禹錫杜牧之雄傑。劉長卿之流利。溫庭筠李商隱之輕豔。以至宋金元明之詩家。稱巨擘者無慮數十百人。各自炫奇翻異。而甫無一不為之開先。此其巧無不到。力無不舉。長盛於千古。不能衰。不可衰者也。今之人固羣然宗杜矣。亦知杜之為杜。乃合漢魏六朝并後代千百年之詩人而陶鑄之者乎。

Here and there among the poets of the Six Dynasties, there were some who were capable of producing lesser mutations, yet they were not capable of showing us a fully individual and living face. Early in the T'ang, poets followed that tradition of clever playfulness and sensuality, with a mechanical parallelism of words and lines that was neither old-style verse nor regulated verse: this was poetry in the extreme of decline. Yet there are blockheads who always say that the early T'ang is poetry in its most perfect norm because it continues the traditions of predecessors. They do not recognize that here the norm has in fact reached its nadir of decline. A major mutation first occurs with the poets of the High T'ang, of the K'ai-yüan and T'ien-pao reigns. And here again those blockheads say that this, too, is poetry in its most perfect norm, not recognizing that in this case poetry had come to the ultimate in decline by following the norm and that now it had come to flourishing once again precisely by a mutation away from that norm.

In regard to the question of whether the poets of the High T'ang were or were not capable of writing old-style verse in the Chien-an manner, my opinion is that the T'ang did indeed produce old-style verse worthy of the name. If this is taken to mean imitating the tone and lines of Han and Wei poetry, then the T'ang did not have that kind of old-style verse—that belonged to the Han and Wei. Moreover, when such critics claim that Ch'en Tzu-ang [661–702] [mistakenly] considered his old-style verse to be authentic old-style verse, what they really mean is that Ch'en Tzu-ang was capable of producing his own old-style verse and thus it is Ch'en Tzu-ang's poetry [rather than a generic old-style verse]. I, on the other hand, would go so far as to say that Ch'en Tzu-ang's poetry followed so closely in the tracks of the Han and Wei poets that he produced some works which are exactly like Juan Chi's [210–263] "Singing My Feelings" (Yung-huai), and that, in doing so, he lost his individual style. Under the circumstances, isn't it strange for those critics to swear that Ch'en Tzu-ang's old-style verse cannot be considered real old-style verse, and then not to accept the old-style verse he wrote in his own manner?

The poetry of Tu Fu encompasses both source and stream, includes both norm and mutation, and nothing that went before him is left out of the scope of his poetry—from the simplicity and ancient dignity of Han and Wei poetry to the lushly ornamental texture of Six Dynasties poetry, or the limpid serenity that is also found in the poetry of that period. However, whatever Tu Fu produced was Tu Fu's own: there was not a word or a line that was not his poetry but the poetry of some predecessor.

After Tu Fu, without even putting our minds to it, we can reckon in the hundreds the number of poets with powerful and shaping talents: the daring strangeness of Han Yü [768–824] and Li Ho [790–816], the outstanding manliness of Liu Yü-hsi [772–842] and Tu Mu [803–852], the smooth fluency of Liu Ch'ang-ch'ing [d. ca. 785], the playful sensuality of Wen T'ing-yün [ca. 812–866] and Li Shang-yin [ca. 813–ca. 858], and from those poets on through the Sung, Chin, Yüan, and Ming. Each was a rare and unique wonder, and yet Tu Fu was the precursor of every single one of them. There was nothing to which his skill could not reach, nothing that his strength could not lift; he flourishes forever, and can neither pass into decline nor be allowed to pass into decline. It is an indisputable fact that the present reverence for Tu Fu is unanimous; but do people realize that what makes Tu Fu unique is his capacity to fuse and shape all the poets of the Han, Wei, and Six Dynasties, along with the poets for a millennium after him?

Despite his doubts about his own contemporaries' understanding of Tu Fu, Yeh Hsieh's explanation of his genius is very much in line with one major lineage of critical evaluation of Tu Fu. Tu Fu is the nexus into which all earlier poetry flows and is remade; at the same time, the variety of Tu Fu's work is the impetus for the variety of poetry in coming centuries.

唐詩為八代以來一大變。韓愈為唐詩之一大變。其力大。其思雄。崛起特為鼻祖。宋之蘇梅歐蘇王黃。皆愈為之發其端。可謂極盛。而俗儒且謂愈詩大變漢魏。大變盛唐。格格而不許。何異居蚯蚓之穴。習聞其長鳴。聽洪鐘之響而怪之。竊竊然議之也。且愈豈不能擁其鼻。肖其吻。而效俗儒為建安開寶之詩乎哉。開寶之詩。一時非不盛。遞至大曆貞元元和之間。沿其影響字句者且百年。此百餘年之詩。其傳者已少殊尤出類之作。不傳者更可知矣。必待有人焉起而撥正之。則不得不改絃而更張之。愈嘗自謂陳言之務去。想其時陳言之為禍。必有出於目不忍見。耳不堪聞者。使天下人之心思智慧。日腐爛埋沒於陳言中。排之者比於救焚拯溺。可不力乎。而俗儒且栩栩然俎豆愈所斥之陳言。以為秘異。而相授受。可不哀耶。

T'ang poetry was the single greatest mutation in eight dynasties, and the poetry of Han Yü was the single greatest mutation in T'ang poetry. His strength was great; his thought had a manly vigor; and he stands out sharply as an important founder. Sung poets such as Su Shun-ch'in, Mei Yao-ch'en, Ou-yang Hsiu, Su Shih, Wang An-shih, and Huang T'ing-chien all had their beginnings from Han Yü; and this can well be said to be flourishing in the highest degree. Conventional scholars, however, think that since Han's poetry represents a major mutation of the Han and Wei legacy, as well as of the High T'ang, his work is totally unacceptable. Such an opinion is no different from living in some insect's hole and growing accustomed to the sounds made there, to think the resonant tones of a great bell are bizarre and mutter criticisms of it. There is no question that Han Yü, had he wanted, could have made himself imitate the accents of the "Chien-an" or "K'ai-yüan and T'ien-pao" poetry that conventional scholars wrote. This is not to say that K'ai-yüan and T'ien-pao poetry did not flourish each in its own time; but by the time of the Ta-li, Chen-yüan, and Yüan-ho reigns [the latter part of the eighth and early ninth centuries] people had been going along with its influence and diction for a century. And of the poems that have been preserved from this period of more than a century, there are very few works that are truly outstanding—we can well imagine the quality of the works that were not preserved! If they had to wait until someone appeared who would prod them back onto the right course (cheng*), it is obvious that this person would have to play in a new key. Han Yü himself said that he should do his utmost to rid himself of commonplace language; when we imagine the harm done by commonplace language at the time, therefore, we realize this statement must have arisen from something he could not bear to see or hear. If the sharpness of mind of everyone in the world is progressively rotting away and sinking into commonplace language, then getting rid of such language can be compared to putting out a fire or rescuing someone from drowning. Isn't it right in such a case to use force? It is indeed a pity that conventional scholars have gleefully taken those very commonplaces denounced by Han Yü as their most treasured antiquities, rare mysteries to be kept close and passed on from one fool to the next.

Although Yeh Hsieh's reverence for Tu Fu follows contemporary critical consensus, the credit that he accords to Han Yü's poetry is singular. A minority of the best literary scholars had always considered Han Yü to be one of the greatest poets of the T'ang, but few would give him the preeminence that Yeh Hsieh accords him here. The aggressively discursive qualities of Han's best poetry were far from the subdued delicacy that was conventionally considered "poetic." Yet this is just what Yeh Hsieh justifies in Han Yü's work: a force necessarily applied to break the inertia of habit.

故晚唐詩人。亦以陳言為病。但無愈之才力。故日趨於尖新纖巧。俗儒即以此為晚唐詬厲。嗚呼。亦可謂愚矣。至於宋人之心手。日益以啟。縱橫鉤致。發揮無餘蘊。非故好為穿鑿也。譬之石中有寶。不穿之鑿之。則寶不出。且未穿未鑿以前。人人皆作模稜皮相之語。何如穿之鑿之之實有得也。如蘇軾之詩。其境界皆開闢古今之所未有。天地萬物。嬉笑怒罵。無不鼓舞於筆端。而適如其意之所欲出。此韓愈後之一大變也。而盛極矣。自後或數十年而一變。或百餘年而一變。或一人獨自為變。或數人而共為變。皆變之小者也。

其間或有因變而得盛者。然亦不能無因變而益衰者。大抵古今作者。卓然自命。必以其才智與古人相衡。不肯稍為依傍。寄人籬下。以竊其餘唾。竊之而似。則優孟衣冠。竊之而不似。則畫虎不成矣。故寧甘作偏裨。自領一隊。如皮陸諸人是也。乃才不及健兒。假他人餘焰。妄自借王稱霸。實則一土偶耳。生機既無。面目塗飾。洪濤一至。疲骨不存。而猶佽口而談。亦何謂耶。惟有明末造。諸稱詩者。專以依傍臨摹為事。不能得古人之興會神理。句剽字竊。依樣葫蘆。如小兒學語。徒有喔呼。聲音雖似。都無成說。令人嘁而卻走耳。乃妄自稱許曰。此得古人某某之法。尊盛唐者。盛唐以後。俱不掛齒。近或有以錢劉為標榜者。舉世從風。以劉長卿為正派。究其實不過以錢劉淺利輕圓。易於摹倣。遂呵宋斥元。

The poets of the late T'ang also held commonplace language to be a serious problem; but they lacked the strength of Han Yü's talent and thus spent their days pursuing clever novelty and fine points of craft. It is this that conventional scholars consider to be the most reprehensible aspect of late-T'ang poetry, and in this again they show their stupidity.

When we reach the style of the Sung poets, we find that they progressively brought more and more into the open; they probed everywhere they could and held everything up for scrutiny so that nothing was kept hidden or in reserve; and they objected to purposeful craft, carving and cutting. One may make an analogy to a jewel in rock: if you don't cut and carve at it, the jewel won't be brought out. Furthermore, the unclear and superficial words that everyone produces before they engage in the craft of cutting and carving cannot compare with the real achievement that comes when a piece is worked on thoroughly.

In the case of Su Shih's poetry, the worlds (ching*-chieh) brought to light in his poetry had never existed before: everything that is in Heaven and Earth, the delights, the laughter, the scorn, and the rage, are all driven to dance on the tip of his brush. And the way his poetry follows his mood wherever it takes him is the single greatest mutation in poetry after Han Yü; it is a flourishing of poetry in the highest degree.

Afterwards a mutation in poetry occurred in intervals ranging from twenty years or so to more than a century. Sometimes a single person produced a mutation all by himself; sometimes several writers joined forces to produce a mutation; but all were minor as far as mutations were concerned. Among these poets there were some who reached the state of flourishing by going along with these mutations; however, there were, of course, some who went along with the mutation and sank even more deeply into decline.

On the whole, when writers of past and present have acted with independence and self-assurance, they have felt it necessary to weigh their intelligence and talents against the greatest older writers; they have been unwilling, even in the slightest way, to be another person's follower or to accept the shelter of another's eminence, to glean the droppings of greatness. If you plunder another writer's work and end up resembling him, then you are like Yu Meng in the borrowed robes of Shu-sun Ao [roughly equivalent to Patroclus in the armor of Achilles]; but if you plunder another writer's work and don't end up resembling your source, then you have the proverbial paper tiger. Such writers are quite happy to be a member of an entourage and lead a regiment: P'i Jih-hsiu and Lu Kuei-meng are examples. But if his talent is not equal to a true warrior's and the writer merely borrows the dying flame of another, falsely usurping the throne and declaring himself overlord, then he is nothing more than a clay statue. Since there is no real life in him, just a painted appearance, once the floods of a heavy rain come, neither flesh nor bone will remain. Even if they make grand and extravagant claims, what does it finally matter?

At last we have the final phase of the Ming dynasty, when everyone who claimed to understand poetry gave their exclusive attention to copying earlier works. Unable to achieve either the intuitive understanding (hsing*-hui) or the principle of spirit (shen*-li*) of the early writers, they tried to mimic them as closely as possible by stolen lines and plundered phrases, like the senseless babbling of a very young child learning to speak: even though the sounds resemble adult speech, they don't mean anything. Such poets make us groan and flee. But they themselves declare in their blind self-admiration, "This work has achieved such and such a method (fa*) of the older writers."

Nothing later than the High T'ang ever passes the lips of those who revere it. Some recent critics have even elevated the poetry of Ch'ien Ch'i [722–780] and Liu Ch'ang-ch'ing [d. ca. 785] as their standard, and an entire generation has been swayed by their influence (feng*) to take Liu Ch'ang-ch'ing as the normative (cheng*) tradition. But the real fact of the matter is that the fluency and facile perfection of Ch'ien Ch'i's and Liu Ch'ang-ch'ing's poetry makes them easy to imitate. And on no better grounds than this, these recent critics will scoff at Sung poetry and dismiss Yüan poetry.

Liu Ch'ang-ch'ing and Ch'ien Ch'i are supremely "minor" poets, and Yeh Hsieh's insight into the reasons for their popularity explains one strain of shockingly bad poetic taste in the Ming and Ch'ing: because the study of poetry was so closely tied to composition, there was a tendency to develop values implicitly based on teachability. A similar force can be seen at work in the admiration for minor ninth-century poets in the Southern Sung.

又推崇宋詩者。竊陸游范成大與元之元好問諸人婉秀便麗之句。以為秘本。昔李攀龍襲漢魏古詩樂府。易一二字便居為己作。今有用陸范及元詩句。或顛倒一二字。或全竊其面目。以盛誇於世。儼主騷壇。傲睨今古。豈惟風雅道衰。抑可窺其術智矣。大凡人無才則心思不出。無膽則筆墨畏縮。無識則不能取舍。無力則不能自成一家。而且謂古人可罔。世人可欺。稱格稱律。推求字句。動以法度緊嚴。扳駁銖兩。內既無具。援一古人為門

戶。藉以壓倒眾口。究之何嘗見古人之真面目。而辨其詩之源流本末正變盛衰之相因哉。
更有竊其腐餘。高自論說。互相祖述。此真詩運之厄。故竊不揣。謹以數千年詩之正變。
盛衰之所以然。略為發明。以俟古人之復起。更列數端於左。

　　或問於余曰。「詩可學而能乎。」曰。「可。」曰。「多讀古人之詩。而求工於詩而
傳焉。可乎。」曰。「否。」曰。「詩既可學而能。而又謂讀古人之詩以求工為未可。竊
惑焉。其義安在。」余應之曰。「詩之可學而能者。盡天下之人皆能讀古人之詩而能詩。
今天下之稱詩者是也。而求詩之工而可傳者。則不在是。何則。大凡天姿人力。次絞先
後。雖有生學困知之不同。而欲其詩之工而可傳。則非就詩以求詩者也。我今與子以詩言
詩。子固未能知也。不若借事物以譬之。而可曉然矣。

But there have also been some who advocate reverence for Sung poetry and
who steal the gentle, comfortably beautiful lines of Lu Yu [1125–1210], Fan
Ch'eng-ta [1126–1193], and Yüan Hao-wen [1190–1257] of the Yüan, taking
these poets as their secret treasures. Earlier Li P'an-lung [1514–1570] imitated
the old-style poetry and *yüeh-fu* [folk ballads] of the Han and Wei by changing
one or two words and then giving it out as his own work. Today we have
people who use Lu Yu, Fan Ch'eng-ta, and Yüan Hao-wen by turning a
phrase around here and there or stealing the overall appearance of one of their
poems; for this such writers have become the talk of the age and lord it over
the world of poetry, casting haughty glances at everyone else, past and present. Not only is this a decline in the Way of poetry (*feng*-*ya**), I don't even
see any particular skill in it.

It is generally true that if a person lacks talent (*ts'ai**), his thoughts (*ssu**)
don't come out readily; if the person lacks courage, then pen and ink shrink
back in anxiety; if the person lacks judgment, then he doesn't know what to
keep and what to discard; if the person lacks force, he can't establish himself as
a fully independent figure. Some people think, however, that the older writers
can be feigned and the present deceived: such people make much of formal
structures (*ko**) and regulations (*lü*); and in trying to get good lines and
phrases, they always apply the most rigidly strict rules and weigh them by the
most minute measures. Lacking what is necessary within themselves, they put
themselves under the protective authority of one of the older writers and use
that writer to impress the crowd to awed silence. But if we look a little more
deeply, we realize that such poets have never really seen the true appearance of
the older writers, nor do they understand the relation between source and
stream, roots and branches, or flourishing and decline. But to go further and
rob the last tatters of flesh from those older writers, to discuss poetic theory in
grandiloquent tones, and to set up these lineages of master and transmitter—
these things suggest that the fate of poetry is in great danger. We must scrupu-
lously examine how norm and mutation and flourishing and decline have
taken place in the past few millennia; by clarifying this in general terms, we

may hope that the kind of poetry produced by the older writers will rise again. I have set forth a few points regarding this in the following sections.

Someone put the question to me whether an ability for poetry might be developed by study, and I responded that it could. But that person went on to ask, "May a person then seek success in poetry and a literary oeuvre worth sharing and preserving by reading much in the poetry of the older writers?" This time I told him "No!" He again: "I'm afraid I don't quite understand what sense there is in admitting that an ability for poetry can be developed by study, but further maintaining that success in poetry cannot be achieved by reading much in the poetry of the older writers."

I answered him thus: You ask why it is that an ability for poetry can be developed by study, so that everyone in the world can read the poetry of the older writers and, by doing so, themselves develop an ability for poetry, such people being the sort who nowadays claim expertise in poetry all over the world. And yet when it comes to the question of seeking success in poetry and something worth sharing and preserving, then the case is different and is not to be accomplished in the same way. In this general question of relative precedence and degree in the relation between natural endowment and what can be accomplished by individual effort, even though innate knowledge and hard-won effort are quite different, the real issue is that if you want true success and something worth preserving, then you cannot seek poetry in poetry. If I were to speak to you right now about poetry in its own terms, there would be no way you could understand; it is better to take some event or object as an example, and then it will be clear.

This passage is almost a touchstone of Yeh Hsieh stylistically, in the structure of his thought, and in the statement of his position. Yeh Hsieh wants essentially to change the grounds of discourse, to shift the question to something that cuts across the common issues of Chinese literary thought. This is hard enough in any language: most people are willing to be reflective about an answer, but they cling passionately to the question. In the tradition of classical Chinese discourse, to reject simple alternatives and redefine the problem was a herculean task.

Yeh Hsieh's interlocutor poses the time-honored question of the relative importance of innate ability as opposed to what can be accomplished by study. In doing so he assumes that "study" refers to poetry as a domain in its own right, separate from all others: the legacy of Yen Yü has reached fruition, and people take for granted what Yen Yü had to say polemically—that poetry is a fully autonomous realm. Yeh Hsieh wants to reply that poetry can be perfected by study in the sense that a person can grow and learn, that a reflective understanding of the world will improve poetry, yet that no amount of the study of poetry per se will contribute to writing major poetry. In short, here and elsewhere, Yeh Hsieh tries to oppose the legacy of Yen Yü; and the most difficult part of such opposition is that he must set aside a whole range of hot critical questions which grew out of positions in "Ts'ang-lang's Remarks on Poetry." He accomplishes this by setting up an apparent paradox, then showing that the paradox is paradoxical only by making certain assumptions; by revealing the assumptions, he is able to call them into question. These concerns are clear in the following passage, which explicitly concerns itself with "ground" or foundations.

今有人焉。擁數萬金而謀起一大宅。門堂樓廡。將無一不極輪奐之美。是宅也。必非憑空結撰。如海上之蜃。如三山之雲氣。以為樓臺。將必有所託基焉。而其基必不於荒江窮壑。負郭僻巷。湫隘卑濕之地。將必於平直高敞。水可舟檝。陸可車馬者。然後始基而經營之。大廈乃可次第而成。我謂作詩者。亦必先有詩之基焉。詩之基。其人之胸襟是也。有胸襟。然後能載其性情智慧。聰明才辨以出。隨遇發生。隨生即盛。

Let us say there is a person with a vast fortune who plans to erect a huge mansion, whose gates and halls and buildings and corridors will all be the ultimate in beauty in height and many chambers. Now such a mansion cannot be constructed on emptiness, like a mirage over the sea or like cumulus clouds resembling mountains. There must be a foundation for the terraces and tall buildings to rest on. Moreover, that foundation cannot be in the flood plain of a river, or in a narrow ravine, or backed up against the outer ramparts of a city wall, or in some back alley, or on low and soggy ground. It must be set on some level, high, and spacious ground, near waters so that it can be reached by boat, and with flatlands for the movement of horse and carriage: only in these circumstances čan you begin the foundation and carry out the construction, completing the great hall in its proper order.

I would say that anyone who would write poetry must first have the foundation for poetry. And the foundation for poetry is in that person's capacity for feeling. Only after there is a capacity for feeling can the person's nature (*hsing*-ch'ing**), his intelligence, his sharpness of wit, and analytical talents be brought forth, coming into being according to what he has experienced (*yü*), and flourishing as they come into being.

"Capacity for feeling," *hsiung-chin*, is analogous to the notion of "sensibility" of late-eighteenth-century England and Europe. It is a fostered capacity to let oneself be moved by things, under the assumption (a questionable assumption) that such capacity for response is "natural," as opposed to the artificial barriers to feeling imposed by social convention.

千古詩人推杜甫。其詩隨所遇之人之境之事之物。無處不發其思君王。憂禍亂。悲時日。
念友朋。弔古人。懷遠道。凡歡愉。幽愁。離合。今昔之感。一一觸類而起。因遇得題。
因題達情。因情敷句。皆因甫有其胸襟以為基。如星宿之海。萬源從出。如鑽燧之火。無
處不發。如肥土沃壤。時雨一過。禾喬百物。隨類而興。生意各別。而無不具足。即如甫
集中樂遊園七古一篇。時甫年纔三十餘。當開寶盛時。使今人為此。必鋪陳颺頌。藻麗雕
繢。無所不極。身在少年場中。功名事業。來日未苦短也。何有乎身世之感。乃甫此詩。
前半即景事無多排場。忽轉「年年人醉」一段。悲白髮。荷皇天。而終之以「獨立蒼
茫」。此其胸襟之所寄託何如也。余又嘗謂晉王羲之獨以法書立極。非文辭作手也。蘭亭
之集。時貴名流畢會。使時手為序。必極力鋪寫。諛美萬端。決無一語稍涉荒涼者。而羲
之此序。寥寥數語。託意於仰觀俯察宇宙萬彙。係之感慨。而極於死生之痛。則羲之之胸
襟。又何如也。

Tu Fu is the most admired poet of all time, and his poems follow directly from
the people, scenes, events, and things he experienced (*yü*); and through these
everywhere there appeared his concern for the ruler, his worries about the
horrors of war and rebellion, his sadness at time's passage, his longing for his
friends, his lament for people of former times, and his thoughts on his far
travels. Everything that touched (*kan**) him—whether delight or melancholy
or separation or reunion or the contrast between past and present—every
single one of these arose through an encounter with something of the same
kind (*lei**) [i.e., an encounter with something that produced a categorical association with those different kinds of feelings]. He found his topics according to
what he experienced and communicated what he felt (*ch'ing**) according to the
topic. All this occurred because Tu Fu had for a foundation [of his poetry] his
own unique capacity for feeling. Like the Sea of Constellations [the source of
the Yellow River] from which ten thousand springs flow; like a fire started by
flint and tinder that breaks out everywhere; like rich soil and loam which, once
the seasonal rains pass over, burgeons with life, each thing arising (*hsing**)
according to its kind (*lei**), and the life in each of those things different, but
every one of them adequate and complete.

From Tu Fu's collected poems take the old-style poem in seven-character
lines, "Lo-yu Park": when Tu Fu wrote it, he was only just over thirty, and it
was the full splendor of the K'ai-yüan and T'ien-pao reigns. Had one of our
modern poets written it, the poem would have been a rhetorical celebration in
the highest degree, with every intricate ornament imaginable. How could such
a writer, finding himself in a world of young men, with an ambition for great
accomplishments and fame, not yet disturbed by the shortness of the days
ahead of him, be stirred (*kan**) by the precarious relation between self and
world? But Tu Fu, in the first half of the poem, describes the scene and the
occasion without great elaboration, then suddenly shifts into the section begin-

ning "every year the person is drunk," where he worries about white-haired old age, feels his debt to Heaven, and ends up "standing all alone in a bleak expanse." The way in which Tu Fu's capacity for feeling is invested (*chi-t'o*) in this is incomparable.

I would also suggest that Wang Hsi-chih [321–379] of the Tsin dynasty set the highest standard in calligraphy, but was not a master of literary composition. The gathering at Orchid Pavilion was an assembly of all the famous and noble men of the age; and when they had Wang Hsi-chih, the greatest master of the age, write the preface for the poems composed at the gathering, surely he would do his utmost to describe the assembly with a thousand points of flattery and praise, and without a single word that touched on anything in the least dark and desolate. Yet in his preface Wang Hsi-chih, with just a few words of somber melancholy, invested that attitude (*t'o-yi**) in the objects of the universe, seen above and below; he continued with the unhappiness that this stirred in him, and concluded with the pain of thoughts of death. Wang Hsi-chih's capacity for feeling was also incomparable.

What strikes Yeh Hsieh most strongly about Tu Fu's poem and Wang Hsi-chih's "Preface for the Orchid Pavilion Gathering" is not so much natural feeling (for the enthusiasm of a social group is also natural feeling) as the ability to violate literary and social expectations and, in doing so, to compel the reader to acknowledge the truth of what was said. The capacity to violate expectations is for Yeh the confirmation of the writer's independence, Yeh Hsieh's highest value. And the natural response defined against social demands always seem to Yeh more "natural" than the natural response that comes in conformity to social demands; the latter is suspect.

由是言之。有是胸襟以為基。而後可以為詩文。不然。雖日誦萬言。吟千首。浮響膚辭。不從中出。如剪綵之花。根蒂既無。生意自絕。何異乎憑虛而作室也。乃作室者。既有其基矣。必將取材。而材非培塿之木。拱把之桐梓。取之近地閭閻村市之間而能勝也。當不憚遠且勞。求荊湘之梗楠。江漢之豫章。若者可以為棟為榱。若者可以為楹為柱。方勝任而愉快。乃免古離屈曲之病。則夫作詩者。既有胸襟。必取材於古人。原本於三百篇楚騷。浸淫於漢魏六朝唐宋諸大家。皆能會其指歸。得其神理。以是為詩。正不傷庸。奇不傷怪。麗不傷浮。博不傷僻。決無剽竊吞剝之病。乃時手每每取捷徑於近代當世之聞人。或以高位。或以虛名。竊其體裁字句。以為秘本。謂既得所宗主。即可以得其人之贊揚獎借。生平未嘗見古人。而才名已早成矣。何異方寸之木。而遽高於岑樓耶。若此等之材。無論不可為大廈。即數椽茅把之居。用之亦不勝任。將見一朝墮地。腐爛而不可支。故有基之後。以善取材為急急也。既有材矣。將用其材。必善用之而後可。得工師大匠指揮之。材乃不枉。為棟為樑。為榱為楹。悉當而無絲毫之憾。非然者。宜方者圓。宜圓者方。枉棟之材而為桷。枉柱之材而為楹。天下斲小之匠人寧少耶。世固有成誦古人之詩數萬首。涉略經史集亦不下數十萬言。逮落筆則有俚俗庸腐。窒板拘牽。隘小膚冗種種諸

習。此非不足於材。有其材而無匠心。不能用而枉之之故也。夫作詩者。要見古人之自命處。着眼處。作意處。命辭處。出手處。無一可苟。而痛去其自己本來面目。如醫者之治結疾。先盡蕩其宿垢。以理其清虛。而徐以古人之學識神理充之。久之而又能去古人之面目。然後匠心而出。我未嘗摹擬古人。而古人且為我役。

Considering the question in the light of these two writers, a person can produce poetry and prose worthy of the name only when the capacity for feeling is present to serve as the foundation [of a writer's work]. Otherwise, even if you compose ten thousand words a day and chant a thousand poems, they will be insubstantial echoes and shallow rhetoric that do not come from within; like flowers cut from colored silk, since they have no roots, there will be no life in them. Is this any different from building a house in empty space?

When building a house, once you have laid the foundation, then you must get timber [ts'ai*, "material," "talent"]. Timber that comes from a tree that grows on a tiny tomb-mound[13] or from some catalpa or pawlonia whose trunk can be encircled with two hands, the sort of wood that can be had close by at gates and village markets, can never bear their weight. You should not shrink from seeking your timber in far places nor from going to great trouble, but rather try to get teak and ebony[14] from the lands of Ching and Hsiang and camphor from the region where the Yangtze meets the Han. Some of this wood can be used for the beams and timbers; the rest can be made into pillars and columns; when you have something that can bear the strain comfortably, then you can avoid the problems of splitting and warping.

In writing poetry, once you have the capacity for feeling, then you should get your materials (ts'ai*) from the older writers: take the *Book of Songs* and the *Li Sao* as your source, and steep yourself in the currents of the great writers of the Han, Wei, Six Dynasties, T'ang, and Sung. Be able to understand the implications in the work of every one of them, and grasp their spiritual principles (shen*-li*). If you write your poetry in this way, it won't be commonplace when it is normative (cheng*); and when it is unusual, you won't run the risk of having it turn out to be merely bizarre; your beauty won't slip into vapid prettiness, and your erudition will avoid obscurity; finally, you will completely escape the problem of plagiarism.

In contrast, the so-called masters of this age always take short-cuts by going to well-known contemporary writers or to writers of recent times, either because of their high social position or because of their baseless reputation. From these they steal the formal structures (t'i*-ts'ai) of poems along with lines and phrases, making those works their secret treasures.[15] Their intention is that, having taken a certain person as an authority, they can obtain that person's praise and encouragement. In their whole lives, they may never have seen the poetry of the older writers; but still they can develop a reputation for talent (ts'ai*) very young. There seems little difference between this and a sapling of an inch in diameter all at once finding itself higher than the pinnacle on which it grows. It goes without saying that material (*ts'ai**) of this sort can't be used to make a great hall; it could not even take the weight of a few rafters and a thatched roof. A day will come when it will collapse to the ground, rotten inside and unable to support anything. Therefore, after laying the foundation, it is of the greatest importance to be good at selecting the right materials.

When you have the material, you must be able to make use of it; for it will be successful only if well used. If you get a master architect to direct the work, the material won't be wasted. The beams, rafters, columns, and pillars will all be exactly right, and there won't be the least cause for dissatisfaction. Otherwise you will find that there are not a few inferior carpenters in the world who round what should be squared and square off what should be rounded, who waste the timbers for making roof beams by making of them rafters for the eaves, and who waste the timber for the upright supports by making them into decorative pillars. In the same way it really does happen in our age that someone will have thoroughly read through tens of thousands of poems by the older writers and will have made his way through hundreds of thousands of words in the Classics, histories, and literary collections, but still when he sets his own brush to paper, he will come out with colloquialisms, weary commonplaces, woodenness, crampedness, narrowness, shallowness, and every kind of bad habit that you can imagine. In this case, it is not that the material was somehow inadequate; the reason is rather that he lacks the master craftsman's mind and, unable to make use of it, wastes the good material he has.

In writing poetry, it is essential to see the projects that the older writers set for themselves, where they focused their attention, where they formed concepts (*yi**), where they determined how to phrase things (*ming-tz'u**), and where they put their intentions into practice. A person who wants to learn to write poetry can't be haphazard in any of these matters, and must painfully get rid of his own original appearance in the work. This is like when a doctor sets out to cure a case of boils, he first washes away the dirt that has collected to make it clean and clear.[16] Gradually that space will be filled with the learning, judgment, and spiritual principles (*shen*-li**) of the older writers. Then, after a long time, he can again get rid of the appearance of the older writers, and only at this point does the mind of the master craftsman emerge. Then the self never imitates the older writers, yet the older writers are always at the service of the self.

This is one, very explicit version of the formation and education of a writer in traditional China: the successful presentation of self in literature is always a return to self, a self mediated and perfected by having been other. The tradition is first assimilated until it replaces the raw, uneducated self; finally the self reemerges with the tradition internalized and organized by this second self. There were many theorists who firmly believed one should never abandon the raw, primary self; but everyone who believed in education believed in some version of the model Yeh Hsieh proposes here. Some theorists failed to articulate the element of return to self strongly enough (among them the Ming archaists), but no one believed in the complete repression of the self in favor of the older writers.

彼作室者。既善用其材而不枉。宅乃成矣。宅成不可無丹艧黝堊之功。一經俗工絢染。徒為有識所嗤。夫詩純淡則無味。純朴則近俚。勢不能如畫家之有不設色。古稱非文辭不為功。文辭者。斐然之章采也。必本之前人。擇其麗而則。典而古者而從事焉。則華實並茂。無夸繢鬬炫之態。乃可貴也。若徒以富麗為工。本無奇意。而飾以奇字。本非異物。而加以異名別號。味如嚼蠟。展誦未竟。但覺不堪。此鄉里小兒之技。有識者不屑為也。故能事以設色布采終焉。然余更有進此。作室者。自始基以至設色。其為宅也。既成而無餘事矣。然自康衢而登其門。於是而堂。而中門。又於是而中堂。而後堂。而閨闥。而曲房。而賓席東廚之室。非不井然秩然也。然使今日造一宅焉如是。明日易一地而更造一宅焉。而亦如是。將百十其宅而無不皆如是。則亦可厭極矣。其道在於善變。變化豈易語哉。終不可易曲房於堂之前。易中堂於樓之後。入門即見廚。而聯賓坐於閨闥也。惟數者一一各得其所。而悉出於天然位置。終無相踵沓出之病。是之謂變化。變化而不失其正。千古詩人。惟杜甫為能。高岑王孟諸子。設色止矣。皆未可語以變化也。夫作詩者。至能成一家之言足矣。此猶清任和三子之聖。各極其至。而集大成。聖而不可知之之謂神。惟夫子。杜甫。詩之神者也。夫惟神乃能變化。子言多讀古人之詩而求工於詩者。乃囿於今之稱詩者論也。

Able to make good use of his material and not waste it, this person who would build a house can now complete the dwelling. But the dwelling, once completed, must now be painted.[17] If it suffers the tawdry decoration of tasteless workmen, it's going to be sneered at by anyone with judgment. In poetry, a pure blandness will lack any flavor (wei*); a pure simplicity will come close to being too rustic; and this disposition (shih*) in poetry does not bear comparison to the way some painters avoid color. In the old days, they said that a work could be considered successful only if it had literary patterning in the language (wen*-tz'u*); and literary patterning in the language means some overt coloration (chang*-ts'ai*).

If you always take your predecessors as the basic, while selecting what is beautiful and normatively standard in their work, taking what is canonical and ancient as your task, then your work will be rich with both fruit and flower, but only truly to be valued if you avoid a gaudy, overwrought manner. If you take mere opulence as skill and achievement, merely with unusual words and nothing unusual in the ideas (yi*) lying at the basis of the work, then the thing itself will not be distinctive, only its name. Its flavor will be like chewing wax:

before you finish reciting it, you feel like you simply can't stand it any more. This is the technique of village children; a person of judgment should be embarrassed to do it. Thus a real master knows when to stop when adding color (*se**) and glitter (*ts'ai**).

I would, moreover, like to extend my analogy a bit further. The person who would build a house has now progressed from laying the foundation to the painting; as a dwelling, it is complete, and there is nothing left to be done. From the street, we enter the gate and there is the hall, then the middle gate, and then the middle hall, the rear hall, and on to the women's apartments and small chambers and rooms for guests and the kitchen: everything is laid out in perfect order. However, if I construct a dwelling on this plan today, and tomorrow construct yet another dwelling in a different place on the same plan, and then construct over a hundred dwellings, every one of which is on exactly the same plan, in that case it would be exceedingly boring. The way here lies in a skill in transformation (*pien**-*hua**). Transformation is not something that is easy to talk about. After all, you can't put the small chambers in front of the halls, or move the middle hall to a place behind the storied buildings, or come into the kitchen when you enter the main gate, with all your guests seated in the women's chambers.[18] What we would call transformation is to have every one of the necessary number of rooms and buildings each in its proper place, all occupying a natural position, yet still to avoid the problem of sameness and repetitiousness. Of all the poets of history, only Tu Fu was really able to achieve transformation without falling away from the normative (*cheng**). Poets such as Kao Shih, Ts'en Shen, Wang Wei, and Meng Hao-jan got no further than the painting; we cannot really talk of transformation in any of them. In writing poetry, it is enough if one reaches the stage of autonomy and distinctive identity.[19] This is like the three disciples who displayed the different sagely qualities of purity, responsibility, and harmony, each reaching the fullest development of his own quality; yet to combine all qualities in a sageliness that cannot be comprehended is what is referred to as divinity or spirit (*shen**), and that was Confucius alone. In the realm of poetry, Tu Fu has that quality of spirit or divinity; and only spirit is capable of transformation. So when you speak of trying to be successful in poetry by reading much in the older writers, you are really just confined within the theories of our contemporaries who claim to understand poetry.

"INNER SECTION"
Chapter 2 (Remainder)

或曰。「先生之論詩。深源於正變盛衰之所以然。不定指在前者為盛。在後者為衰。而謂明二李之論為非是。又以時人之模稜漢魏。貌似盛唐者。熟調陳言。千首一律。為之反覆以開其錮習。發其憒蒙。乍聞之。似乎矯枉而過正。徐思之。真膏肓之針砭也。然則學詩者。且置漢魏初盛唐詩勿即寓目。恐從是入手。未免熟調陳言相因而至。我之心思終於不出也。不若即於唐以後之詩而從事焉。可以發其心思。啟其神明。庶不墮蹈襲相似之故轍。可乎。」

Someone said: "Your discussion of poetry has really examined the fundamental questions of norm (cheng*) and mutation (pien*), and how flourishing and decline occur. I see now that we cannot with certainty single out earlier writing as flourishing and later writing as decline. Moreover, you say that the theories of Li Meng-yang and Li P'an-lung of the Ming are incorrect; and you would reverse the trend by which people these days try to duplicate the Han and Wei or ape the High T'ang with tired commonplaces that make a thousand poems all sound alike. By reversing this trend, you hope to open a space in which poets can move freely and bring them out of confusion and ignorance.

"When I first heard what you were saying, it seemed to me that you were being rash and going too far; but when I reflected on it at leisure, I could see that this was really surgery performed on just the right spot. But then when we study poetry, we should perhaps put away our books of Han, Wei, early- and High T'ang poetry for the time being and not even set eyes on them, lest we not be able to avoid the tired commonplaces that come from reading them, commonplaces that will keep our own thoughts from ever emerging. What would you say to the notion that it would be better to work with the poetry after the T'ang, which may bring out our thoughts and open our intuitive understanding (shen*-ming) so that we can avoid falling into the old rut of imitation?"

Anyone who has ever tried to explain a complex position that demands the listener set aside conventional responses knows that even the grossest misinterpretation, as offered by the imaginary interlocutor here, is not beyond expectation.

余曰。「吁。是何言也。余之論詩。謂近代之習。大桀斥近而宗遠。排變而崇正。為失其中而過其實。故言非在前者之必盛。在後者之必衰。若子之言。將謂後者之居於盛。而前者反居於衰乎。吾見歷來之論詩者。必曰蘇李不如三百篇。建安黃初不如蘇李。六朝不如建安黃初。唐不如六朝。而斥宋者。至謂不僅不如唐。而元又不如宋。惟有明二三作者。高自位置。惟不敢自居於三百篇。而漢魏初盛唐居然兼總而有之而不少讓。平心而論。斯人也。實漢魏唐人之優孟耳。竊以為相似而偽。無寧相異而真。故不必泥前盛後衰為論也。夫自三百篇而下。三千餘年之作者。其間節節相生。如環之不斷。如四時之序。衰旺相循而生物而成物。息息不停。無可或間也。吾前言踵事增華。因時遞變。此之謂也。故不讀「明良」。「擊壤」之歌。不知三百篇之工也。不讀三百篇。不知漢魏詩之工也。不讀漢魏詩。不知六朝詩之工也。不讀六朝詩。不知唐詩之工也。不讀唐詩。不知宋與元詩

之工也。夫惟前者啟之。而後者承之而益之。前者創之。而後者因之而廣大之。使前者未有是言。則後者亦能如前者之初有是言。前者已有是言。則後者乃能因前者之言而另為他言。總之。後人無前人。何以有其端緒。前人無後人。何以竟其引伸乎。譬諸地之生木然。三百篇則其根。蘇李詩則其萌芽由蘗。建安詩則生長至於拱把。六朝詩則有枝葉。唐詩則枝葉垂蔭。宋詩則能開花。而木之能事方畢。自宋以後之詩。不過花開而謝。花謝而復開。其節次雖層層積累。變換而出。而必不能不從根柢而生者也。故無根則由蘗何由生。無由蘗則拱把何由長。不由拱把則何自而有枝葉垂蔭而花開謝乎。

I replied, What are you saying!? In my discussion of poetry I said that it has become a modern habit generally to dismiss what is recent and revere what is remote from us, to set aside all mutation and exalt what is normative. And since I found this view unbalanced and wrong, I said that earlier writing is not *necessarily* in a state of flourishing and that later writing is not *necessarily* in a state of decline. But what you have just suggested amounts to saying that later writing is in a constant state of flourishing, while earlier writing is, conversely, the one in the state of decline!

Virtually everyone I've read who has written about the theory of poetry says that the *Book of Songs* is superior to the poetry of Li Ling and Su Wu, and that Li Ling and Su Wu in turn are superior to the poetry of the Chien-an and Huang-ch'u reigns; the poetry of the Chien-an and Huang-ch'u is superior to the Six Dynasties, and the Six Dynasties is superior to the T'ang. It is even carried to the point that critics who complain loudly about Sung poetry will not only say, as might be expected, that the T'ang is superior to the Sung, they will also add that even the Sung is superior to the Yüan. There are two or three Ming writers [the archaists] who accord themselves the highest position; of course they wouldn't dare set themselves on a par with the *Book of Songs*, but they would say that they have encompassed the full range of the Han, Wei, early and High T'ang, and need not yield to their precursors in the least.

In the more than three millennia since the time of the *Book of Songs*, writers have appeared one after another, as in unbreaking circles or like the cycles of the four seasons. Decline and prospering follow one another, as things are born and brought to completion, continuously and without any intermission. This is what I was referring to when I spoke earlier of improving on what had been done previously and of mutation occurring at the proper time.

If you don't read the archaic songs like "Bright and Good" or "Stick-toss Song," you can't understand the achievement of the *Book of Songs*. In the same way, if you don't read the *Book of Songs*, you can't understand the achievement of Han and Wei poetry. If you don't read the poetry of the Han and Wei, you can't understand the achievement of Six Dynasties poetry, and if you don't read the poetry of the Six Dynasties, you can't understand the achievement of T'ang poetry. If you don't read T'ang poetry, you can't understand the achievement of Sung and Yüan poetry. What is written earlier opens the way; what is written later carries it on and amplifies it. What is written earlier founds something; what is written later follows and broadens it. If there is something that the earlier writers have never said, then a later writer can become like the earlier writers in being the first to say something. On the other hand, if the earlier writers have already said a certain thing, then the later writer can develop what the earlier writers said and say something else. If I may put it in general terms, if later writers lacked predecessors, they would not have any point to start out from; and if those earlier writers didn't have any successors, there would be no way to complete the processes they set in motion.

Compare it to the way in which a tree grows out of the earth. The *Book of Songs* is its roots; the poetry of Li Ling and Su Wu are its first sprouting; the poetry of the Chien-an is its growth into something an armspan in girth; the poetry of the Six Dynasties are its boughs and foliage; the poetry of the T'ang is the shadow cast by its boughs and foliage; in the poetry of the Sung, it is able to flower and all the capacities of the tree are complete. In the poetry after the Sung, the flowers blossom and fade, fade and blossom again; and even though these sequences occur over and over again, each stage appearing out of the mutation of the preceding stage, the life always comes from the root. Had there been no root, how could the first sprout have appeared? And had it not been from the sprout, how could the trunk, an armspan in girth, have grown? And had it not been from the trunk, how could the boughs and foliage have naturally appeared, casting shade and forming flowers that blossom and fade?

This is perhaps the most delightfully misguided elaboration of the tree analogy in traditional literary thought. At some point, botany overwhelms literary history and forces Yeh Hsieh to all sorts of things he really does not want to say. T'ang poetry is reduced to the highly anomalous status of shadow, and real literary history is ended with Sung poetry, after which everything becomes mere repetition (repetition of the stage achieved in the Sung): such a notion of life as repetition without history is precisely the point he has been arguing against.

若曰。審如是。則有其根斯足矣。凡根之所發。不必問也。且有由蘗及拱把成其為木。斯足矣。其枝葉與花。不必問也。則根特蟠於地而具其體耳。由蘗萌芽僅見其形質耳。拱把僅生長而上達耳。而枝葉垂蔭。花開花謝。可遽以已乎。故止知有根芽者。不知木之全用者也。止知有枝葉與花者。不知木之大本者也。由是言之。詩自三百篇以至於今。此中終始相承相成之故。乃豁然明矣。豈可以臆畫而妄斷者哉。大抵近時詩人。其過有二。其一。奉老生之常談。襲古來所云忠厚和平。渾樸典雅。陳陳皮膚之語。以為正始在是。元

音復振。動以道性情。托比興為言。其詩也。非庸則腐。非腐則俚。其人且復鼻孔撩天。搖唇振履。面目與心胸。殆無處可以位置。此真虎豹之鞟耳。其一。好為大言。遺棄一切。掇探字句。。抄集韻脚。覘其成篇。句句可畫。諷其一句。字字可斷。其怪戾則自以為李賀。其濃抹則自以為李商隱。其澀險則自以為皮陸。其拗拙則自以為韓孟。土苴建安。弁髦「初」「盛」。後生小子。詫為新奇。競趨以效之。所云牛鬼蛇神。夔蚿罔兩。揆之風雅之義。風者真不可以風。雅者則已喪其雅。尚可言耶。吾願學詩者。必從先型以察其源流。識其升降。讀三百篇而知其盡美矣。盡善矣。然非今之人所能為。即今之人能為之。而亦無為之之理。終亦不必為之矣。繼之而讀漢魏之詩。美矣善矣。今之人庶能為之。而無不可為之。然不必為之。或偶一為之。而不必似之。又繼之而讀六朝之詩。亦可謂美矣。亦可謂善矣。我可以擇而間為之。亦可以挹而置之。又繼之而讀唐人之詩。盡美盡善矣。我可盡其心以為之。又將變化神明而達之。又繼之而讀宋之詩。元之詩。美之變而仍美。善之變而仍善矣。吾縱其所如。而無不可為之。可以進退出入而為之。此古今之詩相承之極致。而學詩者循序反覆之極致也。

Someone may say, If we consider it from this point of view, then it is quite enough that we have the roots, and we need not concern ourselves with anything that develops from the roots. Or they may say, It is quite enough and the tree is complete when we have the sprout and the trunk, and we need not concern ourselves with boughs, foliage, and flowers. This would leave us with a lot of large roots coiling in the earth as complete forms (*t'i**), or we would only see the plain shapes of sprouts, or nothing more than large trunks growing to full height. Is it all right then to stop before we have boughs and foliage casting their shade and flowers that blossom and fade? To understand only that there are roots and sprouts is not to understand everything that a tree does. In the same way, to understand only that there are boughs, foliage, and flowers is not to understand the great roots of a tree. From this we may conclude that the processes of continuity and completion in the poetry, from the *Book of Songs* to the present, are absolutely clear; and a person may not rashly and willfully separate out some part of the process.

Generally speaking, modern poets err in two different ways. The first sort accept the ordinary opinions of their elders and try to conform closely to various shallow mottoes that have long been in circulation, such as "a steadfast warmth of manner and harmonious evenness," or "primal innocence and authoritative dignity." They take these to be the normative way to begin, and think that in this way poetry's original tones will swell up again; and all the time they make comments about the affections and a person's nature being led forth, or lodging their thoughts in comparisons and affective images (*pi*-hsing**). But as for the poems they write, if they're not utterly ordinary, then they're pedantic; and if not pedantic, then provincial. The men themselves provoke Heaven with their nostrils, flapping their lips and shaking their sandals; yet in the way they present themselves in poetry, as in their hearts, they have hardly any place they can stand securely: it's just as in the old saying that the furless hides of tigers and leopards are no different from those of dogs and sheep.

The second sort love to write in a grandiose manner and abandon any sense of wholeness; writers of this sort gather words and lines and get together their rhyme words. Whenever you look over an entire piece, every line can be divided from every other; and when you recite a line, every word can be split off. They take their harsh and bizarre moments to be like Li Ho, their murky moments to be like Li Shang-yin, their rough and obscure moments to be like P'i Jih-hsiu and Lu Kuei-meng, and their dissonantly clumsy moments to be like Han Yü and Meng Chiao. In their opinion, the poetry of Chien-an is trash, and the poetry of the early T'ang and High T'ang, worthless. Young people and the later-born are beguiled by poems like this, finding them full of fresh wonder, and are all eager to imitate them. If we weigh this "demonic" [demons with ox-heads, spirits with snake bodies, goblins, and spooks] poetry according to the moral values (yi*) of the "Airs" (Feng*) and "Odes" (Ya*), may it not be observed that the aspect of feng* cannot sway (feng*) others, and the aspect of ya* loses all dignity (ya*)?

I wish that those who study poetry would always start with the prior models in order to investigate both poetry's source and the streams that flow from that source, and to be able to judge what is an improvement and what is a falling away. Read the *Book of Songs* and understand that the poems there are indeed both perfectly beautiful and perfectly good, but at the same time that they are not something a modern poet can write. And even if modern poets were able to write them, the natural principle (li*) behind the writing of such poetry is absent, and ultimately we need not try to write it. Next I should read the poetry of the Han and Wei, which is beautiful and good; a modern poet may hope to write such poetry and is in no way prevented from writing it, but he does not have to try to write such poetry. And if someone should chance to write that sort of poetry, his work does not have to closely resemble it.

Next read the poetry of the Six Dynasties, which may indeed be spoken of as beautiful and good; here I can pick and choose and occasionally write this sort of poetry, but I can also ignore it. Next read the poems of the T'ang writers, which are perfectly beautiful and perfectly good; here I can write such poetry by thoroughly knowing their minds, or I can reach it by a spiritual intuition in transformation (pien*-hua* shen*-ming). Then again read the poetry of the Sung and Yüan, where beauty has undergone a mutation but is still beautiful, and goodness has undergone a mutation yet is still good. Here I can do as I please, either trying to write all the different kinds of this poetry or being selective in my judgments in writing it. This is the full extent of the historical tradition of poetry and the full extent of what a student of poetry should follow in sequence and reflect on.

We must observe that the course of the poetic education has now been reduced to poetry through the Sung.

原夫創始作者之人。其興會所至。每無意而出之。即為可法可則。如三百篇中。里巷歌謠。思婦勞人之吟詠居其半。彼其人非素所誦讀講肄推求而為此也。又非有所研精極思腐毫輟翰而始得也。情偶至而感。有所感而鳴。斯以為風人之旨。遂適合於聖人之旨。而刪之為經以垂教。非必謂後之君子。雖誦讀講習。研精極思。求一言之幾於此而不能也。乃後之人。頌美訓訓釋三百篇者。每有附會。而於漢魏初盛唐亦然。以為後人必不能及。乃其弊之流。且有逆而反之。推崇宋元者。菲薄唐人。節取「中」「晚」者。遺置漢魏。則執其源而遺其流者。固已非矣。得其流而棄其源者。又非之非者乎。然則學詩者。使竟從事於宋元近代。而置漢魏唐人之詩而不問。不亦大乖於詩之旨哉。

Originally, the people who first founded the writing of poetry expressed whatever came to their mind in the circumstance (hsing*-hui), and always without prior intent (yi*): this can be taken as a rule (fa*) and as a model. For example, about half the *Book of Songs* is made up of folk lyrics from the villages, the songs of women filled with longing, and toiling men. These were not written by people who constantly recited, read, studied, explained, and racked their brains; and they were not completed only after polishing and brooding, with brushes worn out by draft after draft. The mood (ch'ing*) happened to come to them, and they were stirred (kan*); when they were stirred by something, they sang out: this was the aim of the writers of the "Airs," which subsequently fit in perfectly with the aim of the Sage, Confucius, who edited them as a Classic to transmit his teaching to later ages. I should point out that I am not saying by this that superior people of later times are incapable of coming up with a single phrase that approaches the *Book of Songs*, no matter how much they recite, read, explicate, and practice, polish and give the task their most intense thought. But people of later times always give distorted explanations in their praises and exegeses of the *Book of Songs*; and they treat the Han, Wei, early and High T'ang in exactly the same way, thinking that people of later times can never match this earlier poetry. Then there are the very worst sort, who simply take the antithetical position: some, paying the highest honors to the Sung and Yüan, while belittling the T'ang; others, taking the mid T'ang and late T'ang as their standard while ignoring the Han and Wei. To hold fast to the source while ignoring the streams that flow from it is completely wrong, but to take the streams and reject the source is wrong in the highest degree. So in studying poetry, don't you think it runs quite against the aims of poetry to end up spending your time on the Sung, Yüan, and more recent periods, while ignoring the poetry of Han, Wei, and T'ang writers?

"OUTER SECTION"
Chapter 1 (Selections)

陳熟生新。二者於義為對待。對待之義。自太極生兩儀以後。無事無物不然。日月寒暑晝
夜。以及人事之萬有。生死貴賤。貧富高卑。上下長短。遠近新舊。大小香臭。深淺明
暗。種種兩端。不可枚舉。大約對待之兩端。各有美有惡。非美惡有所偏於一者也。其間
惟生死貴賤貧富香臭。人皆美生而惡死。美香而惡臭。美富貴而惡貧賤。然逢比之盡忠。
死何嘗不美。江總之白首。生何嘗不惡。幽蘭得糞而肥。臭以成美。海木生香則萎。香反
為惡。富貴有時而可惡。貧賤有時而見美。尤易以明。即莊生所云「其成也毀。其毀也
成」之義。對待之美惡。果有常主乎。生熟新舊二義。以凡事物參之。器用以商周為寶。
是舊勝新。美人以新知為佳。是新勝舊。肉食以熟為美者也。果食以生為美者也。反是則
兩惡。推之詩獨不然乎。舒寫胸襟。發揮景物。境皆獨得。意自天成。能令人永言三歎。
尋味不窮。妄其為熟。轉益見新。無適而不可也。若五內空如。毫無寄托。以勦襲浮辭為
熟。搜尋險怪為生。均風雅所擯。論文亦有順逆二義。并可與此參觀發明矣。

Conventionality and novelty constitute an antithetical pair of principles
(*yi**). Even since the Primal Unity (*T'ai-chi*) and the Primal Duality (*liang-yi*,
Yin and Yang), this has been the way of all things (*wu**) and events (*shih**): sun
and moon, heat and cold, day and night, and everything in human affairs, life
and death, nobility and baseness, poverty and wealth, lofty and low, superior
and inferior, long and short, far away and close at hand, new and old, large
and small, sweet-smelling and foul-smelling, deep and shallow, clear and
obscure—there are so many dualities I can't name them all.

Generally speaking, every antithetical pair contains both positive and negative elements, but the positive is not concentrated on one side nor the negative
on the other. In the case of some of these antithetical pairs, we know that
everyone finds life, sweet fragrance, wealth and nobility to be the positive
terms, while their opposites are negative. But Feng Ch'ou-fu [*Tso*, Ch'eng 2]
and Pi Kan represented an utter steadfastness in which death became positive,
while for someone like Chiang Tsung, who survived to old age by serving one
dynasty after another, staying alive should be considered negative. If you put
manure around an orchid, it grows lushly: something foul-smelling becomes a
positive element. There are ocean trees that give off a sweet scent when they
are decaying: sweet fragrance here is negative. And it is exceedingly easy to
show that there are times when wealth and nobility are negative, while poverty and low station are positive. This is the principle behind those words of
Chuang-tzu: "Its fulfillment is its destruction; its destruction, fulfillment."
Finally I doubt if any one term in an antithetical pair has a monopoly on the
positive or the negative.

The opposed principles of freshness and conventionality, or new and old,
may be applied to almost anything; but in antique vessels, it is the Shang and
Chou vessels that are most precious, a case where the old is superior to the

new; in beautiful women, new acquaintance is best, a case in which new is superior to old. Meat is best when it is aged; fruit is best when it is fresh; in both cases the opposites are negative elements. If we extend this to the case of poetry, we find that it is no different. When a person fully expresses what is in his heart, bringing in everything in the scene before him so that the worlds (*ching**) of his poems are his alone and his thoughts (*yi**) are naturally formed, a poetry capable of making others recite it with sighs of admiration and savor its flavor inexhaustibly, then any conventional aspects will be forgotten, and will always seem fresher and newer, apt in every way. In contrast, if there is nothing inside a person and nothing he cares about transmitted through his writing brush, then such conventionality will be nothing more than empty phrases plagiarized from someone else, and this freshness will be nothing more than a strained search for obscurity and striking effects: both are rejected by the art of poetry (*feng**-*ya**). The concepts of forward and retrograde motion in prose theory can be brought in here to clarify this.

. . . .

作詩者在抒寫性情。此語夫人能知之。夫人能言之。而未盡夫人能然之者矣。作詩有性情。必有面目。此不但未盡夫人能然之。并未盡夫人能知之而言之者也。如杜甫之詩。隨舉其一篇與其一句。無處不可見其憂國愛君。憫時傷亂。遭顛沛而不苟。處窮約而不濫。崎嶇兵戈盜賊之地。而以山川景物。友朋盃酒。抒憤陶情。此杜甫之面目也。我一讀之。甫之面目。躍然於前。讀其詩一日。一日與之對。讀其詩終身。日日與之對也。故可慕可樂而可敬也。舉韓愈之一篇一句。無處不可見其骨相稜嶒。俯視一切。進則不能容於朝。退又不肯獨善於野。疾惡甚嚴。愛才若渴。此韓愈之面目也。舉蘇軾之一篇一句。無處不可見其凌空如天馬。游戲如飛仙。風流儒雅。無入不得。好善而樂與。嬉笑怒罵。四時之氣皆備。此蘇軾之面目也。此外諸大家。雖所就各有差別。而面目無不於詩見之。其中有全見者。有半見者。如陶潛。李白之詩。皆全見面目。王維五言則面目見。七言則面目不見。此外面目可見不可見。分數多寡。各各不同。然未有全不可見者。讀古人詩。以此推之。無不得也。余嘗於近代一二聞人。展其詩卷。自始至終。亦未嘗不工。乃讀之數過。卒未能覩其面目何若。竊不敢謂作者如是也。

People can comprehend the truth of the statement that writing poetry resides in describing one's affections and nature (*hsing**-*ch'ing**); people know how to say it, but are not entirely capable of going along with it. If one's nature and affections are in the writing of poetry, then the poem must also have a "face"; in this case, not only are people incapable of going along with it, they can't entirely comprehend the truth of it and articulate it.

Take the poetry of Tu Fu as an example: if you pick a poem or line at random from his work, you will always be able to see his worries about the country, his love for his ruler, and his distress about the times and the civil wars. When he was knocked flat on his face, he did not act rashly and improperly; when he found himself in straitened circumstances, he didn't go to excess; on perilous paths through warring rebel factions, he described his indignation and shaped his nature, writing about the landscape with its seasonal creatures or about friends and a cup of wine. This is Tu Fu's true face. As soon as I read such poems, Tu Fu's true face leaps out before me. If I spend the whole day reading his poems, then I sit face to face with him for the whole day; and if I spend a lifetime reading his poems, I spend every day face to face with him; I can look up to him, take delight in him, and respect him.

If I take up any poem or line by Han Yü, I can see his craggy physiognomy throughout, looking down on everything. When given office, he cannot accommodate himself to the court; out of office, he is not satisfied to practice private virtues in the wilderness. He is fierce in his hatred of evil and loves talent in men as if he were thirsty for them. This is the true face of Han Yü.

If I take up any poem or line by Su Shih, everywhere in it I can see him flying through the sky like one of the horses of Heaven, playing around like one of the immortal beings, a fusion of passionate stylishness (feng*-liu) and Confucian dignity (ya*) that is involved with everything. He loves goodness and has an easy delight in it; and with cheer, laughter, rage, and sharp words of disapproval, he encompasses the full range of moods (ch'i*) of the four seasons. This is Su Shih's true face.

After these three, although each of the great poets goes in his own direction, every one of them shows his true face in his poetry. There are those who show their true face completely, and there are those who show only half of it. In the poetry of T'ao Ch'ien and Li Po we always see the face completely. Wang Wei's face can be seen in his poetry in five-character lines, but not in his poetry in seven-character lines. Besides these poets, everyone differs in how much or little his true face can be seen; but in no one is it true that the face cannot be seen at all. If you read the poetry of the older writers along these lines, then you will grasp everything in them. I have read the poetry collections of several well-known writers of recent times from beginning to end, and always found the poems to be good work; but reading them over several times, I never could make out what their faces looked like. I don't think that this is how a real author should be.[20]

. . . .

詩是心聲。不可違心而出。亦不能違心而出。功名之士。決不能為泉石淡泊之音。輕浮之子。必不能為敦龐大雅之響。故陶潛多素心之語。李白有遺世之句。杜甫興廣廈萬間之願。蘇軾師四海弟昆之言。凡如此類。皆應聲而出。其心如日月。其詩如日月之光。隨其光之所至。即日月見焉。故每詩以人見。人又以詩見。使其人其心不然。勉強造作。而為欺人欺世之語。能欺一人一時。決不能欺天下後世。究之。閱其全帙。其陋必呈。其人既陋。其氣必薾。安能振其辭乎。故不取諸中心而浮慕著作。必無是理也。

Poetry is the voice of mind (*hsin**): it should not come out at odds with mind, and indeed it cannot come out at odds with mind. Men famous for their public accomplishments are utterly incapable of the clear and limpid tones of streams running over stones; those who live a life of carefree sensuality are always incapable of sounds with the honest grandeur of the "Great Odes." In T'ao Ch'ien's words about "many simple-hearted people," in Li Po's lines about leaving the world behind, in Tu Fu's excitement in his desire to build a great mansion of ten thousand rooms [for all the poor scholars of the world], and in Su Shih's statement that all in the world are brothers—in cases like these, the voice always comes out as a response (*ying**). Their minds are like the sun and moon, and their poems are like the light of sun and moon: wherever the light reaches, the sun and moon can be seen. Thus every poem is seen through the person, and, in turn, every person is seen through the poem. Even if the person and his mind are otherwise and they strain to construct words that will fool others and fool the whole world, though they fool one person or one period, they still cannot hope to fool the whole world ever thereafter. If you think about it, that kind of person's ignoble qualities will be evident if you go over the whole corpus of his writings. And since the person is ignoble, his *ch'i** will always give out. And when the *ch'i** gives out, how can his lines stay vital and compelling? Not to find in one's own mind but still to aspire, without real grounds, to be an author—there has never been any such natural principle (*li**).[21]

. . . .

詩道之不能長振也。由於古今人之詩評。雜而無章。紛而不一。六朝之詩。大約沿襲字句。無特立大家之才。其時評詩而著為文者。如鍾嶸。如劉勰。其言不過吞吐抑揚。不能持論。然嶸之言曰。「邇來作者。競須新事。牽攣補衲。蠹文已甚。」斯言為能中當時後世好新之弊。勰之言曰。「沈吟鋪辭。莫先於骨。故辭之待骨。如體之樹骸。」斯言為能探得本原。此二語外。兩人亦無所能為論也。他如湯惠休「初日芙蓉」。沈約「彈丸脫手」之言。差可引伸。然俱屬一斑之見。終非大家體段。其餘皆影響附和。沈淪習氣。不足道也。唐宋以來。諸評詩者。或概論風氣。或指論一人。一篇一語。單辭複句。不可殫數。其間有合有離。有得有失。如皎然曰。「作者須知復變。若惟復不變。則陷於相似。置古集中。視之眩目。何異宋人以燕石為璞。」劉禹錫曰。「工生於才。達生於識。二者相為用。而詩道備。」李德裕曰。「譬如日月。終古常見。而光景常新。」皮日休曰。「才猶天地之氣。分為四時。景色各異。人之才變。豈異於是。」以上數則語。足以啟蒙砭俗。異於諸家悠悠之論。而合於詩人之旨為得之。其餘非戾則腐。如聾如瞶不少。而最厭於聽聞。錮蔽學者耳目心思者。則嚴羽高棅劉辰翁及李攀龍諸人是也。羽之言曰。「學詩者以識為主。入門須正。立意須高。以漢魏晉盛唐為師。不作開元天寶以下人物。若自退屈。即有下劣詩魔。入其肺腑。」夫羽言學詩須識是矣。既有識。則當以漢魏六朝全唐及宋之詩。悉陳於前。彼必自能知所決擇。知所依歸。所謂信手拈來。無不是道。若云漢魏盛唐。則五尺童子三家村塾師之學詩者。亦熟於聽聞得於授受久矣。此如康莊之路。眾所羣趨。即瞽者亦能相隨而行。何待有識而方知乎。吾以為若無識。則一一步趨漢魏盛唐。而無處不是詩魔。苟有識。即不步趨漢魏盛唐。而詩魔悉是智慧。仍不害於漢魏

盛唐也。羽之言。何其謬戾而意且矛盾也。彼楏與辰翁之言。大率類是。而辰翁益覺愉恍
無切實處。詩道之不振。此三人與有過焉。至於明之論詩者無慮百十家。而李夢陽何景明
之徒。自以為得其正而實偏。得其中而實不及。大約不能遠出於前三人之窠臼。而李攀龍
益又甚焉。王世貞詩評甚多。雖祖述前人之口吻。而掇拾其皮毛。然間有大合處。如云。
「剽竊摹擬。詩之大病。割綴古語。痕迹宛然。斯醜已極。」是病也。莫甚於李攀龍。世
貞生平推重服膺攀龍。可謂極至。而此語切中攀龍之隱。昌言不諱。乃知當日之互為推重
者。徒以虛聲倡和。藉相倚以壓倒眾人。而此心之明。自不可掩耳。夫自湯惠休以「初日
芙蓉」擬謝詩。後世評詩者。祖其語意。動以某人之詩如某某。或人或神仙或事或動植
物。造為工麗之辭。而以某某人之詩。一一分而如之。泛而不附。縛而不切。未嘗會於
心。格於物。徒取以為談資。與某某之詩何與。明人遞習成風。其流愈盛。自以為兼總諸
家。而以要言評次之。不亦可哂乎。我故曰。歷來之評詩者。雜而無章。紛而不一。詩道
之不能常振於古今者。其以是故歟。

The reason poetry has been unable to rouse itself to some lasting vitality is
that the criticism of poetry, for its entire history, has been disorganized and
lacking in unity. The poetry of the Six Dynasties was largely caught up in the
close imitation of words and lines, and there was no talent who stood out as a
major poet. The books written on the criticism of poetry during that time,
such as the works of Chung Jung and Liu Hsieh, do not go beyond making a
few evaluative points and are incapable of sustaining an argument. Chung
Jung, however, did say one thing that hit dead center, concerning the love of
novelty that has been such a weakness both in that period and in later ages:
"Writers of recent times try to outdo one another in making novel references;
there is a sense of constant restriction and pieces patched together; this is a
great canker on literature."[22] And Liu Hsieh has some lines that enable a person to find the real source: "Nothing has priority over bone in disposing the
words (tz'u), as one intones them thoughtfully: the way in which the words
depend upon bone is like the way in which the skeleton is set in the human
form (t'i*)."[23] But beyond these two passages, neither critic offers anything
worth considering. Of other critics, there are a few phrases worth quoting,
such as T'ang Hui-hsiu's "lotus in the first frost"[24] or Shen Yüeh's "a shot
[with a sling] leaving the hand"; both, however, are ordinary points of view,
and not the formulations of major figures. Other than these the rest of the
critics of the period all say the same thing and are completely swallowed up by
conventional practice; they are not worth mentioning.

The various critics of poetry from the T'ang and Sung on have either given
general overviews of the question of manner (feng*-ch'i*), or they have
directed their discussion to a single poet. We can't go into every work and
statement, or every comment (given either as single or parallel predicates).
Among these some are apt, and some err; some get it just right, while others
miss the mark. The following examples are statements that set standards, with
the capacity to dispel confusion and heal uncouthness. They get it just right by

setting themselves apart from the vague remoteness of most critics and saying what is apt for the aims of the poets. Take for example Chiao-jan: "An author must understand recurrence and mutation; if there is recurrence without mutation, then the writer falls into the trap of being just like his precursor. But if this happens in the collected works of one of the older writers, it can dazzle the eye—a situation just like the story of the man of Sung who thought that an ordinary rock from the state of Yen was a fine piece of uncut jade." There is Liu Yü-hsi [772–842]: "Skill is born from talent, while attaining your ends comes from judgment. If the two are used to complement one another, then the way of poetry is complete." Another example from Li Tê-yü: "It is like the the sun and moon that have always appeared since the beginning of time, but whose light is always new." Yet another example comes from P'i Jih-hsiu [ca. 834–883]: "Talent is like the way in which the ch'i* of Heaven and Earth is divided into four seasons, each of whose scenes and colors is distinct; the mutations of human talent are no different from this." As for the rest, if they're not strident, then they offer academic commonplaces, and not a few seem deaf and dim-sighted. But the ones with the worst influence are those who try to block up the ears, eyes, and thoughts of a person trying to learn about poetry: here we have Yen Yü, Kao Ping [1350–1423], Liu Chen-weng, Li P'an-lung [1514–1570], and their ilk. Yen Yü writes, "Judgment is the dominant factor in the study of poetry. The beginning must be correct, and your mind must be set on the highest goals. Take for your teacher the poetry of the Han, Wei, and High T'ang; don't act the part of those after the K'ai-yüan and T'ien-pao reigns. If you retreat from this in the least, the vilest poetry demon will enter your breast." Now Yen Yü is quite correct when he says that judgment is an essential requisite in the study of poetry; but when someone has the capacity for judgment, all the poetry from the Han, Wei, Six Dynasties, T'ang, and Sung should be set before him, and he will always know what to choose from them and what to be drawn to: "trusting the hand to pick up the right thing" is always the best way. But this refrain of the "Han, Wei, and High T'ang" is already all too familiar to students of poetry like five-foot adolescents and schoolmasters from small villages, and it has been taught for far too long. This is like a highway thronged with crowds—even a blind man can travel on it simply by following others. There is no need to rely on independent judgment to understand it. It is my feeling that without independent judgment you will meet Yen Yü's "poetry demon" at every step of the way, even following the path of the Han, Wei, and High T'ang. However, if a person does have judgment and does not follow the path of the Han, Wei, and High T'ang, no matter how clever all the poetry demons that he meets on those paths, no harm will be done to the values of the Han, Wei, and High T'ang. Yen Yü's words are strident and misleading; and on top of that, his ideas (yi*) are fraught with problems. The writings of Kao Ping and Liu Chen-weng are pretty much the same, except we realize that Liu Chen-weng has parts that are even more vague and correspond even less to the facts. The excesses of these three critics have made their contribution to the present lifelessness of poetry.

By the Ming, there were well over a hundred theorists of poetry. The group around Li Meng-yang and Ho Ching-ming felt that they had really achieved the norm (cheng*), while in fact their work was skewed; they thought they had found a central position, but they had not. For the most part they did not escape far from the pitfalls into which the three critics previously discussed had fallen. Li P'an-lung was even worse. Wang Shih-chen [1526–1590] wrote a great deal of criticism on poetry; and even though he placed himself in the lineage of the other Ming archaist critics and made use of the external aspects of their work, we still find moments of supreme reasonableness here and there throughout his work. For example, Wang writes, "Plagiarism and imitation are major faults in poetry, and the ugliest thing of all is for a writer to patch together phrases from the older poets, leaving obvious traces." No one is more guilty of this than Li P'an-lung. All his life Wang Shih-chen paid the greatest deference and honor to Li P'an-lung; but in the lines above, he cuts right to the heart of Li P'an-lung's failings: these are clear words that don't flinch from the truth. This makes it clear that the statements of mutual admiration made in those days were only empty sounds sung in harmony; they let them overwhelm ordinary people through their mutual association. Even so Wang Shih-chen could not hide his clear understanding.

Ever since T'ang Hui-hsiu tried to catch the quality of Hsieh Ling-yün's poetry with the phrase "a lotus in first sunlight," critics of poetry in later generations have modeled their comments on the intent (yi*) of his phrase and often describe the poetry of a given writer through some comparison; they take something human or something pertaining to the gods and immortals or some event, animal, or plant, and then fashion it into an elegant phrase, apportioning each one as a metaphor for the work of a particular poet. These are quite arbitrary and never really match the poet in question; never do they coincide with our understanding of the poet nor do they give the true form (ko*) of their object; their only purpose is to provide material for literary chit-chat and have nothing to do with any given poem.

The habits and practice of the Ming critics became the general custom (feng*), and that tradition becomes increasingly widespread; their belief that they have covered all the major writers and that they have given an essential characterization and ranking for each merits only our contempt. It is for these reasons that I have said that the criticism of poetry, for its entire history, has been disorganized and lacking in unity; and that for this reason the way of poetry has been unable to rouse itself to some lasting vitality.

Glossary
of
Basic
Terms

The following glossary is very selective, treating primarily single character terms that are important or recur frequently in the texts treated or both. When these words appear in the translations and commentaries, a romanization with an asterisk (*) is given. Compound usages are often more important in the technical terminology of literary theory: when important compounds appear in the text and commentary, they may be given in romanization and sometimes will be discussed in the commentaries. While many compounds eventually achieved the status of independent words (rather than merely combining the semantic values of their constituent characters), it is important to know the semantic value of their components in order to understand their later meaning. The glossary below is mainly for these primary elements. The reader should keep in mind that the following descriptions only broadly sketch the range of these terms, which change through history and become more semantically determinate in any particular context.

chang 章: the second character in the compound *wen*-chang*, a "literary work," or collectively, "belles lettres." *Chang* has two primary semantic areas: 1) to make evident or manifest, and 2) a unit, stanza, paragraph, or section. Etymological attempts to explain the meaning of *chang* often make reference to the first of these semantic areas; the second, however, is usually the more important in its application to literary contexts. *Chang* is one term for a "stanza" in stanzaic poetry and is also the term for a "paragraph" in prose. In other cases, it is set in opposition to *chü* 句, a "line": *chang* the whole "unit" of which a *chü* is the part. Hence in later poetics, *chü-fa** is the "method for writing lines and couplets"; *chang-fa** is the way in which those parts go together to form a whole poem or work of prose. See especially *Wen-hsin tiao-lung*, "Its Source in the Way" and "Paragraph and Period."

cheng 正: "proper," "upright," "correct," "orthodox," "normative," or "the norm." One antonymn of *cheng* is *hsieh* 邪, "deviant," "warped," "immoral." This primary moral sense of *cheng** sometimes lingers in the background of its most common literary use, as the primordial standard or form against which mutation (*pien**) is measured. Thus, in the *Book of Songs*, there are the *cheng-Feng**, "the Airs proper," "the Airs in their primordial form," "the Airs of a moral society." The subsequent literary phase, according to the "Great Preface" to the *Book of Songs*, will be *pien**-*Feng**, the "mutated Airs," often carrying a strong sense of devolution. *Cheng* and *pien** come to be the most common terms with which to understand literary historical change. Eventually, in certain contexts, these two terms can be used to describe works written in the same period, in which case *cheng* is an ahistorical norm, and *pien** is a "variation on" or "deviation from" such norms. There is a long and idiosyncratic discussion of these terms in the supplementary translations of Yeh Hsieh's "Origins of Poetry."

chi 機: the "trigger" or firing mechanism of a crossbow, and by extension, any mechanism. *Chi* comes to have a rich range of meanings. Sometimes it is "the occasion," like Greek *kairos*, "the right moment." From the sense of "mechanism," *chi* often comes to refer to the presence of "motives" in human action, premeditation; thus to "forget motives," *wang-chi* 忘機 is to act unselfconsciously, without secret motives. One common way *chi* is used in literary theory is as the most subtle, incipient phase of a movement in a natural process; in this case it is best translated as "impulses" or, in the perception of *chi*, "intimations." *Chi* are faintly perceived, but through them one recognizes the ongoing and oncoming processes of Nature. In a somewhat different usage, derived from the sense of "mechanism," *chi* is a "loom," and as such plays a role in the common textile metaphor for poetry.

ch'i 氣: "breath," "air," "steam," "vapor," "humor," "pneuma," "vitality," sometimes translated as "material force" or "psychophysical stuff" (the romanization is generally given in the translations and commentary above). At its most crassly empirical level, the role of *ch'i* in literature and poetry is the breath that comes out when one intones a text; but such venting of *ch'i* is related to its primary function in Chinese physiology; it is a force in the body (coursing through the veins) as well as something appearing in the outer world. *Ch'i* has material (or pseudo-material) aspects, but it always carries other implications of "energy," "vitality," or "impelling force." In the philosophy of Chu Hsi, *ch'i* is the rarified, kinetic essence of matter, appearing in the world structured by some natural principle (*li**). Everyone has *ch'i* within them, but the functioning of *ch'i* is not directly subject to the will: it can only be "fostered" and "stored up." At times in critical writings, *ch'i* is spoken of as a unitary category (e.g., "there is *ch'i* in that"), though this usually means that a work has a strong or vigorous *ch'i*. Sometimes *ch'i* is spoken of in terms of various antithetical qualities, especially the distinction between "clear" *ch'i* and "turbid" or "sluggish" *ch'i*. At other times *ch'i* admits a full range of distinct qualities; for example, a "relaxed" *ch'i*, a "fierce" *ch'i*; in which case it is close to "manner." See especially Ts'ao P'i, "A Discourse on Literature." For a discussion see David Pollard, "*Ch'i* in Chinese Literary Theory," pp. 43–66.

chih 質: "content," "substance" in a piece of writing, as opposed to *wen**, "pattern." *Chih* is also used to characterize style, in which case it is something that is "plain," "direct," and treats the heart of the matter with a minimum of elaboration and ornament. *Chih* exists in the world and is usually not "content" in the sense of authorial intent or concept. Such authorial intent, *yi**, is a private apprehension or structuring of *chih*; *chih* are "the facts."

chih 志: "to be intent upon," "what is intently on the mind." The traditional etymological explanation of *chih* is "that to which the mind goes." It frequently has the political association of "ambition" or the moral sense of "values," "aims," or "goals." Often, however, in poetry *chih* is used in a broader sense of whatever is on the mind intensely and involuntarily. *Chih* is both some content in the mind and a subjective relation to that content. In the "Great Preface" to the *Book of Songs*, *chih* is the prearticulate correlative of a poem, which becomes a poem on becoming external in language. See discussion on pp. 40–41.

chih-yin 知音: literally, "the one who knows the tone," a person who can understand the true significance of a piece of poetry or music by knowing what was in the mind of the producer of the poem or piece of music. The term derives from a famous anecdote of which there are versions in the *Lieh-tzu* 列子 (see above p. 286) and in the *Lü-shih ch'un-ch'iu* 呂氏春秋; and the term was soon extended to mean an "understanding friend," someone who can grasp a person's true nature from various kinds of external evidence. In the *Wen-hsin tiao-lung* the term is used to describe the "critic" or "ideal reader" of a literary work.

ching 景: "scene," a particular scene of the outer world. It often means a scene perceived from a particular place at a particular time, thus implicating the "point of view" of a subject; but it is also often used as broadly and loosely as the English "scene." While a *ching* implicitly locates the perceiver, the term *ching* refers specifically to that aspect of the external world which is independent of a subjective attitude toward it; in this case, it is taken as the complementary antithesis of *ch'ing**, the "affections." Nevertheless, it is often said that every scene, *ching*, implies a particular disposition of the affections, *ch'ing**, towards it. See especially Wang Fu-chih, "Discussions to While Away the Days at Evening Hall." For a discussion see Siu-kit Wong, "*Ch'ing* and *Ching* in the Critical Writings of Wang Fu-chih," pp. 121–150.

ching 境: "world," a term often interchangeable with *ching**, "scene." When a distinction is present, *ching*, "world," tends to be used to emphasize a coherent whole, in contrast to *ching**, "scene" (q.v.), which stresses the particular configuration of the world. In late classical criticism the term *ching* is used in the compound *ching-chieh* 境界, a composite impression of coherence in the presented world evoked by a particular poem or by a collection of poems.

ch'ing 情: the "affections," "emotions," "subjective disposition," "circumstance." This is an exceedingly broad term, often compounded to produce a more restrictive meaning. In some uses, *ch'ing* refers to that aspect of the

affections which would be rendered in English as the "passions." *Wu-ch'ing*
無情, "no passions," "no affections," can refer either to "heartlessness" (in a
romantic situation) or to a dispassionate coolness, in which no subjective
coloring intrudes upon perception. In the compound *ch'ing-hsü* 情緒, it refers
to "feelings" stirred by some particular object or experience. Generally, *ch'ing*
is a much broader term than "emotion" or "passion." In speaking of a line, a
couplet, or a whole poem, *ch'ing* refers to a subjective coloring in a statement or description; or it refers to cases in which a state of mind (or an
action implicating a state of mind) is the topic of discourse. In other cases,
ch'ing refers to the subjectivity or "subjective nature" of a particular person;
in this sense *ch'ing* is very close to *hsing**, "individuating nature," with
which it has been etymologically associated. In addition to being 1) a particular "subjective state" bound to a particular circumstance, and 2) the "subjective disposition" of a particular person, *ch'ing* is also the general category of
"subjectivity," or the human "affections" in general. *Ch'ing* is commonly
used in antithesis to *ching**, "scene." Yeh Hsieh's "Origins of Poetry" draws
on yet another usage of this term, as "circumstance" or the "circumstantial
quality" of external things. For a full discussion, see Siu-kit Wong, "*Ch'ing* in
Chinese Literary Criticism."

ch'ü 趣: "interest," "excitement," some elusive liveliness in poetry, or immediate appeal. Sometimes translated as "flair."

fa 法: "rule," "regulation," "method," also the Chinese term for "law." The term
fa became particularly important in criticism of the Sung dynasty and afterward as "productive method," the "rules" to be observed in composition.
There are general "rules" for writing, and each poet and each kind of poetry
(everything that has a *t'i**) has his, her, or its own *fa*. Tu Fu, for example, is
seen as having his own *fa* and, on a more restrictive scale, his own *fa* for
writing heptasyllabic regulated verse. Although the attention to *fa* was in
some degree simply interpretive, enabling a student to see why Tu Fu wrote
as he did, *fa* was ultimately understood primarily in a productive sense, prom-
ising to enable a later writer who grasped Tu Fu's *fa* to write as Tu Fu did. *Fa*
was a term of common parlance in poetic pedagogy, and most critics used it
unreflectively. In "The Origins of Poetry," however, Yeh Hsieh reinterprets
this term as "organic rule," bound to the particularity of a given poem and
observable only in its particular working out in a given case; in other words,
fa can be observed in a poem and considered necessary, but it cannot be used
as a productive means of future composition.

feng 風: "wind." This is a difficult term with many overlapping semantic areas.
In a generic frame of reference, *feng* can mean "airs" or "songs," following
from its use as a section title in the *Book of Songs*, where *feng* is the short
term for the *Kuo-feng* 國風, the "Airs of the States." In later critical terminology, *feng* is often used to describe poems that are in some way (manner, form,
or presumed intent) like the poems of the *Kuo-feng*. *Feng-Ya**, "Airs and
Odes," is one way to refer to the tradition of poetry in general. *Feng* is sometimes understood as *feng* 諷, meaning to "criticize": the assumption of some
kind of covert social or political critical intent often occurs with the use of the
present term *feng**. Through a commonly used metaphor of grasses bending
in the "wind" (and through the power of *feng* to bring about social change),

feng often carried the sense of "influence" or "affective capacity." When writers speak of the "lingering *feng* of the ancient poets," the reference is both to the survival of the ancient poetry and to its literary or cultural influence. *Ch'i**, "breath," may infuse a poem; but when it is set in motion outward and stirs others, it is "wind," *feng*. When used as a descriptive category, as in the "Wind and Bone" chapter of the *Wen-hsin tiao-lung*, it is some animating force in the text directed outward, the text's capacity to "move" and "move others." See discussion in Donald Gibbs, "Notes on the Wind: The Term '*Feng*' in Chinese Literary Criticism," pp. 285–293.

hsiang 象: "image," the normative visual schematization of a thing or of the embodiment of an idea (such as a phase of change, a hexagram in the *Book of Changes*) in such a schematization. According to the neo-Taoist philosopher Wang Pi 王弼 (226–249), writing in reference to the "Images" section of the *Book of Changes*, *hsiang* is that which necessarily mediates between concepts (*yi**) and language. *Hsiang* is neither the particular thing (though it may be perceived as immanent in particular things) nor the "idea" of a thing, but rather a sensuous schematization of the normative thing. In literary usage, beginning in the Southern Dynasties, *hsiang* becomes strongly associated with "appearances"; and thus the term is sometimes used imprecisely to refer simply to the phenomenal world; for instance, *hsiang-wai* 象外, "beyond *hsiang*," means simply "outside of the sensuous world"; and *wan-hsiang* 萬象, "the myriad images," refers simply to all the phenomena of the sensuous world.

hsin 心: "heart," "mind," the seat of consciousness and of both affective and ratiocinative capacities. *Hsin* is often said to be only a "speck," literally a "square inch," *fang-ts'un* 方寸.

hsing 興: "stir," (sometimes given in romanization in the translations). The use of *hsing* spans the distinction between "stirring," *kan**, and "response," *ying**: something in the outer world may *hsing* a person, and what then occurs in the person is also *hsing*. *Hsing* may be used to refer to the response to a poem; and a poem may be used to *hsing*, to elicit a response from readers. In the tradition of interpretation that grew up around the *Book of Songs*, *hsing* refers to an "affective image" which will elicit a particular response from the reader. Although it is often possible to uncover some underlying metaphorical relation in this process, traditional critics understood *hsing* as being distinct from metaphor: in contrast to "metaphor" or "comparison," *pi**, the relation between *hsing* and its affect must be hidden. Rather than serving as a referential "sign," *hsing* is a relation of process between the image and the emotion (*ch'ing**) stirred. For this reason, *hsing* may properly be linked to T.S. Eliot's notion of an "objective correlative." *Hsing* is also used as a categorical classification in the *Book of Songs*, grouping those poems in which the use of *hsing* is dominant. See especially *Wen-hsin tiao-lung*, "Comparison and Affective Image." For a further discussion of how *hsing* is used in the *Book of Songs*, see Pauline Yu, *The Reading of Imagery in the Chinese Tradition*, pp. 57–65.

hsing 性: "individuating nature," the innate characteristics that distinguish an individual or a class of individuals from others. One may speak of *hsing* as a general concept; one may speak of "human *hsing*" ("human nature"); one may speak of a particular *hsing* belonging to a personality type; a person may speak of his own *hsing* as fully individuated (though its description may be in terms of a normative type). *Hsing* can always be translated as "nature," though the English term "nature" is much broader and encompasses several quite distinct semantic areas in Chinese, only one of which is *hsing*. See especially *Wen-hsin tiao-lung*, "Nature and Form."

hsü 虛: "empty," "plastic." The antonymn of *hsü* is *shih**, "solid." In addition to the meaning of "empty" in the common English sense, *hsü* means "plastic," in the sense of something that takes the form of whatever "solid" it encounters or which contains it, as water or air does. In poetics *hsü* is the attribute of *ch'ing**, the "affections" (which, in "investing" themselves in certain things of the world, take the shape of those things as water might fill a container). *Hsü* is used to characterize certain kinds of lines and passages, those marked with subjectivity. Such "empty" lines are often those which contain *hsü-tzu* 虛字, "empty words," grammatical particles that mark the mediation of a human consciousness in a statement and thus give it a subjective coloring. For instance, the use of *yi*, "already," implies a sense of human time comparison and anticipation that will make the line normally "empty." See especially Chou Pi, "Poetry in Three Forms," prefaces. Paradoxically, in certain compounds such as *ch'ing-hsü* 清虛, "clear and empty," *hsü* may refer to a quality of dispassion and artistic distance.

hua 化: "transform," one of the many words of "change" in Chinese. *Hua* is often used transitively or with transitive implications; and it is sometimes used in a political and ethical sense to refer to the Sage's or ruler's "educating" and "civilizing" the people (or even the natural world).

kan 感: "stir," used both transitively as "to stir something" and passively "to be stirred." The passive is the most common use in poetics. *Kan* is the affect of an encounter, often resulting from some natural bond or sympathetic resonance between the subject and whatever is encountered. It is important to distinguish *kan*, the receptive aspect of an encounter, from *ying**, the "response" to being stirred. Joined as a sequential compound, *kan-ying*, the two terms describe the essential process by which poetry occurs as a response to an experience of the world. For a discussion, see Munakata Kiyohiko, "Concepts of *Lei* and *Kan-lei* in Early Chinese Art Theory," pp. 105–131.

ko 格: *Ko* has two primary senses, one having to do with manner, the other with structure. In the first sense of "manner," "mode," or "style," *ko* unites "character" and general "manner," some integral of characteristics that marks the identity of a person or type in poetry and thus is very close to "style" in one of its English meanings. One can speak of a poet or poem as having one particular quality of *ko* (*ko* being a common category in taxonomies); one can also use the term more generally (something can "have *ko*"). In the second sense of "a pattern of formal structure" or a "fixed form," *ko* is used in technical poetics in the context of adherence to normative models and verse forms.

ku 骨: "bone." One may speak of the distinct qualities of "bone" in any text; or a text may be spoken of as possessing or lacking "bone." *Ku* may be the articulation of structural segments in what would be called in English the "argument" of a text. It is important, however, to distinguish this from the notion of a static and rigid structure: *ku* allows for animation and change in a text on the model of the skeleton in the body. "Possessing bone" suggests a hardness and spareness of style, with a terse and forceful argument. "Lacking bone" suggests a puffiness, lacking a sense of purpose, force, and direction. See especially *Wen-hsin tiao-lung*, "Wind and Bone."

lei 類: "category," "categorical analogy." In Chinese *lei* means that a set of things belong to the same category or inherently share certain properties. In English that relation will often seem to be an "analogy"; that is, since the Western tradition does not see the two terms as belonging to the same class, the fact that they share certain properties will make the relation between them seem merely analogical. It is important to keep this in mind when considering the use of *lei*, and to remember that in Chinese a natural relation is asserted, even if in English that relation seems merely analogical, a speculative or literary association. For a discussion, see Munakata Kiyohiko, "Concepts of *Lei* and *Kan-lei* in Early Chinese Art Theory," pp. 105–131.

li 理: "principle" or "natural principle." *Li* is a central term in Chinese philosophy, and its precise significance at various periods is a matter of dispute. To describe it in a general way for our purposes, *li* is the underlying principle of both synchronic and diachronic structuring in the world; that is, *li* is both the principle of "how things go" as well as of "how they are." *Li* is sometimes spoken of in a unitary sense: a unified *li* that pervades all things. At other times, *li* is spoken of as individuated by category, each thing or category of event having its own *li*. *Li* is immanent in the phenomenal world, knowable in experience and in poems growing out of experience. Thus, in poetry, *li* is sometimes the counterpart of "meaning" as a motive in writing (conveying *li*) and as an end of the epistemological process in reading. It should, however, be stressed that "reading for meaning" is less a part of Chinese reading theory than Western.

li 麗: "beautiful," closely related to *li* 儷, meaning "paired" or "parallel." An allied term is *mei* 美. While *li* as "beauty" and *mei* are spoken of in regard to literature, they are by no means of primary importance, and the English reader should be careful not to invest their appearance with the complex history of "beauty" in Western aesthetics. Although *li* is often given as the determinative quality of poetry and poetic exposition, this is a sensuous beauty and allure rather than an aesthetic beauty of form.

miao 妙: "fine," "subtle," "fine points." Etymologically *miao* is associated with a group of similarly pronounced words involving squinting and seeing what is barely perceptible, either by reason of distance or size. As an aesthetic term, *miao* is an excellence in capturing the details, transferred to subtle evidences of natural process or human mood. Much as in the history of the English term "fine," in late classical criticism *miao* comes to be commonly used as a general term of approbation, though in compounds it often retains its more precise sense.

pi 比: "comparison," "simile," literally "apposition." This is the word we would like to mean "metaphor"; but *pi* is much more restricted in its scope than "metaphor" in its modern usage, and it is of far less importance in the Chinese tradition than "metaphor" is in the Western tradition, both ancient and modern. *Pi* applies primarily to similes, usually in the comparison of nouns. *Pi* and its cognates are also used with *yü* 喻 to describe the process of "allegorical reference" or "topical reference," that is, indirect reference to some political or personal situation. In the *Wen-hsin tiao-lung*, Liu Hsieh distinguishes *hsing** from *pi* on the grounds that the operations of *hsing**, "affective image," are covert and based in *ch'ing**, while the operation of *pi* is overt and based in "natural principle" (*li**).

pien 變: "Mutation," one of the many terms for "change." *Pien* often implies that there has been some norm or primary state which has undergone a change, a "mutation." Unlike "variation," which implies multiple changes around a single norm, *pien* implies serial stages that move ever farther away from the norm or primary state. Like English "mutation," *pien* is a process of change understood in relation to a norm or primary state. Despite the awkwardness and occasional ludicrousness due to the associations of the English term "mutation," I have retained this translation in hopes that the reader will keep in mind the specific kind of change that the word often denotes, especially used as a technical term in literary theory. Sometimes *pien* carries the negative connotation of "devolving." See *cheng**.

shen 神: "Spirit" or "divinity." Originally this term applied to the "gods," but it was early transferred to the incorporeal aspect of the human, the "spirit." Acts of imagination were generally understood as the movement of *shen*; a rich or fantastic "imagination" loosely corresponds to *shen* "moving to remote distances." In later poetics *shen* is used to describe a magical domain in aesthetic experience that eludes analytic comprehension, as in *ju-shen* 入神, "to enter [the realm of] spirit," "divinity," a term originally used in the *Hsi-tz'u chuan* of the *Book of Changes*, and given as the highest poetic value in Yen Yü's "Ts'ang-lang's Remarks on Poetry." See also *Wen-hsin tiao-lung*, "Spirit Thought."

shih 實: "solid," "actual." Sometimes used in opposition to *hsü*, *shih* refers to the fixity of definite form (as opposed to the "plasticity" of *hsü**) and to the external solidity of a *ching**, "scene" (as opposed to the "empty" emotional coloring of the scene). A line is *shih* if it describes external things and has no "empty" words that subordinate the description to the way the subject feels about it or interprets it. To give an example of an early usage, Liu Hsieh writes in the *Wen-hsin tiao-lung*: "The force of one's talent is located within and begins with *ch'i** in the blood; *ch'i** 'solidifies' (*shih*) intent (*chih**)". That is, initially *chih** is "empty," the mere form of an intense relation between the self and some project or goal; that empty form is filled by "material force," *ch'i**, and becomes "solid," *shih*; only through this process can *chih** become definite, forceful, and actual. See especially Chou Pi, "Poetry in Three Forms," prefaces.

shih 勢: "inertial form," "momentum," "force," "vector," "natural bent." In one sense *shih* is used to refer to political power, based not on moral force but on the power to intimidate. This basic meaning of "force" comes to be extended to a wide range of usages. The term was an important one in military theory to describe the dynamics of battle. *Shih* can also be the shape or stance of something with an implicit energy or "line of force": a mountain, for example, may be said to have a *shih* that "thrusts upward" into the sky or "presses down" upon a river. We may decide upon reflection that such qualities finally depend upon the perceiver's interpretation of the scene, but this reflective truth is less important than the fact that the *shih* of something presents itself to a perceiver immediately, as if it inhered in the thing or scene itself. Before its appearance in literary theory, *shih* is an important term in calligraphic theory, brush strokes seeming to have inherent "inertial forms" or "lines of force." *Shih* may be "natural bent," insofar as its "force" is the inherent disposition of a thing interacting with its circumstances. *Shih* may be the directionality of a complete movement (e.g., the flight of an arrow), or it may be the directional force that inheres in a form at any moment in the process of movement (i.e., the arrow at some point mid-flight). Thus in some cases in literary texts, *shih* is a kinetic "manner," the way a particular form (*t'i**) naturally unfolds. In other cases *shih* refers to a quality of movement within the text that would be described in English as "structure" (though it is important to remember that here it would be conceived as a quality of movement rather than a hypostatized set of relations). See especially *Wen-hsin tiao-lung,* "Determination of Momentum."

shih 事: "event," "occurrence," "matter." In technical poetics, "to use an event," *yung-shih* 用事, simply means to make a reference to some story, historical event, or position taken by an earlier writer (and should be distinguished from textual allusion). In some theoretical discussions, however, particularly in Yeh Hsieh's "Origins of Poetry," *shih* is used in a broader and more philosophical sense. In Yeh Hsieh, *shih* is the particular "occurring" of something in the outer world (as opposed to *li**, the general "principle"), which contributes to the determination of the *fa**, the necessary "rule," of a poem.

shu 數: literally "number," used in the *Wen-hsin tiao-lung* as something like "order" or "principle," that is, as that level of distinction (division into enumerated categories) that admits no further significant division.

se 色: "color" or "visage." *Se* is the visual aspect of something independent of its form, although it may be a way to describe shape without resorting to delineated form. Liu Hsieh, for example, says that *se* (and not visible forms) are the medium of painting, suggesting an aggregation of boundariless color areas as in some Expressionist painting. *Se* is also the alluring surface of the things of the world and has strong associations of sensuousness, even of sensuality: to "love *se*," *hao-se* 好色, is the classical phrase for sexual lust. *Se* plays a somewhat different role in the fabric metaphors used to describe poetry. *Pen-se* 本色, "original color," is the native appearance of something: each genre, period, and poet has a *pen-se*, qualities that are inherent in it/him/her and proper to it/him/her. The *pen-se* admits development, but it can be destroyed if excessive or inappropriate other "colors" are added to it. The use of dyes is here the master metaphor: blue added to red gives purple; but if yellow, green, brown, and grey are added, the original color is lost in muddiness. In the same way, the original qualities of a genre, period, or person can be changed or enhanced, but only to a limited degree. See especially *Wen-hsin tiao-lung,* "The Sensuous Colors of Physical Things."

ssu 思: "thought" or more properly "thinking," often with the implication of "longing" or "desire." *Ssu* is distinct from ratiocination; it is the capacity or activity of mind in general, never separated from the emotions. It is rarely hypostatized as "a thought," in the sense of "having a thought."

tao 道: the "Way." The concept of *tao* is as elusive as it is pervasive, and its role in Chinese thought is too large to attempt a full explanation here. There is a Confucian "Way," a Taoist "Way," a Buddhist "Way," a "way" of poetry, "ways" for almost every kind of human activity. It should be stressed that a "way" is not a body of thought, beliefs, or rules, but a course to be followed or which things follow of themselves: insofar as a "way" exists, it exists in potential or actual enactment.

tê 德: "inner power," "virtue". *Tê* is a difficult term, traditionally taken as cognate with another *tê* 得, "to attain." *Tê* is the power, often the moral power, which a person or entity has within, a power that enables that person or entity spontaneously to move or influence other people or the outer world. Liu Hsieh speaks of the *tê* of *wen**: this is the inherent power of *wen** by which it becomes manifest in the world.

t'i 體: "normative form," "embodiment," "body." *T'i* is the word one would use to speak of "the human body," but not the word normally used to speak of a particular person's body (unless speaking of it in terms of the norm). A particular *hsing**, "individuating nature," becomes manifest in a corresponding *t'i*. *T'i* is a very common term in Chinese literary thought, but it crosses several distinctions that seem necessary in Western literary thought, while at the same time making other distinctions that do not exist in the Western tradition. It may be a "genre": poetry, memorials to the throne, letters, and so forth are all distinct *t'i*. "Subgenres" based on thematic or occasional classifications are also *t'i*: for instance, parting poems, banquet poems, and autumn meditations. *T'i* may refer to particular verse forms within a large generic classification, crossing many subgenres and occuring on various levels: regulated verse as a whole, as well as its subdivisions like pentasyllabic or heptasyllabic regulated verse are all *t'i*. For all such usages, the wide and ambiguous word "genre" will serve as an adequate translation; but *t'i* also covers one aspect of the word "style." *T'i* has the sense of a normative style, as when we speak of an "archaic style" or an "exotic style." It does not describe "the style of *this* poem" (although it can identify a categorical, normative style that appears in an individual poem). As a normative style rather than particular stylistic usage, *t'i* is the term used for an author's overall style and for a period style. Finally, *t'i* also applies to normative manners of behavior and personality types ("the type of person he is"). In short, *t'i* is a "normative form," and its importance as a concept bespeaks the interest in identifying what is normative within particulars. Distinctions between genre, subgenre, and style *can* be made by context and by compounds that use *t'i*; but used alone, the word does not make such distinctions. See especially *Wen-hsin tiao-lung*, "Nature and Form."

ts'ai 彩: "coloration," the bright, variegated pattern that seems to be part of the affect of a text, something like "rhetorical flourish," without the pejorative and manipulative associations that attend upon most modern uses of the term "rhetoric." In the standard oppositions between inner and outer qualities, *ts'ai* is a supremely outward quality, a sensuous allure and affective capacity. *Ts'ai* is distinct from the affective power of *feng** in that *ts'ai* has no connotations of moral purposiveness or communication of feeling. See especially *Wen-hsin tiao-lung*, "The Affections and Coloration."

ts'ai 才: "talent," an endowed capacity, essentially identical with another graph *ts'ai* 材, "timber" or "material." In most cases *ts'ai* is spoken of as quantitative, and each person has a fixed amount. In Yeh Hsieh's "Origins of Poetry," however, the anomalous possibility is raised of increasing one's *ts'ai*. See especially the discussion of *ts'ai* in "Ts'ang-lang's Remarks on Poetry."

tsao-hua 造化: "Creation," sometimes freely personified as a "Creator." Because of what the term "creation" has come to mean in the Western tradition, it is perhaps an improper translation: *tsao-hua* is not a purely voluntary making from some prior intent, but rather the initiation and continuous carrying out of structured change in the world. Although *tsao-hua* is many times spoken of in regard to origins, it is continuous and ongoing. "Creation" in the Western sense has been completed; if *tsao-hua* ceased—and there is no eschatology that admits that possibility—the world would simply stop. An analogy between poets or poetry and *tsao-hua* resembles the now dead Western metaphor of literary "creation" and divine creation in its link between literature and cosmogony/cosmology; but the differences between Chinese and Western cosmology are such that the Chinese application of *tsao-hua* to literature means something quite different. It should be added that even though the association of poetry and *tsao-hua* eventually became commonplace, it never became a dead metaphor as the idea of "creation" has.

t'ung 通: "continuous passage through to some point," "continuity," "communicate," "comprehend" (both in the sense of to "include all" and in the sense "understand"), to "make understood." *T'ung* refers to something passing from one stage, position, or time to another. In many cases, *t'ung* is used in opposition to the concept of "blockage." In other cases, as in Liu Hsieh's discussion, *t'ung* means "continuity," and is used in opposition to "mutation," *pien**, to describe the way certain aspects of a literature show continuity through time. See especially *Wen-hsin tiao-lung*, "Continuity and Mutation."

tzu-jan 自然: one of the words commonly translated as "Nature." The most literal translation of *tzu-jan* is "so-of-itself": things being the way they are and events occurring the way they do because that happens to be the way they are or the way they occur. Distinguish *hsing**, "individuating nature," the endowed disposition or nature of a particular entity. A particular *hsing** will follow a certain process of development and will assume certain characteristics according to *tzu-jan*, the larger principle.

tz'u 辭: one of the many words used for "language." Most of the Chinese terms for language are used imprecisely and in overlapping senses, though each has a slightly different center of gravity. *Tz'u* tends to be the external, determinate form of an utterance, translated in various contexts as "diction," "phrasing," or simply "utterance." *Tz'u* sometimes carries the sense of "rhetorical quality," a floridity that aids or endangers the communication (*t'ung**) of basic substance.

wei 味: "flavor," an important master metaphor in describing the aesthetic experience of the text. A complex set of gustatory terms was generated around *wei*. There were several sources of *wei*'s appeal to theorists: it admitted broad shared categories that are held in common (e.g., "salty" or "sour"), while permitting both the cultivation and absolute particularity of individual taste. Another attraction of *wei* is that it lingers after eating, as the *wei* of texts endures, changes, and attenuates after reading. Chinese theorists tended not to speak of disjunctive acts of reflection on the "meaning" of a text, but rather of the "continuation" of the text in the mind after reading is over, a time in which the significance of the text gradually unfolds. See especially Ssu-k'ung T'u, "Letter to Mr Li," pp. 356–357 above.

wen 文: "pattern," "literature," "the written word." *Wen* originally referred to the "pattern" on a piece of jade and was early extended to mean pattern in general. *Wen* is the term for "culture," "refinement," "learning," the "civil" aspect of the state as opposed to the military. "Heaven's *wen*" means "astronomy or astrology"; "Earth's *wen*" means "topography"; in this set, "human *wen*" is "literature," or in a more extended sense, "culture." *Wen* is sometimes simply the written word. In the fifth century, *wen* becomes distinguished from non-literary prose ("non-literary" in a Chinese sense, certainly not in a Western sense); and sometimes *wen* is the term for "prose," as distinguished from poetry. In the common organic tree metaphor for literature, *wen* is the visible outward pattern of the leaves, which, observed carefully, reveals the hidden shape of the trunk and branches: *wen* is the organic external manifestation of some "substance" (*chih**) or "natural principle" (*li**) (e.g., growth or "treeing"). See especially Lu Chi, "The Poetic Exposition on Literature"; and *Wen-hsin tiao-lung*, "Its Origins in the Way."

wu 物: "thing," "phenomenon," and eventually "other" (as in Liu Yi-tsai's use of the term in identifying with another person). *Wu* varies in usage from an "animal" to a "physical thing" to any "object of consciousness." The term "object" is perhaps the English term with the closest semantic range (excluding the meaning of "animal").

ya 雅: "dignity," "elegant," "gracious." One of the major sectional divisions in the *Book of Songs*, the "Odes," translated by Ezra Pound as "elegentiae." As a stylistic category, *ya* suggests dignity, restraint, and a certain archaic quality (this latter quality affirming timelessness and the capacity of literature to transcend the fashions of the day). The antonymn of *ya* is *su* 俗: "mundane," "uncouth," "commonplace," "vulgar," "popular," "low."

yi 意: "concept," "idea," "meaning." *Yi* is perhaps the most difficult technical term of poetics to translate, because it crosses a wide variety of quite distinct English concepts in unexpected ways. *Yi* has a wide range of usage, ranging from the clever interpretation of some material (much like the late-Renaissance *concetto*), to the "general case" (a deduction from or ground for some particular observation), all the way to "import" and "significance." *Yi* is usually spoken of as occurring in the mind rather than in the world. It is often the act of giving relation to the data of the senses. For instance, a poet may see blossoming flowers and feel a breeze: to derive from those two sensory facts the fall of the flowers at the end of spring and implications for things of the same category (*lei**) would be *yi*, an interpretive relation of sensory data. If articulated, the *yi* would be the general category deduced from the particular, such as "late spring." The poem, however, might simply mention the flowers and the breeze, and from that the reader would know the poet's putative *yi*. *Yi* is sometimes "intention" or "will," and in literary usage usually carries some element of intentionality. At other times, *yi* is very broadly used as "the way someone thinks of things." Related to this latter usage are compounds such as *ku-yi* 古意, "the ancient attitude," "on an ancient motif" (a poetic subgenre).

yi 義: "a truth," often a moral truth; "duty," "righteousness," "principles"; "significance," sometimes "meaning." This *yi* is often interchangeable with *yi**, "concept," with which it became homophonous during the Sung. *Yi* is "truth" in the sense of "a truth," and is applied primarily to humans and large universals rather than to things: a tree has its *li**, "natural principle," but there is both *li** and *yi* in the fact that water takes the shape of whatever vessel contains it. *Yi**, "concept," occurs primarily in mind; *yi*, "a truth," is recognized by mind but exists external to it. It is possible to speak of a poet's having *ch'i-yi* 奇意, "a strange concept"; but it is not possible to speak of a poet's articulating *ch'i-yi* 奇義, a "strange truth." Where this *yi* cannot be comfortably translated as "a truth," I have used various other translations, including "significance."

ying 應: "response." See *kan**.

yu 遊: "roam," "wander freely." Although this is not an important technical term, it recurs often in the discussion of literature. It is a verb of going without direction, for one's pleasure.

Notes

INTRODUCTION

1. The term *literary thought* is used here as the broadest possible term to encompass literary theory, poetics, and criticism, while placing literary taxonomies on the margins.

2. *Tzu*, translated here as the "literature of knowledge," was one of the four divisions of traditional Chinese bibliography, the others being Confucian Classics, history, and belles lettres.

3. The terminology of poetics is largely shared by the various languages of the European tradition. This is not to suggest that there are no historical and national differences; but such differences are comprehensible in terms of a history of classical origins and post-classical relations between national literatures; or those words are comprehensible in regard to shared questions from that common background. Though the local pride of various European "national literatures" makes the proponents of each quick to assert that no other literature has a word quite like X, the force of term X can easily be understood in reference to a shared set of questions or issues.

CHAPTER ONE

1. In Yen Yü's "Ts'ang-lang's Remarks on Poetry" the Chinese tradition eventually produced its own version of the "æsthetic," the experience of poetry as essentially separate from all ordinary experience. As we will see in the critique by Wang Fu-chih, however, such a view of poetry could provoke deep hostility.

2. The commentary tradition has taken this passage differently, interpreting *wen** as a "passage" and *tz'u** as the text as a whole. This yields a simple warning not to misunderstand the part by failing to take into account the whole context. Such an interpretation,

while eminently reasonable, ignores the tendency to describe language as a triadic structure of manifestation in many texts of the Confucian school.

3. See Ch'en Shih-hsiang, "In Search of the Beginnings of Chinese Literary Criticism," in *Semitic and Oriental Studies: A Volume Presented to William Popper on the Occasion of His Seventy-fifth Birthday.*

4. The term *chih* 志, translated here as "record," is usually taken to mean a written text.

5. I capitalize the word *images* when referring to the technical category of "Images" in the *Book of Changes*. This technical usage, however, easily blurs into the broader application of "images" in other kinds of language and in the world.

6. A good analogy might be made between a certain mode of Chinese exegesis and the "strict style" for developing a theme in Baroque music: a proposition is elaborated backwards and forwards, its parts filled out, to see what it will yield.

7. For the modern reader, these Images will seem to be mere cultural coding; that is, we see their significance as arbitrarily granted rather than inherently embodied in them (unless, of course, one is a Jungian). But for Wang Pi and others who knew and trusted in the *Book of Changes*, the Images did seem to embody the significance of the hexagrams inherently; and they reasonably assumed that such significance would be universally manifest through the Images. That assumption made the statement of the adequacy of the Image to give the fullness of concept *functionally* true and the modern description of "cultural coding" functionally untrue.

CHAPTER TWO

1. For a discussion of the complicated relation between the "Great Preface" and the "Lesser Prefaces," see Steven Van Zoeren, "Poetry and Personality: A Study of the Hermeneutics of the *Classic of Odes (Shijing)*," Ph.D. diss, Harvard, 1986.

2. For discussions of the tradition, see Van Zoeren, and Pauline Yu, *The Reading of Imagery in the Chinese Tradition* pp. 44–83.

3. The Chinese phrasing is tautological: *feng** is *feng**.

4. "The virtue of the superior person is wind; the virtue of the lesser person is grass; grass in the wind—it will surely bend down" (*Analects* XII.19).

5. It should be noted that this becomes particularly significant in the theory of the "Four Beginnings," *ssu-shih* 四始, an ideal order of the *Book of Songs* involving progress on four distinct levels carried out in the four major sections of the classic.

6. A complete bibliography of English discussions of the "Six Principles" can be found in John Timothy Wixted, "The *Kokinshū* Prefaces: Another Perspective," *Harvard Journal of Asiatic Studies* 43.1:228–229 (1983), footnote 30.

7. For a discussion of *fu*, see Dore J. Levy, "Constructing Sequences: Another Look at the Principle of *Fu* 賦 'Enumeration,'" in *Harvard Journal of Asiatic Studies* 46.2:471–494 (1986).

8. Classical rhetoricians in the West were quite aware of an affective rhetoric, the evocation of a mood for persuasive purposes, similar to the citation of the *Book of Songs* in Warring States oratory. Indian poetics also has a rather different rhetoric of moods. There is a similarity here in the project of moral education in the interpretation of the *Book of Songs*; i.e., language is intentionally "used" to produce a certain response. However, this intentional use of language to shape response largely disappeared from later Chinese poetic theory (with the exception of the theory of *Yüeh-fu*), which was primarily concerned with the involuntary manifestation of the poet in the poem.

9. The graph 樂 has two pronunciations: *lo* meaning "delight" and *yüeh* meaning "music." Hsün-tzu is playing on the visual tautology.

10. In the Chinese, "movement" is *tung-ching*: "movement and rest."

11. "Guided," *tao*, is here written with the same graph as the Way, Tao, and its semantic value in this context is closely related to that larger sense of "according with the Way."

12. "Dissolution" here is *liu*, literally "flow." The notion of things "flowing together," associated with "letting go" and sexual mingling, is the metaphorical danger that besets the Confucian desire to maintain proper distinctions.

13. It is unclear here whether *wen** refers to the verbal texts of the Odes and Hymns or the "patterning" that is given to sounds so that they become musical notes.

14. "Balancer," *ch'i*, is literally "equalizer," that which holds the relations between things in balance. It creates an instinctive sense of when to come forward and when to withdraw, etc., thus maintaining human relations and social relations "on an even keel."

15. Hsün-tzu here returns to the opening statement of the chapter in a new way. In the opening the graph 樂 was "delight," which is "inevitable" in human emotion. Here it is "music" and is something that "cannot be dispensed with" (the Chinese phrasing of "inevitable" and "cannot be dispensed with" is the same).

16. The reading *wen** here is an emendation.

17. The metaphor of liquefaction suggests promiscuous mingling, with overtones of dissolution.

18. *Ch'ing** is an emendation. The original text read *ching* 靜, "calm."

CHAPTER THREE

The text used is found in *chüan* 52 of the *Wen hsüan*.

1. Ts'ao P'i was very proud of the *Authoritative Discourses*; and after he became Emperor of the Wei, in the early 220s he sent copies to Sun Ch'üan, King of Wu, and to the southern literary man Chang Chao, who was Lu Chi's maternal grandfather. See Hayashida Shinnosuke, *Chūgoku chūsei bungaku hyōronshi*, p. 75. Ts'ao Jui, Ts'ao P'i's successor on the Wei throne even had the *Authoritative Discourses*, carved in stone.

2. "A Discourse on Literature" has neither the relatively tight form of a formal essay nor the looser arrangement of most chapters in the large collections of discourses classified as *tzu*, "the literature of knowledge." Its internal structure and the other extant fragments suggest that although it was only part of the original chapter, it was a continuous part.

3. The *Hsün-tzu* would be an early example of such a collection; the *Hsin-lun* 新論 of Huan T'an 桓譚 and the *Lun-heng* 論衡 of Wang Ch'ung 王充 are prominent Eastern Han examples. The *Chung-lun* 中論 of Hsü Kan, referred to at the end of Ts'ao P'i's "Discourse," was the immediate predecessor of the *Authoritative Discourses* and probably Ts'ao P'i's primary model.

4. Fu Yi, writer of prose and *fu*, and Pan Ku, historian and writer, were perhaps the most eminent literary men of the second half of the first century. It is not clear whether the "relation of a younger brother (literally 'middle brother,' implying the existence of others still younger) to an elder brother" refers to a personal friendship or comparison of quality. It is also unclear whether or not some degree of precedence might be implied in the pairing. If it is a comparison of quality, the sequence may suggest, contrary to all later opinion, that Fu Yi was the superior.

5. Chang Huai-chin, *Wen fu yi-chu*, p. 58, interprets the *hsiu* 休 here as "be excellent": thus "he couldn't do a very good job." This makes the point clearer, but violates the common usage of *tzu-hsiu* 自休. Furthermore, Fu Yi's being "unable to stop himself" in writing seems to lead into the next paragraph, with reflection on the motives for such compulsive writing: "people are fond of making themselves known."

6. Some scholars have seen such lines as being directed against Ts'ao P'i's talented younger brother, Ts'ao Chih, with whom Ts'ao P'i felt no little political and literary competitiveness. Ts'ao Chih, as one literary man "belittling" another, was supposed to have mocked Ts'ao P'i's friend Ch'en Lin with the proverb, "A painted tiger cannot go back to being just a dog." See Wang Meng-ou, "Ts'ao P'i Tien-lun lun-wen so-yin," in his *Ku-tien wen-hsüeh lun t'an-so*, p. 62.

7. One finds this model of comprehensive versus partial excellence in early comments on Tu Fu. The movement from comprehensive to partial often appears as a lineage, as in the commonplace that Han Yü united "uprightness" 正 and "strangeness" 奇: of Han's two prose disciples, Li Ao was said to have inherited the "uprightness" but not the strangeness, while Huang-fu Shih inherited the "strangeness" but not the "uprightness." Another variation on such a classification scheme can be seen in the fragmentary *Shih-jen chu-k'o t'u* 詩人主客圖 by Chang Wei 張為 of the late T'ang or Five Dynasties. The first category in this work is a mode of comprehensiveness: *kuang-ta chiao-hua* 廣大教化, within which there

are quantitative degrees of attainment; following the comprehensive category is a series of limited modal categories, each with its own hierarchy of attainment.

8. There is a problem here in the double use of 自見. In the first case, it is clearly *tzu-hsien*, "to make oneself known," as in the passage from the biography of Yü Ch'ing. In the second case, it is *tzu-chien*, "to be self-aware," literally "to see oneself."

9. Literally, "they gallop Yi's and Lu's," the names of two famous steeds of antiquity.

10. *Chün-tzu* 君子, the Confucian "gentleman" or "superior man," originally meant a "lord's son," a "prince." Ts'ao P'i, a *chün-tzu* in the archaic and literal sense, aspires to the role of *chün-tzu* in the Confucian sense.

11. The phrase *ch'i-ch'i* 齊氣 has been the subject of considerable debate. As Li Shan explained it in his commentary to the *Wen hsüan*: "The customary literary style (*wen*-*t'i*) of the Ch'i region is slow and relaxed; this problem appears in Hsü Kan's writing." The Wu-ch'en commentary to the *Wen hsüan* follows Li Shan. Following this interpretation, we translate the sentence: "Hsü Kan has the *ch'i* characteristic of the region of Ch'i; nevertheless he is Ts'an's equal." Modern scholars have shown considerable dissatisfaction with this interpretation and have proposed alternative suggestions, such as "a lofty *ch'i*" and "a proper *ch'i*." On p. 75 of "Shih-lun Ts'ao P'i tsen-yang fa-chien wen-ch'i," in his *Ku-tien wen-hsüeh lun t'an-so*, Wang Meng-ou argues for a similar interpretation, identifying *ch'i* and *chai* 齊. The problem with both these interpretations lies in the *jan* 然 that introduces the apodosis: *jan* should mean "nevertheless," thus suggesting that *ch'i-ch'i* is a negative characteristic. It was no doubt this presumption that led Li Shan to his forced interpretation. I have loosely followed the Li Shan version; but my own opinion is that *ch'i-ch'i* simply means "equal in *ch'i*," i.e., Wang Ts'an's equal. In addition to the beauty of simplicity, this interpretation is favored by the use of *ch'i-tsu* 齊足 earlier in the "Discourse" and by *yin-ch'i* pu ch'i 引氣不齊 later. This interpretation would but weight on the *shih* 時, "at times," leading to the translation "even though Hsü Kan is only occasionally his equal in *ch'i*, still he is Wang Ts'an's match."

12. See the discussion of this principle in regard to "The Poetic Exposition on Literature," p. 75; and in regard to the "The Twenty-four Categories of Poetry," p. 308.

13. *T'i*-*ch'i* can be understood either as an additive compound, *t'i* and *ch'i*, as I have taken it; or *t'i* can modify *ch'i*: "the operation of *ch'i* in the form of his works."

14. It might be noted that later lists of forms (*t'i*), such as we find in Lu Chi, Liu Hsieh, and Yen Yü, tend to grow steadily longer—an ironic and tacit admission that fixed lists do not successfully stem the tendency to divergence.

15. For a discussion of these issues, see John Timothy Wixted, "The Nature of Evaluation in the *Shih-p'in* (Gradings of Poets) by Chung Hung (A.D. 469–518)," in Bush and Murck, eds., *Theories of the Arts in China*, pp. 225–264.

16. Many modern Chinese articles try to determine what kind of *ch'i* or what aspect of *ch'i* is meant here. It is not so much that they give the wrong answers as that they pose the wrong question. At this period *ch'i* had not yet acquired the many determinate and limited applications it was to develop later. Internal structural energy, affective energy, the force of talent, etc., as well as physical "breath," are all present in Ts'ao P'i's *ch'i*.

17. For a discussion of *ch'i*, see David Pollard, "*Ch'i* in Chinese Literary Theory," in Adele Rickett, ed., *Chinese Approaches to Literature from Confucius to Liang Ch'i-ch'ao*, pp. 43–66.

18. *Li Wen-jao wen-chi, wai* 3.4b, in SPTK.

19. See pp. 35–36. There is an intermediate version of this in the *New Discourses*, *Hsin-lun* 新論, of the Eastern Han writer Huan T'an 桓譚: "What is understood alone by one person's mind cannot be handed down from father to son and cannot be taught by an elder brother to a younger." *Ch'üan Hou-Han wen* 全後漢文 15.3a.

20. A similar passage on enduring fame, a passage also using *yeh*, can be found in Wang Ch'ung's *Lun-heng*, in the chapter "Explaining Writing," *Shu-chieh* 書解: "Outstanding men of the past have composed discourses, and by making use of their achievements (*yeh*), have become eminent in their own time. Ordinary educated men of an age may have been highly honored in their own time, but without the writings of the literary scholar, their traces were not handed down." *Lun-heng chi-chieh*, ch. 28, p. 562.

21. From Wang Ch'en's 王沈 *Wei shu* 魏書, cited in P'ei Sung-chih's 裴松之 commentary to the *Annals*, in the *San-kuo chih*, p. 88.

22. Of Hsü Kan, he says that his discourses are "the work of a fully realized writer," *ch'eng yi-chia yen* 成一家言, literally "constitute the words of one household." This is the metaphor of founding a new clan lineage, here done in words, with dependents and successors.

23. We note that of the two successful examples of devotion to writing and subsequent immortality, one was a ruler-to-be and the other, a "Lord Protector": in both Ts'ao P'i might find glorious antecedents for his own situation and that of his father.

CHAPTER FOUR

The text used is found in *chüan* 17 of the *Wen hsüan*.

1. It should be pointed out that there were many different kinds and traditions of the poetic exposition (*fu*) in Lu Chi's time, and some did deal with the local and the occasional experience.

2. For a summary of the dating argument, see Chang Shao-k'ang, *Wen fu chi-shih*, pp. 3–4.

3. Cf. *Shih chi* (Peking, 1964), p. 3314; *Han shu* (Hong Kong, 1970), p. 3509; the "little prefaces" to the *Shih-ching*, passim.

4. Both Fang T'ing-kuei 方廷珪 and Huang K'an 黃侃 take it roughly in this sense: Fang says it is "the intention (*yi**) of the writer"; Huang identifies it with "stating the affections (*ch'ing**)" later in the work. See *Wen fu chi-shih*, p. 2.

5. T'ang Ta-yüan 唐大圓 takes *ch'i ch'ing* as referring to *yung-hsin* in the other sense: "perceive their strenuous efforts." Fang T'ing-kuei refers *ch'i ch'ing* to "beauty and values" in the preceding section, thus "perceiving the situation with regard to the beauty of and values in a work." See *Wen fu chi-shin*, p. 4.

6. Kuo Shao-yü, "Lun Lu Chi 'Wen fu' chung so-wei 'yi,'" in his *Chao-yü-shih ku-tien wen-hsüeh lun-chi*, vol. 2, pp. 138–139.

7. Cf. Fang Hung, in *Wen fu chi-shih*, p. 12.

8. David Lee Clark, ed., *Shelley's Prose*, p. 294.

9. T'ang Ta-yüan, in *Wen-fu chi-shih*, p. 11; and James J. Y. Liu, "The Paradox of Poetics and the Poetics of Paradox," in Lin and Owen, eds., *The Vitality of the Lyric Voice*, p. 60.

10. *TL*; and Chang Huai-chin, *Wen fu yi-chu*.

11. Li Shan, as interpreted by Ch'ien Chung-shu in *Kuan-chü pien*, takes *chung-ch'ü* as *ch'ü-chung* 區中, "in a room," thus referring to the situation of reading. This interpretation is unlikely.

12. Sun Ch'o's (314–371) *Yu T'ien-tai shan fu* gives precisely such a description of a spirit journey as though it were an empirical visit to the T'ien-t'ai Mountains. For a translation, see Burton Watson, *Chinese Rhyme-Prose: Poems in the Fu Form From the Han and Six Dynasties Period*, pp. 80–85.

13. Fang T'ing-kuei takes this couplet as Lu Chi referring to the composition of this poetic exposition itself. This is not impossible, but such initial reference would have to be carried all the way through, creating a delightfully modern self-referentiality, a poetic exposition about its own composition. Unfortunately, poetic expositions that are not explicitly occasional tend to treat the normative rather than the particular case.

14. Only the violation of parallelism weighs against this reading, which is more natural in itself than the reading of the line I have chosen. If we look closely at the rhetoric of the line, however, we note that a *ch'i* 其 has been elided in the parallel line and may be included in this line. Moreover, a descriptive compound such as *fen-yün* 紛緼, here poetically shortened to *fen* 紛, applies to "all things," *wan-wu* 萬物, even more comfortably than to "thoughts." Therefore I take the expanded prose construction of the phrase to be something like: *ssu ch'i fen-yün* 思其紛緼. This preserves parallelism, makes good sense, and more perfectly maintains the rhetorical structure; I think it is the most likely.

15. For the reasons to prefer the reading *hsien-min* 先民 over *hsien-jen* 先人, see *Wen fu chi-shih*, pp. 15, 20.

16. The former interpretation is followed by Li Shan and the Wu-ch'en commentary; the latter interpretation is followed by T'ang Ta-yüan and Ch'eng Hui-ch'ang, the latter taking it as Lu Chi praising his own ancestors. Yü Hsin (513–581) seems to have understood the passage in Ch'eng Hui-ch'ang's sense when he referred to it in the preface to his *Ai Chiang-nan fu*.

17. Ch'ang Huai-chin in *Wen fu yi-chu* takes *t'ou p'ien* as something like "casts himself into writing"; like many interpretations in that work, however, this is inconsistent with good usage. Hsü Fu-kuan offers a more plausible alternative: "lifts up the tablet [with which to write]."

18. Although Hsü Fu-kuan is correct in recognizing that *ssu-wen* had become a general term for "belles lettres," he goes on to identify it with the writings of Lu Chi's literary predecessors; thus it is unclear exactly how he would take this line. Ch'eng Hui-ch'ang and some other scholiasts take *ssu-wen* as "this work"; i.e. the poetic exposition Lu Chi is writing. I agree with Hsü that this is most unlikely.

19. Cited in K'o Ch'ing-ming and Tseng Yung-yi, eds., *Liang-Han Wei Tsin Nan-pei-ch'ao wen-hsüeh p'i-p'ing tzu-liao hui-pien*, p. 214.

20. *Shih chi*, p. 2233.

21. There is something of a debate here as to whether Lu Chi is discussing originality only in phrasing or originality of "concept" (*yi**): see *Wen fu chi-shih*, pp. 38–39 for a summary. T'ang Ta-yüan offers an alternative interpretation here, one which I believe is incorrect: the writer takes material from incomplete or fragmentary works by predecessors and uses them in his own work, then somehow borrows from lost and unrecorded songs for his own writing; in this way he makes use of past writing but avoids the more conventional texts that others use.

22. See Ch'ien Chung-shu, *Kuan-chü pien* pp. 1186–1187, for parallels.

23. A touchstone of the difference is that one can say *ch'i yi* fei* 其意非, "the concept is wrong"; but one cannot say *yi* fei* 義非, "the principle/truth is wrong." Wang Ching-hsien offers an interesting suggestion that *yi** here refers specifically to the "Six Principles" of the *Book of Songs*, each embodying a distinct approach to writing; in selecting one of these, the writer would be adopting some fundamental attitude toward the work.

24. Wang Ching-hsien sees *pu* as the "divisions" (in the Western rhetorical sense) of the larger structure of the text.

25. Li Ch'uan-chia (in *Wen fu chi-shih*) points out many parallel passages in the *Wen-hsin tiao-lung*, to which Chang Shao-k'ang objects on the grounds of the greater complexity of *Wen-hsin tiao-lung* with its relatively precise analytic divisions. Although this is true, both here and elsewhere in "The Poetic Exposition on Literature," it should be pointed out that Lu Chi's phrasings are often much richer, either because of the intense ambiguity of the words, or as with the governmental metaphor beneath the surface here, his terms have greater resonance in other frames of reference. This is the advantage of working early in a tradition, before the formation of a determinate and specialized vocabulary for literary studies.

26. Cf. the discussion of the *Book of Documents* and the *Spring and Autumn Annals* in *Wen-hsin tiao-lung*, "Revering the Classics" (See pp. 197–199).

27. *Shih chi*, p. 3073.

28. Li Shan cites an earlier scholiast who glosses an occurrence of *jao* in another text as "be docile." Chu Chün-sheng changes birds to fish and *lan* to *lien*, "connect" or "continue."

29. Hsü Fu-kuan explains this as the tiger being the dominant concept at the beginning; when it shows itself, all subsidiary aspects of the text (the beasts) fall in line (accepting the old gloss of *jao* as "docile").

30. Chang Huai-chin in *Wen fu yi-chu* offers the anomalous interpretation that *hsing*-nei* here is "within the [human] form": i.e., in the heart or mind.

31. Hsü Fu-kuan takes the act of control in this line as referring to the phrases, each of which has an independent disposition and thus must be mastered by the writer. We should not lightly reinterpret Lu Chi's explicit "things" as "words"; but this interpretation is not entirely without merit, since it would anticipate lines 75–76.

32. *Chu Wen-kung chiao Ch'ang-li hsien-sheng chi*, 16.9b, in SPTK.

33. Wordsworth (though mentioned in only one, critical quotation) and Horace's *Si vis me flere* loom large in the background of Ch'ien Chung-shu's interpretation; at times one

suspects that he reads the lines as he does in order to draw out parallels from Western literary thought.

34. Oscar Wilde, *The Artist as Critic: Critical Writings of Oscar Wilde*, Richard Ellman, ed., p. 389. In the *Wen fu chi-shih*, Chang Shao-k'ang struggles valiantly with the question, trying to offer the modern (but less than contemporary) notion of implicit intent and verbal expression, trying to get away from the traditional notion that the *ch'ing** that are manifested are the actual sentiments of the writer. The problem here is a modern one, not one for Lu Chi: when Lu Chi speaks of *ch'ing** he means real *ch'ing**, regardless of whether it represents the general character of a writer or the shifts of mood when working through some problem. One does not have to be T'ao Ch'ien to feel like T'ao Ch'ien sometimes, or even to get into the mood of T'ao Ch'ien. Most late classical commentators would be closely attentive to the possibility of profound conflict here: someone whose basic disposition was anything but similar to T'ao Ch'ien's, but who could on occasion "get into the mood of" T'ao Ch'ien (a better phrasing than "adopt the mask of" T'ao Ch'ien). However, this question is simply not an issue for Lu Chi.

35. Fang T'ing-kuei offers an interesting paraphrase, although it is not clear how he derives it from the text as it is written: "what language cannot reach, the more it is enlarged, the vaster it gets; what thought cannot reach, the more it is restrained, the deeper it goes."

36. Hsü Fu-kuan not only takes *t'i** as literary forms, he goes on to insist that *wu**, "things," are in fact the "materials" or "contents" of writing, and not things in general. This is interesting because it is symptomatic of the difference between early and modern exegetes. The modern scholar, under the force of certain assumptions in Western literary thought, tries to separate literary questions decisively from the non-literary—what belongs to the rest of the world. To a T'ang commentator, when Lu Chi says "things," he means "things." More than any other Chinese literary theorist before Yen Yü, Lu Chi is inclined to treat literature as a self-contained act of mind. Nevertheless, while different from the T'ang commentators, he is closer to them than he is to a modern exegete like Hsü Fu-kuan. For Lu Chi literature is not an autonomous realm, but an activity within mind as a whole. The "things" he refers to may be objects of consciousness rather than material things, but they are given as an event in mind and not simply the "contents" of a literary work.

37. Hsü Fu-kuan interprets this as "Diction shows the measure of talent."

38. Hsü Fu-kuan, roughly following Li Shan, ignores the *Lao-tzu* passage and takes *ch'i* as "the essentials," "the outline," "the overview." Thus concept has a sense of the larger structure and makes everything else obey.

39. Hsü Fu-kuan paraphrases: "One stands at the juncture between the possibility of shallowness and the possibility of depth; one must go forward boldly to seek the deep."

40. Li Shan cannot endure the dangerous proposition Lu Chi is making here and willfully reinterprets the line as a demand for conformity to the norms.

41. This indicates that Li Shan takes the line as an interrogative: "When one speaks of being in hardship, can there be no impediment?" To resolve the awkwardness of Li Shan's construction, Ch'eng Hui-ch'ang cites a suggested emendation of *wu* 無, "there is no," to *wei* "only."

42. Ch'ien Chung-shu, pp. 1194–1195.

43. There is one further consideration in the interpretation of this couplet. Lines 81 to 82 are closely related to the earlier couplet where words, in a "contest of artfulness," are governed by concept (ll. 75–76). The way in which we take the relation between those lines will shape the way we take the relation between these lines. But on close examination, we find exactly the same latitude there that we have here.

44. See Ssu-k'ung T'u's positive interpretation of this quality in "The Twenty-Four Categories of Poetry,", pp. 321–323.

45. Cf. *Ch'ing*-ts'ai**, "The Affections and Coloration," in the *Wen-hsin tiao-lung*, pp. 239–241.

46. The definition *t'i*-wu** and the quality *liu-liang* suggest that Lu Chi no longer thinks of the poetic exposition as primarily a vehicle for veiled criticism of those in power, the dominant Han interpretation of the form. The late-Ch'ing critic Wang K'ai-yün tries to redeem Lu Chi's description of the genre for that older function, but it is not convincing (even though Wang appeals to the principle announced in line 38, that the genre may "move from the hidden to the manifest").

47. For other interpretations of *hsiang* in this context, see *Wen fu chi-shih*.

48. See James Robert Hightower, "The *Wen hsüan* and Genre Theory," *Harvard Journal of Asiatic Studies* 20.3–4:512–533 (December 1957); David Knechtges, *Wen xuan, or, Selections of Refined Literature*, vol. 1, pp. 1–52; and Ferenc Tökei, *Genre Theory in China in the 3rd–6th Centuries*.

49. Hsü Fu-kuan explains *hui-yi** somewhat differently, as unifying a concept with a particular verbal phrasing. Since the next line takes up the question of language, I think that *hui-yi** here works purely on the level of concept, which is consistent with other uses of the term.

50. K'o Ch'ing-ming and Tseng Yung-yi, p. 196. Lu Yün's letters to his brother are remarkable examples of informal practical criticism from this period.

51. Ibid., p. 195.

52. Here I follow the questionable interpretation of the passage that Lu Chi would have known. See p. 597n2.

53. There are alternative interpretations of *pi* here. Hsü Fu-kuan, for instance, takes its as "thorough."

54. Compare *Wen-hsin tiao-lung*, "Latent and Out-standing" (p. 263): "The latent is the layered significance that lies beyond the literary text...The latent is fully accomplished in complex and multiple concepts."

55. In my opinion the "riding crop" is a line that directs the reader toward the main point, without itself being explicitly a statement of the main point. There are a number of commentators, however, who take this as essentially a forceful statement of the main point. Hsü Fu-kuan even includes *p'ien-yen* here as a "short statement" of the main topic (this misses the real force of *p'ien-yen*, which is one of incompletion and suggestiveness rather than mere terseness).

56. See the discussion in John Timothy Wixted, *Poems on Poetry: Literary Criticism by Yuan Hao-wen (1190–1257)*, pp. 158–160. See also the discussion in Ssu-k'ung T'u's "Letter to Mr Li Discussing Poetry," p. 356.

57. For example, Chiang K'uei 姜夔 (ca. 1155–ca. 1221) writes: "In writing poetry, to seek to be in harmony with the ancients is not as good as to seek to be different from them. To seek to be different from the ancients is not as good as to be unable not to harmonize with and not to differ from them without actually seeking to do so." Translated by Lin Shuen-fu, "Chiang K'uei's Treatises on Poetry and Calligraphy," in Bush and Murck, eds., *Theories of the Arts in China*, p. 296.

58. See the examples cited in Wixted, *Poems on Poetry*, pp. 302–303.

59. Taken out of the structure of a sequence, this pattern "X and not Y" or "X but not Y" became one of the most common verbal formulas for judgments on the manner or quality of something, especially literary style. Sometimes, as above, it is a failing that corresponds to or simply occurs with some virtue. At other time the formula attests the moderate phase of some quality but denies the phase of excess. The source of this second version can be traced back to *Analects* III.20: "He said, 'The *Kuan-chü* [the first poem of the *Book of Songs*] expresses pleasure without being lewd, shows grief without damaging wounds.'"

60. Jao Tsung-yi, "The Relation between Principles of Literary Criticism of the Wei and Tsin Dynasties and Music," paper presented to the Eleventh Conference of Young Sinologues (Padua, 1958); Chinese version "Lu Chi Wen fu li-lun yü yin-yüeh chih kuan-hsi," in *Chūgoku bungaku hō* 14: 22–37 (1961). For a full dicussion in English of the musical issues in the following passage, see Kenneth DeWoskin, "Early Chinese Music and the Origins of Aesthetic Terminology," in Bush and Murck eds., *Theories of the Arts in China*, pp. 198–204.

61. *Wen fu yi-chu* suggests here that "short rhyme" is a kenning for poetry (*shih*).

62. Fang T'ing-kuei offers an interesting, if erroneous interpretation of this passage as a singularity that follows from an absence of allusions and references to earlier writing.

63. The only difficulty in understanding *ying* as "sympathetic resonance" (though the term was clearly used to describe that phenomenon) is the assumption of simultaneity or near simultaneity in "sympathetic resonance." *Ying* presumes sequential relation.

64. Chang Feng-yi interprets the *ai* here in terms of affect: "not causing people to feel love for it."

65. Because it makes little difference in the image and is less awkward, I have used the modern interpretation of *Lao-tzu* V, taking *t'o-yüeh* 橐籥 as simply the "bellows [tubes]." Lu Chi, however, probably would have understood this in the older interpretation with *t'o* as the "bellows" and *yüeh* as a "flute."

66. Hsü Fu-kuan's interpretation here is interesting (though, I suspect, overdeterminate and reflecting late classical and modern notions). Hsü would have the movement of spirit as the "host" or subject and the the poetic content from the material as the "guest" or object. Sometimes the subject stirs and the object responds; sometimes the object stirs and the subject responds. More persuasively, he relates "blockage" and "passage through" to the earlier question of concept's being equal to things, and literary expression's being equal to concepts; i.e., it is in this frame of reference that blockage and passage occur.

67. Hsü Fu-kuan interprets *tun* 頓, "gather," as "worn out"; i.e., though his vital forces are worn out, still he seeks.

68. One commentator, Yü Kuang-hua, tersely notes here "as if there were spiritual (*shen**) aid"; this notion of "spiritual aid" or "divine help," something wondrous coming from outside the self, became important in later aesthetics. Rather than the relation of voice and vessel that we find in the prophets and "Ion," this is a divine collaborator. Yet it should be noted that this is precisely not what Lu Chi is saying; the Chinese is very strong: "this thing is right here in the 'I'."

69. I cannot resist here quoting the comment of Fang T'ing-kuei, who, more than any other commentator, is the voice of late imperial scholasticism: "Probably if he read a lot and composed a lot, he could open [the blockage]; if he reads and composes little, it remains blocked." Of course, this is not at all what Lu Chi is saying; but it does reflect the later solution to this problem: learning assimilated until it becomes second nature, causing the writer to compose easily and with confidence. In his extensive commentary Chang Shao-k'ang builds on the point in a more modern vein, but the response to Lu Chi's statement of involuntarism is essentially the same.

CHAPTER FIVE

The text used in based on Chou Chen-fu's *Wen-hsin tiao-lung chu-shih*, with modifications.

1. There have been numerous studies attempting to date the work precisely. In his *Wen-hsin tiao-lung chu-shih*, Chou Chen-fu favors the year 496–497; Mou Shih-chin in Lu K'an-ju and Mou Shih-chin, *Wen- hsin tiao-lung yi-chu*, favors 501.

2. Apart from *Wen-hsin tiao-lung*, only two works by Liu Hsieh survive, both on Buddhist topics. Even after he found positions in the princely salons, he was best known only for funerary inscriptions for eminent monks. Some scholars suspect his hand in other Buddhist works, while others believe (on questionable grounds) that he was the author of a philosophical tract, the *Liu-tzu* 劉子.

3. Liu Hsieh had been a protégé of the eminent monk Seng-yu and had received a Buddhist education (though clearly including a more standard literary training). Although the jargon and technical vocabulary of Buddhism is virtually absent in *Wen-hsin tiao-lung* (with the exception of a use of *pan-jo, prajnâ,* 般若, in the chapter on "Discourses"), Kōzen Hiroshi has shown the influence of Liu Hsieh's Buddhist training in "Wen-hsin tiao-lung yü Ch'u San-tsang chi chi," in his *Wen-hsin tiao-lung lun-wen chi*, pp. 5–108. Ma Hung-shan has discussed the use of the technical Taoist vocabulary of *hsüan-hsüeh* 玄學 in "Wen-hsin tiao-lung chih Tao pien," in his *Wen-hsin tiao-lung san-lun*, pp. 32–42.

4. For the *Wen hsüan*, its background, and its place in Chinese genre theory, see Hightower, "The *Wen hsüan* and Genre Theory"; and Knechtges, *Wen xuan*, vol. 1, pp. 1–52.

5. Out of more than three hundred pages of citations, references, bibliographical notices, etc., in Yang Ming-chao's *Wen-hsin tiao-lung chiao-chu shih-yi*, there is only one item (on p. 541) from the Southern Dynasties, an unacknowledged citation in the *Chin-lou-tzu* 金樓子.

6. The majority of passages cited by Yang Ming-chao (see previous note) are from the Ch'ing, but there are still numerous references from the T'ang through the Ming. Although it exerted little influence on the tradition of literary theory, the range of such references should vigorously dispel the myth that *Wen-hsin tiao-lung* was ignored before the Ch'ing.

7. One cannot overemphasize the sheer quantity of recent scholarship on *Wen-hsin tiao-lung* in China. With the sole exception of studies on the novel *Hung-lou meng*, the number of articles on *Wen-hsin tiao-lung* far exceeds articles on any poet or prose writer.

8. Lu Chi's "Poetic Exposition on Literature" is also governed by rhetorical expository procedures, but in Lu Chi's work these are much looser and less analytic.

9. It is worth noting that Liu Hsieh's analytic procedures often break down at precisely those points where he does indeed have an opinion or vested interest. An excellent example of this can be found in the opening paragraphs of "The General Technique," where the attempt to assert the superiority of his own critical insight over his predecessors demonstrates quite the opposite.

10. English translations of *Wen-hsin tiao-lung* generally fall into one of two categories: the "literal" translation, such as Vincent Shih's *The Literary Mind and the Carving of Dragons*; and the reconstitution of the title in English abstractions, such as James R. Hightower's *A Serious and Elegant Treatise on (the Art or Secret of) Literature*. For a list of the different English translations and references to where discussions of the translations of the title can be found, see Wixted, "Nature of Evaluation in the *Shih-p'in*," footnote 1, pp. 247–248.

11. In the "Afterword" Liu Hsieh is careful to separate his idea of "carving dragons" from an earlier usage that had potentially negative associations.

12. For a different discussion of the first chapter and others, the reader is encouraged to consult Donald Gibbs, "Literary Theory in the *Wen-hsin tiao-lung*, Sixth Century Chinese Treatise on the Genesis of Literature and Conscious Artistry," Ph.D. dissertation, University of Washington, 1970.

13. For an excellent English commentary on the *Hsi-tz'u chuan*, see Willard J. Peterson, "Making Connections: 'Commentary on the Attached Verbalizations' of the *Book of Change*," in *Harvard Journal of Asiatic Studies* 42.1: 67–116 (1982).

14. This aspect of Liu Hsieh's writing is, of course, impossible to show in translation. I have footnoted only the most important of these references.

15. It is an established ceremony of commentary on the *Wen-hsin tiao-lung* to explain the range of the reference of *wen** at this point. *Wen** is "literature," "prose" as opposed to poetry (though not used in this way in *Wen-hsin tiao-lung*), "rhymed writing" as opposed to unrhymed writing, "cultivation," "learning," "decoration" and often when applied to literary style "ornamentation." Finally, in the context of this chapter *wen** is used in the broadest sense of all, as "pattern." In classical Chinese two-character compounds often serve to delimit the scope of semantic reference, while the choice of uncompounded characters gradually comes to be used, as here, to blur the distinctions made by compounds, to assert some fundamental identity between things that common usage puts asunder. The very fact that Liu Hsieh must make this complex argument shows that the identification between universal "pattern" and "literature" (as the human version of such pattern) was not taken for granted. We might also note that in its early usages (as in the *Hsiao-hsü* hexagram of the *Book of Changes* and *Chiang-Han* in the *Book of Songs*), *wen**-*tê** had a broad cultural meaning, something like "the moral power (*tê**) to transform the people by cultural (*wen**) influence."

16. The Chinese has literally: "[Of] purple and brown, colors are mixed; [by] round and square forms divide." The metonymic associations of "Heaven" and "Earth" have been added to make the translation comprehensible. Heaven's basic color is *hsüan*, a blackish-purple, and its shape is circular, assumed by its rotation; Earth is *huang*, "brown" or "yellow" (the English distinction between these colors not being made in classical Chinese); its shape is square, thus it stays at rest.

17. "Cleave" is the accepted interpretation of *li* 麗 in this context; but Shiba Rokurō offers an attractive interpretation using *li* in its more common sense as "beautiful": the Images "give beauty to" the heavens. Although philology compels us to accept "cleave" as the primary sense here, it seems that in a context like this it would be impossible for Liu Hsieh to use *li* without some play on its more common meaning of "beauty." The "images of Heaven" are the configurations of sun, moon, stars, and planets. This is of some help in understanding the quality of the Chinese term *hsiang** or "image": it is a schematic pattern with relatively few details, given on a more general level than the determinacy of things of the empirical world, but elusively immanent within them.

18. Toda Kōkyō (*Bunshin chōryū*) and Chou Chen-fu (*Wen-hsin tiao-lung chu-shih*) stress the root sense of *li** here, as a pattern in jade; rather than the sense of "order," they take it as "give pattern." Obviously both aspects of *li** are drawn together here, and the weight given the term depends largely on the interpretation of the source passage in the *Hsi-tz'u chuan* of the *Book of Changes*; unfortunately, the early commentaries do not specify the sense of *li** there, but the subcommentary, the *Cheng-yi* 正義 (completed in the T'ang, but based on classical scholarship from the third through sixth centuries), takes it as "order."

19. Compare the bald phrasing in the *Liu-tzu*, "Caution in Words": "Sun and moon are the pattern of Heaven; rivers and mountains are the pattern of Earth; language is the pattern of humankind." Lin Ch'i-hsien and Ch'en Feng-chin, eds., *Liu-tzu chi-chiao*, p. 176. Although there are indeed many striking parallels between *Wen-hsin tiao-lung* and the *Liu-tzu*, the floridity of the former and the flatness of the latter make it very difficult to believe that both works are by the same hand.

20. The interpretation of "beauty" for *chang** (usually "section" or "manifest") follows from the Wang Pi gloss for the term in commenting on the source passage in the hexagram *K'un* 坤 in the *Book of Changes*. Other commentators link this to the *wan- hsiang** 萬象, the "ten thousand images [of things]" immanent in the world of the Earth. The term translated as "inhere" is *han* 含: to "hold within," with the implication of "holding back almost out of sight."

21. The "two standards," *liang-yi*, are Heaven and Earth, whose large categorical difference became manifest through the investigation of the patterns inhering in each.

22. *Hsing*-ling* is the "magic spark" of humanity, associated with spirit, consciousness, the capacity of understanding.

23. *Hsiu* is literally a high ear of grain, conventionally extended to whatever is "outstanding." The term is applied to a particular mode of language in chapter 40, "Latent and Out-standing." The association in this context is both with something very rare and also the entelechy of the elements. "The elements" (*wu-hsing*) are literally the "five processes": water, fire, metal, wood, and earth, whose constant interchange accounts for the processes and forms of nature. Both of these statements are paraphrases of passages in the *Book of Rites*.

24. This may follow from the famous statement by Yang Hsiung 揚雄 in the *Fa-yen* 法言 that "language is the sound of mind."

25. We should note here the first occurrence of the recurring motif denigrating not only ornamental craft but also the *mimêsis* of external shapes.

26. I.e., winds blowing through the empty spaces of the earth associated with the "piping of Earth" in the *Ch'i-wu lun* 齊物論 chapter of the *Chuang-tzu*.

27. *T'ai-chi*, the Ultimate, the primordial state from which the differentiated world came into being.

28. "Patterned Words" is the treatise *Wen*-yen**, one of the "Wings" of the *Book of Changes*, which is devoted to a discussion of the two primary hexagrams *Ch'ien* 乾 (Heaven) and *K'un* 坤 (Earth).

29. There was a legend that the trigrams, the core elements of the hexagrams of the *Book of Changes*, first appeared in a diagram carried by a dragon that emerged from the Yellow River.

30. Another legend had it that when Yü was controlling the great flood, a sacred tortoise appeared in the Lo River, which carried the "Nine Divisions," nine sets of enumerated categories which comprehended the operations of nature and the state. They appear in the "Great Plan," *Hung-fan* 洪範, chapter of the *Book of Documents*.

31. Ts'ang Chieh, the "recorder" of the Yellow Emperor, came up with the idea for written characters by observing the tracks of birds; prior to this, knotted cords had been used for keeping records.

32. Both Yen-ti and Shen-nung were mythical Sage Emperors of high antiquity. The "Three Monuments" were legendary lost texts of high antiquity.

33. See *Analects* VIII.19.

34. The quotation is from the *Book of Documents*.

35. *Analects* III.24: "The border guard at Yi asked to meet him [Confucius], and said 'When a superior person reaches this point, I always get to meet him.' Confucius' followers

brought him to meet [the Master], and when he went out, he said, 'You two or three disciples, why do you think it so terrible that he has lost his office? The world has been without the Way for a long time indeed, but Heaven intends to make the Master its wooden bell-clapper.'"

36. *Tz'u**, the "comments" given in the *Book of Changes*, and a particular "phrasing."

37. *Tsung*, translated as "revere," was originally associated with the honor given to ancestors, and often carries the implication of "to consider as a source," an implication that is strongly present here.

38. The reader may consult the two following studies of the *Shih-p'in*: Wixted, "The Nature of Evaluation in the *Shih-p'in*"; and Yeh Chia-ying and Jan Walls, "Theory, Standards, and Practice of Criticizing Poetry in Chung Hung's *Shih-p'in*" in Ronald Miao, ed. *Studies in Chinese Poetry and Poetics*. There is an English translation of the prefaces and the first and second categories in John Timothy Wixted, "The Literary Criticism of Yüan Hao-wen," Ph.D. dissertation, Oxford, 1976, Appendix A.

39. I.e., their capacity for transformation. Or "imitate the spirits and gods."

40. Either their atemporal order or, more likely, their seasonal progressions.

41. But note the exception in the "Four Things Taught" (note 70 below), where *wen** is "placed at the head."

42. The "Primordial Reigns" are those of Fu-hsi, Shen-nung, and Huang-ti, the Yellow Emperor (or in other versions Fu-hsi, Nü-wa, and Shen-nung: Huang-ti was included in the Five Emperors). Again there are various lists of the Five Emperors, e.g., Huang-ti, Chuan-hsü, Ti-k'u, and the better known Yao and Shun. The original parts of the *Book of Changes* were attributed to Fu-hsi and earliest antiquity. Parts of the *Book of Documents* were attributed to the time of Yao and Shun.

43. The "Eight Investigations" are most commonly linked to the eight trigrams of the *Book of Changes*, though there are other explanations of the term.

44. Supposedly related to the nine regions into which archaic China was divided.

45. I.e., the ten original commentary sections on the *Book of Changes*.

46. According to an apocryphal tradition, Confucius said that through the *Book of Documents*, one could consider Virtue, Fellow-Feeling, Sincerity, Measure, Events, Governance, and Beauty.

47. These are the four sections of the *Songs*: the *Feng**, Lesser and Greater *Ya**, and the Hymns (or *Sung*).

48. Sacrificial, Funeral, Court Reception, Military, and the "excellent rites," weddings and coming-of-age ceremonies.

49. These are five different principles involved in how events are presented. See *Tso chuan* (Ch'eng 14).

50. This is an emendation from the Tun-huang manuscript version; the printed editions read *chi* 極, "give the ultimate in."

51. A quotation from the *Book of Songs*.

52. *Analects* XIX.23: [The disciple Tzu-kung, having heard that he was praised at Confucius' expense, compares Confucius' teaching to a great mansion, saying,] "My walls reach only to a person's shoulders; one can peer in and see whatever good there is in the chambers. But the Master's wall is several cubits high: if you don't go in by the front gate, you will not see the beauty of the ancestral temple or the richness of its officers. Few are those indeed who find the front gate." The point here is that Confucian learning is not something that can be immediately appreciated, despite the fact that the Classics are the basis of all learning. "What is given forth and received there" refers to the Confucian teachings.

53. This is a paraphrase of a passage in the *Hsi-tz'u chuan* 繫辭傳. The *Book of Changes* penetrates into the realm of mystery, that which operates the world but which is ordinarily invisible to human perception; then the principles of the world of spirit are ascertained and brought back for application in the human realm, so that people can know how events have occurred and will occur. One can see how closely analogous this is to modern theoretical economics.

54. *Historical Records*, "Genealogical Records of Confucius."

55. I.e., the mysterious place where Confucius discovered what was precious. This image is from the *Lieh-yü-k'ou* 列禦寇 chapter of *Chuang-tzu*.

56. Liu Hsieh would have understood this in terms of the apocryphal division between

the ancient Historian of the Right, who recorded acts, and the Historian of the Left, who recorded words. Since much of the *Book of Documents* consists of proclamations and recorded dialogues and addresses, it belongs to the domain of the Historian of the Left.

57. This quotation comes from the *Shang-shu ta-chuan* 尚書大傳 cited in *Yi-wen lei-chü* 藝文類聚, *chüan* 55 (Taipei: Wen-kuang ch'u-pan-she, 1974), p. 990.

58. Literally "displays the *feng** and forms the *hsing**": commentators generally agree that all of the Six Principles (*liu-yi**) are intended here.

59. "Suggestive" is *yü* 喻, having hidden referents, particularly to social and ethical referents which were understood as the motives for the composition of the *Songs*.

60. This was a commonplace of criticism of the *Spring and Autumn Annals*, found in various phrasings in a variety of sources.

61. This refers to one of the touchstone passages in the *Spring and Autumn Annals* (though what was long taken as a touchstone of Confucius' careful choice of words now is more a touchstone of exegetical ingenuity). First we have the passage from the sixteenth year of Duke Hsi: "Spring, the king's first month, at the very beginning of the month there fell stones [meteors] in Sung, five of them; that month six albatrosses flew in reverse, passing the capital of Sung." With regret we bypass the *Kung-yang* commentary with its delightful explanation for the sequence of the numbers (in the case of the meteors, the thing enumerated precedes the number because the meteors were seen first and the number only discovered later; in the case of the albatrosses, first the number was recognized, then the fact that they were albatrosses). However, Liu Hsieh is referring here to the *Ku-liang* commentary, which addresses the question of why the exact day is given in the case of the meteors and not with the albatrosses: "The Master said, 'Stones are things without understanding; albatrosses are things with a little understanding.' Since stones lack understanding, he gave the day; since albatrosses have a little understanding, he noted it by the month. When the superior person deals with things, nothing is done thoughtlessly. Since [the situations in regard to] meteors and albatrosses were so fully expressed in his words, imagine how it would be in regard to people. Had he not written as he did about the five stones and six albatrosses, the Royal Way would not have been upheld." Toda Kōkyō cites the subcommentary on the *Ku-liang* commentary by Fan Ning (339–401), which sheds some light on this exegetical passage, which is more cryptic than the classical text it purports to explain: according to Fan, since the meteors lacked understanding, their falling was an act of Heaven and thus merited the mention of the day; the same was not true of the albatrosses. What is important here is that Fan Ning used these terms, "giving the details," *hsiang* 詳, and "omitting the details," *lüeh* 略 (though these were part of the vocabulary of word usage in exegesis of the *Spring and Autumn Annals*). See the discussion of this passage by Ch'eng Ya-lin, "Wu-shih liu-yi chü t'an-wei," in *Ku-tai wen- hsüeh li-lun yen-chiu* 6 (Shanghai, 1982).

62. *Spring and Autumn Annals*, the second year of Duke Ting: "Summer, the fifth month, the day *jen-ch'en*: Chih Gate and its two watchtowers burned down." The *Kung-yang* commentary says that this would have been phrased differently if the fire had begun in the gate and spread to the watchtowers; but since it began in the watchtowers and spread to the gate, why is the gate mentioned first? The answer is, of course, to show that the gate was more important (and to avoid suggesting that something important was catastrophically affected by two unimportant things).

63. These are two of the five principles by which the *Spring and Autumn Annals* were composed: see note 49.

64. We might also note that the text which becomes pellucid, the *Book of Documents*, ultimately reveals *li** ("natural principle") to the reader; in contrast, the text that becomes difficult, the *Spring and Autumn Annals*, ultimately reveals *yi** ("concept," "significance"), implying human "motive" or "intention" (other semantic areas of *yi**). The presumption of individual motives in the words of a text—especially the motives of that most subtle human being, the Sage—creates the difficulties that require a more serious hermenetics than philological glosses.

65. "Cultural instruction," *chiao-hua* 教化, was often described with images of fecundity, especially rains that make the land fertile.

66. The *lun*, *shuo*, and *hsü* were recognized genres of classical prose; several forms were known as *tz'u*, and it is not altogether clear to which of these, if any, Liu Hsieh is referring here. The reason the *Book of Changes* is singled out as the source of these genres is

due to the names of several of the Ten Wings, the early adjuncts or "commentaries" on the *Book of Changes*: there we find the *Hsi-tz'u chuan* 繫辭傳 ("the tradition of appended comments"); the *Shuo-kua* 說卦 ("exposition of the trigrams"); and the *Hsü-kua* 序卦 ("sequences of the trigrams," *hsü*, being literally "sequence" or "explanation," but later becoming the fixed generic term for "preface" or "afterword"). The *Hsi-tz'u chuan* itself would also serve well as an early example of *lun*. Note that of these only the *shuo* of *Shuo-kua* is used in a way identical to the later generic term.

67. I.e., there is an inexhaustible store in each.

68. The term *liu-yi** here does not refer to the "Six Principles" of the *Book of Songs*.

69. This refers to a passage in the *Fa-yen* 法言 of Yang Hsiung (58B.C.–A.D.18) in which someone said to Yang Hsiung: "What do you say to the claim that 'As the best jade is not carved, so lovely words are not patterned (*wen**)'?" Yang Hsiung answered: "If the jade is left uncarved, the finest *yü-fan* jade cannot be made into a vessel; if words are not patterned, the authoritative canons cannot make a Classic."

70. *Analects* VII.24: "He taught four things: *wen**, [right] action, loyalty, trustworthiness."

71. Although there are precedents for the use of the term "spirit thought" (*shen**-*ssu**), these earlier usages are rather different. The term seems to have been part of Southern Dynasties discourse on literature; for example, in the discussion of the "Biographies of Literary Men" in the official *History of the Southern Ch'i*, Hsiao Tzu-hsien 蕭子顯 (489–537) writes, "In the Way of literary composition, the event (*shih**) follows from spirit thought."

72. This line comes originally from the *Jang-wang* 讓王 chapter of *Chuang-tzu*; it originally referred to the inability to escape political attachments, even while ostensibly living in retirement. As many commentators have pointed out, Liu Hsieh used the line in total disregard of its original context. Chuang-tzu was less interested in the disjunction between the movements of mind and empirical circumstance than he was in the haunting compulsion of ambition.

73. *Mencius* II.A.2.9 offers a clear explanation of the relation between *chih** and *ch'i**: "*Chih** is the leader of *ch'i**; *ch'i** is what stuffs the body (*t'i**) full; *chih** is in operation first, then *ch'i** follows." The point here is that *chih** is direction of interest; *ch'i** in varying degrees may energize and actualize that direction.

74. The clause here can be taken as a general condition ("spirit thought is subtle, and . . .") or as a restrictive condition ("when spirit thought is subtle, . . .").

75. Commentators all cite a similar passage in *Chuang-tzu*, the *Chih pei-yu* 知北遊 chapter. This language of inner purification for spiritual events became a common part of Neo-Taoist jargon.

76. This sentence refers to two parables in *Chuang-tzu* of craftsmen who work by intuition; these exemplars serve much the same function here that reference to Wheelwright Pien served in "The Poetic Exposition of Literature." The first of these, the story of Butcher Ting, is found in the *Yang-sheng* 養生 chapter. Butcher Ting explains to Lord Wen-hui, who has expressed admiration of Ting's skills in cutting up an ox, that he does it by the unconscious operations of spirit, by moving through the empty interstices in the body of the ox. Other cooks, who actually cut with their knives, have to change knives often; but Ting has used his knife for nineteen years without ever needing to sharpen it. There is a problem here with the term *hsüan-chieh* (懸解, here written 玄解). This occurs elsewhere in the *Yang-sheng* chapter in the meaning "released from spiritual bondage." However, since *chieh* is also the term used in the story of Butcher Ting for cutting apart the ox, it seems almost certain that Liu Hsieh has recalled the phrase, forgotten its proper context, and misapplied it to the Butcher Ting anecdote. From this comes the translation above, "cuts things apart mysteriously." The "uniquely discerning carpenter" is Carpenter Shih, referred to in the *Hsü-wu-kuei* 徐无鬼 chapter of *Chuang-tzu*. Carpenter Shih was famous for being able to swing his ax and remove a speck of plaster from the nose of his friend. Although the terms Liu Hsieh uses clearly refer to the story of Carpenter Shih, it is not impossible that Liu Hsieh has the story of Wheelwright Pien in mind. The stories of Butcher Ting and Carpenter Shih differ from the story of Wheelwright Pien, however, in that the former two possess almost miraculous skills, achieved by a unique spiritual mastery whereas Wheelwright Pien is merely a very good wheelwright whose intuitive skill comes from experience.

77. Here I am following the interpretation of Chou Chen-fu, that the manifold possibilities that appear in the operation of spirit thought are still indeterminate and not yet selected and put into literary form. This is one of those points where the commentators gloss over serious problems of interpretation; only those forced to offer paraphrases and translations show the real differences in the way this sentence is understood. Li Yüeh-kang has the writer giving form in the emptiness and carrying out craftsmanship in the formless. Lu K'an-ju and Mou Shih-chin are close in having the writer give form *to* what is empty and practice cutting and carving **on** what is formless. Vincent Shih and Toda Kōkyō offer an attractive and entirely different interpretation that here formal rules are empty positions transcended by the writer and that there is no form of careful craftsmanship—as later critics say, no "traces of the ax."

78. It is interesting to note that both Chou Chen-fu and Lu K'an-ju, when they translate this passage, qualify Liu Hsieh's statement by saying, "When the writer *thinks of* climbing a mountain/viewing the sea..." While this is not in the original text, they are absolutely correct here: the question in this chapter is the experience of mind, not empirical experience.

79. See Wang Fu-chih in Chapter Ten, pp. 472–478.

80. See commentary to "The Poetic Exposition on Literature," l. 76.

81. See "The Poetic Exposition on Literature," ll. 57–58. This antithesis recurs throughout *Wen-hsin tiao-lung* in different forms, e.g., the organizational antithesis between those who work straight through from beginning to end as opposed to those who join sections together; see "Fluency and Coherence," p. 270.

82. "Great accomplishment" is literally "forming a vessel," conventionally referring to something with capacity, value, and use.

83. Yi Yin, who was to become the minister of King T'ang of the Shang dynasty, was originally a cook and, by legend, is said to have been unable to explain the secrets of his art.

84. "Mutations of the affections" is *ch'ing-pien**. Toda Kōkyō (p. 405), interprets: "The affections are where mutations are generated." The supporting verses are willfully cryptic and no interpretation can be said to be absolute.

85. The reference here is to General Chang Liang, who won great victories by staying in his tent and planning.

86. This line is a rephrasing of the line in the "Great Preface" to the *Book of Songs*: "The affections (*ch'ing**) are stirred within and take on form (*hsing**) in words (*yen**)." The translation "form" has been used to keep these concepts broad in English, but here an essential distinction exists in the Chinese: *hsing** stresses determinate externality; *t'i** stresses normative quality.

87. This is the process referred to in "The Poetic Exposition on Literature," l. 39, and in Ssu-ma Ch'ien's 司馬遷 comment on the *Book of Changes* at the end of "The Biography of Ssu-ma Hsiang-ju" in the *Historical Records*.

88. *Feng**-*ch'ü** is an interesting term and only very lamely translated as "manner." It is "manner" in the way it affects others, a quality of presence and influence, the way in which the energy that is *ch'i** moves out and touches the outside.

89. "The paths followed," *kuei-t'u*, is literally the "paths to return," appropriate since Liu Hsieh is "moving back" from infinite variation to a limited set of norms.

90. Most commentators associate the "mysterious doctrines" with the Taoists.

91. One might associate this with the presumed intentions of Confucius in writing the *Spring and Autumn Annals*.

92. This clearly echoes "The Poetic Exposition on Literature," l. 100. Note how the broad semantic range of *t'i** makes it possible to apply one proposition in many frames of reference: in the source line in "The Poetic Exposition on Literature" *t'i** meant either literary genres or the normative forms of the things of the world; Liu Hsieh here easily transfers this to categories of style or manner. Moreover, in this context we have not the slightest indication of the level on which these shifts or variations are supposed to occur: it might be within a single piece, from one work to another, from one author to another, or through various periods of literary history.

93. "*Ch'i** solidifies that upon which one is intent; and that upon which one is intent determines language" is a quotation from the *Tso chuan* (Chao 9).

94. Reading *ching* 競 for *jui* 銳, with Chou Chen-fu.

95. The hub of the wheel and the center of the ring were commonplace images in early Taoism.

96. *Analects* XVII.18: "He said, 'I hate how the color purple robs the vermilion [of its beauty]; I hate how the music of Cheng confuses the *Ya** music; I hate how a facile tongue topples states and families.'"

97. See Lin Wen-yüeh, "The Decline and Revival of *Feng-ku* (Wind and Bone): On the Changing Poetic Styles from the Chien-an Era through the High T'ang Period," in Lin and Owen, eds., *The Vitality of the Lyric Voice*; and Donald Gibbs, "Notes on the Wind: The Term '*Feng*' in Chinese Literary Criticism," in Buxbaum and Mote, eds., *Transition and permanence*, pp. 285–293.

98. This passage harks back to the affective function of the *Book of Song* described in the "Great Preface." "Counterpart," *fu-ch'i*, is the broken contractual tally whose edges fit together.

99. The term *ch'en-yin* later came to mean simply "to brood," but most commentators agree that the original sense of *yin* as "intone" is still present in this passage.

100. Reading *sheng* 生, "be born," rather than *ch'ing* 清, "clear."

101. *Sheng*, translated as "resonance," is literally "sound" and is taken by most commentators to refer to the "tone" of a work in reference to its capacity to stir a person. It could also refer to reputation.

102. "Argument" here is literally *hsi-tz'u*, the "analysis of words." *Hsi-tz'u* refers specifically to exposition based on dividing compounds, properly aggregating associated terms, and amplifying concepts. It is closer to Aristotelian formal procedures of analysis than to a modern notion of "argument."

103. It is by no means certain that Liu Hsieh understood the phrase *ch'i ch'i** in the same way that Li Shan did, the interpretation adopted above. See Chapter Three, note 11 above.

104. This comment appears in the letter to Wu Chih rather than in "A Discourse on Literature."

105. Reading *pin* 馪 here; an alternate character *ch'eng* 騁 is the original reading, interpreted as "speeds" (i.e, his literary talent speeds ahead).

106. Sometimes scholars have argued strenuously for one interpretation or another. The *Hsi-tz'u chuan* clearly uses *t'ung** and *pien** in both senses. *T'ung** is both a principle in the structure of a hexagram opposed to *pien**, and it is also the verb used to "carry through" a "mutation." This opens the attractive notion that *t'ung** is ultimately achieved by *pien**.

107. Or "endure long by a continuity achieved through mutation."

108. Most of the earlier commentators take *ku-shih** ("prior substance") as I have, as some definite basis in the world outside literature that determines the existence and nature of each form; but both Chou Chen-fu and Lu K'an-ju interpret it as "earlier works."

109. It is unclear whether this principle applies to different trees, to the parts of one tree, or to the development of a single tree through time. This ambiguity in the analogy opens a wide variety of possible applications to literature.

110. I have accepted the emendation *pieh*, "differ," here. The original text, followed by Chou Chen-fu, Lu K'an-ju, and others, reads *tse* 則, "standards," thus giving a translation something like "what the mind was intent upon matched the standards of writing."

111. This was a "song" in two-character lines on the origins of archery: a filial son, who could not endure to see his parents' corpses eaten by wild beasts, invented the bow to protect them. Like the other examples that Liu Hsieh gives of poetry prior to the *Book of Songs*, this song is, in fact, a concoction of later ages.

112. If this is correctly identified with a ceremonial song contained in the *Book of Rites*, then it is the more "extensive," both in its elaboration and in being in a four-character line.

113. Compare Ts'ao P'i's "Discourse on Literature," p. 64, where the opposite problem is raised: "Ordinary people value what is far away and feel contempt for what is close at hand."

114. *K'ua-chang* carries associations of hyperbole.

115. This probably means a broad sense of what should constitute a literary work, though there are slight variations among the commentators here.

116. See "Spirit Thought." p. 202.

117. A more simplistic literary use of *shih** (a use more suited to practical poetics and closer to the term's use in the criticism of calligraphy) can be seen in the list of "Seventeen *Shih**" in the *Bunkyō hifuron* of the T'ang, in which poetic structure is described in terms of qualities of momentum.

118. *Li*, "advantage," translated as the "path of least resistance," is the direction or course of action most natural in the circumstance. This is close to the passage from the *Hsi-tz'u chuan* cited in "Continuity and Mutation": "Mutation and continuity occur according to the requirements of the moment."

119. Later, in the "Seventeen *Shih*" of the *Bunkyō hifuron*, *shih** is treated as a kinetic principle of poetic structure, each poem embodying a quality of movement that can be achieved by careful compositional technique. This would support an interpretation identifying *shih** as the internal "movement" of the text. Liu Hsieh's discussion makes it seem equally likely, however, that *shih** is the way in which the normative and as yet unrealized *t'i** unfolds into determinate and particular qualities.

120. *Tien-ya**, given as the first of the normative forms in "Nature and Form."

121. *Yün-chieh*, an early member of a group of compounds that become important in later theory, implying both "reserve," and a breadth and fullness in the text or personality behind the text which is yet to be known.

122. These two similes correspond to the problems suggested above: the swift waters that form no ripples refer to the "shallowness" of a person without "reserve"; the barren tree that gives no shade matches a style that "fails in abundance."

123. Note that here, as elsewhere, a pair of antonymns includes the full range of variation between.

124. "Eine solche Art des Ausdrucks, wo das Zeichen ganz in dem Bezeichneten verschwindet und wo die Sprache den Gedanken, den sie ausdrückt, noch gleichsam nackend lässt, da ihn die andre nie darstellen kann, ohne ihn zugleich zu verhüllen, ist es, was man in der Schreibart vorzugsweise genialisch und geistreich nennt": *Über naive und sentimentalische Dichtung*, Johannes Beer, ed., p. 20.

125. The term *ch'i-hui* presents serious problems of interpretation; I have followed Toda's interpretation, but Chou Chen-fu and Lu K'an-ju takes it as differences that follow from "matching the demands of the moment."

126. The original text of this line is such that all modern commentators suspect textual corruption. A wide variety of emendations have been proposed; I have followed Chou Chen-fu's, proposed on what seems to me excellent evidence.

127. No one knows to whom Liu Chen was referring here.

128. Note that in this case *t'i** is being used for "period style." "Momentum" in this sense is very close to English "trend."

129. This echoes a passage in the *Tso chuan* (Hsüan 15): "When literature inverts the proper, it is wanting." The statement is based on the old forms of the characters, in which "proper," *cheng**, turned upside down resembled the character for "wanting."

130. *Ch'i*, translated here as "extraordinary," became an important and problematic evaluative term. In some cases it meant "strange" in a potentially derogatory sense; in other cases it meant simply "excellent."

131. See the discussion of meteors and albatrosses in "Revering the Classics," note 61.

132. We should note that there were ways of phrasing the sentence as a "proper" sequence in order to stress different aspects; for example, if one wished to stress the investigation of causes, one might come up with a form roughly translated into English as "the fact that the boy hit the ball was because he had practiced."

133. "Closest," *chin*, is also "recent": hence the application of the principle in the following lines.

134. "A talent trained in the old ways" may also be interpreted as "a talent with long training."

135. This refers to a parable of natural versus self-conscious action in the *Ch'iu-shui* 秋水 chapter of *Chuang-tzu*: "Are you the only one who hasn't heard about the boy of Shou-ling who went to Han-tan [the capital of the state of Chao] to learn how to walk: not only did he not master that particular skill of the city [the 'Han-tan walk'], he even forgot the way he had walked before and ended up going home on his hands and knees."

136. In reference to this passage, commentators often cite *Analects* V.12: "Tzu-kung said, 'We have the opportunity to hear of the Master's wen*-chang* . . .'" Originally wen*-chang* probably meant something like "external behavior, manner, and cultivation." As the phrase came to mean "literary works," the *Analects* usage was taken in that sense. Liu Hsieh's apparently odd conclusion, that this is "bright coloration," can be explained by the Ho Yen gloss to the *Analects*, quoted in Lu K'an-ju: "*Chang** means "bright"; *wen** means "coloration" (ts'ai*)." The glosses of Classical commentators, especially those from roughly Liu Hsieh's period, often provide the key to why Liu Hsieh cites or alludes to a particular passage from the Classics as an authority (although at this period the status of the *Analects* as a Classic was not yet confirmed).

137. This refers to a comment by the disciple Tzu-kung in *Analects* XII.8: "Substance (chih*) is like pattern (wen*), and pattern is like substance: the bare hide of a tiger or leopard is like the bare hide of a dog or sheep."

138. This involves a complicated allusion to the *Tso chuan* (Hsüan 2) in which red lacquer was necessary to turn hides into armor. Hence the external coloration is necessary to what the thing "is."

139. "Ample delineation of the images of things" probably refers specifically to "poetic expositions," *fu*.

140. Note that hsing*, "individuating nature," and ch'ing* "the affections," are etymologically linked and sometimes interchangeable. The proper term here is the "five ch'ing*; but for the sake of variation, Liu Hsieh uses five hsing*, out of which the affections arise.

141. This nice piece of sophistry of course does not follow logically, but it is a good example of how antithetical exposition shapes conclusions: a statement, "at funerals language is not patterned" tends to produce a parallel member, "other than at funerals language is not plain."

142. This is a direct quotation from *Lao-tzu* LXXXI, the second clause of which is "and trustworthy words are not beautiful."

143. *Chuang-tzu*, the *T'ien-tao* chapter. The use of the term "adorn," *tiao*, "add craft by carving" (the same term used in the title of *Wen-hsin tiao-lung*), is so perplexing here and so unlike the usual opposition to artfulness in the *Chuang-tzu* that emendations have been proposed. By the way he takes it in the subsequent lines, Liu Hsieh seems to be reading this passage as expressing disapproval.

144. Liu Hsieh is misquoting the proper text of the *Han Fei-tzu* here (or using a variant text), reading ts'ai* for another character.

145. There is a play on *cheng* 正 and *hsieh* 邪, which may refer literally to the linear straightness and crookedness of paths, but which also, as the "proper" and "deviant," carry a strong sense of value judgment.

146. Quoting and paraphrasing the "Great Preface" to the *Book of Songs*.

147. This refers to a beautiful passage in the *Ch'i-wu-lun* chapter of the *Chuang-tzu*, in which the self is described as an aggregate of constantly shifting affections, followed by reflection on the existence of some entity, some center of identity, who is truly "in charge" of all this.

148. An aphorism quoted in the biography of Li Kuang 李廣 in the *Historical Records*. It suggests that what is attractive in itself need not seek admiration, but rather that others will be drawn to it spontaneously. Here Liu Hsieh twists the sense of the proverb somewhat to stress that the attraction is due to the fact that peach and plum bear "fruit," shih*, playing on the reference of the word to what is "substantial" in writing. It might be noted, parenthetically, that Liu Hsieh, who always berates his contemporaries for ignoring the past in their quest for novelty, is himself always twisting the sense of the sources he quotes.

149. This bit of what seems to be folklore is quoted in the *Huai-nan-tzu* 准南子.

150. This is an anecdote in the now lost *Ch'üeh-tzu* 闕子, cited in the encyclopedia *T'ai-p'ing yü-lan* 大平御覽, chüan 834: "Once there was an avid fisherman of Lu who used cassia as bait, cast gold for a hook and inlaid it with silver and jade, and threw out a line of kingfisher feathers [presumably tied to the line]. The way he held the pole and the spot he chose were fine, but he didn't catch many fish."

151. "Pattern and substance in perfect balance" is the descriptive binome *pin-pin* from *Analects* VI.16: "He said, 'When substance dominates pattern we have crudeness; when

pattern dominates substance, we have clerkishness; only when pattern and substance are in perfect balance (wen* chih* pin-pin) do we have a superior person.'"

152. The reference is to *Tso chuan* (Hsiang 25).

153. Because it blossoms at dawn and the flowers fall by the same evening.

154. This is an excellent example of how Liu Hsieh makes use of the authority of the Classics in subtle ways. Here he has taken a line from the *Hsi-tz'u chuan* of the *Book of Changes* and inserted the terms of his literary argument in place of the cosmological terms of the source text. The original reads: "When the places are established for Heaven and Earth, the changes move in their midst."

155. This sentence is a verbatim quotation from the *Hsi-tz'u chuan*, cited earlier in the commentary to "Continuity and Mutation." "Firm" and "yielding" are technical terms for the unbroken and broken lines respectively in the hexagrams of the *Book of Changes*. Implied here is that the process by which a literary work grows or by which literary history occurs is identical to the schematized development of an archetypal situation in a hexagram, developing from the bottom line to the top line.

156. The metallurgical analogy wobbles here. Liu Hsieh's point is simply that the normative form should be a model for the particular shape of the work.

157. This passage is largely a quotation from the beginning of the *P'ien-mu* chapter in the *Chuang-tzu*. The point of the image in the *Chuang-tzu* is an unnecessary excess of attention to cultivation (wen*) and the fine points of behavior.

158. *Shih** is an "event" or "matter." The same term is used for the source phrases by which reference may be made to historical events, persons, anecdotes, famous opinions, and the like. By the pairing or grouping of such shih* ("matching categories") a discourse is developed. Thus the line refers to gathering the material from earlier texts. Liu Hsieh has a chapter on this aspect of composition.

159. The phrase in quotation marks derives from a passage in the *P'ien-mu* chapter of *Chuang-tzu*, pejoratively describing one who is "webbed toed in argumentation."

160. There are native Chinese traditions for such discourse, but Liu Hsieh's Buddhist training would have exposed him to far more rigorous traditions of argumentation.

161. Both the notion of descriptive completeness in an orderly set of antithetical balances and the movement of serial compensation can perhaps be traced back to the *Book of Changes*. The *Book of Changes* is probably the supreme example of a text that claims to include all "points."

162. Although this is true of most of the terms used to describe a lush style, the use of the quotation from *Chuang-tzu*, "a mind wandering at its leisure through intricately carved sentences," is a particularly fine example of a pejorative phrase forced to do service as a positive description.

163. Although there was a primitive semiotics developing in the pre-Ch'in period, these interests were largely abandoned in the Western Han. From the Han until the nineteenth century, the description of language (appearing primarily in Classical studies and poetics) was not separated from larger questions of rhetoric and argumentation. This very loose, unsystematic tradition bears little similarity to its two Western counterparts: Grammar and Rhetoric. Most of the functions of grammar were treated on the lexical level. There were a few broad categories such as "helping words" (particles), and from the Sung on, "solid" and "empty" words, "living" and "dead" words; however, the most common categories of reference were semantic catergories, derived from lexicographical traditions (i.e., instead of "nouns," we have "flora," "human affairs," etc.). Syntax was not distinguished from larger-scale questions of the organization of discourse (taxis). Both syntax and *taxis* were described by a flexible vocabulary of sequencing, using terms such as "forward motion," "inverse motion," "reversal," "winding," and so on. In short, the purely formal features of language were not distinguished from the meaning of the particular utterance.

164. I.e., bounded units to contain them.

165. It is unclear whether the positions are those of the characters within a *chü* or of the *chü* within a *chang*.

166. Very similar formulations are found in the K'ung Ying-ta *cheng-yi*, 正義, the scholiastic subcommentaries on the Classics which reached their final form in the early T'ang, but which are a compendium of classical scholarship between the third century

and the T'ang. See Cheng Tien and Mai Mei-ch'iao, *Ku-Han-yü yü-fa-hsüeh tzu-liao hui-pien*, pp. 208ff.

167. Perhaps the closest analogy in English can be found in editing Shakespeare's sonnets, where wonders can be worked in the understanding of lines by moving commas.

168. The T'ang Classical scholar Ch'eng Po-yü distinguishes a "phrase" (*yen*) from a *chü* as follows: "We call it a *chü* only when there is something said afterward that continues it, just as there are bends and curves in roads and alleys." See *Mao-Shih chih-shuo* 毛詩指說 (*Ssu-k'u ch'üan-shu* ed.), 9b.

169. This is peculiar to *Wen-hsin tiao-lung*, though consonant with the description of *chü* in Classical studies. Later scholars sometimes speak of *chü*, as units of meaning.

170. "Sets down language," *li-yen*, is literally "establishes language," and is one of the "three things that do not decay" (see Ts'ao P'i' "Discourse on Literature," p. 70 above). It is a phrase fraught with promise.

171. See "Revering the Classics," pp. 198–199.

172. See "Revering the Classics," pp. 198–199, and "Determination of Momentum," pp. 237–238.

173. This refers to a practice in early recitation and application of the *Book of Songs* (not in their composition), a practice by which someone would recite lines from one of the *Songs* out of context to make a point. An excellent example of this is Hsien-ch'iu Meng's citation of a stanza from the *Book of Songs*, to whose interpretation Mencius so strongly objected (see pp. 24–26 above). Liu Hsieh treats this phenomenon as if it were part of the original composition. Considering the immense ingenuity which exegetes of the *Book of Songs* devoted to proving the perfect integrity of every word and the absolute necessity of every line to contribute to the whole, this comment is most peculiar.

174. This is a phrase in the *Hsi-tz'u chuan* describing the virtues of the *Book of Changes*.

175. See "The Poetic Exposition on Literature" ll. 143–150 and 169–174 for a similar vision of the loneliness of the word or line that does fit in with its society. "Proper sequence," *tz'u*, may also be read as "place to lodge."

176. The history of the interpretation of *pi* and *hsing* is treated extensively in Pauline Yu, *The Reading of Imagery in the Chinese Tradition*.

177. The Mao commentary to the *Book of Songs* does not note the presence of *fu* or *pi**, only of *hsing**.

178. There are numerous explanations of this sentence. The omission of any mention of the Odes, *Ya**, or Hymns, *Sung*, of the "Six Principles" is one problem, though perhaps, as Chou Chen-fu suggests, these are implicit in the mention of *Feng**. The point of the sentence seems to be that all of the "Six Principles" are obvious to readers except for *hsing**, and for that reason it was necessary for Mao to note the presence of that mode in his commentary.

179. 譬, *pi*, cognate with the *pi** under discussion.

180. The use of this second *pi* 譬 in reference to *hsing** probably derives from one of the commonplace phrases used to explain *hsing** in Classical scholarship, *ch'ü pi yin lei* 取譬引類, "to get a comparison and draw in categorical analogy." For a discussion of these definitions, see Yu, *Reading of Imagery*, pp. 58–59. However, this phrase is often linked with other explanations: "to entrust a matter to a thing," *t'o shih** *yü wu** 託事於物 and "to stir the mind," (variously phrased in Chinese). "Circling," *huan* 環, was a favorite term of Liu Hsieh and is often associated with what is covert (*yin* 隱): the comparison "bends around out of sight."

181. It might be pointed out that in the paragraph above *t'o* 託 is given as a variant for "record" 記, and has been preferred by many modern commentators.

182. This is one of the modes of expression given in the *Tso chuan* (Ch'eng 15). See "Revering the Classics," pp. 195 and 608n49.

183. This is a phrase from the *Hsi-tz'u chuan*, describing the way the hexagrams work. Liu Hsieh probably has the Images in mind particularly here.

184. "*Kuan* sing the ospreys" refers to *Book of Songs* 1; the above is a reference to *Book of Songs* 20. Both of these poems use bird images that are taken to refer to the virtuous qualities of women. The images are classed by Mao as *hsing** the quality of the two birds "resembling" (the terms used are *fang* 方 and *hsiang** 象) those of the ladies in question.

185. A quotation from *Tso chuan* (Chao 5), here applied to understanding the *hsing** in these poems.

186. All of these are similes and metaphors from the *Book of Songs*.

187. These are also lines from the *Book of Songs*.

188. This distinction will be more fully elaborated in the seventeenth-century writings of Wang Fu-chih and Yeh Hsieh.

189. There is a text that contains what purports to be the missing section of the chapter. Virtually all scholars consider this to be a Ming forgery. In recent years Chan Ying, one of the leading specialists in *Wen-hsin tiao-lung*, has made a forceful argument for this section's authenticity. See Chan Ying, *Wen-hsin tiao-lung te feng-ko hsüeh*, pp. 78–105. A refutation of Chan Ying's arguments can be found in Yang Ming-chao, *Hsüeh-pu-yi chai tsa-chu*, pp. 501–516.

190. I hyphenate the translation of *hsiu* as "out-standing" to recall something of the etymological force of *hsiu* (something that "stands out" or is "salient"), and further to suggest excellence without the translation's disappearing entirely into the vagueness of the category of "excellence."

191. The metaphor of the "ear of grain standing lofty" is close to the earliest semantic value of *hsiu*, from which other, more comon meanings were extended.

192. Chang Hsieh, *Sui-han-t'ang shih-hua*, in Ting Fu-pao, ed., *Li-tai shih-hua hsü-pien*, p. 456.

193. One might note that "latency" was a property of *hsing**, "affective image." Although *hsiu* was not explicitly associated with *pi**, "comparison," the passages that Liu Hsieh cited as examples of *pi**, would be considered *hsiu-chü*, "out-standing lines."

194. The passage cited might just as easily be understood as a *hu-wen*, a common rhetorical recombination ("A and B are X and Y" is recast "A is X and B is Y"), by which the passage would mean simply "giving fluency and coherence to the words and the truths."

195. Chou Chen-fu and Lu K'an-ju both interpret this as harmony between the sections of a piece.

196. This is associated with judging the propriety of ornamentation. Purple and brown were the two primary colors, referring to Heaven and Earth respectively.

197. "From a general point of view" (*ta-t'i**) in this context can also be interpreted literally as "a work with a large scope," its magnitude being the condition of the organizational principles described subsequently.

198. This line is a free expansion of a statement attributed to Confucius in the *Hsi-tz'u chuan*.

199. In Chinese these pores will be associated with *wen**, a "pattern" covering the body. The tin is for hardness; the gold is for malleability; together they form the alloy for a good sword. The original text reads something like "as beans join with yellow," a proposition that makes no sense even to the most learned commentators (with the exception of Lu K'an-ju who offers an ingenious explanation from medical lore on the use of beans in curing jaundice). The translation given above is based on one of the emendations proposed.

200. This simile is based on a couplet from the *Book of Songs* 218.

201. Mixed metaphors were not considered a fault in Chinese rhetoric, but this comparison of a hand holding reins to the spokes meeting at the axel is as unfortunate as it is visually effective. We have one metaphor of a moving carriage piled upon another metaphor of a moving carriage.

202. "Goes off or lingers" develops from the metaphor of carriage driving, though in the literary context it would be natural to read this as "getting rid of or keeping" something in a composition.

203. "Tight or loose" is also "long and short," referring to the length of the composition, its parts, or its rhythms.

204. The four characters translated as "will send something off with it" is a guess. It is suspected that the text as we have it is corrupt.

205. This is the judgment on one of the lines in the hexagram *kuai*, a negative hexagram, suggesting blockage in the final stages of a process.

206. This refers to a famous statement by the great Han writer Yang Hsiung that "Language is the voice of mind."

207. For a full discussion of these issues see Pauline Yu, "Formal Distinctions in

Chinese Literary Theory," in Bush and Murck, eds., *Theories of the Arts in China*, pp. 27–53.

208. See p. 29.

209. I.e., later works like the *Li chi*, "Record of Rites," and the *Tso chuan*, "Tso Tradition."

210. Literally "I would like to snatch away his spear, then strike his own shield with it."

211. Despite Liu Hsieh's many assertions of the filiation of contemporary literary genres to the Classics, this sharp dissociation of the Classics from issues in contemporary literary discussion anticipates Hsiao T'ung's decision to leave the Classics in a separate category and exclude them from the *Wen hsüan*.

212. See p. 84 above.

213. See Lu Chi, "Poetic Exposition on Literature," ll. 115–116, and elsewhere.

214. This combines two versions of a story about King Ching of Chou, one in the *Tso chuan* (Chao 21) and the other in the *Kuo-yü* 國語 (Chou-yü). King Ching wanted to cast a bell; his advisors told him not to, but he went ahead against their advice. When the bell was completed, a professional musician told him it was in harmony with the note he was seeking; but a more honest musician informed him that it was not, the reason being that the king's government was not in sufficient harmony to permit Heaven to give that note.

215. I have accepted Chou Chen-fu's very persuasive emendation in the first part of this line, based on a passage from the *Shuo-yüan* 說苑 on Yung-men-tzu tuning his zither.

216. This comes from an anecdote in the *Chan-kuo ts'e* 戰國策: the person who proposed the journey of a thousand leagues had everything perfect except for one thing: the rope he was using for his horse was too long.

217. Of course, he has not at all set them out in this chapter. Chou Chen-fu would like to take *p'ien* here not as "chapter" but as the second half of the *Wen-hsin tiao-lung*. It is an attractive solution although it twists the usage.

218. In an untranslated chapter, "The Measure of the Vessel," *Ch'eng-ch'i* 程器, Liu Hsieh addresses the question of innate ability.

219. Attention to both of these phenomena comes from the almanacs, included in several early works. Under the headings of each month such almanacs list the seasonal changes in plants and animals and the proper activities for human beings.

220. These lines are a direct quotation from *Tso chuan* (Chao 9).

221. This echoes a famous line from *Huai-nan-tzu*: "We see one leaf fall and know that the year is coming toward its end."

222. Literally "drawing forth mind" (*hsin**).

223. Because Liu Hsieh goes on to cite descriptive phrases from the *Book of Songs*, the primary reference here is probably to the poets of the *Book of Songs*; but the statement is paradigmatic for all who write poetry.

224. See "Spirit Thought," p. 203.

225. It is unclear here whether "giving the fullness of principle" refers to the quality of the physical thing or their conceptual associations from the standard commentary to the *Book of Songs*. The "gleaming sun" is that which will reveal whether a person is trustworthy or not; it is the witness in an oath which the speaker of the song swears. The "faint stars" are the ladies of the harem, who accept their subordinate position.

226. Cf. Longinus, *Peri Hupsous* X.6, describing a passage of Homer in which danger is "stamped into" the language.

227. English has no exact equivalent of the descriptive binomial expressions that play such a large role in both literary and spoken Chinese. However, there are some colloquial examples that can serve as rough analogies: in a colloquial usage such as "wishy-washy," we are given some integral of manner. Any attempt at defining "wishy-washy" ("the manner of not being assertive, of not having bold and definite opinions") is somehow unequal to the richness of the application of the phrase. For most words, a synonymn or a periphrastic explanation can serve as an adequate, if imperfect substitute. But the attempt to define "wishy-washy" becomes mildly comic in the difference between the primary term and the definition: in such a case the primary thing we notice in the act of "definition," however correct, is its inadequacy. This should give us some sense of why Liu Hsieh felt that these binomial expressions offered some irreducible perfection in the description of the quality of

a thing. In English such phrases are "unliterary"; in Chinese they are intensely literary. Literary Chinese has thousands of such compounds, each of which is associated with some precise integral of quality, often of sensuous quality (though there are many which, like "wishy-washy," describe spiritual quality of manner). Even modern Chinese literary essays can seriously debate whether a particular poem is "wishy-washy" or "namby-pamby": these moments are a translator's despair.

228. Cf. the discussion of "shallow" color in "Latent and Out-standing," p. 266.

229. For a discussion of this passage and its relevance to contemporary poetry, see Kang-i Sun Chang, "Description of Landscape in Early Six Dynasties Poetry," in Lin and Owen, eds., *The Vitality of the Lyric Voice*, pp. 105–131.

230. This was the phrase conventionally used by critics to define what a poetic exposition (*fu*) did: it was used by Lu Chi and by Liu Hsieh himself in his chapter on the poetic exposition.

231. Modern commentators tend to reconcile such conflicting positions as if such reconciliations were implicit in the original. This process of reconciliation, which is so natural for modern intellectuals, both Chinese and Western, may be anachronistic when imposed on a "theorist" like Liu Hsieh.

232. See Ssu-k'ung T'u, "The Twenty-Four Categories of Poetry," pp. 326–329 above.

233. See Ts'ao P'i's "Discourse on Literature," p. 59 above.

234. See ibid., p. 58.

235. This anxiety was expressed by the Han writer Liu Hsin 劉歆 regarding Yang Hsiung's 揚雄 imitation of the *Book of Changes*, the *T'ai-hsüan* 太玄. Liu Hsin was worried about the lack of discernment in the modern reading public.

236. The first of these examples is the famous story in the *Tso chuan* (Ai 14) when the people of Lu captured a unicorn and thought it was a roebuck with horns. At this, Confucius gave up composing the *Spring and Autumn Annals*.

237. "Apprehends" is *chao*, literally "shines on and shows."

238. *Chuang-tzu, Tien-ti*: "The supreme music never enters the villagers' ears, but when it's 'Breaking the Willow Branch' or the 'Gleaming Flowers,' they smile and chortle."

239. This was a common story, first appearing in the "Responses to the Questions of the King of Ch'u" (*Tui Ch'u-wang wen* 對楚王問) attributed to Sung Yü 宋玉: someone on the marketplace of the Ch'u capital Ying first sang the popular song *Hsia-li Pa-jen*, and thousands joined in; but when he sang the noble song "White Snow," only ten or twenty people joined in. Thus "White Snow" became a standard example of something whose excellence is appreciated by few.

240. The music of the state of Cheng was the standard example of arts that were vulgar, easily appreciated, and morally pernicious.

241. Chüan-tzu was supposedly a Taoist and disciple of Lao-tzu. The now lost *Ch'in-hsin** in three sections was probably a philosophical treatise on zither playing.

242. The *Wang-sun-tzu* was a work, now extant only in a few fragments, that supposedly belonged to the Confucian school.

243. Tsou Shih was a pre-Ch'in literary figure who earned the nickname "Dragon-Carver Shih" because he was supposed to have embellished things with figures that looked like dragons. This passage may either be pejorative, not wanting to be a mere ornamenter, or it may simply be saying that his use of the term here is not necessarily a reference to Tsou Shih.

244. Toda Kōkyō cites an ironic parallel usage from the treatise on astronomy from the *Chin shu* 晉書: "The years and generations go on and on forever, but literary texts are not transmitted."

245. "Treatise on Laws and Punishments" in the *Han shu*: "Man's outward appearance bears a likeness to Heaven and Earth; he holds within him the Five Constants." This and the rest of the line make various reference to the human being as microcosm, a commonplace in Han thought.

246. See Ts'ao P'i's "A Discourse on Literature" pp. 68–70 above.

247. The sentence is a quotation from *Mencius* III.B.9, with the first person pronoun removed.

248. Literally "the time to establish myself," an allusion to the *Analects* II.4: "At thirty I established myself."

249. The implication is that he has become a disciple of Confucius.

250. This is a slightly misquoted line from *Mencius* II.A.2.

251. Ma Jung and his disciple Cheng Hsüan were the two greatest classical scholars of the Eastern Han. Although Classical scholarship in the Southern Dynasties had undergone significant changes, it was still considered basically an activity of "subcommentary," amplifying the work of Ma and Cheng.

252. Some of the Five Rites (Sacrificial, Funeral, Court Reception, Military, and the "excellent rites," weddings and coming-of-age ceremonies) did require the composition of literary works (for example, the temple hymns of the dynasty and funerary eulogies). For most of the other rites, certain pieces were recited or sung. As for the "Six Bureaus" (an archaic term here referring to government offices), many of the prose forms discussed in *Wen-hsin tiao-lung* were primarily for government use.

253. The implication is that literary forms have degenerated. Toda Kōkyō cites a nice parallel from the Bibliography (*Yi-wen chih* 藝文志) of the *Han shu* on the "works of thought" (*chu-tzu* 諸子): "Now we have gone far from the Sage, the skills of the Way have been lost, and we have no place to find them again."

254. The term *tz'u-jen* here may refer to writers in general, but it probably is based on the famous distinction by Yang Hsiung in his *Fa-yen*: "The *fu* as used by the poets of the *Book of Songs* (*Shih-jen*) used beauty to give a normative standard; the *fu* [poetic expositions] of the rhapsodes (*tz'u-jen*) used beauty to seduce us." See also "The Sensuous Colors of Physical Things," p. 281 above.

255. This comes from a story in the *Lieh-yü-k'ou* 列禦寇 chapter of *Chuang-tzu* in which Yeh Ho criticizes Confucius for decorating feathers with painting; i.e., adding superfluous adornment to what is already naturally beautiful.

256. This refers to a passage in the *Kua-chien* 寡見 chapter of Yang Hsiung's 楊雄 *Fa-yen* 法言 in which he criticizes contemporary scholars for this practice. As in the preceding reference, this is superfluous ornament.

257. The passage is from the *Pi-ming* 畢命 chapter of the *Book of Documents*: "In governance it is important to have constants; in language value bringing out the essentials; do not be fond of the unusual."

258. *Analects* II.16: "Applying oneself to unusual principles brings great harm."

259. There are serious problems with the interpretation of this sentence, in no small part because the word for "different," *yi*, is the same word used for "unusual" in the passage from the *Analects* quoted above. I have followed Lu K'an-ju and Mou Shih-chin here; it is an uninspired interpretation, but one can see how they derived it from the words. In Chou Chen-fu's *Wen-hsin tiao-lung hsüan-yi*, he takes the passage as a *hu-wen* 互文, a rhetorical form in which the parts of two sentences can be exchanged: "he set forth his teaching on dislike of strangeness; it discussed language in terms of bringing out the essentials." Vincent Shih allows Liu Hsieh to play with the word *yi*, in this sentence used as "unique" or "extraordinary," rather than the pejorative "unusual": "The uniqueness of the *tz'u* and the *hsün* is due to this emphasis on the essential."

260. This is an overview of the specialized writings on literature between Ts'ao P'i and Liu Hsieh's own time. Ts'ao P'i's "Discourse on Literature" survives largely intact; Lu Chi's "Poetic Exposition" survives; some of Ts'ao Chih's writings on literature survive. Fragments of Chih Yü and Li Ch'ung survive; the Ying Ch'ang work is lost, unless Liu Hsieh meant Ying's "Discourse on *Wen** and *Chih**," *Wen-chih lun* 文質論, which has nothing directly to do with literature.

261. The term translated as "suggestive" is *mi*, meaning essentially "kept secret." In this period (and indeed earlier in Ts'ao P'i's "Discourse on Literature" itself; see p. 62) *mi* often implies profundity and depth hidden beneath the surface.

262. For this distinction between *wen** and *pi*, see Chapter 44, "The General Technique."

263. This comment is based on the numerology of the *Book of Changes*: in the *Hsi-tz'u chuan*, the number fifty is given as the totality of basic divisions within which Change occurs: the Ultimate (*T'ai-chi* 太極), Heaven and Earth, the sun, moon, and four seasons, the five Elements (or Phases), the twelve months, and the twenty-four kinds of *ch'i**. However, only forty-nine of these function: the Ultimate stands apart from function. For this reason in some forms of divination there are fifty bamboo slips, but only forty-nine are actually

used. Liu Hsieh is describing the structure of his book on this model, with the "Afterword" in the supernumerary fiftieth position, corresponding to the Ultimate, the T'ai-chi, the center around which all changes are generated.

264. Note the similarity between this disclaimer and that in the preface of Lu Chi's "Poetic Exposition on Literature."

265. See p. 31.

266. "Fixed standards" are literally the carpenter's compass and ruler. "Pitcher and pipe" are proverbial images for limited capacity. Liu Hsieh is being uncharacteristically modest here.

267. Taking the emendation hsi 洗, "cleanse." Chou Chen-fu accepts the original reading ch'en 沉, producing a translation "What I have heard leaves me deeply immersed in past ages"; Chou supports this with a quotation from the Chan-kuo-ts'e: "Scholars become deeply immersed in what they hear."

CHAPTER SIX

The text used is based on that in Kuo Shao-yü's Shih-p'in chi-chieh.

1. For a discussion of the problem of unity and distinction in the structure, see Chiang Kuo-chen, Ssu-k'ung Piao-sheng yen-chiu, pp. 175–186.

2. See Lü Hsing-ch'ang, Ssu-k'ung T'u shih-lun yen-chiu, pp. 21–44. Lü's study contains an excellent discussion of the T'ang and pre-T'ang traditions informing "The Twenty-Four Categories of Poetry," traditions characterizing manner, painting, and calligraphy. I draw heavily from her work in the following discussion.

3. The tetrasyllabic verse form in which Ssu-k'ung T'u writes is, by its tradition and by its nature, more elliptical and ambiguous than the pentasyllabic and heptasyllabic verse of ordinary poetry, where there are strong thematic, generic, and structural expectations that allow a reader to construe the lines. The commentaries on the "The Twenty-Four Categories of Poetry," of course, differ in the interpretation of individual words, but most disturbing, they offer a dazzling variety of interpretations on whether the first two characters of a line are the protasis and the second two characters the apodosis, or the line is a single predicate, or each pair of characters is a coordinate predicate, or the line as a whole is the protasis of the following line. For some lines, exegetes offer virtually every kind of conjunction imaginable to unify a given line internally or join it with the following line, yet, of course, any decision has consequences for how one takes the next and following lines.

4. For example, see Maureen Robertson, " . . . To Convey What Is Precious: Ssu-k'ung T'u's Poetics and the Erh-shih-ssu Shih P'in," in Buxbaum and Mote, eds., Transition and Permanence; and Pauline Yu, "Ssu-k'ung T'u's Shih-p'in: Poetic Theory in Poetic Form," in Ronald C. Miao, ed., Studies in Chinese Poetry and Poetics, vol. 1.

5. The work is referred to in colophons by Cheng Man 鄭鄤 (1594–1638) and the bibliophile Mao Chin 毛晉 (1599–1659), quoted in Kuo Shao-yü's Shih-p'in chi-chieh, p. 57. The lateness of the work's appearance understandably raises questions regarding its authenticity. Absence of comment on the work is surprising only in the context of its later position of central importance in traditional poetics. "The Twenty-Four Categories of Poetry" originally belonged to a class of specialized T'ang works on poetics (including taxonomies and technical manuals) that were not at all widely circulated between the eleventh and seventeenth centuries (some probably seemed naive, while others probably seemed simply daffy); nearly all resurfaced only at the end of the Ming and early Ch'ing; thus they all have problematic textual histories (the late Ming was a particularly fertile era for forgery). In his bibliography of the Ssu-k'u ch'üan-shu 四庫全書, Chi Yün 紀昀 doubts the attribution of all such works with the sole exception of "The Twenty-Four Categories of Poetry" (though he does not state his grounds). The rediscovery of the Bunkyō hifuron, a compendium of works of T'ang technical poetics preserved in Japan, has shown that although we cannot reliably trace the full textual history of such works of T'ang technical poetics in the Chinese bibliographical tradition, in their present form at least some do contain genuine T'ang material. Lü Hsing-ch'ang tries to show that "The Twenty-Four Categories of Poetry" is deeply embedded in the authenticated traditions of T'ang poetics. Although I have not discussed the matter with him, I have heard that Achilles Fang has long been working to prove that "The Twenty-Four Categories of Poetry" is a forgery. This hint raised my own suspicions; and during the long

years of the present work's preparation, I have come to believe that "The Twenty-Four Categories of Poetry" might well be a forgery. Perhaps the most telling evidence against the work's authenticity is the use of many popular terms of aesthetics that came into currency only in the Sung. If this is, indeed, the source of such usages, we would expect that the work would have been more widely read and referred to. I cannot, however, disprove that the work is late T'ang. Therefore readers, while reserving large room for suspicion, may conditionally grant that "The Twenty-Four Categories of Poetry" is the work of Ssu-k'ung T'u. If the work is, in fact, a forgery, it is surely one of the most enduring, influential, and successful forgeries in the Chinese literary tradition. And it has so shaped the understanding of the history of poetics that it has earned its position in the present volume.

6. In the eleventh entry of "Interpretations of Poetry" (which is not translated in Chapter Ten), Wang Fu-chih gives his own illustrations of how this couplet should be understood. Instead of billowing clouds, Wang suggests more misty, elusive scenes: "If you can understand the subtlety (miao*) of: 'Pool and pond grow with spring plants,' and 'Butterflies flutter in the southern garden,' [both by Hsieh Ling-yün] then you can understand that the lines [from the *Book of Songs*]: 'Willows and poplars, a blur,' and, 'Falleth rain, misting down,' are sages in poetry. This is what Ssu-k'ung T'u meant by 'The norm [misquoted] lies beyond the images,/and attains the center of the ring.'"

7. See *Wen-hsin tiao-lung*, "Nature and Form": "If you attain the center of the ring, all the spokes meet there to make the wheel" (p. 217). Liu Hsieh is referring to the necessity of being able to master all particular forms.

8. *Hsiung-hun* later became a relatively common stylistic characterization, often no more than a general "grandeur"; and it was applied to a great variety of different kinds of poetic styles. Several examples are cited in Chao Fu-t'an, pp. 7–9. To give one such example, in the *Ssu-ming shih-hua* 四溟詩話 the Ming critic Hsieh Chen 謝榛 observes:

Han Yü praised Chia Tao's couplet,

Birds spend the night in the trees by the pool,
A monk knocks at the gate in the moonlight,

But this cannot match the 'potent, undifferentiated' quality of the atmosphere (ch'i*-hsiang*) in [Chia's]:

The autumn wind blows over the river Wei,
And falling leaves fill Ch'ang-an.

9. Here is one of the best examples of the difference between *ching**, "scene," and *ching**, "a world." The first eight lines present a unified "world" without presenting a unified "scene," which would imply some temporally or spatially unified act of perception. These couplets are discontinuous "scenes," even though they might all belong to the same valley landscape; however, they have a unity of quality which creates the impression that they belong together (from which we suspect they are scenes within the "world" of the valley).

10. These lines may specifically recall the famous couplet from a poem attributed to Su Wu 蘇武 on parting from Li Ling 李陵:

Since all men in the world are brothers,
Who is a traveler on the roads?

11. Quoted in Kuo Shao-yü, *Shih-p'in chi-chieh*, p. 7.

12. "For the most part he wrote only from his natural *élan* and was not restrained by forms (ko*). He was willing to set his brush to paper only if something flowed out from his own breast. From time to time his feelings and the scene would meet in perfect accord, and in an instant there were a thousand words, like rivers pouring eastward, causing people's spirits to be swept away. Among these writings there are both excellent spots and faults, but even his faults are full of phrases of his own making and his original color (pen-se). Thus for my part I find the greatest delight in his faults; what are called his excellent spots cannot

avoid being in some way repellent by their adornment and imitative qualities—these, I think, have not entirely escaped the manner and practice of literary men of recent times" (from "On the Poems of Hsiao-hsiu"): Yüan Hung-tao, *Yüan Hung-tao chi chien-chiao*, Ch'ien Po-ch'eng, ed., pp. 187–188. See also Jonathan Chaves, "The Panoply of Images: A Reconsideration of Literary Theory of the Kung-an School," in Bush and Murck, eds., *Theories of the Arts in China*.

13. Prior to Ssu-k'ung T'u, *han-hsü* 含蓄 had been used in poems by Tu Fu and Han Yü to describe a murky atmosphere. However, both components of the compound were very commonly used in the T'ang as verbs describing emotion "held back" (*han*) and "stored up" (*hsü*). The compound term is notably absent in modal taxonomies of both this and earlier periods; indeed this verse seems to be its earliest use as a modal quality. Since *han-hsü* came into common use in the Sung, and since there is no evidence that "The Twenty-Four Categories of Poetry" was read (except by Su Shih), we must make the not unreasonable assumption that it appeared in the late T'ang in oral discourse on aesthetics. Or, if we have a skeptical disposition, we may use it as a piece of evidence that "The Twenty-Four Categories of Poetry" is a later forgery.

14. See *Wen-hsin tiao-lung*, "Spirit Thought," pp. 205–206 above.

15. The couplet cited by Ch'i-chi sounds nothing at all like the mode as described by Ssu-k'ung T'u: it is offhand and extempore, closer to "fresh" in the colloquial English sense. Among the collateral passages cited in Chao Fu-t'an, we might note that the poet Wei Chuang 韋莊 (836–910) used *ch'ing-ch'i* to describe the finely crafted poetry of the early-ninth-century poet Hsü Hun 許渾, a style that could be reconciled with Ssu-k'ung T'u's description of the mode. But then in his 1058 preface to the *Yang-ch'un chi* 陽春集, Ch'en Shih-hsiu 陳世修 used *ch'ing-ch'i* to describe the rather languid songs of Feng Yen-ssu 馮延巳 (903–960); moreover, Ch'en compounded the description of Feng's talent as *ch'ing-ch'i piao-yi*, the latter element being Category 22, "Drifting Aloof." I cite these examples to suggest how little agreement there was on the application of these terms, and how easily they might be combined.

16. Of course, if "The Twenty-Four Categories of Poetry" is a Ming forgery, this would be merely repeating a commonplace value.

17. *Tsin shu* (Peking, 1974), p. 2384.

18. This may have been something of a commonplace in the second half of the ninth century. See the first couplet of Tu Hsün-ho's 杜荀鶴 (846–904) quatrain "On Reading the Poets" (*Tu chu-chia shih* 讀諸家詩):

Of belles lettres and poetic expositions the masters are few,
But for the most difficult among difficult things nothing surpasses poetry.

19. See the commentary to "The Poetic Exposition on Literature," ll. 127–128.

20. From this point on I have followed the *Ssu-pu ts'ung-k'an* edition; instead of more seven-character couplets, Kuo Shao-yü's *Shih-p'in chi-chieh* offers quatrains in five- and seven-syllable lines.

21. Accepting Kuo Shao-yü's suggested emendation from *jih-jih*, 日日 to *tan-jih* 旦日.

22. This sentence is added in some editions.

CHAPTER SEVEN

The text used is the *Liu-yi shih-hua* edited by Cheng Wen.

1. However offensive the distinction between "high" and "low" may be to the modern sensibility, in the Chinese tradition (as in the Western tradition) there was a strong sense of hierarchy in genres and styles. It was perceived as a hierarchy of status, and upon this hierarchy were superimposed various sets of antithetical values: serious and frivolous; important (i.e., worthy of preservation) and disposable; archaic, allusive language and vernacular diction; public and private; elegant (*ya**) and vulgar (*su*). The use of the language of relative elevation is meant in no way to suggest that "high" is better than "low"; it simply reflects the relative gradations from the most conventional cultural standards. Indeed there was an enduring strain in the Chinese literary and cultural tradition that claimed, either explicitly or implicitly, that the "low" was superior to the "high."

2. For an excellent general study of Ou-yang Hsiu's literary works, the reader is encouraged to consult Ronald C. Egan, *The Literary Works of Ou-yang Hsiu*. When Egan uses the term "informal prose," he means works such as prefaces and letters that would be included in an author's official collection. I use the term "informal prose" differently, to refer to writings such as miscellanies, random notes, and informal letters—genres that were usually excluded from a writer's official collection.

3. See Jonathan Chaves, "Ko Li-fang's Subtle Critiques on Poetry," *Bulletin of Sung-Yüan Studies* 14: 39–49 (1979).

4. *Jade Chips of the Poets* arranges *shih-hua* quotations around useful terms in technical poetics, then gives a chronological survey of major poets with *shih-hua* comments (though the chronological anthology of comments on major poets precedes the late Southern Sung). There is a German translation of *Shih-jen yü-hsieh* by Volker Klöpsch: *Die Jadesplitter der Dichter: Die Welt der Dichtung in der Sicht eines Klassikers der chinesischen Literaturkritik.*

5. In the major rewriting of the history of traditional Chinese literary criticism that has occurred in this century, one of the most striking events has been the new importance accorded to works in the genres of thought. The most striking example is the new prestige of *Wen-hsin tiao-lung* (although its rehabilitation had begun in the Ch'ing). Yeh Hsieh's "Origins of Poetry" is another example. Both of these texts were worthy of renewed attention; but at the same time the remarkably simple-minded comments in the *Lun-heng*, by the Eastern Han writer Wang Ch'ung, have received undue prominence because, utterly wanting in nuance, they offer an easy contribution to the "history of ideas." Wisely, the *Lun-heng* was generally ignored in traditional criticism.

6. Since the ability of the written text to authentically present the person was an important issue, we often find critical comments asserting the opposite case, occasions of inauthenticity and the failure of writing to reveal the true person. One case in the "Remarks on Poetry" is the untranslated entry XXVI on the scholarly but unusually taciturn Chao Shih-min. After citing an exuberant couplet on spring by Chao, Ou-yang Hsiu comments: "This is not at all characteristic of the kind of person he is." I am not suggesting that Chinese writers on literature naively believed that the quality of the person was embodied in the text; rather it was a concern of paramount importance and one that dominates many of the entries in "Remarks on Poetry." A particularly bald inversion of understanding the person through the poem can be found in Yüan Hao-wen's 元好問 (1190–1257) criticism of P'an Yüeh 潘岳 (247–300), which begins by denying Yang Hsiung's famous statement that "Spoken language is the sound of mind; written words are the marks [or pictures] of mind." Since P'an Yüeh wrote eloquently of the life of retirement while pursuing public position, Yüan Hao-wen begins his epigram: "Poetic 'sounds and pictures of the mind' are generally untrue,/One can scarcely know a man from his writing." The translation is from Wixted, *Poems on Poetry*, p. 63.

7. The "mocking verse," *ch'ao*, was usually composed in ordinary verse lines. This exchange, however, is in rhythmic prose: the sally and the perfectly matched parallel retort are each in two periods of seven and four syllables.

8. The verb *kuo* was also used for paying a brief and casual social visit, like the colloquial English "stops by."

9. In his *Shih-lin shih-hua* 石林詩話 (second or third decade, twelfth century) Yeh Meng-tê 葉夢得 articulates this principle quite directly: "Everyone in the world understands perfectly well that poets achieve success by the use of single words." But Yeh goes on to exempt Tu Fu, whose stylistic transformations are such that there is no single point where one can see the artistically chosen word.

10. See Yu-shih Chen, "The Literary Theory and Practice of Ou-yang Hsiu," in Adele Rickett, ed., *Chinese Approaches to Literature*, pp. 79–80.

11. Ironically, the first couplet Ou-yang Hsiu attributes to Chou P'u is also attributed, on better evidence, to the poet Tu Hsün-ho, a near contemporary of Chou P'u. Chou P'u may have written his finest couplet through a slip in Ou-yang Hsiu's memory; and it is amusing that Ou-yang Hsiu's authority has led later critics to insist that the couplet is indeed by Chou P'u rather than Tu Hsün-ho.

12. On reasonably good authority Mei Yao-ch'en is credited with the *Hsü chin-chen shih-ko* 續金針詩格, of which portions still survive. The *Hsü chin-chen shih-ko* is repre-

sentative of the T'ang tradition of technical poetics by which the compositional proprieties of regulated verse were taught.

13. For a comparison of this practice in *shih-hua* with Matthew Arnold's "touchstones," see Wai-leung Wong, "Selections of Lines in Chinese Poetry Talk Criticism—With a Comparison between the Selected Couplets and Matthew Arnold's 'Touchstone,'" in John J. Deeny, ed., *Chinese-Western Comparative Literature*, pp. 33–44.

14. This capacity to "meet" the scene in the poet's mind is reminiscent of Chung Tzu-ch'i's ability to see what was in the mind of Po-ya when he played his zither: see pp. 286–287. Ultimately this concept of understanding can be traced back to Mencius' expanation of how to understand the *Book of Songs*; see pp. 24–26.

15. For a discussion of the relation between couplets and class-concepts in Chinese, see Stephen Owen, *Traditional Chinese Poetry and Poetics*, pp. 78–103.

16. Note that the above exegesis could be done very differently; for instance, the tracks could be the poet's own as he sets out. The reading above comes from numerous Sung echoes of this couplet.

17. For a full discussion of Mei Yao-ch'en's poetry, see Jonathan Chaves, *Mei Yao-ch'en and the Development of Early Sung Poetry*.

18. The historical veracity of Ou-yang Hsiu's claim is questionable: there is no evidence that Su Shun-ch'in's poetry was more widely appreciated than Mei Yao-ch'en's (indeed there is evidence to the contrary). But Ou-yang Hsiu is deep in his own myth of misunderstood plainness and protective of his role as the unique *chih-yin*.

19. Entry XVIII is clearly Ou-yang Hsiu's complement to Mei Yao-ch'en's comment in entry XV (note the use of "also"). The two intervening entries treat totally disparate topics: one on the gleaning of historical information from the "Palace Poems" of the late-eighth-century poet Wang Chien 王建, the other on the use of some interesting colloquialisms in poetry. These have been left untranslated to spare the patience of the English reader. If we can trust the present order of entries in the "Remarks on Poetry," this is an excellent example of the *shih-hua*'s value of randomness. Entries XV and XVIII are the most closely related entries in the work (though it is easy to read entry XII as the first of a sequence of Mei Yao-ch'en's comments on technical poetics). By breaking them apart, Ou-yang Hsiu preserves the appearance of the casual remark, randomly recalled. At the same time he keeps the two (or three) entries in sequence so that they can still work together in the proper way. It should be added, however, that some scholars would probably consider the obvious connection between XII, XV, and XVIII to be evidence that the present order of the text is not the original order.

20. Beneath the surface of "Remarks on Poetry" there is an exceedingly complicated literary historical relation between Ou-yang Hsiu and Mei Yao-ch'en. Ou-yang Hsiu was Mei Yao-ch'en's most ardent supporter, but he had a very clear notion of the kind of poet he wanted Mei to be. Although Mei Yao-ch'en often played the role Ou-yang Hsiu had given him, Mei also had other poetic values (like those expressed in entry XII) that had no place in the literary historical drama Ou-yang Hsiu was organizing. The Mei Yao-ch'en of modern literary histories and anthologies is Ou-yang Hsiu's Mei Yao-ch'en. But writing outside the context of Ou-yang Hsiu and his circle, Mei often produced couplets like those Yen Shu so admired. We must accept the "Remarks on Poetry" as we have it, but I suspect Mei Yao-ch'en had been quite proud of his couplets and Yen Shu's praise, until Ou-yang Hsiu "expressed his doubts." Ou-yang Hsiu "doubts" and Mei Yao-ch'en obligingly confirms his opinion, strengthening Ou-yang Hsiu's conviction that he is the only one who truly understands Mei Yao-ch'en.

CHAPTER EIGHT

The text used is based on Kuo Shao-yü's *Ts'ang-lang shih-hua chiao-shih*.

1. Ts'ang-lang was Yen Yü's psudonymn.

2. In Yen's "Letter to Wu Ling," published in Kuo Shao-yü, *Ts'ang-lang shih-hua chiao-shih*, p. 234.

3. This version is translated in Klöpsch, *Die Jadesplitter der Dichter*.

4. Another consequence, given as a seed in Yen Yü's work and fulfilled by the Ming

archaists, was the restoration of the importance of pre-T'ang poetry, which, with the notable exception of T'ao Ch'ien, had been widely ignored in the Sung.

5. See Richard Lynn, "Orthodoxy and Enlightenment—Wang Shih-chen's Theory of Poetry and its Antecedents" in Wm. Theodore de Bary, ed., *The Unfolding of Neo-Confucianism*, pp. 217–269. In this chapter, I have taken the position that the most significant aspect of "Ts'ang-lang's Remarks on Poetry" is neither Yen Yü's concepts in themselves nor their lineage, but rather his critical voice and the way in which he deploys concepts. Where I discuss the concepts themselves, my treatment overlaps with that of Lynn, certainly the most learned and subtle expositor of Yen Yü and his legacy in English. For a fuller discussion of Yen Yü, I recommend that the reader consult Lynn's various writings on the subject.

6. To some degree the *Book of Songs* had been such an immutable standard, but it never offered a serious alternative to contemporary poetic practice. In the eighth and ninth centuries, the "old style," *ku-feng**, was for some writers such a historically realized standard, but it remained a poetics opposed to contemporary practice, never entirely supplanting it.

7. Lynn, "Orthodoxy and Enlightenment"; and Richard Lynn, "Alternate Routes to Self-Realization in Ming Theories of Poetry", in Bush and Murck, eds., *Theories of the Arts in China*, pp. 319–340.

8. Such a polemical articulation of values can be traced back to the proto-orthodoxy of Han Yü 韓愈 (768–824); but Han Yü's writing, as a whole, shows a tolerance that subverts any rigid application of his archaist values. The rhetoric of contempt figures in some *shih-hua* comments, most notably in those attributed to the supremely intolerant Wang An-shih; but these were not situated in a coherent program of literary orthodoxy.

9. There is much scholarship on both the sources of this analogy and its appearance in earlier poetry. Discussions in English can be found in Wixted, *Poems on Poetry*, pp. 239–241. The standard Chinese article on the subject is by Kuo Shao-yü, "'Ts'ang-lang shih-hua' yi-ch'ien chih shih ch'an shuo," reprinted in his *Chao-yü-shih ku-tien wen-hsüeh lun-chi*, vol. 1. The preceding scholars all focus on Sung antecedents of the analogy. Wang Meng-ou has traced elements of the analogy back to the T'ang in "Yen Yü yi ch'an yü shih shih-chieh," in his *Ku-tien wen-hsüeh lun t'an-so*.

10. For discussions of this question, see Jonathan Chaves, "Not the Way of Poetry: The Poetics of Experience in the Sung Dynasty," *Chinese Literature: Essays, Articles, and Reviews* 4.2 (1982); and especially Stuart Sargent, "Can Latecomers Get There First? Sung Poets and T'ang Poetry," *Chinese Literature: Essays, Articles, and Reviews* 4.2 (1982).

11. Chang Chien, *Ts'ang-lang shih-hua yen-chiu* (Taipei, 1966), p. 11.

12. There are several arrangements of the first chapter of "Ts'ang-lang's Remarks on Poetry." Here I have followed Kuo Shao-yü's arrangement in *Ts'ang-lang shih-hua chiao-shih*. For a discussion of the text, see Kuo Shao-yü, "Shih ts'e 'Ts'ang-lang shih-hua' te pen-lai mien-mao," reprinted in his *Chao-yü-shih ku-tien wen-hsüeh lun-chi*, vol. 2.

13. "Retreat," *t'ui-ch'ü*, was a term commonly used in Buddhist texts in reference to progress along the path to enlightenment; to "retreat" under certain circumstances was sometimes recommended and sometimes not. Although the tone of this passage is distinctly that of a Ch'an master, no Ch'an text I have seen ever suggests such total failure following "retreat." The secret subtext of Yen Yü's argument is probably not Ch'an at all but the famous passage in *Mencius* I.A.3, in which Mencius uses the example of the equal culpability of soldiers who have fled different distances on the field of battle to show the existence of an absolute standard of virtue that finally admits no distinction in degrees of approximation. A "poetry demon," *shih-mo*, was a popular way of accounting for the passion for poetry, but was usually associated with bad or voluminous writing.

14. Literally "from the top to the bottom," echoing the paradigm of history as descent. There is no implication that the end of this course of study, the High T'ang, is in any way inferior to the beginning.

15. Since there are many Han *yüeh-fu*, it is uncertain which are intended here. In his *Ts'ang-lang shih-hua chiao-shih*, Kuo Shao-yü cites Wang Yün-hsi 王運熙 as taking these as the four old *yüeh-fu* in the Wu-ch'en edition of *Wen hsüan*.

16. This is the terminology of Buddhist enlightenment, literally "becoming aware and entering," an awareness that leads immediately to the heart of things.

17. These are all Ch'an catch-phrases for the doctrine of instant enlightenment.

18. See pp. 65–67 (Ts'ao P'i) and pp. 457–458 (Wang Fu-chih).

19. In his article "Orthodoxy and Enlightenment," Richard Lynn has suggested at least one parallel between Yen Yü's description of the right path in poetic studies and Ch'eng Yi on classical studies. Throughout the opening section, there are numerous parallels with Sung theories of reading the Confucian Classics: comparative reading of passages, self-evident judgment following from reading, and the spontaneous internalization of judgment into praxis.

20. A good example of the Romantic version of poetic historicism is found in Friedrich Schlegel's "Epochen der Dichtkunst" in his *Gespräch über die Poesie*. At the end of this discourse, German poets are urged to follow the example of Goethe in assimilating all previous poetry as a series of possibilities.

21. In later, Ming versions of this poetic orthodoxy, there were different historical moments that embodied the perfection of different genres.

22. This model created absurd divisions between the ideal history of poetry and the implicit judgments of the reading public; for example, speaking from a literary historical point of view, we would be forced to conclude that a High T'ang poet like Li Ch'i was a "better" poet than the late-T'ang poet Li Shang-yin, even though Li Shang-yin was obviously more widely read, more appreciated, and more influential. Even today many Chinese literary histories give disproportionate attention to minor High T'ang poets over major mid- and late-T'ang poets.

23. For an excellent discussion of these terms and Chinese theories of literary history in general, see Maureen Robertson, "Periodization in the Arts and Patterns of Change in Traditional Chinese Literary History," in Bush and Murck, eds., *Theories of the Arts in China*, pp. 3–26.

24. One may contrast the formulation of the "study of poetry" in the slightly earlier, anonymous *Man-chai yü-lu* 漫齋語錄 (between 1186 and 1206). Note the absence of the historical curriculum and the weaker sense of the gap of final understanding (the following translation reflects the colloquial quality of this work): "When you want to study poetry, you've got to read the old poets thoroughly and look for the spots where they paid particular attention—there's hardly a careless line or a careless phrase. After reading like this, you've got to put your own brush to paper and try to emulate them. It doesn't matter whether you succeed or not—just study like this, and after a time you'll get it right. I'm afraid it's absurd, the way in which people these days won't either study or watch the way the old writers handled things—and yet they still want to be as famous as the old writers . . ."

25. It should be pointed out that these technical terms are quite vague, and there is latitude of interpretation on their scope of reference.

26. Though the phrase was commonly used in reference to literature and the other arts, it has its origins in the *Hsi-tz'u chuan* of the *Book of Changes*.

27. The "eye of the law", *fa*-yen* is a Buddhist techinical term; it is that by which one can correctly perceive the operations of Dharma, the laws governing Buddhist reality.

28. "Original color", *pen*-se** is an important critical term referring to the qualities that are inherent in a thing; variation and change are possible, but it is a falling away from the original state.

29. Lynn, "Orthodoxy and Enlightenment," p. 222.

30. For antecedents to this opinion see, for example, Lü Pen-chung's 呂本中 (1084–1145) comment on Ts'ao Chih 曹植: "In breadth and depth works like [Ts'ao Chih's] *Ch'i-ai shih* 七哀詩 can no longer be attained by people who write poetry: this is surely because at that point there was not yet any attention (*yi**) to language." Cited in Hu Tzu, *T'iao-hsi yü-yin ts'ung-hua*, p. 332.

31. A similar interplay between authority and the transcendence of authority can also be found in Ch'an. The Ch'an master, too, demands unswerving obedience from the disciple—but the Ch'an master does not anticipate the disciple's disobedience, nor does he "protest too much" in laying claim to his authority.

32. This alludes to the famous passage on language in the *Wai-wu* 外物 chapter of the *Chuang-tzu*: "The reason for the trap is the fish; when you catch the fish, you forget the trap. The reason for the snare is the rabbit; when you catch the rabbit, you forget the snare. The reason for words is the concept (*yi**); when you grasp [catch] the concept, you forget the words. Ah, how may I catch a man who has forgotten words to have a word with him!"

33. "To sing what is in the heart" is *yin-yung ch'ing*-hsing**, a quotation from the "Great Preface."

34. See the "Record of Music," p. 53.

35. For a discussion of *p'ing-tan*, see Chaves, *Mei Yao-ch'en*, pp. 114–125; and Egan, *Ou-yang Hsiu* pp. 82–85. One cannot help noticing that every T'ang poet mentioned in Yen Yü's list is a mid-T'ang or late-T'ang poet. Wang An-shih, the ardent admirer of the High T'ang poet Tu Fu, is unmentioned.

36. In popular poetics, *ts'ai* was quite simply the "materials" a poet could use. For example, the *T'ang-tzu-hsi yü-lu* observes: "Whenever you want to write poetry, you have to gather poetic material (*shih-ts'ai*) in your daily life to make use of"; and "You've got to read the 'Explanations of the *Yüeh-fu*'—there's a lot of poetic material in it." Cited in Ho Wen, *Chu-ch'uang shih-hua* (1206), Ch'ang Chen-kuo and Chiang Yü, eds. p. 7.

37. We might recall here that the alternation between these two grounds for poetry—world and written tradition—had been the rhetorical antithesis that governed much of the structure of Lu Chi's "Poetic Exposition on Literature."

38. A T'ang analogy to Yen Yü's rejection of *li** can be found in the first line (in the most popular of its various readings) of Ssu-k'ung T'u's "Encomium on Poetry and Poetic Expositions" (*Shih fu tsan* 詩賦贊): "Understanding the Way is not poetry" *Chih Tao Jei shih* 知道非詩. It is possible Yen Yü had this in mind (though unlikely). Ssu-k'ung T'u's statement, while carrying a rhetorical force similar to Yen Yü's, is so vague as to be unobjectionable: no reasonable person would claim that "understanding the Way" and poetry were identical. Yen Yü's statement is radical because it is more precise.

39. One should note how Western aesthetics clearly distinguishes aesthetic interest from understanding. This is already essential to Kant's argument in the *Critique of Judgment*, and is elaborated into a distinction between the aesthetic drive and the drive to understanding in Johann Gottlieb Fichte's "On the Spirit and the Letter in Philosophy" translated in David Simpson, ed., *German Aesthetic and Literary Criticism*. It is not a problem that can be easily resolved, nor disregarded simply because we do not approve of it. Hans-Georg Gadamer's 1964 essay "Aesthetics and Hermeneutics" begins by restating the same division adumbrated by Yen Yü: "If we define the task of hermeneutics as the bridging of personal or historical distance between minds, then the experience of art would seem to fall entirely outside its province." See Hans-Georg Gadamer, *Philosophical Hermeneutics*, David E. Linge, tr., p. 95.

40. Indeed the influence of Yen Yü was such that this phrase is often cited as if these were Yen Yü's own words and not a quotation.

41. Ch'ien Chung-shu, *T'an yi lu*, rev. ed., pp. 306–307, gives a series of precedents for several of these images in Buddhist texts. See also Ch'en Kuo-ch'iu, "Lun shih-lun shih shang yi-ko ch'ang-chien te hsiang-yü: ching-hua shui-yüeh," *Ku-tai wen-hsüeh li-lun yen-chiu* 9 (1984).

42. Injunctions against *su* were commonplace in *shih-hua*; for example, the early Southern Sung writer Hsü Tu 徐度 in his *Ch'üeh-sao pien* 卻掃編 cites one Ts'ui Tê-fu 崔德符 instructing the young poet Ch'en Yü-yi 陳與義: "In writing poetry the question is not skill or awkwardness—the absolute essential is nothing more than to hate uncouthness": cited in Wang Ta-p'eng et al., *Chung-kuo li-tai shih-hua hsüan*, p. 537. Although "Ts'ang-lang's Remarks on Poetry" is often observed to be directed against the Chiang-hsi School, this principle of "hating uncouthness" was a basic tenet of the Chiang-hsi School.

43. J. D. Schmidt, *Yang Wan-li*, pp. 56–77.

CHAPTER NINE

The text used for the *San-t'i shih* is the one in Murakami Tetsumi's *Santaishi*. The text used in Yang Tsai's "Poetic Rules of the Masters" is a composite of the texts in *Li-tai shih-hua* and that in Chu Fu's *Ming-chia shih-fa hui-pien*.

1. Alternately entitled *T'ang san-t'i shih* 唐三體詩, *T'ang-shih san-t'i chia-fa* 唐詩三體家法, and *T'ang-hsien san-t'i shih-fa* 唐賢三體詩法.

2. We may recall that Ou-yang Hsiu had criticized the second couplet of this poem for being empirically incorrect (see p. 383). The question whether a midnight bell was or was not rung at Cold Mountain Temple became a favorite topic for *shih-hua*, "re-

marks on poetry." Chou Pi's and Ou-yang Hsiu's citations of this couplet differ textually; here and in subsequent examples from *Poetry in Three Forms*, I follow Chou Pi's texts, though they are often not the best texts of the poems.

3. During the first period of the (pentasyllabic) quatrain's development, from the end of the fifth through the sixth centuries, such closure with a parallel couplet was not at all uncommon (and may have been related to the quatrain as a unit in early linked verses).

4. Murakami Tetsumi, *Santaishi*, vol. 2, p. 427.

5. The *shih** in this and the preceding category are identical. In the first case, in the phrase *shu-shih** 書事, it refers to taking current "matters" as the topic of a poem. The second usage is the more common technical term *yung-shih** 用事, making reference to some situation in the past.

6. The section in brackets is not included in the standard *Li-tai shih-hua* edition, but it is included in the otherwise incomplete *Ming-chia shih-fa hui-pien* 名家詩法匯編 edition. Chu Fu, *Ming-chia shih-fa hui-pien* (preface, 1577; rpt. Taipei, 1973), p. 92.

7. The portions of the first two sentences in parentheses appear in the *Ming-chia shih-fa* edition and not in the *Li-tai shih-hua* edition.

8. This passage is included in the *Ming-chia shih-fa* edition, but omitted from the *Li-tai shih-hua* edition.

CHAPTER TEN

The text used is that in Tai Hung-sen's *Chiang-chai shih-hua chien-chu*.

1. The excellent annotated modern edition, the *Chiang-chai shih-hua chien-chu*, by Tai Hung-sen, combines the *Hsi-t'ang yung-jih hsü-lun* with Wang's *shih-hua* on the *Book of Songs*, the *Shih yi* 詩譯, and with another collection of random comments, the *Nan-ch'uang man-chi* 南窗漫記. In order to bring together Wang's scattered comments, Tai Hung-sen often appends passages from Wang's anthologies and commentaries to each *shih-hua* entry. Some of these will be included in the following commentary.

2. An excellent example might be the third of the "Nineteen Old Poems," in which the speaker goes off to the great cities of the Eastern Han and tells of the feasting and high living of the powerful and wealthy. Traditional commentators could not decide whether the speaker was complaining about having been excluded from such celebrations, or was criticizing such extravagance, or was joining in with wholehearted abandon. Slight adjustments in tone and presumed pronominal referents (left unstated in the Chinese) could produce any of these readings quite naturally. If the poem were sung in different situations, it could have easily been seen to express any of these contradictory states of mind.

3. Tai Hung-sen, p. 4.

4. The *Analects* passage continues, suggesting that the *Songs* can be of use in the service of one's parents or prince, and that that can teach one much about "the names of birds, beasts, plants, and trees."

5. In the following passages I summarize some of the conclusions of Steven Van Zoeren's *Poetry and Personality: Reading, Exegesis, and Hermeneutics in Traditional China*, tracing the hermeneutics of the *Book of Songs* up through Chu Hsi.

6. It should be noted, however, that the determinate affective quality was not necessarily the direct "meaning" of the words of the *Song*: the putative authors of the "mutated *Feng**," the "historians of the States" ("Great Preface"), were supposed to have intended that many of their poems be read ironically, contrasting the ideal evoked with the circumstances of their own times. The presumptions of Confucius' editorial intentions produced similar ironies.

7. This is an inappropriate use of the term "secular"; I simply use it to refer to all poetry that did not have the sanction of belonging to the Confucian Classics. It should be noted that the poetry is also historically later, so that its deviation from the model of the *Book of Songs* is also, to some degree, a falling away from perfection.

8. See Tai Hung-sen, p. 7.

9. See Tai Hung-sen, p. 46.

10. See Tai Hung-sen, p. 46.

11. Chao Ch'ih-hsin, *T'an-lung-lu chu-shih*, pp. 6–7.

12. Tai Hung-sen, p. 51.

13. Tai Hung-sen, p. 55.

14. The text usually given as the primary source of this passage is an entry in the late-Sung "Night Chats Facing My Bed" (*Tui-ch'uang yeh-yü*) by Fan Hsi-wen. Using examples from Tu Fu's poetry, Fan distinguishes cases of the alternation of couplets of scene and affections, affections-within-scene, scene within affections, and fusion of scene and affection so that they cannot be distinguished.

15. Tai Hung-sen, pp. 72–73.

16. The couplets quoted are the two middle couplets of an eight-line regulated verse.

17. "However, it is to be noted that the Words denoting the Passions do not, for the most part, raise up in us any Degree of the Passions themselves, but only the Ideas of the associated Circumstances." David Hartley, *Observations on Man, His Frame, His Duty, and His Expectations*, p. 276.

18. Classical Chinese uses the weapon metaphor of a "[blade-] point" in a way similar to English "making a point" (though the latter derives from fencing vocabulary). In saying that "Tu Fu hid the sharp point even more effectively [than Hsieh] and did not let it become obvious, gathering things together limitlessly," Wang means that Tu Fu did not reveal his purposes, what he was aiming at, within the text, but rather drew a wide variety of matters in, conveying the "point" implicitly.

19. Liu I-ching, *A New Account of Tales of the World* [Shih-shuo hsin-yü], Richard B. Mather, tr., p. 118.

CHAPTER ELEVEN

The text used is that in Ting Fu-pao, *Ch'ing shih-hua*.

1. Though sometimes relatively systematic, works of popular poetics tended to be amplifications of a more or less received "outline" of standard topics. In contrast, Yeh Hsieh's "Inner Chapters" offer a relatively tight argument in response to the questions posed by an imaginary interlocutor.

Wu Hung-yi sees a close relation between the systematic treatise of Yeh Hsieh and the expansion of the *shih-hua* entry into a short essay, as witnessed in Li Yi's *Ch'iu-hsing-ko shih-hua* 秋星閣詩話. Wu takes note that this *shih-hua* is dedicated to beginning students. Yeh Hsieh's tone is clearly magistral in "The Origins of Poetry"; but his interlocutor (representing the level his audience is to rise above), though sometimes foolish, is no beginner. See Wu Hung-yi, *Ch'ing-tai shih-hsüeh ch'u-t'an*, p. 158.

2. One might recall here that Liu Hsieh had offered a similar criticism of his own great predecessor Lu Chi. In fairness to Liu Hsieh, it should be observed that Chinese argumentation had changed substantially since Liu Hsieh's time. Liu Hsieh's rhetorical "division" of a topic (closely analogous to the formal division in the Western "art of the sermon" *ars predicandi*) was linked to a profound confidence in the identity of the rhetorical order and the order of nature: see Owen, *Traditional Chinese Poetry*, pp. 78–86.) By the seventeenth century, this older rhetoric survived primarily in the ossified form of the *pa-ku-wen* 八股文, required for the state examination system; and such exposition, based on division and amplification of terms, had come to sound stilted, artificial, and discontinuous when compared with the more "modern" argumentation practiced by Yeh Hsieh. In "modern" argumentation an author was required to make an "individual" point in a sequential form, with each stage contingent on what had been said previously in the argument.

3. Yen Yü believed that ultimately what made poetry great was ineffable, that one should be able to "recognize" or "judge" (*shih**) greatness in the best poets, but that such greatness was beyond a reflective understanding of poetic principles. In short, Yen Yü claimed that one could judge "that" a poem was great without being able to judge "why" it was great, and without knowing the grounds of such judgment. To this Yeh Hsieh objects strongly.

4. The internal disputes of poetic theory in this period are so loud that it is easy to overlook what they have in common, and how different that ground of agreement is from older concerns with the poem as a manifestation of the quality of an age or of a particular personality.

5. Here following the text in Ting Fu-pao, *Ch'ing shih-hua*. Kuo Shao-yü's *Chung-kuo*

li-tai wen-lun hsüan reads: "He again doesn't know why he should agree to study the late T'ang, Sung, and Yüan."

6. One reason Yeh Hsieh raises this final question is the popular association between "talent" ("capacity") and a facility in composition.

7. James Harry Smith and Edd Winfield Parks, eds., *The Great Critics: An Anthology of Literary Criticism*, pp. 411–412.

8. This cheerfully ahistorical view of the relation between precursors and later poets cannot readily be reconciled with Yeh Hsieh's views on literary history, presented in the supplement to this chapter: there the later poet must differ from the predecessor, completing and complementing his work.

9. Immanuel Kant, *Critique of Judgment*, section 49.

10. In parallel with the even stranger matching line of the couplet ("Its metal pedestals [for catching the dew] lie beside the unitary [universal] *ch'i**"), it is preferable to read this line as translated above. However, this line seems to suggest reading the line "Outside the first chill of its emerald tiles."

11. There are two ways to understand this query: one may take the alternative translation suggested in the preceding note; or one may presume a courtyard, interpreting "within" as the space enclosed by the roof tiles (rather than within the tiles themselves).

12. It is hoped the reader will forgive this most imperfect translation "much" for Tu Fu's perfect *to*. *To* is the simplest word of quantitative magnitude, a sudden and direct impression of the moon and its light that turns away from the conventionally "poetic" descriptive possibilities to a most simple word—but not the most obvious word (not a "big" moon, or "bright" light).

13. From an old aphorism in the *Tso chuan* that pines and cypresses do not grow on small tumuli.

14. Literally "*pien* and *nan* wood."

15. *Mi-pen*, here, a book containing secret teaching, not known to the world and not to be seen by all.

16. *Ch'ing-hsü*: "clean and clear," or in the context of the psyche, "pure and empty," would be both cleaning the area of an infection and "emptying oneself" to receive the spirit of the ancients. Cf. the injunctions to "emptiness within" in the "Poetic Exposition on Literature" and the "Spirit Thought" chapter of *Wen-hsin tiao-lung*.

17. The reference here is to the ubiquitous red plaster of late imperial architecture.

18. As the reader no doubt realizes by this point, the constituent parts of a Chinese upper-class residence contained a more or less fixed number of elements on a relatively fixed plan. American houses seem different only because we take the structure for granted; however, imagine a front door that led into the main bedroom, from which you had to walk through the bathroom to get to the kitchen, on the other side of which was the living room.

19. Literally "form your own household," a standard metaphor for a writer who has a distinct personality.

20. See *Wen-hsin tiao-lung*, "The One Who Knows the Tone," p. 290 above.

21. The presumptions here are one of the most explicit literary elaborations of Mencius' "understanding language"; see pp. 22–24 above.

22. Yeh Hsieh's quotation is inexact. The original reads, "In modern times Jen Fang [460–508], Wang Jung [467–493], and others have not cared about the truly remarkable in their diction, but instead try to outdo one another in making novel references. Writers of recent times are gradually becoming more and more vulgar; thus in their lines there are no 'empty' phrases, and in their phrases, no 'empty' words; there is a sense of constant restriction and pieces patched together; this is a great canker on literature." The "restrictiveness" of which Chung Jung is speaking is the density of poetic diction unrelieved by "empty" words, i.e., particles.

23. See p. 219 above.

24. There are times when Yeh Hsieh's vanity overcomes his scholarship. The T'ang Hui-hsiu passage was cited under the entry on Yen Yen-chih in Chung Jung's "Categories of Poets" as a description of the qualities of Hsieh Ling-yün's poetry; the exact phrase, however, is *fu-jung ch'u-shui* 芙蓉初水, "a lotus emerging from the water," and not *ch'u-jih fu-jung* as Yeh Hsieh gives it.

Selected Analytical Bibliography

I. WORKS IN CHINESE AND JAPANESE

The following bibliography consists of both general works on Chinese literary thought and a selection of scholarship on works treated in the present volume. As in all bibliography, here a certain lore is presumed; those who wish and are able to look up the references will understand.

CHINESE LITERARY THOUGHT (I.A)

General Works and Histories (I.A.1)

Aoki Masaru 青木正兒. *Shina bungaku shishōshi* 支那文學思想史 (A History of Chinese Literary Thought). Tokyo: Iwanami shoten, 1943.

Chao Tse-ch'eng 趙則誠 et at., eds. *Chung-kuo ku-tai wen-hsüeh li-lun tz'u-tien* 中國古代文學理論辭典 (A Dictionary of Early Chinese Literary Theory). Ch'i-lin: Ch'-lin wen-shih ch'u-pan-she, 1985.

Chou Chen-fu 周振甫. *Shih-tz'u li-hua* 詩詞例話 (Exemplary Discussions of Poems and Lyrics). Peking, 1962; reprint, Peking: Chung-kuo ch'ing-nien ch'u-pan-she, 1980.

Chung-kuo wen-hsüeh p'i-p'ing shih 中國文學批評史 (History of Chinese Literary Criticism). Compiled by the Chinese department of Fudan University. Shanghai: Shang-hai ku-chi ch'u-pan-she, vol. 1, 1964; vol. 2, 1981; vol. 3, 1985.

Hayashida Shinnosuke 林田慎元助. *Chūgoku chūsei bungaku hyōronshi* 中國中世

文學批評史 (A History of Critical Discussion in the Chinese Middle Ages). Tokyo: Sōbunsha, 1979.

Huang Pao-chen 黃保真, Ts'ai Chung-hsiang 蔡鐘翔, and Ch'eng Fu-wang 成復旺. *Chung-kuo wen-hsüeh li-lun shih* 中國文學理論史 (A History of Chinese Literary Theory). 5 vols. Peking: Pei-ching ch'u-pan-she, 1987.

Kuo Shao-yü 郭紹虞. *Chung-kuo wen-hsüeh p'i-p'ing shih* 中國文學批評史 (History of Chinese Literary Criticism). Shanghai, 1956; reprint, Shanghai: Shanghai ku-chi ch'u-pan-she, 1979.

Li Tse-hou 李澤厚 and Liu Kang-chi 劉綱紀. *Chung-kuo mei-hsüeh shih* 中國美學史 (History of Chinese Aesthetics). 2 vols. Peking: Chung-kuo she-hui k'o-hsüeh ch'u-pan-she, 1986–1987. The first two volumes cover the period through the Six Dynasties in a projected history of Chinese aesthetics.

Lo Ken-tse 羅根澤. *Chung-kuo wen-hsüeh p'i-p'ing shih* 中國文學批評史 (History of Chinese Literary Criticism). Shanghai, 1958–1962; reprinted Shanghai: Shang-hai ku-chi ch'u-pan-she, 1983. Goes only through the Sung.

Matsushita Tadashi 松下忠. *Min Shin no sanshisetsu* 明清の三詩說 (The Three Poetic Theories of the Ming and Ch'ing). Tokyo: Meiji shoin, 1978.

Min Tse 敏澤. *Chung-kuo wen-hsüeh li-lun p'i-p'ing shih* 中國文學理論批評史 (History of Chinese Literary Theory and Criticism). Peking: Jen-min wen-hsüeh ch'u-pan-she, 1981.

Suzuki Toraō 鈴木虎雄. *Shina shironshi* 支那詩論史 (History of Chinese Discussion of Poetry). 1927; reprint, Tokyo: Kōbundō shobō, 1967.

Ts'ai Ying-chün 蔡英俊. *Pi-hsing wu-se yü ch'ing-ching chiao-jung* 比興物色與情景交融 (Comparison, Affective Image, the Appearances of Things and the Fusion of Scene and Affection). Taipei: Ta-an ch'u-pan-she, 1986.

Yeh Lang 葉朗. *Chung-kuo mei-hsüeh shih ta-kang* 中國美學史大綱 (An Outline History of Chinese Aesthetics). Taipei: Ts'ang-lang ch'u-pan-she, 1986.

Yü Yüan 鬱沅. *Chung-kuo ku-tien mei-hsüeh ch'u-pien* 中國古典美學初編. Hu-pei: Ch'ang-chiang wen-yi ch'u-pan-she, 1986.

Collections (I.A.2)

THE SUNG AND YÜAN COLLECTIONS (I.A.2.a)

Hu Tzu 胡仔. *T'iao-hsi yü-yin ts'ung-hua* 苕溪漁隱叢話 (The Collected Chats of the Fisherman Recluse of T'iao Creek). First series in 60 *chüan*, 1148; second series in 40 *chüan*, 1167. Typeset edition, Peking: Jen-min wen-hsüeh ch'u-pan-she, 1962. See Yves Hervouet, *A Sung Bibliography* (Hong Kong, The Chinese University Press, 1978), p. 450.

Juan Yüeh 阮閱. [*Tseng-hsiu*] *shih-hua tsung-kuei* 增修詩話總龜 ([Amplified and Corrected] General Source for Remarks on Poetry). First series in 48 *chüan*, 1123; second series (not by Juan Yüeh) in 50 *chüan* after 1167. A problematic Ming version is our sole extant source for the present edition (photo-reprint in *Ssu-pu ts'ung-k'an*, first series). See Hervouet, *A Sung Bibliography*, p. 449.

Ts'ai Cheng-sun 蔡正孫. *Shih-lin kuang-chi* 詩林廣記 (Broad Records of the Forest of Poems). Two series, each in 10 *chüan*, second series 1289 (Yüan). Typeset edition, Peking: Chung-hua shu-chü, 1982. The full title is *Ching-hsüan ku-chin ming-hsien ts'ung-hua shih-lin kuang-chi* 精選古今名賢叢話詩林廣記. See Hervouet, *A Sung Bibliography*, p. 455.

Wang Kou 王構. *Hsiu-tz'u chien-heng* 修辭鑑衡 (The Mirror and Measure of Fine Words). Yüan work. Shanghai: Chung-hua shu-chü, 1958.

Wei Ch'ing-chih 魏慶之. *Shih-jen yü-hsieh* 詩人玉屑 (The Jade Chips of the Poets). First published in 1244. Typeset edition, Shanghai: Ku-tien wen-hsüeh ch'u-pan-she, 1958. New edition, Shanghai: Chung-hua shu-chü, 1959. See Hervouet, *A Sung Bibliography*, p. 455. There is a German translation by Volker Klöpsch, *Die Jadesplitter der Dichter* (II. H below).

SOURCES FOR WORKS ON TECHNICAL POETICS (I.A.2.b)
Ko-chih ts'ung-shu 格致叢書 (Collectanea on Forms). 1608.
Shih-hsüeh chih-nan 詩學指南 (The Compass of the Study of Poetry). Preface 1759. Photo-reprint, Taipei: Kuang-wen shu-chü, 1970.

THE SHIH-HUA COLLECTIONS (I.A.2.c)
Ho Wen-huan 何文煥. *Li-tai shih-hua* 歷代詩話 (Remarks on Poetry through the Ages). Preface 1770. Typeset edition, Shanghai: Chung-hua shu-chü, 1958. Helmut Martin has compiled an *Index to the Ho Collection of Twenty-Eight Shih-hua* (Taipei: Chinese Materials and Research Aids Service Center, 1973). This contains a punctuated reprint of the woodblock edition with an index of authors cited and a concordance of quoted passages. The Chung-hua shu-chü edition has an index of authors cited.
Ting Fu-pao 丁福保. *Hsü li-tai shih-hua* 續歷代詩話 (Continuation of Remarks on Poetry through the Ages). 1915; typeset edition, Peking: Chung-hua shu-chü, 1983 as *Li-tai shih-hua hsü-pien* 歷代詩話續編, with index of authors cited.
———. *Ch'ing shih-hua* 清詩話 (Ch'ing Remarks on Poetry). 1916; typeset edition, Shanghai: Chung-hua shu-chü, 1963. Ting's texts are not always the best.
Kuo Shao-yü 郭紹虞. *Ch'ing shih-hua hsü-pien* 清詩話續編 (Continuation of Ch'ing Remarks on Poetry). 4 vols. Shanghai: Shang-hai ku-chi ch'u-pan-she, 1983.
T'ang Kuei-chang 唐圭璋. *Tz'u-hua ts'ung-pien* 詞話叢編 (General Collection of Remarks on Lyric). Nanking, 1935; typeset edition, Peking, Chung-hua shu-chü, 1986.

MODERN SERIES OF EDITIONS (I.A.2.d)
Chung-kuo ku-tien wen-hsüeh li-lun p'i-p'ing ch'uan-chu hsüan-chi 中國古典文學理論批評專著選輯 (A Selection of Individual Works of Early Chinese Literary Theory and Criticism), under the general editorship of Kuo Shao-yü, published by Jen-min wen-hsüeh ch'u-pan-she from 1960 through the present. This is an ongoing series of editions of important works of traditional criticism. Works in this series are typeset, sometimes in critical editions and sometimes with annotation.
Ku-chin shih-hua ts'ung-pien 古今詩話叢編 (A General Collection of Ancient and Modern Remarks on Poetry). Put out by Kuang-wen shu-chü in Taipei. These are photo-reprints of early editions. Although they often contain serious textual problems and are often unclear, the great virtue of this series lies in reprinting many rare works which would be otherwise impossible to obtain, including several works in manuscript.
Li-tai shih-shih ch'ang-pien 歷代詩史長編 (An Extensive Collection of the History of Poetry through the Ages). Put out by Ting-wen in Taipei under the general editiorship of Yang Chia-lo.

MODERN ANTHOLOGIES OF CRITICAL COMMENTS (I.A.2.e)
Ch'ang Chen-kuo 常振國 et al. *Li-tai shih-hua lun tso-chia* 歷代詩話論作家 (The Discussion of Individual Writers in Remarks on Poetry through the Ages). 2 vols. Ch'ang-sha: Hu-nan wen-yi, 1986. Volume 1 contains comments from the Sung and earlier; volume 2 contains post-Sung comments.
Cheng Tien 鄭奠 and Mai Mei-ch'iao 麥梅翹 *Ku-Han-yü yü-fa-hsüeh tzu-liao hui-pien* 古漢語語法學資料彙編 (A Compendium of Materials on Early Chinese Language Study). Peking: Chung-hua shu-chü, 1972.
Cheng Tien and T'an Ch'üan-chi 譚全基 *Ku-Han-yü hsiu-tz'u-hsüeh tzu-liao hui-*

pien 古漢語修辭學資料彙編 (A Compendium of Materials on Early Chinese Rhetorical Study). Peking: Shang-wu yin-shu-kuan, 1980.

Chou Wei-tê 周維德. *Shih-wen ssu-chung* 詩問四種 (Four Dialogues on Poetry). Chi-nan: Ch'i-Lu shu-she, 1985.

Chung-kuo ku-tai wen-yi li-lun tzu-liao mu-lu hui-pien 中國古代文藝理論資料目錄滙編 (An Index of Materials on Early Chinese Theories of Literary Arts). Compiled by the Chinese Department of Shantung University. Chi-nan: Ch'i-Lu shu-she, 1983.

Chung-kuo li-tai shih-hua hsüan 中國歷代詩話選 (An Anthology of Chinese Remarks on Poetry through the Ages). Compiled by the Study Committe on the Theory of the Arts of the Chinese Social Science Research Council. 2 vols. Ch'ang-sha: Yüeh-lu shu-she, 1985. Covers the period through Yüan.

Chung-kuo wen-hsüeh p'i-p'ing tzu-liao hui-pien 中國文學批評資料彙編 (Compendium of Materials on Chinese Literary Criticism). 11 vols. Taipei: Ch'eng-wen ch'u-pan-she, 1978–1979. A typeset compendium of critical materials drawn from poetry and classical prose (i.e., prefaces, letters, colophons, etc.); independent treatises such as *Wen-hsin tiao-lung*, *shih-hua*, and technical works are excluded. Sources are given. The works are:

K'o Ch'ing-ming 柯慶明 and Tseng Yung-yi 曾永義, eds. *Liang-Han Wei Tsin Nan-pei-ch'ao wen-hsüeh p'i-p'ing tzu-liao hui-pien* 兩漢魏晉南北朝文學批評資料彙編.

Lo Lien-t'ien 羅聯添, ed. *Sui T'ang Wu-tai* . . . 隋唐五代 . . .

Huang Ch'i-fang 黃啟方, ed. *Pei-Sung* . . . 北宋 . . .

Chang Chien 張健, ed. *Nan-Sung* . . . 南宋 . . .

Lin Ming-te 林明德, ed. *Chin-tai* . . . 金代 . . .

Tseng Yung-yi 曾永義, ed. *Yüan-tai* . . . 元代 . . . 2 vols.

Yeh Ch'ing-ping 葉慶炳 and Shao Hung 邵紅. *Ming-tai* . . . 明代 . . . 2 vols.

Wu Hung-yi 吳宏一 and Yeh Ch'ing-ping 葉慶炳, ed. *Ch'ing-tai* . . . 清代 . . . 2 vols.

Ku-tien wen-hsüeh yen-chiu tzu-liao hui-pien 古典文學研究資料滙編 (A Compendium of Materials on the Study of Early Literature). This series was originally issued by Chung-hua shu-chü in Peking between 1961 and 1964, and resumed again in recent years. The volumes contain collections of traditional critical comments on individual writers: the Ts'ao's; T'ao Ch'ien (2 vols, one general and one on particular poems); Tu Fu (through Sung only); Po Chü-yi; Han Yü; Liu Tsung-yüan, Tu Mu, Huang T'ing-chien and the Chiang-hsi school (2 vols.); Lu Yu, Yang Wan-li, Fan Ch'eng-ta, and *Hung-lou meng*.

Kung Chao-chi 龔兆吉. *Li-tai tz'u-lun hsin-pien* 歷代詞論新編 (A New Collection of Discussion of Lyric through the Ages). Peking: Pei-ching shih-fan ta-hsüeh ch'u-pan-she, 1984.

Kuo Shao-yü 郭紹虞. *Chung-kuo li-tai wen-lun hsüan* 中國歷代文論選 (An Anthology of Chinese Discussions of Literature through the Ages). Peking: Chung-hua shu-chü, 1962–1963, and often reprinted.

Li-tai shih-hua tz'u-hua hsüan 歷代詩話詞話選 (An Anthology of Remarks on Poetry and Remarks on Lyric through the Ages). Compiled by the Chinese Department of Wu-Han University. Wu-Han: Wu-Han ta-hsüeh ch'u-pan-she, 1984.

Sung Chin Yüan wen-lun hsüan 宋金元文論選 (An Anthology of Discussions of Literature in the Sung, Chin, and Yüan). Compiled by Jen-min wen-hsüeh ch'u-pan-she. Peking: Jen-min wen-hsüeh ch'u-pan-she, 1984.

T'an Ling-yang 譚令仰. *Ku-tai wen-lun ts'ui-pien* 古代文論萃編 (A Gathering of Early Discussions of Literature). 2 vols. Peking: Shu-mu wen-hsien ch'u-pan-she, 1986.

Wang Ta-chin 王達津 and Ch'en Hung 陳洪. *Chung-kuo ku-tien wen-lun-hsüan* 中國古典文論選 (An Anthology of Chinese Classical Discussions of Literature). Shen-yang: Liao-ning chiao-yü ch'u-pan-she, 1988.

Wu Shih-ch'ang 吳世常. *Lun-shih chüeh-chü erh-shih-chung chi-chu* 論詩絕句二十四種輯注 (Twenty Series of Quatrains on Poetry, With Collected Commentaries). Hsi-an: Shen-hsi jen-min ch'u-pan-she, 1984.

Yang Ch'ung-ch'iu 羊春秋 et al. *Li-tai lun-shih chüen-chü hsüan* 歷代論詩絕句選 (An Anthology of Quatrains of Poetry through the Ages). Ch'ang-sha: Hu-nan jen-min ch'u-pan-she, 1981.

Yeh Kuang-ta 葉光大, et al. *Li-tai ming-chu hsü-pa hsüan-chu* 歷代名著序跋選注 (An Annotated Anthology of Prefaces and Colophons on Famous Works through the Ages). Lan-chou: Kan-su jen-min ch'u-pan-she, 1986.

Yü Chung-shan 于忠善. *Li-tai wen-jen lun wen-hsüeh* 歷代文人論文學 (Discussions of Literature by Literary Men through the Ages). Peking: Wen-hua yi-shu ch'u-pan-she, 1985.

Collected Articles (I.A.3)

Chang Chien 張健. *Chung-kuo wen-hsüeh p'i-p'ing lun-chi* 中國文學批評論集 (A Collection of Articles on Chinese Literary Criticism). Taipei: T'ien-hua ch'u-pan shih-yeh kung-ssu, 1979.

Chang Wen-hsün 張文勛. *Chung-kuo ku-tai wen-hsüeh li-lun lun-kao* 中國古代文學理論論稿 (Draft Articles on Early Chinese Literary Theory). Shanghai: Shang-hai ku-chi ch'u-pan-she, 1984.

Chao Sheng-te 趙盛德, ed. *Chung-kuo ku-tai wen-hsüeh li-lun ming-chu t'an-so* 中國古代文學理論名著探索 (Researches into Famous Works of Early Chinese Literary Theory). Kuei-lin: Kuang-hsi shih-fan ta-hsüeh ch'u-pan-she, 1989.

Chu Tung-jun 朱東潤. *Chung-kuo wen-hsüeh lun-chi* 中國文學論集 (A Collection of Articles on Chinese Literature). Peking: Chung-hua shu-chü, 1983.

Ku-tai wen-hsüeh li-lun yen-chiu 古代文學理論研究. An irregular journal put out by the Association for Early Chinese Literary Theory based in Shanghai, beginning 1979.

Kuo Shao-yü 郭紹虞. *Chao-yü-shih ku-tien wen-hsüeh lun-chi* 照隅室古典文學論集 (A Collection of Articles on Old Literature from Chao-yü Lodge). 2 vols. Shanghai: Shang-hai ku-chi ch'u-pan-she, 1983.

Lu K'an-ju 陸侃如. *Lu K'an-ju ku-tien wen-hsüeh lun-wen chi* 陸侃如古典文學論文集 (A Collection of Lu K'an-ju's Articles on Old Literature). Shanghai: Shang-hai ku-chi ch'u-pan-she, 1987.

Mou Shih-chin 牟世金. *Tiao-lung chi* 雕龍集 (The Dragon Carving Collection). Peking: Chung-kuo k'o-hsüeh ch'u-pan-she, 1983.

Wang Meng-ou 王夢鷗. *Ku-tien wen-hsüeh lun t'an-so* 古典文學論探索 (Researches into Old Discussions of Literature). Taipei: Cheng-chung shu-chü, 1984.

Wang Ta-chin 王達津 *Ku-tai wen-hsüeh li-lun yen-chiu lun-wen-chi* 古代文學理論研究論文集 (A Collection of Articles on the Study of Early Literary Theory). T'ien-chin: Nan-k'ai ta-hsüeh ch'u-pan-she, 1985.

Wu Tiao-kung 吳調公. *Ku-tai wen-lun chin-t'an* 古代文論今探 (Modern Investigations of Ancient Discussions on Literature). Hsi-an: Shen-hsi jen-min ch'u-pan-she, 1982.

Yang Ming-chao 楊明照. *Hsüeh-pu-yi-chai tsa-chu* 學不已齋雜著 (Various Writings from Hsüeh-pu-yi Studio). Shanghai: Shang-hai ku-chi ch'u-pan-she, 1985.

Yang Sung-nien 楊松年. *Chung-kuo ku-tien wen-hsüeh p'i-p'ing lun-chi* 中國文學批評論集 (A Collection of Articles an Old Chinese Literary Theory). Hong Kong: San-lien shu-chü, 1987.

Early Literary Theory (I.B.1)

Chang Heng 張亨. "Lun-yü lun Shih" 論語論詩 (The Discussion of the Poems in the *Analects*), *Wen-hsüeh p'ing-lun* 6 (1980).

Chang Shao-k'ang 張少康. "Lun Chuang-tzu te wen-yi ssu-hsiang chi ch'i ying-hsiang" 論莊子的文藝思想及其影響 (On Chuang-tzu's Thought on the Arts and Its Influence), *Ku-tien wen-hsüeh lun-ts'ung* 3 (Chi-nan, 1982).

Chang Wen-hsün 張文勛. "K'ung-tzu wen-hsüeh-kuan chi ch'i ying-hsiang te tsai p'ing-chia" 孔子文學觀及其影響的再評價 (A Further Critical Evaluation of Confucius' View of Literature and Its Influence), *Ku-tai wen-hsüeh li-lun yen-chiu* 1 (1979; see I.A.3 above). Reprinted in Chang Wen-hsün, *Chung-kuo ku-tai wen-hsüeh li-lun lun-kao* (see I.A.3 above).

———. "Lao-Chuang te mei-hsüeh ssu-hsiang chi ch'i ying-hsiang" 老莊的美學思想及其影響 (The Aesthetic Thought of Lao-tzu and Chuang-tzu and Their Influence), in his *Chung-kuo ku-tai wen-hsüeh li-lun lun-kao* (see I.A.3 above).

———. "Yüeh-chi lun chung-ho chih mei" 樂記論中和之美 (The Discussion of Mellow Beauty in "The Record of Music"), in his *Chung-kuo ku-tai wen-hsüeh li-lun lun-kao* (see I.A.3 above).

Chu Tzu-ch'ing 朱自清. "Shih yen chih pien" 詩言志辨 (An Analysis of the Idea that Poetry Articulates What Is on the Mind Intently). Reprinted in *Chu Tzu-ch'ing ku-tien wen-hsüeh ch'uan-chi* 朱自清古典文學專集, vol. 1. Shanghai, 1980. One of the most important works on the most basic concepts of Chinese poetics.

Hsiao Hua-jung 蕭華榮. "Ch'un-ch'iu ch'eng Shih yü K'ung-tzu shih-lun" 春秋稱詩與孔子詩論 (The Recitation of the Poems in the Spring and Autumn Annals and Confucius' Theory of Poetry), *Ku-tai wen-hsüeh li-lun yen-chiu* 5 (1981; see I.A.3 above).

Juan Kuo-hua 阮國華. "Meng-tzu shih-shuo fu-yi" 孟子詩說復議 (A Reconsideration of Mencius' Discussion of the Poems), *Ku-tai wen-hsüeh li-lun yen-chiu* 9 (1984; see I.A.3 above).

Kuo Shao-yü. "Hsien-Ch'in ju-chia chih wen-hsüeh-kuan" 先秦儒家之文學觀 (The View of Literature of Pre-Ch'in Traditionalists), in his *Chao-yü-shih ku-tien wen-hsüeh lun-chi*, vol. 1 (see I.A.3 above).

———. "Hsing kuan ch'ün yüan shuo p'ou-hsi" 興觀羣怨說剖析 (An Analysis of the Theory of 'Stir,' 'Observe,' 'Express Fellowship,' 'Show Resentment'), in his *Chao-yü-shih ku-tien wen-hsüeh lun-chi*, vol. 2 (see I.A.3 above).

———. "Ju-Tao erh-chia lun shen yü wen-hsüeh p'i-p'ing chih kuan-hsi" 儒道二家論神與文學批評之關係 (The Discussion of Spirit between the Traditionalists and the Taoists and Its Relation to Literary Criticism), in his *Chao-yü-shih ku-tien wen-hsüeh lun-chi*, vol. 1 (see I.A.3 above).

Lü Yi 呂藝. "K'ung-tzu hsing kuan ch'ün yüan pen-yi tsai-t'an" 孔子興觀羣怨本義再探 (A Further Discussion of the Original Meaning of Confucius' 'Stir,' 'Observe,' 'Express Fellowship,' 'Show Resentment'), *Wen-hsüeh yi-ch'an* 1985.4.

Han to Sui, Excluding Wen fu, Wen-hsin tiao-lung, Etc. (I.B.2).

Chang Ching-erh 張靜二. "Wang Ch'ung te wen-hsüeh li-lun—ts'ung ch'i te kuan-nien shuo-ch'i" 王充的文學理論：從氣的觀念說起 (Wang Ch'i's Literary Theory—Beginning from His Point of View on Ch'i), *Chung-wai wen-hsüeh* 70–71 (1978).

Chang Jen-ch'ing 張仁青. *Wei Chin Nan-pei-ch'ao wen-hsüeh ssu-hsiang shih*

魏晉南北朝文學思想史 (A History of Literary Thought in the Wei, Chin, and Southern Dynasties). Taipei: Wen-shih-che ch'u-pan-she, 1978.

Chang Wen-hsün. "Lun liu-ch'ao wen-hsüeh li-lun fa-ta te yüan-yin" 論六朝文學理論發達的原因 (On the Reasons for the Development of Literary Thought in the Six Dynasties), in his Chung-kuo ku-tai wen-hsüeh li-lun lun-kao (see I.A.3 above).

Chao Ch'ang-p'ing 趙昌平. "Wen-chang ch'ieh hsü fang-tang pien" 文章且須放蕩辨 (A Discussion of the Principle That in Literature There Should Be a Letting Go), Ku-tai wen-hsüeh li-lun yen-chiu 9 (1984; see I.A.3 above). On Liang Chieng-wen-ti.

Chou Hsün-ch'u 周勛初. "Liang-tai wen-lun san-p'ai shu-yao" 梁代文論三派述要 (The Essentials of the Three Factions in the Discussion of Literature in the Liang Dynasty), in his Wen-shih t'an-wei 文史探微 (Explorations of the Subtleties of Literature and History). Shanghai, 1987.

———. "Wang Ch'ung yü Liang-Han wen-feng" 王充與兩漢文風 (Wang Ch'ung and the Literary Currents of the Han), in his Wen-shih t'an-wei (see previous entry).

Chu Jung-chih 朱榮智. Liang-Han wen-hsüeh li-lun chih yen-chiu 兩漢文學理論之研究 (A Study of Literary Theory in the Han Dynasty). Taipei: Lien-ching ch'u-pan shih-yeh kung-ssu, 1982.

Ch'u Yü-lung 褚玉龍. "P'ei Tzu-yeh wen-hsüeh ssu-hsiang lun-hsi" 裴子野文學思想論析 (A Discourse on the Literary Thought of P'ei Tzu-yeh), Ku-tien wen-hsüeh lun-ts'ung 3 (Chi-nan: Ch'i-Lu shu-she, 1982).

Hayashida Shinnosuke 林田慎之助. "Hai Shiya Chōchūron kōsho—Rikuchō ni okeru fukko bungakuron no kōzō" (Research on P'ei-Tzu-yeh's "Discourse on Insect Carving"—A Study of the Theory of Return to Antiquity in the Six Dynasties), in Nihon Chūgoku gakkai hō 20 (1968).

Kuo Shao-yü "Wen pi shuo k'ao-pien" 文筆說考辨 (An Analysis of the Theory of Wen and Pi), in his Chao-yü-shih ku-tien wen-hsüeh lun-chi, vol. 2 (see I.A.3 above).

Liao Tung-liang 寥棟樑. "Liu-ch'ao shih-p'ing chung te hsing-hsiang p'i-p'ing" 六朝詩評中的形象批評 (Imagistic Criticism in Poetic Criticism of the Six Dynasties), Wen-hsüeh p'ing-lun 8 (1984).

Liao Wei-ch'ing 寥蔚卿. Liu-ch'ao wen-lun 六朝文論 (A Study of the Discourse on Literature in the Six Dynasties). Taipei: Lien-ching ch'u-pan shih-yeh kung-ssu, 1978.

Liu Wen-chung 劉文忠. "Shih-shuo hsin-yü chung te wen-lun kai-shu" 世說新語中的文論概述 (An Overview of the Discussion of Literature in "A New Account of Tales of the World"), Ku-tai wen-hsüeh li-lung yen-chiu 3 (1981; see I.A.3 above).

Lu Ch'in-li 逯欽立. "Shuo wen pi" 說文筆 (On Wen and Pi), in his Han Wei liu-ch'ao wen-hsüeh lun-chi 漢魏六朝文學論集 (A Collection of Essays on the Literature of the Han, Wei, and Six Dynasties). Hsi-an: Shen-hsi jen-min ch'u-pan-she, 1984.

T'ai Ching-nung 台靜農. "Wei Chin wen-hsüeh ssu-hsiang shu-lun" 魏晉文學思想史論 (A Discussion of Literary Thought in the Wei and Chin), in his Ching-nung lun-wen chi 靜農論文集 (Ching-nung's Collected Essays). Taipei: Lien-ching ch'u-pan-she, 1989.

Ts'ao Shun-ch'ing 曹順慶. Liang-Han wen-lun yi-chu 兩漢文論譯注 (Translation and Commentary on Discussions of Literature in the Han). Peking: Pei-ching ch'u-pan-she, 1988.

Wang Meng-ou. "Kuei-yu wen-hsüeh yü liu-ch'ao wen-t'i-te yen-pien"

貴遊文學與六朝文體的演變 (The Literature of Aristocratic Activities and the Evolution of Literary Genres in the Six Dynasties), in his *Ku-tien wen-hsüeh lun t'an-so* (see I.A.3).

Wang Yün-hsi 王運熙 and Yang Ming 楊明. *Wei Chin Nan-pei-ch'ao wen-hsüeh p'i-p'ing shih* 魏晉南北朝文學批評史 (A History of Literary Criticism in the Wei, Chin, and Northern and Southern Dynasties). Shanghai: Shang-hai ku-chi ch'u-pan-she, 1990.

Yang Ming-chao 楊明照. "Ko Hung te wen-hsüeh chu-chang" 葛洪的文學主張 (Literary Principles Advocated by Ko Hung). *Hsüeh-pu-yi-chai tsa-chu* (see I.A.3 above).

Yüan Hsing-p'ei 袁行霈. "Wen Chin hsüan-hsüeh-chung te yen-yü chih pien yü Chung-kuo ku-tai wen-yi li-lun" 魏晉玄學中的語言之辨與中國古代文藝理論 (The Dispute on Language and Meaning in the "Dark Learning" of the Wei and Chin and Early Chinese Theory of the Literary Art), *Ku-tai wen-hsüeh li-lun yen-chui* 1 (1979; see I.A.3 above).

TS'AO PI'S "DISCOURSE ON LITERATURE" (LUN-WEN) (I.C)

Commentaries to the *Lun-wen* begin with the Li Shan and the Wu-ch'en commentaries to the *Wen hsüan*. Some important scholarship on *Lun-wen* can be found in the later tradition of *Wen hsüan* studies (see the introduction to David Knechtges, *Wen xuan, or, Selections of Refined Literature*; II.F.4 below). Modern commentaries can be found in various collections, one of the most useful of which is *Wei Chin Nan-pei-ch'ao wen-hsüeh shih ts'an-k'ao tzu-liao* 魏晉南北朝文學史參考資料 (Reference Materials for the Literary History of the Wei, Chin, and Northern and Southern Dynasties) (Peking: Chung-hua shu-chü, 1962). A commentary on the *Lun-wen* is also found in Chang Huai-chin, *Wen fu yi-chu* (see I.D.1 below).

Ch'en Chih-e 陳值鍔. "Ts'ao P'i wen-ch'i shuo tang-yi" 曹丕文氣說當議 (A Discussion of Ts'ao P'i's Theory of *Ch'i* in Writing), *Wen-hsüeh yi-ch'an* 1981.4.

Chih Yang 志洋. "Shih 'Ch'i ch'i'" 釋齊氣 (An Explanation of the Phrase *Ch'i-ch'i*), *Wen-hsüeh yi-ch'an* 339 (20 November 1960).

Hsiu Ch'uan 秀川. "Tui Ts'ao P'i te wen-hsüeh p'i-p'ing piao-chun chi yu-kuan wen-t'i" 對曹丕的文學批評標準及有關問題 (On Ts'ao P'i's Standards of Literary Criticism and Related Questions), *Ku-tai wen-hsüeh li-lun yen-chiu* 5 (1981; see I.A.3 above).

Ping Ch'en 炳宸. "Ts'ao P'i te wen-hsüeh li-lun" 曹丕的文學理論 (Ts'ao P'i's Literary Theory), *Wen-hsüeh yi-ch'an* 232 (26 October 1958).

Wang Meng-ou. "Shih-lun Ts'ao P'i tsen-yang fa-hsien wen-ch'i" 試論曹丕怎樣發見文氣 (An Essay on How Ts'ao P'i Discovered Ch'i in Writing), in his *Ku-tien wen-hsüeh lun t'an-so* (see I.A.3 above).

———. "Ts'ao P'i Tien-lun Lun-wen so-yin" 曹丕典論論文索隱 (An Exposition of the Problems in Ts'ao P'i's Discourse on Literature in the *Canonical Discourses*), in his *Ku-tien wen-hsüeh lun t'an-so* (see I.A.3 above).

THE POETIC EXPOSITION ON LITERATURE (WEN FU) (I.D.)

Commentaries (I.D.1)

Commentaries to the *Wen fu* begin with the Li Shan and the Wu-ch'en commentaries to the *Wen hsüan*. Some important scholarship on *Wen fu* is contained in the later tradition of *Wen hsüan* studies (see the introduction to David Knechtges,

Wen Xuan, or, *Selection of Refined Literature*; II.F. 4 below). Modern commentaries exist both in larger works, such as the excellent commentary in *Wei Chin Nan-pei-ch'ao wen-hsüeh shih ts'an-k'ao tzu-liao* (see I.C headnote), and in independent works.

Chang Huai-chin 張懷瑾. *Wen fu yi-chu* 文賦譯注 (A Translation and Commentary on the Poetic Exposition on Literature). Peking: Pei-ching ch'u-pan-she, 1984.

Chang Shao-k'ang 張少康. *Wen fu chi-shih* 文賦集釋 (Collected Explanations on the Poetic Exposition on Literature). Shanghai: Shang-hai ku-chi ch'u-pan-she, 1984.

Ch'ien Chung-shu 錢鐘書. *Kuan-chü pien* 管錐編 (The Pipe Awl Collection), vol. 3. Peking: Chung-hua shu-chü, 1979. Pp. 1176–1209.

Hsü Fu-kuan 徐復觀 "Lu Chi Wen fu shu-shih ch'u-kao" 陸機文賦疏釋初稿 (An Initial Draft of an Exegesis on Lu Chi's "Poetic Exposition on Literature"), *Chung-wai wen-hsüeh* 97 (1980).

Wang Ching-hsien 王靖獻. "Lu Chi Wen fu chiao-shih" 陸機文賦校釋 (Collations and Explanations of Lu Chi's Poetic Exposition on Literature), *Wen shih che* 32 (1983). Building on Ch'en Shih-hsiang's English translation and Hsü Fu-kuan's exegesis.

Wen fu chi-shih. See Chang Shao-k'ang above.

Studies (I.D.2)

Chang Heng 張亨. "Lu Chi lun wen-hsüeh te ch'uang-tso kuo-ch'eng" 陸機論文學的創作過程 (Lu Chi's Discussion of the Creative Process in Literature), *Chung-wai wen-hsüeh* 8 (1973).

Chou Hsün-ch'u 周勛初. "Wen fu hsieh-tso nien-tai hsin-t'an" 文賦寫作年代新探 (A New Investigation on the Year in which "The Poetic Exposition on Literature" was Written), *Wen-hsüeh yi-ch'an tseng-k'an* 14 (Peking, 1982).

Kuo Shao-yü 郭紹虞. "Kuan-yü 'Wen fu' te p'ing-chia" 關於文賦的評價 (Regarding the Critical Value of "The Poetic Exposition on Literature"), in his *Chao-yü-shih ku-tien wen-hsüeh lun-chi*, vol. 2 (see I.A.3 above).

———. "Lun Lu Chi 'Wen fu' chung so-wei 'yi'" 論陸機文賦中所謂意 (On What is Called "Concept" in Lu Chi's "Poetic Exposition on Literature"), in his *Chao-yü-shih ku-tien wen-hsüeh lun-chi*, vol. 2 (see I.A.3 above).

Lu Ch'in-li 逯欽立. "Wen fu chuan-chu nien-tai k'ao" 文賦撰著年代考 (A Study of the Year of Composition of "The Poetic Exposition of Literature"), in his *Han Wei liu-ch'ao wen-hsüeh lun-chi* (see Lu Ch'in-li in I.B.1 above).

Mou Shih-chin. "Wen fu te chu-yao kung-hsien ho-tsai" 文賦的主要貢獻何在 (Wherein Lies the Important Contribution of "The Poetic Exposition on Literature"), in his *Tiao-lung chi* (see I.A.3 above).

Wang Meng-ou. "Lu Chi Wen fu so tai-piao-te wen-hsüeh kuan-nien" 陸機文賦所代表的文學觀念 (The View of Literature Represented in Lu Chi's "Poetic Exposition on Literature"), in his *Ku-tien wen-hsüeh lun t'an-so* (see I.A.3 above).

Wu Tiao-kung. "Wen fu te yi-shu kou-ssu lun" 文賦的藝術構思論 (A Discussion of the Conception of Art in "The Poetic Exposition on Literature"), in his *Ku-tai wen-lun chin-t'an* (see I.F. below).

WEN-HSIN TIAO-LUNG (I.E)

There has been a vast amount of scholarship on the *Wen-hsin tiao-lung* in recent years. The following bibliography is in no way complete, but represents only some of the standard works and a sampling of recent scholarship.

Huang Shu-lin 黃叔林 (issued under various titles). This is the standard premodern commentary, 1738, reissued in 1833 with critical comments by Chi
Yün 紀昀. This commentary has often been reprinted. The Huang commentary with Chi Yün's comments was issued in the *SPPY* and reprinted as *Wen-
hsin tiao-lung chi-chu* 文心雕龍集注 (Gathered Commentary on *Wen-hsin tiao-
lung*), Peking: Chung-hua shu-hü, 1957. The standard modern typeset edition
was issued as *Wen-hsin tiao-lung chiao-chu* 文心雕龍校注 (Collation and Commentary on *Wen-hsin tiao-lung*), Shanghai: Ku-tien wen-hsüeh ch'u-pan-she,
1958. This contains the Huang edition and commentary, with a supplementary commentary by the Ch'ing scholar Li Hsiang 李祥 and the modern
scholar Yang Ming-chao 楊明照.

Fan Wen-lan 范文瀾. *Wen-hsin tiao-lung chu* 文心雕龍注 (Commentary on *Wen-
hsin tiao-lung*). Peking: Jen-min wen-hsüeh ch'u-pan-she, 1958. First issued
in 1925 as *Wen-hsin tiao-lung chiang-su . . .* 講疏; reprinted with present title
1929, 1936. The 1958 edition contains various revisions. Three works of supplement and correction have been done:

    Shiba Rokurō 斯波六郎. *Wen-hsin tiao-lung Fan-chu pu-cheng . . .* 范注補正
    (Emendations and Corrections on Fan's Commentary to . . .). Hiroshima:
    Hiroshima University Press, 1952.

    Wang Keng-sheng 王更生. *Wen-hsin tiao-lung Fan-chu po-cheng . . .* 范注駁正
    (Refutations of Fan's Commentary to . . .). Taipei: Hua-cheng shu-chü,
    1970.

    Yang Ming-chao 楊明照. *Fan Wen-lan Wen-hsin tiao-lung chu chü-cheng
    . . .* 范文瀾注舉正 (Corrections of Fan Wen-lan's Commentary to . . .). *Wen-
    hsüeh nien-pao* 1937.3.

Wang Li-ch'i 王利器. *Wen-hsin tiao-lung hsin-shu . . .* 新書 (A New Text of *Wen-
hsin tiao-lung*). Peking: Université de Paris Centre d'Etudes Sinologiques de
Pékin, 1951. This is a critical text, without commentary, and is printed with
Wang Li-ch'i's concordance, *Wen-hsin tiao-lung t'ung-chien . . .* 通檢. The concordance is geared to the *hsin-shu*. There is a colophon, "Wen-hsin tiao-lung
hsin-shu pa-wei" . . . 新書跋尾, in *Ku-tien wen-hsüeh lun-ts'ung* 1 (Chi-nan,
1980).

Liu Yung-chi 劉永濟. *Wen-hsin tiao-lung chiao-shih . . .* 校釋 (Collations and Explanations of *Wen-hsin tiao-lung*). Shanghai: Chung-hua shu-chü ch'u-pan-
she, 1962.

Li Yüeh-kang 李日剛. *Wen-hsin tiao-lung chiao-ch'üan . . .* 斠詮 (Comprehensive
Commentary and Collation on *Wen-hsin tiao-lung*). Taipei: Kuo-li pien-yi-
kuan ch'u-pan-she, 1982.

Yang Ming-chao 楊明照. *Wen-hsin tiao-lung chiao-chu shih-yi . . .* 校注拾遺 (Supplements to the Collation and Commentary on *Wen-hsin tiao-lung*). Shang-
hai: Shang-hai ku-chi ch'u-pan-she, 1982.

Chiang Shu-ko 姜書閣. *Wen-hsin tiao-lung yi-chih . . .* 繹旨 (The Essential Conclusions of *Wen-hsin tiao-lung*). Chi-nan: Ch'i-Lu shu-she, 1984.

Chu Ying-p'ing 朱迎平. *Wen-hsin tiao-lung so-yin* 文心雕龍索引 (Indices to *Wen-
hsin tiao-lung*). Shanghai: Shang-hai ku-chi ch'u-pan-she, 1987. This work is
not a true concordance; it consists of three sections: an index of sentences, an
index of books and works, and an index of terms deemed important in literary
theory. These indices are correlated to a text given at the end of the book.

Chan Ying 詹鍈. *Wen-hsin tiao-lung yi-cheng* 文心雕龍義證 (Proofs of the Meaning
of *Wen-hsin tiao-lung*). 3 vols. Shanghai: Shang-hai ku-chi ch'u-pan-she,
1989.

Vernacular Commentaries and Translations (I.E.2)

Vernacular commentaries and translations are very numerous and differ greatly in quality and originality; the following are the most important.

Chou Chen-fu 周振甫. *Wen-hsin tiao-lung chu-shih*... 注釋 (Commentary to and Explanations of *Wen-hsin tiao-lung*). Peking: Jen-min wen-hsüeh ch'u-pan-she, 1981. There is a good review by Ch'en Hsin 陳新 in *Wen-hsüeh yi-ch'an* 1982.2:145–150.

———. *Wen-hsin tiao-lung hsüan-yi*... 選譯 (Selected Translations from *Wen-hsin tiao-lung*). Peking: Chung-hua shu-chü, 1980. This is somewhat different from the preceding work and seems to have been intended for a wider audience. It contains thirty-five of the most important chapters with a brief introduction, a vernacular translation, and notes.

Lu K'an-ju 陸侃如 and Mou Shih-chin 牟世金. *Wen-hsin tiao-lung yi-chu*... 譯注 (Translation and Commentary on *Wen-hsin tiao-lung*). Chi-nan: Ch'i-Lu shu-she, 1981. This supplants the earlier anthologies of chapters *Wen-hsin tiao-lung hsüan-yi*... 選譯 (Chi-nan: Shan-tung Jen-min ch'u-pan-she, 1962–1963); and *Liu Hsieh lun ch'uang-tso* 劉勰論創作 (Ho-fei: An-hui jen-min ch'u-pan-she, 1963).

Tsu Pao-chüan 祖保泉. *Wen-hsin tiao-lung hsüan-hsi* 文心雕龍選析 (Analytical Anthology of *Wen-hsin tiao-lung*). Ho-pei: An-hui chiao-yü, 1985.

Japanese Translations and Commentaries (I.E.3)

Kōzen Hiroshi 興膳宏. *Bunshin chōryū* 文心雕龍 (*Wen-hsin tiao-lung*), in *Sekai koten bungaku zenshū*, no. 25. Tokyo: Chikuma shobō, 1968. No text and minimal notes.

Mekada Makoto 目加田誠. *Bunshin chōryū* 文心雕龍 (*Wen-hsin tiao-lung*), in *Bungaku geijutsu ronshū*, in *Chūgoku koten bungaku taikei*, no. 54. Tokyo: Iwanami shoten, 1974.

Toda Kōkyō 戸田浩曉. *Bunshin chōryū* 文心雕龍 (*Wen-hsin tiao-lung*), in *Shinyaku kambun taisei*. 2 vols. Tokyo: Meiji shoin, 1976.

Studies (I.E.4)

The sheer mass of scholarship on *Wen-hsin tiao-lung* is overwhelming. One bibliography of works from the People's Republic of China lists ten pages of articles from 1981 to 1982. The following omits articles and gives only a selection of books. Mention here should be made of the irregular journal put out by the *Wen-hsin tiao-lung hsüeh-hui*, the *Wen-hsin tiao-lung hsüeh-k'an* 文心雕龍學刊, published by Ch'i-Lu shu-she in Chi-nan.

Chan Ying 詹鍈. *Liu Hsieh yü Wen-hsin tiao-lung* 劉勰與文心雕龍 (Liu Hsieh and the *Wen-hsin tiao-lung*). Peking: Chung-hua shu-chü, 1980.

———. *Wen-hsin tiao-lung te feng-ko hsüeh*... 的風格學 (The Study of Style in *Wen-hsin tiao-lung*). Peking: Jen-min wen-hsüeh ch'u-pan-she, 1982.

Ch'en Ssu-ling 陳思苓. *Wen-hsin tiao-lung yi-lun* 文心雕龍臆論 (Conjectural Discussions of *Wen-hsin tiao-lung*). Ch'eng-tu: Pa-Shu shu-she, 1986.

Chiang Tsu-yi 蔣祖怡. *Wen-hsin tiao-lung lun-ts'ung*... 論叢 (A Collection of Discussions of *Wen-hsin tiao-lung*). Shanghai: Shang-hai ku-chi ch'u-pan-she, 1985.

Hsü Fu-kuan 徐復觀 "Wen-hsin tiao-lung te wen-t'i lun" 文心雕龍的文體論 (The Discussion of Genre in *Wen-hsin tiao-lung*), in his *Chung-kuo wen-hsüeh lun-chi* 中國文學論集 (Collected Essays on Chinese Literature). 3rd ed. Taipei: Hsüeh-sheng shu-chü, 1976. A long and important article by one of the major modern Chinese aestheticians. Pp. 385–444 of this collection contain a series of short articles on selected articles on various topics in *Wen-hsin tiao-lung* entitled "Wen-hsin tiao-lung chien-lun" . . . 箋論.

Huang Ch'un-kuei 黃春貴. *Wen-hsin tiao-lung chih ch'uang-tso lun* 文心雕龍之創作論 (The Theory of Creativity in *Wen-hsin tiao-lung*). Taipei: Wen-shih-che ch'u-pan-she, 1978.

Huang K'an 黃侃. *Wen-hsin tiao-lung cha-chi* 文心雕龍札記 (Notes on *Wen-hsin tiao-lung*). Shanghai, 1962; reprint Taipei: Wen-shih-che ch'u-pan-she, 1973. This work, with a complicated history, has been very influential in *Wen-hsin tiao-lung* studies.

Kōzen Hiroshi 興膳宏. *Wen-hsin tiao-lung lun-wen-chi* 文心雕龍論文集 (A Collection of Articles on *Wen-hsin tiao-lung*). Chi-nan: Ch'i-Lu shu-she 1984. Kōzen Hiroshi is a major scholar, both of the period and of *Wen-hsin tiao-lung*; his articles are scattered through various Japanese journals and Festschrifts. The above is a collection of Kōzen's articles translated by P'eng En-hua 彭恩華. P'eng's anthology contains a bibliography of Kōzen's important works.

Lu K'an-ju 陸侃如 and Mou Shih-chin 牟世金. *Liu Hsieh ho Wen-hsin tiao-lung* 劉勰和文心雕龍. Shanghai: Shang-hai ku-chi ch'u-pan-she, 1978.

Ma Hung-shan 馬宏山. *Wen-hsin tiao-lung san-lun* 文心雕龍散論 (Random Discussions on *Wen-hsin tiao-lung*). Urumchi: Hsin-chiang jenmin ch'u-pan-she, 1982.

Tu Li-chün 杜黎均. *Wen-hsin tiao-lung wen-hsüeh li-lun yen-chiu ho yi-shih* 文心雕龍文學理論研究和譯釋 (A Study and Interpretive Explanation of Literary Theory in *Wen-hsin tiao-lung*). Peking: Pei-ching ch'u-pan-she, 1981.

Wang Chin-ling 王金淩. *Wen-hsin tiao-lung wen-lun shu-yü hsi-lun* 文心雕龍文論術語析論 (An Analytical Discussion of the Technical Terms in the Discussion of Literature in *Wen-hsin tiao-lung*). Taipei: Hua-cheng shu-chü, 1981.

Wang Yüan-hua 王元化. *Wen-hsin tiao-lung ch'uang-tso lun* 文心雕龍創作論 (A Discussion of Creativity in *Wen-hsin tiao-lung*). Shanghai: Shang-hai ku-chi ch'u-pan-she, 1979.

Wang Yün-hsi 王運熙. *Wen-hsin tiao-lung t'an-so* 文心雕龍探索 (An Exploration of *Wen-hsin tiao-lung*). Shanghai: Shang-hai ku-chi ch'u-pan-she, 1986.

Yang Ming-chao. *Hsüeh-pu-yi-chai tsa-chu*. See I.A.3.

Yi Chung-t'ien 易中天. *Wen-hsin tiao-lung mei-hsüeh ssu-hsiang lun-kao* 文心雕龍美學思想論稿 (A Draft Discussion of Aesthetic Thought in *Wen-hsin tiao-lung*). Shanghai: Shang-hai wen-yi, 1988.

Yü K'o-k'un 禹克坤. *Wen-hsin tiao-lung yü shih-p'in* 文心雕論與詩品 (*Wen-hsin tiao-lung* and the "Gradations of Poetry"). Peking: Jen-min ch'u-pan-she, 1989.

"THE TWENTY-FOUR CATEGORIES OF POETRY" (I.F)

Commentaries (I.F.1)

Chao Fu-t'an 趙福壇. *Shih-p'in hsin-shih* 詩品新釋 (A New Interpretation of the Categories of Poetry). Kuang-chou: Hua-ch'eng ch'u-pan-she, 1986.

Ch'iao Li 喬力. *Erh-shih-ssu Shih-p'in t'an-wei* 二十四詩品探微 (Investigating the Subtleties of "The Twenty-Four Categories of Poetry"). Chi-nan: Ch'i-Lu shu-she, 1983.

Kuo Shao-yü 郭紹虞. *Shih-p'in chi-chieh* 詩品集解 (Collected Explanations of "The Categories of Poetry"), with *Hsü shih-p'in chu* 續詩品注 (A Commentary on [Yüan Mei's] "Continuation of the Categories of Poetry"), etc., included. Peking: Jen-min wen-hsü ch'u-pan-she, 1963.

Lo Chung-ting 羅仲鼎 et al. *Shih-p'in chin-hsi* 詩品今析 (A New Analysis of "The

Categories of Poetry"). N.p.: Chiang-su jen-min ch'u-pan-she, 1983.

Lü Hsing-ch'ang 呂興昌. *Ssu-k'ung T'u shih-lun yen-chiu* 司空圖詩品研究 (A Study of Ssu-k'ung T'u's Theory of Poetry). Taipei: Hung-ta ch'u-pan-she, 1980.

Sun Ch'ang-hsi 孫昌熙 et al., eds. *Ssu-k'ung T'u 'Shih-p'in' chieh-shuo erh-chung* 司空圖詩品解說二種 (Two Explanations of Ssu-k'ung T'u's "Twenty-four Categories of Poetry"). Chi-nan: Shan-tung jen-min ch'u-pan-she, 1962. New edition, Chi-nan: Ch'i-Lu shu-she, 1980. This contains the complete *Shih-p'in yi-shuo* 詩品臆說 (Conjectural Theories on "The Categories of Poetry") by Sun Lien-k'uei 孫聯奎 and the *Erh-shih-ssu Shih-p'in chien-chieh* 二十四詩品淺解 (Shallow Notes on "The Twenty-four Categories of Poetry") by Yang T'ing-chih 楊廷芝.

Sun Lien-k'uei. *Shih-p'in yi-shuo*. See Sun Ch'ang-hsi, previous entry.

Tsu Pao-ch'üan 祖保泉. *Ssu-k'ung T'u Shih-p'in chieh-shuo* 司空圖詩品解說 (Explanation of Ssu-k'ung T'u's "Categories of Poetry"). Ho-fei: An-hui jen-min ch'u-pan-she, 1964; revised edition 1980. Early edition has only vernacular notes and translation; revised edition adds discussion of each category.

Tu Li-chün 杜黎均. *Erh-shih-ssu shih-p'in yi-chu p'ing-hsi* 二十四詩品譯注評析 (Translation, Commentary, Critical Comment and Analysis of "The Twenty-four Categories of Poetry"). Peking: Pei-ching ch'u-pan-she, 1988.

Wang Chi-heng 王濟亨 and Kao Chung-chang 高仲章. *Ssu-k'ung T'u hsüan-chi chu* 司空圖選集注 (An Annotated Anthology of Ssu-k'ung T'u). T'ai-yüan: Shan-hsi jen-min, 1989.

Yang T'ing-chih. *Erh-shih-ssu Shih-p'in chien-chieh*. See Sun Ch'ang-hsi above.

Studies (I.F.2)

Chiang Kuo-chen 江國貞. *Ssu-k'ung Piao-sheng yen-chiu* 司空表聖研究 (A Study of Ssu-k'ung Piao-sheng [T'u]). Taipei: Wen-chin ch'u-pan-she, 1978.

Tsu Pao-ch'üan 祖保泉. *Ssu-k'ung T'u te shih-ko li-lun* 司空圖的詩歌理論. Shanghai: Shang-hai ku-chi ch'u-pan-she, 1984.

Wu Tiao-kung 吳調公. *Ku-tai wen-lun chin-t'an* 古代文論今探 (Modern Investigations of Ancient Theories of Literature). Hsi-an: Shen-hsi jen-min ch'u-pan-she, 1982.

SUNG *SHIH-HUA* (I.G)

Chang Pao-ch'üan 張葆全. *Shih-hua ho tz'u-hua* 詩話和詞話 (Remarks on Poetry and Remarks on Song Lyric). Shanghai: Shang-hai ku-chi ch'u-pan-she, 1983.

Ch'ien Chung-lien 錢仲聯. "Sung-tai shih-hua niao-k'an" 宋代詩話鳥瞰 (A Bird's-eye View of Remarks on Poetry in the Sung dynasty), *Ku-tai wen-hsüeh li-lun yen-chiu* 3 (1981; see I.A.3 above).

Kuo Shao-yü 郭紹虞. *Pei-Sung shih-hua k'ao* 北宋詩話考 (A Study of Northern Sung Remarks on Poetry). Hong Kong: Ch'ung-wen shu-tien, 1971. A reprint of 1937 and 1939 articles in *Yen-ching hsüeh-pao*, including an appended discussion of Southern Sung *shih-hua*.

———. *Sung shih-hua chi-yi* 宋詩話輯佚 (Gathered Fragments of Sung Remarks on Poetry). Peking: Chung-hua shu-chü, 1980.

TS'ANG-LANG'S REMARKS ON POETRY (I.H.)

Commentaries (I.H.1)

Hu Ts'ai-fu 胡才甫. *Ts'ang-lang shih-hua chu* 滄浪詩話注 (A Commentary to Ts'ang-lang's Remarks on Poetry). Peking, 1937; photo-reprint, Taipei: Kuang-wen shu-chü, 1972.

Kuo Shao-yü 郭紹虞. *Ts'ang-lang shih-hua chiao-shih* 滄浪詩話校釋 (Collations and Annotations on Ts'ang-lang's Remarks on Poetry). Peking: Jen-min wen-hsüeh ch'u-pan-she, 1961.

Japanese Translations (I.H.2)

Arai Ken 荒井健. *Sōrō shiwa* 滄浪詩話 (Ts'ang-lang's Remarks on Poetry), in *Bungaku ronshū* in *Chūgoku bunmei sen*, no. 13. Tokyo: Asahi shimbunsha, 1972.

Ichino Sawatorao 市野澤寅雄. *Sōro shiwa* 滄浪詩話 (T'ang-lang's Remarks on Poetry). Tokyo: Meitoku shuppansha, 1976.

Books and Articles (I.H.3)

Chang Chien 張健. *Ts'ang-lang shih-hua yen-chiu* 滄浪詩話研究. Taipei: Kuo-li T'ai-wan ta-hsüeh wen-shih ts'ung-k'an, 1966.

Ch'en Kuo-ch'iu 陳國球. "Lun shih-lun shih shang yi-ko ch'ang-chien te hsiang-yü: ching-hua shui-yüeh" 論詩論史上一個常見的象喻: 鏡花水月 (On a Lasting Image in the History of Poetic Theory: Flowers in the Mirror and Moonlight on the Water), *Ku-tai wen-hsüeh li-lun yen-chiu* 9 (1984; see I.A.3 above).

Kuo Shao-yü. "Shih ts'e 'Ts'ang-lang shih-hua' te pen-lai mien-mao" 試測滄浪詩話的本來面貌 (An Attempt to Uncover the Original Appearance of Ts'ang-lang's Remarks on Poetry), in his *Chao-yü-shih ku-tien wen-hsüeh lun-chi*, vol. 2 (see I.A.3 above).

———. "Ts'ang-lang shih-hua yi-ch'ien chih shih ch'an shuo" 滄浪詩話以前之詩禪說 (On the Theory of Poetry as Ch'an Before Ts'ang-lang's Remarks on Poetry), in his *Chao-yü-shih ku-tien wen-hsüeh lun-chi*, vol. 1 (see I.A.3 above). An important article on the comparison of poetry to Ch'an prior to Yen Yü.

Wang Meng-ou. "Yen Yü yi ch'an yü shih shih-chieh" 嚴羽以禪喻詩試解 (An Attempt to Explain Yen Yü's Use of Ch'an as a Figure for Poetry), in his *Ku-tien wen-hsüeh lun t'an-so* (see I.A.3 above).

Wu Tiao-kung. "Pieh-ts'ai ho pieh-ch'ü: Ts'ang-lang shih-hua te ch'uang-tso lun ho chien-shang lun" 別才和別趣: 滄浪詩話的創作論和鑒賞論 (Distinct Material and Distinct Interest: The Theory of Creation and the Theory of Appreciation in Ts'ang-lang's Remarks on Poetry), in his *Ku-tai wen-lun chin-t'an* (see I.A.3 above).

Yen Yü hsüeh-shu yen-chiu lun-wen hsüan 嚴羽學術研究論文選 (Anthology of Articles Studying the Scholarship of Yen Yü). Compiled by the Chinese Department of Fu-chien shih-fan ta-hsüeh. Hsia-men: Lu-chiang ch'u-pan-she, 1987.

POETRY IN THREE FORMS (*SAN-T'I SHIH*) (I.I)

Murakami Tetsumi 村上哲見. *Santaishi* 三體詩 (Poetry in Three Forms). 2 vols. Tokyo: Asahi shimbunsha, 1966.

WANG FU-CHIH (I.J)

Ch'ien Chung-lien 錢仲聯. "Wang Ch'uan-shan shih-lun hou-an" 王船山詩論後案 (A Later Opinion on the Poetic Theories of Wang Fu-chih), in his *Men-t'iao-an Ch'ing-tai wen-hsüeh lun-chi* 夢苕庵清代文學論集. Chi-nan: Ch'i-Lu shu-she, 1983.

Kuo Ho-ming 郭鶴鳴. "Wang Ch'uan-shan shih-lun t'an-wei" 王船山詩論探微 (On the Subtleties of the Poetic Theories of Wang Fu-chih), *Kuo-li Shih-fan Ta-hsüeh kuo-wen yen-chiu-so chi-k'an* 23 (1979).

Lan Hua-tseng 藍華增. "Ku-tien shu-ch'ing shih te mei-hsüeh" 古典抒情詩的美學 (The Aesthetics of Early Poetry Expressing Emotion), *Ku-tai wen-hsüeh li-lun yen-chiu* 10 (1985).

Liu Ch'ang 劉暢. "Wang Ch'uan-shan shih-ko mei-hsüeh san-t'i" 王船山詩歌美學三題 (Various Topics in the Poetic Aesthetics of Wang Fu-chih), *Wen-hsüeh yi-ch'an* 1985.3.

Liu Heng-k'uei 柳亨奎. "Wang Fu-chih shih-p'ing ch'u t'an" 王夫之詩評初探 (An Initial Discussion of the Poetic Criticism of Wang Fu-chih), *Wen-hsüeh p'ing-lun* 8 (1984).

Tai Hung-sen 戴鴻森. *Chiang-chai shih-hua chien-chu* 薑齋詩話箋注 (Notes and Annotation on Chiang-chai's [Wang Fu-chih] Remarks on Poetry). Peking: Jen-min wen-hsüeh ch'u-pan-she, 1981.

Ts'ai Ying-chün. *Pi-hsing wu-se yü ch'ing-ching chiao-jung.* See I.A.1.

Yü Yüan 鬱沅. "Wang Fu-chih te shih-ko yi-shu-lun kai-kuan" 王夫之的詩歌藝術論概觀 (A General View of the Theory of the Poetic Art in Wang Fu-chih), *Ku-tai wen-hsüeh li-lun yen-chiu* 3 (1981; see I.A.3 above).

YEH HSIEH (I.K)

Chang Wen-hsün 張文勛. "Yeh Hsieh te shih-ko li-lun" 葉燮的詩歌理論 (Yeh Hsieh's Theory of Poetry), *Ku-tai wen-hsüeh li-lun yen-chiu* 3 (1981; see I.A.3 above).

Ch'en Hui-feng 陳惠豐. "Yeh Hsieh shih-lun yen-chiu" 葉燮詩論研究 (A Study of Yeh Hsieh's Theory of Poetry). M.A. thesis, Taiwan shih-fan ta-hsüeh, 1976.

Ch'eng Fu-wang 成復旺. "Tui Yeh Hsieh shih-ko ch'uang-tso-lun te ssu-k'ao" 對葉燮詩歌創作論的思考 (Pondering Yeh Hsieh's Theory of Poetic Creation), *Wen-hsüeh yi-ch'an* 1986.5.

Chiang Fan 蔣凡. *Yeh Hsieh ho Yüan-shih* 葉燮和原詩 (Yeh Hsieh and "The Origins of Poetry"). Shanghai: Shang-hai ku-chi ch'u-pan-she, 1985.

———."Yeh Hsieh 'Yüan shih' te li-lun t'e-se chi kung-hsien" 葉燮原詩的理論特色及貢獻 (The Contribution and Distinguishing Characteristics of Theory in Yeh Hsieh's "Origins of Poetry"), *Wen-hsüeh yi-ch'an* 1984.2.

Huo Sung-lin 霍松林. *Yüan shih* 原詩 (The Origins of Poetry). Peking: Jen-min wen-hsüeh ch'u-pan-she, 1979. Basic minimal annotation.

Lan Hua-tseng 藍華增. "Yen-chih p'ai ho yüan-ch'ing p'ai te li-lun chi-ch'u" 言志派和緣情派的理論基礎 (The Theoretical Basis of the Group that Believes that Poetry Articulates What Is On the Mind Intently and of the Group that Believes that Poetry Follows From the Affections), *Ku-tien wen-hsüeh lun-ts'ung*, 2 (Chi-nan, 1981).

II. SELECTED ENGLISH READINGS

GENERAL (II.A)

Books (II.A.1)

Bush, Susan, and Christian Murck, eds. *Theories of the Arts in China.* Princeton: Princeton University Press, 1983. A collection of essays, some of which are listed individually below.

Liu, James J. Y. *Chinese Theories of Literature.* Chicago: University of Chicago Press, 1975. An attempt to transcend the limitations of treating individual works by grouping areas of concern in traditional theory under the following headings: metaphysical theories, deterministic and expressive theories, technical theories, aesthetic theories, and pragmatic theories.

Rickett, Adele, ed. *Chinese Approaches to Literature from Confucius to Liang Ch'i-ch'ao*. Princeton: Princeton University Press, 1978. A collection of essays, some of which are listed individually below.

Tökei, Ferenc. *Genre theory in China in the 3rd–6th Centuries (Liu Hsieh's Theory on Poetic Genres)*. Budapest: Akademiei Kiado, 1971.

Wong, Siu-kit. "*Ch'ing* in Chinese Literary Criticism," Ph.D. dissertation, Oxford University, 1969.

Wong, Siu-kit. *Early Chinese Literary Criticism*. Hong Kong: Joint Publishing Company, 1983. A set of translations of pieces through the Six Dynasties: the "Great Preface," Wang Yi's preface to the Li Sao, Ts'ao P'i's "Discourse," Ts'ao Chih's letter to Yang Te-tsu, the *Wen fu*, the fragments of the *Wen-chang liu-pieh lun*, the Li Ch'ung preface, Shen Yüeh's biography of Hsieh Ling-yün, the *Shih-p'in* preface, two sections of *Wen-hsin tiao-lung*, the letter to the Prince of Hsiang-tung by Hsiao Kang, and the *Wen hsüan* preface.

Yu, Pauline. *The Reading of Imagery in the Chinese Tradition*. Princeton: Princeton University Press, 1987. This an important study of reading traditions and contains many translations.

Articles (II.A.2)

DeWoskin, Kenneth. "Early Chinese Music and the Origins of Aesthetic Terminology," in Bush and Murck, eds. *Theories of the Arts in China*. (see II.A.1 above).

Munakata, Kiyohiko. "Concepts of *Lei* and *Kan-lei* in Early Chinese Art Theory, in Bush and Murck, eds., *Theories of the Arts in China* (see II.A.1 above).

Rickett, Adele. "The Anthologist as Literary Critic in China," *Literature East and West* 19:146–165 (1975).

Robertson, Maureen. "Periodization in the Arts and Patterns of Change in Traditional Chinese Literary History," in Bush and Murck, eds., *Theories of the Arts in China* (see II.A.1 above).

TEXTS FROM THE EARLY PERIOD (II.B)

Ch'en Shih-hsiang, "In Search of the Beginnings of Chinese Literary Criticism" in *Semitic and Oriental Studies: A Volume Presented to William Popper on the Occasion of His Seventy-fifth Birthday*. University of California Publications in Semitic Philology 11. Berkeley; University of California Press, 1951.

Holzman, Donald. "Confucius and Ancient Chinese Literary Criticism," in Adele Rickett, ed., *Chinese Approaches to Literature* (see II.A.1 above).

Ma Yau-woon. "Confucius and Ancient Chinese Literary Criticism: A Comparison with the Early Greeks," in *Essays in Chinese Studies Dedicated to Professor Jao Tsung-i*. Hong Kong, 1970.

Shih, Vincent. "Literature and Art in 'The Analects,'" C. Y. Hsu, tr., *Renditions* 8:5–38 (Autumn, 1977).

THE GREAT PREFACE (II.C)

Translation in Wong, Siu-kit, *Early Chinese Literary Criticism* (see II.A.1 above).

Levy, Dore J. "Constructing Sequences: Another Look at the Principle of *Fu* 'Enumeration,'" *Harvard Journal of Asiatic Studies* 46.2:471–494 (1986).

Van Zoeren, Steven. *Poetry and Personality: Reading, Exegesis, and Hermeneutics in Traditional China*. Stanford: Stanford University Press, 1991.

Wixted, John Timothy. "The *Kokinshū* Prefaces: Another Perspective," *Harvard Journal of Asiatic Studies* 43.1:215–238 (1983). Not only does this contain an extensive discussion of the "Great Preface" and its transmission to Japan, footnote 4 contains a list of translations of the "Great Preface."

A DISCOURSE ON LITERATURE (II.D)

Complete translations: E. R. Hughes, *The Art of Letters: Lu Chi's "Wen fu" A.D. 302* (New York: Pantheon Books, 1951), pp. 231–234; Ronald C. Miao, "Literary Criticism at the End of the Eastern Han," *Literature East and West* 16:1016–1026 (1972); and Donald Holzman, "Literary Criticism in China in the Early Third Century A.D." (see next entry); Siu-kit Wong, *Early Chinese Literary Criticism*, pp. 19–25 (see II.A.1).

Holzman, Donald. "Literary Criticism in China in the Early Third Century A.D.," *Asiatische studien/Études asiatiques* 28.2:113–149 (1974).
Miao, Ronald C. "Literary Criticism at the End of the Eastern Han," *Literature East and West* 16 (1972).
Pollard, David. "Ch'i in Chinese Literary Theory," in Adele Rickett, ed., *Chinese Approaches to Literature* (see II.A.1 above).

THE POETIC EXPOSITION ON LITERATURE (II.E)

The two most important translations of the *Wen fu* into English are Ch'en Shih-hsiang's "Essay on Literature" (Portland, Maine, 1953), reprinted in Cyril Birch, ed., *Anthology of Chinese Literature, From Earliest Times to the Fourteenth Century* (New York: Grove Press, 1965), pp. 222–232; and Achilles Fang, "Rhymeprose on Literature: The *Wen-fu* of Lu Chi," *Harvard Journal of Asiatic Studies* 14 (1951), reprinted in John L. Bishop, ed., *Studies in Chinese Literature* (Cambridge: Harvard University Press, 1965). The latter translation contains valuable textual notes. There are other translations by E. R. Hughes, *The Art of Letters: Lu Chi's "Wen fu" A.D. 302* (New York: Pantheon Books 1951); and Siu-kit Wong, *Early Chinese Literary Criticism* pp. 39–60 (see II.A.1 above). There is a French translation by Georges Margouliès in his *Anthologie raisonnée de la littérature chinoise* (Paris: Payot, 1948), pp. 419–425.

Chou Ju-ch'ang, "An Introduction to Lu Chi's *Wen fu*," *Studia Serica* 9 (1950).
DeWoskin, Kenneth. "Early Chinese Music and the Origins of Aesthetic Terminology," in Bush and Murck, eds., *Theories of the Arts in China*, pp. 198–204 (see II.A.1 above). Contains a discussion of an important passage in the *Wen fu*.
Jao Tsung-yi. "The Relation Between Principles of Literary Criticism of the Wei and Tsin Dynasties and Music." Paper presented to the Eleventh Conference of Young Sinologues, Padua, 1958. Chinese version as "Lu Chi Wen fu li-lun yü yin-yüeh chih kuan-hsi" 陸機文賦理論與音樂之關係, in *Chūgoku bungaku ho* 14:22–37 (1961).
Knoerle, Sister Mary Gregory, "The Poetic Theories of Lu Chi with a Brief Comparison with Horace's 'Ars Poetica,'" *Journal of Aesthetics and Art Criticism* 25.2:137–143 (1966).

WEN-HSIN TIAO-LUNG (II.F)

Translations of Wen-hsin tiao-lung (II.F.1)

Shih, Vincent Y.C. *The Literary Mind and the Carving of Dragons*. New York: Columbia University Press, 1959. Bilingual reprint, Taipei: T'ai-wan chung-hua shu-chü, 1970.

Yang Hsien-yi and Gladys Yang. "Carving a Dragon at the Core of Literature," *Chinese Literature* 1962.8:58–71. Translation of five chapters.

Translations can also be found in Siu-kit Wong, *Early Chinese Literary Criticism*, chapters 26 and 50 (see II.A.1 above); in Ferenc Tökei, *Genre Theory in China* (see II.A.1 above); and in Donald Gibbs, "Literary Theory in the *Wen-hsin tiao-lung*" (see II.F.2 below).

Articles (II.F.2)

Chi Ch'iu-lang. "Liu Hsieh as a Classicist and His Concepts of Tradition and Change," *Tamkang Review.* 4.1:89–108 (1973).

Gibbs, Donald. "Literary Theory in the *Wen-hsin tiao-lung*, Sixth Century Chinese Treatise on the Genesis of Literature and Conscious Artistry." Ph.D. dissertation, University of Washington, 1970.

———. "Liu Hsieh, Author of the *Wen-hsin tiao-lung*," *Monumenta Serica* 29:117–141 (1970–1971).

———. "Notes on the Wind: The Term '*Feng*' in Chinese Literary Criticism," in David C. Buxbaum and Frederick W. Mote, eds., *Transition and Permanence: A Festschrift in Honor of Dr. Hsiao Kung-ch'üan*. Hong Kong: Cathay Press, 1972.

Liu Shou-sung, "Liu Hsieh on Writing," *Chinese Literature* (1962).

Shih, Vincent Y. C. "Classicism in Liu Hsieh's "*Wen-hsin tiao-lung*," *Asiatische studien/Études asiatiques* 7 (1953).

———. "Liu Hsieh's Conception of Organic Unity," *Tamkang Review* 4.2:1–10 (1973).

Yu, Pauline. "Formal Distinctions in Chinese Literary Theory," in Bush and Murck, eds., *Theories of the Arts in China*, pp. 27–53 (see II.A.1 above). On the issue of *wen* and *pi*.

Chung Jung's Shih-p'in (II.F.3)

There is an English translation of the prefaces and the first and second categories in John Timothy Wixted, "The Literary Criticism of Yüan Hao-wen" (Ph.D. dissertation, Oxford, 1976), Appendix A; and a translation of the preface in Siu-kit Wong, *Early Chinese Literary Criticism* (see II.A.1 above).

Brooks, E. Bruce. "A Geometry of the *Shr Pin*," in Chow Tse-tsung, ed., *Wen-lin: Studies in the Chinese Humanities*. Madison: University of Wisconsin Press, 1968.

Cha Chu Whan. "On Enquiries for Ideal Poetry: An Instance of Chung Hung," *Tamkang Review* 6.2–7.1:43–54 (October 1975–April 1976).

Wilhelm, Hellmut. "A Note on Chung Hung and his *Shih-p'in*," in Chow Tse-tsung, ed., *Wen-lin: Studies in the Chinese Humanities*. Madison: University of Wisconsin Press, 1968.

Wixted, John Timothy. "The Nature of Evaluation in the *Shih-p'in* (Gradings of Poets) by Chung Hung (A.D. 469–518)," in Bush and Murck, eds., *Theories of the Arts in China* (see II.A.1 above).

Yeh Chia-ying and Jan Walls. "Theory, Standards, and Practice of Criticizing Poetry in Chung Hung's *Shih-p'in*," in Ronald C. Miao, ed., *Studies in Chinese Poetry and Poetics*, vol. 1. San Francisco: Chinese Material Center, 1978. Chinese version by Yeh Chia-ying in *Chung-wai wen-hsüeh* 4.4:4–24 (1975).

Other Six Dynasties Criticism (II.F.4)

Allen, Joseph. "Chih Yü's *Discussions of Different Types of Literature*," *Parerga* 3:3–36 (1976). Collection and translation of the fragments.

Chang, Kang-i Sun, "Chinese 'Lyric Criticism' in the Six Dynasties," in Bush and Murck, eds., *Theories of the Arts in China* (see II.A.1 above).

Fisk, William Craig. "Formal Themes in Medieval Chinese and Modern Western Literary Theory: Mimesis, Intertextuality, Figurativeness, and Foregrounding." Ph.D. dissertation. University of Wisconsin, 1976.

Hightower, James Robert. "Some Characteristics of Parallel Prose," in John L. Bishop, eds., *Studies in Chinese Literature*. Cambridge: Harvard University Press, 1965. Translation of the preface to *Yü-t'ai hsin-yung*.

————. "The *Wen hsüan* and Genre Theory," *Harvard Journal of Asiatic Studies* 20.3–4:512–533 (December 1957). Reprinted in John L. Bishop, ed., *Studies in Chinese Literature* (Cambridge: Harvard University Press, 1965). With translation of preface.

Knechtges, David. *Wen Xuan, or, Selection of Refined Literature*, vol. 1: *Rhapsodies on Metropolises and Capitals*. Princeton: Princeton University Press, 1982. Translation of preface with discussion.

Marney, John. "P'ei Tzu-yeh: A Minor Literary Critic of the Liang Dynasty," in *Selected Papers in Asian Studies*, vol. 1. Western Conference for the Association for Asian Studies, Boulder, Colorado, October, 1975. Albuquerque, 1976.

Mather, Richard B. *The Poet Shen Yüeh (441–513): The Reticent Marquis*. Princeton: Princeton University Press, 1988. Mather's chapter, "The Flowering of the Yung-ming Style," accurately translates and discusses Shen's "Postface" to the "Biography of Hsieh Ling-yün" along with his exchange of letters with Lu Chüeh.

Yu, Pauline. *The Reading of Imagery in the Chinese Tradition*, pp. 118–167 (see II.A.1 above).

Wong, Siu-kit. *Early Chinese Literary Criticism* (see II.A.1 above). A set of translations of Ts'ao Chih's letter to Yang Te-tsu; the *Wen-chang liu-pieh lun*, the Li Ch'ung preface, Shen Yüeh's biography of Hsieh Ling-yün, the letter to the Prince of Hsiang-tung by Hsiao Kang, and the *Wen hsüan* Preface.

THE TWENTY-FOUR CATEGORIES OF POETRY (II.G)

Translations of the "The Twenty-Four Categories of Poetry" can be found in Herbert Allen Giles, *A History of Chinese Literature*, with a supplement on the modern period, by Liu Wu-chi (New York: F. Ungar, 1967); in L. Cranmer-Byng, *A Lute of Jade: Being Selections from the Classical Poets of China*, 2nd ed., New York: E. P. Dutton, 1911; and in the Yu and Robertson articles below.

Bodman, Richard W. "Poetics and Prosody in Early Medieval China: A Study and Translation of Kūkai's *Bunkyō hifuron*." Ph.D. dissertation, Cornell, 1978. The translation is not a complete one, but this is a very useful work. It does not treat Ssu-k'ung T'u, but contains much background in T'ang technical poetics.

Robertson, Maureen. " . . . To Convey What Is Precious: Ssu-k'ung T'u's Poetics and the *Erh-shih-ssu Shih P'in*," in David C. Buxbaum and Frederick W. Mote, eds., *Translation and Permanence: A Festschrift in Honor of Dr. Hsiao Kung-ch'üan*. Hong Kong: Cathay Press, 1972.

Yu, Pauline, "Ssu-k'ung T'u's *Shih-p'in*: Poetic Theory in Poetic Form," in Ronald C. Miao, ed., *Studies in Chinese Poetry and Poetics*, vol. 1. San Francisco: Chinese Materials Center, 1978.

OU-YANG HSIU AND OTHER SUNG *SHIH-HUA* (II.H)

Chaves, Jonathan. "Ko Li-fang's Subtle Critiques on Poetry," in *Bulletin of Sung-Yüan Studies* 14:39–49 (1979).

Ch'en Yu-shih. "The Literary Theory and Practice of Ou-yang Hsiu," in Adele Rickett, ed., *Chinese Approaches to Literature* (see II.A.1 above).

Egan, Ronald. *The Literary Works of Ou-yang Hsiu.* Cambridge: Cambridge University Press, 1983.

Klöpsch, Volker. *Die Jadesplitter der Dichter: Die Welt der Dichtung in der Sicht eines Klassikers der chinesischen Literaturkritik.* Bochum, 1983.

Rickett, Adele. "Method and Intuition: The Poetic Theories of Huang T'ing-chien," in Adele Rickett, ed., *Chinese Approaches to Literature* (see II.A.1 above).

Wong, Wai-leung. "Chinese Impressionistic Criticism: A Study of the Poetry Talk (*Shih-hua tz'u-hua*) Tradition." Ph.D. dissertation, Ohio State University, 1976.

———. "Selection of Lines in Chinese Poetry Talk Criticism—With a Comparison between the Selected Couplets and Matthew Arnold's 'Touchstones,'" in William Tay, Ying-hsiung Chou, and Heh-hsiang Yuan, eds., *China and the West: Comparative Literature Studies.* Hong Kong: Chinese University Press, 1980.

"TS'ANG-LANG'S REMARKS ON POETRY" (II.I)

English translations can be found in the works by Lynn and Yip given below. Debon's work is a complete German translation.

Debon, Gunther. *Ts'ang-langs Gespräche über die Dichtung: ein Beitrag zur chinesischen Poetik.* Wiesbaden: Franz Steiner Verlag, 1962.

Lynn, Richard John. "Orthodoxy and Enlightenment—Wang Shih-chen's Theory of Poetry and its Antecedents," in Wm. Theodore de Bary, ed., *The Unfolding of Neo-Confucianism.* New York: Columbia University Press, 1975.

Yip, Wai-lim. "Yen Yü and Poetic Theories in the Sung Dynasty," *Tamkang Review* 1.2:183–200 (1970).

WANG FU-CHIH (II.J)

Wong, Siu-kit. "*Ch'ing* and *Ching* in the Critical Writings of Wang Fu-chih," in Adele Rickett, ed., *Chinese Approaches to Literature* (see II.A.1 above). Contains translations.

SUPPLEMENTARY READINGS IN LATER CHINESE CRITICISM (II.K)

Chaves, Jonathan. "Not the Way of Poetry: The Poetics of Experience in the Sung Dynasty," *Chinese Literature: Essays, Articles, and Reviews* 4.2:199–212 (1982).

———. "The Panoply of Images: A Reconsideration of Literary Theory of the Kung-an School," in Bush and Murck, eds., *Theories of the Arts in China* (see II.A.1 above).

Lin Shuen-fu. "Chiang K'uei's Treatises on Poetry and Calligraphy," in Bush and Murck, eds., *Theories of the Arts in China* (see II.A.1 above).

Lynn, Richard John. "Alternate Routes to Self-Realization in Ming Theories of Poetry," in Bush and Murck, eds., *Theories of the Arts in China* (see II.A.1 above).

————. "Tradition and Individual: Ming and Ch'ing Views of Yüan Poetry," in Ronald C. Miao, ed., *Chinese Poetry and Poetics*. San Francisco: Chinese Materials Center, 1978.

————. "Tradition and Synthesis: Wang Shih-chen as Poet and Critic." Ph.D. dissertation, Stanford, 1961.

Stuart Sargent. "Can Latecomers Get There First? Sung Poets and T'ang Poetry," *Chinese Literature: Essays, Articles, and Reviews.* 4.2:165–198 (1982).

Wixted, John Timothy. "The Literary Criticism of Yüan Hao-wen." Ph.D. dissertation, Oxford, 1976. Mammoth, meticulously researched works that touches incidentally on many facets of Chinese literature and literary thought.

————. *Poems on Poetry: Literary Criticism by Yüan Hao-wen (1190–1257).* Wiesbaden: Franz Steiner Verlag, 1982. Book version of the above, with some of the supplementary material removed.

Alphabetical List of Works Cited

For works that appear in the Selected Analytical Bibliography, reference to the appropriate section is given; for others, bibliographical data are given below.

Bodman, Richard W. "Poetics and Prosody in Early Medieval China: A Study and Translation of Kūkai's *Bunkyō hifuron*." II.G.

Bush, Susan, and Christian Murck. *Theories of the Arts in China*. II.A.1.

Chan Ying. *Wen-hsin tiao-lung te feng-ko hsüeh*. I.E.4.

Chang Feng-yi 張鳳翼. *Wen hsüan tsuan-chu* 文選纂注 (Compiled Commentaries on the *Wen hsüan*), in Chang Shao-k'ang, *Wen fu chi-shih*. I.D.1.

Chang Hsieh 張戒. *Sui-han-t'ang shih-hua* 歲寒堂詩話 (Remarks on Poetry from the Cold-of-the-year Hall), in Ting Fu-pao 丁福保, ed., *Li-tai shih-hua hsü-pien* 歷代詩話續編 (Remarks on Poetry through the Ages: Second Series). Peking: Chung-hua shu-chü, 1983.

Chang Huai-chin. *Wen fu yi-chu*. I.D.1.

Chang, Kang-i Sun. "Description of Landscape in Early Six Dynasties Poetry," in Lin and Owen, eds., *The Vitality of the Lyric Voice* (q.v.).

Chang Shao-k'ang. *Wen fu chi-shih*. I.D.1.

Chang Wen-hsün. *Chung-kuo ku-tai wen-hsüeh li-lun lun-kao*. I.A.3.

Chao Fu-t'an. *Shih-p'in hsin-shih*. I.F.1.

Chao Chih-hsin 趙執信. *T'an-lung-lu chu-shih* 談龍錄注釋 (Commentary on and Explanations of "Records of Chat about Dragons"). Commentary by Chao Wei-chih 趙蔚芝 and Liu Yü-hsin 劉聿鑫. Chi-nan: Ch'i Lu shu-she, 1987.

Chaves, Jonathan. "Ko Li-fang's Subtle Critiques on Poetry." II.H.

————. *Mei Yao-ch'en and the Development of Early Sung Poetry*. New York: Columbia University Press, 1971.

————. "Not the Way of Poetry: The Poetics of Experience in the Sung Dynasty." II.K.

————. "The Panoply of Images: A Reconsideration of Literary Theory of the Kung-an School," in Bush and Murck, eds., *Theories of the Arts in China* (q.v.).

Chen, Yu-shih. "The Literary Theory and Practice of Ou-yang Hsiu," in Adele Rickett, ed., *Chinese Approaches to Literature* (q.v.).

Ch'en Kuo-ch'iu. "Lun shih-lun shih shang yi-ko ch'ang-chien te hsiang-yü: ching-hua shui-yüeh." I.H.3.

Ch'en Shih-hsiang. "In Search of the Beginnings of Chinese Literary Criticism." II.B.

Cheng Tien and Mai Mei-ch'iao. *Ku-Han-yü yü-fa-hsüeh tzu-liao hui-pien*. I.A.2.e.

Ch'eng Ya-lin 程亞森. "Wu-shih liu-yi chü t'an-wei" 五石六鶂句探微 (Investigating the Fine Points of the Line on Five Stones and Six Albatrosses), *Ku-tai wen-hsüeh li-lun yen-chiu* 6 (1982). For *Ku-tai wen-hsüeh li-lun yen-chiu*, see I.A.3.

Chiang Kuo-chen. *Ssu-k'ung Piao-sheng yen-chiu*. I.F.2.

Ch'iao Li. *Erh-shih-ssu Shih-p'in t'an-wei*. I.F.1.

Ch'ien Chung-shu. *Kuan-chü pien*. I.D.1.

————. *T'an yi lu* 談藝錄 (Record of Chats on Art). Rev. ed. Peking: Chung-hua shu-chü, 1984.

Chou Chen-fu. *Wen-hsin tiao-lung chu-shih*. I.E.2.

Chu Fu 朱紱. *Ming-chia shih-fa hui-pien* 名家詩法彙編 (A Compilation of Rules for Poetry by Famous Authors). Preface, 1577; reprint, Taipei: Kuang-wen shu-chü, 1973.

Chu Wen-kung chiao Ch'ang-li hsien-sheng chi 朱文公校昌黎先生集, in *SPTK*.

Chu Ying-p'ing. *Wen-hsin tiao-lung so-yin*. I.E.1.

Clark, David Lee. *Shelley's prose; or, The trumpet of a prophecy*. Albuquerque, University of New Mexico Press, 1954.

DeWoskin, Kenneth. "Early Chinese Music and the Origins of Aesthetic Terminology." II.A.2.

Egan, Ronald C. *The Literary Works of Ou-yang Hsiu*. II.H.

Fang T'ing-kuei 方廷珪, *Chao-ming Wen hsüan ta-ch'eng* 昭明文選大成 (A Compendium on Chao-ming's *Wen hsüan*), cited in Chang Shao-k'ang, *Wen fu chi-shih*. I.D.1.

Fichte, Johann Gottlieb. "On the Spirit and the Letter in Philosophy," in David Simpson, tr., *German Aesthetic and Literary Criticism: Kant, Fichte, Schelling, Schopenhauer, Hegel*. Cambridge: Cambridge University Press, 1984.

Gadamer, Hans-Georg. *Philosophical Hermeneutics*, David E. Linge, tr. Berkeley: University of California Press, 1976.

Gibbs, Donald, "Literary Theory in the *Wen-hsin tiao-lung*, Sixth Century Chinese Treatise on the Genesis of Literature and Conscious Artistry." II.F.2.

————. "Notes on the Wind: The Term 'Feng' in Chinese Literary Criticism." II.F.2.

Han shu 漢書 (History of the Han Dynasty). Hong Kong: Chung-hua shu-chü, 1964.

Hartley, David. *Observations on Man, His Frame, His Duty, and His Expectations*. London: Printed by S. Richardson, 1749.

Hayashida Shinnosuke. *Chūgoku chūsei bungaku hyōronshi*. I.A.1.

Hervouet, Yves. *A Sung Biography.* Hong Kong: The Chinese University Press, 1978.

Hightower, James Robert. "The *Wen hsüan* and Genre Theory." II.F.4.

Ho Wen 何汶. *Chu-ch'uang shih-hua* 竹莊詩話 (Bamboo Village Remarks on Poetry; 1206). Ch'ang Chen-kuo 常振國 and Chiang Yün 絳雲, eds. Peking: Chung-hua shu-chü, 1984.

Hsü Fu-kuan. "Lu Chi Wen fu shu-shih ch'u-kao." I.D.1.

Hu Tzu. *T'iao-hsi yü-yin ts'ung-hua.* I.A.2.a.

Huang K'an 黃侃, *Wen hsüan p'ing-tien* 文選評點 (Critical Comments and Pointings on *Wen hsüan*), cited in Chang Shao-k'ang, *Wen fu chi-shih.* I.D.1.

Klöpsch, Volker. *Die Jadesplitter der Dichter.* II.H.

Knechtges, David. Wen Xuan *or Selections of Refined Literature.* II.F.4.

K'o Ch'ing-ming and Tseng Yung-yi. *Liang-Han Wei Tsin Nan-pei-ch'ao wen-hsüeh p'i-p'ing tzu-liao hui-pien.* See *Chung-kuo wen hsüeh p'i-p'ing tzu-liao hui-pien* in I.A.2.e.

Kōzen Hiroshi. *Wen-hsin tiao-lung lun-wen-chi.* I.E.4.

Kuo Shao-yü. "Lun Lu Chi 'Wen fu' chung so-wei 'yi.'" I.D.2.

———. *Shih-p'in chi-chieh.* I.F.1.

———. "Shih ts'e 'Ts'ang-lang shih-hua' te pen-lai mien-miao." I.H.2.

———. *Ts'ang-lang shih-hua chiao-shih.* I.H.1.

———. "'Ts'ang-lang shih-hua' yi-ch'ien chih shih ch'an shuo." I.H.2.

Levy, Dore J. "Constructing Sequences: Another Look at the Principle of *Fu* 'Enumeration.'" II.C.

Li Ch'uan-chia 李全佳. *Wen fu yi-cheng* 文賦義證 (Verifications of Meaning in "The Poetic Exposition on Literature"), cited in Chang Shao-k'ang, *Wen fu chi-shih.* I.D.1.

Li Wen-jao wen-chi 李文饒文集 (Li Wen-jao's Collected Works), in *SPTK.*

Li Yüeh-kang. *Wen-hsin tiao-lung chiao-ch'uan.* I.E.1.

Lin Ch'i-hsien 林其錟 and Ch'en Feng-chin 陳鳳全, eds. *Liu-tzu chi-chiao* 劉子集校 (Collected Collations on the *Liu-tzu*). Shanghai: Shang-hai ku-chi ch'u-pan-she, 1985.

Lin Shuen-fu and Stephen Owen, eds. *The Vitality of the Lyric Voice: Shih Poetry from the late Han to T'ang.* Princeton: Princeton University Press, 1986.

Lin Wen-yüeh. "The Decline and Revival of *Feng-ku* (Wind and Bone): On the Changing Poetic Styles from the Chien-an Era through the High T'ang Period," in Lin and Owen, eds. *The Vitality of the Lyric Voice* (q.v.).

Liu I-ching. *A New Account of Tales of the World.* Richard B. Mather, tr. Minneapolis: University of Minnesota Press, 1976.

Liu, James J. Y. "The Paradox of Poetics and the Poetics of Paradox," in Lin and Owen, eds., *The Vitality of the Lyric Voice* (q.v.).

Liu-yi shih-hua 六一詩話 (Liu-yi's Remarks on Poetry). Cheng Wen 鄭文, ed. Peking: Jen-min wen-hsüeh ch'u-pan-she, 1983.

Lu K'an-ju and Mou Shih-chin. *Wen-hsin tiao-lung yi-chu.* I.E.2.

Lü Hsing-ch'ang. *Ssu-k'ung T'u shih-lun yen-chiu.* I.F.1.

Lynn, Richard. "Alternate Routes to Self-Realization in Ming Theories of Poetry," in Bush and Murck, eds., *Theories of the Arts in China* (q.v.).

———. "Orthodoxy and Enlightenment—Wang Shih-chen's Theory of Poetry and its Antecedents," in Wm. Theodore de Bary, ed., *The Unfolding of Neo-Confucianism.* New York: Columbia University Press, 1975.

Ma Hung-shan. *Wen-hsin tiao-lung san-lun.* I.E.4.

Munakata, Kiyohiko. "Concepts of *Lei* and *Kan-lei* in Early Chinese Art Theory." II.A.2.

Murakami Tetsumi. *Santaishi*. I.I.

Owen, Stephen. *Traditional Chinese Poetry and Poetics: Omen of the World.* Madison: University of Wisconsin Press, 1985.

Peterson, Willard J. "Making Connections: 'Commentary on the Attached Verbalizations' of the *Book of Change,*" *Harvard Journal of Asiatic Studies* 42.1:67–116 (1982).

Pollard, David. "*Ch'i* in Chinese Literary Theory." II.D.

Rickett, Adele, ed. *Chinese Approaches to Literature from Confucius to Liang Ch'i-ch'ao.* II.A.1.

Robertson, Maureen. " . . . To Convey What is Precious: Ssu-k'ung T'u's Poetics and the *Erh-shih-ssu Shih P'in.*" II.G.

———. "Periodization in the Arts and Patterns of Change in Traditional Chinese Literary History," in Bush and Murck (q.v.).

San-kuo chih 三國志 (Account of the Three Kingdoms). Peking: Chung-hua shu-chü, 1959.

Sargent, Stuart. "Can Latecomers Get There First? Sung Poets and T'ang Poetry." II.K.

Schiller, Friedrich von. *Über naive and sentimentalische Dichtung.* Johannes Beer, ed. 1795; Stuttgart: Reclam, 1975.

Schmidt, J. D. *Yang Wan-li.* Boston: Twayne, 1976.

Shiba Rokurō. *Wen-hsin tiao-lung Fan-chu pu-cheng.* See Fan Wen-lan, I.E.1.

Shih chi 史記 (Historical Records). Peking: Chung-hua shu-chü, 1964.

Shih, Vincent Y. C. *The Literary Mind and the Carving of Dragons.* II.F.1.

Smith, James Harry, and Edd Winfield Parks, eds. *The Great Critics: An Anthology of Literary Criticism.* New York: W. W. Norton, 1951.

SPTK: Ssu-pu ts'ung-k'an 四部叢刊. A modern series photo-reprinting good early editions; it has appeared at various times and places.

SPPY: Ssu-pu pei-yao 四部備要.

Tai Hung-sen. *Chiang-chai shih-hua chien-chu.* I.J.

T'ang Ta-yüan 唐大圓, *Wen-fu chu* 文賦注 (Commentary on "The Poetic Exposition on Literature") cited in *Wen-fu chi-shih* (q.v.).

Ting Fu-pao. *Ching shih-hua.* I.A.2.c.

TL: Wei Chin Nan-pei-ch'ao wen-hsüeh shih ts'an-k'ao tzu-liao. I.D.1.

Toda Kōkyō. *Bunshin chōryū.* I.E.3.

Tōkei, Ferenc. *Genre Theory in China in the 3rd–6th Centuries.* II.A.1.

Tsu Pao-ch'üan. *Ssu-k'ung T'u Shih-p'in chieh-shuo.* I.F.1.

Van Zoeren, Steven. *Poetry and Personality: Reading, Exegesis, and Hermeneutics in Traditional China.* II.C.

———. "Poetry and Personality: A Study of the Hermeneutics of the *Classic of Odes (Shijing).* Ph.D. dissertation, Harvard, 1986.

Wang Ching-hsien. "Lu Chi Wen fu chiao-shih." I.D.1.

Wang Ch'ung 王充. *Lun-heng chi-chieh* 論衡集解 (Collected Explanations of the *Lun-heng*). Liu P'an-sui 劉盼遂, ed. Peking: Chung-hua shu-chü, 1959.

Wang K'ai-yün 王闓運. *Hsiang-ch'i-lou lun wen-chang t'i-fa* 湘綺樓論文章體法, cited in *Wen-fu chi-shih* (q.v.).

Wang Meng-ou. "Shih-lun Ts'ao P'i tsen-yang fa-chien wen-ch'i." I.C.

———. "Ts'ao P'i Tien-lun lun-wen so-yin." I.C.

———. "Yen Yü yi ch'an yü shih shih-chieh." I.H.2.

Wang Ta-p'eng 王大鵬 et al. *Chung-kuo li-tai shih-hua hsüan* 中國歷代詩話選. Ch'ang-sha: Yüeh-lu shu-she 1985.

Watson, Burton. *Chinese Rhyme-Prose: Poems in the Fu Form from the Han and Six Dynasties Period.* New York: Columbia University Press, 1971.

Wen-fu chi-shih. See Chang Shao-k'ang, I.D.1.

Wen-fu yi-chu. See Chang Huai-chin, I.D.1.

Wilde, Oscar. *The Artist as Critic: Critical Writings of Oscar Wilde.* Richard Ellmann, ed. New York: Random House, 1969.

Wilhelm, Hellmut. "A Note on Chung Hung and his *Shih-p'in.*" II.F.3.

Wixted, John Timothy. "The *Kokinshū* Prefaces: Another Perspective. " II.C.

———. "The Literary Criticism of Yüan Hao-wen." II.K.

———. "The Nature of Evaluation in the *Shih-p'in* (Grading of Poets) by Chung Hung (A.D. 469–518)." II.F.3.

———. *Poems on Poetry: Literary Criticism by Yuan Hao-wen (1190–1257).* II.K.

Wong, Siu-kit. "*Ch'ing* and *Ching* in the Critical Writings of Wang Fu-chih," in Adele Rickett, ed., *Chinese Approaches to Literature* (q.v.).

———. "*Ch'ing* in Chinese Literary Criticism." II.A.1.

Wong, Wai-leung. "Selections of Lines in Chinese Poetry Talk Criticism—With a Comparison between the Selected Couplets and Matthew Arnold's 'Touchstones.'" II.H.

Wu Hung-yi 吳宏一. *Ch'ing-tai shih-hsüeh ch'u-t'an* 清代詩學初探 Taipei: Hsüeh-sheng shu-chü, 1986.

Yang Ming-chao. *Hsüeh-pu-yi-chai tsa-chu.* I.A.3.

———. *Wen-hsin tiao-lung chiao-chu shih-yi.* I.E.1.

Yang T'ing-chih. *Erh-shih-ssu Shih-p'in chien-chieh.* I.F.1.

Yeh Chia-ying and Jan Walls. "Theory, Standards, and Practice of Criticizing Poetry in Chung Hung's *Shih-p'in.*" II.F.3.

Yu, Pauline. "Formal Distinctions in Chinese Literary Theory," in Bush and Murck, eds., *Theories of the Arts in China* (q.v.).

———. *The Reading of Imagery in the Chinese Tradition.* II.A.1.

———. "Ssu-k'ung T'u's *Shih-p'in*: Poetic Theory in Poetic Form." II.G.

Yü Hsin 庾信 *Ai Chiang-nan fu* 哀江南賦.

Yüan Hung-tao 袁宏道. *Yüan Hung-tao chi chien-chiao* 袁宏道集箋校. Ch'ien Po-ch'eng 錢伯城, ed. Shanghai: Shang-hai ku-chi ch'u-pan-she, 1981.

Index
of Terms
and
Concepts

225, 305; modes of, 446–447. See also
Normative form; Shape
Formal school, 496
Four Beginnings (*Ssu-shih*), 48–49
Fu. See Exposition; Poetic Exposition

Going far/lasting long, words and texts, 46,
64, 180, 195, 245, 285, 366–367, 480

Han dynasty, 55, 57–58, 200, 226, 227, 395,
565. See also Chien-an period; High
T'ang
Han-hsü. See Reserve
Hao-fang. See Swaggering abandon
Harmony (*ho*), 62, 161, 164–165, 306–307
Hexagrams, 63, 156, 224, 264–265, 308;
Ch'ien, 33, 191, 305, 308, 321, 505;
Images and, 31, 33; *K'un*, 191, 308, 505
High T'ang, 392, 399, 429, 540, 555–556;
Han, Wei and, poetry of, 397, 402, 407,
437; in study of poetry, 395, 398–399.
See also T'ang dynasty
Ho. See Harmony
Hsi-k'un style, 369–371, 386
Hsi-lien. See Washed and refined
Hsiang. See Image; Images
Hsieh-nung. See Delicate-fresh and rich-
lush
Hsin. See Mind
Hsing. See Affective Image; Nature; Shape;
Stirring
Hsiung-hun. See Potent, undifferentiated
Hsü. See Empty
Hsüan-lan. See Observe in darkness
Hsüan-yen poetry, 300–301
Huo-fa. See Vital method
Hymns (*sung*), 45, 49–50, 191, 197

Image, 109, 187–188, 210, 532; in language
and poetry, 34, 279, 371
Images (of the *Book of Changes*), 31–32, 33,
180, 190–191, 193, 265, 598 ch1n7;
"beyond the Images," 304–305
Imitation, 151, 175–176
Individuality, of poets, 212–213, 217–218,
411
Influence (*feng*), 200, 307
Inspiration, 173–174, 176
Intent (*chih*), ch'i and, 202–204, 214–215,
219–220, 610n73; conception, language/
literature and, 24-26, 29, 30, 31, 176, 207;
definition of, 28, 30, 83; in definition of
shih, poetry, 26–29, 40–44, 59, 68, 130–
131, 197; stirring of mind and, 87, 89, 91
Intentionality, gap of, 508, 510

Interior and exterior correspondences, 39,
310, 477, 533–534; affections and coloration as version of 239, 242, 268; conceptions, external world, language/literature
and, 30, 32, 41, 64, 82–83, 92, 114, 192–
193, 210–211, 216, 240, 305, 448; mind,
expression and, 116–117, 278–280, 291;
nature, self, external world and, 29–30,
206, 213, 337, 464–466, 521–523, 529.
See also Scenes and affections
Intertextuality, 409–410, 484–485
Intricate beauty (*ch'i-li*), 321–323, 328,
331, 335–336
Involuntarism. See Voluntarism

Ju-shen. See Divinity
Judgment (*shih*); principle, event, circumstance and, 495–496, 512–519; in study
of poetry, 394–395, 580, 630n3; talent,
courage, force and 526–528, 560

Kan. See Stirring
Kao-ku. See Lofty and ancient
Knowing, 20; and being, 398–399; con-
scious knowledge, 53–54; how to write,
396; vs. judgment, 395; knowing people,
31, 34–35, 62, 68, 286, 388–389. See also
One Who Knows the Tone
Ku. See Bone
Kuang-ta. See Expansive contentment

Language (*yen*), 29, 30, 82, 207, 212, 237,
268, 477–478; definitions of, 129, 143–
144, 272. See also Understanding language
Latent (*yin*), 108, 199, 262–266
Learning, 212–215, 217–218, 408
Li. See Natural Principle
Lien lei. See Categorical associations
Limpid and calm (*ch'ung-tan*), 306–308
Lines, 439, 447; closing, 432, 437, 441; dead
and vital, 417, five- and seven-character,
441–443, 444; opening, 433, 437, 442
Literary factionalism, 540–541
Literary patterning/literature (*wen*), 24–25,
46, 58, 80–81, 192, 200, 232, 247–248,
289, categories and definitions of, 64,
272–277, 294, 606n15; functions of, 179;
going far, 29–30; mind, self, and 30, 178,
185, 210; principle and, 179–180, 267–
268. See also Patterning
Literary thought, traditions of, 3–5. See
also Chinese literary theory; Chinese
literary theory vs. Western theory
Literature of knowledge (*tzu*), 8–9

Index

of Authors

and Titles

Cross-references to the Index of Terms and Concepts are included.

Index
of Sources

This index lists those pages where a passage from one Chinese text is shown to be the source of a later text.